广州统计年鉴

GUANGZHOU STATISTICAL YEARBOOK

2020

（总第32期 NO. 32）

广　州　市　统　计　局　编
国家统计局广州调查队
Guangzhou Municipal Statistics Bureau
Guangzhou Survey Office of National Bureau of Statistics

中国统计出版社
China Statistics Press

图书在版编目（CIP）数据

广州统计年鉴. 2020 = Guangzhou Statistical Yearbook 2020 : 汉英对照 / 广州市统计局，国家统计局广州调查队编.
-- 北京 : 中国统计出版社，2020.9
ISBN 978-7-5037-9238-0

Ⅰ. ①广…
Ⅱ. ①广… ②国…
Ⅲ. ①统计资料—广州—2020—年鉴—汉、英
Ⅳ. ①C832.651-54

中国版本图书馆 CIP 数据核字(2020)第 153578 号

广州统计年鉴-2020

作　　者/ 广州市统计局　国家统计局广州调查队
责任编辑/ 郭　栋
装帧设计/ 广州市人民印刷厂股份有限公司
出版发行/ 中国统计出版社有限公司
地　　址/ 北京市丰台区西三环南路甲 6 号
邮政编码/ 100073
电　　话/ 邮购（010）63376909　书店（010）68783171
网　　址/ http://www.zgtjcbs.com
印　　刷/ 广州星河印刷有限公司
经　　销/ 新华书店
开　　本/ 890mm×1240mm　1/16
字　　数/ 1484 千字
印　　张/ 35
版　　别/ 2020 年 9 月第 1 版
版　　次/ 2020 年 9 月第 1 次印刷
定　　价/ 398 元　Price: 398 (RMB)

本书附同版本 CD-ROM 一张，光盘内容以书面文字为准。
如有印装差错，由本社发行部调换。

编者说明

EDITOR'S NOTE

一、《2020广州统计年鉴》是一本全面反映广州经济和社会发展的资料工具书。本书通过大量的统计数据，全面客观地记录了2019年及重要历史年份广州市经济、社会的发展情况。

二、全书内容分为18个篇目，即：1. 综合；2. 人口；3. 从业人员和工资；4. 固定资产投资；5. 能源和环保；6. 财政和金融；7. 价格指数；8. 人民生活；9. 城市建设；10. 农业；11. 工业；12. 建筑业；13. 运输和邮电；14. 国内贸易；15. 对外经济贸易和旅游；16. 规模以上服务业；17. 科技；18. 教育、文化、体育、卫生、社会福利和其他。在附录部分，收集了全国、广东省及香港特别行政区、澳门特别行政区主要经济指标。

三、本年鉴资料主要来自广州市的政府各级统计局、国家统计局广州调查队的各种定期统计报表和抽样调查资料，部分资料来自省属、市属各主管部门。

四、2014年广州市行政区划有调整，原黄埔区和原萝岗区合并为新黄埔区，原增城市和原从化市撤市设区。从2015年起，我市行政区划包括荔湾区、越秀区、海珠区、天河区、白云区、黄埔区、番禺区、花都区、南沙区、从化区和增城区等11个区，无县级市。

五、从2014年起广州市实施城乡一体化分市县住户调查制度，住户调查统计指标体系有较大变动。

六、根据《国家统计局关于执行新国民经济行业分类国家标准的通知》（国统字〔2017〕142号）要求，新《国民经济行业分类》从2017年统计年报和2018年定期统计报表统一开始使用。本资料中凡是涉及到分行业的表式（除个别部门提供的数据仍按旧行业分类，表中有注明），均按照新的行业分类《国民经济行业分类GB/T4754-2017》作调整。

七、从2018年起，新增《规模以上服务业》篇。

八、本年鉴总量指标计算所采用的价格除注明外均为当年价格。

九、读者在使用历年资料时，凡与本年鉴有出入的，均以本年鉴为准。

十、本年鉴中部分数据合计数或相对数由于单位取舍不同而产生的计算误差，均未作机械调整。

十一、本年鉴表中的符号使用说明：“空格”表示该项统计指标数据不详或无该项数据；“…”表示数不足本表最小单位数；“#”表示其中的主要项。

2019年，根据第四次全国经济普查结果，对2008-2018年度地区生产总值、2010-2017年度工业、2011-2018年度年末全社会从业人员和1992-2018年度社会消费品零售总额数据进行了修订。

编者说明

EDITOR'S NOTE

Ⅰ. Guangzhou Statistical Yearbook 2020 (abbreviation as the Yearbook below)is an annual statistics publication, reflecting comprehensively the economic and social development of Guangzhou. It covers maily statistics in 2019 and some selected major data series in historically important years, at municipal level and local level of district.

Ⅱ. The Yearbook contains the following 18 chapters: 1. Gerneral Survey; 2. Population; 3. Employment and Wages; 4. Investment in Fixed Assets; 5. Energy and Environment; 6. Government Finance and Banking; 7. Price Indices; 8. People's Livelihood; 9. City Construction; 10. Agriculture; 11. Industry; 12. Construction; 13. Transport, Postal and Telecommunication Services; 14. Domestic Trade; 15. Foreign Economy and Tourism; 16. Service Industry above Scale; 17. Science and Technology; 18. Education, Culture, Sports, Public Health, Social Welfare and Others. The data listed in the Appendix are main economic indicators of China, Guangdong province, Hongkong Special Administrative Region and Macao Administrative Region.

Ⅲ. The data in the Yearbook are mainly obtained from regular ststistical reports and sample surveys conducted by statistics bureaus of all levels of government and the Surney office of the National Bureau of statistics in Guangzhou. Some data are collected from the departments of the provincial and municipal government.

Ⅳ. Since 2014 Guangzhou administrative division has been adjusted. The original Huangpu and Luogang districts have been merged into the new Huangpu district. The former Zengcheng City and the former Conghua City are divided into districts. Since 2015, Guangzhou city administrative division has included 11 districts, which are Liwan district, Yuexiu district, Haizhu district, Tianhe district, Baiyun district, Huangpu district, Panyu district, Huadu district, Nansha district, Conghua district and Zengcheng district, excluding county-level cities.

Ⅴ. From 2014 urban and rural integrated household survey is carried out in Guangzhou, statistical indicator system of urban and rural integrated household survey is changed greatly.

Ⅵ. According to the notice of the National Bureau of Statistics on the implementation of the new national standard of national economic industry classification (2017) 142, the new national economic industry classification has been used from the statistical annual report of 2017 and the periodic statistical report of 2018. In this data, all the tables related to sub-industries (except the data provided by individual departments are classified according to the old industry, as indicated in the table), are adjusted according to the new industry classification & GB/T4754-2017 of national economy.

Ⅶ. Starting from 2018, a new chapter entitled "Service Industry above scale" has been added.

Ⅷ. The prices used in calculation in the Yearbook are current prices except noted.

Ⅸ. In any case the data of this book shall be deemed as the authoritative ones.

Ⅹ. In the Yearbook all caculating errors of some total and regular figures for the differency of measuring units haven't been adjusted.

Ⅺ. Notations in this book: blank space indicates data are not available; "…" indicates not large enough to be rounded into the least unit of measurement; "#" indicates major item in a category.

In 2019, according to the results of the fourth national economic census, the 2008-2018 regional GDP, the 2010-2017 industry, the entire society's employees at the end of 2011-2018, and the total retail sales of consumer goods in 1992-2018 were revised.

综合
GENERAL SURVEY

地区生产总值（亿元）
[Gross Domestic Product (100 million yuan)]

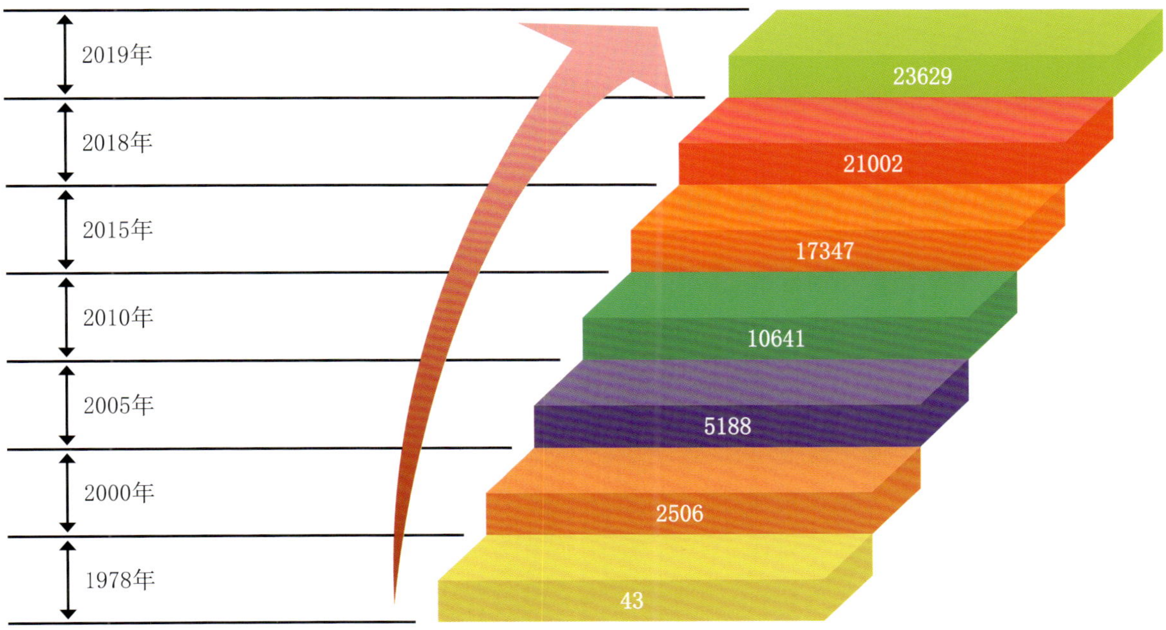

地区生产总值构成（%）
[Proportions in GDP (%)]

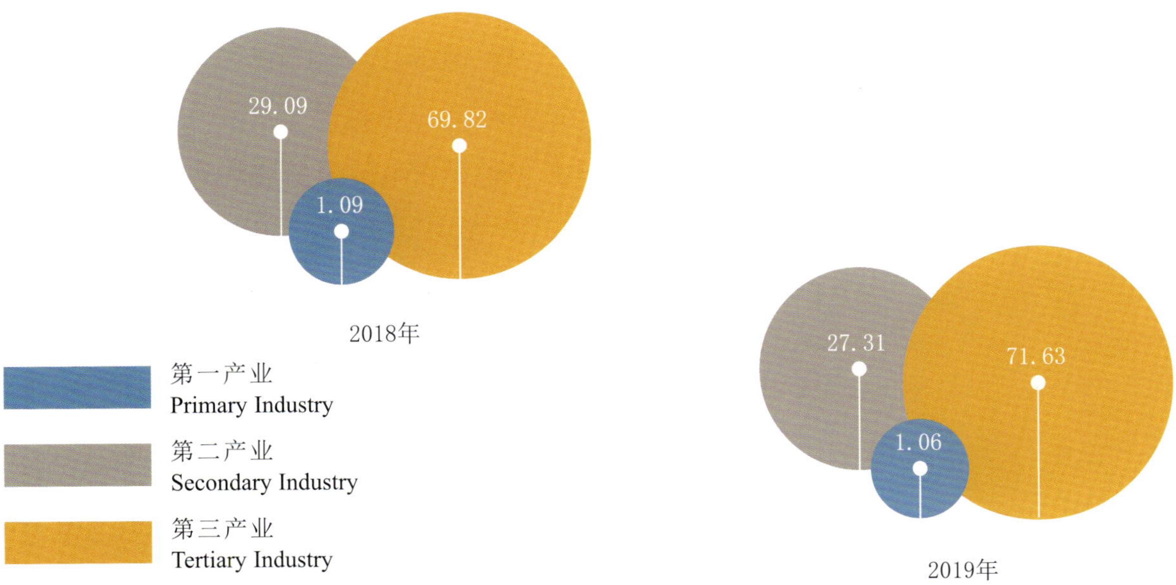

人口
POPULATION

年末户籍总人口（万人）
[Total Registered Permanent Residents at Year-end (10000 persons)]

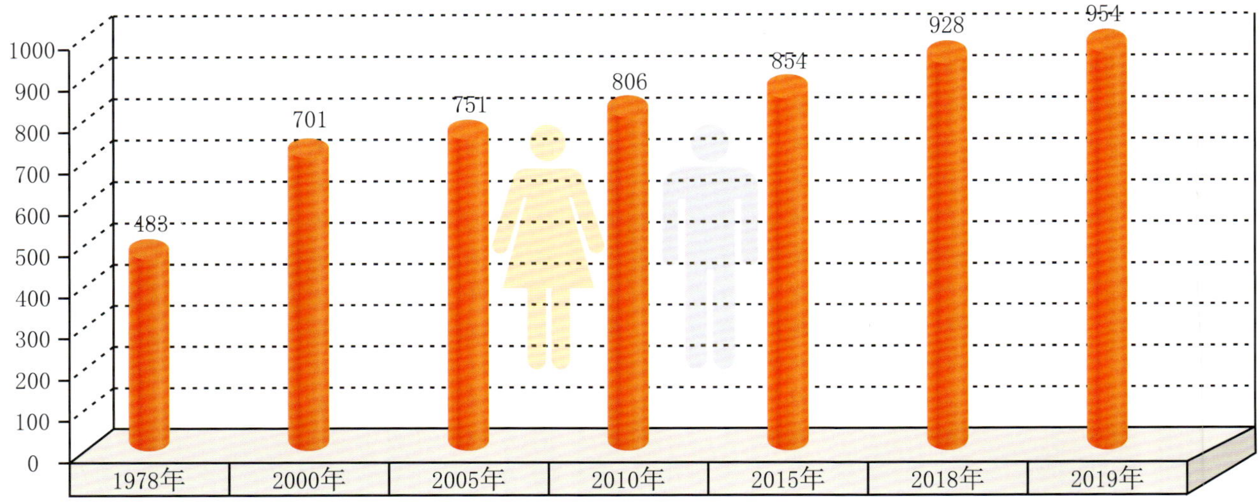

户籍人口自然增长率（‰）
[Natural Growth Rate of Registered Population (‰)]

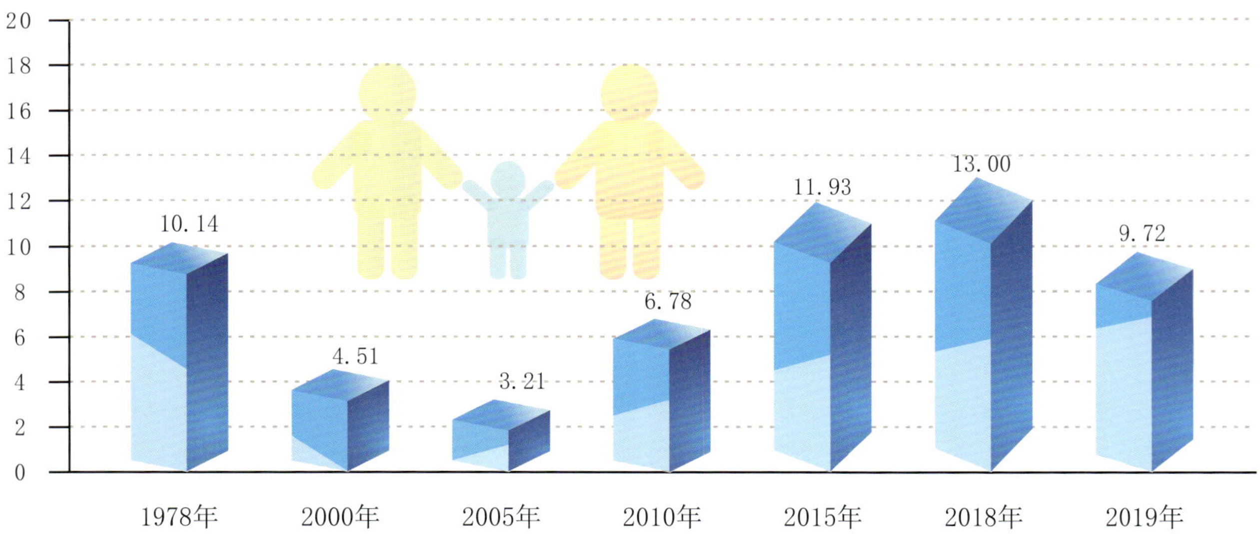

从业人员和工资
EMPLOYMENT AND WAGES

社会从业人员（万人）
[Number of Employed Persons (10000 persons)]

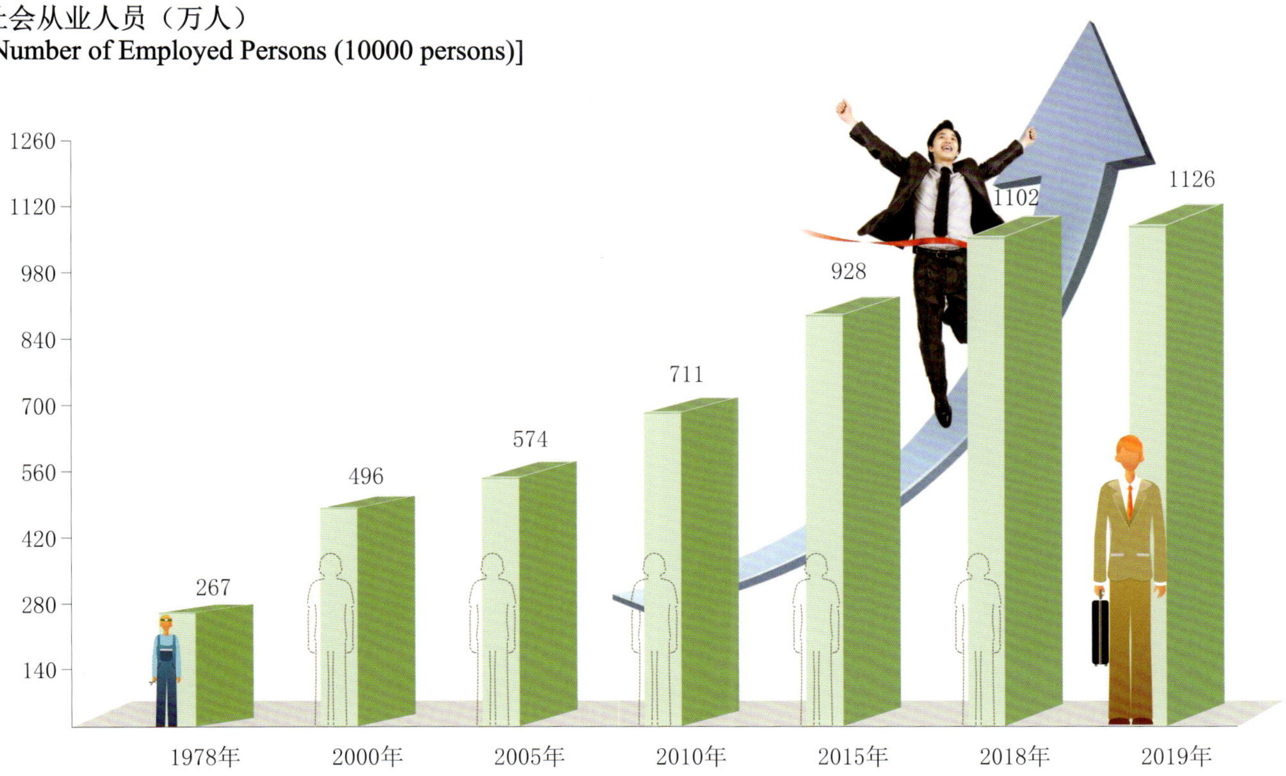

城镇非私营单位在岗职工年平均工资（元）
[Average Wage of Fully Employed Staff and Workers in Urban Units (yuan)]

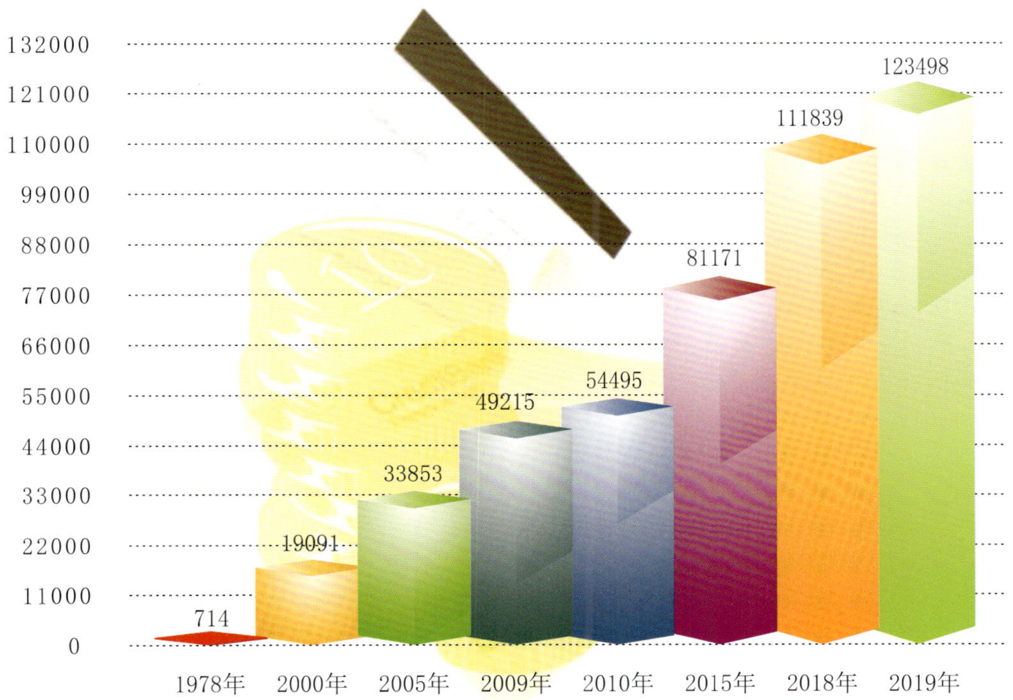

固定资产投资
INVESTMENT IN FIXED ASSETS

固定资产投资额（亿元）
[Total Investment in Fixed Assets (100 million yuan)]

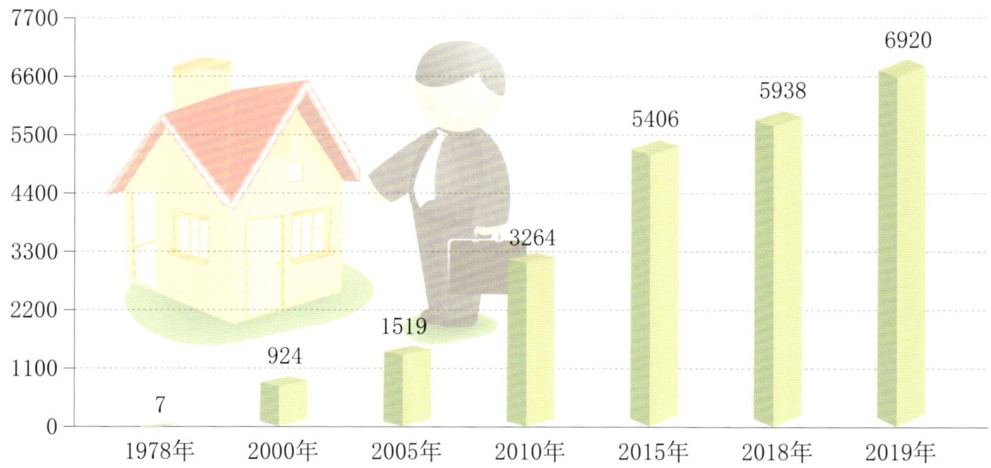

固定资产投资额三次产业构成（%）
[Compositions of Investment in Fixed Assets Classified by Three Strata of Industries (%)]

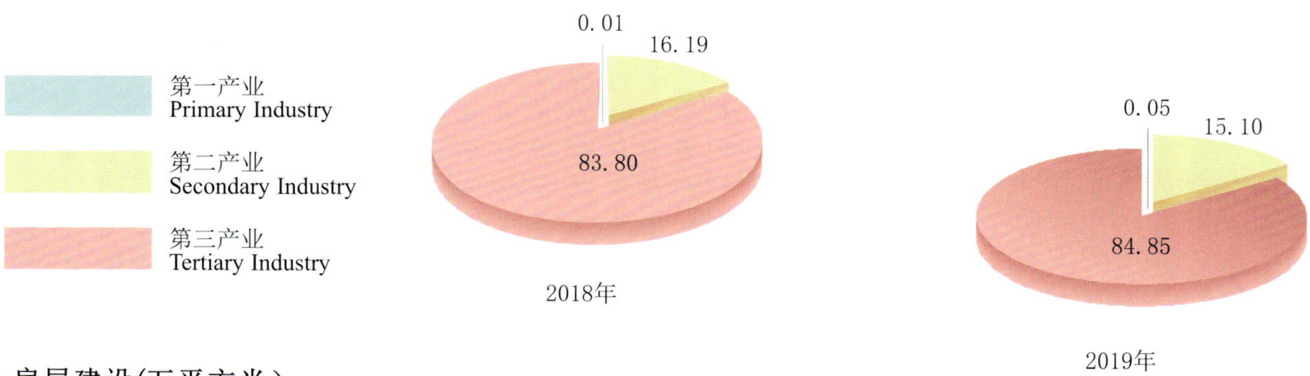

房屋建设(万平方米)
[Real Estate Development (10000 sq.m)]

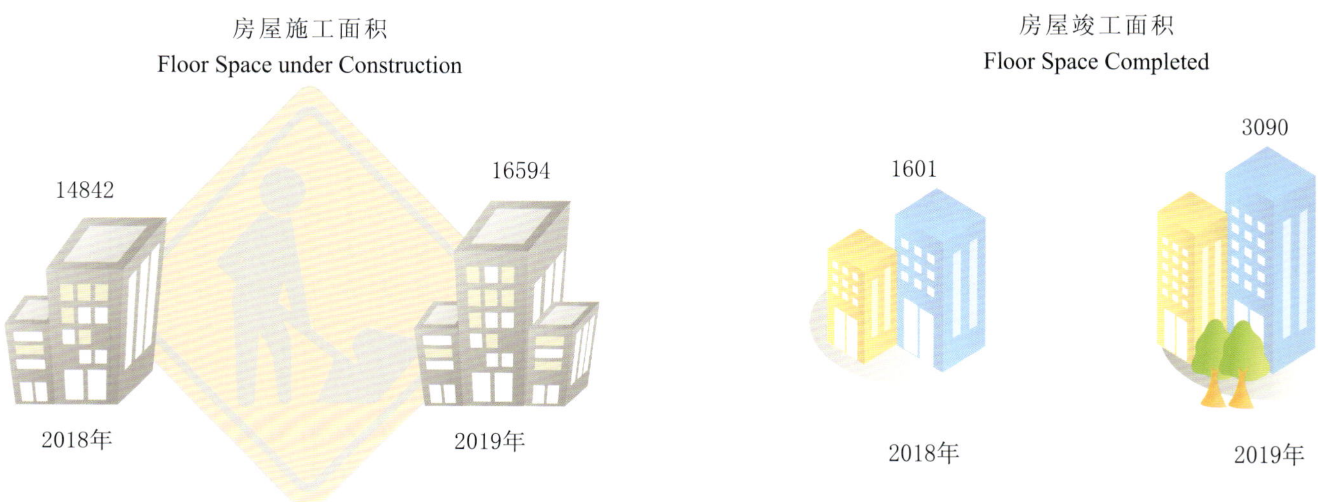

能源
ENERGY

能源消费总量（万吨标准煤）
[Total Energy Consumption (10000 tons of SCE)]

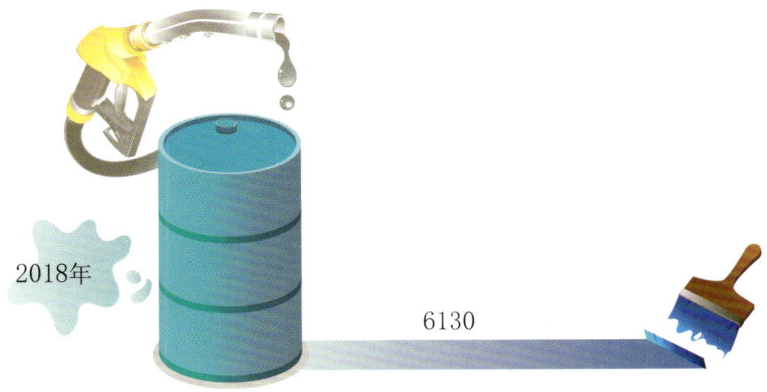

能源消费总量构成（%）（2019 年）
[Proportions of Total Energy Consumption (%) (2019)]

第一产业
Primary Industry

第二产业
Secondary Industry

第三产业
Tertiary Industry

生产消费
Production Consumption

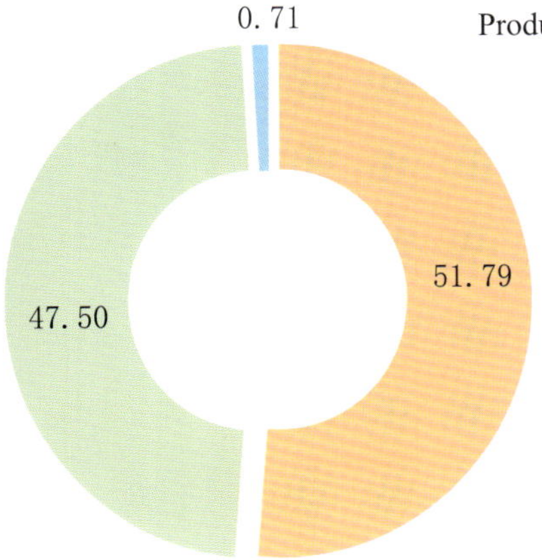

生活消费
Living Consumption

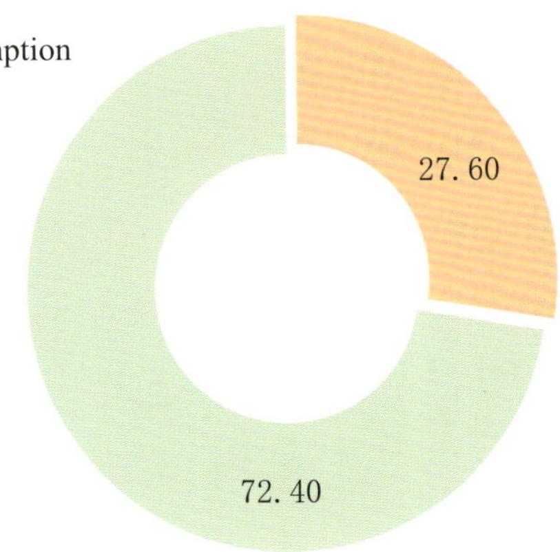

城镇
Urban Area

乡村
Rural Area

财政收支（按当年口径、亿元）
[Revenue and Expenditure of Local Government (at the Coverage of Current Year,100 million yuan)]

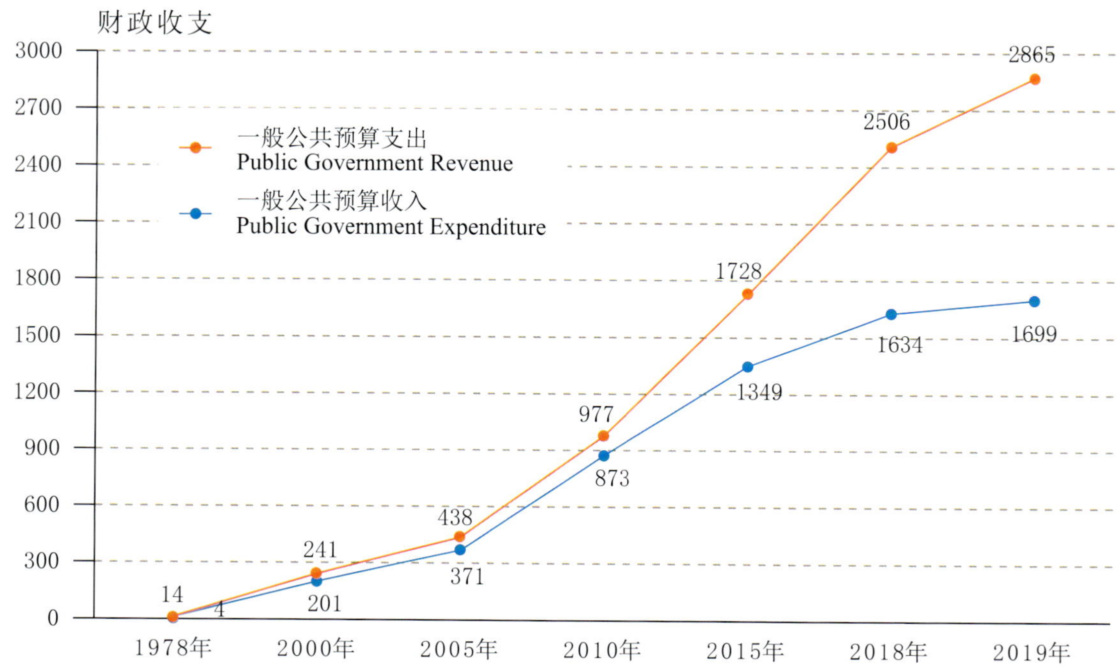

金融机构人民币存、贷款余额（亿元）
[RMB Saving Deposit and Loan of Financial Institutions (100 million yuan)]

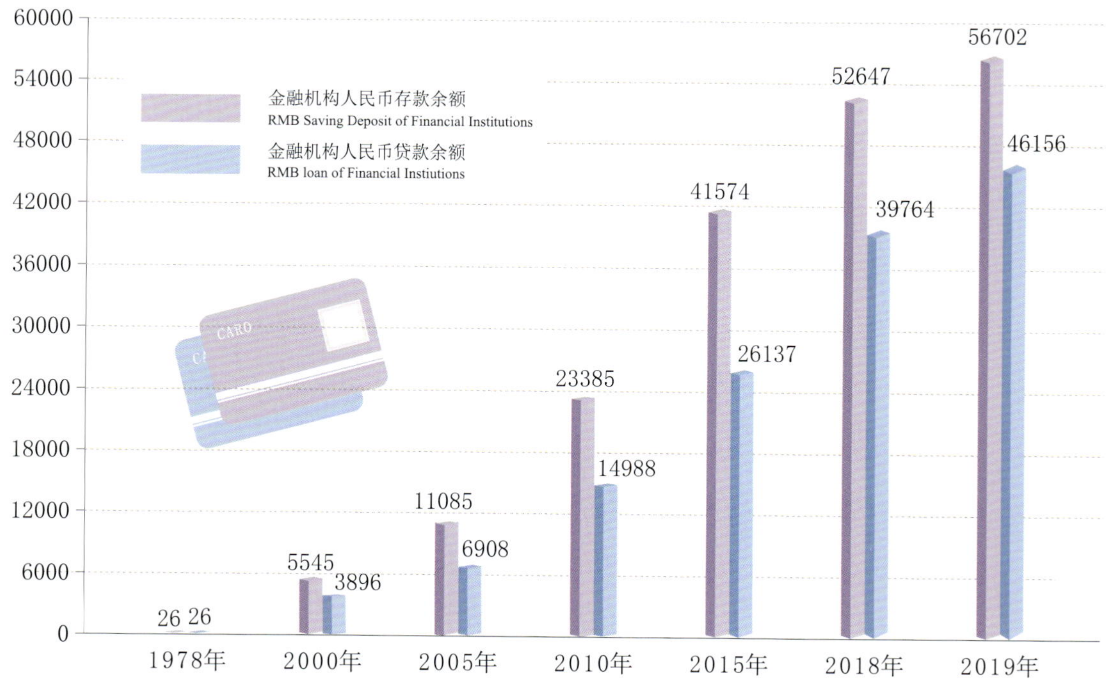

价格指数
PRICE INDICES

城市居民消费价格指数（以1978年价格为100）
[Urban Residents Consumer Price Indices (the price of 1978=100)]

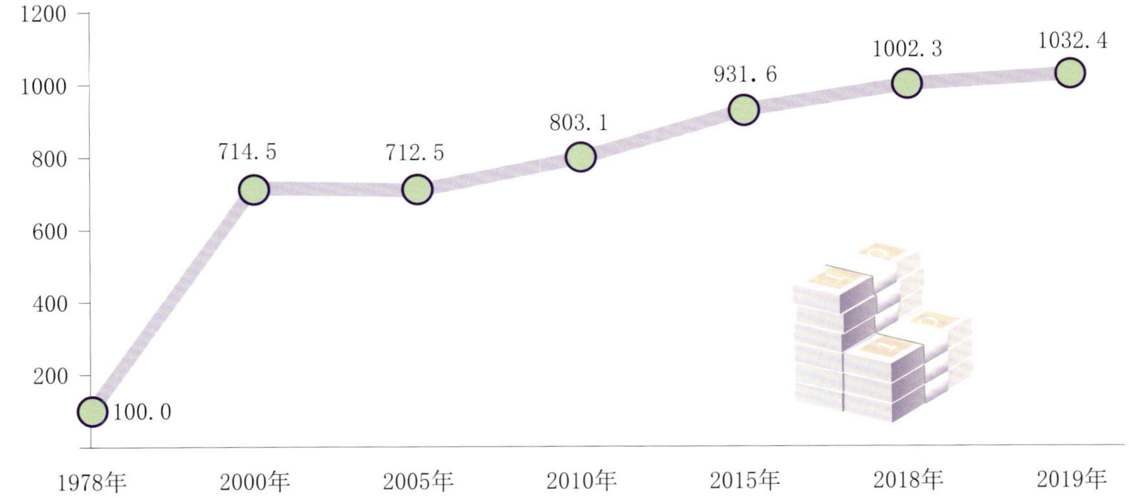

城市商品零售价格指数（以1978年价格为100）
[Urban Retail Price Indices in Main Years (the price of 1978=100)]

□ 城市居民年人均可支配收入（元）
[Per Capita Annual Disposable Income of Urban Residents (yuan)]

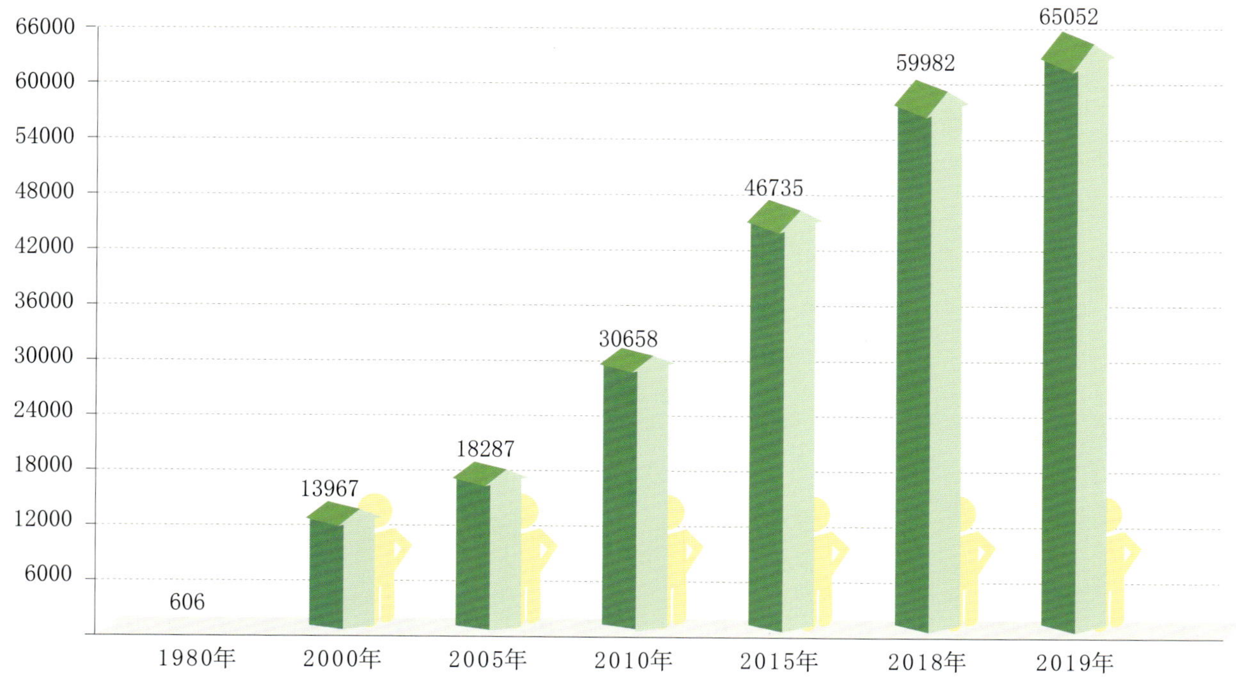

□ 农村居民年人均可支配收入（元）
[Per Capita Annual Net Income of Rural Residents (yuan)]

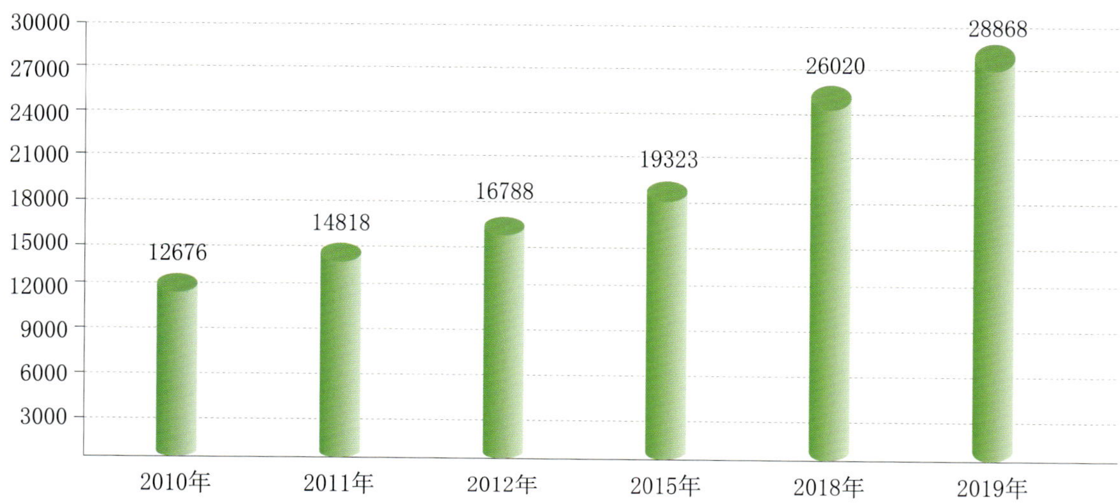

城市建设
CITY CONSTRUCTION

◻ 城市市政公用设施建设固定资产投资（亿元）
[Investment in Fixed Assets in Public Facilities in Urban Districts (100 million yuan)]

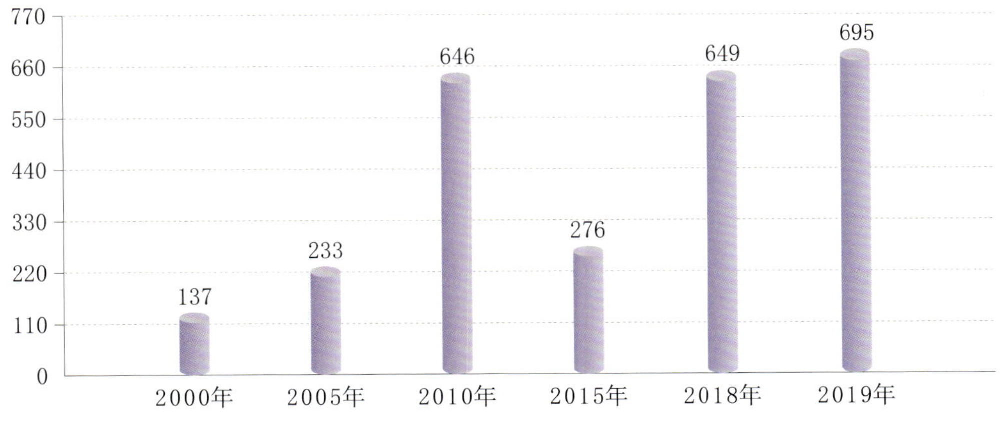

◻ 城市道路面积（万平方米）
[Roads Area in Urban Districts (10000 sq.m)]

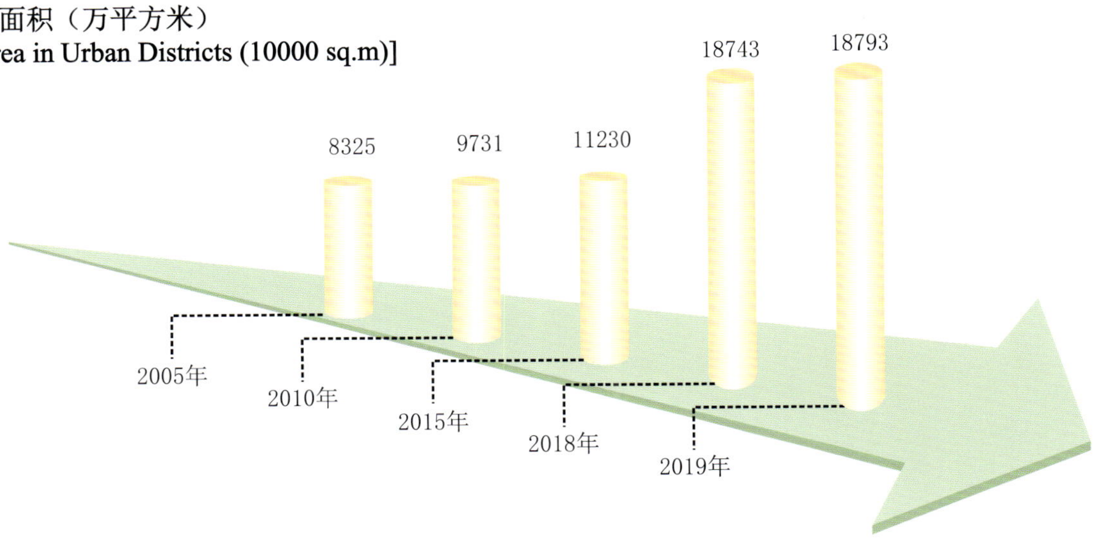

◻ 绿地面积（公顷）
[Area of Green Areas (hectare)]

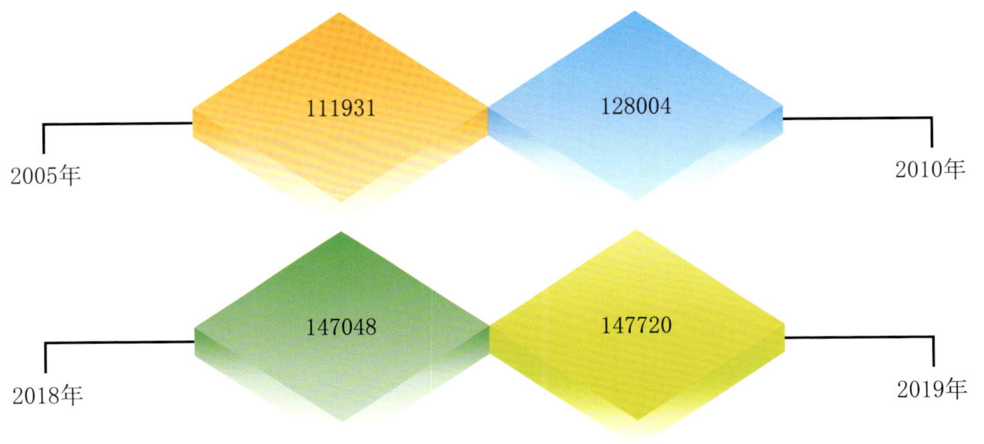

农、林、牧、渔业总产值及增加值（亿元）
[Gross Output Value and Added Value of Agriculture (100 million yuan)]

农、林、牧、渔业总产值
Gross Output Value of Agriculture

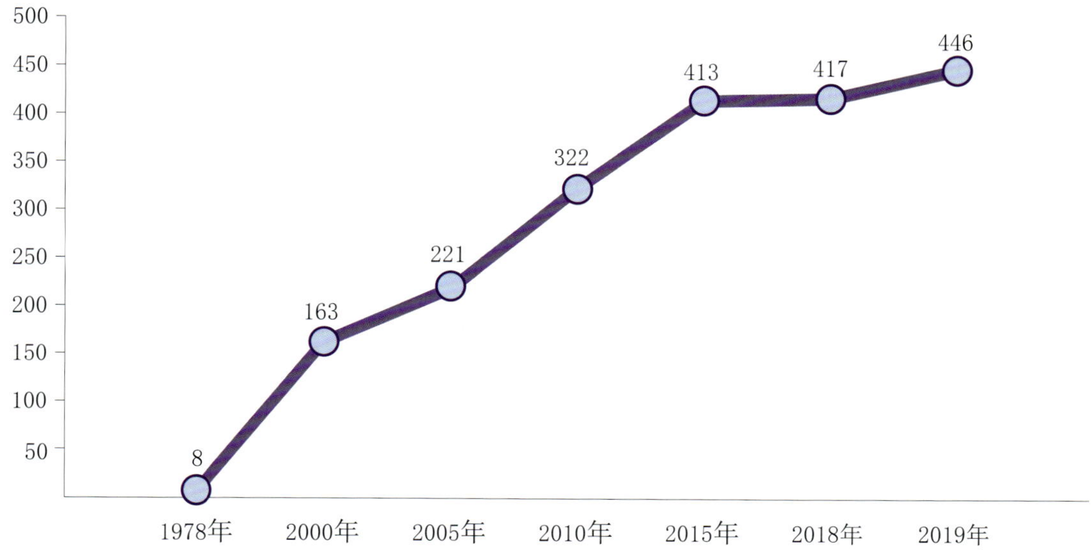

农、林、牧、渔业增加值
Added Value of Agriculture

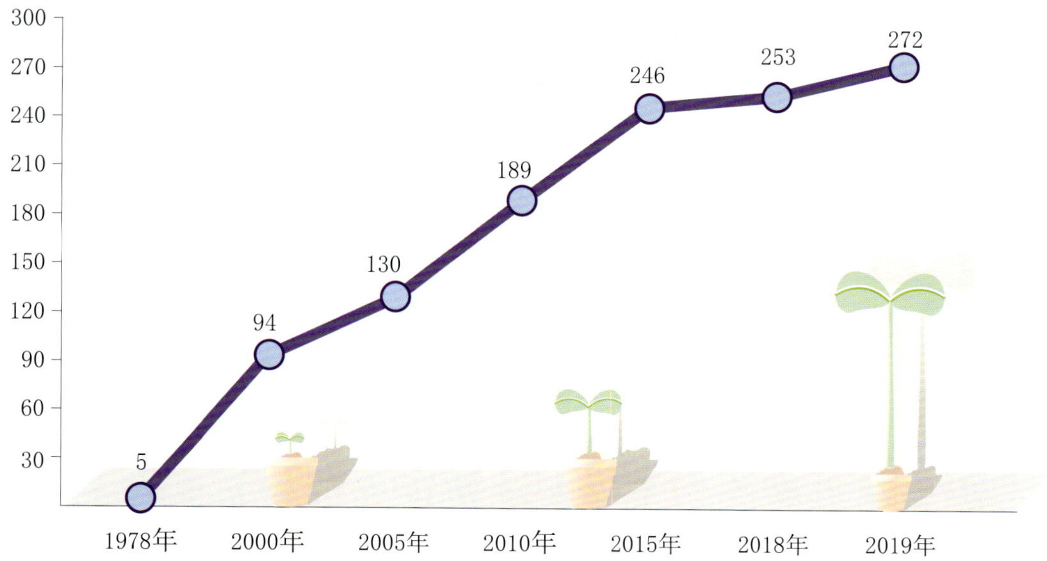

工 业
INDUSTRY

工业总产值（亿元）
[Gross Output Value of Industry (100 million yuan)]

规模以上工业总产值构成（%）（2019）
[Proportions in Gross Output Value of Industry Enterprises above Designated Size(%) (2019)]

按规模分
by Scale

按轻重工业分
by Light and Heavy Industries

建筑业
CONSTRUCTION

建筑业总产值（亿元）
[Gross Output Value (100 million yuan)]

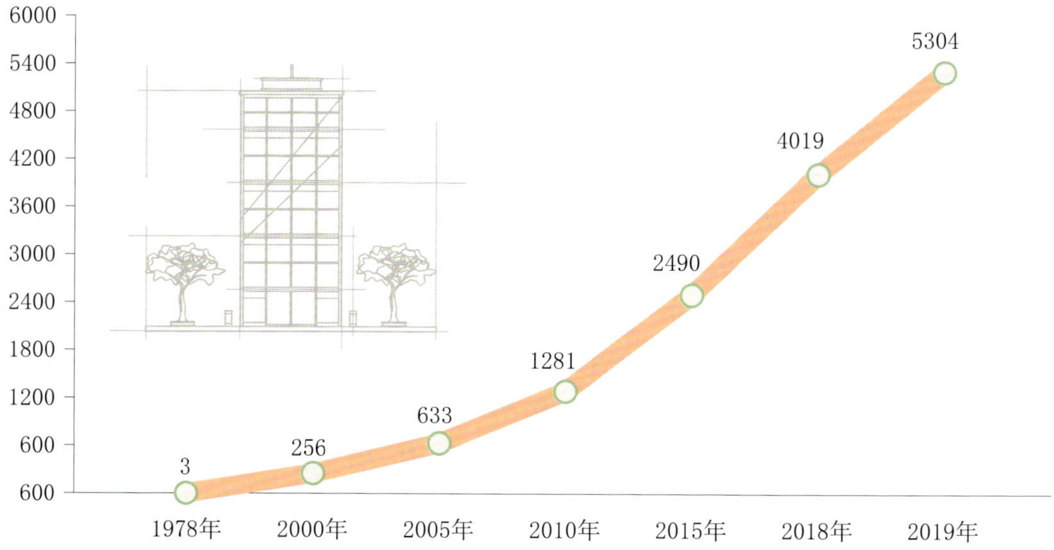

运输和邮电
TRANSPORT, POSTAL AND TELECOMMUNICATION SERVICES

邮电业务收入（亿元）
[Revenue of Postal and Telecommunication Services (100 million yuan)]

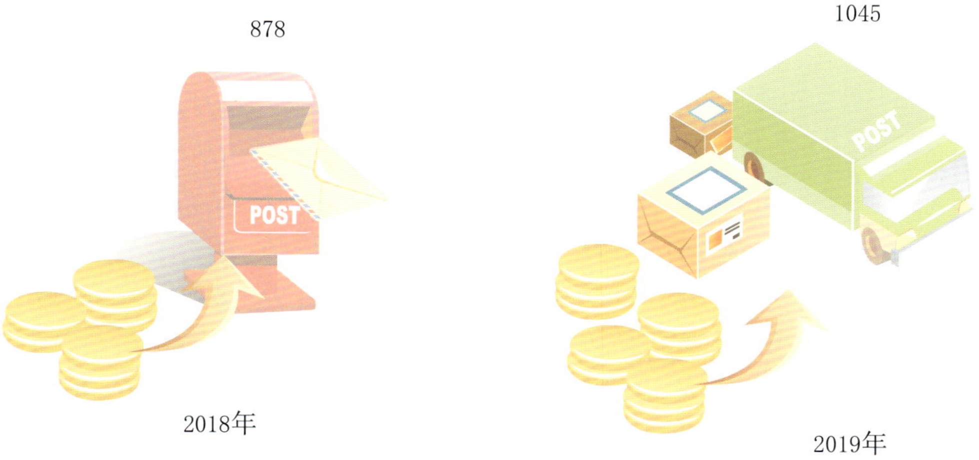

国内贸易
DOMESTIC TRADE

社会消费品零售总额（亿元）
[Retail Sale of Consumer Goods (100 million yuan)]

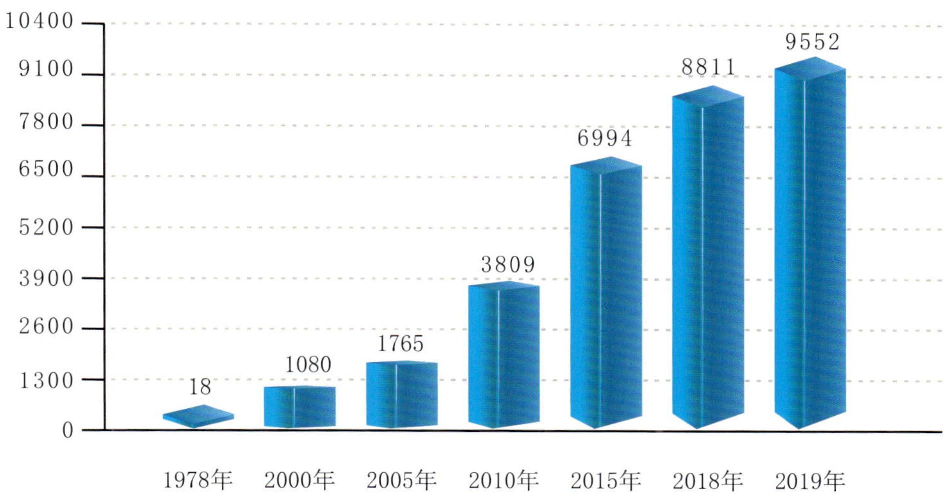

社会消费品零售总额构成（%）
[Proportions in Retail Sale of Consumer Goods (%)]

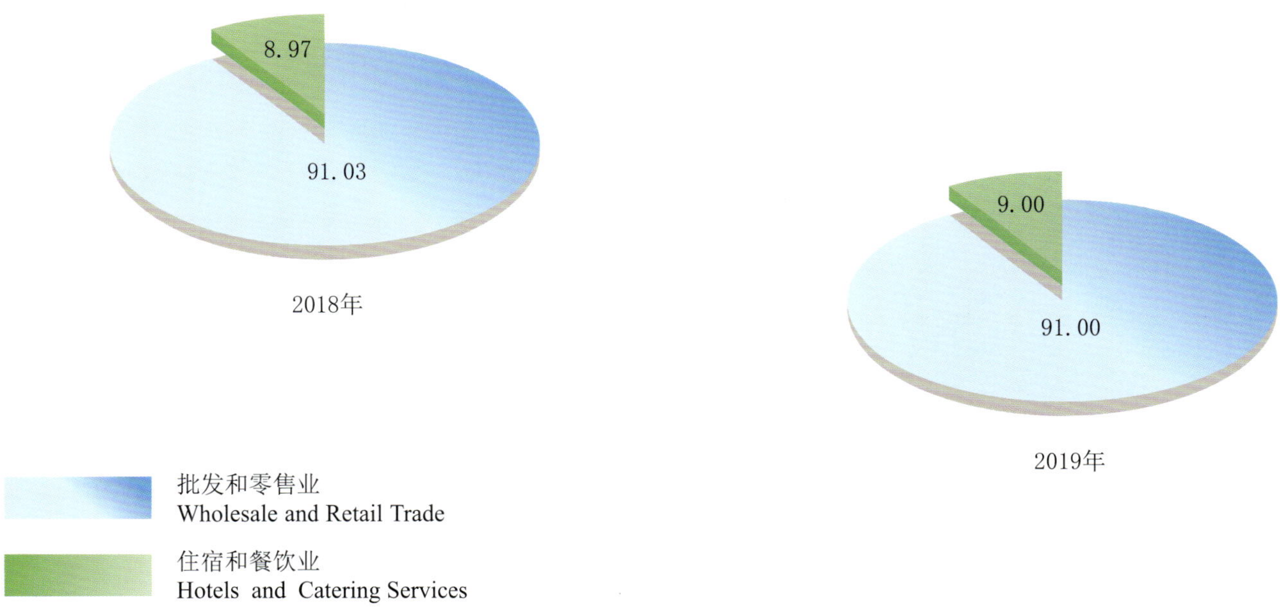

海外旅游者（万人次）
[International Tourists (10000 person-times)]

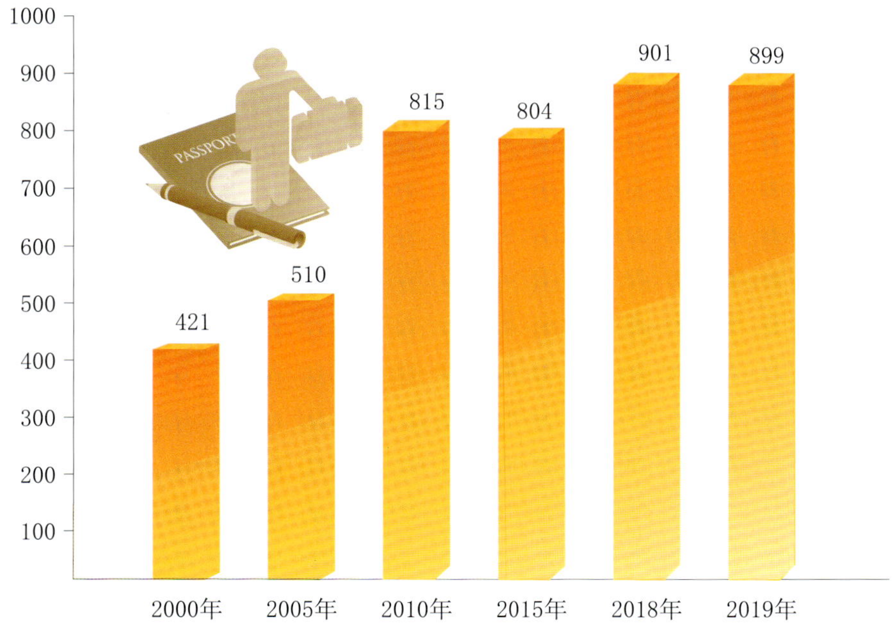

商品出口总值构成（%，以人民币计价）
[Proportions in Total Value of Export Comodities (%，Valuation in RMB)]

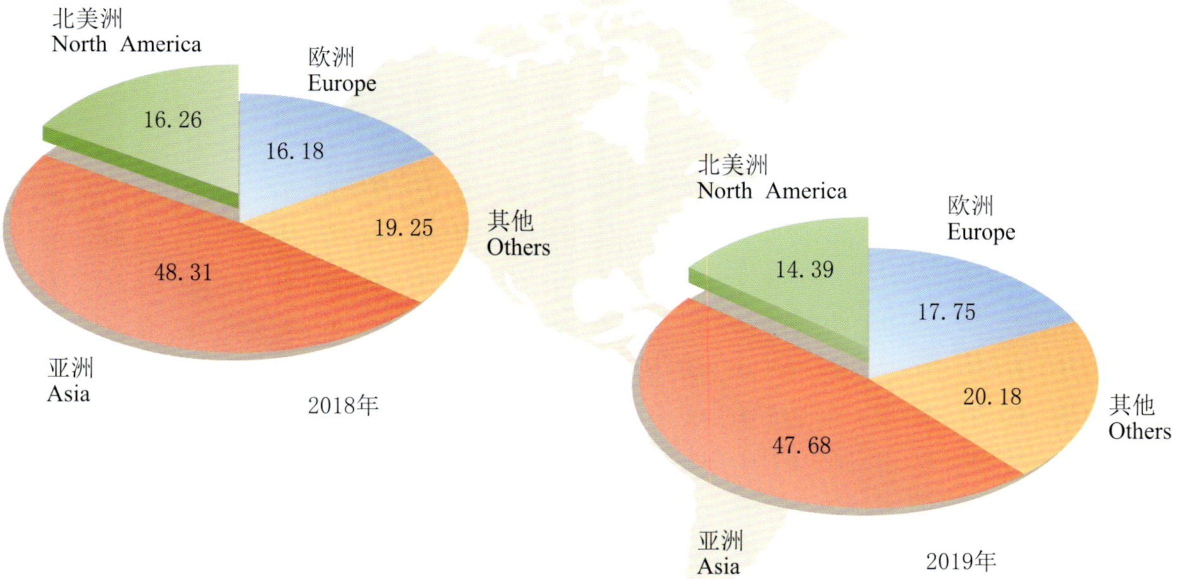

专利申请量和专利授权量
[Patent Applications and Patent Certified]

专利申请量（件）
Patent Applications (item)

专利授权量（件）
Patent Certified (item)

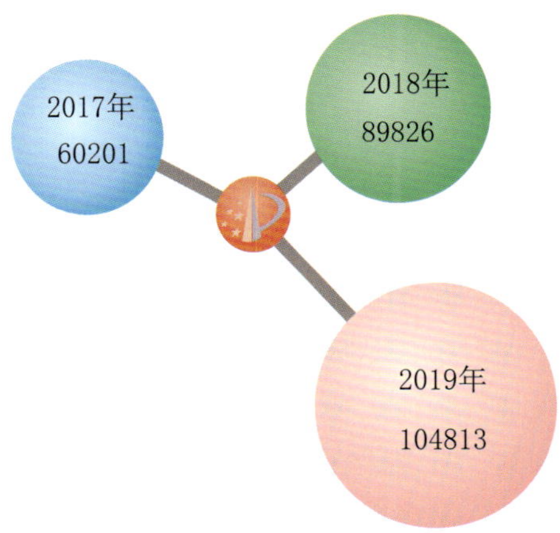

教育、文化、体育、卫生、社会福利和其他

EDUCATION, CULTURE, SPORTS, PUBLIC HEALTH, SOCIAL WELFARE AND OTHERS

各类学校及在校学生数
[Number of Schools and Enrolled Students]

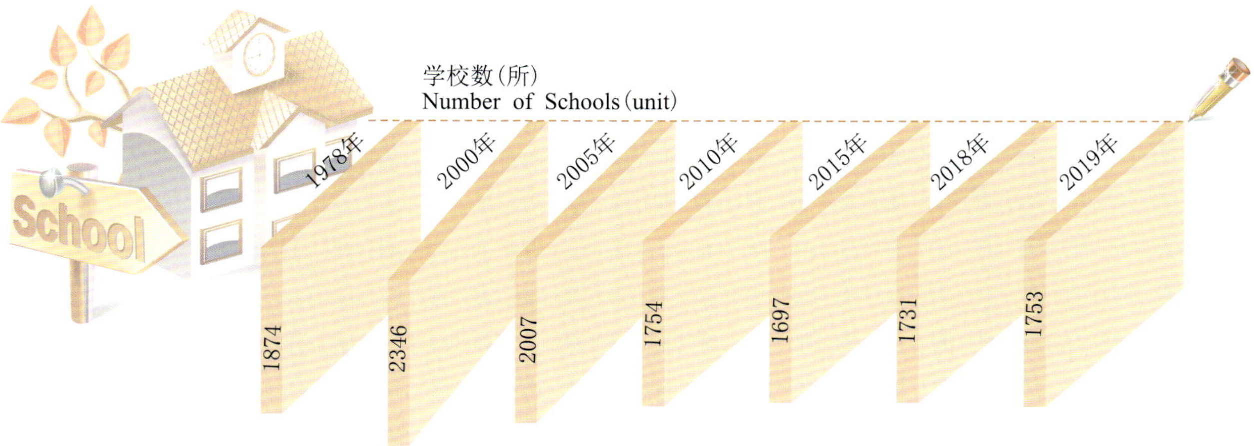

卫生事业机构床位数（张）
[Number of Beds in Health Institutions (unit)]

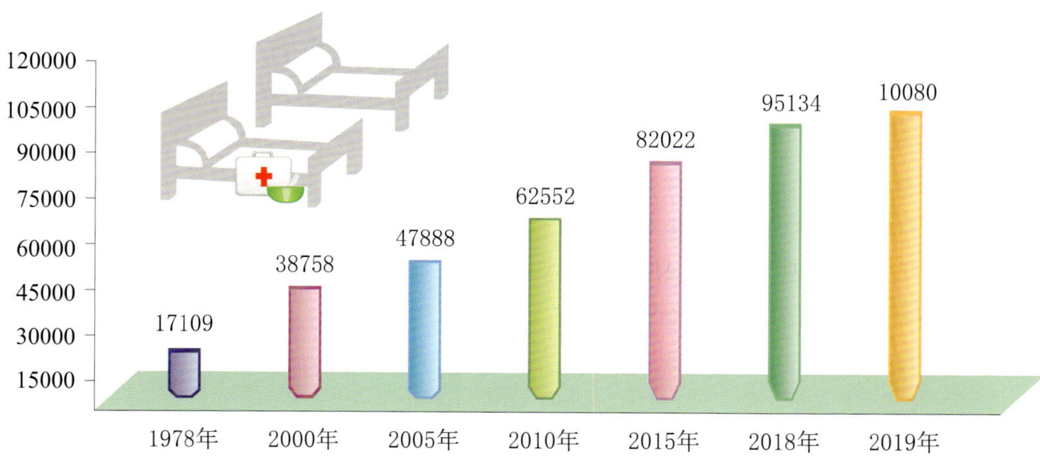

第一篇 综 合
General Survey

简要说明 …… 2
Brief Introduction

1-1 行政区划 (2019年末) …… 3
Administrative Divisions (Year-end of 2019)

1-2 各月平均温度、湿度 (2019年) …… 4
Monthly Average Temperature and Humidity (2019)

1-3 各月降雨量、日照时数 (2019年) …… 4
Monthly Precipitation and Sunshine Hours (2019)

1-4 行政区域面积和人口密度 (2019年) …… 5
Land Area and Population Density (2019)

1-5 法人和产业活动单位数 …… 6
Number of Corporate Units and Industrial Establishments

1-6 按登记注册类型分组的法人单位数 (2018 年) …… 10
Number of Corporate Units by Sector and by Status of Registration (2018)

1-7 按登记注册类型分组的法人单位数 (2019 年) …… 14
Number of Corporate Units by Sector and by Status of Registration (2019)

1-8 国民经济和社会发展总量与速度指标 …… 18
Principal Aggregate Indicators on National Economic and Social Development and Growth Rates

1-9 各时期主要指标平均每年增长速度 …… 22
Average Annual Growth Speed of Main Indicators in Different Periods

1-10 全市产业及主要结构情况 …… 23
Basic Statistics on Industries and Main Structure of Guangzhou

1-11 主要年份人民物质文化生活水平 …… 24
Material and Culture Life of the People in Main Years

1-12 主要年份地区生产总值 …… 26
Gross Domestic Product in Main Years

1-13 主要年份地区生产总值指数 (上年 =100) …… 27
Indices of Gross Domestic Product in Main Years (Preceding Year=100)

1-14 主要年份地区生产总值构成 …… 28
Composition of Gross Domestic Product in Main Years

1-15 地区生产总值 …… 29
Gross Domestic Product

1-16 各时期地区生产总值和平均每年增长速度 …… 30
Gross Domestic Product and Annual Average Growth Speed in Different Periods

1-17 三次产业对地区生产总值增长的贡献率 (1990-2019年) …… 31
Share of the Contributions of the Three Strata of Industry to the Growth of GDP (1990-2019)

1-18 三次产业对地区生产总值增长的拉动 (1990-2019年) …… 32
Contribution of the Three Strata of Industry to the Growth of GDP (1990-2019)

1-19 全市国有土地使用权出让、划拨情况 …… 33
Total City Lease and Administrative Allocation of the Right to the Use of the State-owned Land
1-20 全市房地产市场交易情况 …… 34
Transactions in Total Real Estate Market
1-21 劳动力市场情况 …… 35
Statistics on Labor Force Market
1-22 技术市场交易情况 …… 35
Statistics on Transactions in Technological Market
1-23 各区国民经济主要指标 (2019 年) …… 36
Main Indicators of National Economic by District (2019)
1-24 广州开发区国民经济主要指标 …… 38
Main Indicators of National Economy of Guangzhou Development Zone
1-25 广州保税区国民经济主要指标 …… 39
Main Indicators of National Economy of Guangzhou Bonded Zone
1-26 广州高新技术产业开发区国民经济主要指标 …… 39
Main Indicators of National Economy of Guangzhou Hi-tech Development Zone
1-27 私营企业基本情况 (2019 年末，按行业分) …… 40
Basic Statistics on Private Enterprises (Year-end of 2019, by Sector)
1-28 私营企业基本情况 (2019 年末，按地区分) …… 42
Basic Statistics on Private Enterprises (Year-end of 2019, by Region)
1-29 个体工商户情况 …… 43
Basic Statistics on Individual Business
1-30 个体工商户情况 (2019 年末，按行业分) …… 44
Basic Statistics on Individual Business (Year-end of 2019, by Sector)
1-31 内资企业基本情况 (2019 年末) …… 46
Basic Statistics on Domestic-Funded Enterprises (Year-end of 2019)
主要统计指标解释 …… 48
Explanatory Notes on Main Statistical Indicators

第二篇 人 口
Population

简要说明 …… 54
Brief Introduction
2-1 主要年份全市年末户籍总户数、总人口数 …… 55
Total Registered Households and Population at Year-end in Main Years
2-2 主要年份全市年末户籍常住户口户数、常住户口人口数 …… 56
Permanent Registered Households and Population at Year-end in Main Years
2-3 主要年份全市户籍总人口自然变动情况 …… 57
Statistics on Natural Changes of Total Registered Population in Main Years
2-4 各区、县级市年末人口数 (2005-2014 年) …… 58
Population at Year-end by District and County-level City (2005-2014)

2-5 主要年份各区年末人口数 …… 59
Population at Year-end by District in Main Years
2-6 各区户籍总人口自然变动状况 (2019 年) …… 60
Statistics on Natural Changes of Total Registered Population by District (2019)
2-7 各区户籍人口迁移状况 (2019 年) …… 61
Statistics on Migration of Registered Population by District (2019)
2-8 各区计划生育情况 (2019 年) …… 62
Statistics on Family Planning by District (2019)
2-9 各区户籍人口年龄构成 (2019) …… 63
The Registered Population Age Composition by District (2019)
2-10 主要年份各区常住人口城镇人口比重 (2010-2019 年) …… 64
The Proportion of Urban Population in the Permanent Population by District in Main Years (2010-2019)
主要统计指标解释 …… 65
Explanatory Notes on Main Statistical Indicators

第三篇 从业人员和工资
Employment and Wages

简要说明 …… 68
Brief Introduction
3-1 社会就业情况主要指标 …… 69
Main Indicators of Social Employment Situation
3-2 主要年份全社会从业人员人数 …… 70
Number of Employed Persons in Main Years
3-3 主要年份三次产业从业人员及构成 …… 71
Employed Persons and Composition by Three strata of Industry in Main Years
3-4 三次产业全社会从业人员及构成 (2019 年末) …… 72
Employed Persons and Composition by Three Strata of Industry (Year-end of 2019)
3-5 全市全社会从业人员 (2019 年末) …… 73
Number of Employed Persons (Year-end of 2019)
3-6 主要年份城镇非私营单位从业人员数及工资 …… 74
Number and Wages of Employed Persons in Urban Units in Main Years
3-7 主要年份城镇非私营单位在岗职工工资总额及指数 …… 75
Total Wages of Fully Employed Staff and Workers in Urban Units and Related Indices in Main Years
3-8 城镇非私营单位从业人数与工资 (2019 年) …… 77
Number and Wages of Employed Persons in Urban Units (2019)
3-9 全市城镇非私营单位在岗职工人数与工资 (2019 年) …… 78
Number and Wages of Fully Employed Staff and Workers in Urban Units (2019)
3-10 城镇国有单位在岗职工人数与工资 (2019 年) …… 82
Number and Wages of Fully Employed Staff and Workers in Urban State-owned Units (2019)
3-11 城镇集体单位在岗职工人数与工资 (2019 年) …… 84
Number and Wages of Fully Employed Staff and Workers in Urban Collective-owned Units (2019)

3-12 城镇非私营其他单位在岗职工人数与工资 (2019 年) ………… 86
Number and Wages of Fully Employed Staff and Workers in Urban Other Types of Ownership (2019)
3-13 城镇非私营单位从业人员女性年末人数 (2019 年) ………… 88
Number of Female Staff and Workers at Year-end in Urban Units (2019)
主要统计指标解释 ………… 90
Explanatory Notes on Main Statistical Indicators

第四篇 固定资产投资 Investment in Fixed Assets

简要说明 ………… 92
Brief Introduction
4-1 固定资产投资主要经济指标 ………… 93
Main Indicators of Total Investment in Fixed Assets
4-2 主要年份按经济类型分固定资产投资额 ………… 94
Total Investment in Fixed Assets in Main Years by Type of Ownership
4-3 主要年份按经济类型分固定资产投资额指数 (上年 =100) ………… 96
Indices of Total Investment in Fixed Assets in Main Years by Type of Ownership (preceding year=100)
4-4 主要年份按投资类别分固定资产投资额 ………… 97
Total Investment in Fixed Assets in Main Years by Type of Investment
4-5 主要年份按投资类别分固定资产投资额指数 (上年 =100) ………… 98
Indices of Total Investment in Fixed Assets in Main Years by Type of Investment (preceding year=100)
4-6 各时期按投资类别分固定资产投资额 ………… 99
Total Investment in Fixed Assets in Different Periods by Type of Investment
4-7 各时期按投资类别分固定资产投资额平均每年增长速度 ………… 100
Average Growth Rate of Investment in Fixed Assets in Different Periods by Type of Investment
4-8 主要年份按三次产业分固定资产投资额 ………… 101
Total Investment in Fixed Assets and its Construction in Main Years by Three Strata of Industries
4-9 主要年份按构成分固定资产投资额 ………… 102
Total Investment in Fixed Assets in Main Years by Use of Funds
4-10 主要年份房屋建设情况 ………… 103
Total Investment in Fixed Assets and Building Construction in Main Years
4-11 固定资产投资额 (2019 年) ………… 104
Total Investment in Fixed Assets (2019)
4-12 各区固定资产投资主要指标 (2019 年，按项目所在地分) ………… 108
Main Indicators of Investment in Fixed Assets by Districts (2019, by Tegion of Item)
4-13 民间固定资产投资情况 (2019 年) ………… 110
Investment in Fixed Assets by Private Units (2019)
4-14 工业及工业技术改造固定资产投资情况 (2019 年) ………… 111
Investment in Fixed Assets in Industrial and Technological Renovation (2019)
4-15 住宅投资建设情况 (2019 年) ………… 112
Housing Investment and Construction (2019)

4-16 主要年份基础设施投资额 …… 113
Total Investment of Infrastructure in Main Years
4-17 基础设施固定资产投资情况（2019 年）…… 114
Infrastructure Fixed Assets Investment (2019)
4-18 新增固定资产（2019 年）…… 115
Total Newly Increased Fixed Assets (2019)
4-19 固定资产投资资金来源（2019 年）…… 117
The Funds Sources of Fixed Assets Investment (2019)
4-20 房地产开发与经营（2019 年，按法人单位办公所在地分）…… 118
Real Estate Development and Management (2019, by the Locations of the Offices of Corporate Units)
4-21 房地产开发与经营（2019 年，按项目所在地分）…… 120
Real Estate Development and Management (2019, by Region of Item)
4-22 房地产开发投资额和新增固定资产（2019 年）…… 122
Investment and Newly Increased Fixed Assets in Real Estate Development (2019)
4-23 房地产开发房屋面积（2019 年）…… 124
Floor Space of Buildings in Real Estate Development (2019)
4-24 房地产开发资金来源（2019 年）…… 126
Real Estate Development by Source of Funds (2019)
4-25 房地产开发主要财务指标（2019 年）…… 128
Main Financial Indicators of Real Estate Development (2019)
主要统计指标解释 …… 130
Explanatory Notes on Main Statistical Indicators

第五篇 能源和环境
Energy and Environment

简要说明 …… 132
Brief Introduction
5-1 能源生产量 …… 133
Energy Production
5-2 主要年份能源消耗基本情况 …… 134
Energy Consumption in Main Years
5-3 能源消费总量 …… 135
Total Consumption of Energy
5-4 规模以上工业企业能源加工转换效率 …… 135
Efficiency of Energy Conversion by Industrial Enterprises above the Designated Size
5-5 规模以上工业企业分行业主要能源消费量（2019 年）…… 136
Consumption of Main Energy by Industrial Sector above the Designated Size (2019)
5-6 主要年份全市用电量 …… 140
Total Electricity Supply in Main Years
5-7 全市分行业用电量 …… 142
Electricity Consumption by Industrial Sector

5-8 主要年份环境保护基本情况 …… 144
Fundamental State of Environment Protection in Main Year
5-9 环境保护基本情况 …… 146
Fundamental State of Environment Protection
主要统计指标解释 …… 148
Explanatory Notes on Main Statistical Indicators

第六篇 财政和金融
Government Finance and Banking

简要说明 …… 150
Brief Introduction
6-1 财政和金融业主要经济指标 …… 151
Main Indicators of Government Finance and Financial Intermediation
6-2 主要年份地方财政收支 …… 152
Local Government Revenue and Expenditure in Main Years
6-3 地方财政收入 …… 153
Revenue of Local Government
6-4 地方财政支出 …… 154
Expenditure of Local Government
6-5 主要年份金融机构（含外资）存贷款余额 …… 155
Deposits and Loans in All Financial Institutions (Foreign Currencies) in Main Years
6-6 中外资金融机构本外币存贷款年末余额 …… 156
Deposits and Loans in Renminbi and Foreign Currencies of All Financial Institutions at Year-end
6-7 中外资金融机构外币存贷款年末余额 …… 157
Deposits and Loans in Foreign Currencies of All Financial Institutions at Year-end
6-8 中外资金融机构存贷款年末余额（折人民币，2008-2019 年） …… 158
Deposits and Loans of All Financial Institutions at Year-end (converted into RMB, at the end of year from 2008 to 2019)
6-9 中外资金融机构人民币信贷资金平衡表 …… 159
Credit Funds Balance Sheet of Financial Institutions
6-10 中资金融机构人民币各项存贷款年末余额 …… 160
Deposits and Loans in Renminbi of Chinese Financial Institutions at Year-end
6-11 上市公司及新三板概况（2011-2019 年） …… 160
Listed Companies and NEEQ-listed Companies (2011-2019)
6-12 证券市场股票筹资概况（2011-2019 年） …… 161
Equity Financing of Securities Market (2011-2019)
6-13 证券市场交易额概况（2011-2019 年） …… 161
Turnover of Securities Market (2011-2019)
6-14 主要年份原保险保费收入和赔款及给付支出 …… 162
Premium of Primary Insurance and Payment in Main Years
6-15 保险公司主要业务指标（2019 年） …… 163
Major Business Indicators of Insurance Companies (2019)

6-16 财产保险公司主要指标 ………… 163
Main Indicators of Property Insurance Companies
6-17 人身保险公司主要指标 ………… 164
Main Indicators of Personal Insurance Companies
6-18 主要外资金融机构及代表处一览表 ………… 166
List of Main Foreign Financial Institutions and Representative Offices
6-19 外资保险公司及代表处一览表 ………… 168
List of Foreign Insurance Companies and Representative Offices
6-20 金融机构人民币法定存款利率 ………… 169
Official Interest Rates of Deposits of Financial Institutions
6-21 金融机构人民币法定贷款利率 ………… 170
Official Interest Rates of Loans of Financial Institutions
主要统计指标解释 ………… 171
Explanatory Notes on Main Statistical Indicators

第七篇 价格指数
Price Indices

简要说明 ………… 174
Brief Introduction
7-1 主要年份城市居民消费价格指数 ………… 175
Urban Residents Consumer Price Indices in Main Years
7-2 城市居民消费价格分类指数 (上年 =100) ………… 176
Urban Residents Consumer Price Indices by Category (Preceding Year=100)
7-3 主要年份城市商品零售价格指数 ………… 177
Urban Retail Price Indices in Main Years
7-4 城市商品零售价格指数 (上年 =100) ………… 178
Urban Retail Price Indices by Category (Preceding Year=100)
7-5 主要食品平均价格 ………… 179
Average Price of Major Food
7-6 主要年份工业生产者价格指数 (上年＝100) ………… 180
Price Indices for Industrial Products in Main Years (Preceding Year=100)
7-7 工业生产者出厂价格指数 (上年＝100) ………… 181
Producer Price Index for Industrial Products (Preceding Year=100)
7-8 按工业行业分工业生产者出厂价格指数 ………… 182
Producer Price Indices for Industrial Products by Sector
7-9 工业生产者购进价格指数(上年＝100) ………… 183
Purchasing Price Index for Industrial Producers (Preceding Year=100)
7-10 固定资产投资价格指数 (上年 =100) ………… 184
Prices Indices of Investment in Fixed Assets (Preceding Year=100)
7-11 各月住宅销售价格指数 (2019 年,上年同期 =100) ………… 185
Sales Prices Indices of Residence Buildings (2019,Preceding Year=100)

主要统计指标解释 …… 186
Explanatory Notes on Main Statistical Indicators

第八篇 人民生活 People's Livelihood

简要说明 …… 188
Brief Introduction
8-1 城乡居民人均全年可支配收入和消费支出情况 …… 189
Per Capita Annual Disposable Income and Expenditure for Consumption of Urban and Rural Residents
8-2 城乡居民家庭平均每百户年末耐用消费品拥有量 …… 190
Ownership of Major Durable Consumer Goods per 100 Urban and Rural Households at Year-end
8-3 城市居民家庭基本情况（2019 年） …… 191
Basic Conditions of Urban Households (2019)
8-4 按收入五等份分组的城市居民人均收支及构成（2019 年） …… 192
Per Capita Income and Expenditure of Urban Residents Grouped by Five Income Parts and Their Composition (2019)
8-5 城市居民人均可支配收入、恩格尔系数及人均住房建筑面积 …… 194
Per Capita Annual Disposable Income，Engel's Coefficient and Per Capita Housing Construction Area of Urban Households
8-6 城市居民家庭年末居住情况（2019 年） …… 195
Housing Conditions of Urban Households at Year-end (2019)
8-7 主要年份农村居民人均可支配收入、恩格尔系数及人均住房建筑面积 …… 196
Per Capita Annual Disposable Income，Engel's Coefficient and Per Capita Housing Construction Area of Rural Households in Main Years
8-8 农村居民家庭基本情况（2019 年） …… 197
Basic Conditions of Rural Households (2019)
8-9 按收入五等份分组的农村居民人均收支及构成（2019 年） …… 198
Per Capita Income and Expenditure of Rural Residents Grouped by Five Income Parts and Their Composition (2019)
主要统计指标解释 …… 200
Explanatory Notes on Main Statistical Indicators

第九篇 城市建设 City Construction

简要说明 …… 202
Brief Introduction
9-1 城市市政设施 …… 203
Public Facilities in Urban Districts
9-2 城市供水 …… 204
Water Supply in Urban Districts
9-3 城市燃气供应 …… 205
Gas Supply in Urban Districts
9-4 城市市政公用设施建设固定资产投资额 …… 205
Investment in Fixed Assets in Public Facilities in Urban Districts

9-5 城市园林绿化 …… 206
Parks, Gardens and Green Areas in Urban Districts
9-6 城市市容环境卫生 …… 206
City Appearance and Environmental Sanitation
主要统计指标解释 …… 207
Explanatory Notes on Main Statistical Indicators

第十篇 农 业
Agriculture

简要说明 …… 210
Brief Introduction
10-1 农业主要指标 …… 211
Major Indicators of Agriculture
10-2 主要年份年末耕地面积 …… 212
Area of Cultivated Land at Year-end in Main Years
10-3 耕地面积及变动情况 (2019 年) …… 213
Statistics on Area of Cultivated Land and Its Changes (2019)
10-4 农村基层基本情况 (2019 年) …… 214
Basic Statistics on Rural Grassroots Units (2019)
10-5 农林牧渔业生产经营户及从业人员情况 (2019 年) …… 216
Number of Households and Laborers Engaging in Agriculture, Forestry, Animal Husbandry and Fishery (2019)
10-6 主要年份农林牧渔业总产值 …… 218
Gross Output Value of Agriculture, Forestry, Animal Husbandry and Fishery in Main Years
10-7 主要年份农林牧渔业总产值指数 …… 219
Indices of Gross Output Value of Agriculture, Forestry, Animal Husbandry and Fishery in Main Years
10-8 农林牧渔业总产值、增加值和商品产值 (2019 年) …… 220
Gross Output Value, Value-added and Commodity Output Value of Agriculture, Forestry, Animal Husbandry and Fishery (2019)
10-9 按历史时期分农林牧渔业总产值 …… 222
Gross Output Value of Agriculture, Forestry, Animal Husbandry and Fishery by History Period
10-10 渔业生产情况 (2019 年) …… 223
Statistics on Fishery Production (2019)
10-11 畜牧业生产情况 (2019 年) …… 224
Statistics on Animal Husbandry Production (2019)
10-12 农村电力、化肥用量和农田水利建设情况 (2019 年) …… 226
Statistics on Electricity, Chemical Fertilizer Consumption and Construction of Water Conservancy Works in Rural Areas (2019)
10-13 农业机械总动力和拥有量 (2019 年) …… 228
Total Power and Possession of Major Agricultural Machinery (2019)
10-14 主要农作物及水果种植面积和产量 (2019 年) …… 230
Sown Area and Output of Major Farm Crops and Fruits (2019)
10-15 主要农产品产量与建国以来最高年份比较 (2019 年) …… 232
Output of Major Farm Products in Comparison with that of Peak Year since 1949 (2019)

10-16 农业生产水平 …… 233
Production Level of Agriculture, Animal Husbandry and Fishery
10-17 建制镇社会经济发展基本情况 (2019 年) …… 234
Basic Statistics on Social and Economic Development of Towns (2019)
10-18 全市村委会社会经济基本情况 (2019 年) …… 236
Social and Economic Information of Village Committees (2019)
10-19 都市农业主要指标 …… 240
Main Economic Indicators of Urban Agriculture
主要统计指标解释 …… 241
Explanatory Notes on Main Statistical Indicators

第十一篇 工 业
Industry

简要说明 …… 244
Brief Introduction
11-1 工业总产值 …… 245
Gross Output Value of Industry
11-2 主要年份工业总产值及工业总产值指数 …… 247
Gross Output Value and Indices of Industry in Main Years
11-3 按历史时期分工业总产值 …… 248
Gross Output Value of Industry by History Periods
11-4 规模以上工业企业单位数 …… 249
Number of Industrial Enterprises above the Designated Size
11-5 规模以上工业销售产值 …… 251
Sales Value of Industrial Enterprises above the Designated Size
11-6 主要年份规模以上工业企业出口交货值及比重 …… 251
Delivery Value of Exports and Proportion of Industrial Enterprises above the Designated Size in Main Years
11-7 规模以上工业企业出口交货值 (2019 年) …… 252
Delivery Value of Exports of Industrial Enterprises above the Designated Size (2019)
11-8 工业三大支柱产业主要指标 (2019 年) …… 254
Major Indicators of Three Pillar Industrial Industries (2019)
11-9 主要工业产品产量 (2019 年) …… 255
Output of Major Industrial Products (2019)
11-10 主要年份规模以上工业企业全员劳动生产率 …… 257
Overall Labor Productivity of Industrial Enterprises above the Designated Size in Main Years
11-11 规模以上工业企业全员劳动生产率(2019 年，按行业分) …… 258
Overall Labor Productivity of Industrial Enterprises above the Designated Size (2019, by Sector)
11-12 主要年份规模以上工业企业主要经济指标 …… 260
Main Indicators of Industrial Enterprises above the Designated Size in Main Years
11-13 规模以上工业企业主要经济指标 (2019 年) …… 262
Main Indicators of Industrial Enterprises above the Designated Size (2019)

11-14 规模以上工业企业主要经济指标（2019 年，按轻重工业分）…… 264
Main Indicators of Industrial Enterprises above the Designated Size (2019, by Light and Heavy Industry)
11-15 规模以上工业企业主要经济指标（2019 年，按经济类型分）…… 266
Main Indicators of Industrial Enterprises above the Designated Size (2019, by Type of Ownership)
11-16 规模以上工业企业主要经济指标（2019 年，按企业规模分）…… 268
Main Indicators of Industrial Enterprises above the Designated Size (2019, by Size of Enterprises)
11-17 规模以上工业企业主要经济指标（2019 年，按行业分）…… 270
Main Indicators of Industrial Enterprises above the Designated Size (2019, by Sector)
11-18 规模以上大中型工业企业主要经济指标（2019 年，按轻重工业分）…… 276
Major Indicators of Large and Medium-sized Industrial Enterprises above the Designated Size (2019, by Light and Heavy Industry)
11-19 规模以上大中型工业企业主要经济指标（2019 年，按经济类型分）…… 278
Major Indicators of Large and Medium-sized Industrial Enterprises above the Designated Size (2019, by Type of Ownership)
11-20 规模以上工业企业主要经济效益指标 …… 280
Main Indicators on Economic Benefit of Industrial Enterprises above the Designated Size
11-21 规模以上工业企业主要经济效益指标（2019 年，按轻重工业分）…… 282
Main Indicators on Economic Benefit of Industrial Enterprises above the Designated Size (2019, by Light and Heavy Industry)
11-22 规模以上工业企业主要经济效益指标（2019 年，按经济类型分）…… 284
Main Indicators on Economic Benefit of Industrial Enterprises above the Designated Size (2019, by Type of Ownership)
11-23 规模以上工业企业主要经济效益指标（2019 年，按企业规模分）…… 286
Main Indicators on Economic Benefit of Industrial Enterprises above the Designated Size (201, by Size of Enterprises)
11-24 规模以上工业企业分组主要指标（2019 年）…… 288
Major Indicators of Industrial Enterprises above the Designated Size by Group (2019)
主要统计指标解释 …… 289
Explanatory Notes on Main Statistical Indicators

第十二篇 建筑业
Construction

简要说明 …… 292
Brief Introduction
12-1 资质以上建筑业企业主要经济指标 …… 293
Major Indicators of Grade Construction Enterprises
12-2 主要年份建筑业主要指标 …… 294
Major Indicators of Construction Sector in Main Years
12-3 资质以上建筑业企业签订合同情况（2019 年）…… 295
Statistics on Construction Contracts of Grade Construction Enterprises (2019)
12-4 资质以上建筑业企业生产情况（2019 年）…… 296
Statistics on Production of Grade Construction Enterprises (2019)
12-5 资质以上建筑业企业承包工程完成情况（2019 年）…… 300
Statistics on Contracted Projects of Grade Construction Enterprises (2019)

12-6 资质以上建筑业企业财务指标 (2019 年) …… 302
Financial Indicators of Grade Construction Enterprises (2019)
12-7 资质以上建筑业企业盈亏情况 (2019 年) …… 308
Statistics on Profits and Losses of Grade Construction Enterprises (2019)
主要统计指标解释 …… 310
Explanatory Notes on Main Statistical Indicators

第十三篇 运输和邮电
Transport, Postal and Telecommunication Services

简要说明 …… 312
Brief Introduction
13-1 运输邮电主要指标 …… 313
Basic Statistics of Transport and Post
13-2 公路和航道线路基本情况 …… 314
Basic Statistics on Highways and Waterways
13-3 民用车辆拥有量 (2019 年) …… 315
Possession of Civil Vehicles (2019)
13-4 营业性民用运输轮驳船拥有量 …… 316
Possession of Business Civil Transport Vessels
13-5 主要年份客货运输 (吞吐量)和邮电业务收入 …… 317
Total Passenger and Freight Traffic and Revenue of Postal and Telecommunication Services in Main Years
13-6 民航运输主要指标 …… 319
Main Indicators on Civil Aviation
13-7 民航航线及飞机年末数 …… 320
Number of Civil Aviation Routes and Civil Aircraft at Year-end
13-8 白云国际机场吞吐量 …… 321
Volume Handled in Baiyun International Airport
13-9 输油 (气)管道基本情况 (2019 年) …… 322
Basic Statistics on Pipelines (2019)
13-10 港口码头泊位数 …… 322
Number of Berths in Ports
13-11 港口吞吐量及货物分类 (2019 年) …… 323
Volume Handled in Ports and Type of Freight (2019)
13-12 港口标准集装箱吞吐量 (2019 年) …… 324
Cargo Handled in International Standard Containers (2019)
13-13 邮政电信网 …… 325
Network of Postal and Telecommunication Services
13-14 邮政业务主要指标 …… 326
Main Indicators on Post
13-15 电信业务主要指标 …… 327
Main Indicators on Telecommunication Services

13-16 邮电业务收入 …… 328
Revenue of Postal and Telecommunication Services
13-17 城市公共交通 (2019 年) …… 329
Public Traffic in City (2019)
13-18 规模以上运输邮电企业财务指标 (2019 年) …… 330
Finance Indicators of Transport, Postal and Telecommunication Services Enterprises above the Designated Size (2019)
主要统计指标解释 …… 332
Explanatory Notes on Main Statistical Indicators

第十四篇 国内贸易
Domestic Trade

简要说明 …… 334
Brief Introduction
14-1 主要年份社会消费品零售总额 …… 335
Total Retail Sales of Consumer Goods in Main Years
14-2 主要年份社会消费品零售总额指数 …… 336
Indices of Total Retail Sales of Consumer Goods in Main Years
14-3 各时期社会消费品零售总额 …… 337
Total Retail Sales of Consumer Goods in Different Periods
14-4 社会消费品零售总额 …… 338
Total Retail Sales of Consumer Goods
14-5 限额以上批发和零售业法人企业商品分类销售总额 (2019 年) …… 339
Total Sales Value of Enterprises above Designated Size in Wholesale and Retail Trade by Category of Commodities (2019)
14-6 限额以上批发业法人企业商品购、销、存总额 (2019 年) …… 340
Total Purchases, Sales and Stock of Enterprises above Designated Size in Wholesale Trade (2019)
14-7 限额以上零售业法人企业商品购、销、存总额 (2019 年) …… 342
Total Purchases, Sales and Stock of Enterprises above Designated Size in Retail Trade (2019)
14-8 限额以上批发业法人企业财务状况 (2019 年) …… 344
Financial Situation of Enterprises above Designated Size in Wholesale Trade (2019)
14-9 限额以上零售业法人企业财务状况 (2019 年) …… 350
Financial Situation of Enterprises above Designated Size in Retail Trade (2019)
14-10 限额以上住宿业法人企业基本情况 (2019 年) …… 356
Basic Statistics of Enterprises above Designated Size of Hotels (2019)
14-11 限额以上餐饮业法人企业基本情况 (2019 年) …… 358
Basic Statistics of Enterprises above Designated Size of Catering Sevices (2019)
14-12 限额以上住宿业法人企业财务状况 (2019 年) …… 360
Financial Situation of Enterprises above Designated Size of Hotels (2019)
14-13 限额以上餐饮业法人企业财务状况 (2019 年) …… 366
Financial Situation of Enterprises above Designated Size of Catering Services (2019)
14-14 连锁店 (公司)基本情况 (2019 年) …… 372
Statistics on Chain Stores (Companies) (2019)

14-15 亿元以上商品交易市场成交情况 (2019 年) ······ 374
Statistics on Commodity Exchange Markets with Total Sale over 100 Million Yuan (2019)
主要统计指标解释 ······ 375
Explanatory Notes on Main Statistical Indicators

第十五篇 对外经济贸易和旅游 Foreign Economy and Tourism

简要说明 ······ 378
Brief Introduction
15-1 主要年份商品进出口总值和商品进出口总值指数 ······ 379
Total Value and Indices of Import and Export Commodities in Main Years
15-2 商品进出口总值 (人民币计价) ······ 380
Total Value of Import and Export Commodities through Customs (Renminbi-denominated)
15-3 商品进出口总值 (美元计价) ······ 384
Total Value of Import and Export Commodities through Customs (U.S.dollar-denominated)
15-4 商品进出口总值 (2019 年，按地区分) ······ 388
Total Value of Import and Export Commodities through Customs (2019, by Region)
15-5 主要进口商品数量和金额 ······ 390
Main Import Commodities in Volume and Value
15-6 主要出口商品数量和金额 ······ 392
Main Export Commodities in Volume and Value
15-7 进出口商品分类金额 (按人民币计价) ······ 394
Value of Imports and Exports by Category of Commodities (Renminbi-denominated)
15-8 进出口商品分类金额 (按美元计价) ······ 400
Value of Imports and Exports by Category of Commodities (U.S.dollar-denominated)
15-9 广州地区口岸进出口商品总值 ······ 406
Commodity Value of Imports and Exports through Ports in Guangzhou Area
15-10 软件出口和技术进口情况 ······ 406
Software Export and Technology Import
15-11 历年利用外资情况 ······ 407
Statistics on Utilization of Foreign Capital in Main Years
15-12 历年利用外资项目 (企业)个数、合同外资金额、实际使用外资金额指数 (上年 =100) ······ 408
Indices of Contracts Number, Contracted Foreign Capital and Foreign Capital Actually Used in Main Years (Preceding Year=100)
15-13 外商直接投资情况 ······ 409
Statistics on Foreign Direct Investment
15-14 外商直接投资情况 (按地区分) ······ 410
Statistics on Utilization of Foreign Direct Investment Capital (by Region)
15-15 外商直接投资项目分类 (2019 年) ······ 411
Amount of Foreign Direct Investment Capital Actually Used by Category (2019)

15-16 境外企业情况 (2019 年) …… 413
Statistics on Overseas Enterprises Funded by Domestic Capital (2019)
15-17 对外劳务合作业务情况 (2019 年) …… 415
Statistics on Labor Cooperation with Foreign Countries or Territories (2019)
15-18 主要年份对外经济合作业务情况 …… 416
Contracted Projects and Labor Cooperation with Foreign Countries or Territories in Main Years
15-19 旅游业总收入、外汇收入情况 (2019 年) …… 416
Total Income from Tourism and Foreign Exchange Earnings (2019)
15-20 城市接待过夜旅游者情况 …… 417
Tourists Staying Overnight in Guangzhou
15-21 主要宾馆 (酒店) 基本情况 …… 418
Statistics on Main Hotels
15-22 旅行社基本情况 …… 419
Statistics on Travel Agencies
15-23 主要年份人民币对主要外币年平均汇价 …… 420
Average Exchange Rates of RMB Against Main Convertible in Main Years
15-24 外商投资企业及分支机构工商登记情况 (2019) …… 421
Statistics on Foreign Funded Enterprises Registered by Departments of Industry and Commerce (2019)
15-25 广州市与国外结成友好城市一览 (2019 年末) …… 422
List of Foreign Friendly Cities with Guangzhou (Year-end of 2019)
15-26 各国驻广州总领事馆一览 (2019 年末) …… 423
List of Consulate General in Guangzhou (Year-end of 2019)
主要统计指标解释 …… 425
Explanatory Notes on Main Statistical Indicators

第十六篇 规模以上服务业
Service Enterprise above the Designated Size

简要说明 …… 428
Brief Introduction
16-1 规模以上服务业企业主要财务指标 …… 429
Main Financial Indicators of Service Enterprises above the Designated Size
16-2 规模以上服务业企业主要财务指标 (2019 年，按行业分) …… 430
Main Financial Indicators of Service Enterprises above the Designated Size (2019, by Sector)
16-3 规模以上服务业企业主要财务指标 (2019 年，按地区分) …… 434
Main Financial Indicators of Service Enterprises above the Designated Size (2019, by Region)
16-4 规模以上服务业企业主要财务指标 (2019 年，按登记注册类型分) …… 436
Main Financial Indicators of Service Enterprises above the Designated Size (2019, by Registration Status)
16-5 规模以上服务业企业主要财务指标 (2019 年，按控股情况分) …… 440
Main Financial Indicators of Service Enterprises above the Designated Size (2019, by Type of Ownership)
16-6 规模以上服务业企业营业收入 (2019年，按行业分) …… 442
Business Revenue of Service Enterprises above the Designated Size (2019, by Sector)

16-7 规模以上服务业企业营业收入 (2019 年，按地区分) …… 444
Business Revenue of Service Enterprises above the Designated Size (2019, by District)
16-8 规模以上服务业企业营业收入 (2019 年，按登记注册类型和控股情况分) …… 445
Business Revenue of Service Enterprises above the Designated Size (2019, by Registration Status and Type of Ownership)
主要统计指标解释 …… 446
Explanatory Notes on Main Statistical Indicators

第十七篇 科 技
Science and Technology

简要说明 …… 448
Brief Introduction
17-1 科技监测主要指标 …… 449
Main Indicators of Scientific and Technological Monitoring
17-2 各类科学研究与开发机构基本情况 …… 450
Basic Statistics of Scientific Research and Development Institutions
17-3 获得省级以上科技成果奖励情况 …… 451
Statistics on Provincial Prizes and Above for Scientific and Technological Research Achievements
17-4 科协基本情况 (2019 年) …… 452
Basic Statistics on Associations for Science and Technology (2019)
17-5 专利申请量和专利授权量 …… 454
Patent Applications and Patent Certified
17-6 主要年份研究与试验发展(R&D)投入情况 …… 454
Research and Experimental Development (R&D) in Main Years
17-7 研究与试验发展(R&D)投入基本情况 …… 455
Basic situation of Research and Experimental Development (R&D)
17-8 规模以上工业企业研发情况 …… 456
Research and Experimental Development (R&D) of Industrial Enterprises above the Designated Size
17-9 资质以上建筑业企业研发情况 …… 457
Research and Experimental Development (R&D) of Grade Construction Enterprises
17-10 规模以上服务业企业研发情况 …… 458
Research and Experimental Development (R&D) of Service Enterprises above the Designated Size
17-11 各区研究与试验发展 (R&D) 投入情况 (2019 年) …… 459
Research and Experimental Development (R&D) by District (2019)
17-12 高新技术产品情况 (2019 年) …… 459
Statistics on High-tech Products (2019)
17-13 规模以上工业企业高新技术产品情况 (2019 年) …… 460
Statistics on High-tech Products of Industrial Enterprisesa Above the Designated Size (2019)
17-14 服务业企业高新技术产品情况 (2019 年) …… 462
Statistics on High-tech Products of Enterprises in Service Sector Enterprises (2019)
主要统计指标解释 …… 464
Explanatory Notes on Main Statistical Indicators

第十八篇 教育、文化、体育、卫生、社会福利和其他
Education, Culture, Sports, Public Health, Social Welfare and Others

简要说明 …… 466
Brief Introduction
18-1 主要年份教育事业基本情况 …… 467
Basic Statistics on Education in Main Years
18-2 主要年份每万人口在校学生数、每个教师负担学生数 …… 469
Students Enrollment per 10000 Persons and Students Taught by Every Teacher in Main Years
18-3 主要年份各级各类学校在校学生数 …… 470
Students Enrollment by Various Schools in Main Years
18-4 主要年份研究生基本情况 …… 472
Basic Statistics on Postgraduates in Main Years
18-5 普通高等院校各类专业本科学生数 (2019 年) …… 474
Students Enrollment in Regular Institutions of Higher Education by Field of Study (2019)
18-6 普通高等院校专科分学科学生数 (2019 年) …… 475
Students Enrollment in Regular Institutions of Higher Education for Junior College by Field of Study (2019)
18-7 普通高等院校本专科基本情况 (2019 年) …… 476
Basic Statistics on Regular Institutions of Higher Education (2019)
18-8 高中、初中、小学毕业生升学情况 …… 480
Statistics on Graduates of Senior, Junior Secondary Schools and Primary Schools Entering Higher Level Schools
18-9 普通中学专任教师学历情况 (2019 年) …… 481
Diploma Qualifications of Full-time Teachers in Regular Secondary Schools (2019)
18-10 各类学校教职工人数及专任教师数 …… 482
Staff and Workers and Full-time Teachers by Type of School
18-11 小学教育情况 …… 483
Statistics on Primary Education
18-12 成人高等教育基本情况 …… 483
Basic Statistics on Adult Higher Education
18-13 成人高等教育在校学生数 …… 484
Number of Students Enrolled in Adult Higher Education by Level
18-14 民办普通中小学及幼儿园情况 (2019 年) …… 484
Statistics on Regular Secondary Schools, Primary Schools and Kindergartens Run by Society (2019)
18-15 幼儿园基本情况 …… 485
Basic Statistics on Kindergartens
18-16 体育事业基本情况 …… 485
Basic Statistics on Sports
18-17 文化主要指标 …… 486
Main Indicators of Culture
18-18 主要年份卫生事业基本情况 …… 488
Basic Statistics on Public Health in Main Years
18-19 医疗卫生机构数 …… 489
Number of Health Institutions

18-20 医疗卫生机构床位数 (2019 年) …… 490
Number of Beds in Medical and Health Institutions (2019)
18-21 医疗卫生机构工作人员 (2019 年) …… 491
Number of Employed Personnel in Medical and Health Institutions (2019)
18-22 医疗卫生机构基本情况 (2019 年，按地区分) …… 492
Basic Statistics on Medical and Health Institutions (2019, by District)
18-23 民营医疗机构基本情况 (2019 年，按地区分) …… 493
Basic Statistics on Private Medical and Health Institutions (2019, by District)
18-24 医疗资源与服务情况 (2019 年，按经济类型和设置主办单位分) …… 494
Resources and Services on Medical Institutions (2019，By Economic Type and Setting Organizer)
18-25 医疗资源与服务情况 (2019 年，按机构类型分) …… 495
Resources and Services on Medical Institutions (2019，By Organization Type)
18-26 村卫生室基本情况 …… 495
Statistics on Rural Health Institutions
18-27 卫生事业其他指标 …… 496
Other Indicators of Health Care
18-28 律师、公证、基层司法基本情况 …… 497
Basic Statistics on Lawyers, Notarization and Grassroots Judicial Work
18-29 社会治安主要指标 …… 498
Main Indicators of Public Security
18-30 结婚和离婚对数 …… 499
Couples of Marriage and Divorce
18-31 社会保险情况 …… 500
Conditions of Social Insurance
18-32 优抚和社会救助、福利事业情况 …… 501
Statistics on Special Care, Social Relief and Social Welfare
18-33 社会组织机构情况 …… 502
Social Organization Structure
主要统计指标解释 …… 503
Explanatory Notes on Main Statistical Indicators

附 录
Appendix

附 1 全国国民经济主要指标 …… 506
Appendix Ⅰ. Main Indicators of National Economy of China
附 2 广东省国民经济主要指标 …… 507
Appendix Ⅱ. Main Indicators of National Economy of Guangdong Province
附 3 中国香港特别行政区主要统计指标 …… 508
Appendix Ⅲ. Main Indicators of Hong Kong Special Administrative Region
附 4 中国澳门特别行政区主要统计指标 …… 510
Appendix Ⅳ. Main Indicators of Macao Special Administrative Region

第一篇 CHAPTER 1

综合

GENERAL SURVEY

简要说明
Brief Introduction

第一篇　综　合

一、本篇资料反映广州国民经济和社会发展的综合情况以及国民经济核算情况，分别由广州市统计局综合统计处和国民经济核算处整理提供。

二、综合统计资料是根据广州市统计局各专业统计年报资料以及广州市有关部门提供的统计资料加工整理而成。

三、国民经济核算资料主要包括广州市地区生产总值及其有关资料。地区生产总值是根据不同产业部门、不同支出构成的特点和资料来源情况而采用不同方法计算的。2019年，根据第四次全国经济普查结果，我市对2008-2018年度地区生产总值数据进行了修订。

地区生产总值是一个价值量指标，其价值的变化受价格变化和物量变化两大因素影响。不变价地区生产总值是把按当期价格计算的地区生产总值换算成按某个固定期（基期）价格计算的价值，从而使两个不同时期的价值进行比较时，能够剔除价格变化的影响，以反映物量变化，反映生产活动成果的实际变动。地区生产总值指数就是根据两个时期不变价地区生产总值计算得到的。随着经济的不断发展，各行业的价格结构也会不断发生变化，为了更好的反映这种变化对于经济的影响，计算不变价地区生产总值需要每隔若干年调整一次基期。我国自开始核算国内生产总值以来，共有1952年、1957年、1970年、1980年、1990年、2000年、2005年、2010年、2015年9个不变价基期，目前的基期是2015年。2015-2017年的不变价地区生产总值是按照2015年价格计算的。

四、根据《国家统计局关于执行新国民经济行业分类国家标准的通知》（国统字〔2017〕142号）要求，新《国民经济行业分类》从2017年统计年报和2018年定期统计报表统一开始使用。本资料中凡是涉及到分行业的表式（除个别部门提供的数据仍按旧行业分类，表中有注明），均按照新的行业分类《国民经济行业分类GB/T4754-2017》作调整。

五、资料来源

1．行政区划资料由广州市民政局提供；

2．城市房地产市场交易情况、国有土地使用权出让、划拨情况由广州市规划和自然资源局提供；

3．气象资料由广州市气象局提供；

4．劳动力市场情况由广州市人力资源和社会保障局提供；

5．技术市场交易情况由广州市科学技术局提供；

6．私营企业、城乡个体工商企业资料由广州市市场监督管理局提供。

1 General Survey

I. The summary data in this chapter reflect the national economy and social development of Guangzhou and also cover the data on its national economic accounts. The data are prepared and provided by the Division of Comprehensive Statistics and the Division of National Accounts of Guangzhou Municipal Bureau of Statistics respectively.

II. The summary data are processed and prepared in the light of the annual reports of various specialized fields provided by Guangzhou Municipal Bureau of Statistics and data provided by some related departments of Guangzhou Municipality.

III.The data on the national economic accounts mainly cover the gross domestic Product (GDP)and related data of Guangzhou. The regional gross domestic product is calculated by different methods according to the characteristics and sources of different industrial sectors and different expenditure components. The GDP data of 2008-2018 are revised in 2019,according to the data of the fourth national economic census.

Regional GDP is an index of value, and the change of value is influenced by two factors: price change and material quantity change. The regional GDP at constant prices is converted to the value calculated at a fixed (base period) price at current prices, so that when comparing the values of two different periods, the effects of price changes can be excluded. In order to reflect the volume of change, reflect the actual changes in the results of production activities. Regional GDP index is based on two periods of constant price region GDP calculation. With the continuous development of economy, the price structure of various industries will change constantly. In order to better reflect the impact of this change on the economy, the base period should be adjusted once every several years to calculate the gross domestic product in the constant price area. Since the beginning of our gross domestic product (GDP) accounting, there have been nine constant price base periods in 1952, 1957, 1970, 1980, 1990, 2000, 2005, 2010 and 2015. The current base period is 2015. Gross domestic product in constant prices for 2015-2017 is calculated at 2015 prices.

IV. According to the notice of the National Bureau of Statistics on the implementation of the new national standard of national economic industry classification (2017) 142, the new national economic industry classification has been used from the statistical annual report of 2017 and the periodic statistical report of 2018. In this data, all the tables related to sub-industries (except the data provided by individual departments are classified according to the old industry, as indicated in the table), are adjusted according to the new industry classification & GB/T4754-2017 of national economy.

V. Data Resources comes as follows:

The data on administrative divisions are provided by Guangzhou Municipal Bureau of Civil Affairs.

The data on transaction in urban real estate, lease and administrative allocation of the use right of state-owned land are provided by Guangzhou Municipal Planning and Resources Bureau.

The data on meteorological phenomena are provided by Guangzhou Municipal Bureau Meteorology.

The data on labor force markets are provided by Guangzhou Municipal Science and Technology Bureau.

The data on transactions in technology markets are provided by Guangzhou Science Technology and Innovation Commission.

The data on private enterprises and individuals are provided by Guangzhou Municipal Market Regulatory Administration.

1-1 行政区划（2019年末）
Administrative Divisions (Year-end of 2019)

单位:个 (unit)

地 区	Districts	街道办事处 Street Communities	镇 Towns	社区居委会 Community Committees	村民委员会 Villagers' Committees
合 计	**Total**	**140**	**34**	**1596**	**1144**
荔湾区	Liwan	22		191	
越秀区	Yuexiu	18		222	
海珠区	Haizhu	18		265	
天河区	Tianhe	21		220	
白云区	Baiyun	18	4	281	118
黄埔区	Huangpu	16	1	112	28
番禺区	Panyu	11	5	98	177
花都区	Huadu	4	6	64	188
南沙区	Nansha	3	6	33	128
从化区	Conghua	3	5	53	221
增城区	Zengcheng	6	7	57	284

注：本表数据由广州市民政局提供。
Note: The data in this table are provided by Guangzhou Municipal Civil Affairs Bureau.

1-2　各月平均温度、湿度（2019年）

Monthly Average Temperature and Humidity (2019)

月　份	Month	平均温度(℃) Average Temperature (℃)					平均相对湿度(%) Average Humidity (%)
		全　市 Total	番禺站 Panyu	花都站 Huadu	从化站 Conghua	增城站 Zengcheng	全　市 Total
全　年	**Annual Total**	**23.1**	**24.2**	**23.4**	**22.1**	**22.9**	**78.4**
一　月	January	15.2	16.3	15.1	13.9	15.5	75.3
二　月	February	18.1	19.3	17.5	17.0	18.6	83.7
三　月	March	19.6	20.4	19.5	18.9	19.8	85.2
四　月	April	23.5	24.6	23.5	22.8	23.4	88.7
五　月	May	25.2	25.8	25.4	24.7	25.0	86.6
六　月	June	28.2	29.2	28.6	27.5	27.7	85.4
七　月	July	28.9	29.7	29.4	28.2	28.6	84.5
八　月	August	28.9	29.8	29.5	28.1	28.4	83.9
九　月	September	27.5	29.0	28.2	26.2	27.1	75.4
十　月	October	24.9	26.6	24.9	23.8	24.6	72.6
十一月	November	20.5	22.2	21.5	19.0	20.1	66.3
十二月	December	16.7	18.0	17.3	15.5	16.5	53.6

注：本表数据由广州市气象局提供。
Note: The data in this table are provided by Guangzhou Meteorological Bureau.

1-3　各月降雨量、日照时数(2019年)

Monthly Precipitation and Sunshine Hours (2019)

月　份	Month	降　雨　量（毫米） Precipitation (millimeter)					日　照　时　数（小时） Sunshine Hours (hour)				
		全　市 Total	#番禺站 Panyu	#花都站 Huadu	#从化站 Conghua	#增城站 Zengcheng	全　市 Total	#番禺站 Panyu	#花都站 Huadu	#从化站 Conghua	#增城站 Zengcheng
全　年	**Annual Total**	**2336.0**	**2060.6**	**2136.4**	**2281.0**	**2739.7**	**1650.1**	**1589.6**	**1631.4**	**1622.4**	**1762.3**
一　月	January	2.7	1.6	2.2	4.4	3.5	107.8	108.5	109.4	99.7	121.4
二　月	February	103.5	88.9	85.2	85.6	92.5	49.8	57.9	53.4	45.5	59.9
三　月	March	199.5	154.6	194.4	230.1	237.5	63.8	65.7	63.8	66.1	66.3
四　月	April	492.5	268.6	636.0	529.7	615.1	52.2	63.6	56.0	30.5	67.1
五　月	May	354.1	383.7	217.9	413.1	406.1	63.4	49.0	69.1	69.5	67.9
六　月	June	428.8	283.6	333.2	412.4	654.9	120.0	134.6	112.4	121.9	116.8
七　月	July	271.8	362.9	276.6	232.0	227.1	145.8	149.0	143.8	147.8	152.1
八　月	August	330.5	267.5	267.9	253.8	382.7	177.2	165.9	181.7	170.5	181.4
九　月	September	111.4	156.2	97.0	115.4	83.3	235.3	228.5	222.8	236.4	244.3
十　月	October	39.8	93.0	26.0	4.5	36.0	209.5	195.5	193.6	207.3	229.1
十一月	November	0.1				0.2	257.9	228.8	258.2	257.4	275.6
十二月	December	1.3				0.8	167.4	142.6	167.2	169.8	180.4

注：本表数据由广州市气象局提供。
Note: The data in this table are provided by Guangzhou Meteorological Bureau.

1-4 行政区域面积和人口密度(2019年)
Land Area and Population Density (2019)

各 区	Districts	行政区域面积(平方公里) Administrative Area (sq.km)	年末常住人口(万人) Permanent Population at Year-end (10000 person)	年末户籍人口(万人) Registered Permanent Residents at Year-end (10000 person)	常住人口密度(人/平方公里) Permanent Population Density (person/sq.km)	户籍人口密度(人/平方公里) Population Density by Registered Permanent Residents (person/sq.km)
全 市	**Total**	**7434.40**	**1530.59**	**953.72**	**2059**	**1283**
荔湾区	Liwan	59.10	101.20	75.59	17124	12790
越秀区	Yuexiu	33.80	120.97	117.29	35790	34701
海珠区	Haizhu	90.40	172.42	106.73	19073	11806
天河区	Tianhe	96.33	178.85	96.57	18566	10025
白云区	Baiyun	795.79	277.96	108.02	3493	1357
黄埔区	Huangpu	484.17	115.12	56.22	2378	1161
番禺区	Panyu	529.94	182.78	103.35	3449	1950
花都区	Huadu	970.04	110.72	81.13	1141	836
南沙区	Nansha	783.86	79.61	46.33	1016	591
从化区	Conghua	1974.50	64.95	64.17	329	325
增城区	Zengcheng	1616.47	126.01	98.32	780	608

注：本表行政区域面积数据由广州市民政局提供，户籍人口数据由广州市公安局提供。

Note: The data of administrative area in this table are provided by Guangzhou Municipal Civil Affairs Bureau, and registered permanent residents data are provided by Guangzhou Public Security Bureau.

1-5 法人和产业活动单位数

单位:个

项 目	Item
总 计	**Total**
按产业分	**Grouped By Industry**
第一产业	Primary Industry
第二产业	Secondary Industry
第三产业	Tertiary Industry
按行业分	**Grouped By Sector**
农、林、牧、渔业	Agriculture, Forestry, Animal Husbandry and Fishery
采矿业	Mining
制造业	Manufacturing
电力、热力、燃气及水生产和供应业	Production and Supply of Electricity, Heat,Gas and Water
建筑业	Construction
批发和零售业	Wholesale and Retail Trade
交通运输、仓储和邮政业	Transport, Storage and Post
住宿和餐饮业	Hotels and Catering Services
信息传输、软件和信息技术服务业	Information Transmission, Software and Information Technology
金融业	Financial Intermediation
房地产业	Real Estate
租赁和商务服务业	Leasing and Business Services
科学研究和技术服务业	Scientific Research and Technical Services
水利、环境和公共设施管理业	Management of Water Conservancy, Environment and Public Facilities
居民服务、修理和其他服务业	Service to Households, Repair and Other Services
教 育	Education
卫生和社会工作	Health and Social Service
文化、体育和娱乐业	Culture, Sports and Entertainment
公共管理、社会保障和社会组织	Public Management, Social Security and Social Organizations

注：2018年农、林、牧、渔业行业只含从事农、林、牧、渔专业及辅助性活动和兼营第二、三产业活动的农、林、牧、渔业法人单位。

Number of Corporate Units and Industrial Establishments

(unit)

2018			2019		
法人单位 Corporate Units	产业活动单位 Industrial Establishments	其中：多产业法人所属的产业活动单位 Establishments belonging to Multi-industry Corporation	法人单位 Corporate Units	产业活动单位 Industrial Establishments	其中：多产业法人所属的产业活动单位 Establishments belonging to Multi-industry Corporation
751580	**803118**	**59650**	**782731**	**829627**	**59098**
2			2375	2406	54
103217	106101	3957	107540	109926	4003
648361	697017	55693	672816	717295	55041
606	615	12	2989	3030	68
56	59	4	56	57	3
76363	77565	1869	79760	80753	1925
658	854	216	688	852	193
27401	28935	1927	28324	29594	1943
260746	278704	20023	272131	288802	19731
19029	21993	3473	20019	22749	3389
15923	19471	4050	16253	19564	4077
58137	60309	2604	60164	61964	2450
5150	9515	4682	4807	9126	4575
30396	35079	5686	31171	35597	5768
124005	131125	8101	131585	137734	7936
69008	71214	2741	70328	72112	2706
2202	2288	115	2362	2426	124
13264	14415	1370	16165	17321	1547
2844	2969	160	12846	13601	995
15689	16795	1298	3583	3815	314
15118	15513	519	19190	19653	679
12250	12962	791	10310	10877	675

Note: Number of legal entities and industrial establishments of agriculture,forestry, animal husbandry and fishery in 2018 refers to those engaged in professional and support activities for agriculture, forestry, animal husbandry and fishery as well as also engaged in the secondary and teriary industries at part time .

1-5 续表

单位:个

项　　目	Item
总　计	**Total**
按地区分	**Grouped By District**
荔湾区	Liwan
越秀区	Yuexiu
海珠区	Haizhu
天河区	Tianhe
白云区	Baiyun
黄埔区	Huangpu
番禺区	Panyu
花都区	Huadu
南沙区	Nansha
从化区	Conghua
增城区	Zengcheng
按注册类型分	**Grouped by Registration Status**
内资	Domestic Funded
国有	State-owned
集体	Collective-owned
股份合作	Cooperative
联营企业	Joint Ownership Enterprises
有限责任公司	Limited Liability Corporations
股份有限公司	Share-holding Corporations Ltd.
私营企业	Private Enterprises
其他	Others
港、澳、台商投资企业	Enterprises with Funds from Hong Kong, Macao and Taiwan Investors
与港、澳、台商合资经营企业	Joint-venture Enterprises
与港、澳、台商合作经营企业	Cooperative Enterprises
港、澳、台商独资经营企业	Enterprises with Sole Funds
港、澳、台商投资股份有限公司	Share-holding Corporations Ltd.
其他港、澳、台商投资企业	Other Enterprises with Funds from Hong Kong, Macao and Taiwan
外商投资企业	Foreign Funded Enterprises
中外合资经营企业	Joint-venture Enterprises
中外合作经营企业	Cooperative Enterprises
外资企业	Enterprises with Sole Foreign Funds
外商投资股份有限公司	Share-holding Corporations Ltd.
其他外商投资企业	Other Foreign Funded Enterprises

continued

(unit)

2018			2019		
法人单位 Corporate Units	产业活动单位 Industrial Establishments	其中：多产业法人所属的产业活动单位 Establishments belonging to Multi-industry Corporation	法人单位 Corporate Units	产业活动单位 Industrial Establishments	其中：多产业法人所属的产业活动单位 Establishments belonging to Multi-industry Corporation
751580	**803118**	**59650**	**782731**	**829627**	**59098**
28233	31482	3790	30019	33063	3766
61445	68596	8743	65109	71650	8609
54966	60585	6810	55912	60923	6067
189342	201892	14231	192612	203653	13899
133242	139052	7087	136736	142290	7027
47393	49924	2888	51408	53601	3105
86271	92415	6605	91737	97377	7024
39381	42571	3529	41836	44792	3523
62916	64594	1915	65489	67078	2086
12019	12991	1089	13093	14030	1138
36372	39016	2963	38780	41170	2854
736148	780861	52136	766146	806668	51823
8312	10550	2478	8464	10704	2613
12256	13171	1050	12371	13239	1024
1798	1969	237	1945	2365	493
274	309	40	309	355	53
54773	63464	10208	47082	54931	9782
4111	8573	4759	3788	7591	4131
641347	669375	33176	677602	702635	33427
13277	13450	188	14585	14848	300
9500	12308	3183	10208	12837	3150
1450	2048	670	1578	2144	673
369	469	115	402	495	113
7434	9335	2183	7917	9686	2153
101	145	49	110	155	48
146	311	166	201	357	163
5932	9949	4331	6377	10122	4125
1130	1877	830	1223	1938	805
87	111	31	108	136	37
4237	7054	3019	4542	7148	2865
139	261	132	157	261	116
339	646	319	347	639	302

1-6 按登记注册类型分组的法人单位数（2018年）

单位:个

项　　目	Item	总　计 Total
总　　计	**Total**	**751580**
按地区分	**Grouped By District**	
荔湾区	Liwan	28233
越秀区	Yuexiu	61445
海珠区	Haizhu	54966
天河区	Tianhe	189342
白云区	Baiyun	133242
黄埔区	Huangpu	47393
番禺区	Panyu	86271
花都区	Huadu	39381
南沙区	Nansha	62916
从化区	Conghua	12019
增城区	Zengcheng	36372
按产业分	**Grouped By Industry**	
第一产业	Primary Industry	2
第二产业	Secondary Industry	103217
第三产业	Tertiary Industry	648361
按行业分	**Grouped By Sector**	
农、林、牧、渔业	Agriculture, Forestry, Animal Husbandry and Fishery	606
采矿业	Mining	56
制造业	Manufacturing	76363
电力、热力、燃气及水生产和供应业	Production and Supply of Electricity, Heat,Gas and Water	658
建筑业	Construction	27401
批发和零售业	Wholesale and Retail Trade	260746
交通运输、仓储和邮政业	Transport, Storage and Post	19029
住宿和餐饮业	Hotels and Catering Services	15923
信息传输、软件和信息技术服务业	Information Transmission, Software and Information Technology	58137
金融业	Financial Intermediation	5150
房地产业	Real Estate	30396
租赁和商务服务业	Leasing and Business Services	124005
科学研究和技术服务业	Scientific Research and Technical Services	69008
水利、环境和公共设施管理业	Management of Water Conservancy, Environment and Public Facilities	2202
居民服务、修理和其他服务业	Service to Households, Repair and Other Services	13264
教　育	Education	2844
卫生和社会工作	Health and Social Service	15689
文化、体育和娱乐业	Culture, Sports and Entertainment	15118
公共管理、社会保障和社会组织	Public Management, Social Security and Social Organizations	12250

Number of Corporate Units by Sector and by Status of Registration (2018)

(unit)

内资 Domestic Funded	国有 State-owned	集体 Collective-owned	股份合作 Cooperative	联营企业 Joint Ownership Enterprises	有限责任公司 Limited Liability Corporations	股份有限公司 Share-holding Corporations Ltd.	私营企业 Private Enterprises	其他 Others
736148	**8312**	**12256**	**1798**	**274**	**54773**	**4111**	**641347**	**13277**
27217	559	368	387	10	1642	313	23220	718
58240	1664	422	586	35	5428	514	47759	1832
54123	683	514	498	25	4400	407	46556	1040
186556	1205	346	109	51	18320	1326	163588	1611
132428	766	2095	120	56	6919	453	120574	1445
45913	485	809	31	19	4428	342	39265	534
84814	763	590	41	34	4004	222	78184	976
38727	672	2022	10	17	1622	76	33514	794
60617	381	224	8	9	5407	279	53482	827
11611	541	1454	2	3	790	77	6466	2278
35902	593	3412	6	15	1813	102	28739	1222
2							1	1
100335	213	342	377	30	5270	523	93580	
635811	8099	11914	1421	244	49503	3588	547766	13276
593	12	8			58	3	453	59
55					9	2	44	
73646	136	245	351	26	3308	381	69199	
623	22	22			143	16	420	
27257	62	80	31	4	1876	126	25078	
255987	247	437	778	41	14582	1057	238640	205
18563	104	77	33	5	1444	99	16795	6
15615	119	47	166	6	1307	115	13852	3
57295	84	13	9		5692	396	51058	43
4657	65	1	5		1076	219	3286	5
29292	328	1744	68	31	4239	184	22468	230
120767	514	8706	96	50	10820	675	97439	2467
68046	591	100	44	12	6233	506	60245	315
2182	288	30		4	223	21	1565	51
13174	91	85	141	10	839	70	11807	131
2811	28	18	14	1	190	22	2504	34
15612	2020	388	26	25	1019	92	9565	2477
15012	433	45	23	8	1344	108	12451	600
12226	3168	210	13	51	371	19	4478	3916

1-6 续表

单位:个

项　　目	Item	港、澳、台商投资企业 Enterprises with Funds from Hong Kong, Macao and Taiwan Investors	与港、澳、台商合资经营企业 Joint-venture Enterprises
总　计	**Total**	**9500**	**1450**
按地区分	**Grouped By District**		
荔湾区	Liwan	484	27
越秀区	Yuexiu	1791	175
海珠区	Haizhu	437	58
天河区	Tianhe	1744	245
白云区	Baiyun	390	57
黄埔区	Huangpu	729	130
番禺区	Panyu	981	146
花都区	Huadu	406	49
南沙区	Nansha	1856	490
从化区	Conghua	352	21
增城区	Zengcheng	330	52
按产业分	**Grouped By Industry**		
第一产业	Primary Industry		
第二产业	Secondary Industry	1789	280
第三产业	Tertiary Industry	7711	1170
按行业分	**Grouped By Sector**		
农、林、牧、渔业	Agriculture, Forestry, Animal Husbandry and Fishery	12	2
采矿业	Mining	1	
制造业	Manufacturing	1676	261
电力、热力、燃气及水生产和供应业	Production and Supply of Electricity, Heat,Gas and Water	16	7
建筑业	Construction	104	15
批发和零售业	Wholesale and Retail Trade	2405	175
交通运输、仓储和邮政业	Transport, Storage and Post	289	45
住宿和餐饮业	Hotels and Catering Services	190	35
信息传输、软件和信息技术服务业	Information Transmission, Software and Information Technology	606	60
金融业	Financial Intermediation	368	187
房地产业	Real Estate	787	132
租赁和商务服务业	Leasing and Business Services	2233	399
科学研究和技术服务业	Scientific Research and Technical Services	597	86
水利、环境和公共设施管理业	Management of Water Conservancy, Environment and Public Facilities	11	4
居民服务、修理和其他服务业	Service to Households, Repair and Other Services	51	4
教　育	Education	21	3
卫生和社会工作	Health and Social Service	47	13
文化、体育和娱乐业	Culture, Sports and Entertainment	69	16
公共管理、社会保障和社会组织	Public Management, Social Security and Social Organizations	17	6

continued

(unit)

与港、澳、台商合作经营企业 Cooperative Enterprises	港、澳、台商独资经营企业 Enterprises with Sole Funds	港、澳、台商投资股份有限公司 Share-holding Corporations Ltd.	其他港、澳、台商投资企业 Other Share-holding Corporations Ltd.	外商投资企业 Foreign Funded Enterprises	中外合资经营企业 Joint-venture Enterprises	中外合作经营企业 Cooperative Enterprises	外资企业 Enterprises with Sole Foreign Funds	外商投资股份有限公司 Share-holding Corporations Ltd.	其他外商投资企业 Other Share-holding Corporations Ltd.
369	**7434**	**101**	**146**	**5932**	**1130**	**87**	**4237**	**139**	**339**
21	422	4	10	532	40	3	467	2	20
111	1470	11	24	1414	164	18	1160	18	54
26	336	6	11	406	80	7	270	15	34
42	1399	19	39	1042	181	12	696	49	104
24	292	10	7	424	60	5	305	17	37
27	558	9	5	751	208	16	480	18	29
34	769	21	11	476	120	6	325	5	20
19	331	2	5	248	53	5	178	3	9
28	1297	12	29	443	167	8	234	10	24
5	319	4	3	56	15	2	38	1	
32	241	3	2	140	42	5	84	1	8
65	1404	26	14	1093	294	23	718	19	39
304	6030	75	132	4839	836	64	3519	120	300
	10			1			1		
	1								
55	1324	26	10	1041	270	21	702	15	33
1	8			19	12	1	3	1	2
9	76		4	40	16	1	16	3	4
16	2152	21	41	2354	201	5	1979	48	121
89	153	2		177	46	11	109	5	6
13	137	4	1	118	30	3	74	4	7
6	524	9	7	236	58		159	2	17
4	173		4	125	66		54	3	2
132	509	6	8	317	111	26	144	20	16
24	1739	22	49	1005	153	6	734	23	89
6	479	10	16	365	127	5	194	10	29
1	6			9	3	1	2		3
5	40		2	39	5	2	28	3	1
	16		2	12	4		7		1
1	32		1	30	9	3	13		5
5	47		1	37	17	2	14	2	2
2	8	1		7	2		4		1

1-7 按登记注册类型分组的法人单位数（2019年）

单位:个

项　　目	Item	总　计 Total
总　　计	**Total**	**782731**
按地区分	**Grouped By District**	
荔湾区	Liwan	30019
越秀区	Yuexiu	65109
海珠区	Haizhu	55912
天河区	Tianhe	192612
白云区	Baiyun	136736
黄埔区	Huangpu	51408
番禺区	Panyu	91737
花都区	Huadu	41836
南沙区	Nansha	65489
从化区	Conghua	13093
增城区	Zengcheng	38780
按产业分	**Grouped By Industry**	
第一产业	Primary Industry	2375
第二产业	Secondary Industry	107540
第三产业	Tertiary Industry	672816
按行业分	**Grouped By Sector**	
农、林、牧、渔业	Agriculture, Forestry, Animal Husbandry and Fishery	2989
采矿业	Mining	56
制造业	Manufacturing	79760
电力、热力、燃气及水生产和供应业	Production and Supply of Electricity, Heat,Gas and Water	688
建筑业	Construction	28324
批发和零售业	Wholesale and Retail Trade	272131
交通运输、仓储和邮政业	Transport, Storage and Post	20019
住宿和餐饮业	Hotels and Catering Services	16253
信息传输、软件和信息技术服务业	Information Transmission, Software and Information Technology	60164
金融业	Financial Intermediation	4807
房地产业	Real Estate	31171
租赁和商务服务业	Leasing and Business Services	131585
科学研究和技术服务业	Scientific Research and Technical Services	70328
水利、环境和公共设施管理业	Management of Water Conservancy, Environment and Public Facilities	2362
居民服务、修理和其他服务业	Service to Households, Repair and Other Services	16165
教　育	Education	12846
卫生和社会工作	Health and Social Service	3583
文化、体育和娱乐业	Culture, Sports and Entertainment	19190
公共管理、社会保障和社会组织	Public Management, Social Security and Social Organizations	10310

Number of Corporate Units by Sector and by Status of Registration (2019)

(unit)

内资 Domestic Funded	国有 State-owned	集体 Collective-owned	股份合作 Cooperative	联营企业 Joint Ownership Enterprises	有限责任公司 Limited Liability Corporations	股份有限公司 Share-holding Corporations Ltd.	私营企业 Private Enterprises	其他 Others
766146	**8464**	**12371**	**1945**	**309**	**47082**	**3788**	**677602**	**14585**
28949	575	389	438	11	1772	314	24701	749
61679	1768	449	625	32	5707	495	50625	1978
55008	672	531	504	28	4740	425	47062	1046
189604	1207	331	108	62	11656	1084	173398	1758
135903	779	2125	144	54	4911	328	125980	1582
49778	509	828	54	26	5324	418	41957	662
90169	766	600	35	35	2369	154	85139	1071
41136	676	2028	12	23	1967	81	35469	880
63000	393	223	12	11	5691	295	55446	929
12647	529	1462	4	6	926	84	7203	2433
38273	590	3405	9	21	2019	110	30622	1497
2342	12	18	1	2	167	18	1536	588
104503	220	376	401	32	4803	514	98079	78
659301	8232	11977	1543	275	42112	3256	577987	13919
2942	24	26	1	3	221	20	1997	650
55					11	1	43	
76888	138	267	370	29	3168	390	72457	69
652	22	27			148	18	437	
28182	66	87	35	3	1539	108	26334	10
267064	273	460	844	57	11976	970	252153	331
19525	89	79	41	7	1340	103	17841	25
15916	123	49	174	5	1082	95	14360	28
59242	84	11	10		4832	365	53871	69
4280	64	3	5	1	881	198	3105	23
29976	316	1697	68	32	4029	159	23429	246
128067	574	8794	118	62	9450	621	105847	2601
69290	629	99	51	14	5184	449	62522	342
2335	310	34	2	4	210	20	1707	48
16029	101	95	161	9	760	79	14651	173
12772	1602	304	21	19	599	61	7988	2178
3559	522	108	5	6	316	22	1858	722
19062	364	30	39	5	1330	107	16880	307
10310	3163	201		53	6	2	122	6763

1-7 续表

单位:个

项　　目	Item	港、澳、台商投资企业 Enterprises with Funds from Hong Kong, Macao and Taiwan Investors	与港、澳、台商合资经营企业 Joint-venture Enterprises
总　计	**Total**	**10208**	**1578**
按地区分	**Grouped By District**		
荔湾区	Liwan	518	34
越秀区	Yuexiu	1920	184
海珠区	Haizhu	472	66
天河区	Tianhe	1867	280
白云区	Baiyun	405	56
黄埔区	Huangpu	805	154
番禺区	Panyu	1038	150
花都区	Huadu	435	49
南沙区	Nansha	2006	522
从化区	Conghua	384	26
增城区	Zengcheng	358	57
按产业分	**Grouped By Industry**		
第一产业	Primary Industry	28	3
第二产业	Secondary Industry	1869	287
第三产业	Tertiary Industry	8311	1288
按行业分	**Grouped By Sector**		
农、林、牧、渔业	Agriculture, Forestry, Animal Husbandry and Fishery	41	5
采矿业	Mining	1	
制造业	Manufacturing	1755	268
电力、热力、燃气及水生产和供应业	Production and Supply of Electricity, Heat,Gas and Water	19	8
建筑业	Construction	103	14
批发和零售业	Wholesale and Retail Trade	2581	216
交通运输、仓储和邮政业	Transport, Storage and Post	296	40
住宿和餐饮业	Hotels and Catering Services	208	38
信息传输、软件和信息技术服务业	Information Transmission, Software and Information Technology	662	81
金融业	Financial Intermediation	410	208
房地产业	Real Estate	851	143
租赁和商务服务业	Leasing and Business Services	2394	411
科学研究和技术服务业	Scientific Research and Technical Services	641	88
水利、环境和公共设施管理业	Management of Water Conservancy, Environment and Public Facilities	16	6
居民服务、修理和其他服务业	Service to Households, Repair and Other Services	82	13
教　育	Education	45	9
卫生和社会工作	Health and Social Service	15	7
文化、体育和娱乐业	Culture, Sports and Entertainment	88	23
公共管理、社会保障和社会组织	Public Management, Social Security and Social Organizations		

continued

(unit)

与港、澳、台商合作经营企业 Cooperative Enterprises	港、澳、台商独资经营企业 Enterprises with Sole Funds	港、澳、台商投资股份有限公司 Share-holding Corporations Ltd.	其他港、澳、台商投资企业 Other Share-holding Corporations Ltd.	外商投资企业 Foreign Funded Enterprises	中外合资经营企业 Joint-venture Enterprises	中外合作经营企业 Cooperative Enterprises	外资企业 Enterprises with Sole Foreign Funds	外商投资股份有限公司 Share-holding Corporations Ltd.	其他外商投资企业 Other Share-holding Corporations Ltd.
402	**7917**	**110**	**201**	**6377**	**1223**	**108**	**4542**	**157**	**347**
26	445	5	8	552	43	2	485	2	20
126	1569	12	29	1510	170	20	1238	22	60
27	361	6	12	432	92	8	276	17	39
51	1474	22	40	1141	198	20	774	51	98
24	306	12	7	428	60	7	312	19	30
25	607	11	8	825	230	18	513	24	40
31	828	18	11	530	128	11	367	7	17
23	355	2	6	265	53	4	193	4	11
29	1365	15	75	483	187	10	252	9	25
6	346	3	3	62	17	3	41		1
34	261	4	2	149	45	5	91	2	6
2	22		1	5	1	2	2		
68	1470	31	13	1168	312	27	772	23	34
332	6425	79	187	5204	910	79	3768	134	313
2	32	1	1	6	2	2	2		
	1								
59	1387	30	11	1117	289	25	752	20	31
1	9	1		17	10	1	4	2	
8	78		3	39	16	1	18	1	3
18	2275	21	51	2486	226	9	2082	56	113
90	163	2	1	198	54	13	117	4	10
16	148	3	3	129	32	4	83	4	6
5	557	11	8	260	72	2	165	5	16
5	191		6	117	60	1	51	3	2
154	537	5	12	344	116	30	162	19	17
25	1867	24	67	1124	163	7	823	27	104
4	507	10	32	397	138	6	209	11	33
2	7	1		11	1		7		3
4	61		4	54	12	2	36	3	1
1	35			29	11	2	11		5
	7		1	9	6	2			1
8	55	1	1	40	15	1	20	2	2

1-8 国民经济和社会发展总量与速度指标

指　　标		Item		1978	2000	2005	2010
人口和劳动力		**Population and Employment**					
年末户籍人口	（万人）	Year-end Registered Permanent Residents	(10000 persons)	482.90	700.69	750.53	806.14
年末常住人口	（万人）	Year-end Permanent Population	(10000 persons)	482.90	994.80	949.68	1270.96
年末全社会从业人员	（万人）	Year-end Employment	(10000 persons)	266.90	496.26	574.46	711.07
城镇非私营单位从业人员年末人数	（万人）	Number of Employed Persons at Year-end in Urban Units	(10000 persons)	147.36	175.55	199.76	246.37
地区生产总值	**（亿元）**	**Gross Domestic Product**	**(100 million yuan)**	**43.09**	**2505.58**	**5187.85**	**10640.67**
第一产业		Primary Industry		5.03	94.37	130.22	168.62
第二产业		Secondary Industry		25.24	1029.94	2067.00	4053.30
第三产业		Tertiary Industry		12.82	1381.27	2990.63	6418.75
人均地区生产总值	（元）	Per Capita GDP	(yuan)	907	25758	54160	86582
农业生产		**Agriculture**					
农林牧渔业总产值	（亿元）	Gross Output Value of Agriculture, Forestry, Animal Husbandry and Fishery	(100 million yuan)	7.99	163.05	220.81	322.13
主要农业产品产量		Output of Major Farm Products					
粮　食	（万吨）	Grain	(10000 tons)	111.06	88.11	51.73	43.04
园林水果	（万吨）	Fruits	(10000 tons)	5.17	32.97	48.87	39.92
蔬　菜	（万吨）	Vegetable	(10000 tons)	55.68	306.49	348.89	325.99
肉　类	（万吨）	Meat	(10000 tons)	5.05	32.77	32.03	32.36
水产品	（万吨）	Aquatic Products	(10000 tons)	3.16	32.52	38.83	44.14
工业生产		**Industry**					
工业总产值	（亿元）	Gross Industrial Output Value	(100 million yuan)	75.39	3100.02	6767.96	14438.99
主要工业产品产量		Output of Major Industrial Products					
汽　车	（万辆）	Motor Vehicles	(10000 unit)	0.23	3.81	41.35	135.84
新能源汽车	（辆）	New Energy Automobile	(unit)				
摩托车整车	（万辆）	Motorcycles	(10000 units)		60.31	196.57	441.05
家用电冰箱	（万台）	Household Refrigerators	(10000 sets)		58.14	146.29	179.14
智能电视	（万台）	Smart TV	(10000 sets)				
房间空气调节器	（万台）	Air Conditioners	(10000 sets)	0.32	103.43	292.71	636.78
原电池及原电池组	（亿只）	Primary Cells and Batteries	(100 million units)	2.69	18.89	39.35	22.90
锂离子电池	（亿只）	Lithium Ion Battery	(10000 units)				
光缆	（芯千米）	Optical Cable	(Core Km)				
工业机器人	（套）	Industrial Robot	(set)				
工业自动调节仪表与控制系统	（万套）	Industrial Automatic Regulating Instrument and Control System	(10000 sets)				
粗　钢	（万吨）	Crude Steel	(10000 tons)	18.46	151.16	308.71	403.17
固定资产投资		**Investment in Fixed Assets**					
固定资产投资	（亿元）	Total Investment in Fixed Assets	(100 million yuan)	7.26	923.67	1519.16	3263.57
# 住　宅		Residential Buildings		0.90	325.03	377.70	572.71
社会消费品零售总额	**（亿元）**	**Total Retail Sales of Consumer Goods**	**(100 million yuan)**	**17.63**	**1079.59**	**1765.01**	**3809.04**

注：1.本表地区生产总值和工业总产值指数按照可比口径计算。
2.2016、2017年农业生产相关数据经过修订，绝对数沿用历史数，相对数以调整后数据为基期进行计算。
3.2019年，根据第四次全国经济普查结果，对2008—2018年度地区生产总值和1992—2018年社零数据进行了修订。

Principal Aggregate Indicators on National Economic and Social Development and Growth Rates

2015	2018	2019	速度指标(%) Indices and Growth Rates (%)									
			指数(2019为以下各年) Index(2019 as percentage of the following years)						平均增长速度 Average Annual Growth Rate			
			1978	2000	2005	2010	2015	2018	1979–2019	2001–2019	2006–2019	2011–2019
854.19	927.69	953.72	197.5	136.1	127.1	118.3	111.7	102.8	1.7	1.6	1.7	1.9
1350.11	1490.44	1530.59	317.0	153.9	161.2	120.4	113.4	102.7	2.9	2.3	3.5	2.1
927.91	1102.36	1125.89	421.8	226.9	196.0	158.3	121.3	102.1	3.6	4.4	4.9	5.2
320.31	348.65	400.22	271.6	228.0	200.4	162.4	124.9	114.8	2.5	4.4	5.1	5.5
17347.37	**21002.44**	**23628.60**	**14051.7**	**756.8**	**395.5**	**209.5**	**130.1**	**106.8**	**12.8**	**11.2**	**10.3**	**8.6**
206.52	229.18	251.37	620.8	169.0	129.7	129.2	113.3	103.9	4.6	2.8	1.9	2.9
5777.17	6109.95	6454.00	14910.6	699.6	348.2	190.0	122.8	105.5	13.0	10.8	9.3	7.4
11363.68	14663.31	16923.23	18507.9	825.1	438.1	222.9	134.1	107.5	13.6	11.7	11.1	9.3
130522	142860	156427	4797.9	487.3	250.8	170.4	114.5	103.9	9.9	8.7	6.8	6.1
413.46	416.69	446.28	680.1	170.6	135.3	120.7	108.7	103.2	4.7	2.7	2.2	2.1
44.09	13.01	13.20	11.9	15.0	25.5	30.7	29.9	101.5	-5.1	-9.5	-9.3	-12.3
48.58	60.57	64.26	1242.9	194.9	131.5	161.0	132.3	106.1	6.3	3.6	2.0	5.4
369.10	368.79	385.32	692.0	125.7	110.4	118.2	104.4	104.5	4.8	1.2	0.7	1.9
22.86	13.52	11.49	227.5	35.1	35.9	35.5	50.3	85.0	2.0	-5.4	-7.1	-10.9
48.39	45.42	46.52	1472.2	143.1	119.8	105.4	96.1	102.4	6.8	1.9	1.3	0.6
17935.16	20314.23	21366.49	25466.5	935.3	403.9	194.2	121.5	106.0	14.5	12.5	10.5	7.7
220.99	296.52	292.26	127070.0	7670.9	706.8	215.2	132.3	98.6	19.0	25.7	15.0	8.9
2613	28228	60606					2319.4	214.7				
363.77	230.78	218.41		362.1	111.1	49.5	60.0	94.6		7.0	0.8	-7.5
349.74	329.84	309.50		532.3	211.6	172.8	88.5	93.8		9.2	5.5	6.3
568.39	609.91	536.78					94.4	88.0				
1154.23	732.32	813.20	254125.1	786.2	277.8	127.7	70.5	111.0	21.1	11.5	7.6	2.8
2.26	0.89	0.95	35.3	5.0	2.4	4.1	42.0	106.7	-2.5	-14.6	-23.4	-29.8
1.18	1.81	2.56					217.2	141.7				
13960	9851	7963					57.0	80.8				
1737	4188	4200					241.8	100.3				
30.17	182.67	166.80					552.9	91.3				
101.44	160.43	159.63	864.7	105.6	51.7	39.6	157.4	99.5	5.4	0.3	-4.6	-9.8
5405.95	5938.40	6920.21	114038.1	895.2	544.4	261.8	143.9	116.5	18.7	12.2	12.9	11.3
1406.81	1746.66	2099.90	233471.9	645.5	556.0	366.5	149.2	120.2	20.8	10.3	13.0	15.5
6994.42	**8810.91**	**9551.57**	**52796.5**	**884.8**	**541.3**	**250.9**	**136.6**	**108.4**	**16.5**	**12.2**	**12.8**	**10.8**

Note: I. Indices of gross domestic product and gross industrial output value are calculated at comparable coverage.

II. The relevant data of agricultural production in 2016 and 2017 have been revised, and the absolute number follows the historical number. The relative number is calculated on the basis of adjusted data.

III.The GDP data of 2008-2018 and the total retail sales of consumer goods in 1992-2018 are revised in 2019, according to the data of the fourth national economic census.

1-8 续表

指　　标	Item	1978	2000	2005	2010
运输邮电	**Transport, Post and Telecommunication**				
货运量 (万吨)	Total Freight Traffic (10000 tons)		27972	38153	57369
#铁　路	Railway		5398	6379	6689
公　路	Highway		12549	20601	39696
水　路	Waterway		9569	10710	10169
民　航	Civil Aviation		27	63	90
客运量 (万人次)	Total Passenger Traffic (10000 person-times)		26097	40524	62595
#铁　路	Railway		4848	6356	9362
公　路	Highway		19964	30782	47296
水　路	Waterway		190	104	273
民　航	Civil Aviation		1095	3282	5664
港口货物吞吐量 (万吨)	Volume of Freight Handled at Ports (10000 tons)	1950	12455	27283	42526
邮电业务收入 (亿元)	Postal and Telecommunication Services (100 million yuan)	0.24	138.48	222.06	290.09
对外贸易、外经	**Foreign Trade and Economic Cooperation**				
商品进口总值 (亿美元)	Total Imports through Customs (USD 100 million)		115.60	268.07	553.89
商品出口总值 (亿美元)	Total Exports through Customs (USD 100 million)		117.91	266.68	483.79
外商直接投资实际使用金额 (亿美元)	Amount of Foreign Direct Investment Capital Actually Used (USD 100 million)		29.89	26.49	39.79
财　政	**Government Finance**				
一般公共预算收入 (亿元)	General Budgetary Revenue (100 million yuan)	13.65	200.55	371.26	872.65
一般公共预算支出 (亿元)	General Budgetary Expenditure (100 million yuan)	3.87	240.72	438.41	977.32
价格指数 (上年=100)	**Price Indices (preceding year =100)**				
城市居民消费价格总指数	Urban Residents Consumer Price Index	100.3	102.8	101.5	103.2
人民生活	**People's Livelihood**				
城镇非私营单位从业人员年平均工资 (元)	Average Wage of Employed Persons in Urban Units (yuan)	714	19091	33853	54495
城镇非私营单位在岗职工年平均工资 (元)	Average Wage of Fully Employed Staff and Workers in Urban Units (yuan)		19674	34328	54807
城市居民年人均可支配收入 (元)	Per Capita Annual Disposable Income of Urban Households (yuan)	442	13967	18287	30658
农村居民年人均可支配收入 (元)	Per Capita Annual Disposable Income of Rural Households (yuan)	250	6086	7080	12676
教育文化	**Education and Culture**				
普通高等学校所数 (所)	Number of Regular Institutions of Higher Education (unit)	15	31	59	77
普通高等学校在校学生数 (万人)	Number of Students Enrollment of Regular Institutions of Higher Education (10000 persons)	2.17	18.51	55.43	84.39
普通中学所数 (所)	Number of Regular Secondary Schools (unit)	234	388	448	475
普通中学在校学生数 (万人)	Number of Students Enrollment of Regular Secondary Schools (10000 persons)	38.43	42.53	55.03	57.23
小学学校所数 (所)	Number of Primary Schools (unit)	1515	1626	1283	1004
小学学校在校学生数 (万人)	Number of Students Enrollment of Primary Schools (10000 persons)	56.92	75.70	90.34	82.48
卫　生	**Health Care**				
医院病床数 (万张)	Hospital Beds (10000 units)	1.44	3.37	3.94	5.32
卫生技术人员 (万人)	Medical Technical Personnel (10000 persons)	3.15	5.57	6.42	9.55
#医　生	Doctors	1.20	2.35	2.59	3.36

注：1.国家统计局对2012年城市居民可支配收入统计方法有所调整，绝对值按新口径，增长幅度按可比口径计算。
2.2019年起，港口统计口径和部分货类吞吐量的计算方法有所调整，同时对2018年同期数据进行了调整。

continued

2015	2018	2019	速度指标(%) Indices and Growth Rates (%)									
			指数(2019为以下各年) Index(2019 as percentage of the following years)						平均增长速度 Average Annual Growth Rate			
			1978	2000	2005	2010	2015	2018	1979-2019	2001-2019	2006-2019	2011-2019
100124	127752	136165		521.9	382.3	254.5	145.7	106.6		9.1	10.1	10.9
4811	1989	2105		109.6	92.8	88.6	123.1	105.8		0.5	-0.5	-1.3
71284	82032	88352		748.2	455.5	236.5	131.7	107.7		11.2	11.4	10.0
23007	42608	44571		465.2	416.1	438.3	193.6	104.6		8.4	10.7	17.8
116	137	140		517.8	221.9	155.3	120.5	102.0		9.0	5.9	5.0
106082	48048	49819		515.2	331.9	215.0	126.8	103.7		9.0	8.9	8.9
13647	13355	14530		399.7	305.1	207.2	142.1	108.8		7.6	8.3	8.4
85109	25725	25625		493.0	319.9	207.9	115.5	99.6		8.8	8.7	8.5
281	55	33		95.5	174.4	66.5	64.5	60.1		-0.2	4.1	-4.4
7045	8913	9630		879.5	293.5	170.1	136.7	108.0		12.1	8.0	6.1
52096	55669	62687	3540.7	554.4	253.0	162.4	132.5	112.6	9.1	9.4	6.9	5.5
540.01	877.90	1045.06	438021.7	759.2	473.4	362.4	194.7	119.7	22.7	11.3	11.7	15.4
527.01	636.55	687.96		596.4	257.0	124.4	130.6	108.1		9.9	7.0	2.5
811.67	848.50	762.23		645.5	285.2	157.3	93.8	89.8		10.3	7.8	5.2
54.16	66.11	71.43		612.0	269.9	179.6	132.0	108.1		10.0	7.4	6.7
1349.47	1634.22	1699.04	12447.2	847.2	457.6	194.7	125.9	104.0	12.5	11.9	11.5	7.7
1727.72	2506.18	2865.33	74039.5	1190.3	653.6	293.2	165.8	114.3	17.5	13.9	14.3	12.7
101.7	102.4	103.0	1032.4	144.5	144.9	128.5	110.8	103.0	5.9	2.0	2.7	2.8
79534	109879	119453	16730.1	625.7	352.9	219.2	150.2	108.7	13.3	10.1	9.4	9.1
81171	111839	123498		627.7	359.8	225.3	152.1	110.4		10.2	9.6	9.4
46735	59982	65052	18620.8	589.7	391.3	233.4	139.4	108.5	13.6	9.8	10.2	9.9
19323	26020	28868	16021.9	657.5	480.7	268.6	149.4	110.9	13.2	10.4	14.4	11.6
81	82	81	540.0	261.3	137.3	105.2	100.0	98.8	4.2	5.2	2.3	0.6
104.32	108.64	114.09	5257.6	616.4	205.8	135.2	109.4	105.0	10.1	10.0	5.3	3.4
510	527	534	228.2	137.6	119.2	112.4	104.7	101.3	2.0	1.7	1.3	1.3
51.52	51.44	52.62	136.9	123.7	95.6	91.9	102.1	102.3	0.8	1.1	-0.3	-0.9
941	965	980	64.7	60.3	76.4	97.6	104.1	101.6	-1.1	-2.6	-1.9	-0.3
93.79	105.85	110.47	194.1	145.9	122.3	133.9	117.8	104.4	1.6	2.0	1.4	3.3
7.33	8.60	9.09	631.3	269.7	230.7	170.9	124.0	105.7	4.6	5.4	6.2	6.1
12.67	15.65	16.81	533.7	301.8	261.8	176.0	132.7	107.4	4.2	6.0	7.1	6.5
4.25	5.41	5.87	489.2	249.8	226.6	174.7	138.1	108.5	3.9	4.9	6.0	6.4

Note: I. Since 2012, the coverage of per capita annual disposable income of urban households has been adjusted, the grow rate of which being calaulated at comparable coverage.

II. Since 2019, port statistical caliber and the calculation methods of some cargo throughput have been adjusted, and the data of the same period in 2018 have been adjusted.

1-9 各时期主要指标平均每年增长速度
Average Annual Growth Speed of Main Indicators in Different Periods

单位：% (%)

时 期	Period	地区生产总 值 Gross Domestic Product	工 业 总产值 Gross Output Value of Industry	农林牧渔业 总 产 值 Gross Output Value of Agriculture	社会消费品零售总额 Total Retail Sales of Consumer Goods	一般公共预算收入 Genera Budgetary Revenue
"六五"时期	6th Five-year Plan Period	12.7	12.8	6.2	21.2	13.3
"七五"时期	7th Five-year Plan Period	10.8	13.1	4.6	14.5	5.1
"八五"时期	8th Five-year Plan Period	20.2	26.1	10.0	30.4	21.3
"九五"时期	9th Five-year Plan Period	13.2	15.7	5.9	13.6	23.6
"十五"时期	10th Five-year Plan Period	13.9	18.3	5.8	10.3	18.1
"十一五"时期	11th Five-year Plan Period	13.6	15.8	2.3	16.6	18.6
"十二五"时期	12th Five-year Plan Period	10.0	9.8	2.1	12.9	9.1
1979-2019	1979-2019	12.8	14.5	4.7	16.5	12.5
2001-2019	2001-2019	11.2	12.5	2.7	12.2	11.9
2006-2019	2006-2019	10.3	10.5	2.2	12.8	11.5
2011-2019	2011-2019	8.6	7.7	2.1	10.8	7.7

注：2019年，根据第四次全国经济普查结果，对2008—2018年度地区生产总值和1992—2018年度社会消费品零售总额数据进行了修订。

Note: In 2019, according to the results of the fourth national economic census, the 2008-2018 regional GDP and the total retail sales of consumer goods in 1992-2018 were revised.

1-10 全市产业及主要结构情况

Basic Statistics on Industries and Main Structure of Guangzhou

项　　目	Item	2018	2019
地区生产总值 (亿元)	Gross Domestic Product (100 milllion yuan)	21002.44	23628.60
# 服务业增加值	Service Industry Added Value	14663.31	16923.23
现代服务业增加值 (亿元)	Modern Service Added Value (100 milllion yuan)	9467.43	11150.25
规模以上工业增加值 (亿元)	Added Value of Industry above Designated Size (100 milllion yuan)	4209.48	4347.79
先进制造业增加值 (亿元)	Added Value of Advanced Manufacturing Industry (100 milllion yuan)	2531.34	2466.38
高技术制造业增加值 (亿元)	Added Value of High-technology Industry (100 milllion yuan)	576.44	592.87
民营经济增加值 (亿元)	Added Value of Private Economy (100 milllion yuan)	8394.38	9532.60
规模以上民营工业增加值 (亿元)	Added Value of Private Industry above Designated Size (100 milllion yuan)	907.26	1022.33
固定资产投资 (亿元)	Total Investment in Fixed Assets (100 milllion yuan)	5938.40	6920.21
民间投资 (亿元)	Private Investment in Fixed Assets (100 milllion yuan)	2194.73	2805.56
出口 (亿元)	Exports (100 milllion yuan)	5607.50	5258.36
现代服务业增加值占服务业增加值比重 (%)	Modern Service Added Value Accounts for Service Industry Added Value (%)	64.57	65.89
先进制造业增加值占规模以上工业增加值的比重 (%)	Added Value of Advanced Manufacturing Industry Accounts for Added Value of Industry above Designated Size (%)	60.13	57.03
高技术制造业增加值占规模以上工业增加值的比重 (%)	Added Value of High-technology Industry Accounts for Added Value of Industry above Designated Size (%)	13.69	13.71
民营经济增加值占GDP比重 (%)	Added Value of Private Economy Accounts for Gross Domestic Product (%)	39.97	40.34
规模以上民营工业增加值占规模以上工业增加值比重 (%)	Added Value of Private Industry above Designated Size Accounts for Added Value of Industry above Designated Size (%)	21.55	23.64
民间投资占固定资产投资比重 (%)	Private Investment in Fixed Assets Accounts for Total Investment in Fixed Assets (%)	36.96	40.54
工业品内销占工业销售产值的比重 (%)	Domestic Sales of Industrial Products Accounts for Sales Value of Industry (%)	85.35	85.48
私营企业出口占全市出口的比重 (%)	Private Sector Exports Accounts for Total Exports (%)	52.74	52.42
一般贸易出口占全市出口的比重 (%)	General Trade Exports Accounts for Total Exports (%)	36.85	41.98
加工贸易出口占全市出口的比重 (%)	Processing Trade Exports Accounts for Total Exports (%)	28.46	28.17

1-11 主要年份人民物质文化生活水平
Material and Culture Life of the People in Main Years

项　目	Item	2018	2019
城镇非私营单位在岗职工年平均工资　(元)	Average Wage of Fully Employed Staff and Workers in Urban Units (yuan)	111839	123498
城市居民年人均可支配收入　(元)	Per Capita Annual Disposable Income of Urban Residents (yuan)	59982	65052
农村居民年人均可支配收入　(元)	Per Capita Annual Disposable Income of Rural Residents (yuan)	26020	28868
社会消费品零售总额　(亿元)	Total Retail Sales of Consumer Goods (100 million yuan)	8810.91	9551.57
储　蓄	**Savings Deposits**		
住户存款余额　(亿元)	Deposits of Households (100 million yuan)	16042.06	17980.56
平均每人储蓄额　(元)	Per Capita Savings Deposits (yuan)	109119	119036
交　通	**Transportation**		
每万人拥有公交车辆　(辆)	Possession of Buses per 10000 Persons (unit)	16.55	16.36
公交车辆平均每日乘客人数　(万人次)	Average Daily Passengers by Buses (10000 person-times)	627.73	613.95
每万人拥有出租汽车　(辆)	Possession of Taxis per 10000 Persons (unit)	24.60	21.50
出租车平均每日乘客人数　(万人次)	Average Daily Passengers by Taxi (10000 person-times)	165.84	146.57
通讯、电信	**Postal and Telecommunication Services**		
城市电话普及率(含移动电话)　(部/百人)	Possession of Telephones per 100 Persons in Urban Areas (including mobile telephones) (sets/100 persons)	472.00	265.01
每人每年函件交寄　(件)	Per Capita Annual Number of Letters Mailed (unit)	568	687
供　气	**Gas Supply**		
居民燃气普及率　(%)	Popularization Rate of Residents with Access to Gas (%)	99.10	99.20
自来水	**Tap Water**		
人均日生活用水量　(升)	Per Capita Daily Water Used (liter)	261.36	263.86

注：2019年，根据第四次全国经济普查结果，对1992—2018年度社会消费品零售总额数据进行了修订。
Note: In 2019, according to the results of the fourth national economic census, the total retail sales of consumer goods in 1992-2018 were revised.

1-11 续表 continued

项　　目	Item	2018	2019
教　育	**Education**		
每万人拥有在校大学生　（人）	Number of University and College Students Enrollment per 10000 Persons (person)	1171	1209
适龄儿童入学率　(%)	Percentage of School-age Children Enrolled (%)	100.00	100.00
卫　生	**Public Health**		
每万人拥有医院床位　（张）	Number of Hospital Beds per 10000 Persons (unit)	58	59
每万人拥有医生　（人）	Number of Doctors per 10000 Persons (person)	36	38
就　业	**Employment**		
城镇每一就业者负担人口　（人）	Number of Dependents per Employee in Urban Areas (person)	1.71	1.71
绿　化	**Green Areas**		
建成区绿化覆盖率　(%)	Coverage Rate of Green Areas in Developed Land Area (%)	39.22	39.91
人均公园绿地面积　（平方米）	Per Capita Garden (sq.m)	17.30	17.96
居民家庭耐用消费品拥有量	**Number of Durable Consumer Goods Owned**		
每百户城市居民家庭拥有	Owned by per 100 Urban Households		
彩色电视机　（台）	Color TV Sets (set)	131	128
计算机　（台）	Computers (set)	122	123
洗衣机　（台）	Washing Machines (set)	102	103
电冰箱　（台）	Refrigerators (set)	103	104
空调器　（台）	Air Conditioners (set)	239	244
每百户农村居民家庭拥有	Owned by Per 100 Rural Household		
彩色电视机　（台）	Color TV Sets (set)	145	146
计算机　（台）	Computers (set)	87	88
洗衣机　（台）	Washing Machines (set)	105	107
电冰箱　（台）	Refrigerators (set)	109	110
空调器　（台）	Air Conditioners (set)	221	237

1-12 主要年份地区生产总值

Gross Domestic Product in Main Years

单位:万元 (10000 yuan)

年 份 Year	地区生产总值 Gross Domestic Product	第一产业 Primary Industry	第二产业 Secondary Industry	第三产业 Tertiary Industry	地区生产总值中 In GDP: 工 业 Industry	建筑业 Construction	人均地区生产总值（元）Per Capita GDP (yuan)	人均地区生产总值(美元) Per Capita GDP (USD)
1978	430947	50287	252479	128181	243585	8894	907	
1980	575497	62438	313734	199325	295337	18397	1160	
1985	1243623	120449	658130	465044	577048	81082	2302	784
1986	1395466	132079	701074	562313	608511	92563	2536	734
1987	1732050	156794	794127	781129	693003	101124	3092	831
1988	2400818	227772	1141606	1031440	972078	169528	4205	1130
1989	2878733	243187	1296309	1339237	1093864	202445	4953	1315
1990	3195952	257288	1362975	1575689	1180978	181997	5418	1133
1991	3866741	281734	1799166	1785841	1582970	216196	5956	1119
1992	5107027	356399	2413129	2337499	2120096	293033	7521	1364
1993	7443455	475960	3512607	3454888	3050098	462509	10481	1819
1994	9853082	606222	4556278	4690582	3870183	686095	13264	1539
1995	12603097	734606	5787475	6081016	4941140	846335	16222	1943
1996	14706621	811630	6736549	7158442	5791501	945048	18098	2179
1997	16828743	857155	7642990	8328598	6635562	1007428	19800	2389
1998	19004058	888763	8245913	9869382	7113774	1132139	21378	2582
1999	21492534	928522	9375989	11188023	8044065	1331924	23116	2792
2000	25055794	943718	10299412	13812664	8861172	1438240	25758	3112
2001	28579151	972806	11228325	16378020	9657735	1570590	28700	3468
2002	32243283	1030721	12245382	18967180	10638507	1606875	32544	3932
2003	37804451	1099080	15000699	21704672	13279574	1721125	38621	4666
2004	44773511	1171452	18054293	25547766	16111365	1942928	46182	5579
2005	51878466	1302159	20670012	29906295	18652577	2017435	54160	6612
2006	61242011	1285022	24689504	35267485	22538389	2151115	62930	7894
2007	72029498	1495247	28665860	41868391	26428369	2237491	70284	9243
2008	83660227	1548659	32750141	49361427	30240254	2565556	77165	11110
2009	91467431	1558600	34601705	55307126	31772238	2898289	79457	11629
2010	106406742	1686203	40532998	64187541	37021616	3601957	86582	12753
2011	121996914	1800454	46326780	73869680	42089867	4407184	95830	14756
2012	131946870	1854415	47731922	82360533	43383733	4617236	103123	16337
2013	150504031	1961339	53184480	95358212	48209169	5170729	116825	18802
2014	161359536	2008134	56478499	102872903	51217728	5385230	124088	20200
2015	173473724	2065218	57771661	113636845	52329802	5576564	130522	20927
2016	185597316	2160317	58134525	125302474	52701453	5763975	134761	20302
2017	198716679	2204517	59006069	137506093	53407784	5978984	139246	20624
2018	210024435	2291770	61099495	146633170	54874446	6620846	142860	21588
2019	236285953	2513711	64540005	169232237	57229397	7736290	156427	23639

注：1．本表数据按当年价格计算。
2．从1991年起，人均地区生产总值按常住人口计算。
3．人均地区生产总值(美元)按当年年平均汇率换算。
4．2019年，根据第四次全国经济普查结果，对2008—2018年度地区生产总值数据进行了修订。

Note: I. The data in this table are calculated at current prices.
II. Since 1991 the per capita GDP are calculated by resident population.
III. The Per Capita GDP (USD) are calculated at current annual average exchange rate.
IV. The GDP data of 2008-2018 are revised in 2019,according to the data of the fourth national economic census.

1-13 主要年份地区生产总值指数（上年=100）

Indices of Gross Domestic Product in Main Years (Preceding Year=100)

年 份 Year	地区生产总值 Gross Domestic Product	第一产业 Primary Industry	第二产业 Secondary Industry	第三产业 Tertiary Industry	地区生产总值中: In Gross Domestic Product 工业 Industry	建筑业 Construction	人均地区生产总值 Per Capita GDP
1978	110.3	100.1	108.5	117.6	108.7	105.0	108.8
1980	115.4	114.6	119.0	110.3	117.4	154.8	113.2
1985	118.3	107.4	124.3	111.7	123.1	135.7	116.3
1986	105.7	100.5	101.3	114.1	101.3	101.3	103.7
1987	115.2	99.0	108.2	128.9	108.6	104.5	113.2
1988	117.8	104.6	126.3	109.0	125.1	137.2	115.6
1989	104.7	100.7	100.6	111.4	101.0	96.9	102.9
1990	111.3	103.7	107.8	116.9	109.6	92.1	109.7
1991	116.3	109.1	127.2	108.0	128.6	118.2	114.6
1992	123.3	120.4	128.1	118.8	128.7	123.3	117.9
1993	126.4	102.1	133.6	122.4	132.1	144.0	120.9
1994	118.8	112.6	123.2	114.5	121.0	137.3	113.6
1995	116.5	104.1	117.1	117.5	118.8	107.0	111.4
1996	112.5	105.3	113.5	112.1	115.7	99.5	107.6
1997	113.5	105.5	113.0	115.0	114.8	99.7	108.5
1998	113.2	104.0	112.7	114.7	113.0	110.2	108.2
1999	113.3	110.4	115.7	110.6	115.4	118.2	108.3
2000	113.4	101.7	111.9	116.3	112.5	106.7	108.4
2001	112.8	102.2	111.0	114.9	111.2	109.5	110.2
2002	113.3	109.8	112.5	114.1	113.9	103.9	113.9
2003	115.2	104.5	121.4	111.3	124.3	101.6	116.6
2004	115.1	105.4	117.2	113.9	118.6	105.7	116.2
2005	113.0	105.6	113.0	113.3	113.8	105.6	114.3
2006	115.0	95.7	116.6	114.7	117.9	104.4	113.2
2007	115.5	102.8	114.2	116.9	115.5	100.6	109.7
2008	112.6	95.2	111.1	114.3	112.0	102.6	106.5
2009	111.7	104.0	109.6	113.3	109.5	111.6	105.2
2010	113.0	103.1	113.0	113.2	112.5	119.0	105.8
2011	111.4	103.0	111.9	111.2	111.8	114.1	107.5
2012	110.4	103.3	108.4	111.8	109.0	102.8	109.8
2013	111.5	102.9	111.2	111.9	111.9	102.3	110.8
2014	108.5	101.8	107.4	109.3	107.8	102.4	107.5
2015	108.3	102.4	106.8	109.3	107.0	104.8	105.9
2016	107.6	100.6	105.6	108.8	106.2	104.0	103.9
2017	106.7	102.2	104.6	107.9	105.2	99.2	103.0
2018	106.0	106.0	105.4	106.4	105.5	104.1	102.9
2019	106.8	103.9	105.5	107.5	104.8	112.4	103.9

注：1.本表数据按可比价格计算。
　　2.2019年，根据第四次全国经济普查结果，对2008—2018年度地区生产总值数据进行了修订。

Note: I.The data in this table are calculated at comparable prices.
　　II. The GDP data of 2008-2018 are revised in 2019,according to the data of the fourth national economic census.

1-14 主要年份地区生产总值构成

Composition of Gross Domestic Product in Main Years

单位：% (%)

年 份 Year	地区生产总值 Gross Domestic Product	第一产业 Primary Industry	第二产业 Secondary Industry	第三产业 Tertiary Industry	地区生产总值中：In Gross Domestic Product 工 业 Industry
1978	100.00	11.67	58.59	29.74	56.52
1980	100.00	10.85	54.51	34.64	51.32
1985	100.00	9.69	52.92	37.39	46.40
1986	100.00	9.46	50.24	40.30	43.61
1987	100.00	9.05	45.85	45.10	40.01
1988	100.00	9.49	47.55	42.96	40.49
1989	100.00	8.45	45.03	46.52	38.00
1990	100.00	8.05	42.65	49.30	36.95
1991	100.00	7.29	46.53	46.18	40.94
1992	100.00	6.98	47.25	45.77	41.51
1993	100.00	6.39	47.19	46.42	40.98
1994	100.00	6.15	46.24	47.61	39.28
1995	100.00	5.83	45.92	48.25	39.21
1996	100.00	5.52	45.81	48.67	39.38
1997	100.00	5.09	45.42	49.49	39.43
1998	100.00	4.68	43.39	51.93	37.43
1999	100.00	4.32	43.62	52.06	37.43
2000	100.00	3.77	41.11	55.12	35.37
2001	100.00	3.40	39.29	57.31	33.79
2002	100.00	3.20	37.98	58.82	32.99
2003	100.00	2.91	39.68	57.41	35.13
2004	100.00	2.62	40.32	57.06	35.98
2005	100.00	2.51	39.84	57.65	35.95
2006	100.00	2.10	40.31	57.59	36.80
2007	100.00	2.08	39.80	58.12	36.69
2008	100.00	1.85	39.15	59.00	36.15
2009	100.00	1.70	37.83	60.47	34.74
2010	100.00	1.58	38.09	60.33	34.79
2011	100.00	1.48	37.97	60.55	34.50
2012	100.00	1.41	36.17	62.42	32.88
2013	100.00	1.30	35.34	63.36	32.03
2014	100.00	1.24	35.00	63.76	31.74
2015	100.00	1.19	33.30	65.51	30.17
2016	100.00	1.16	31.32	67.52	28.40
2017	100.00	1.11	29.69	69.20	26.88
2018	100.00	1.09	29.09	69.82	26.13
2019	100.00	1.06	27.32	71.62	24.22

注：本表数据按当年价格计算。

Note: The data in this table are calculated at comparable prices.

1-15 地区生产总值

Gross Domestic Product

单位：万元 (10000 yuan)

项目	Item	2018	2019	2019年比2018年增长(%) Growth Rate in 2019 over 2018 (%)
地区生产总值	Gross Domestic Product	210024435	236285953	6.8
按产业分	Grouped By Industry			
第一产业	Primary Industry	2291770	2513711	3.9
第二产业	Secondary Industry	61099495	64540005	5.5
第三产业	Tertiary Industry	146633170	169232237	7.5
按行业分	Grouped By Sector			
农、林、牧、渔业	Agriculture, Forestry, Animal Husbandry and Fishery	2537526	2763118	3.7
工　业	Industry	54874446	57229397	4.8
建筑业	Construction	6620846	7736290	12.4
批发和零售业	Wholesale and Retail Trade	29136669	32376773	6.3
交通运输、仓储和邮政业	Transport, Storage and Post	12633314	13726416	5.4
住宿和餐饮业	Hotels and Catering Services	4031834	4491180	2.7
金融业	Financial Intermediation	17575099	20418743	8.2
房地产业	Real Estate	21022963	26489185	8.8
其他服务业	Other Services	61591738	71054851	8.3
信息传输、软件和信息技术服务业	Information Transmission, Software and Information Technology	11607458		
租赁和商务服务业	Leasing and Business Services	10489356		
科学研究和技术服务业	Scientific Research and Technical Services	6733426		
水利、环境和公共设施管理业	Management of Water Conservancy, Environment and Public Facilities	1031183		
居民服务、修理和其他服务业	Service to Households, Repair and Other Services	3967915		
教　育	Education	10292874		
卫生和社会工作	Health and Social Work	5943456		
文化、体育和娱乐业	Culture, Sports and Entertainment	2591692		
公共管理、社会保障和社会组织	Public Management, Social Security and Social Organizations	8934378		

注：1.本表数据绝对值按当年价格计算，增长速度按可比价格计算；
2.2019年为年快报数据，其他服务业数据无法细分。

Note: I. The level data in this table are calculated at current prices while the growth rates at comparable prices.
II.2019 is the annual express data, and other service industry data can not be subdivided.

1-16 各时期地区生产总值和平均每年增长速度

Gross Domestic Product and Annual Average Growth Speed in Different Periods

时 期	Period	地区生产总值 Gross Domestic Product	第一产业 Primary Industry	第二产业 Secondary Industry	第三产业 Tertiary Industry	地区生产总值中: In Gross Domestic Product	
						工 业 Industry	建筑业 Construction
绝对值 (万元)	Absolute Figure (10000 yuan)						
"六五"时期	6th Five-year Plan Period	4373327	459872	2395362	1518093	2137482	257880
"七五"时期	7th Five-year Plan Period	11603019	1017120	5296091	5289808	4548434	747657
"八五"时期	8th Five-year Plan Period	38873402	2454921	18068655	18349826	15564487	2504168
"九五"时期	9th Five-year Plan Period	97087750	4429788	42300853	50357109	36446074	5854779
"十五"时期	10th Five-year Plan Period	195278862	5576218	77198711	112503933	68339758	8858953
"十一五"时期	11th Five-year Plan Period	414805909	7573731	161240208	245991970	148000866	13454408
"十二五"时期	12th Five-year Plan Period	739281075	9689560	261493342	468098173	237230299	25156943
1950-1978	1950-1978	5578418	753734	3146791	1677893	2999275	147516
1979-2019	1979-2019	2332990739	40485524	811356774	1481148441	731034962	82963859
1991-2019	1991-2019	2315951381	38894533	803081863	1473974985	723794564	81929346
1996-2019	1996-2019	2277077979	36439612	785013208	1455625159	708230077	79425178
2001-2019	2001-2019	2179990229	32009824	742712355	1405268050	671784003	73570399
2003-2019	2003-2019	2119167795	30006297	719238648	1369922850	651487761	70392934
平均每年增长 (%)	Annual Average Growth Speed (%)						
"六五"时期	6th Five-year Plan Period	12.7	7.6	13.6	12.5	12.5	27.6
"七五"时期	7th Five-year Plan Period	10.8	1.7	8.4	15.9	8.8	5.3
"八五"时期	8th Five-year Plan Period	20.2	9.5	25.7	16.1	25.8	25.3
"九五"时期	9th Five-year Plan Period	13.2	5.4	13.4	13.7	14.3	6.6
"十五"时期	10th Five-year Plan Period	13.9	5.4	15.0	13.5	16.3	5.2
"十一五"时期	11th Five-year Plan Period	13.6	0.1	12.9	14.5	13.4	7.4
"十二五"时期	12th Five-year Plan Period	10.0	2.7	9.1	10.7	9.5	5.2
1950-1978	1950-1978	9.2	3.8	12.7	9.5	12.7	13.1
1979-2019	1979-2019	12.8	4.6	13.0	13.6	13.1	12.1
1991-2019	1991-2019	13.1	4.4	13.7	12.9	14.2	9.0
1996-2019	1996-2019	11.6	3.3	11.3	12.2	12.0	5.9
2001-2019	2001-2019	11.2	2.8	10.8	11.7	11.4	5.7
2003-2019	2003-2019	11.0	2.4	10.7	11.4	11.2	5.6

注:1.本表数据绝对值按当年价格计算，增长速度按可比价格计算；

2.2019年，根据第四次全国经济普查结果，对2008—2018年度地区生产总值数据进行了修订，因此对应的数据也进行了调整。

Note: I. The level data in this table are calculated at current prices while the growth rates at comparable prices.

II. The GDP data of 2008-2018 are revised in 2019, according to the data of the fourth national economic census. Therefore, the corresponding data has also been adjusted.

1-17　三次产业对地区生产总值增长的贡献率(1990-2019年)

Share of the Contributions of the Three Strata of Industry to the Growth of GDP (1990-2019)

单位：%　　(%)

年　份 Year	地区生产总值 Gross Domestic Product	第一产业 Primary Industry	第二产业 Secondary Industry	第三产业 Tertiary Industry	地区生产总值中：In Gross Domestic Product 工　业 Industry
1990	100.0	1.7	37.1	61.2	41.0
1991	100.0	4.2	71.3	24.5	64.9
1992	100.0	6.2	56.3	37.5	50.4
1993	100.0	0.5	61.6	37.9	51.8
1994	100.0	3.7	63.0	33.3	49.8
1995	100.0	1.3	54.7	44.0	51.5
1996	100.0	2.0	57.4	40.6	57.7
1997	100.0	1.8	51.8	46.4	51.9
1998	100.0	1.2	51.5	47.3	47.3
1999	100.0	2.9	62.8	34.3	55.5
2000	100.0	0.5	48.4	51.1	45.7
2001	100.0	0.7	35.3	64.0	31.1
2002	100.0	2.5	38.1	59.4	36.4
2003	100.0	1.0	56.7	42.3	56.1
2004	100.0	1.1	48.4	50.5	46.7
2005	100.0	1.2	43.4	55.4	41.6
2006	100.0	-0.7	44.1	56.6	42.9
2007	100.0	0.4	37.0	62.6	36.9
2008	100.0	-0.7	35.1	65.6	35.0
2009	100.0	0.5	32.4	67.1	29.8
2010	100.0	0.4	38.6	61.0	34.6
2011	100.0	0.4	39.9	59.7	36.1
2012	100.0	0.4	31.1	68.5	30.4
2013	100.0	0.3	36.5	63.2	35.6
2014	100.0	0.3	32.7	67.0	31.7
2015	100.0	0.3	30.5	69.2	28.9
2016	100.0	0.1	24.6	75.3	24.4
2017	100.0	0.4	22.3	77.3	23.0
2018	100.0	1.1	28.5	70.4	26.7
2019	100.0	0.6	25.2	74.2	20.6

注：1．本表数据按可比价格计算。
　　2．三次产业贡献率指各产业增加值增量与GDP增量之比。

Note: I. The data of this table are calculated at comparable prices.
　　II. Share of the contributions of the three strata of industry to the growth of GDP refers to the proportion of the increment of the Value-added of each Industry to the increment of GDP.

1-18 三次产业对地区生产总值增长的拉动（1990-2019年）

Contribution of the Three Strata of Industry to the Growth of GDP (1990-2019)

单位：百分点 (percentage points)

年 份 Year	地区生产 总 值 Gross Domestic Product	第一产业 Primary Industry	第二产业 Secondary Industry	第三产业 Tertiary Industry	地区生产总值中： In Gross Domestic Product 工 业 Industry
1990	11.3	0.2	4.2	6.9	4.6
1991	16.3	0.7	11.6	4.0	10.6
1992	23.3	1.4	13.1	8.8	11.7
1993	26.4	0.1	16.3	10.0	13.7
1994	18.8	0.7	11.8	6.3	9.4
1995	16.5	0.2	9.0	7.3	8.5
1996	12.5	0.2	7.2	5.1	7.2
1997	13.5	0.2	7.0	6.3	7.0
1998	13.2	0.2	6.8	6.2	6.2
1999	13.3	0.4	8.3	4.6	7.4
2000	13.4	0.1	6.5	6.8	6.1
2001	12.8	0.1	4.5	8.2	4.0
2002	13.3	0.3	5.1	7.9	4.8
2003	15.2	0.2	8.6	6.4	8.5
2004	15.1	0.2	7.3	7.6	7.0
2005	13.0	0.2	5.6	7.2	5.4
2006	15.0	-0.1	6.6	8.5	6.4
2007	15.5	0.1	5.7	9.7	5.7
2008	12.6	-0.1	4.4	8.3	4.4
2009	11.7	0.1	3.8	7.8	3.5
2010	13.0	0.1	5.0	7.9	4.5
2011	11.4	0.1	4.5	6.8	4.1
2012	10.4	0.1	3.2	7.1	3.2
2013	11.5		4.2	7.3	4.1
2014	8.5		2.8	5.7	2.7
2015	8.3		2.6	5.7	2.4
2016	7.6		1.9	5.7	1.9
2017	6.7		1.5	5.2	1.5
2018	6.0	0.1	1.7	4.2	1.6
2019	6.8		1.8	5.0	1.4

注：1．本表数据按可比价格计算。

2．三次产业拉动指GDP增长速度与各产业贡献率之乘积。

Note: I. The data of this table are calculated at comparable prices.

II. Contribution of the three strata of industry to the growth of GDP refers to the growth rate of GDP multiplied by the contribution share of each industry.

1-19 全市国有土地使用权出让、划拨情况

Total City Lease and Administrative Allocation of the Right to the Use of the State-owned Land

项　　目	Item	2018	2019
国有土地使用权出让	**Lease of the Right to the Use of the State-owned Land**		
出让小计	Lease Sub-total		
出让地块 (宗)	Number of Plots (piece)	353	438
出让面积 (公顷)	Areas (hectare)	2212.27	2406
成交价款 (万元)	Value of Transactions (10000 yuan)	15355745	16142769
# 公开出让	Lease by Public		
出让地块 (宗)	Number of Plots (piece)	207	234
出让面积 (公顷)	Areas (hectare)	1243.03	1448.82
成交价款 (万元)	Value of Transactions (10000 yuan)	15234114	16133632
国有土地使用权划拨	**Allocation of the Right to the Use of the State-owned Land**		
划拨地块 (宗)	Number of Plots (piece)	146	204
划拨面积 (公顷)	Areas (hectare)	969.24	957.53

注：1. 本表数据由广州市规划和自然资源局提供。
2. 本表数据已剔除被解除合同数据。
3. 本表统计范围为全市口径。

Note: I. The data in this table are provided by Guangzhou Municipal Planning and Natural Resources Bureau.
II. The data in this table has excluded the part of terminated contracts.
III.The statistical scale of this table is total city scale.

1-20 全市房地产市场交易情况

Transactions in Total Real Estate Market

项　目		Item		2018	2019
新建商品房现售		**Newly-constructed Commercial Buildings Sold out**			
成交面积	(万平方米)	Transacted Floor Space	(10000 sq.m)	344.84	451.60
#住　宅		Residential Buildings		165.66	222.16
成交金额	(万元)	Transacted Value	(10000 yuan)	6574067	8535974
#住　宅		Residential Buildings		3634625	4998899
住宅成交套数	(套)	Number of Transacted Flats	(flat)	13931	19436
新建商品房预售		**Newly-constructed Commercial Buildings Sold in Advance**			
成交面积	(万平方米)	Transacted Floor Space	(10000 sq.m)	971.53	934.91
#住　宅		Residential Buildings		816.34	738.78
成交金额	(万元)	Transacted Value	(10000 yuan)	19518311	23343240
#住　宅		Residential Buildings		16235378	19314416
住宅成交套数	(套)	Number of Transacted Flats	(flat)	78006	70636
存量房买卖		**Sales of Buildings in Stock**			
成交面积	(万平方米)	Transacted Floor Space	(10000 sq.m)	1083.11	1002.15
#住　宅		Residential Buildings		882.49	790.70
成交金额	(万元)	Transacted Value	(10000 yuan)	20080639	19793400
#住　宅		Residential Buildings		17974625	17550669
住宅成交套数	(套)	Number of Transacted Flats	(flat)	102384	92222

注:1.本表数据由广州市住房和城乡建设局提供。
2.新建商品房现售和新建商品房预售为网签数据，存量房买卖为交易登记数据。
3.本表统计口径为全市口径。

Note: I. The data in this table are provided by Guangzhou Housing and Urban-Rural Construction Committee.
II.The Data of Newly-constructed Commercial Buildings Sold out and Newly-constructed Commercial Buildings Sold in Advance is Net Registered Data.The Data of Buildings in Stock is Transaction Registered Data.
III.The statistical scale of this table is total city scale.

1-21 劳动力市场情况
Statistics on Labor Force Market

项　目	Item	2018	2019
全市经人力资源社会保障部门批准的人力资源服务机构(个)	Number of Employment Service Institutions Approved by Human Resources and Social Security Department (unit)	1308	1523
劳动部门所属	Run by Labor Departments	199	195
非劳动部门所属	Run by Non-labor Departments	1109	1328

注：本表数据由广州市人力资源和社会保障局提供。
Note: The data in this table are provided by Guangzhou Municipal Bureau of Human Resources and Social Security.

1-22 技术市场交易情况
Statistics on Transactions in Technological Market

项　目	Item	2018		2019	
		合同数(项) Numbers of Contracts (unit)	金额(万元) Value (10000 yuan)	合同数(项) Numbers of Contracts (unit)	金额(万元) Value (10000 yuan)
买方市场	**Buyers' Market**	**12158**	**7193802**	**21074**	**12733644**
机关法人	Official Organ as Juridical Person	1655	590830	3927	1924584
事业法人	Institution as Juridical Person	1463	242745	1837	697307
社团法人	Mass Organization as Juridical Person	58	56155	72	4892
企业法人	Corporate as Juridical Person	8767	6256247	14663	9607637
自然人	Natural Person	74	15618	290	460511
其他组织	Others	141	32207	285	38712
卖方市场	**Sellers' Market**	**12158**	**7193802**	**21074**	**12733644**
机关法人	Official Organ as Juridical Person	2	400	13	2054
事业法人	Institution as Juridical Person	2759	181232	4266	762178
社团法人	Mass Organization as Juridical Person	238	527070	154	4384
企业法人	Corporate as Juridical Person	9049	6472745	16536	11948826
自然人	Natural Person	66	9660	87	12141
其他组织	Others	44	2696	18	4061

注：本表数据由广州市科学技术局提供。
Note: The data in this table are provided by Guangzhou Municipal Science and Technology Bureau.

1-23 各区国民经济主要指标（2019年）

项　　目		Item	
土地面积	（平方公里）	Total Land Area	(sq.km)
年末户籍人口	（人）	Year-end Population by household registered	(person)
街道办事处	（个）	Street Communities	(unit)
镇	（个）	Towns	(unit)
社区居委会	（个）	Community Committees	(unit)
村民委员会	（个）	Village Committees	(unit)
地区生产总值	（万元）	Gross Domestic Product	(10000 yuan)
第一产业	（万元）	Primary Industry	(10000 yuan)
第二产业	（万元）	Secondary Industry	(10000 yuan)
第三产业	（万元）	Tertiary Industry	(10000 yuan)
地区生产总值中：工业	（万元）	Industry In Gross Domestic Product	(10000 yuan)
年末全社会从业人员	（人）	Total Number of Employed Persons at Year-end	(person)
# 城镇非私营单位在岗职工年末人数	（人）	Number of Fully Employed Staff and Workers in Urban Units at Year-end	(person)
城镇非私营单位在岗职工工资总额	（万元）	Total Wages of Fully Employed Staff and Workers in Urban Units	(10000 yuan)
城镇非私营单位在岗职工年平均工资	（元）	Average Wages of Fully Employed Staff and Workers in Urban Units	(yuan)
固定资产投资额(按项目所在地分)	（万元）	Investment in Fixed Assets (by project location)	(10000 yuan)
# 建筑和安装工程	（万元）	Construction and Erection Engineering	(10000 yuan)
新增固定资产(按项目所在地分)	（万元）	Newly-increased Investment in Fixed Assets (by Tegion of Item)	(10000 yuan)
一般公共预算收入	（万元）	General Budgetary Revenue	(10000 yuan)
一般公共预算支出	（万元）	General Budgetary Expenditure	(10000 yuan)
农林牧渔业总产值	（万元）	Gross Output Value of Agriculture	(10000 yuan)
社会消费品零售总额	（万元）	Total Retail Sales of Consumer Goods	(10000 yuan)
实际使用外商直接投资金额	（万美元）	Foreign Direct Capital Actually Utilized	(USD 10000)
普通中学学校数	（所）	Number of Regular Secondary Schools	(unit)
普通中学在校学生数	（人）	Number of Students Enrolled in Regular Secondary Schools	(person)
小学学校数	（所）	Number of Primary Schools	(unit)
小学在校学生数	（人）	Number of Students Enrolled in Primary Schools	(person)
幼儿园数	（所）	Number of Kindergartens	(unit)
幼儿园在园人数	（人）	Number of Children Enrolled	(person)
各类卫生机构数	（个）	Number of Health Institutions	(unit)
# 医　院		Hospitals	
各类卫生机构床位数	（张）	Number of Beds	(unit)
# 医　院		Hospitals	
卫生技术人员	（人）	Medical Technical Personnel	(person)
# 执业(助理)医师		Licensed (Assistant) Doctors	

Main Indicators of National Economic by District (2019)

荔湾区 Liwan	越秀区 Yuexiu	海珠区 Haizhu	天河区 Tianhe	白云区 Baiyun	黄埔区 Huangpu	番禺区 Panyu	花都区 Huadu	南沙区 Nansha	从化区 Conghua	增城区 Zengcheng
59.10	33.80	90.40	96.33	795.79	484.17	529.94	970.04	783.86	1974.50	1616.47
755852	1172926	1067334	965694	1080194	562203	1033474	811299	463274	641737	983170
22	18	18	21	18	16	11	4	3	3	6
				4	1	5	6	6	5	7
191	222	265	220	281	112	98	64	33	53	57
				118	28	177	188	128	221	284
11044931	31354734	19351165	50473850	22118231	35024717	20795015	15627599	16832250	3558558	10104903
41617		15397	11830	315592	44082	336746	379258	561346	266344	541499
2759698	1326519	3972651	4007221	4446764	21300997	7288342	7086608	7086712	1268823	3995670
8243616	30028215	15363117	46454799	17355875	13679638	13169927	8161733	9184192	2023391	5567734
2490443	297656	2675209	3152402	3522071	20892095	6413908	7074210	6143484	1090240	3477679
463263	1074143	1015757	2202307	1661773	1046965	1246085	772969	643373	379099	753206
157070	571091	309185	810514	344142	552456	285214	197491	315287	75330	133919
1797789	7747392	4091626	11108300	4169859	6885416	3153867	1778853	2935119	728768	1467835
115631	136855	134474	138534	121233	124912	110524	90997	97491	95638	110514
3308390	886181	3465576	5010135	8655863	13987178	7586224	4563192	7545803	2056823	12136722
1615720	382925	1419806	2338603	3649264	7103631	3786937	2317241	3959022	1093336	4357600
1865982	896209	1844914	4891132	3688460	3236571	3465257	1929354	2776750	797094	2178755
506007	578312	546746	771240	623417	1811949	1026943	832514	839991	285907	1057641
1095664	1245835	1165491	1511256	1817742	3437265	1828300	1446524	2492822	868347	2236147
68758		24002	79317	640997	78139	539587	654360	939402	477266	960976
6028161	12854578	10994359	19240047	11113715	9969456	12455013	5275372	2277866	1203090	4104042
17032	24636	51115	62636	31348	228097	50128	2448	186311	10449	47310
42	35	38	51	70	36	71	81	28	25	57
40811	60239	44400	50733	62247	32271	73751	57221	23653	30534	50362
51	49	82	76	173	61	138	107	62	68	113
65866	71075	90401	118154	165989	72932	155831	145224	51156	58050	110036
109	120	163	208	360	129	344	123	123	90	197
27406	31791	43446	48807	94299	36356	91152	36133	30731	27220	60307
230	401	328	776	734	368	521	527	238	382	588
30	33	18	46	52	21	24	13	12	8	12
7121	24777	10819	13000	21391	4360	6650	4148	1437	2887	3490
6921	22994	10235	12596	19787	3975	5839	2969	1279	2057	2288
10675	44710	17781	26667	24444	7141	12700	9064	2955	4139	7780
3904	14252	6008	9750	8301	2557	4923	3416	1156	1467	2937

1-24 广州开发区国民经济主要指标

Main Indicators of National Economy of Guangzhou Development Zone

项　目	Item	2018	2019
年末社会从业人员　(规模以上)	Year-end Employed Persons (person)	497801	560512
# 工业从业人员	Employed Persons in Industry	304224	325153
地区生产总值 (万元)	Gross Domestic Product (10000 yuan)	27953856	29788922
第一产业	Primary Industry	53897	51050
第二产业	Secondary Industry	18007001	18978796
第三产业	Tertiary Industry	9892958	10759076
地区生产总值中:	In Gross Domestic Product		
工　业	Industry	16624948	17791438
建筑业	Construction	1382053	1187358
固定资产投资额 (万元)	Investment in Fixed Assets (10000 yuan)	10380710	12743236
# 基础(公共)设施	Infrastructure	2815721	3244837
工业项目	Industry	3466771	3448987
利润总额 (万元)	Total Profits (10000 yuan)	9010001	10164101
# 工业利润　(规模以上)	Industrial Profit	5799355	6024695
地方可支配财力 (万元)	Local Disposable Financial Resources (10000 yuan)	5256501	5474698
地方财政支出 (万元)	Local Government Financial Expenditure (10000 yuan)	4110926	4857454
工业总产值 (万元)	Gross Industrial Output Value (10000 yuan)	57967316	59344162
# 港澳台企业产值	Enterprises with Funds from Hong Kong, Macao and Taiwan	10301076	11351879
工业销售产值 (万元)	Output Value of Industrial Products Sold (10000 yuan)	56672998	58721176
商品销售总额 (万元)	Total Sales of Industrial Products (10000 yuan)	53483921	84828536
外贸出口总值 (万美元)	Total Exports (USD 10000)	1667944	1642555
外贸进口总值 (万美元)	Total Imports (USD 10000)	2153756	2127827
利用外资项目(合同)数 (个)	Number of Projects (Contracts) for Utilization of Foreign Capital (unit)	172	166
合同利用外资金额 (万美元)	Contracted Value of Foreign Capital to be Utilized (USD 10000)	414493	200884
外商直接投资实际使用外资金额(万美元)	Total Amount of Foreign Capital Actually Used (USD 10000)	224705	228097

注：1.广州开发区包括广州经济技术开发区、广州保税区、广州高新技术产业开发区和广州出口加工区；
2.2018年区内税收、地方可支配财力和地方财政支出等指标为黄埔区口径数据。

Note: I. The indicators include Guangzhou economic and technological development zone, Guangzhou bonded zone,Guangzhou hi-tech development zone and Guangzhou exportance manufacturing district.

II. The tax,local disposable financial resources and government financial expenditure indicators in 2018 are the caliber data of Huangpu District.

1-25 广州保税区国民经济主要指标

Main Indicators of National Economy of Guangzhou Bonded Zone

项　　目	Item	2018	2019
工业增加值（万元）	Value-added of Industry (10000 yuan)	146662	133140
工业总产值（万元）	Gross Industrial Output Value (10000 yuan)	549295	595033
固定资产投资额（万元）	Investment in Fixed Assets (10000 yuan)	12721	49576
进出区货物总值（万美元）	Total Value of Imports and Exports (USD 10000)	1329514	1318203
利润总额（万元）	Total Profits (10000 yuan)	77932	127808

1-26 广州高新技术产业开发区国民经济主要指标

Main Indicators of National Economy of Guangzhou Hi-tech Development Zone

项　　目	Item	2018	2019
营业总收入（万元）	Revenue (10000 yuan)	105407811	1172456923
工业总产值（万元）	Gross Industrial Output Value (10000 yuan)	68808200	74082459
高新区企业数（个）	Number of Enterprises in Development Zone (unit)	72888	107433
认定高新技术企业数（个）	Number of Enterprises Certified (unit)	3544	3599
港澳台企业数（个）	Number of Enterprises with Funds from Hong Kong, Macao and Taiwan (unit)	127	72
职工人数（人）	Number of Staff and Workers (person)	731682	845249
利润总额（万元）	Total Profits (10000 yuan)	9407206	10108142
合同利用外资（万美元）	Foreign Capital to be Utilized in the Signed Agreements and Contracts (USD 10000)	414493	200884
外商直接投资实际使用外资金额（万美元）	Foreign Capital Actually Utilized (USD 10000)	224705	228097

1-27 私营企业基本情况（2019年末，按行业分）

项　　目	Item
总　计	**Total**
农林牧渔业	Agriculture, Forestry, Animal Husbandry and Fishing
采矿业	Mining
制造业	Manufacturing
电力、热力、燃气及水生产和供应业	Production and Supply of Electricity, Heat,Gas and Water
建筑业	Construction
批发和零售业	Wholesale and Retail Trade
交通运输、仓储和邮政业	Transport, Storage and Post
住宿和餐饮业	Hotels and Catering Services
信息传输、软件和信息技术服务业	Information Transmission, Software and Information Technology
金融业	Financial Intermediation
房地产业	Real Estate
租赁和商务服务业	Leasing and Business Services
科学研究和技术服务业	Scientific Research and Technical Services
水利、环境和公共设施管理业	Management of Water Conservancy, Environment and Public Facilities
居民服务、修理和其他服务业	Service to Households, Repair and Other Services
教育	Education
卫生和社会工作	Health and Social Service
文化、体育和娱乐业	Culture, Sports and Entertainment
其他	Others

注：本表数据由广州市市场监督管理局提供。

Basic Statistics on Private Enterprises (Year-end of 2019, by Sector)

全　市 Total		#城　镇 Urban Areas	
户　数 (户) Number of Enterprises (unit)	年末投资者人数 (人) Number of Investors at Year-end (person)	户　数 (户) Number of Enterprises (unit)	年末投资者人数 (人) Number of Investors at Year-end (person)
1147324	**2001363**	**1115566**	**1928837**
4557	8459	4405	8078
55	100	55	100
84767	139102	78992	123838
401	936	390	905
49438	84486	47925	81566
451269	715169	439846	690999
23926	37906	22980	36040
15810	25193	15313	22562
92540	172994	91910	171537
3768	11729	3714	11610
26867	47105	25695	44973
169259	341755	165208	333071
168557	316685	164176	307622
1488	2933	1429	2822
13406	20972	12856	19266
2720	4749	2675	4628
1899	3804	1865	3595
36596	67284	36131	65623
1	2	1	2

Note: Data in this table are provided by Guangzhou Municipal Market Regulatory Administration.

1-28 私营企业基本情况（2019年末，按地区分）

Basic Statistics on Private Enterprises (Year-end of 2019, by Region)

地 区	District	年末户数（户）Number of Enterprises at Year-end (unit)	年末投资者人数（人）Number of Investors at Year-end (person)
合 计	**Total**	**1147324**	**2001363**
#荔湾区局	Liwan District Bureau	38042	65951
越秀区局	Yuexiu District Bureau	84867	151224
海珠区局	Haizhu District Bureau	71883	124917
天河区局	Tianhe District Bureau	290186	507528
白云区局	Baiyun District Bureau	201075	331254
黄埔区局	Huangpu District Bureau	96778	169893
番禺区局	Panyu District Bureau	113807	195108
花都区局	Huadu District Bureau	47788	75888
南沙区局	Nansha District Bureau	111957	186719
从化区局	Conghua District Bureau	10795	18371
增城区局	Zengcheng District Bureau	47724	78050

注：本表数据按注册地区分，由广州市市场监督管理局提供。

Note: Data in this table are provided by Guangzhou Municipal Market Regulatory Administration according to the registered area.

1-29 个体工商户情况

Basic Statistics on Individual Business

年 份 Year	期末户数 (户) Number of Year-end Enterprises (unit)	从业人数 (人) Number of Employees (person)
2000	226016	380941
2001	250672	427923
2002	245505	415817
2003	230229	360809
2004	244756	375349
2005	285557	446874
2006	308655	492191
2007	417392	633234
2008	469128	710642
2009	552031	858694
2010	596854	953510
2011	661026	1031588
2012	675449	1055281
2013	716711	1127338
2014	739923	1169148
2015	799583	1256776
2016	862631	1357477
2017	933528	1480664
2018	1006472	1597471
2019	1050639	1668684

注：本表数据由广州市市场监督管理局提供。
Note: Data in this table are provided by Guangzhou Municipal Market Regulatory Administration.

1-30 个体工商户情况(2019年末，按行业分)

项　　目	Item
总　　计	**Total**
# 农林牧渔业	Agriculture, Forestry, Animal Husbandry and Fishing
采矿业	Mining
制造业	Manufacturing
电力、热力、燃气及水生产和供应业	Production and Supply of Electricity, Heat,Gas and Water
建筑业	Construction
批发和零售业	Wholesale and Retail Trade
交通运输、仓储和邮政业	Transport, Storage and Post
住宿和餐饮业	Hotels and Catering Services
信息传输、软件和信息技术服务业	Information Transmission, Software and Information Technology
金融业	Financial Intermediation
房地产业	Real Estate
租赁和商务服务业	Leasing and Business Services
科学研究和技术服务业	Scientific Research and Technical Services
水利、环境和公共设施管理业	Management of Water Conservancy, Environment and Public Facilities
居民服务、修理和其他服务业	Service to Households, Repair and Other Services
教育	Education
卫生和社会工作	Health and Social Service
文化、体育和娱乐业	Culture, Sports and Entertainment

注:本表数据由广州市市场监督管理局提供。

Basic Statistics on Individual Business
(Year-end of 2019, by Sector)

户 数 (户) Number of Enterprises (unit)	# 城 镇 Urban Areas	从业人员 (人) Number of Employed Persons (person)	# 城 镇 Urban Areas
1050639	**899954**	**1668684**	**1420626**
5835	4774	13957	11236
1	1	1	1
73487	65346	231147	205836
98	34	202	79
6183	5202	11500	9760
682909	594208	882783	762490
11631	9865	18520	15610
160279	129503	316811	256523
1381	1039	1912	1449
47	37	73	60
1638	1353	2789	2329
19216	15113	32221	25421
5794	4777	9795	8088
61	45	186	77
73018	61128	129068	106709
1285	1216	2731	2604
1531	1275	4240	3599
6245	5038	10748	8755

Note: Data in this table are provided by Guangzhou Municipal Market Regulatory Administration.

1-31 内资企业基本情况（2019年末）

项　　目	Item
总　　计	**Total**
按行业分	**Grouped by Sector**
农林牧渔业	Agriculture, Forestry, Animal Husbandry and Fishing
采矿业	Mining
制造业	Manufacturing
电力、热力、燃气及水生产和供应业	Production and Supply of Electricity, Heat,Gas and Water
建筑业	Construction
批发和零售业	Wholesale and Retail Trade
交通运输、仓储和邮政业	Transport, Storage and Post
住宿和餐饮业	Hotels and Catering Services
信息传输、软件和信息技术服务业	Information Transmission, Software and Information Technology
金融业	Financial Intermediation
房地产业	Real Estate
租赁和商务服务业	Leasing and Business Services
科学研究和技术服务业	Scientific Research and Technical Services
水利、环境和公共设施管理业	Management of Water Conservancy, Environment and Public Facilities
居民服务、修理和其他服务业	Service to Households, Repair and Other Services
教育	Education
卫生和社会工作	Health and Social Service
文化、体育和娱乐业	Culture, Sports and Entertainment
其他	Others

注：1. 本表数据由广州市市场监督管理局提供。
　　2. 本表不包括私营企业。

Basic Statistics on Domestic-Funded Enterprises (Year-end of 2019)

企业数 (户) Numbers of Enterprises (unit)	# 国有企业 Stated-owned Enterprises	# 集体企业 Collective-owned Enterprises	# 公司 Corporations	# 其他企业 Other Enterprises
96057	**2199**	**3970**	**86557**	**3331**
586	39	84	457	6
25		1	24	
4443	202	629	2873	739
469	15	41	411	2
3159	125	181	2776	77
20001	670	1735	16163	1433
3209	293	136	2692	88
2478	122	75	1986	295
6791	4	9	6768	10
5220	13		5204	3
7661	124	535	6940	62
21965	364	308	21136	157
13900	146	97	13551	106
334	17	19	293	5
1208	26	80	832	270
586	7	15	551	13
1168		4	1161	3
2851	32	21	2736	62
3			3	

Note: I.Data in this table are provided by Guangzhou Municipal Market Regulatory Administration.
II. This table excludes private enterprises.

【地区生产总值(GDP)】 指一个地区所有常住单位在一定时期内生产活动的最终成果。国内生产总值有三种表现形态，即价值形态、收入形态和产品形态。从价值形态看，它是所有常住单位在一定时期内生产的全部货物和服务价值与同期投入的全部非固定资产货物和服务价值的差额，即所有常住单位的增加值之和；从收入形态看，它是所有常住单位在一定时期内创造的各项收入之和，包括劳动者报酬、生产税净额、固定资产折旧和营业盈余；从产品形态看，它是所有常住单位在一定时期内最终使用的货物和服务价值与货物和服务净出口价值之和。在实际核算中，国内生产总值有三种计算方法，即生产法、收入法和支出法。三种方法分别从不同的方面反映国内生产总值及其构成。

【三次产业】 三产业的划分是世界上较为常用的产业结构分类，但各国的划分不尽一致。根据《国民经济行业分类》（GB/T 4754-2011），我国的三次产业划分是：

第一产业是指农、林、牧、渔业（不含农、林、牧、渔服务业）。

第二产业是指采矿业（不含开采辅助活动），制造业（不含金属制品、机械和设备修理业），电力、热力、燃气及水生产和供应业，建筑业。

第三产业即服务业，是指除第一产业、第二产业以外的其他行业。

【劳动者报酬】 指劳动者从事生产活动应获得的全部报酬，既包括货币形式的报酬，也包括实物形式的报酬。主要包括工资、奖金、津贴和补贴，单位为其员工交纳的社会保险费、补充社会保险费和住房公积金、行政事业单位职工的离退休金、单位为其员工提供的其他各种形式的福利和报酬等。

【生产税净额】 指生产税减生产补贴后的差额。其中，生产税指政府对生产单位从事生产、销售和经营活动，以及因从事生产活动使用某些生产要素（如固定资产和土地等）所征收的各种税收、附加费和其他规费。生产税分为产品税和其他生产税，产品税主要有：增值税、消费税、进口关税、出口税等；其他生产税主要有：房产税、车船使用税、城镇土地使用税等。生产补贴则相反，它是政府为影响生产单位的生产、销售及定价等生产活动而对其提供的无偿支付，包括农业生产补贴、政策亏损补贴、进口补贴等。生产补贴作为负生产税处理。

【固定资产折旧】 指由于自然退化、正常淘汰或损耗而导致的固定资产价值下降，用以代表固定资产通过生产过程被转移到其产出中的价值。原则上，固定资产折旧应按照固定资产的重置价值计算。

【营业盈余】 指常住单位创造的增加值扣除劳动者报酬、生产税净额和固定资产折旧后的余额。

【支出法国内生产总值】 是从最终使用的角度反映一个国家(或地区)一定时期内生产活动最终成果的一种方法，包括最终消费支出、资本形成总额及货物和服务净出口三部分。计算公式为：

支出法国内生产总值=最终消费支出+资本形成总额+货物和服务净出口

【最终消费支出】 指常住单位为满足物质、文化和精神生活的需要，从本国经济领土和国外购买的货物和服务的支出。它不包括非常住单位在本国经济领土内的消费支出。最终消费支出分为居民消费支出和政府消费支出。

【居民消费支出】 指常住住户在一定时期内对于货物和服务的全部最终消费支出。居民消费支出除了直接以货币形式购买的货物和服务的消费支出外，还包括以其他方式获得的货物和服务的消费支出，即所谓的虚拟消费支出。居民虚拟消费支出包括如下几种类型：单位以实物报酬及实物转移的形式提供给劳动者的货物和服务；住户生产并由本住户消费了的货物和服务，其中的服务仅指住户的自有住房服务；金融机构提供的金融媒介服务。

【政府消费支出】 指政府部门为全社会提供的公共服务的消费支出和免费或以较低的价格向居民住户提供的货物和服务的净支出，前者等于政府服务的产出价值减去政府单位所获得的经营收入的价值，后者等于政府部门免费或以较低价格向居民住户提供的货物和服务的市场价值减去向住户收取的价值。

【资本形成总额】 指常住单位在一定时期内获得减去处置的固定资产和存货的净额，包括固定资本形成总额和存货变动两部分。

【固定资本形成总额】 指常住单位在一定时期内获得的固定资产减处置的固定资产的价值总额。固定资产是通过生产活动生产出来的，且其使用年限在一年以上、单位价值在规定标准以上的资产，不包括自然资产、耐用消费品、小型工器具。固定资本形成总额包括住宅、其他建筑和构筑物、机器和设备、培育性生物资源、知识产权产品（研发支出、矿藏的勘探、计算机软件）的价值获得减处置。

【存货变动】 指常住单位在一定时期内存货实物量变动的市场价值，即期末价值减期初价值的差额，再扣除当期由于价格变动而产生的持有收益。存货变动可以是正值，也可以是负值，正值表示存货上升，负值表示存货下降。存货包括生产单位购进的原材料、燃料和储备物资等存货，以及生产单位生产的产成品、在制品和半成品等存货。

【可比价格】 指在不同时期的价值指标对比时，扣除了价格变动的因素，以确切反映物量的变化。按可比价格计算有两种方法：一种是直接用产品产量乘某一年的不变价格计算；另一种是用价格指数换算。

【平均增长速度】 表明社会经济现象在一个较长的时期内逐期平均增长变化的程度，它不能根据各个环比增长速度直接求得，但与平均发展速度之间存在着一定的数量关系：平均增长速度＝平均发展速度－1。

平均发展速度是一种根据环比发展速度计算的序时平均数，由于各时期对比的基础不同，所以计算平均发展速度不能采用一般的序时平均数的计算方法，计算方法分为水平法和累计法。水平法，又称几何平均法，即将环比发展速度按连乘法用几何平均数公式计算。累计法，也称方程法，根据一段时期内各年发展水平总和与基期水平的关系，列出方程式计算平均发展速度。水平法着重考虑最后一年所达到的发展水平；累计法着重考虑整个时期累计发展水平的总量。

本《年鉴》内所列的平均增长速度，除固定资产投资用

"累计法"计算外，其余均用"水平法"计算。从某年到某年平均增长速度的年份，均不包括基期年在内。如1979年平均增长速度是以1978年为基期计算的，余类推。

【国有企业】指企业全部资产归国家所有，并按《中华人民共和国企业法人登记管理条例》规定登记注册的非公司制的经济组织。不包括有限责任公司中的国有独资公司。

【集体企业】指企业资产归集体所有，并按《中华人民共和国企业法人登记管理条例》规定登记注册的经济组织。

【股份合作企业】指以合作制为基础，由企业职工共同出资入股，吸收一定比例的社会资产投资组建，实行自主经营，自负盈亏，共同劳动，民主管理，按劳动分配与按股分红相结合的一种集体经济组织。

【联营企业】指两个及两个以上相同或不同所有制性质的企业法人或事业单位法人，按自愿、平等、互利的原则，共同投资组成的经济组织。联营企业包括国有联营企业、集体联营企业、国有与集体联营企业和其他联营企业。

【有限责任公司】指根据《中华人民共和国公司登记管理条例》规定登记注册，由2个以上，50个以下的股东共同出资，每个股东以其所认缴的出资额对公司承担有限责任，公司以其全部资产对其债务承担责任的经济组织。有限责任公司包括国有独资公司以及其他有限责任公司。

【股份有限公司】指根据《中华人民共和国公司登记管理条例》规定登记注册，其全部注册资本由等额股份构成并通过发行股票筹集资本，股东以其认购的股份对公司承担有限责任，公司以其全部资产对其债务承担责任的经济组织。

【私营企业】指由自然人投资设立或由自然人控股，以雇佣劳动为基础的营利性经济组织。包括按照《公司法》、《合伙企业法》、《私营企业暂行条例》以及《个人独资企业法》规定登记注册的私营有限责任公司、私营股份有限公司、私营合伙企业、私营独资企业和个人独资企业。

【其他企业】指国有企业、集体企业、股份合作企业、联营企业、有限责任公司、股份有限公司和私营企业之外的其他内资经济组织。

【合资经营企业（港或澳、台资）】指港澳台地区投资者与内地企业依照《中华人民共和国中外合资经营企业法》及有关法律的规定，依照合作合同的约定进行投资或提供条件设立、分配利润、分担风险和亏损的企业。

【合作经营企业（港或澳、台资）】指港澳台地区投资者与内地企业依照《中华人民共和国中外合作经营企业法》及有关法律的规定，依照合作合同的约定进行投资或提供条件设立、分配利润和分担风险的企业。

【港澳台商独资经营企业】指依照《中华人民共和国外资企业法》及有关法律的规定，在内地由港澳台地区投资者全额投资设立的企业。

【港澳台商投资股份有限公司】指根据国家有关规定，经商务部（原外经贸部）依法批准设立，其中港、澳、台商的股本占公司注册资本的比例达25%以上的股份有限公司。凡其中港、澳、台商的股本占公司注册资本的比例小于25%的，属于内资企业中的股份有限公司。

【其他港澳台商投资企业】指在中国境内参照《外国企业或个人在中国境内设立合伙企业管理办法》和《外商投资合伙企业登记管理规定》，依法设立的港、澳、台商投资合伙企业。

【中外合资经营企业】指外国企业或外国人与中国内地企业依照《中华人民共和国中外合资经营企业法》及有关法律的规定，按合同规定的比例投资设立、分享利润和分担风险的企业。

【中外合作经营企业】指外国企业或外国人与中国内地企业依照《中华人民共和国中外合作经营企业法》及有关法律的规定，依照合作合同的约定进行投资或提供条件设立、分享利润和分担风险的企业。

【外资企业】指依照《中华人民共和国外资企业法》及有关法律的规定，在中国内地由外国投资者全额投资设立的企业。

【外商投资股份有限公司】指根据国家有关规定，经商务部（原外经贸部）依法批准设立，其中外资的股本占公司注册资本的比例达25%以上的股份有限公司。凡其中外资股本占公司注册资本的比例小于25%的，属于内资企业中的股份有限公司。

【其他外商投资企业】指在中国境内依照《外国企业或个人在中国境内设立合伙企业管理办法》和《外商投资合伙企业登记管理规定》，依法设立的外商投资合伙企业。

【法人单位】指同时具备以下条件的单位：（1）依法成立、有自己的名称、组织机构和场所、能够独立承担民事责任；（2）独立拥有和使用（或授权使用）资产或者经费、承担负债、有权与其它单位签订合同；（3）具有包括资产负债表在内的账户，或者能够根据需要编制账户。法人单位包括企业法人、事业单位法人、机关法人、社会团体法人、民办非企业法人和其他法人。

【单产业法人】指只在一个地点，主要从事一种生产经营活动的法人单位。

【多产业法人】指坐落于两个及两个以上地点或主要从事两种及两种以上生产经营活动的，按照单位划分规定可以划分为两个或两个以上的产业活动单位的法人单位。

【产业活动单位】是法人单位的组成部分。产业活动单位应同时具备下列条件：（1）在一个场所从事一种或主要从事一种社会经济活动；（2）相对独立组织生产活动或经营活动；（3）能够提供收入和支出等相关资料。

【Gross Domestic Product (GDP)】 refers to the final products produced by all resident units in a country during a certain period of time. Gross domestic product is expressed in three different perspectives, namely value, income, and products respectively. GDP in its value perspective refers to the balance of total value of all goods and services produced by all resident units during a certain period of time, minus the total value of input of goods and services of the nature of non-fixed assets; in other words, it is the sum of the value-added of all resident units. GDP from the perspective of income refers to the sum of all kinds of revenue, including Compensation of Employees, Net Taxes on Production, Depreciation of Fixed Assets, and Operating Surplus. GDP from the perspective of products refers to the value of all goods and services for final demand by all resident units plus the net exports of goods and services during a given period of time. In the practice of national accounting, gross domestic product is calculated from three approaches, namely production approach, income approach and expenditure approach, which reflect gross domestic product and its composition from different angles.

【Three Strata of Industry】 Classification of economic activities into three strata of industry is a common practice in the world, although the grouping varies to some extent from country to country. In China, according to Industrial classification for National Economic Activities (GB/T 4754-2011) and Dividing Basis of Three Industries, economic activities are categorized into the following three strata of industry:

Primary industry refers to agriculture, forestry, animal husbandry and fishery industries (not including services in support of agriculture, forestry, animal husbandry and fishery industries).

【Secondary industry】 refers to mining and quarrying(not including support activities for mining), manufacturing(not including repair service of metal products, machinery and equipment), production and supply of electricity, heat, gas and water, and construction.

Tertiary industry refers to all other economic activities not included in the primary or secondary industries.

【Compensation of Employees】 refers to the total payment of various forms to employees for the productive activities they are engaged in. It includes the employees earn in cash or in kind. It mainly include: wages, bonuses and allowances, subsidies, social insurance paid by company or unit for its staff, supplementary social insurance, housing fund, the pension for the employees of the administrative institution, other forms of welfare and remuneration provide by the units for its employees.

【Net Taxes on Production】 refers to taxes on production less subsidies on production. The taxes on production refers to the various taxes, extra charges and fees levied on the production units on their production, sale and business activities as well as on the use of some factors of production, such as fixed assets, land etc. in the production activities they are engaged in. Taxes on production are divided into product tax and other kinds of taxes on production, product tax mainly includes: value-added tax, consumption tax, import duty, export duty; other taxes on production mainly include: House Property Tax, Tax on Vehicles and Boat Operation, Urban Land Use Tax, etc. In contrast to taxes on production, subsidies on production refer to the payment by the government for free to the production units to influence production activities of production units such as production, sales and pricing, which include agricultural production subsidies, subsidies for policy losses, import subsidies, etc. Subsidies on production are therefore regarded as negative taxes on production.

【Depreciation of Fixed Assets】 Refers to the decline of the value of fixed assets due to natural deterioration, normal elimination or loss, it reflects the value of transfer of the fixed assets in the production of the current period. In principle, the depreciation of fixed assets should be calculated on the basis of the re-purchased value of the fixed assets.

【Operating Surplus】 refers to the balance of the value added created by the resident units after deducting the labourers remuneration, net taxes on production and the depreciation of fixed assets.

【GDP by Expenditure Approach】 refers to the method of measuring the final results of production activities of a country (region) during a given period from the perspective of final uses. It includes final consumption expenditure, gross capital formation and net export of goods and services. The formula for computation is:

GDP by expenditure approach = final consumption expenditure + gross capital formation + net export of goods and services.

【Final Consumption Expenditure】 refers to the total expenditure of resident units for purchases of goods and services from both the domestic economic territory and abroad to meet the needs of material, cultural and spiritual life. It does not include the expenditure of non-resident units on consumption in the economic territory of the country. The final consumption expenditure is broken down into household consumption expenditure and government consumption expenditure.

【Household Consumption Expenditure】 refers to the total expenditure of resident households on the final consumption of goods and services. In addition to the consumption of goods and services bought by the households directly with money, the household consumption expenditure also includes expenditure on goods and services obtained by the households in other ways, i.e. the latter so-called imputed consumption expenditure, which mainly includes: (a) the goods and services provided to households by employers in the form of payment in kind and transfer in kind; (b) goods and services produced and consumed by the households themselves (such as self produced agricultural products); (c) financial intermediate services provided by banking and insurance institutions.

【Government Consumption Expenditure】 refers to the consumption expenditure spent for the provision of public services provided by the government to the whole country and the net expenditure on the goods and services provided by the government to households free of charge or at reduced prices. The former equals to the output value of the government services minus the value of operating income obtained by the government departments. The latter equals to the market value of the goods and services provided by the government free of charge or at reduced prices to the households minus the value received by the government from the households.

【Gross Capital Formation】 refers to the fixed assets acquired less disposals and the net value of inventory, thus including gross fixed capital formation and changes in inventories.

【Gross Fixed Capital Formation】 refers to the value of acquisitions less those disposals of fixed assets during a given period. Fixed assets are the assets produced through production activities with unit value above a specified amount and which could be used for over one year. Natural assets, consumer durables, small instruments are not included. Gross Fixed Capital Formation includes the value of housing, other buildings and structure, equipment and machinery, breeding biological resources, intellectual property right product (expenditure for R&D, the prospecting of minerals and the acquisition of computer software) minus the disposal of them.

【Changes in Inventories】 refers to the market value of the change in the physical volume of inventory of resident units during a given period, i.e. the difference between the values at the beginning and at the end of the period minus the gains due to the change in prices. The changes in inventories can have a positive or a negative value. A positive value indicates an increase in inventory while a negative value indicates a decrease in inventory. The inventory includes raw materials, fuels and reserve materials purchased by the production units as well as the inventory of finished products, semi-finished products and work-in-progress.

【Comparable price】 refers to when the value index is compared in different periods, the factors of price change are deducted to reflect the change of material quantity. There are two methods to calculate the comparable price: one is to calculate the product output directly by the constant price of a certain year, and the other is to convert by the price index.

【Average Annual Growth Rate】 shows the average growth rate of social and economic development during a longer period. It can not be directly calculated by chain based growth rate. The relation is:

Average Annual Growth Rate = Average Speed of Development - 1

Average speed of development is the time series average of speed which calculated by chain based. Because the reference bases during the different periods are not same, average speed of development can not be calculated by the general method. Level approach and accumulative approach for calculating average speed of development rate are applied. The "level approach", or the method of calculating the geometric average, is derived by the formula of geometric average of the chain-based speeds of development, or comparing the level of the last year of the interval with that of the beginning year; the other is called the "accumulative approach" or the "algebraic average", "equation" method, which is derived by the summation of the actual figure of each year in the interval divided by the figure in the base year. The level approach focuses on the level of the last year, while the accumulative approach emphasizes the aggregate development in the duration.

The average annual growth rates listed in the Yearbook are calculated by the level approach except for the growth rate of investment in fixed assets. The base year is not listed in the duration for which average annual growth rates are computed. For example, the average growth rate in 1979 is calculated on the basis of 1978, and so on.

【The state-owned enterprises】 are economic organizations whose assets are solely owned by the state and whose registrations are made according to "Regulations of the People's Republic of China for Controlling the Registration of Enterprises as legal Persons." Excluding the state-owned solely enterprises of liability limited companies.

【The collective-owned enterprises】 are economic organizations whose assets are owned by the collective and whose registration are made according to"Regulations of the People's Republic of China for Controlling the Registration of Enterprises as Legal Persons."

【Joint stock cooperative enterprises】 are a kind of collective economic organizations based on a cooperative system. In addition to the shares bought by their workers and staff, the enterprises also absorb a certain percentage of social capital. They enjoy staff, the autonomy in operation and take care of their own losses and profits. The shareholding work together, conduct democratic management, and combine distribution according to one's performance with sharing out profits according to shares.

【Joint operation enterprises】 refer to economic organizations set up with joint investment from legal persons of two or more enterprises of different ownerships or institutions according to principle of voluntary participation, equality and mutual benefit. They include state-owned joint operation enterprises, collective joint operation enterprises, state-collective joint operation enterprises and other types of joint operation enterprises.

【Company with limited liability】 is a company registered in accordance with the "Regulations of the People's Republic of China on Administration of Company Registration."Its investment comes from more than 2 and less than 50 shareholders. Each shareholder assumes limited liability for the company according to his subscription to capital stock. The company assumes liabilities for its debts according to all its assets. Such economic organizations include solely state invested companies and other types of companies with limited liability.

【The joint stock company limited】 refers to economic organizations registered in accordance with the"Regulations of the People's Republic of China on Administration of Company

Registration."All its registered capital is composed of shares of equal value and its capital is collected through share issuing. The shareholders bear limited liability for the company according to the amount of shares they have bought from the company and the company assumes liabilities for its debts according to all its assets.

【Private enterprise】 refers to profit making economic organizations set up with investment from natural persons or with controlling interest in the hands of natural persons who employ laborers for operation. Such enterprises include private companies with limited liability, private joint stock companies limited, private partnership enterprises and solely individual invested enterprises, which are registered according to the "Company Law","Partnership Enterprises Law","Temporary Regulations of Private Enterprises" and "Individual Proprietorship Enterprise Law".

【Other companies】 refers to other economic organizations exclude the state-owned enterprises, the collective-owned enterprises, joint stock cooperative enterprises, joint operation enterprises, company with limited liability, the joint stock company limited, private enterprise.

【Joint Venture Enterprises(Funds are from Hong Kong, Macao or Taiwan.) 】 are enterprises established by investors from Hong Kong, Macao and Taiwan with enterprises in the mainland of China in accordance with the Law of the People's Republic of China on Sino-foreign Equity Joint Ventures and other relevant laws, where the establishment of the investment and the sharing of profits and risks are stipulated under joint venture contracts.

【Cooperative Enterprises(Funds are from Hong Kong, Macao or Taiwan.)】 established by investors from Hong Kong, Macao and Taiwan with enterprises in the mainland of China in accordance with the Law of the People's Republic of China on Sino-foreign Contractual Joint Venture and other relevant laws, where the investment or provision of facilities and the sharing of profits and risks are stipulated under cooperative contracts.

【Solely invested Hong Kong, Macao and Taiwan enterprises】 refer to enterprises set up on the mainland according to the "Law of the People's Republic of China on Foreign Capital Enterprises and solely invested by investors from Hong Kong, Macao and Taiwan."

【The joint stock company limited funded by investors from Hong Kong, Macao and Taiwan】 refers to any joint stock company limited that is set up according relevant state regulations and is approved by the Ministry of Commerce of PRC (former Ministry of Foreign Economic Relations and Trade). The investment from Hong Kong, Macao and Taiwan investors must account more than 25 percent of the company's total capital. If such investment is less than 25 percent, it shall be classified as a joint stock company limited invested by domestic investors.

【Other Enterprises with Funds From Hong Kong, Macao and Taiwan】 refer to partnership enterprises with investments from Hong Kong, Macao and Taiwan established within the territory of China in accordance with Administrative Measures on the Establishment of Partnership Enterprises in China by Foreign Enterprises or Foreign Individuals and Regulations for the Administration of the Registration of Foreign-invested Partnership Enterprises.

【The Sino foreign joint ventures】 refers to any enterprise that is jointly set up by foreign enterprises or foreigners with Chinese enterprises in accordance with the "Law of the People's Republic of China on Joint Ventures with Chinese and Foreign Investment." The investors shall put in investment, share profits and risks according to the contract on the joint venture.

【The foreign capital enterprise】 refers to any enterprise that is set up on the Chinese mainland according to the "Law of the People's Republic of China on Foreign Capital Enterprises" and with all its investment coming from foreign investors.

【The foreign-invested joint stock company limited】 refers to any joint stock company limited that is set up according to relevant state regulations and is approved by the Ministry of Foreign Economic Relations and Trade. The foreign investment must account more than 25 percent of the company's total capital .If such investment is less than 25 percent, it shall be classified as a joint stock company limited invested by Chinese investors.

【Other foreign capital enterprises】 refer to the foreign capital enterprises set up on the mainland according to the Ministry of Commerce of PRC (former Ministry of Foreign Economic Relations and Trade) on Foreign enterprises or individuals to establish a partnership enterprises"and "Foreign-invested Partnership Enterprise Registration Regulations".

【Legal entities】 Refers to a unit meet the following conditions at the same time: Established by law, it has its own name, organization and location, ability to independently bear civil liability; Independently owned and use (or authorize the use of) assets or funds, assume liabilities, and entitled to sign contracts with other units; Having accounts including balance sheet, including, or can prepare accounts according to needs. Legal entities including corporate, legal institutions, corporate bodies, corporate social groups, private non-enterprise legal persons and other legal entities.

【Single-industry Legal entities】 refers to the legal entities at only one location and mainly one production and business activities .

【Multi-industry Legal entities】 refers to the legal entities located in two or more locations or mainly engaged in two kinds and two or more production and business activities, in accordance with the provisions of the unit can be divided into two or more of the industrial units of legal entities.

【Industrial units】 is part of Legal entities. Industrial units should also meet the following conditions: engaged in a place or primarily in a social economic activities; a relatively independent production activities or operating activities; the ability to provide income and expenditure and other related information.

第二篇 CHAPTER 2

人 口

POPULATION

第二篇 人 口

一、本篇资料由广州市统计局人口和社会科技统计处整理提供。

二、本篇资料2-4表中2006-2009年的常住人口数根据2010年第六次全国人口普查结果进行了修正。2-6表中的婴儿死亡率和2-8表数据由广州市卫生健康委员会提供，其他资料均由广州市公安局提供。

三、本篇资料中的农业与非农业人口统计，2003年以前按户口性质分类。2003-2014年，非农业人口的统计口径根据省公安厅《转发公安部办公厅关于修改人口统计年报表等有关问题的通知》（广公（办）字[2003]146号）调整为：设区市的区和不设区市的市区所辖街道办事处区域内的常住人口和市辖镇、县辖镇所辖居民委员会或镇政府驻地村委会区域内的常住人口按非农业人口统计。表2-2中2003-2014年的农业人口和非农业人口均按此口径列出。从2015年开始，按户籍人口所在区域城乡属性分为城镇人口和乡村人口。

2 Population

I. The data in this chapter are prepared by the Division of Population, Social, Science and Technology Statistics of Guangzhou Statistics Bureau.

II. The resident population data for 2006- 2009 of table 2-4 in this chapter has been revised, according to the Sixth National Census in 2010. The death rate of infants in table 2-6 and table 2-8 is provided by Guangzhou Municipal Health Commission, the other data on household population are provided by the Public Security Bureau of Guangzhou Municipality.

Ⅲ. The agricultural population and nonagricultural population in this chapter were cataloged by residence registration before 2003. From 2003 to 2014 the statistical coverage of nonagricultural population has been adjusted in accordance with The Notice about Some Items on Changing the Annual Reporting Tables of Population Statistics Transmitted from the Ministry of Public Security stipulated by Guangdong Provincial Bureau of Public Security. The permanent population living in the region of sub-district offices under the jurisdiction of districts, neighborhood committees under the jurisdiction of towns and village committees where town governments seat are cataloged to non-agricultural population. The agricultural population and nonagricultural population from 2003 to 2014 in table 2-2 are cataloged on this coverage. Since 2015, urban population and rural population are divided by the registered region of registered population.

2-1 主要年份全市年末户籍总户数、总人口数

Total Registered Households and Population at Year-end in Main Years

年 份 Year	总户数 (户) Total Households (household)	总人口 (人) Total Population (person)	男 Male	女 Female	性别比 (女=100) Sex Ratio (Female=100)
1978	1145925	4828961	2454010	2374951	103.33
1980	1162717	5018638	2549801	2468837	103.28
1985	1369661	5449820	2786389	2663431	104.62
1986	1414794	5554073	2844443	2709630	104.98
1987	1462530	5650761	2898250	2752511	105.29
1988	1514705	5769101	2964697	2804404	105.72
1989	1565517	5854265	3009581	2844684	105.80
1990	1641840	5942534	3055107	2887427	105.81
1991	1675951	6022186	3096991	2925195	105.87
1992	1722833	6122016	3151204	2970812	106.07
1993	1825541	6236647	3210324	3026323	106.08
1994	1832571	6370241	3284477	3085764	106.44
1995	1871894	6467115	3334356	3132759	106.44
1996	1905998	6560508	3380751	3179757	106.32
1997	1945905	6664862	3432921	3231941	106.22
1998	2007082	6741400	3469164	3272236	106.02
1999	2044756	6850024	3522913	3327111	105.89
2000	2100434	7006896	3605481	3401415	106.00
2001	2135837	7125979	3670177	3455802	106.20
2002	2162532	7206229	3705036	3501193	105.82
2003	2202851	7251888	3722168	3529720	105.45
2004	2259730	7376720	3779757	3596963	105.08
2005	2302890	7505322	3839680	3665642	104.75
2006	2346536	7607220	3883760	3723460	104.31
2007	2382491	7734787	3942645	3792142	103.97
2008	2425582	7841695	3990328	3851367	103.61
2009	2474396	7946154	4036898	3909256	103.27
2010	2526804	8061370	4089885	3971485	102.98
2011	2595686	8145797	4125784	4020013	102.63
2012	2646091	8222969	4158292	4064677	102.30
2013	2706068	8323096	4201393	4121703	101.93
2014	2765020	8424169	4244403	4179766	101.55
2015	2802675	8541913	4293289	4248624	101.05
2016	2871024	8704901	4366737	4338164	100.66
2017	2950211	8978717	4493885	4484832	100.20
2018	3059851	9276914	4628811	4648103	99.58
2019	3138455	9537157	4749376	4787781	99.20

2-2 主要年份全市年末户籍常住户口户数、常住户口人口数

Permanent Registered Households and Population at Year-end in Main Years

年 份 Year	总户数 (户) Total Households (household)	人口数 (人) Total Population (person)	农业人口(乡村人口) Agricultural Population	非农业人口(城镇人口) Non-agricultural Population
1978	1145925	4815417	2500559	2314858
1980	1162717	5000658	2444826	2555832
1985	1369170	5431487	2475329	2956158
1986	1414007	5532926	2485169	3047757
1987	1461719	5632622	2492576	3140046
1988	1513715	5750293	2484339	3265954
1989	1564202	5837019	2475068	3361951
1990	1641063	5918462	2504602	3413860
1991	1674843	5997893	2514973	3482920
1992	1721098	6095547	2537164	3558383
1993	1784571	6204135	2450263	3753872
1994	1831663	6338332	2465936	3872396
1995	1871173	6433241	2480482	3952759
1996	1905305	6532967	2500263	4032704
1997	1945526	6629339	2520700	4108639
1998	2006279	6704699	2531875	4172824
1999	2042447	6807635	2551340	4256295
2000	2090384	6939568	2578513	4361055
2001	2127840	7058885	2548091	4510794
2002	2162199	7171300	2297622	4873678
2003	2202124	7226882	990540	6236342
2004	2251393	7348972	828510	6520462
2005	2294825	7466206	784226	6681980
2006	2330293	7573939	782154	6791785
2007	2361299	7701900	787611	6914289
2008	2402885	7802474	760735	7041739
2009	2450739	7917646	806140	7111506
2010	2510473	8042445	820905	7221540
2011	2580335	8129427	806652	7322775
2012	2646091	8222969	782640	7440329
2013	2706068	8323096	792254	7530842
2014	2765020	8424169	761300	7662869
2015	2802675	8541913	1731646	6810267
2016	2871024	8704901	1762341	6942560
2017	2950211	8978717	1823858	7154859
2018	3059851	9276914	1875737	7401177
2019	3138455	9537157	1916742	7620415

注：2003—2014年，农业人口、非农业人口资料口径与以前口径不同，详细情况见第二篇简要说明。2015年开始，户籍人口按所在区域城乡属性分为城镇人口和乡村人口。

Note: 2003-2014 agricultural population and non-agricultural population has been calculated on different coverage. Since 2015, urban population and rural population are divided by the registered region of registered population.

2-3 主要年份全市户籍总人口自然变动情况

Statistics on Natural Changes of Total Registered Population in Main Years

单位:人、‰ (person, ‰)

年 份 Year	年平均人数 Annual Average Population	出 生 Birth 人 数 Population	出 生 Birth 出生率 Birth Rate	死 亡 Death 人 数 Population	死 亡 Death 死亡率 Death Rate	自然增长率 Natural Growth Rate
1978	4753314	73470	15.46	25283	5.32	10.14
1980	4959822	80604	16.25	27643	5.57	10.68
1985	5402904	89630	16.59	28968	5.36	11.23
1986	5501946	91522	16.63	27839	5.06	11.57
1987	5602417	89106	15.90	28794	5.14	10.76
1988	5709931	86032	15.07	30265	5.30	9.77
1989	5811683	91402	15.73	30910	5.32	10.41
1990	5898400	88289	14.97	32388	5.49	9.48
1991	5982360	78680	13.15	30476	5.09	8.06
1992	6072101	79592	13.11	33588	5.53	7.58
1993	6179332	82515	13.35	34619	5.60	7.75
1994	6303444	78614	12.47	33349	5.29	7.18
1995	6418678	75867	11.82	35735	5.57	6.25
1996	6513812	78339	12.03	37216	5.71	6.32
1997	6612685	75184	11.37	35696	5.40	5.97
1998	6703131	67695	10.10	40981	6.11	3.99
1999	6795712	81485	11.99	39176	5.76	6.23
2000	6928460	71248	10.28	39987	5.77	4.51
2001	7066438	67542	9.56	37641	5.33	4.23
2002	7166104	61929	8.64	39673	5.54	3.10
2003	7229059	57277	7.92	41082	5.68	2.24
2004	7314304	69928	9.56	41961	5.74	3.82
2005	7441021	65840	8.85	41949	5.64	3.21
2006	7556271	67662	8.95	40936	5.42	3.53
2007	7671004	71332	9.30	42548	5.55	3.75
2008	7788241	79130	10.16	44420	5.70	4.46
2009	7893925	76482	9.69	42746	5.42	4.27
2010	8003762	99779	12.47	45571	5.69	6.78
2011	8103584	87024	10.74	44130	5.45	5.29
2012	8184383	101782	12.44	50538	6.17	6.27
2013	8273033	115813	14.00	44966	5.44	8.56
2014	8373633	113926	13.61	46767	5.59	8.02
2015	8483041	150403	17.73	49158	5.79	11.94
2016	8623407	137275	15.92	47145	5.47	10.45
2017	8841809	200958	22.73	60947	6.89	15.84
2018	9127816	170997	18.73	52293	5.73	13.00
2019	9407036	139773	14.86	48317	5.14	9.72

2-4 各区、县级市年末人口数(2005-2014年)

Population at Year-end by District and County-level City (2005-2014)

单位:万人 (10000 person)

地 区	District	2005	2006	2007	2008	2009	2010	2011	2012	2013	2014
户籍人口	**Registered Population**										
全 市	**Total**	**750.53**	**760.72**	**773.48**	**784.17**	**794.62**	**806.14**	**814.58**	**822.30**	**832.31**	**842.42**
荔湾区	Liwan	70.47	70.53	70.48	70.61	70.65	70.93	71.04	71.20	71.56	71.96
越秀区	Yuexiu	115.06	115.15	115.84	116.33	116.69	116.97	117.17	117.21	117.52	117.55
海珠区	Haizhu	87.70	89.05	90.79	92.31	93.73	95.28	96.75	97.74	98.89	99.81
天河区	Tianhe	61.97	64.54	69.00	71.66	74.53	77.06	78.51	79.63	80.95	82.43
白云区	Baiyun	76.07	76.77	77.65	78.99	80.65	83.19	84.66	86.31	88.15	89.83
黄埔区	Huangpu	19.27	19.36	19.55	19.71	19.85	19.97	20.15	20.42	20.64	20.93
番禺区	Panyu	93.08	94.76	97.51	98.92	99.92	100.39	100.86	80.81	82.06	83.57
花都区	Huadu	63.03	63.67	63.93	64.62	65.16	66.19	66.93	67.71	68.73	69.56
南沙区	Nansha	14.26	14.76	14.86	15.05	15.23	15.41	15.68	36.74	37.23	37.74
萝岗区	Luogang	16.37	16.73	17.16	17.63	18.27	18.90	19.57	20.20	20.91	21.58
增城市	Zengcheng	79.43	81.06	81.80	82.66	83.36	83.98	84.58	84.77	85.44	86.46
从化市	Conghua	53.82	54.34	54.91	55.68	56.58	57.87	58.68	59.56	60.23	61.00
常住人口	**Permanent Population**										
全 市	**Total**	**949.68**	**996.66**	**1053.01**	**1115.34**	**1186.97**	**1270.96**	**1275.14**	**1283.89**	**1292.68**	**1308.05**
荔湾区	Liwan	71.08	73.80	77.11	80.74	84.91	89.82	89.15	89.31	88.92	89.14
越秀区	Yuexiu	98.34	100.66	103.69	107.03	110.98	115.73	114.89	114.95	114.09	114.65
海珠区	Haizhu	122.07	127.01	132.99	139.56	147.09	155.92	156.63	157.58	158.34	159.98
天河区	Tianhe	104.56	110.34	117.19	124.74	133.34	143.37	143.65	144.66	148.43	150.61
白云区	Baiyun	155.45	165.46	177.24	190.27	205.16	222.48	223.67	225.20	226.57	228.89
黄埔区	Huangpu	27.52	30.19	33.34	36.89	41.00	45.83	46.10	46.47	46.67	47.43
番禺区	Panyu	142.36	147.26	153.31	159.95	167.61	176.65	177.64	143.75	144.86	146.75
花都区	Huadu	67.93	71.91	76.61	81.79	87.70	94.59	94.86	95.64	96.48	97.51
南沙区	Nansha	17.80	19.03	20.46	22.06	23.89	26.01	26.77	62.33	62.51	63.53
萝岗区	Luogang	19.60	22.10	25.08	28.51	32.57	37.41	38.06	38.67	39.61	40.58
增城市	Zengcheng	75.70	79.88	84.83	90.29	96.51	103.76	104.14	104.92	105.18	106.97
从化市	Conghua	47.27	49.02	51.16	53.51	56.21	59.39	59.58	60.41	61.02	62.01

注：2006年～2009年常住人口数根据2010年第六次全国人口普查结果进行了修正。2015年行政区划调整，数据见表2-5。

Note: The permanent population from 2006 to 2009 are revised according to the Sixth National Population Census.The district has been adjusted in 2015, data in Form 2-5.

2-5 主要年份各区年末人口数

Population at Year-end by District in Main Years

单位:万人 (10000 person)

地 区	District	2015	2016	2017	2018	2019
户籍人口	**Registered Population**					
全 市	**Total**	**854.19**	**870.49**	**897.87**	**927.69**	**953.72**
荔湾区	Liwan	72.10	72.69	73.59	74.54	75.59
越秀区	Yuexiu	117.48	117.44	117.82	117.79	117.29
海珠区	Haizhu	101.05	102.26	104.03	105.59	106.73
天河区	Tianhe	84.46	86.77	90.28	93.92	96.57
白云区	Baiyun	91.78	94.36	98.92	103.34	108.02
黄埔区	Huangpu	43.95	45.75	48.94	52.76	56.22
番禺区	Panyu	85.57	88.65	93.45	98.94	103.35
花都区	Huadu	70.68	72.38	74.90	78.24	81.13
南沙区	Nansha	38.35	39.26	41.54	43.93	46.33
从化区	Conghua	61.52	61.85	62.63	63.49	64.17
增城区	Zengcheng	87.25	89.08	91.77	95.15	98.32
常住人口	**Permanent Population**					
全 市	**Total**	**1350.11**	**1404.35**	**1449.84**	**1490.44**	**1530.59**
荔湾区	Liwan	92.17	92.50	95.00	97.00	101.20
越秀区	Yuexiu	115.68	116.11	116.38	117.89	120.97
海珠区	Haizhu	161.37	163.79	166.31	169.36	172.42
天河区	Tianhe	154.57	163.10	169.79	174.66	178.85
白云区	Baiyun	240.34	244.19	257.24	271.43	277.96
黄埔区	Huangpu	89.85	108.26	109.10	111.41	115.12
番禺区	Panyu	154.41	164.11	171.93	177.70	182.78
花都区	Huadu	101.58	105.49	107.55	109.26	110.72
南沙区	Nansha	65.58	68.74	72.50	75.17	79.61
从化区	Conghua	62.53	63.53	64.21	64.71	64.95
增城区	Zengcheng	112.03	114.53	119.83	121.85	126.01

2-6 各区户籍总人口自然变动状况（2019年）
Statistics on Natural Changes of Total Registered Population by District (2019)

单位：人、‰ (person, ‰)

地 区	District	年平均人数 Annual Average Population	出 生 Birth		死 亡 Death		
			人 数 Population	出生率 Brith Rate	人 数 Population	死亡率 Death Rate	#婴 儿 Infant
全 市	**Total**	**9407036**	**139773**	**14.86**	**48317**	**5.14**	**2.37**
荔湾区	Liwan	750649	7328	9.76	5938	7.91	2.77
越秀区	Yuexiu	1175414	9582	8.15	8037	6.84	1.85
海珠区	Haizhu	1061628	10606	9.99	7041	6.63	2.55
天河区	Tianhe	952448	13065	13.72	3083	3.24	2.34
白云区	Baiyun	1056803	17968	17.00	4959	4.69	2.72
黄埔区	Huangpu	544914	11853	21.75	2157	3.96	1.89
番禺区	Panyu	1011414	17854	17.65	3929	3.88	1.98
花都区	Huadu	796825	14223	17.85	2979	3.74	2.44
南沙区	Nansha	451270	8497	18.83	2343	5.19	2.03
从化区	Conghua	638315	10369	16.24	3241	5.08	3.15
增城区	Zengcheng	967356	18428	19.05	4610	4.77	2.31

2-7 各区户籍人口迁移状况（2019年）
Statistics on Migration of Registered Population by District (2019)

单位：人、‰ (person, ‰)

地　区	District	迁入人数 Number of Immigration	迁入率 Immigration Rate	迁出人数 Number of Emigration	迁出率 Emigration Rate	净增人数 Number of Net Migration	净增率 Net Migration Rate
全　市	**Total**	**210518**	**22.38**	**42952**	**4.57**	**167566**	**17.81**
荔湾区	Liwan	8433	11.23	1474	1.96	6959	9.27
越秀区	Yuexiu	17463	14.86	6266	5.33	11197	9.53
海珠区	Haizhu	15745	14.83	4787	4.51	10958	10.32
天河区	Tianhe	37982	39.88	12118	12.72	25864	27.16
白云区	Baiyun	26204	24.80	3411	3.23	22793	21.57
黄埔区	Huangpu	19094	35.04	1667	3.06	17427	31.98
番禺区	Panyu	32442	32.08	7286	7.20	25156	24.87
花都区	Huadu	17125	21.49	1839	2.31	15286	19.18
南沙区	Nansha	12785	28.33	547	1.21	12238	27.12
从化区	Conghua	3743	5.86	1716	2.69	2027	3.18
增城区	Zengcheng	19502	20.16	1841	1.90	17661	18.26

2-8 各区计划生育情况（2019年）
Statistics on Family Planning by District (2019)

单位：人、%　　(person, %)

地　区	District	已婚育龄妇女人数 Married Women at Childbearing Age	女性初婚人数 Number of Women First Married	晚婚率 Late Married Rate	政策生育率 Family Planning Rate	一孩率 One-child Rate	二孩率 Two-child Rate	多孩率 More Than One-child Rate	出生人口性别比 Sex Ratio of Birth Population
全　市	**Total**	**1790288**	**45561**	**89.28**	**94.02**	**43.20**	**48.60**	**8.20**	**114.83**
荔湾区	Liwan	110756	2098	94.33	96.99	49.41	45.33	5.27	110.63
越秀区	Yuexiu	178680	4839	97.40	97.31	49.87	45.54	4.59	111.42
海珠区	Haizhu	172840	3819	95.81	97.22	49.84	45.16	5.00	112.40
天河区	Tianhe	190416	6385	97.21	95.72	47.52	46.26	6.22	116.76
白云区	Baiyun	219453	5245	88.45	93.35	41.39	50.21	8.40	117.73
黄埔区	Huangpu	123946	3161	88.71	94.14	41.96	49.54	8.50	116.47
番禺区	Panyu	217722	4833	92.36	96.36	43.56	51.40	5.04	113.16
花都区	Huadu	163725	3841	86.54	93.09	38.13	52.24	9.63	115.20
南沙区	Nansha	95077	2407	81.18	97.47	43.62	51.19	5.19	113.71
从化区	Conghua	122925	3280	73.84	84.75	36.90	45.04	18.06	111.16
增城区	Zengcheng	194748	5653	79.78	90.12	38.91	48.52	12.56	118.72

2-9 各区户籍人口年龄构成（2019年）

The Registered Population Age Composition by District (2019)

地 区	District	人口数（人） Total Population (person)			占总人口比重（%） The Proportion of the Total Population (%)		
		18岁以下 Under 18	18-60岁 Between 18 and 60	60岁以上 Above 60	18岁以下 Under 18	18-60岁 Between 18 and 60	60岁以上 Above 60
总 计	**Total**	**1977291**	**5804792**	**1755074**	**20.73**	**60.87**	**18.40**
荔湾区	Liwan	109725	431032	215095	14.51	57.03	28.46
越秀区	Yuexiu	173466	692377	307083	14.79	59.03	26.18
海珠区	Haizhu	172620	619948	274766	16.17	58.08	25.75
天河区	Tianhe	202766	625883	137045	21.00	64.81	14.19
白云区	Baiyun	248810	650976	180408	23.03	60.27	16.70
黄埔区	Huangpu	143489	344569	74145	25.52	61.29	13.19
番禺区	Panyu	248472	643317	141685	24.04	62.25	13.71
花都区	Huadu	194203	492747	124349	23.94	60.74	15.32
南沙区	Nansha	100462	288051	74761	21.69	62.17	16.14
从化区	Conghua	150783	404342	86612	23.50	63.00	13.50
增城区	Zengcheng	232495	611550	139125	23.65	62.20	14.15

2-10 主要年份各区常住人口城镇人口比重（2010-2019年）
The Proportion of Urban Population in the Permanent Population by District in Main Years (2010-2019)

单位:%　　(%)

地 区	District	2010	2011	2012	2013	2014	2015	2016	2017	2018	2019
全 市	**Total**	**83.78**	**84.13**	**85.02**	**85.27**	**85.43**	**85.53**	**86.06**	**86.14**	**86.38**	**86.46**
荔湾区	Liwan	96.70	96.81	97.68	98.02	100.00	100.00	100.00	100.00	100.00	100.00
越秀区	Yuexiu	100.00	100.00	100.00	100.00	100.00	100.00	100.00	100.00	100.00	100.00
海珠区	Haizhu	100.00	100.00	100.00	100.00	100.00	100.00	100.00	100.00	100.00	100.00
天河区	Tianhe	99.61	99.72	100.00	100.00	100.00	100.00	100.00	100.00	100.00	100.00
白云区	Baiyun	78.13	78.47	79.95	80.21	80.26	80.53	80.73	80.93	81.02	81.04
黄埔区	Huangpu	90.37	90.77	91.39	91.45	91.47	91.56	91.58	91.58	91.65	91.66
番禺区	Panyu	80.06	82.55	83.94	84.24	84.28	85.04	88.49	89.07	89.13	89.28
花都区	Huadu	64.54	64.91	66.21	66.53	66.59	66.85	67.26	67.26	68.80	69.02
南沙区	Nansha	68.83	70.59	71.99	72.11	72.19	72.33	72.47	72.50	72.79	72.89
从化区	Conghua	38.61	41.33	43.09	44.31	44.49	44.79	44.81	45.01	45.08	45.11
增城区	Zengcheng	68.47	69.32	70.95	71.67	71.86	71.88	71.90	72.12	73.10	73.16

【常住人口】常住人口是指实际经常居住在某地区一定时间（指半年以上）的人口。按人口普查和人口变动抽样调查规定，主要包括：1、除离开本地半年以上（不包括在国外工作或学习的人）的全部常住本地的户籍人口；2、户口在外地，但在本地居住半年以上者，或离开户口地半年以上而调查时在本地居住的人口；3、调查时居住在本地，但在任何地方都没有登记常住户口，如手持户口迁移证、出生证、退伍证、劳改劳教释放证等尚未办理常住户口的人。

【户籍人口】户籍人口是指公民依照《中华人民共和国户口登记条例》，已在其经常居住地的公安户籍管理机关登记了常住户口的人。这类人口不管其是否外出，也不管外出时间长短，只要在某地注册有常住户口，则为该地区的户籍人口。户籍人口数一般是通过公安部门的经常性统计月报或年报取得。

【晚婚率】指在一定时期内(通常为一年)的女性初婚人口中23岁以上人数占当年女性初婚人数的比例，一般用百分比表示。计算公式：

晚婚率=本年23岁以上女性初婚人数/本年女性初婚人数×100%

【出生率(又称粗出生率)】指在一定时期内(通常为一年)一定地区的出生人数与同期平均人数(或期中人数)之比，一般用千分率表示。计算公式:

$$出生率 = \frac{年出生人数}{年平均人数} \times 1000‰$$

出生人数是指活产婴儿，即胎儿脱离母体时(不管怀孕月数)，有过呼吸或其他生命现象。年平均人数是年初、年底人口数的平均数，也可用年中人口数代替。

【死亡率(又称粗死亡率)】 指在一定时期内(通常为一年)一定地区的死亡人数与同期平均人数(或期中人数)之比，一般用千分率表示。计算公式:

$$死亡率 = \frac{年死亡人数}{年平均人数} \times 1000‰$$

【人口自然增长率】 指在一定时期内(通常为一年)人口自然增加数(出生人数减死亡人数)与该时期内平均人数(或期中人数)之比,一般用千分率表示。计算公式:

$$人口自然增长率 = \frac{本年出生人数-本年死亡人数}{年平均人数} \times 1000‰$$

人口自然增长率 = 人口出生率-人口死亡率

【The population of permanent residents】 The population of permanent residents refers to the population who actually and usually lives in a given area for a certain time (above half a year). According to the provisions of the population census and the sampling survey of population, the population of permanent residents mainly includes the following types: 1.All registered population who usually live in one certain place, excluding the person who leave away above half a year, including persons working or studying abroad. 2.The population who has lived in a certain place above half a year and whose household registration at other place, or living at a certain place at the survey moment, and leaving the household registered location for half a year. 3.The population who live at a certain place at the survey moment, but without registered permanent residence certificate everywhere, for example the person who has not gained registered permanent residence certificate, and with registration movement certificate, birth certificate,retirement certificate,or prisoners released certificate.

【The registered population】 According to the household registration ordinance of the People's Republic of China, the registered population refers to the citizens who have registered in the household registration department where the citizens usually live. No matter going out or not, no matter how long dose he go out, as long as the person has gained the permanent residence registration, the person is the region's registered population. Registered population data is generally gained from the regular statistical monthly or annual report of republic security department.

【Late Marriage Rate】 refers to the proportion of women who are over 23 years old in the number of first marriage women in a certain period (usually one year), which is generally expressed as a percentage. Calculation formula:

Late Marriage Rate = Number of first marriage of women over 23 years of age / number of first marriage of women in this year × 100%

【Birth Rate (or Crude Birth Rate)】 means the ratio between the number of births in a certain period (usually a year)and the average population in the same period (or mid-year figure).It is usually calculated in terms of permillage and its calculating formula is:

$$\text{Birth Rate} = \frac{\text{Number of Births}}{\text{Average Number of Population}} \times 1000‰$$

Number of Births refers to live births,when babies have showed any vital phenomena regardless of the length of pregnancy.

Average Number of Population is the average of the number of population at the beginning of the year and,at the end of the year and sometimes is substituted for with mid-year population.

【Death Rate(or Crude Death Rate)】 refers to the ratio of number of deaths to the average population (or mid-year population)during a certain period of time (usually a year),which is often presented as perminvar.its calculating formula is:

$$\text{Death Rate} = \frac{\text{Number of Deaths}}{\text{Average Number of Population}} \times 1000‰$$

【Natural Growth Rate of Population】 refers to the ratio of natural increase in population (number of births minus number of deaths) in a certain period of time (usually a year) to the average population (or mid-year population) of the same period,which is often presented as perminvar.The following formula are applied:

$$\text{Number of Growth of Population} = \frac{\text{Number of Births} - \text{Number of Deaths}}{\text{Average Number of Population}} \times 1000‰$$

Natural Growth Rate of Population = Birth Rate-Death Rate

第三篇 CHAPTER 3

从业人员和工资

EMPLOYMENT AND WAGES

第三篇　从业人员和工资

一、本篇资料反映广州市社会从业人员总量及构成、城镇单位就业与工资等基本情况。

二、本篇资料由广州市统计局人口和社会科技统计处整理提供。

三、本篇资料中的城镇非私营单位在岗职工及工资统计范围只包括城镇以上国有、集体及其他经济类型单位，不包括乡镇企业、私营单位和个体工商户。

四、本篇资料中的社会从业人员主要包括本市劳动力以及外来劳动力。

五、1998年，劳动统计年报中对全部调查单位改按企业登记注册类型分组，使统计口径发生变化，即国有单位中不再包括国有联营和有限责任公司中的国有独资公司；城镇集体单位中不再包括集体联营和股份合作企业；其他单位则包括国有联营和有限责任公司中的国有独资公司，集体联营和股份合作企业。

3 Employment and Wages

I. The data in this chapter show the basic conditions of social composition of employees, employment and wages in urban units of Guangzhou.

II. The data in this chapter are prepared and provided by the Division of Population, Social, Science and Tech1ology Statistics of Guangzhou Statistical Bureau.

Ⅲ. The statistical coverage of staff and worker urban units and wages in this chapter only includes the state-owned units, the collective -owned units and other economic ownership in urban areas, not including township enterprises, private institutions and individual businesses.

Ⅳ. The employed persons in this chapter mainly include the labor resources of Guangzhou origin and the migrant labors.

V. Since 1998,the statistical coverage of the annual reports of labor statistics has been adjusted, in which all the survey units are grouped by registration ownership of the enterprises, i.e. the state-owned units excludes the exclusively state-invested companies in state-owned joint ownership units and limited liability companies, the urban collective units excludes the collective-owned joint ownership units and share-holding cooperative operation and the other units include the exclusively state-invested companies in state-owned joint ownership units and limited liability companies, the collective-owned jointed owner-ship units and share-holding cooperative operation.

3-1 社会就业情况主要指标

Main Indicators of Social Employment Situation

项　　目	Item	2019	2019年比2018年增长(%) Growth Rate in 2019 over 2018 (%)
全社会从业人员 (人)	Total Number of Employed Persons at Year-end (person)	11258940	2.1
第一产业	Primary Industry	622398	3.2
第二产业	Secondary Industry	2665507	-3.1
第三产业	Tertiary Industry	7971035	3.9
城镇非私营单位从业人员 (人)	Number of Employed Persons in Urban Units at Year-end (person)	4002180	14.8
国有单位	State-owned Units	801129	11.9
集体单位	Urban Collective-owned Units	71312	20.8
其他单位	Units of Other Types of Ownership	3129739	15.4
# 外商及港澳台投资单位	Enterprises with Funds from Foreign Countries, Hong Kong,Macao and Taiwan	1045137	8.3
私营、个体和其他从业人员 (人)	Employed Persons in Private Enterprises and Self-employed Individuals at Year-end (person)	7256760	-3.7
城镇非私营单位从业人员工资总额(万元)	Total Wages of Employed Persons in Urban Units (10000 yuan)	47497456	24.9
国有单位	State-owned Units	13933964	33.5
集体单位	Urban Collective-owned Units	475010	37.3
其他单位	Units of Other Types of Ownership	33088482	21.4
# 外商及港澳台投资单位	Enterprises with Funds from Foreign Countries, Hong Kong,Macao and Taiwan	10678695	18.3
城镇非私营单位从业人员年平均工资(元)	Average Wage of Employed Persons in Urban Units (yuan)	119453	8.7
国有单位	State-owned Units	175585	19.9
集体单位	Urban Collective-owned Units	67245	16.3
其他单位	Units of Other Types of Ownership	106325	4.9
# 外商及港澳台投资单位	Enterprises with Funds from Foreign Countries, Hong Kong,Macao and Taiwan	101175	7.4
城镇非私营单位在岗职工年平均工资(元)	Average Wage of Fully Employed Staff and Workers in Urban Units (yuan)	123498	10.4
国有单位	State-owned Units	179244	20.6
集体单位	Urban Collective-owned Units	70585	17.8
其他单位	Units of Other Types of Ownership	109901	6.7
# 外商及港澳台投资单位	Enterprises with Funds from Foreign Countries, Hong Kong,Macao and Taiwan	105879	9.9
年末城镇登记失业人员 (人)	Number of Registered Unemployed Persons in Urban Areas (person)	35350	1.6
城镇登记失业率 (%)	Registered Unemployment Rate in Urban Areas (%)	2.15	0.25 (个百分点)

注：1. 私营、个体和其他从业人员指全社会从业人员中扣除城镇非私营单位从业人员外的部分。
　　2. 城镇登记失业人员及城镇登记失业率由广州市人力资源和社会保障局提供。

Note: I. Employed persons in private enterprises and self-employed individuals are refer to employed persons other than employed persons in urban units.

II. Data on number of registered unemployed persons in urban areas and registered unemployment rate in urban areas are provided by Guangzhou Municipal Bureau of Labor and Social Security.

3-2 主要年份全社会从业人员人数

Number of Employed Persons in Main Years

单位：人 (person)

年 份 Year	合 计 Total	城镇非私营单位从业人员 Employed Persons in Urban Units	私营、个体和其他从业人员 Employed Persons in Private Enterprises, Self-employed Individuals and others
1978	2668989	1473615	1195374
1980	2750467	1565533	1184934
1985	3134739	1756497	1378242
1990	3411513	1893944	1517569
1995	4077775	2082361	1995414
2000	4962579	1755512	3207067
2001	5029338	1686900	3342438
2002	5070216	1755779	3314437
2003	5210706	1880184	3330522
2004	5407087	1943955	3463132
2005	5744550	1997579	3746971
2006	5994973	2071574	3923399
2007	6236312	2236902	3999410
2008	6529045	2255380	4273665
2009	6791495	2351538	4439957
2010	7110695	2463713	4646982
2011	7644827	3102356	4542471
2012	7945771	3268488	4677283
2013	8251070	3245858	5005212
2014	8749630	3263983	5485647
2015	9279096	3203134	6075962
2016	9800359	3252340	6548019
2017	10371691	3291696	7079995
2018	11023598	3486454	7537144
2019	11258940	4002180	7256760

注：1．2000年以前，城镇非私营单位从业人员统计口径为城镇单位职工口径。
2．2006—2010年数据根据第六次全国人口普查结果作了相应调整。
3．2011—2018年数据根据第四次全国经济普查结果作了相应调整。

Note: I.The statistical scale of employed persons in urban units is the statistical scale of staff and workers before 2000.
II. The data from year 2006 to 2010 are revised according to the Sixth National Population Census.
III. The data from year 2011 to 2018 are revised according to the Fourth National Economic Census.

3-3 主要年份三次产业从业人员及构成

Employed Persons and Composition by Three strata of Industry in Main Years

年 份 Year	从业人员（人） Employed Persons (person)	第一产业 Primary Industry	第二产业 Secondary Industry	第三产业 Tertiary Industry	构成 (%) Composition (%) 第一产业 Primary Industry	第二产业 Secondary Industry	第三产业 Tertiary Industry
1978	2668989	1165987	857527	645475	43.69	32.13	24.18
1980	2750467	1106432	922756	721279	40.23	33.55	26.22
1985	3134739	979869	1180526	974344	31.26	37.66	31.08
1990	3411513	963548	1241813	1206152	28.24	36.40	35.36
1995	4077775	924969	1583686	1569120	22.68	38.84	38.48
2000	4962579	956596	1982905	2023078	19.27	39.96	40.77
2001	5029338	969793	1960309	2099236	19.28	38.98	41.74
2002	5070216	949624	1953095	2167497	18.73	38.52	42.75
2003	5210706	958819	2001677	2250210	18.40	38.42	43.18
2004	5407087	901318	2046552	2459217	16.67	37.85	45.48
2005	5744550	869141	2222177	2653232	15.13	38.68	46.19
2006	5994973	831303	2335315	2828355	13.87	38.95	47.18
2007	6236312	774596	2477232	2984484	12.42	39.72	47.86
2008	6529045	730174	2625645	3173226	11.18	40.22	48.60
2009	6791495	733557	2733281	3324657	10.80	40.25	48.95
2010	7110695	590223	2736424	3784048	8.30	38.48	53.22
2011	7644827	629012	2916585	4099230	8.23	38.15	53.62
2012	7945771	646030	3008191	4291550	8.13	37.86	54.01
2013	8251070	646758	2839653	4764659	7.84	34.42	57.74
2014	8749630	627996	3033806	5087828	7.18	34.67	58.15
2015	9279096	629254	3066200	5583642	6.78	33.04	60.18
2016	9800359	621426	3066503	6112430	6.34	31.29	62.37
2017	10371691	620657	2966789	6784245	5.98	28.60	65.42
2018	11023598	603377	2751831	7668390	5.47	24.96	69.57
2019	11258940	622398	2665507	7971035	5.53	23.67	70.80

注：1.2006—2010年数据根据第六次全国人口普查结果作了相应调整。

2.2011—2018年数根据第四次全国经济普查结果作了相应调整。

Note:I. The data from year 2006 to 2010 are revised according to the sixth National Population Census.

II. The data from year 2011 to 2018 are revised according to the Fourth National Economic Census.

3-4 三次产业全社会从业人员及构成（2019年末）

Employed Persons and Composition by Three Strata of Industry (Year-end of 2019)

项　目	Item	从业人员（人）Employed Persons (person)	构成（%）Composition (%)
合　计	**Total**	**11258940**	**100.00**
按产业分	**Grouped By Industry**		
第一产业	Primary Industry	622398	5.53
第二产业	Secondary Industry	2665507	23.67
第三产业	Tertiary Industry	7971035	70.80
按行业分	**Grouped By Sector**		
农、林、牧、渔业	Agriculture, Forestry, Animal Husbandry and Fishery	623062	5.53
工　业	Industry	1951697	17.34
建筑业	Construction	726718	6.45
批发和零售业	Wholesale and Retail Trade	1994784	17.73
交通运输、仓储和邮政业	Transport, Storage and Post	558806	4.96
住宿和餐饮业	Hotels and Catering Services	566354	5.03
信息传输、软件和信息技术服务业	Information Transmission, Software and Information Technology	572124	5.08
金融业	Financial Intermediation	834752	7.41
房地产业	Real Estate	487607	4.33
租赁和商务服务业	Leasing and Business Services	952584	8.46
科学研究和技术服务业	Scientific Research and Technical Services	534878	4.75
水利、环境和公共设施管理业	Management of Water Conservancy, Environment and Public Facilities	82925	0.74
居民服务、修理和其他服务业	Service to Households, Repair and Other Services	315246	2.80
教　育	Education	400691	3.56
卫生和社会工作	Health and Social Work	233434	2.07
文化、体育和娱乐业	Culture, Sports and Entertainment	132991	1.18
公共管理、社会保障和社会组织	Public Management, Social Security and Social Organizations	290287	2.58

3-5 全市全社会从业人员（2019年末）

Number of Employed Persons (Year-end of 2019)

单位：人 (person)

项目	Item	合计 Total	城镇非私营单位从业人员 Number of Employed Persons in Urban Units	私营、个体和其他从业人员 Employed Persons in Private Enterprises, Self-employed Individuals and Others
总计	**Total**	11258940	4002180	7256760
按国民经济行业分	**Grouped by Economic Sector**			
农、林、牧、渔业	Agriculture, Forestry, Animal Husbandry and Fishery	623062	1963	621099
采矿业	Mining	415	117	298
制造业	Manufacturing	1907867	747315	1160552
电力、热力、燃气及水生产和供应业	Production and Supply of Electricity, Heat, Gas and Water	43415	35665	7750
建筑业	Construction	726718	272761	453957
批发和零售业	Wholesale and Retail Trade	1994784	337563	1657221
交通运输、仓储和邮政业	Transport, Storage and Post	558806	295798	263008
住宿和餐饮业	Hotels and Catering Services	566354	147830	418524
信息传输、软件和信息技术服务业	Information Transmission, Software and Information Technology	572124	226695	345429
金融业	Financial Intermediation	834752	182239	652513
房地产业	Real Estate	487607	273655	213952
租赁和商务服务业	Leasing and Business Services	952584	412569	540015
科学研究和技术服务业	Scientific Research and Technical Services	534878	172161	362717
水利、环境和公共设施管理业	Management of Water Conservancy, Environment and Public Facilities	82925	65214	17711
居民服务、修理和其他服务业	Service to Households, Repair and Other Services	315246	30259	284987
教育	Education	400691	313544	87147
卫生和社会工作	Health and Social Service	233434	194223	39211
文化、体育和娱乐业	Culture, Sports and Entertainment	132991	40011	92980
公共管理、社会保障和社会组织	Public Management, Social Security and Social Organizations	290287	252598	37689

3-6 主要年份城镇非私营单位从业人员数及工资

Number and Wages of Employed Persons in Urban Units in Main Years

年 份 Year	城镇非私营单位从业人员年末人数（人） Number of Employed Persons in Urban Units at Year-end (person)	城镇非私营单位从业人员工资总额（万元） Total Wages of Employed Persons in Urban Units (10000 yuan)	城镇非私营单位从业人员年平均工资（元） Average Wage of Employed Persons in Urban Units (yuan)
2000	1755512	3489371	19714
2005	1997579	6772629	34171
2006	2071574	7532573	36566
2007	2236902	8961040	40280
2008	2255380	10251127	45368
2009	2351538	11439796	49054
2010	2463713	13354746	54091
2011	3102356	17486373	56618
2012	3268488	20305943	62598
2013	3245858	21724541	68594
2014	3263983	23881767	73131
2015	3203134	25674928	79534
2016	3252340	28537980	88136
2017	3291696	31983933	97522
2018	3486454	38035167	109879
2019	4002180	47497456	119453

3-7 主要年份城镇非私营单位在岗职工工资总额及指数

Total Wages of Fully Employed Staff and Workers in Urban Units and Related Indices in Main Years

年 份 Year	在岗职工工资总额(万元) Total Wages of Fully Employed Staff and Workers in Urban Units (10000 yuan)	国有单位 State-owned Units	集体单位 Urban Collective-owned Units	其他单位 Units of Other Types of Ownership	# 外商及港澳台投资单位 Enterprises with Funds from Foreign Countries,Hong Kong,Macao and Taiwan	在岗职工年平均工资(元) Average Wage of Fully Employed Staff and Workers in Urban Units (yuan)
1978	101809	76913	24896			714
1980	142243	108015	34228			941
1985	278892	208829	65660	4403	3127	1621
1990	656434	487524	121441	47469	41198	3504
1991	783043	565974	148783	68286	61119	4022
1992	971335	690135	183771	97429	89978	4792
1993	1316773	941475	226929	148369	106957	6342
1994	1815428	1277944	308933	228551	183030	8623
1995	2146245	1481375	344494	320376	263343	10317
1996	2395597	1672483	348629	374485	313623	11813
1997	2615842	1798987	338388	478467	404483	13118
1998(原口径) 1998 (Original Standards)	2831440	1900631	344677	586132	454061	14318
1998(新口径) 1998 (New Standards)	2831440	1758088	322399	750953	454061	14318
1999	3085768	1917375	296558	871835	507875	16202
2000	3480880	2188085	289750	1003045	586413	19091
2001	3878065	2401471	216967	1259627	691639	22141
2002	4534911	2817578	229015	1488318	838420	25583
2003	5335484	3185006	243455	1907023	1097924	28237
2004	5983255	3529828	240966	2212461	1251256	31025
2005	6653196	3837476	233643	2582077	1464470	33853
2006	7389676	3967484	238729	3183463	1718714	36321
2007	8770687	4448123	254851	4067713	2228358	40187
2008	10053742	4970189	261939	4821614	2655221	45365
2009	11180296	5345813	276463	5558020	2889870	49215
2010	13044801	6053212	284742	6706846	3565786	54495
2011	17008733	7040246	274165	9694322	5332522	57473
2012	19695115	7944452	356403	11394260	5950277	63752
2013	21107782	5536325	408310	15163147	6568426	69692
2014	23049712	6233018	414591	16402103	6773266	74245
2015	24874876	6690706	361441	17822729	7250138	81171
2016	27703134	7457706	357722	19887706	7595025	89096
2017	31032760	8704188	327055	22001517	7945622	98612
2018	37005944	10292371	320460	26393113	8741982	111839
2019	45864824	13706998	453982	31703845	10337458	123498

注：1. 本表数据2011年以前为城镇单位职工工资总额，2011年起为城镇非私营单位在岗职工工资总额。
2. 城镇非私营单位职工含劳务派遣人员。

Note: I. The name of Total Wages of Fully Employed Staff and Workers in Urban Units is adjusted to Total Wages of Staff and Workers in Urban Units since 2011.

II. Fully employed staff and workers in urban units contain labor dispatching personnel .

3-7 续表 continued

指数(上年=100) Indices (preceding year=100)

年 份 Year	在岗职工工资总额(上年=100) Total Wages of Fully Employed Staff and Workers in Urban Units (preceding year=100)	国有单位 State-owned Units	集体单位 Urban Collective-owned Units	其他单位 Units of Other Types of Ownership	# 外商及港澳台投资单位 Enterprises with Funds from Foreign Countries,Hong Kong,Macao and Taiwan	在岗职工年平均工资(上年=100) Average Wage of Fully Employed Staff and Workers in Urban Units (preceding year=100)
1978	116.2	121.3	102.8			105.0
1980	139.7	140.4	137.5			114.8
1985	123.2	122.0	124.3	190.7	236.4	121.2
1990	107.7	106.1	105.4	137.1	152.4	107.1
1991	119.3	116.1	122.5	143.9	148.4	114.8
1992	124.1	121.9	123.5	142.7	147.2	119.1
1993	135.6	136.4	123.5	152.3	118.9	132.4
1994	137.9	135.7	136.1	154.0	171.1	136.0
1995	118.2	115.9	111.5	140.2	143.9	119.7
1996	111.6	112.9	101.2	116.9	119.1	114.5
1997	109.2	107.6	97.1	127.8	129.0	111.1
1998	108.2	105.7	101.9	122.5	112.3	109.2
1999	109.0	109.1	92.0	116.1	111.9	113.2
2000	112.8	114.1	97.7	115.1	115.5	117.8
2001	111.4	109.8	74.9	125.6	117.9	116.0
2002	116.9	117.3	105.6	118.2	121.2	115.6
2003	117.7	113.0	106.3	128.1	131.0	110.4
2004	112.1	110.8	99.0	116.0	114.0	109.9
2005	111.2	108.7	97.0	116.7	117.0	109.1
2006	111.1	103.4	102.2	123.3	117.4	107.3
2007	118.7	112.1	106.8	127.8	129.7	110.6
2008	114.6	111.7	102.8	118.5	119.2	112.9
2009	111.2	107.6	105.5	115.3	108.8	108.5
2010	116.7	113.2	103.0	120.7	123.4	110.7
2011	130.4	116.3	96.3	144.5	149.6	111.6
2012	115.8	112.8	130.0	117.5	111.6	110.9
2013	107.2	69.7	114.6	133.1	110.4	109.3
2014	109.2	112.6	101.5	108.2	103.1	106.5
2015	107.9	107.3	87.2	108.7	107.0	109.3
2016	111.4	111.5	99.0	111.6	104.8	109.8
2017	112.0	116.7	91.4	110.6	104.6	110.7
2018	119.2	118.2	98.0	120.0	110.0	113.4
2019	123.9	133.2	141.7	120.1	118.3	110.4

注：1. 本表数据2011年以前为城镇单位职工工资总额指数，2011年起为城镇非私营单位在岗职工工资总额指数。
2. 2011年城镇非私营单位在岗职工年平均工资指数按可比口径计算。

Note: I. The name of Total Wages of Fully Employed Staff and Workers in Urban Units is adjusted to Total Wages of Staff and Workers in Urban Units since 2011.

II. The data of 2011 are calculated at comparable coverage.

3-8 城镇非私营单位从业人数与工资（2019年）

Number and Wages of Employed Persons in Urban Units (2019)

项　　目	Item	2018	2019
城镇非私营单位从业人员年末人数（人）	**Number of Employed Persons in Urban Units at Year-end (person)**	**3486454**	**4002180**
国有单位	State-owned Units	716136	801129
集体单位	Urban Collective Owned Units	59038	71312
其他单位	Units of Other Types of Ownership	2711280	3129739
# 外商及港澳台投资单位	Enterprises with Funds from Foreign Countries, Hong Kong, Macao and Taiwan	964632	1045137
城镇非私营单位从业人员年平均人数（人）	**Average Number of Employed Persons in Urban Units (person)**	**3461542**	**3976238**
国有单位	State-owned Units	712598	793572
集体单位	Urban Collective Owned Units	59834	70639
其他单位	Units of Other Types of Ownership	2689110	3112027
# 外商及港澳台投资单位	Enterprises with Funds from Foreign Countries, Hong Kong, Macao and Taiwan	958075	1055466
城镇非私营单位从业人员工资总额（万元）	**Total Wages of Employed Persons in Urban Units (10000 yuan)**	**38035167**	**47497456**
国有单位	State-owned Units	10439713	13933964
集体单位	Urban Collective Owned Units	345959	475010
其他单位	Units of Other Types of Ownership	27249495	33088482
# 外商及港澳台投资单位	Enterprises with Funds from Foreign Countries, Hong Kong, Macao and Taiwan	9027434	10678695
城镇非私营单位从业人员年平均工资（元）	**Average Wage of Employed Persons in Urban Units (yuan)**	**109879**	**119453**
国有单位	State-owned Units	146502	175585
集体单位	Urban Collective Owned Units	57820	67245
其他单位	Units of Other Types of Ownership	101333	106325
# 外商及港澳台投资单位	Enterprises with Funds from Foreign Countries, Hong Kong, Macao and Taiwan	94225	101175

3-9 全市城镇非私营单位在岗职工人数与工资（2019年）

项　　目	Item
合　计	**Total**
按隶属关系分	**Grouped by Subordination**
中央单位	Units Subordinated to Central Government
地方单位	Units Subordinated to Provincial Government
其他单位	Units Subordinated to Municipal Government
按执行会计制度类别分	**Grouped by Accounting Regulation Implemented**
企　业	Enterprises
事业单位	Institutions
行政单位	Agencies & Organizations
民间非营利组织	Civil Nonprofit Organizations
其　他	Others
按国民经济行业分	**Grouped by Economic Sector**
农、林、牧、渔业	Agriculture, Forestry, Animal Husbandry and Fishery
#农、林、牧、渔专业及辅助性活动	Services for Agriculture, Forestry, Animal Husbandry and Fishery
采矿业	Mining
制造业	Manufacturing
#食品制造业	Manufacture of Foods
纺织服装、服饰业	Manufacture of Textile Wearing Apparel, Clothing
皮革、毛皮、羽毛及其制品和制鞋业	Manufacture of Leather, Fur, Feather and Related Products and Footwear
文教、工美、体育和娱乐用品制造业	Manufacture of Culture and Education,Art and Crafts,Sports and Entertainment Supplies
化学原料和化学制品制造业	Manufacture of Raw Chemical Materials and Chemical Products
医药制造业	Manufacture of Medical
通用设备制造业	Manufacture of General Purpose Machinery
汽车制造业	Manufacture of Automobile
铁路、船舶、航空航天和其他运输设备制造业	Manufacture of Railway, Ship, Aerospace and Other Transportation Equipment
电气机械和器材制造业	Manufacture of Electrical Machinery and Equipment
计算机、通信和其他电子设备制造业	Manufacture of Computers, Communications and Other Electronic Equipment
电力、热力、燃气及水生产和供应业	Production and Supply of Electricity, Heat,Gas and Water
建筑业	Construction
房屋建筑业	Housing Industry
土木工程建筑业	Civil Engineering Construction
建筑安装业	Architectural Installation
建筑装饰和其他建筑业	Building Decoration and Other Construction
批发和零售业	Wholesale and Retail Trade
批发业	Wholesale
零售业	Retail Trade
交通运输、仓储和邮政业	Transport, Storage and Post
铁路运输业	Railway Transport
道路运输业	Highway Transport

Number and Wages of Fully Employed Staff and Workers in Urban Units (2019)

单位数 (个) Number of Units (unit)	在岗职工年末人数 (人) Number of Fully Employed Staff and Workers in Urban Units at Year-end (person)	在岗职工年平均人数 (人) Average Number of Fully Employed Staff and Workers in Urban Units (person)	在岗职工工资总额 (万元) Total Wages of Fully Employed Staff and Workers in Urban Units (10000 yuan)	在岗职工年平均工资 (元) Average Wages of Fully Employed Staff and Workers in Urban Units (yuan)
46205	**3751699**	**3713798**	**45864824**	**123498**
735	431937	429945	6812107	158441
8598	1211874	1197981	17343477	144773
36872	2107888	2085872	21709240	104078
38419	2994581	2964754	32901902	110977
4118	469463	463919	8553280	184370
1502	217948	216794	3895760	179699
2008	65246	63888	466147	72963
158	4461	4443	47735	107440
73	1951	1937	16350	84408
34	964	969	9741	100526
3	117	115	3647	317104
4152	738962	747761	7323124	97934
128	46784	46938	566970	120791
342	28578	29543	188394	63769
180	22300	24246	132224	54534
207	30398	33108	203464	61454
386	40925	40711	501691	123232
125	30361	30113	340198	112974
257	35762	36470	362004	99261
243	123307	122633	1582656	129056
47	16376	16803	166737	99231
247	54354	53321	436638	81889
341	134980	134628	1225615	91037
161	35645	35578	592773	166612
1178	249076	246387	2374324	96366
218	115152	114948	847351	73716
208	97182	96007	1200276	125020
313	20933	20501	215184	104963
439	15809	14931	111513	74686
9754	313527	309741	2973253	95992
7649	206560	201757	2137204	105930
2105	106967	107984	836049	77423
1265	286058	284698	3365879	118226
5	2766	2767	34365	124197
494	131039	130456	1358057	104101

3-9 续表

项 目	Item
水上运输业	Waterway Transport
航空运输业	Air Transport
管道运输业	Pipeline Transport
多式联运和运输代理业	Handing and Transportation Agents
装卸搬运和仓储业	Storage
邮政业	Post
住宿和餐饮业	Hotels and Catering Services
住宿业	Hotels Services
餐饮业	Catering Services
信息传输、软件和信息技术服务业	Information Transmission, Software and Information Technology
电信、广播电视和卫星传输服务	Telecommunications, Broadcasting, TV Transmission and Satellite Services
互联网和相关服务	Networks Related Services
软件和信息技术服务业	Software and Information Technology Services
金融业	Financial Intermediation
# 货币金融服务	Monetary Financial Services
资本市场服务	Capital Market Services
保险业	Insurance
房地产业	Real Estate
租赁和商务服务业	Leasing and Business Services
租赁业	Leasing Services
商务服务业	Business Services
科学研究和技术服务业	Scientific Research and Technical Services
研究与试验发展	Research and Experimental Development
专业技术服务业	Professional Skill Services
科技推广和应用服务业	Science and Technology Popularization and Application Services
水利、环境和公共设施管理业	Management of Water Conservancy, Environment and Public Facilities
水利管理业	Management of Water Conservancy
生态保护和环境治理业	Ecological Protection and Environmental Governance Industry
公共设施管理业	Management of Public Facilities
土地管理业	Land Management
居民服务、修理和其他服务业	Service to Households, Repair and Other Services
教 育	Education
卫生和社会工作	Health and Social Work
卫 生	Health
社会工作	Social Work
文化、体育和娱乐业	Culture, Sports and Entertainment
新闻和出版业	Press and Publishing Industry
广播、电视、电影和影视录音制作业	Radio,Television,Movie and Recording Manufacturing
文化艺术业	Culture and Art
体 育	Sports
娱乐业	Entertainment
公共管理、社会保障和社会组织	Public Management, Social Security and Social Organizations
# 社会保障	Social Security

continued

单位数 (个) Number of Units (unit)	在岗职工年末人数 (人) Number of Fully Employed Staff and Workers in Urban Units at Year-end (person)	在岗职工年平均人数 (人) Average Number of Fully Employed Staff and Workers in Urban Units (person)	在岗职工工资总额 (万元) Total Wages of Fully Employed Staff and Workers in Urban Units (10000 yuan)	在岗职工年平均工资 (元) Average Wages of Fully Employed Staff and Workers in Urban Units (yuan)
77	13000	13521	247219	182841
15	83899	84079	1203861	143182
1	467	428	6257	146187
435	16176	16407	170858	104137
209	9688	9495	87127	91761
29	29023	27545	258135	93714
1232	114155	112972	674434	59699
416	33601	33494	225204	67237
816	80554	79478	449230	56523
2886	216465	214040	3594088	167917
79	31898	32121	545447	169810
324	37708	37395	713397	190773
2483	146859	144524	2335244	161582
1112	125669	126364	2982730	236043
485	82444	82894	2095036	252737
202	6525	6516	223332	342744
376	35060	35264	611920	173525
4186	264050	260186	2447919	94083
6369	374820	356901	3277579	91834
303	6923	6836	65416	95693
6066	367897	350065	3212163	91759
3714	166319	162647	2638022	162193
985	33667	32897	558391	169739
1689	116139	112966	1868152	165373
1040	16513	16784	211479	126001
468	61884	60603	453707	74865
64	2510	2493	43678	175204
87	3752	3654	52093	142565
298	55212	54052	351463	65023
19	410	404	6473	160220
954	28928	28756	198498	69029
3993	299542	294609	4561536	154834
1114	189103	186537	3545540	190072
708	171600	169472	3372098	198977
406	17503	17065	173442	101636
1132	37343	37246	559364	150181
112	7503	7692	131737	171264
199	10075	10192	152863	149982
395	7924	7919	106801	134869
181	7117	7235	125580	173573
245	4724	4208	42383	100719
2459	248085	246720	4282057	173559
32	1474	1456	21145	145224

3-10 城镇国有单位在岗职工人数与工资（2019年）

项　　目	Item
总　计	**Total**
按执行会计制度类别分	**Grouped by Accounting Regulation Implemented**
企　业	Enterprises
事业单位	Institutions
行政单位	Agencies & Organizations
民间非营利组织	Civil Nonprofit Organizations
其　他	Others
按国民经济行业分组	**Grouped by Economic Sector**
农、林、牧、渔业	Agriculture, Forestry, Animal Husbandry and Fishery
采矿业	Mining
制造业	Manufacturing
电力、热力、燃气及水生产和供应业	Production and Supply of Electricity, Heat,Gas and Water
建筑业	Construction
批发和零售业	Wholesale and Retail Trade
交通运输、仓储和邮政业	Transport, Storage and Post
住宿和餐饮业	Hotels and Catering Services
信息传输、软件和信息技术服务业	Information Transmission, Software and Information Technology
金融业	Financial Intermediation
房地产业	Real Estate
租赁和商务服务业	Leasing and Business Services
科学研究和技术服务业	Scientific Research and Technical Services
水利、环境和公共设施管理业	Management of Water Conservancy, Environment and Public Facilities
居民服务、修理和其他服务业	Service to Households, Repair and Other Services
教　育	Education
卫生和社会工作	Health and Social Service
文化、体育和娱乐业	Culture, Sports and Entertainment
公共管理、社会保障和社会组织	Public Management, Social Security and Social Organizations

Number and Wages of Fully Employed Staff and Workers in Urban State-owned Units (2019)

单位数 (个) Number of Units (unit)	在岗职工年末人数 (人) Number of Fully Employed Staff and Workers in Urban Units at Year-end (person)	在岗职工年平均人数 (人) Average Number of Fully Employed Staff and Workers in Urban Units (person)	在岗职工工资总额 (万元) Total Wages of Fully Employed Staff and Workers in Urban Units (10000 yuan)	在岗职工年平均工资 (元) Average Wages of Fully Employed Staff and Workers in Urban Units (yuan)
6165	**772067**	**764712**	**13706998**	**179244**
1002	115518	114654	1667591	145445
3604	436716	431391	8109052	187975
1455	216159	215009	3873175	180140
100	2932	2916	37106	127250
4	742	742	20074	270539
15	680	700	8924	127483
53	3564	3661	40165	109711
15	5645	5581	69585	124682
37	6264	6173	57926	93837
109	2834	2867	29940	104429
70	17607	17790	226108	127098
87	8763	9037	64327	71182
40	1595	1614	26506	164222
113	17786	17615	412578	234220
173	4380	4385	44356	101155
266	28810	28295	273697	96730
446	45900	45157	970004	214807
257	29332	29164	272868	93563
81	5392	5439	51602	94873
1539	180870	178709	3509287	196369
447	154317	151215	3136687	207432
226	15903	16209	290001	178914
2191	242425	241101	4222437	175131

3-11 城镇集体单位在岗职工人数与工资（2019年）

项　　目	Item
总　计	**Total**
按执行会计制度类别分	**Grouped by Accounting Regulation Implemented**
企　业	Enterprises
事业单位	Institutions
行政单位	Agencies & Organizations
民间非营利组织	Civil Nonprofit Organizations
其　他	Others
按国民经济行业分组	**Grouped by Economic Sector**
农、林、牧、渔业	Agriculture, Forestry, Animal Husbandry and Fishery
采矿业	Mining
制造业	Manufacturing
电力、热力、燃气及水生产和供应业	Production and Supply of Electricity, Heat,Gas and Water
建筑业	Construction
批发和零售业	Wholesale and Retail Trade
交通运输、仓储和邮政业	Transport, Storage and Post
住宿和餐饮业	Hotels and Catering Services
信息传输、软件和信息技术服务业	Information Transmission, Software and Information Technology
金融业	Financial Intermediation
房地产业	Real Estate
租赁和商务服务业	Leasing and Business Services
科学研究和技术服务业	Scientific Research and Technical Services
水利、环境和公共设施管理业	Management of Water Conservancy, Environment and Public Facilities
居民服务、修理和其他服务业	Service to Households, Repair and Other Services
教　育	Education
卫生和社会工作	Health and Social Service
文化、体育和娱乐业	Culture, Sports and Entertainment
公共管理、社会保障和社会组织	Public Management, Social Security and Social Organizations

Number and Wages of Fully Employed Staff and Workers in Urban Collective-owned Units (2019)

单位数 (个) Number of Units (unit)	在岗职工年末人数 (人) Number of Fully Employed Staff and Workers in Urban Units at Year-end (person)	在岗职工年平均人数 (人) Average Number of Fully Employed Staff and Workers in Urban Units (person)	在岗职工工资总额 (万元) Total Wages of Fully Employed Staff and Workers in Urban Units (10000 yuan)	在岗职工年平均工资 (元) Average Wages of Fully Employed Staff and Workers in Urban Units (yuan)
1950	**65050**	**64317**	**453982**	**70585**
1626	51230	50591	312333	61737
146	8652	8659	110636	127770
10	225	224	3166	141335
106	3804	3715	21915	58991
62	1139	1128	5932	52590
6	222	221	1141	51615
101	10694	11684	71902	61539
9	206	206	1697	82354
41	2615	2693	24580	91274
189	1845	1751	14586	83303
42	795	802	3508	43734
34	1029	1036	5435	52462
4	32	41	483	117707
1	2	2	5	25500
589	13336	13313	73400	55134
472	18140	16566	95369	57570
48	673	649	11100	171029
23	1573	1563	11418	73050
50	844	832	5394	64828
269	8951	8841	74706	84501
46	3635	3662	55515	151596
13	71	71	522	73563
13	387	384	3221	83885

3-12 城镇非私营其他单位在岗职工人数与工资（2019年）

项　目	Item
总　计	**Total**
按登记注册类型分	**Grouped by Registration Status**
股份合作	Cooperative Enterprises
联　营	Joint Ownership Enterprises
有限责任公司	Limited Liability Corporations
股份有限公司	Share Holding Enterprises
内资其他	Other Enterprises
港澳台投资	Enterprises with Funds from Hong Kong, Macao and Taiwan
外商投资	Foreign Funded Enterprises
按国民经济行业分	**Grouped by Economic Sector**
农、林、牧、渔业	Agriculture, Forestry, Animal Husbandry and Fishery
采矿业	Mining
制造业	Manufacturing
电力、热力、燃气及水生产和供应业	Production and Supply of Electricity, Heat,Gas and Water
建筑业	Construction
批发和零售业	Wholesale and Retail Trade
交通运输、仓储和邮政业	Transport, Storage and Post
住宿和餐饮业	Hotels and Catering Services
信息传输、软件和信息技术服务业	Information Transmission, Software and Information Technology
金融业	Financial Intermediation
房地产业	Real Estate
租赁和商务服务业	Leasing and Business Services
科学研究和技术服务业	Scientific Research and Technical Services
水利、环境和公共设施管理业	Management of Water Conservancy, Environment and Public Facilities
居民服务、修理和其他服务业	Service to Households, Repair and Other Services
教　育	Education
卫生和社会工作	Health and Social Service
文化、体育和娱乐业	Culture, Sports and Entertainment
公共管理、社会保障和社会组织	Public Management, Social Security and Social Organizations

注：城镇非私营其他单位指城镇非私营单位中扣除国有单位和集体单位外的其他各种类型单位。

Number and Wages of Fully Employed Staff and Workers in Urban Other Types of Ownership (2019)

单位数 (个) Number of Units (unit)	在岗职工年末人数 (人) Number of Fully Employed Staff and Workers in Urban Units at Year-end (person)	在岗职工年平均人数 (人) Average Number of Fully Employed Staff and Workers in Urban Units (person)	在岗职工工资总额 (万元) Total Wages of Fully Employed Staff and Workers in Urban Units (10000 yuan)	在岗职工年平均工资 (元) Average Wages of Fully Employed Staff and Workers in Urban Units (yuan)
38090	**2914582**	**2884769**	**31703845**	**109901**
1201	13405	13386	104326	77936
108	3981	3915	52814	134901
22183	1387661	1360276	14120836	103809
2439	402689	400404	5896849	147272
3200	133454	130438	1191562	91351
5124	446717	453439	4476303	98719
3835	526675	522911	5861155	112087
52	1049	1016	6285	61864
3	117	115	3647	317104
3998	724704	732416	7211058	98456
137	29794	29791	521491	175050
1100	240197	237521	2291818	96489
9456	308848	305123	2928727	95985
1153	267656	266106	3136263	117858
1111	104363	102899	604672	58764
2842	214838	212385	3567100	167954
998	107881	108747	2570146	236342
3424	246334	242488	2330163	96094
5631	327870	312040	2908512	93210
3220	119746	116841	1656918	141810
188	30979	29876	169421	56708
823	22692	22485	141503	62932
2185	109721	107059	977543	91309
621	31151	31660	353338	111604
893	21369	20966	268841	128227
255	5273	5235	56399	107735

Note: Other types of units in urban are refer to units other than state-owned units and collective-owned units.

3-13 城镇非私营单位从业人员女性年末人数（2019年）

行 业	Sector
合 计	**Total**
农、林、牧、渔业	Agriculture, Forestry, Animal Husbandry and Fishery
采矿业	Mining
制造业	Manufacturing
电力、热力、燃气及水生产和供应业	Production and Supply of Electricity, Heat,Gas and Water
建筑业	Construction
批发和零售业	Wholesale and Retail Trade
交通运输、仓储和邮政业	Transport, Storage and Post
住宿和餐饮业	Hotels and Catering Services
信息传输、软件和信息技术服务业	Information Transmission, Software and Information Technology
金融业	Financial Intermediation
房地产业	Real Estate
租赁和商务服务业	Leasing and Business Services
科学研究和技术服务业	Scientific Research and Technical Services
水利、环境和公共设施管理业	Management of Water Conservancy, Environment and Public Facilities
居民服务、修理和其他服务业	Service to Households, Repair and Other Services
教 育	Education
卫生和社会工作	Health and Social Service
文化、体育和娱乐业	Culture, Sports and Entertainment
公共管理、社会保障和社会组织	Public Management, Social Security and Social Organizations

Number of Female Staff and Workers at Year-end in Urban Units (2019)

年末人数 (人)			女性从业人员比重 (%) Proportion of Female Staff and Workers (%)		
Number of Staff and Workers at Year-end (person)	#国 有 State-owned Units	#集 体 Urban Collective-owned Units	合 计 Total	#国 有 State-owned Units	#集 体 Urban Collective-owned Units
1697263	385484	33242	42.41	48.12	46.61
606	117	50	30.87	17.13	22.12
31			26.50		
292577	918	8064	39.15	25.49	75.34
8365	1785	33	23.45	31.61	16.02
43671	1226	448	16.01	17.57	13.24
175802	1445	931	52.08	48.02	49.52
85332	4693	267	28.85	26.12	33.50
82346	4513	539	55.70	48.81	51.98
85089	609	10	37.53	34.66	30.30
100622	9022		55.21	48.51	
104063	1568	4926	38.03	35.01	30.01
164624	6540	6496	39.90	19.07	32.52
59959	16370	283	34.83	34.32	39.97
28636	12735	700	43.91	39.85	40.39
16056	2471	249	53.06	44.60	28.79
206022	116516	7555	65.71	61.56	82.46
135123	110169	2496	69.57	69.71	67.28
18285	7795	42	45.70	47.63	54.55
90054	86992	153	35.65	35.36	38.54

【从业人员】指在各类法人单位工作中，由单位支付劳动报酬的人员，包括在岗职工、劳务派遣人员和其他就业人员。这一指标反映了一定时期内全部劳动力资源的实际利用情况，是研究我国基本国情国力的重要指标。

【在岗职工】指在本单位工作且与本单位签订劳动合同，并由单位支付各项工资和社会保险、住房公积金的人员，以及上述人员中由于学习、病伤、产假等原因暂未工作仍由单位支付工资的人员。

【劳务派遣人员】根据《中华人民共和国劳动合同法》规定，指与劳务派遣单位签订劳动合同；并被劳务派遣单位派遣到实际用工单位工作；且劳务派遣单位与实际用工单位签订《劳务派遣协议》的人员。无论用工单位是否直接支付劳动报酬，劳务派遣人员均由实际用工单位填报，而劳务派遣单位（派出单位）不填报这些人员。

【工资总额】根据《关于工资总额组成的规定》，工资总额是指本单位在报告期内（季度或年度）直接支付给本单位人员的劳动报酬总额。包括计时工资、计件工资、奖金、津贴和补贴、加班加点工资、特殊情况下支付的工资。

工资总额是税前工资，包括单位从个人工资中直接为其代扣或代缴的房费、个人所得税、水费、电费、住房公积金和社会保险基金个人缴纳部分等。

工资总额不论是计入成本的还是不计入成本的，不论是以货币形式支付的还是以实物形式支付的，均应列入工资总额的计算范围。

工资总额由基本工资、绩效工资、工资性津贴和补贴、其他工资四部分组成。工资总额不包括病假、事假等情况的扣款。

【在岗职工平均工资】指企业、事业、机关单位的在岗职工在一定时期内平均每人所得的货币工资额。它表明一定时期在岗职工工资收入的高低程度，是反映在岗职工工资水平的主要指标。

计算公式为：在岗职工平均工资=报告期实际支付的全部在岗职工工资总额/报告期全部在岗职工平均人数。

【Practitioners】refers to employees in various legal person units, paid by the unit labor remuneration, including on-the-job, labor dispatch personnel and other employees. This indicator reflects all the actual utilization of labor resources at a certain period of time, is an important index to study the basic situation of our country national strength.

【Staff and workers 】refers to the staff work in the unit and the unit signed labor contracts, and by the unit to pay the wages and social insurance, housing provident fund staff, and the staff in learning, because of injuries and other reasons not to work on maternity leave, still receive wages from their working units.

【Dispatch Personnel】refers to personnel signed labor contracts with the labor dispatch unit,and by the labor dispatch unit sent to the actual labor units, and the labor dispatch unit and the actual labor units signed “labor dispatch agreement” ,according to the "Labor contract law provisions of the people's Republic of China". No matter whether the direct labor units to pay labor remuneration, labor dispatch personnel are filled by the actual labor units.

【Total Wages】according to the “Regulations on the payroll” the composition of total wages, payroll is refers to the unit paid directly to the total remuneration of the staff during the reporting period (quarterly or annual). Including hourly wages, piece-rate wages, bonuses, allowances and subsidies, overtime pay overtime wages, special circumstances wages.

Total wages is pre-tax wages, including the unit from individual pay directly for its withholding or paying rent, personal income tax, water, electricity, housing provident fund and the social insurance fund individual pay part etc.

Wages regardless of whether it is included in the cost was not included in the cost, whether in monetary form of payment or payment in kind, should be included in the scope of calculation of total wages.

Four parts of Total wages including the basic salary, performance salary, wages and allowances and subsidies, and other wages. Total wages not including deduction of sick leave and personal leave.

【Average Wage of Fully Employed Staff and Workers】refer to the average wage in monetary terms per person during a certain period of time for fully employed staff and workers in enterprises, institutions and government agencies, which reflects the general level of wage income of fully employed staff and workers during a certain period of time and is calculated as follows:

Average Wage of Fully Employed Staff and Workers =Total Wages of Fully Employed Staff and Workers at the Report Period/Average Number of Fully Employed Staff and Workers at the Report Period

第四篇 CHAPTER 4

固定资产投资
INVESTMENT IN FIXED ASSETS

第四篇　固定资产投资

一、本篇资料反映广州市固定资产投资的基本情况。

二、本篇资料由广州市统计局固定资产投资统计处整理提供。

三、固定资产投资统计的资料来源主要为全面统计报表。按照现行的固定资产投资统计报表制度，从2011年起固定资产投资项目统计起报点由计划总投资50万元及以上提高到500万元及以上，固定资产投资不再称全社会固定资产投资。固定资产投资按经济类型分为：国有经济、集体经济、联营经济、股份制经济、私营经济、港澳台投资经济、外商投资经济、其他经济和个体经济。

从2012年起民间投资包含内容有所调整，民间投资是指工商登记注册类型为：集体、股份合作、私营独资、私营合伙、私营有限责任公司、个体户、个人合伙等纯民间主体的固定资产投资及混合经济成分中由集体、私营、个体控股的投资主体单位的全部固定资产投资。

4 Investment in Fixed Assets

I. The data in this chapter show the basic conditions of the total investment in fixed assets of Guangzhou .

II. The data in this chapter are prepared and provided by the Division of Investment and Construction Statistics of Guangzhou Municipal Bureau of Statistics.

Ⅲ. The data sources for the statistics of investment in fixed assets mainly come from the complete statistical report forms. According to the present regulations in the reporting scheme on the statistics of the investment in fixed assets, the statistics report point of the fixed assets investment projects has been increased from a planned total investment of 500,000 yuan and above to 5,000,000 yuan and above since 2011. The investment in fixed assets is no longer called the whole society investment in fixed assets. The investment in fixed assets is classified by the following types of ownership: state-owned economy, collective-owned economy, joint-owned economy, share-holding economy, private economy, economy funded by the enterprises from Hong Kong, Macao and Taiwan, foreign funded economy, individual investment and the economy of other types of ownership.

The content of non-state-owned investment has been adjusted since 2012, and non-state-owned investment refers to the industrial and commercial registration type: collective, cooperative, private, private partnership, private limited liability company, the self-employed, private partnership of pure folk subject of investment in fixed assets and mixed by the collective, private, individual holdings investment main body unit of economic composition the total investment in fixed assets.

4-1 固定资产投资主要经济指标

Main Indicators of Total Investment in Fixed Assets

单位：万元 (10000 yuan)

项 目	Item	2019	2019年比2018年增长(%) Growth Rate in 2019 over 2018 (%)
固定资产投资额	**Total Investment in Fixed Assets**	**69202087**	**16.5**
按投资类别分	Grouped by Type of Investment		
#房地产开发	Real Estate Development	31022573	14.8
按登记注册类型分	Grouped by Registration Status		
内资企业	Domestic Funded Enterprises	60089185	24.9
国有企业	State-owned Enterprises	13232574	13.6
集体企业	Collective-owned Enterprises	486241	29.6
股份合作企业	Cooperative Enterprises	8043	-91.2
联营企业	Joint Ownership Enterprises	2598	1667.3
国有联营企业	State Joint Ownership Enterprises		
集体联营企业	Collective Joint Ownership Enterprises		
国有与集体联营企业	Joint State-collective Enterprises	1500	
其他联营企业	Other Joint Ownership Enterprises	1098	646.9
有限责任公司	Limited Liability Corporations	31786969	32.7
国有独资公司	State Sole Funded Corporations	7787751	105.5
其他有限责任公司	Other Limited Liability Corporations	23999218	19.0
股份有限公司	Share-holding Corporations Ltd.	3975912	1.2
私营企业	Private Enterprises	10162745	29.9
其他企业	Other Enterprises	434103	56.9
港、澳、台商投资企业	Enterprises with Funds from Hong Kong, Macao and Taiwan	3124994	3.2
#与港、澳、台商合资经营企业	Joint-venture Enterprises	954469	26.7
与港、澳、台商合作经营企业	Cooperative Enterprises	581995	44.9
港、澳、台商独资经营企业	Enterprises with Sole Funds	1583851	-13.8
港、澳、台商投资股份有限公司	Share-holding Corporations Ltd.	3632	-82.3

注：1．机关、事业、社会团体及其他依法成立的单位固定资产投资登记注册类型参照企业登记注册类型划分。
2．从2011年起，固定资产投资项目统计起报点由计划总投资50万元及以上提高到500万元及以上，增速按可比口径计算。
3．从2012年起，"国家预算内资金"改称为"国家预算资金"，"国家预算资金"和"自筹资金"有所调整。故与上年不可比(下同)。
4．2017年固定资产投资增速按可比口径计算。(下同)

Note: I. The registration status of agencies, institutions, social organizations and other units established according to law is divided referring to the registration status of enterprises.
II. Since 2011, the cut-off point of investment in fixed assets is changed from a minimum of 50000 yuan to a minimum of 5000000 yuan. The growth rates in this table are calculated at comparable prices.
III. Since 2012, the coverage of state budget and self-raising funds have been changed. So the data in 2012 is not comparable with the pervious year(the same as below).
IV. Fixed asset investment growth rate in 2017 is calculated by comparable caliber. (the same as below)

4-1 续表 continued

单位：万元 (10000 yuan)

项 目	Item	2019	2019年比2018年增长(%) Growth Rate in 2019 over 2018 (%)
外商投资企业	Foreign Funded Enterprises	5982327	-27.5
# 中外合资经营企业	Joint-venture Enterprises	4702695	62.3
中外合作经营企业	Cooperative Enterprises	116327	16.0
外资企业	Enterprises with Sole Foreign Funds	1092886	-63.5
外商投资股份有限公司	Share-holding Corporations Ltd.	7645	-99.7
个体经营	Self-employed Individual	5581	264.8
按构成分	Grouped by Use of Funds		
建安工程	Construction and installation project	32024085	17.5
设备工器具购置	Purchases of Equipment and Instruments	9049938	-0.4
其他费用	Others	28128064	22.1
房屋建筑面积 （平方米）	**Floor Space of Buildings (sq.m)**		
施工面积	Floor Space under Construction	165942363	11.8
# 住 宅	Residential Buildings	73812646	3.0
竣工面积	Floor Space Completed	30898209	93.0
# 住 宅	Residential Buildings	16494655	89.2
本年新增固定资产	New fixed assets in this year	27570478	80.8
本年实际到位资金合计	**Total Actually Funds Provided This Year**		
上年末结余资金	Surplus Fund from Year-end of Preceding Year	33102916	26.1
本年实际到位资金小计	Subtotal Actually Funds Provided This Year	83544709	24.2
# 国家预算资金	State Budget	6731947	-3.3
国内贷款	Domestic Loans	19988058	31.6
债 券	Bonds	149952	41.9
利用外资	Foreign Investment	177136	-30.2
自筹资金	Self-raising Funds	29685110	26.4
其他资金	Others	5810835	46.2

注：本年新增固定资产、本年实际到位资金合计统计口径为5000万元及以上固定资产投资项目和房地产开发项目。

Note: The statistical caliber of newly added fixed assets and actually funds provided in this year is 50 million yuan and above in fixed assets investmei projects and real estate development projects.

4-2 主要年份按经济类型分固定资产投资额

Total Investment in Fixed Assets in Main Years by Type of Ownership

单位：万元 (10000 yuan)

年份 Year	合计 Total	国有经济 State-owned Units	集体经济 Collective-owned Units	联营经济 Joint Ownership Economic Units	股份经济 Share Holding Economic Units	私营经济 Private Economic Units	外商及港澳台经济 Economic Units with Funds from Foreign Regions,Hong Kong, Macao and Taiwan Investors	其他经济 Others	个体经济 Individual Investment
1978	72641	68584	1755						2302
1980	99565	89823	2934						6808
1985	436197	346000	44788						45409
1986	524813	434240	42264						48309
1987	584140	468967	64131						51042
1988	902161	703117	105514						93530
1989	933326	780946	84009						68371
1990	905937	761738	73172						71027
1991	1037424	850310	99147						87967
1992	1881379	1520508	230316						130555
1993	3733976	1885582	676520	15912	72334		842469	5870	235289
1994	5257053	2701653	835384	20679	132421		1234395		332521
1995	6182515	3324871	724898	62755	280004	2157	1464489		323341
1996	6389360	3172138	662454	69611	213638	5617	1947862		318040
1997	6565767	3543369	556536	30949	369066	66960	1720070		278817
1998	7588283	3803451	685243	35596	444474	123884	2210943		284692
1999	8782586	4514598	784507	23172	764251	286732	2129471	2959	276896
2000	9236676	4830889	619778	2579	1326102	534456	1514900	45197	362775
2001	9782093	4475639	368690	5930	1330108	1007708	2311811	10684	271523
2002	10092421	3529709	492329	6974	1986469	1304823	2502251	27560	242306
2003	11751668	4469885	452236	21451	2353980	1391787	2814567	24940	222822
2004	13489283	5371055	308617	37673	2298098	2135297	3183159	19930	135454
2005	15191582	5612243	295243	46941	3326313	1872079	3881748	26366	130649
2006	16963824	6070411	309514	17087	3876752	1904587	4646403	63002	76068
2007	18633437	6802190	440692	41760	4168899	2385743	4655795	20552	117806
2008	21055373	7972112	566318	56254	3881865	3260658	5225525	11599	81042
2009	26598516	12724805	698449	80059	4517995	3444249	5018306	9301	105352
2010	32635731	15528450	711201	54940	6832917	3253895	6055481	4042	194805
2011	34122005	12858860	807709	29504	9432487	4461680	6475334	18585	37846
2012	37583868	12330573	1941043	1836	10077974	4749672	8272350	156227	54193
2013	44545508	11979522	3333867	80244	13579487	6547526	8862572	9755	152535
2014	48895026	13918358	3453080	16779	15251803	7345376	8854921	53056	1653
2015	54059522	13013007	2793087	33652	19220207	9502398	9419157	62785	15229
2016	57035860	13109710	1433043		22249191	8457260	11141497	642515	2644
2017	59198316	13559790	831905	636	25209923	8625918	10154609	812757	2778
2018	59384003	15439768	466026	147	24091060	7823441	11285343	276688	1530
2019	69202087	21020325	494284	2598	27975130	10162745	9107321	434103	5581

4-3 主要年份按经济类型分固定资产投资额指数（上年=100）

Indices of Total Investment in Fixed Assets in Main Years by Type of Ownership (preceding year =100)

年 份 Year	合 计 Total	国有经济 State-owned Units	集体经济 Collective-owned Units	联营经济 Joint Ownership Economic Units	股份经济 Share Holding Economic Units	私营经济 Private Economic Units	外商及港澳台经济 Economic Units with Funds from Foreign Regions,Hong Kong, Macao and Taiwan Investors	其他经济 Others	个体经济 Individual Investment
1978	99.2	95.9	103.1						
1980	134.0	130.4	182.4						179.5
1985	145.8	141.0	231.5						131.4
1986	120.3	125.5	94.4						106.4
1987	111.3	108.0	151.7						105.7
1988	154.4	149.9	164.5						183.2
1989	103.5	111.1	79.6						73.1
1990	97.1	97.5	87.1						103.9
1991	114.5	111.6	135.5						123.9
1992	181.4	178.8	232.3						148.4
1993	198.5	124.0	203.4						180.2
1994	140.8	143.3	140.2	130.0	183.1		146.5		141.3
1995	117.6	123.1	78.1	303.5	211.5		118.6		97.2
1996	103.4	95.4	88.2	110.9	76.3	260.4	133.0		98.4
1997	102.8	111.7	84.0	44.5	172.8	1192.1	88.3		87.7
1998	115.6	107.3	123.1	115.0	120.4	185.0	128.5		102.1
1999	115.7	118.7	114.5	65.1	172.0	231.5	96.3		97.3
2000	105.2	107.0	79.0	11.1	173.5	186.4	71.1	1527.4	131.0
2001	105.9	92.7	59.5	229.9	100.3	188.6	152.6	23.6	74.9
2002	103.2	78.9	133.5	117.6	149.4	129.5	108.2	258.0	89.2
2003	116.4	126.6	91.9	307.6	118.5	106.7	112.5	90.5	92.0
2004	114.8	120.2	68.2	175.6	97.6	153.4	113.1	79.9	60.8
2005	112.6	104.5	95.7	124.6	144.7	87.7	122.0	132.3	96.5
2006	111.7	108.2	104.8	36.4	116.6	101.7	119.7	239.0	58.2
2007	109.8	112.1	142.4	244.4	107.5	125.3	100.2	32.6	154.9
2008	113.0	117.2	128.5	134.7	93.1	136.7	112.2	56.4	68.8
2009	122.3	150.4	123.3	142.3	113.6	105.6	96.0	80.2	130.0
2010	122.7	122.0	101.8	68.6	151.2	94.5	120.7	43.5	184.9
2011	110.0	89.4	161.1	53.7	138.5	139.1	107.6	690.6	84.3
2012	110.2	95.9	240.3	6.2	106.8	106.5	127.8	840.6	143.2
2013	118.5	97.2	171.8	4370.6	134.7	137.9	107.1	6.2	281.5
2014	114.5	123.7	109.9	22.3	115.7	117.5	102.2	579.3	1.2
2015	110.6	93.5	80.9	200.6	126.0	129.4	106.4	118.3	921.3
2016	108.0	100.7	51.3		115.8	89.0	118.3	1023.4	17.4
2017	105.7	103.4	58.1		113.3	102.0	91.1	126.5	105.1
2018	108.2	129.5	58.7	23.1	98.2	93.5	133.7	34.1	55.1
2019	116.5	136.1	106.1	1767.3	116.1	129.9	80.7	156.9	364.8

4-4 主要年份按投资类别分固定资产投资额

Total Investment in Fixed Assets in Main Years by Type of Investment

单位：万元 (10000 yuan)

年 份 Year	合 计 Total	建设改造投资 Construction and Innovation	房地产开发 Real Estate Development
1978	72641	72641	
1980	99565	99565	
1985	436197	389725	46472
1986	524813	472248	52565
1987	584140	514109	70031
1988	902161	762070	140091
1989	933326	780967	152359
1990	905937	788518	117419
1991	1037424	881075	156349
1992	1881379	1483959	397420
1993	3733976	2481589	1252387
1994	5257053	3362533	1894520
1995	6182515	4091379	2091136
1996	6389360	4097720	2291640
1997	6565767	4191544	2374223
1998	7588283	4894594	2693689
1999	8782586	5823559	2959027
2000	9236676	5680860	3555816
2001	9782093	5911886	3870207
2002	10092421	5828523	4263898
2003	11751668	7556862	4194806
2004	13489283	8718968	4770315
2005	15191582	10110736	5080846
2006	16963824	11395931	5567893
2007	18633437	11595406	7038031
2008	21055373	13421349	7634024
2009	26598516	18425067	8173449
2010	32635731	22799149	9836582
2011	34122005	21068400	13053605
2012	37583868	23879357	13704511
2013	44545508	28821219	15724289
2014	48895026	30733497	18161529
2015	54059522	32683631	21375891
2016	57035860	31627311	25408549
2017	59198316	32169381	27028935
2018	59384003	32364680	27019323
2019	69202087	38179514	31022573

4-5 主要年份按投资类别分固定资产投资额指数(上年=100)

Indices of Total Investment in Fixed Assets in Main Years by Type of Investment (preceding year =100)

年 份 Year	合 计 Total	建设改造投资 Construction and Innovation	房地产开发 Real Estate Development
1978	99.2	99.2	
1980	134.0	134.0	
1985	145.8	152.0	108.3
1986	120.3	121.2	113.1
1987	111.3	108.9	133.2
1988	154.4	148.2	200.0
1989	103.5	102.5	108.8
1990	97.1	101.0	77.1
1991	114.5	111.7	133.2
1992	181.4	168.4	254.2
1993	198.5	167.2	315.1
1994	140.8	135.5	151.3
1995	117.6	121.7	110.4
1996	103.4	100.2	109.6
1997	102.8	102.3	103.6
1998	115.6	116.8	113.5
1999	115.7	119.0	109.9
2000	105.2	97.5	120.2
2001	105.9	104.1	108.8
2002	103.2	98.6	110.2
2003	116.4	129.7	98.4
2004	114.8	115.4	113.7
2005	112.6	116.0	106.5
2006	111.7	112.7	109.6
2007	109.8	101.8	126.4
2008	113.0	115.7	108.5
2009	122.3	137.3	107.1
2010	122.7	123.7	120.4
2011	110.0	99.4	132.7
2012	110.2	113.3	105.0
2013	118.5	120.7	114.7
2014	114.5	113.9	115.5
2015	110.6	106.3	117.7
2016	108.0	96.8	118.9
2017	105.7	105.1	106.4
2018	108.2	116.2	持平
2019	116.5	118.0	114.8

4-6 各时期按投资类别分固定资产投资额

Total Investment in Fixed Assets in Different Periods by Type of Investment

单位：万元 (10000 yuan)

时 期	Period	合 计 Total	建设改造投资 Construction and Innovation	房地产开发 Real Estate Development
“六五”时期	6th Five-year Plan Period	1310742	1221368	89374
“七五”时期	7th Five-year Plan Period	3850377	3317912	532465
“八五”时期	8th Five-year Plan Period	18092347	12300535	5791812
“九五”时期	9th Five-year Plan Period	38562672	24688277	13874395
“十五”时期	10th Five-year Plan Period	60307047	38126975	22180072
“十一五”时期	11th Five-year Plan Period	115886881	77636902	38249979
“十二五”时期	12th Five-year Plan Period	219205929	137186104	82019825
1950-2019	1950-2019	702912129	429694827	273217302
1979-2019	1979-2019	702210114	428992812	273217302
1991-2019	1991-2019	696875142	424279679	272595463
2001-2019	2001-2019	640220123	387290867	252929256

4-7 各时期按投资类别分固定资产投资额平均每年增长速度

Average Growth Rate of Investment in Fixed Assets in Different Periods by Type of Investment

单位：% (%)

时 期	Period	合 计 Total	建设改造投资 Construction and Innovation	房地产开发 Real Estate Development
"六五"时期	6th Five-year Plan Period	34.2	31.6	
"七五"时期	7th Five-year Plan Period	19.6	18.3	29.1
"八五"时期	8th Five-year Plan Period	50.4	40.7	89.2
"九五"时期	9th Five-year Plan Period	7.5	6.3	9.6
"十五"时期	10th Five-year Plan Period	9.0	10.0	7.5
"十一五"时期	11th Five-year Plan Period	14.4	14.7	14.0
"十二五"时期	12th Five-year Plan Period	12.7	10.5	16.8
1951-2019	1951-2019	17.4	16.7	
1979-2019	1979-2019	18.7	17.4	
1991-2019	1991-2019	16.8	15.6	21.2
2001-2019	2001-2019	12.2	12.4	12.1

4-8 主要年份按三次产业分固定资产投资额
Total Investment in Fixed Assets and its Composition in Main Years by the Three Strata of Industries

年 份 Year	合 计 (万元) Total (10000 yuan)	第一产业 Primary Industry	第二产业 Secondary Industry	第三产业 Tertiary Industry	比 重 (%) Composition (%)	第一产业 Primary Industry	第二产业 Secondary Industry	第三产业 Tertiary Industry
1978	72641	4317	32100	36224	100.00	5.94	44.19	49.87
1980	99565	4953	39722	54890	100.00	4.97	39.90	55.13
1985	436197	13672	143702	278823	100.00	3.13	32.94	63.93
1990	905937	14268	346872	544797	100.00	1.57	38.29	60.14
1995	6182515	42433	1698901	4441181	100.00	0.69	27.48	71.83
2000	9236676	66584	1411261	7758831	100.00	0.72	15.28	84.00
2001	9782093	17789	1419209	8345095	100.00	0.18	14.51	85.31
2002	10092421	24625	1913745	8154051	100.00	0.24	18.96	80.80
2003	11751668	14657	2265387	9471624	100.00	0.12	19.28	80.60
2004	13489283	30084	2863780	10595419	100.00	0.22	21.23	78.55
2005	15191582	9816	4379347	10802419	100.00	0.06	28.83	71.11
2006	16963824	17999	4632303	12313522	100.00	0.11	27.30	72.59
2007	18633437	11541	4015821	14606075	100.00	0.06	21.55	78.39
2008	21055373	16269	4510845	16528259	100.00	0.08	21.42	78.50
2009	26598516	34894	5454577	21109045	100.00	0.13	20.51	79.36
2010	32635731	34280	6262773	26338678	100.00	0.10	19.19	80.71
2011	34122005	39223	5529978	28552804	100.00	0.11	16.21	83.68
2012	37583868	71881	5998727	31513260	100.00	0.19	15.96	83.85
2013	44545508	107320	7169083	37269105	100.00	0.24	16.09	83.67
2014	48895026	151898	7174196	41568932	100.00	0.31	14.67	85.02
2015	54059522	337727	7795480	45926315	100.00	0.62	14.42	84.96
2016	57035860	211577	7320025	49504258	100.00	0.37	12.83	86.80
2017	59198316	105089	7515079	51578148	100.00	0.18	12.69	87.13
2018	59384003	7998	9615139	49760866	100.00	0.01	16.19	83.80
2019	69202087	31996	10450955	58719136	100.00	0.05	15.10	84.85

4-9 主要年份按构成分固定资产投资额

Total Investment in Fixed Assets in Main Years (by Use of Funds)

单位：万元 (10000 yuan)

年份 Year	合计 Total	建安工程 Construction and installation project	建筑工程 Construction Project	安装工程 Installation Project	设备工器具购置 Purchases of Equipment and Instruments	其他费用 Others
1995	6182515	3380428	3066640	313788	1474613	1327474
1996	6389360	3645509	3225327	420182	1501358	1242493
1997	6565767	3761130	3230953	530177	1475112	1329525
1998	7588283	4238753	3805530	433223	1465162	1884368
1999	8782586	4983134	4443801	539333	1520186	2279266
2000	9236676	5351968	4862795	489173	1284866	2599842
2001	9782093	5744072	4943427	800645	1792544	2245477
2002	10092421	6045582	5043136	1002446	1735461	2311378
2003	11751668	6596074	5926676	669398	1907214	3248380
2004	13489283	7996258	7167180	829078	2328974	3164051
2005	15191582	9087325	7899596	1187729	2749875	3354382
2006	16963824	9724062	8375238	1348824	3657839	3581923
2007	18633437	10891409	9571281	1320128	3299746	4442282
2008	21055373	12807649	11296603	1511046	3227977	5019747
2009	26598516	16750826	15003807	1747019	3798896	6048794
2010	32635731	21513034	18964747	2548287	4866404	6256293
2011	34122005	20887886	18138348	2749538	6193268	7040851
2012	37583868	24731081	21468095	3262986	6003316	6849471
2013	44545508	29692453	25879973	3812480	6995873	7857182
2014	48895026	31495401	27760295	3735106	7380551	10019074
2015	54059522	34965551	30635972	4329579	8300480	10793491
2016	57035860	32761129	28524666	4236463	9297170	14977561
2017	59198316	31970283	28275166	3695117	8947522	18280511
2018	59384003	27259894			9088439	23035670
2019	69202087	32024085			9049938	28128064

注：2018年起，500—5000万固定资产投资项目情况表取消建筑工程和安装工程分组，合并为建安工程。

Note: Since 2018, 5-50 million fixed assets investment project table canceled the construction and installation project group, merged into constructior and installation project.

4-10 主要年份房屋建设情况

Total Investment in Fixed Assets and Building Construction in Main Years

年份、时期 Year and Period	房屋施工面积 (万平方米) Floor Space under Construction (10000 sq.m)	#住宅 Residential Buildings	房屋竣工面积 (万平方米) Floor Space Completed (10000 sq.m)	#住宅 Residential Buildings
1978	429.55	173.09	184.97	84.82
1980	610.94	334.12	269.07	163.33
1985	1448.87	820.45	796.96	531.33
1990	1681.89	970.81	879.68	537.36
1995	4958.58	2840.92	1847.86	1212.84
2000	6152.47	3789.88	2404.81	1539.43
2001	6612.84	3916.82	2138.40	1304.28
2002	6376.80	3809.32	2129.56	1392.66
2003	6540.20	3643.26	2243.10	1317.25
2004	7263.32	3817.60	2308.23	1045.58
2005	7165.93	3836.53	2405.30	1091.48
2006	6895.68	3751.36	1677.24	918.05
2007	8113.99	4049.79	2243.77	1001.43
2008	8272.29	3986.32	1849.70	865.15
2009	8690.90	3740.54	2208.57	965.85
2010	10114.91	4279.53	2388.95	950.10
2011	11555.51	5083.07	2804.28	938.38
2012	12381.69	5152.06	2957.66	940.44
2013	13959.31	5753.99	3683.50	897.97
2014	13995.56	6410.68	3699.66	1266.35
2015	13129.83	6461.25	2712.01	1031.79
2016	11563.90	6228.81	1642.25	832.98
2017	12044.84	6427.97	1496.38	832.80
2018	14841.71	7166.30	1601.19	871.70
2019	16594.23	7381.27	3089.81	1649.46
"六五"时期 6th Five-year Plan Period			3328.10	2352.34
"七五"时期 7th Five-year Plan Period			4454.23	2772.75
"八五"时期 8th Five-year Plan Period			7045.41	4339.71
"九五"时期 9th Five-year Plan Period			10112.06	6673.86
"十五"时期 10th Five-year Plan Period			11224.59	6151.25
"十一五"时期 11th Five-year Plan Period			10368.23	4700.58
"十二五"时期 12th Five-year Plan Period			15857.11	5074.93
1950-2019			72768.52	37261.35
1979-2019			70681.22	36514.42
1991-2019			62437.03	31127.27
2001-2019			45279.56	20113.70

4-11 固定资产投资额(2019年)

单位：万元

项 目	Item
总 计	**total**
按登记注册类型分	**Grouped by Registration Status**
内资企业	Domestic Funded Enterprises
国有企业	State-owned Enterprises
集体企业	Collective-owned Enterprises
股份合作企业	Cooperative Enterprises
联营企业	Joint Ownership Enterprises
国有联营企业	State Joint Ownership Enterprises
集体联营企业	Collective Joint Ownership Enterprises
国有与集体联营企业	Joint State-collective Enterprises
其他联营企业	Other Joint Ownership Enterprises
有限责任公司	Limited Liability Corporations
国有独资公司	State Sole Funded Corporations
其他有限责任公司	Other Limited Liability Corporations
股份有限公司	Share-holding Corporations Ltd.
私营企业	Private Enterprises
其他企业	Other Enterprises
港、澳、台商投资企业	Enterprises with Funds from Hong Kong, Macao and Taiwan
# 与港、澳、台商合资经营企业	Joint-venture Enterprises
与港、澳、台商合作经营企业	Cooperative Enterprises
港、澳、台商独资经营企业	Enterprises with Sole Funds
港、澳、台商投资股份有限公司	Share-holding Corporations Ltd.
外商投资企业	Foreign Funded Enterprises
# 中外合资经营企业	Joint-venture Enterprises
中外合作经营企业	Cooperative Enterprises
外资企业	Enterprises with Sole Foreign Funds
外商投资股份有限公司	Share-holding Corporations Ltd.
个体经营	Self-employed Individual
按隶属关系分	**According to affiliation**
中央	Center
地方	Local
其他	Other

Total Investment in Fixed Assets (2019)

(10000 yuan)

合 计 Total	#建设改造 Construction and Transformation
69202087	**38179514**
60089185	32232302
13232574	12228996
486241	473451
8043	8043
2598	2598
1500	
1098	
31786969	12633645
7787751	6111921
23999218	6521724
3975912	3834326
10162745	2728263
434103	322980
3124994	1562047
954469	512453
581995	183986
1583851	860929
3632	
5982327	4379584
4702695	3432134
116327	59177
1092886	855558
7645	
5581	5581
8009692	6550045
21713422	17570245
39478973	14059224

4-11 续表 1

单位：万元

项　　目	Item
按建设性质分	**Grouped by Type of Construction**
#新　建	New Construction
扩　建	Expansion
改建和技术改造	Renovation and Technical Transformation
单纯购置	Simple Purchase
按构成分	**Grouped by Composition**
建安工程	Construction and Installation Project
设备工器具购置	Equipment and Appliance Purchase
其他费用	Other Expenses
按行业分	**Grouped by Sector**
农、林、牧、渔业	Agriculture, Forestry, Animal Husbandry and Fishery Industry
采矿业	Mining
制造业	Manufacturing
电力、热力、燃气及水生产和供应业	Production and Supply of Electricity, Heat,Gas and Water
建筑业	Construction
批发和零售业	Wholesale and Retail Trade
交通运输、仓储和邮政业	Transport, Storage and Post
住宿和餐饮业	Hotels and Catering Services
信息传输、软件和信息技术服务业	Information Transmission, Software and Information Technology
金融业	Financial Intermediation
房地产业	Real Estate
租赁和商务服务业	Leasing and Business Services
科学研究和技术服务业	Scientific Research and Technical Services
水利、环境和公共设施管理业	Management of Water Conservancy, Environment and Public Facilities
居民服务、修理和其他服务业	Service to Households, Repair and Other Services
教　育	Education
卫生和社会工作	Health and Social Service
文化、体育和娱乐业	Culture, Sports and Entertainment
公共管理、社会保障和社会组织	Public Management, Social Security and Social Organizations
国际组织	Internationale Organizations

continued

(10000 yuan)

合 计 Total	#建设改造 Construction and Transformation
58330033	27307460
2313783	2313783
5045673	5045673
3401653	3401653
32024085	21170476
9049938	8917737
28128064	8091301
45478	45478
7443263	7443263
2936260	2936260
93451	93451
332289	332289
11190873	11190873
326576	326576
1686117	1686117
115258	115258
33014287	1991714
1121666	1121666
404060	404060
7171219	7171219
24813	24813
1735850	1735850
998972	998972
291432	291432
270223	270223

4-12 各区固定资产投资主要指标

（2019年，按项目所在地分）

项　　目	Item	全　市 Total	荔湾区 Liwan	越秀区 Yuexiu
固定资产投资额（万元）	Total Investment in Fixed Assets (10000 yuan)	69202087	3308390	886181
按登记注册类型分	**Grouped by Registration Status**			
# 国有经济投资	State-owned Investment	21020325	631922	435247
民间投资	Investment by Non-state-owned Units	28055607	1536694	85117
港澳台商经济投资	Investment from Hong Kong, Macao and Taiwan	3124994	104662	234845
外商经济投资	Foreign Investment	5982327	40670	
按构成分	**Grouped by Use of Funds**			
# 建筑安装工程合计	Construction and Installation Project	32024085	1615720	382925
新增固定资产（万元）	Newly Increased Fixed Assets (10000 yuan)	27570478	1865982	896209
房屋施工面积（平方米）	Floor Space under Construction (sq.m)	165942363	10718920	2039985
房屋竣工面积（平方米）	Floor Space Completed (sq.m)	30898209	2211487	997599

注：国有经济投资包括国有企业、国有联营企业、国有独资公司的投资额。民间投资是指工商登记注册类型为：集体、股份合作、私营独资、私营合伙、私营有限责任公司、个体户、个人合伙等纯民间主体的固定资产投资及混合经济成分中由集体、私营、个体控股的投资主体单位的全部固定资产投资(下同)。

Main Indicators of Investment in Fixed Assets

(2019, by Tegion of Item)

海珠区 Haizhu	天河区 Tianhe	白云区 Baiyun	黄埔区 Huangpu	番禺区 Panyu	花都区 Huadu	南沙区 Nansha	从化区 Conghua	增城区 Zengcheng
3465576	5010135	8655863	13987178	7586224	4563192	7545803	2056823	12136722
1293843	1458387	3699347	4434832	2020316	836387	3812038	412027	1985979
1747087	1553213	1934434	5710500	3573068	2743630	2423201	886240	5862423
127576	433120	151458	572534	370053	191973	446656	163224	328893
81817	38958	24178	2075646	357288	174437	695522	20403	2473408
1419806	2338603	3649264	7103631	3786937	2317241	3959022	1093336	4357600
1844914	4891132	3688460	3236571	3465257	1929354	2776750	797094	2178755
10627012	12116852	8604448	25514165	22914404	20070752	20444394	8123397	24768034
2407685	3996095	1182842	2338790	4896325	4548457	3819477	1631537	2867915

Note: The state-owned investment refers to the investment from state-ownered enterprises, state joint ownership enterprises and sole state-funded corporations. The investment by non-state-owned units refers to the total investment excluding the investment from state-owned enterprises, state joint ownership enterprises, sole state-funded corporations, enterprises with funds from foreign regions,Hong Kong, Macao and Taiwan. The investment by private enterprises refers to private holding investment and individual investment of the investment from collective-owned enterprises, other cooperative enterprises, other limited liability corporations,private enterprises, other domestic funded enterprises and share holding corporations. The same as in the following tables.

4-13 民间固定资产投资情况(2019年)

Investment in Fixed Assets by Private Units (2019)

单位：万元　　(10000 yuan)

指标名称	Item	2019年	2019年比2018年增长(%) Growth Rate in 2019 over 2018 (%)
合计	**Total**	**28055607**	**27.8**
按投资类别分	**Grouped by Type of Investment**		
建设改造	Construction and Transformation	6279175	18.2
房地产开发	Real Estate Development	21776432	30.9
按主要领域分	**Grouped by Main Sector**		
其中：基础设施	Infrastructure investment	571621	-3.5
工业投资	Industrial investment	2281178	45.0
其中：工业技术改造	Industry technical renovation	672929	-3.5
按构成分	**Grouped by Use of Funds**		
建安工程	Construction and Installation Project	10321836	-3.8
设备工器具购置	Purchases of Equipment and Instruments	1192971	13.7
其他费用	Others	16540800	62.7
按三次产业分	**Grouped By Industry**		
第一产业	Primary Industry	22939	612.4
第二产业	Secondary Industry	2281646	45.1
第三产业	Tertiary Industry	25751022	26.4
按国民经济行业分	**Grouped by Sector**		
农、林、牧、渔业	Agriculture, Forestry, Animal Husbandry and Fishery Industry	22939	612.4
采矿业	Mining		
制造业	Manufacturing	2092517	35.7
电力、热力、燃气及水生产和供应业	Production and Supply of Electricity, Heat,Gas and Water	188661	503.9
建筑业	Construction	3475	
批发和零售业	Wholesale and Retail Trade	291451	-23.0
交通运输、仓储和邮政业	Transport, Storage and Post	637427	33.3
住宿餐饮业	Hotels and Catering Services	302088	131.9
信息传输、软件和信息技术服务业	Information Transmission, Software and Information Technology	345920	-39.5
金融业	Financial Intermediation	58305	45.5
房地产业	Real Estate	22506865	29.6
租赁和商务服务业	Leasing and Business Services	775600	28.6
科学研究和技术服务业	Scientific Research and Technical Services	82997	-50.5
水利、环境和公共设施管理业	Management of Water Conservancy, Environment and Public Facilities	105572	-47.5
居民服务、修理和其他服务业	Service to Households, Repair and Other Services	11335	1913.3
教育	Education	220140	152.9
卫生和社会工作	Health and Social Service	257876	61.7
文化、体育和娱乐业	Culture, Sports and Entertainment	145320	-20.1
公共管理、社会保障和社会组织	Public Management, Social Security and Social Organizations	7119	691.0
国际组织	International Organizations		

4-14 工业及工业技术改造固定资产投资情况(2019年)

Investment in Fixed Assets in Industrial and Technological Renovation(2019)

单位：万元 (10000 yuan)

项目	Item	工业投资 Industrial Investment	#工业技术改造 Industrial Technological Transformation
合计	**Total**	**10379523**	**3676924**
其中：汽车制造业	Automobile Manufacturing	1781646	1226708
其中：汽车零配件	Auto Parts Manufacturing	895680	355237
电子产品制造业	Electronic Appliance Manufacturing	3387035	407694
石油化工制造业	Petrochemical Manufacturing	271507	161337
其中：高技术制造业	High-tech Manufacturing Industry	3825899	529913
医药制造业	Pharmaceutical Manufacturing Industry	439698	113906
航空航天及设备制造业	Aerospace and Equipment Manufacturing Industry	33820	15407
电子及通信设备制造	Manufacturing Industry of Electronic and Communication Equipment	3070688	346679
计算机及办公设备制造业	Computer and Office Equipment Manufacturing Industry	49380	12878
医疗设备及仪器仪表制造业	Manufacturing Industry of Medical Equipment and Instruments	79613	41043
信息化学品制造	Information Chemicals Manufacturing Industry	152700	
按工业行业分	**By industry**		
农副食品加工业	Processing of Food from Agricultural Products	56051	52826
食品制造业	Manufacture of Foods	91984	31579
酒、饮料和精制茶制造业	Manufacture of Wine, Beverages and Refined Tea	43199	12910
烟草制品业	Manufacture of Tobacco	1632	1632
纺织业	Manufacture of Textile	13409	10073
纺织服装、服饰业	Manufacture of Textile Wearing Apparel, Clothing	53487	9277
皮革、毛皮、羽毛及其制品和制鞋业	Manufacture of Leather, Fur, Feather and Related Products, Footwear	47578	15210
木材加工和木、竹、藤、棕、草制品业	Processing of Timber, Manufacture of Wood, Bamboo, Rattan, Palm and Straw Products	2086	1348
家具制造业	Manufacture of Furniture	54586	18304
造纸和纸制品业	Manufacture of Paper and Paper Products	97793	59165
印刷和记录媒介复制业	Printing, Reproduction of Recording Media	94376	25852
文教、工美、体育和娱乐用品制造业	Manufacture of Culture and Education, Arts and Crafts, Sports and Entertainment Supplies	31871	20026
石油煤炭及其他燃料加工业	Processing of Petroleum, Coking, Processing of Nuclear Fuel	82296	82296
化学原料和化学制品制造业	Manufacture of Raw Chemical Materials and Chemical Products	341911	79041
医药制造业	Manufacture of Medicines	439698	113906
化学纤维制造业	Manufacture of Chemical Fibers		
橡胶和塑料制品业	Manufacture of Rubber	124083	72646
非金属矿物制品业	Manufacture of Non-metallic Mineral Products	184205	23914
黑色金属冶炼和压延加工业	Smelting and Pressing of Ferrous Metals	4958	4958
有色金属冶炼和压延加工业	Smelting and Pressing of Non-Ferrous Metals	64022	19733
金属制品业	Manufacture of Metal Products	48744	34733
通用设备制造业	Manufacture of General Purpose Machinery	206745	92888
专用设备制造业	Manufacture of Special Purpose Machinery	139412	69513
汽车制造业	Manufacture of Automobile	1781646	1226708
铁路、船舶、航空航天和其他运输设备制造业	Manufacture of Railway, Ship, Aerospace and Other Transportation Equipment	30218	7436
电气机械和器材制造业	Manufacture of Electrical Machinery and Equipment	275988	113438
计算机、通信和其他电子设备制造业	Manufacture of Computers, Communication Equipment and Other Electronic Equipment	3072303	343324
仪器仪表制造业	Manufacture of Instrments and Meters	32705	16812
其他制造业	Other Manufactures	1392	1392
废弃资源综合利用业	Comprehensive Utilization of Waste	2866	2376
金属制品、机械和设备修理业	Manufacture of Metal Products, Machinery and Equipment Maintenance	22019	19051
电力、热力生产和供应业	Production and Supply of Electric Power and Heat Power	1324446	236170
燃气生产和供应业	Production and Supply of Gas	52647	
水的生产和供应业	Production and Supply of Water	1559167	858387

4-15 住宅投资建设情况（2019年）
Housing Investment and Construction (2019)

项　　目	Item	固定资产投资额（万元）Investment in Fixed Assets (10000 yuan)	房屋施工面积（平方米）Floor Space under Construction (sq.m)	房屋竣工面积（平方米）Floor Space Completed (sq.m)
总　计	**Total**	**20998985**	**73812646**	**16494655**
按登记注册类型分	**Grouped by Registration Status**			
内资企业	Domestic Funded Enterprises	19302720	60805924	12643570
国有企业	State-owned Enterprises	751530	2406221	696070
集体企业	Collective-owned Enterprises	62789	165090	560
股份合作企业	Cooperative Enterprises			
联营企业	Joint Ownership Enterprises			
有限责任公司	Limited Liability Corporations	12787732	41245947	8393075
股份有限公司	Share-holding Corporations Ltd.	93859	671673	
私营企业	Private Enterprises	5523776	16112647	3520827
其他企业	Other Enterprises	83034	204346	33038
港、澳、台商投资企业	Enterprises with Funds from Hong Kong, Macao and Taiwan	772789	9070533	2999962
外商投资企业	Foreign Funded Enterprises	923476	3936189	851123
个体经营	Self-employed Individual			
按投资类别分	**By investment category**			
# 房地产开发	Real estate development	20870742	71611021	16457746

4-16 主要年份基础设施投资额

Total Investment of Infrastructure in Main Years

单位：万元 (10000 yuan)

年份 Year	基础设施投资额合计 Total Investment in Infrastructure	电力、热力、燃气及水生产和供应业 Production and Supply of Electricity, Heat, Gas and Water	交通运输、仓储和邮政业 Transport, Storage and Post	信息传输、软件和信息技术服务业 Information Transmission, Software and Information Technology	水利、环境和公共设施管理业 Management of Water Conservancy, Environment and Public Facilities
2006	5486487	1027261	2584536	323481	1551209
2007	5396237	823335	2395913	231485	1945504
2008	6058585	721278	2993037	310452	2033818
2009	10205364	1921535	3755212	1018626	3509991
2010	13322053	2300961	4498051	898385	5624656
2011	9977291	891065	4274037	1864116	2948073
2012	10650125	1241487	4568369	1229343	3610926
2013	11371899	1016015	5935429	1037231	3383224
2014	12466576	1227907	6707111	1251867	3279691
2015	13390770	1105701	6316844	1816401	4151824
2016	15164507	1603562	7922729	1110701	4527515
2017	16842963	1573871	8832349	1060190	5376553
2018	17619987	1665621	9140573	1002888	5810905
2019	21934686	2936260	10609024	1218183	7171219

注：基础设施投资是指为社会生产和生活提供基础性、大众性服务的工程和设施。因此表中的交通运输、仓储和邮政业不包括通用仓储、低温仓储、危险品仓储和谷物、棉花等农产品仓储业；信息传输、软件和信息技术服务业不包括软件和信息技术服务业。与其他表的国民经济行业分类略有不同。

Note: Infrastructure investment refers to projects and facilities that provide basic and popular services for social production and life.Therefore the transportation, storage and postal services in the tables do not include general storage, low temperature storage, dangerous goods storage and storage of agricultural products such as grain and cotton; information transmission,software and information technology services do not include software and information technology services. The industry classification of national economy is slightly different from other tables.

4-17 基础设施固定资产投资情况(2019年)
Infrastructure Fixed Assets Investment (2019)

单位：万元 (10000 yuan)

项 目	Item	2019年	2019年比2018年增长(%) Growth Rate in 2019 over 2018 (%)
合 计	**Total**	**21934686**	**24.5**
按行业分	**By Sector**		
电力、热力生产和供应业	Production and Supply of Electric Power and Heat Power	1324446	7.4
燃气生产和供应业	Production and Supply of Gas	52647	-3.2
水的生产和供应业	Production and Supply of Water	1559167	311.9
铁路运输业	Railway Transportation Industry	2584868	29.5
道路运输业	Road Transportation Industry	5342618	25.5
水上运输业	Water Transportation Industry	416078	21.6
航空运输业	Aviation Transportation Industry	2197198	-11.2
管道运输业	Pipeline Transportation Industry	540	-9.4
多式联运和运输代理业	Multimodal Transport and Transport Agent Industry	66997	-2.5
装卸搬运	Handling and handling		
邮政业	Post Industry	725	-64.6
电信、广播电视和卫星传输服务	Telecommunications, Radio and Television, Satellite Transmission Services	1146941	22.7
互联网和相关服务	Internet and Related Services	71242	4.5
水利管理业	Management of Water Conservancy	475684	41.0
生态保护和环境治理业	Ecology Protection and Environment Control	870612	104.5
公共设施管理业	Management of Public Facilities	5824923	15.4

4-18 新增固定资产（2019年）

Total Newly Increased Fixed Assets (2019, by Type of Investment)

单位：万元 (10000 yuan)

项　　目	Item	合　计 Total	#建设改造 Construction and Transformation
总　　计	**Total**	**27570478**	**10797980**
按登记注册类型分	**Grouped by Registration Status**		
内资企业	Domestic Funded Enterprises	21466847	9488417
国有企业	State-owned Enterprises	3051319	2723302
集体企业	Collective-owned Enterprises	90450	82161
股份合作企业	Cooperative Enterprises	7851	7851
联营企业	Joint Ownership Enterprises		
国有联营企业	State Joint Ownership Enterprises		
集体联营企业	Collective Joint Ownership Enterprises		
国有与集体联营企业	Joint State-collective Enterprises		
其他联营企业	Other Joint Ownership Enterprise		
有限责任公司	Limited Liability Corporations	11287366	2966633
国有独资公司	State Sole Funded Corporations	2559813	1202002
其他有限责任公司	Other Limited Liability Corporations	8727553	1764631
股份有限公司	Share Holding Corporations Ltd.	3375666	3375666
私营企业	Private Enterprises	3615194	293803
其他企业	Other Enterprises	39001	39001
港、澳、台商投资企业	Enterprises with Funds from Hong Kong, Macao and Taiwan	4127250	156736
#与港、澳、台商合资经营企业	Joint-venture Enterprises	1988243	52223
与港、澳、台商合作经营企业	Cooperative Enterprises	1043223	460
港、澳、台商独资经营企业	Enterprises with Sole Funds	1095784	104053
港、澳、台商投资股份有限公司	Share-holding Corporations Ltd.		
外商投资企业	Foreign Funded Enterprises	1976381	1152827
#中外合资经营企业	Joint-venture Enterprises	1235200	668739
中外合作经营企业	Cooperative Enterprises	108209	5519
外资企业	Enterprises with Sole Foreign Funds	526935	473389
外商投资股份有限公司	Share-holding Corporations Ltd.	5180	5180
个体经营	Self-employed Individual		
按隶属关系分	**Grouped by Jurisdiction of Management**		
中央	Central Investment	5325436	4135991
地方	Local Investment	7969391	4445842
其他	Others	14275651	2216147

4-18 续表 continued

单位：万元 (10000 yuan)

项目	Item	合计 Total	#建设改造 Construction and Transformation
按建设性质分	**Grouped by Type of Construction**		
# 新　建	New Construction	21992423	5219925
扩　建	Expansion	906279	906279
改建和技术改造	Reconstruction	1535832	1535832
单纯购置	Purchase	3124197	3124197
按行业分	**Grouped by Economic Sector**		
农、林、牧、渔业	Agriculture, Forestry, Animal Husbandry and Fishery	4914	4914
采矿业	Mining		
制造业	Manufacturing	1710731	1710731
电力、热力、燃气及水生产和供应业	Production and Supply of Electricity, Heat,Gas and Water	1585703	1585703
建筑业	Construction	113317	113317
批发和零售业	Wholesale and Retail Trade	56580	56580
交通运输、仓储和邮政业	Transport, Storage and Post	4015871	4015871
住宿和餐饮业	Hotels and Catering Services	73656	73656
信息传输、软件和信息技术服务业	Information Transmission, Software and Information Technology	861894	861894
金融业	Financial Intermediation	234901	234901
房地产业	Real Estate	16935886	163388
租赁和商务服务业	Leasing and Business Services	171783	171783
科学研究和技术服务业	Scientific Research and Technical Services	103944	103944
水利、环境和公共设施管理业	Management of Water Conservancy, Environment and Public Facilities	874509	874509
居民服务、修理和其他服务业	Service to Households, Repair and Other Services		
教　育	Education	295559	295559
卫生和社会工作	Health and Social Service	322545	322545
文化、体育和娱乐业	Culture, Sports and Entertainment	98919	98919
公共管理、社会保障和社会组织	Public Management, Social Security and Social Organizations	109766	109766
国际组织	International Organization		

4-19 固定资产投资资金来源（2019年）
The Funds Sources of Fixed Assets Investment (2019)

单位：万元 (10000 yuan)

项　　目	Item	合 计 Total	# 建设改造 Construction and Transformation
本年实际到位资金合计	Total Actually Funds Provided This Year	116647625	36785118
上年末结余资金	Surplus Fund from Year-end of Preceding Year	33102916	3276014
本年实际到位资金小计	Subtotal Actually Funds Provided This Year	83544709	33509104
# 国家预算资金	State Budget	6731947	6731947
国内贷款	Domestic Loans	19988058	9813449
债　　券	Bonds	149952	149952
利用外资	Foreign Investment	177136	177136
自筹资金	Self-raising Funds	29685110	12997979
其他资金	Others	5810835	3638641
本年各项应付款合计	Total Payment This Year	12964076	4168244
# 工程款	Payment Against Projects	3468604	730581

注：国家制度修订，统计口径为5000万元及以上固定资产投资项目和房地产开发项目。

Note: The statistical caliber adjusts 50 million yuan and above in fixed assets investment projects and real estate development projects according to the national statistical system.

4-20 房地产开发与经营(2019年，按法人单位办公所在地分)

项　　目	Item	全　市 Total	荔湾区 Liwan	越秀区 Yuexiu
企业个数 (个)	Number of Enterprises (unit)	1306	46	72
年末从业人数 (人)	Employed Persons at Year-end (person)	49160	1343	2065
本年完成投资 (万元)	Total Investment Completed This Year (10000 yuan)	31022573	1727132	401464
#住　宅	Residential Buildings	20870742	1254523	135846
办公楼	Office Buildings	3278582	35685	133300
商业营业用房	Houses for Business Use	2974561	318653	97017
房屋施工面积 (平方米)	Floor Space of Buildings under Construction (sq.m)	119859143	6232804	3303166
#住　宅	Residential Buildings	71611021	4118084	1836924
办公楼	Office Buildings	13508722	92509	332442
商业营业用房	Houses for Business Use	12747017	574065	354319
#新开工面积	Floor Space of Newly Started Buildings	22205110	1218950	1350391
#住　宅	Residential Buildings	14070224	850344	686697
办公楼	Office Buildings	2210777	22905	103307
商业营业用房	Houses for Business Use	1389355	115345	71871
房屋竣工面积 (平方米)	Floor Space of Buildings Completed (sq.m)	28991942	1354975	1018226
#住　宅	Residential Buildings	16457746	866760	730374
办公楼	Office Buildings	4040388	35571	61952
商业营业用房	Houses for Business Use	3414649	74653	72595
商品房销售面积 (平方米)	Floor Space of Buildings Actually Sold This Year (sq.m)	14646364	859311	65035
现房销售面积	Floor Space of Existing Buildings with Contracts Signed	4697805	153293	47655
#住　宅	Residential Buildings	3034518	91750	43087
办公楼	Office Buildings	584026		
商业营业用房	Houses for Business Use	444683	41695	2585
期房销售面积	Floor Space of Buildings Presold This Year	9948559	706018	17380
#住　宅	Residential Buildings	8031245	619617	4426
办公楼	Office Buildings	954115	15015	
商业营业用房	Houses for Business Use	621134	39815	12910
商品房销售合同金额(万元)	Contracted Value of Buildings Actually Sold This Year(10000 yuan)	32753538	3742676	373601
现房销售合同金额	Contracted Value of Existing Buildings with Contracts Signed	7321971	592568	288018
#住　宅	Residential Buildings	5019577	417447	275151
办公楼	Office Buildings	889580		
商业营业用房	Houses for Business Use	780636	138573	8084
期房销售合同金额	Contracted Value of Buildings Presold	25431567	3150108	85583
#住　宅	Residential Buildings	21555096	2907661	27072
办公楼	Office Buildings	2179861	50843	
商业营业用房	Houses for Business Use	1366290	140756	58408

Real Estate Development and Management

(2019, by the Locations of the Offices of Corporate Units)

海珠区 Haizhu	天河区 Haizhu	白云区 Baiyun	黄埔区 Huangpu	番禺区 Panyu	花都区 Huadu	南沙区 Nansha	从化区 Conghua	增城区 Zengcheng
136	206	80	110	159	115	121	69	192
3107	12780	2232	5180	6841	3402	3371	1739	7100
1883990	2295682	1900936	4614494	3805902	2652540	3180473	1026861	7533099
977320	775066	1467018	2910321	2658990	1990876	1990672	835981	5874129
381996	581864	113333	808385	292409	50526	470726	12869	397489
339113	682334	102789	219286	376373	264289	251975	64215	258517
8134109	12465538	6177100	17179135	15192872	12199229	15379469	5700440	17895281
4049103	5510853	3748126	11394244	8417221	7380217	8870811	4355605	11929833
1579911	2950447	704777	2375835	1534596	660995	2231136	185170	860904
1377370	1839927	406234	1229257	2078992	1802513	1350770	350671	1382899
980323	1488412	1423166	2618017	2162571	2675638	3259208	998826	4029608
246555	400523	1276293	1571570	1597237	1759439	1908575	653791	3119200
334276	691265		464310	91426	56808	311517	27560	107403
204870	111313	31867	194645	119800	207898	179073	44162	108511
3260932	4445285	1002454	2116985	4107403	3798616	3814417	1442406	2630243
1922135	1231552	596797	1196443	2470488	2351069	2104870	1124619	1862639
458208	1663674	154088	368114	438624	228147	579950		52060
472780	858591	90073	111574	639410	444198	387684	39936	223155
487156	805422	602592	2458557	1415675	1335550	2151806	481775	3983485
227800	311353	171117	876454	366823	644573	281285	92129	1525323
101282	133578	141766	601203	157552	308164	70388	72061	1313687
71542	50484	9621	107258	68594	240307	34117		2103
50233	83020	9326	50175	49693	43853	39891	6035	68177
259356	494069	431475	1582103	1048852	690977	1870521	389646	2458162
155221	329059	342179	1126506	794138	459874	1530459	344290	2325476
76911	130156	44286	184620	171282	101726	196231	11137	22751
27224	27803	37953	48979	61986	117739	125581	27590	93554
1852312	2924602	2600044	4885926	3978417	2317397	4212153	684917	5181493
592332	844445	789890	1012118	929292	988317	317473	120112	847406
474787	436956	743252	698477	547256	545048	94840	96551	689812
52306	103216	11812	155073	163115	341307	55768		6983
61754	160749	24697	78553	108721	65272	73668	3574	56991
1259980	2080157	1810154	3873808	3049125	1329080	3894680	564805	4334087
799845	1592823	1585062	3195244	2474769	992018	3301431	508325	4170846
361676	356493	96701	413901	400079	152806	308773	10999	27590
98459	110143	119768	93369	150877	174397	268712	37042	114359

4-21 房地产开发与经营（2019年，按项目所在地分）

项　目	Item	全　市 Total	荔湾区 Liwan	越秀区 Yuexiu
本年完成投资　（万元）	Total Investment Completed This Year (10000 yuan)	31022573	1747648	354651
#住　宅	Residential Buildings	20870742	1275590	78377
办公楼	Office Buildings	3278582	35064	137078
商业营业用房	Houses for Business Use	2974561	318180	101151
房屋施工面积　（平方米）	Floor Space of Buildings under Construction (sq.m)	119859143	7443282	1969717
#住　宅	Residential Buildings	71611021	5008233	732164
办公楼	Office Buildings	13508722	117004	517437
商业营业用房	Houses for Business Use	12747017	627889	357841
#新开工面积	Floor Space of Newly Started Buildings	22205110	1249878	245058
#住　宅	Residential Buildings	14070224	881018	45652
办公楼	Office Buildings	2210777	22669	103543
商业营业用房	Houses for Business Use	1389355	115345	48101
房屋竣工面积　（平方米）	Floor Space of Buildings Completed (sq.m)	28991942	2149676	997599
#住　宅	Residential Buildings	16457746	1549530	461854
办公楼	Office Buildings	4040388	15882	212736
商业营业用房	Houses for Business Use	3414649	77419	106281
商品房销售面积（平方米）	Floor Space of Buildings Actually Sold This Year (sq.m)	14646364	931538	57480
现房销售面积	Floor Space of Existing Buildings with Contracts Signed	4697805	171968	33389
#住　宅	Residential Buildings	3034518	103715	27135
办公楼	Office Buildings	584026		
商业营业用房	Houses for Business Use	444683	46119	1738
期房销售面积	Floor Space of Buildings Presold This Year	9948559	759570	24091
#住　宅	Residential Buildings	8031245	673169	11181
办公楼	Office Buildings	954115	15015	
商业营业用房	Houses for Business Use	621134	39815	12910
商品房销售合同金额(万元)	Contracted Value of Buildings Actually Sold This Year(10000 yuan)	32753538	4044538	338224
现房销售合同金额	Contracted Value of Existing Buildings with Contracts Signed	7321971	652498	219891
#住　宅	Residential Buildings	5019577	470339	201057
办公楼	Office Buildings	889580		
商业营业用房	Houses for Business Use	780636	143649	9976
期房销售合同金额	Contracted Value of Buildings Presold	25431567	3392040	118333
#住　宅	Residential Buildings	21555096	3149593	59925
办公楼	Office Buildings	2179861	50843	
商业营业用房	Houses for Business Use	1366290	140756	58408

Real Estate Development and Management (2019, by Region of Item)

海珠区 Haizhu	天河区 Tianhe	白云区 Baiyun	黄埔区 Huangpu	番禺区 Panyu	花都区 Huadu	南沙区 Nansha	从化区 Conghua	增城区 Zengcheng
1813187	2052688	2033228	4753552	3852016	2675170	3180473	1026861	7533099
902314	611499	1549467	3043725	2699444	2009544	1990672	835981	5874129
381869	587262	104770	808485	292536	50434	470726	12869	397489
338237	655619	120126	224329	377504	264708	251975	64215	258517
6595904	10181012	6048362	18072888	17044923	13527865	15379469	5700440	17895281
2859477	3974110	3683590	12269719	9636346	8291133	8870811	4355605	11929833
1431476	3096310	488973	2381348	1534696	664268	2231136	185170	860904
1285611	1780432	423315	1234918	2115348	1837323	1350770	350671	1382899
1046021	984093	1861787	2618017	3236976	2675638	3259208	998826	4029608
283597	81618	1558156	1571570	2207608	1759439	1908575	653791	3119200
334276	691265		464310	91426	56808	311517	27560	107403
204870	102824	40356	194645	143570	207898	179073	44162	108511
2066096	3784960	1150627	2220793	4587481	4147644	3814417	1442406	2630243
973292	980672	792672	1281973	2880189	2445436	2104870	1124619	1862639
306622	1784615	38252	373627	438724	237920	579950		52060
443682	801250	98843	117235	640657	478507	387684	39936	223155
408389	784129	557719	2483739	1423980	1382324	2151806	481775	3983485
201245	260045	186872	901636	375084	668829	281285	92129	1525323
74671	117737	148517	625734	160184	320689	70388	72061	1313687
71542	48722	9621	107258	68594	242069	34117		2103
50233	73299	11185	50175	49693	48138	39891	6035	68177
207144	524084	370847	1582103	1048896	713495	1870521	389646	2458162
103009	315460	331600	1126506	794138	475957	1530459	344290	2325476
76911	140090	34352	184620	171282	101726	196231	11137	22751
27224	61483	4273	48979	61986	117739	125581	27590	93554
1517593	2933002	2532481	4950316	3994098	2364723	4212153	684917	5181493
491713	791148	845824	1076508	944870	1014528	317473	120112	847406
373982	432044	782656	762088	555005	561203	94840	96551	689812
52306	101877	11812	155073	163115	342646	55768		6983
61754	145614	28598	78553	108721	69538	73668	3574	56991
1025880	2141854	1686657	3873808	3049228	1350195	3894680	564805	4334087
565745	1527649	1595944	3195244	2474769	1005625	3301431	508325	4170846
361676	380864	72330	413901	400079	152806	308773	10999	27590
98459	212643	17268	93369	150877	174397	268712	37042	114359

4-22 房地产开发投资额和新增固定资产（2019年）

单位：万元

项目	Item	企业数（个）Number of Enterprises (unit)
全 市	**Total**	**1306**
按企业登记注册类型分	**Grouped by Registration Status**	
内资企业	Domestic Funded Enterprises	1052
国有企业	State-owned Enterprises	22
集体企业	Collective-owned Enterprises	14
股份合作企业	Cooperative Enterprises	1
联营企业	Joint Ownership Enterprises	2
# 国有联营企业	State Joint Ownership Enterprises	
集体联营企业	Collective Joint Ownership Enterprises	
国有与集体联营企业	Joint State-collective Enterprises	
有限责任公司	Limited Liability Corporations	591
# 国有独资公司	State Sole Funded Corporations	43
股份有限公司	Share-holding Corporations Ltd.	14
私营企业	Private Enterprises	407
其他企业	Other Enterprises	1
港、澳、台商投资企业	Enterprises with Funds from Hong Kong, Macao and Taiwan	184
# 与港、澳、台商合资经营企业	Joint-venture Enterprises	31
与港、澳、台商合作经营企业	Cooperative Enterprises	61
港、澳、台商独资经营企业	Enterprises with Sole Funds	92
港、澳、台商投资股份有限公司	Share-holding Corporations Ltd.	
外商投资企业	Foreign Funded Enterprises	70
# 中外合资经营企业	Joint-venture Enterprises	23
中外合作经营企业	Cooperative Enterprises	11
外资企业	Enterprises with Sole Foreign Funds	33
外商投资股份有限公司	Share-holding Corporations Ltd.	
按资质分	**Grouped by Grade**	
一级资质	Grade One	13
二级资质	Grade Two	70
三级资质	Grade Three	387
四级以下(含四级)	Grade Four and below	836
按隶属关系分	**Grouped by Jurisdiction of Management**	
中央	Central Investment	26
地方	Local Investment	230
其他	Other Investment	1050

Investment and Newly Increased Fixed Assets in Real Estate Development (2019)

(10000 yuan)

投资额合计 Total Investment	住 宅 Residential Buildings	办公楼 Office Buildings	商业营业用房 Houses for Business Use	其他用房 Other Buildings	新增固定资产 Newly Increased Fixed Assets
31022573	**20870742**	**3278582**	**2974561**	**3898688**	**16772498**
27856883	19175532	2774128	2489736	3417487	11978430
1003578	744298	47941	27264	184075	328017
12790	10707	120	336	1627	8289
19153324	12739193	2273331	1680226	2460574	8320733
1675830	1048727	253037	150072	223994	1357811
141586	93859	37750	7088	2889	
7434482	5516516	414986	764681	738299	3321391
111123	70959		10141	30023	
1562947	771734	325792	283260	182161	3970514
442016	177308	91113	153806	19789	1936020
398009	206700	87766	54577	48966	1042763
722922	387726	146913	74877	113406	991731
1602743	923476	178662	201565	299040	823554
1270561	786912	108766	128986	245897	566461
57150	25122	22867	315	8846	102690
237328	108309	17630	68826	42563	53546
414178	380461	4016	10589	19112	1705041
942555	644627	15405	71530	210993	2260464
2734566	1941982	226597	267716	298271	3619213
26931274	17903672	3032564	2624726	3370312	9187780
1459647	1157830	148063	46512	107242	1189445
4143177	2687719	560994	309837	584627	3523549
25419749	17025193	2569525	2618212	3206819	12059504

4-23 房地产开发房屋面积（2019年）

单位:平方米

项目	Item
全 市	**Total**
按企业登记注册类型分	**Grouped by Registration Status**
内资企业	Domestic Funded Enterprises
国有企业	State-owned Enterprises
集体企业	Collective-owned Enterprises
股份合作企业	Cooperative Enterprises
联营企业	Joint Ownership Enterprises
# 国有联营企业	State Joint Ownership Enterprises
集体联营企业	Collective Joint Ownership Enterprises
国有与集体联营企业	Joint State-collective Enterprises
有限责任公司	Limited Liability Corporations
# 国有独资公司	State Sole Funded Corporations
股份有限公司	Share-holding Corporations Ltd.
私营企业	Private Enterprises
其他企业	Other Enterprises
港、澳、台商投资企业	Enterprises with Funds from Hong Kong, Macao and Taiwan
# 与港、澳、台商合资经营企业	Joint-venture Enterprises
与港、澳、台商合作经营企业	Cooperative Enterprises
港、澳、台商独资经营企业	Enterprises with Sole Funds
港、澳、台商投资股份有限公司	Share-holding Corporations Ltd.
外商投资企业	Foreign Funded Enterprises
# 中外合资经营企业	Joint-venture Enterprises
中外合作经营企业	Cooperative Enterprises
外资企业	Enterprises with Sole Foreign Funds
外商投资股份有限公司	Share-holding Corporations Ltd.
按资质分	**Grouped by Grade**
一级资质	Grade One
二级资质	Grade Two
三级资质	Grade Three
四级以下(含四级)	Grade Four and below
按隶属关系分	**Grouped by Jurisdiction of Management**
中央	Central Investment
地方	Local Investment
其他	Other Investment

Floor Space of Buildings in Real Estate Development (2019)

(sq.m)

施工面积 Floor Space of Buildings under Construction	#住宅 Residential Buildings	竣工面积 Floor Space of Buildings Completed	#住宅 Residential Buildings	商品房销售面积 Floor Space of Buildings Actually Sold	#住宅 Residential Buildings
119859143	**71611021**	**28991942**	**16457746**	**14646364**	**11065763**
95104071	58628299	20930081	12606661	12482972	9591583
3624802	2367231	860699	696070	363055	286941
167046	114097			45157	39783
3600					
64315822	39368139	13755629	8392723	9415105	7045987
7183258	4685904	2899376	2184192	1851971	1539040
1186142	671673			201842	192713
25678596	16031518	6313753	3517868	2443895	2012241
128063	75641			13918	13918
17299527	9046533	6119611	2999962	1434919	960497
5008752	2031989	2059650	479292	323512	154554
5481320	3439121	1882997	1262566	381366	284074
6809455	3575423	2176964	1258104	730041	521869
7455545	3936189	1942250	851123	728473	513683
3885220	1938553	1325407	429055	314321	245819
837174	516369	278507	242715	28681	23331
2262137	1398135	206273	179353	294681	240183
5256801	3777253	3840980	2634292	163039	46207
9463057	6052387	2612358	1873910	968911	884450
24058982	13745599	7411617	3794618	2161391	1570553
81080303	48035782	15126987	8154926	11353023	8564553
6543559	4853612	2782027	2158261	390414	260054
19444560	11762591	5131073	3617031	2135187	1550313
93871024	54994818	21078842	10682454	12120763	9255396

4-24 房地产开发资金来源（2019年）

单位：万元

项　　目	Item
全　市	**Total**
按企业登记注册类型分	**Grouped by Registration Status**
内资企业	Domestic Funded Enterprises
国有企业	State-owned Enterprises
集体企业	Collective-owned Enterprises
股份合作企业	Cooperative Enterprises
联营企业	Joint Ownership Enterprises
# 国有联营企业	State Joint Ownership Enterprises
集体联营企业	Collective Joint Ownership Enterprises
国有与集体联营企业	Joint State-collective Enterprises
有限责任公司	Limited Liability Corporations
# 国有独资公司	State Sole Funded Corporations
股份有限公司	Share-holding Corporations Ltd.
私营企业	Private Enterprises
其他企业	Other Enterprises
港、澳、台商投资企业	Enterprises with Funds from Hong Kong, Macao and Taiwan
# 与港、澳、台商合资经营企业	Joint-venture Enterprises
与港、澳、台商合作经营企业	Cooperative Enterprises
港、澳、台商独资经营企业	Enterprises with Sole Funds
港、澳、台商投资股份有限公司	Share-holding Corporations Ltd.
外商投资企业	Foreign Funded Enterprises
# 中外合资经营企业	Joint-venture Enterprises
中外合作经营企业	Cooperative Enterprises
外资企业	Enterprises with Sole Foreign Funds
外商投资股份有限公司	Share-holding Corporations Ltd.
按资质分	**Grouped by Grade**
一级资质	Grade One
二级资质	Grade Two
三级资质	Grade Three
四级以下(含四级)	Grade Four and below
按隶属关系分	**Grouped by Jurisdiction of Management**
中央	Central Investment
地方	Local Investment
其他	Other Investment

注：本表资金来源为本年发生额。

Real Estate Development by Source of Funds (2019)

(10000 yuan)

合 计 Total	国内贷款 Domestic Loans	利用外资 Foreign Investment	自筹资金 Self-raising Funds	定金及预收款 Deposit and Advance Payment	个人按揭贷款 Personal Mortgage Loan	其他资金 Others
50035605	**10174609**		**16687131**	**17038155**	**3963516**	**2172194**
42530614	9483041		15180863	12426063	3336529	2104118
867810	147903		659828			60079
12891			12891			
29886399	6158258		10508351	10236209	2907993	75588
2760436	260972		1928027	495211	17251	58975
509859	252333		44683	173266	39577	
11216408	2904547		3950610	2006846	388959	1965446
37247	20000		4500	9742		3005
4777347	419762		826231	3213702	253540	64112
1743553	44870		257443	1308167	80313	52760
1468783	45243		172365	1165506	85667	2
1565011	329649		396423	740029	87560	11350
2727644	271806		680037	1398390	373447	3964
1619469	107500		346784	949399	211822	3964
162327	35252		63892	52661	10522	
856635	105000		269361	331171	151103	
3582239	937707		650471	185650	4258	1804153
3511971	509510		204049	2451053	347359	
4861389	886467		1239819	2184635	512604	37864
38080006	7840925		14592792	12216817	3099295	330177
2932268	621457		1488872	468333	300456	53150
7348461	1244109		2311361	2979157	769767	44067
39754876	8309043		12886898	13590665	2893293	2074977

Note: The source of funds in this table refers to the amount in current year.

4-25 房地产开发主要财务指标（2019年）

单位：万元

项 目	Item
全 市	**Total**
按企业登记注册类型分	**Grouped by Registration Status**
内资企业	Domestic Funded Enterprises
国有企业	State-owned Enterprises
集体企业	Collective-owned Enterprises
股份合作企业	Cooperative Enterprises
联营企业	Joint Ownership Enterprises
# 国有联营企业	State Joint Ownership Enterprises
集体联营企业	Collective Joint Ownership Enterprises
国有与集体联营企业	Joint State-collective Enterprises
有限责任公司	Limited Liability Corporations
# 国有独资公司	State Sole Funded Corporations
股份有限公司	Share-holding Corporations Ltd.
私营企业	Private Enterprises
其他企业	Other Enterprises
港、澳、台商投资企业	Enterprises with Funds from Hong Kong, Macao and Taiwan
# 与港、澳、台商合资经营企业	Joint-venture Enterprises
与港、澳、台商合作经营企业	Cooperative Enterprises
港、澳、台商独资经营企业	Enterprises with Sole Funds
港、澳、台商投资股份有限公司	Share-holding Corporations Ltd.
外商投资企业	Foreign Funded Enterprises
# 中外合资经营企业	Joint-venture Enterprises
中外合作经营企业	Cooperative Enterprises
外资企业	Enterprises with Sole Foreign Funds
外商投资股份有限公司	Share-holding Corporations Ltd.
按资质分	**Grouped by Grade**
一级资质	Grade One
二级资质	Grade Two
三级资质	Grade Three
四级以下(含四级)	Grade Four and below
按隶属关系分	**Grouped by Jurisdiction of Management**
中央	Central Investment
地方	Local Investment
其他	Other Investment

Main Financial Indicators of Real Estate Development (2019)

(10000 yuan)

资产总计 Total Assets	所有者权益 Owners′ Equity	营业收入 Business Revenue	营业成本 Cost of Business	利润总额 Total Profits
434684215	**84333091**	**31529039**	**18470059**	**10972458**
322841541	65538120	25298049	15672269	9553497
1154811	881203	28793	6883	30188
355720	118606	14567	5776	-931
35882	2817	1203		-142
11427	-4082	715	71	-106
239889304	54336050	20266604	12598344	8556780
51035178	11154328	1740592	1454481	518276
19238219	2641207	398275	195530	46650
62144280	7563657	4587846	2865665	921210
11898	-1338	46		-152
72598668	12602899	4072891	1768401	1119381
8633538	4089906	1390654	633803	445602
12195758	3216804	1456068	595315	283027
51769373	5296189	1226169	539284	390751
39244006	6192072	2158099	1029389	299580
24501359	3232947	1448813	692070	254242
2091184	957888	175175	59545	60072
10603106	1470517	430223	246637	-96601
133263422	25628396	854635	223361	4247561
25715173	6046913	2452795	1229085	424868
56637737	17192227	6726486	3710502	1535355
219067883	35465555	21495123	13307111	4764674
38843141	5704030	732098	374182	372483
103522035	32917599	6789129	3840866	5893222
292319039	45711462	24007812	14255011	4706753

【固定资产投资额】以货币形式表现的在一定时期内建造和购置固定资产的工作量以及与此有关的费用的总称。该指标是反映固定资产投资规模、结构和发展速度的综合性指标，又是观察工程进度和考核投资效果的重要依据。

【房地产开发投资】各种登记注册类型的房地产开发公司、商品房建设公司及其他房地产开发单位统一开发的包括统代建、拆迁还建的住宅、厂房、仓库、饭店、宾馆、度假村、写字楼、办公楼等房屋建筑物和配套的服务设施、土地开发工程，如道路、给水、排水、供电、供热、通讯、平整场地等基础设施工程的投资。包括实际从事房地产开发或经营活动的附营房地产开发单位。不包括单纯的土地交易活动。

【房屋施工面积】指报告期内施工的全部房屋建筑面积。包括本期新开工的面积和上期开工跨入本期继续施工的房屋面积，以及上期已停建在本期复工的房屋面积。本期竣工和本期施工后又停缓建的房屋，其建筑面积仍计入本期房屋施工面积中。

【房屋竣工面积】指在报告期内房屋建筑按照设计要求已全部完工，达到住人和使用条件，经验收鉴定合格（或达到竣工验收标准），可正式移交使用的各栋房屋建筑面积的总和。

【Total Investment in Fixed Assets】 refers to the volume of activities in construction and purchases of fixed assets and related fees, expressed in monetary terms. It is a comprehensive indicator which shows the size, structure and growth of the investment in fixed assets, providing basis for observing the progress of construction projects and evaluating results of investment.

【Investment in Real Estate Development】It includes the investment by the real estate development companies, commercial buildings construction companies and other real estate development units of various types of ownership in the construction of house buildings, such as residential buildings, factory buildings, warehouses, hotels, guesthouses, holiday villages, office buildings, and the complementary service facilities and land development projects, such as roads, water supply, water drainage, power supply, heating, telecommunications, land leveling and other projects of infrastructure. It covers the activities of the non-real estate companies in real estate development or management, but excludes the activities in simple land transactions.

【Floor Space under Construction】 refers to total floor space of all buildings under construction during the reference period, including floor space of newly started buildings during the reference period, floor space of construction extended from the previous period to the current period, and floor space of construction suspended during the previous period but resumed in the current period. Floor space of construction completed in the current period and floor space of construction started and then suspended in the current period are still included in floor space under construction.

【Floor Space of Buildings Completed】 refer to the floor space of housing construction in accordance with the design requirements have been completed In the reporting period, to live and the conditions of use, have been checked or reach the completion acceptance criteria, of housing construction put to use.

第五篇 CHAPTER 5

能源和环境
ENERGY AND ENVIRONMENT

第五篇　能源和环境

一、本篇资料反映广州市能源和环境综合情况。

（一）能源部分主要包括：能源生产、消费基本情况，规模以上工业企业能源加工转换效率和工业企业分行业主要能源消费量，全市用电量等。

1. 能源统计资料取自广州市能源与生产、销售与库存、工业企业能源购进、消费与库存，及能源加工转换与回收利用表等。

2. 统计口径与计算说明：

⑴ 5-1表至5-3表及5-6表和5-7表的统计口径均为全社会口径；5-4表和5-5表的统计口径均为年主营业务收入2000万元及以上工业企业法人单位。

⑵ 计算能源消费指标涉及的地区生产总值、工业增加值均采用可比口径。

⑶ 5-2表和5-3表的能源消费总量及分行业能源消费量中的电力按等价值计算；5-4表能源加工转换效率表中的电力按当量值计算，即每千瓦时折0.1229千克标准煤。

3. 本篇的5-2表、5-6表、5-7表电力数据来自广东电网有限责任公司广州供电局。

（二）环境部分主要包括水环境、大气环境、固体废物、生态环境、自然灾害、城市环境、农村环境等。

环境资料由市生态环境局、水务局、规划和自然资源局、住房城乡建设局、应急管理局、农业农村局、林业和园林局等单位提供。

二、本篇资料由广州市统计局能源统计处整理提供。

5 Energy and Environment

I. This paper reflects the comprehensive situation of energy and environment in Guangzhou.

1.The energy part mainly includes: the energy production, the consumption basic situation, the scale above industrial enterprise energy processing conversion efficiency and the industrial enterprise by profession main energy consumption, the whole city electricity consumption and so on.

1.1 Energy statistics from Guangzhou energy production, sales and inventory, industrial enterprises energy purchase, consumption and inventory, and energy processing conversion and recycling tables.

1.2 Statistical caliber and calculation description:

1.2.1 The statistical caliber of 5-1 table to 5-3 table and 5-6 table to 5-7 table are all the whole social caliber, and the statistical caliber of 5-4 table to 5-5 table are all 20 million yuan of annual main business income and corporate unit of industrial enterprise above.

1.2.2 Calculation of energy consumption indicators related to the regional gross domestic product, industrial value added using comparable caliber.

1.2.3 The total energy consumption in table 5-2 and table 5-3 and the energy consumption in each industry are calculated by equal value, and the power in the table of conversion efficiency of energy processing in table 5-4 is calculated at an equal value, that is, 0.1229 kg of standard coal per kilowatt-hour.

1.3 The 5-2, 5-6, 5-7 tables are from Guangzhou Power Supply Bureau of Guangdong Power Grid Co., Ltd.

2. The environmental part mainly includes water environment, atmosphere environment, solid waste, ecological environment, natural disaster, urban environment, rural environment and so on.

The environmental information is provided by Guangzhou Municipal Ecological Environmental Bureau, Water Authority, Planning and Natural Resources Bureau, Emergency Management Bureau, Agriculture and Rural Affairs Bureau, Forestry and Landscaping Bureau and so on.

II. The data in this chapter is collected and provided by Guangzhou Bureau of Statistics Energy Statistics Department.

5-1 能源生产量

Energy Production

项目		Item		2018	2019
原油加工量	（万吨）	Crude Oil Processing	(10000 tons)	1261.37	1186.01
汽　油	（万吨）	Gasoline	(10000 tons)	303.56	313.46
煤　油	（万吨）	Kerosine	(10000 tons)	197.32	205.23
柴　油	（万吨）	Diesel Oil	(10000 tons)	363.60	346.00
燃料油	（万吨）	Fuel Oil	(10000 tons)	0.11	0.14
液化石油气	（万吨）	Liquefied Petroleum	(10000 tons)	58.26	50.28
发电量	（万千瓦·时）	Electricity Production	(10000 kWh)	3410895	3481000
#火力发电量		Thermal Power Generation		3074533	3093285
#燃煤发电量		Fossil Fired Power Generation		2459270	2352278
余热余压发电量		Waste Heat and Pressure Power Generation			3178
燃气发电量		Gas Power Generation		497955	535745
垃圾焚烧发电量		Waste Incineration Power Generation		109459	187935
生物质发电量		Biomass Power Generation		7849	14149
水力发电量		Hydroelectric Generation		276762	313500
#抽水蓄能发电量		Pumped Storage Power Generation		245162	254800
太阳能发电量		Solar Power Generation		59600	74215
热力	（百万千焦）	Heating Power	(MkJ)	29509168	29322760
#生物质能供热		Biomass Heating		1750219	1948433
化石燃料供热		Fossil Fuel Heating		27758949	27374327

注：1.本表能源生产量为全社会口径。

2.水力发电量包括抽水蓄能发电量，2018年数据同口径调整。

Note: I.The energy production data in this table is of full coverage.

II.Hydroelectric generation includes pumped storage power generation, with the same adjustment for 2018 data.

5-2 主要年份能源消耗基本情况
Energy Consumption in Main Years

年份 Year	能源消费总量（万吨标准煤）Total Energy Consumption (10000 tons SCE)	万元地区生产总值能耗下降率(%) Desent rate of Energy Consumption per Unit of GDP (%)	万元地区生产总值电耗下降率(%) Desent rate of Electricity Consumption per Unit of GDP (%)	工业增加值能耗下降率(%) Desent rate of Energy Consumption of Industrial Value-added (%)	工业增加值电耗下降率(%) Desent rate of Electricity Consumption of Industrial Value-added (%)
2006	4122.58	4.62	4.05	9.68	4.11
2007	4395.38	4.44	2.29	5.46	6.28
2008	4577.54	4.56	7.98	8.34	9.70
2009	4673.27	4.01	6.96	8.81	8.73
2010	4775.60	4.60	2.53	11.09	-0.28
2011	5013.40	4.91	4.74	9.98	7.48
2012	5163.45	4.94	4.59	12.13	7.12
2013	5333.57	5.14	8.21	13.24	8.74
2014	5496.46	3.52	0.77	8.46	2.15
2015	5688.89	4.52	6.13	3.53	4.66
2016	5852.60	4.96	2.36	6.56	0.42
2017	5961.97	4.81	1.32	5.78	0.34
2018	6129.55	3.24	2.27	5.62	5.10
2019	6294.20	3.86	-0.50	4.49	0.88

5-3 能源消费总量
Total Consumption of Energy

单位：万吨标准煤 (10000 tons of SCE)

项 目	Item	2018 数量 Consumption Volume	2018 构成(%) Composition (%)	2019 数量 Consumption Volume	2019 构成(%) Composition (%)
合 计	**Total**	**6129.55**	**100.00**	**6294.20**	**100.00**
生产消费	Production Consumption	5126.63	83.64	5258.33	83.54
第一产业	Primary Industry	37.56	0.61	37.46	0.60
第二产业	Secondary Industry	2486.50	40.57	2497.78	39.68
第三产业	Tertiary Industry	2602.57	42.46	2723.09	43.26
生产消费中：	In Production Consumption:				
工 业	Industry	2349.90	38.34	2352.29	37.37
生活消费	Residential Consumption	1002.92	16.36	1035.87	16.46
城 镇	Urban Areas	731.58	11.93	749.92	11.92
乡 村	Rural Areas	271.34	4.43	285.95	4.54

5-4 规模以上工业企业能源加工转换效率
Efficiency of Energy Conversion by Industrial Enterprises above the Designated Size

项 目	Item	火力发电 Thermal Power Generation		供热 Heating		炼油 Petroleum Refining	
		2018年	2019年	2018年	2019年	2018年	2019年
投入量合计 (万吨标准煤)	Total Input (10000 tons of SCE)	935.14	943.93	136.83	129.53	1956.36	1866.64
产出量合计 (万吨标准煤)	Total Output (10000 tons of SCE)	376.27	373.70	117.06	110.86	1920.46	1848.40
加工转换损失量(万吨标准煤)	Losses in Energy Conversion (10000 tons of SCE)	558.87	570.23	19.77	18.67	35.90	18.24
加工转换效率 (%)	Efficiency of Energy Conversion (%)	40.24	39.59	85.55	85.59	98.16	99.02

5-5 规模以上工业企业分行业主要能源消费量（2019年）

行　　业	Sector
工　业	**Industry**
按轻重工业分	**Grouped by Light & Heavy Industries**
轻工业	Light Industry
重工业	Heavy Industry
按工业行业分	**Grouped by Sector**
采矿业	Mining
制造业	Manufacturing
农副食品加工业	Processing of Food from Agricultural Products
食品制造业	Manufacture of Foods
酒、饮料和精制茶制造业	Manufacture of wine,Beverages and Refined Tea
烟草制品业	Manufacture of Tobacco
纺织业	Manufacture of Textile
纺织服装、服饰业	Manufacture of Textile Wearing Apparel,Clothing
皮革、毛皮、羽毛及其制品和制鞋业	Manufacture of Leather,Fur,Feather and Related Products and Footwear
木材加工和木、竹、藤、棕、草制品业	Processing of Timber,Manufacture of Wood, Bamboo, Rattan, Plam and Straw Products
家具制造业	Manufacture of Furniture
造纸和纸制品业	Manufacture of Paper and Paper Products
印刷和记录媒介复制业	Printing, Reproduction of Recording Media
文教、工美、体育和娱乐用品制造业	Manufacture of Culture and Education, Arts and Crafts, Sports and Entertainment Supplies
石油、煤炭及其他燃料加工业	Petroleum, Coal and Other Fuel Proccessing
化学原料和化学制品制造业	Manufacture of Raw Chemical Materials and Chemical Products

Consumption of Main Energy by Industrial Sector above the Designated Size (2019)

煤　炭 (吨) Coal (ton)	燃料油 (吨) Fuel Oil (ton)	汽　油 (吨) Gasoline (ton)	柴　油 (吨) Diesel Oil (ton)	热　力 (百万千焦) Heating (million kJ)	电　力 (万千瓦·时) Electricity (10000 kWh)
12593086	**12057**	**55256**	**118670**	**23564173**	**3971163**
417122	2495	16237	24383	16099103	733101
12175964	9562	39019	94287	7465070	3238062
			39		1063
1378723	11764	52555	105807	23537214	2383772
47385	9	402	1261	2134353	40104
		1103	3104	1571693	59400
		496	630	1430262	38634
		43	2		7102
341843	661	1147	666	7488325	66582
7882		1355	1192	55049	20677
75		1312	478		19981
		204	435		7762
		1237	1132	7521	20232
3686	31	1376	2894	2508904	69207
		364	398		23517
	876	710	1167	5201	27701
368577	1434	3075	2126	39957	144840
79299	742	4016	11485	5795936	193805

5-5 续表

行　　业	Sector
医药制造业	Manufacture of Medicines
化学纤维制造业	Manufacture of Chemical Fibers
橡胶和塑料制品业	Manufacture of Rubber
非金属矿物制品业	Manufacture of Non-metallic Mineral Products
黑色金属冶炼和压延加工业	Smelting and Pressing of Ferrous Metals
有色金属冶炼和压延加工业	Smelting and Pressing of Non-Ferrous Metals
金属制品业	Manufacture of Metal Products
通用设备制造业	Manufacture of General Purpose Machinery
专用设备制造业	Manufacture of Special Purpose Machinery
汽车制造业	Manufacture of Automobile
铁路、船舶、航空航天和其他运输	Manufacture of Railway, Ship, Aerospace and Other Transportation
设备制造业	Equipment
电气机械和器材制造业	Manufacture of Electrical Machinery and Equipment
计算机、通信和其他电子设备制造业	Manufacture of Computers, Communications and Other Electronic Equipment
仪器仪表制造业	Manufacture of Instrument
其他制造业	Other Manufacturing
废弃资源综合利用业	Comprehensive Utilization of Waste Resources
金属制品、机械和设备修理业	Metal Products, Machinery and Equipment Repair
电力、热力、燃气及水生产和供应业	Production and Supply of Electricity,Heat,Gas and Water
电力、热力生产和供应业	Production and Supply of Electric Power and Heat Power
燃气生产和供应业	Production and Supply of Gas
水的生产和供应业	Production and Supply of Water

注：本表电力消费量包含法人单位自产自用电量。

continued

煤 炭 (吨) Coal (ton)	燃料油 (吨) Fuel Oil (ton)	汽 油 (吨) Gasoline (ton)	柴 油 (吨) Diesel Oil (ton)	热 力 (百万千焦) Heating (million kJ)	电 力 (万千瓦·时) Electricity (10000 kWh)
		755	649	395138	40468
		83	93	27700	5154
2865	858	2417	4324	751057	177131
527111	5345	821	44547	107136	122984
	18	167	1646	395384	180384
	147	302	1034		25599
	25	2388	4133	34922	85278
		3707	4365	31021	61749
		3370	1390	95601	36569
	35	12139	5043	529086	319963
	1519	930	3089		24779
	2	4023	3055	41279	95807
	40	3896	1922	91689	431282
		289	141		17217
		164	274		4596
		22	529		5530
	22	242	2603		9738
11214363	293	2701	12824	26959	1586328
11214363	293	1561	12127	26959	1438910
		449	285		1089
		691	412		146329

Note: The electricity consumption in the table includes electricity generated and used by enterprise itself.

5-6 主要年份全市用电量

Total Electricity Supply in Main Years

单位：万千瓦·时 (10000 kWh)

年 份 Year	用电总量 Consumption	各行业用电 Total Electricity Consumption of Industry	#工 业 Industry	生活用电 Power Consumed by Urbanites
1978	229680		183814	
1979	273124		217438	
1980	302175		228544	
1981	314537		229280	
1982	335533		237124	
1983	376334		261924	
1984	375693		247131	
1985	403864		251572	
1986	425740		266993	
1987	528671	468372	353019	60299
1988	570888	497403	367882	73485
1989	588073	510252	381924	77821
1990	651907	551870	402427	100037
1991	850413	729858	557693	120555
1992	988361	844301	641685	144060
1993	1194668	1013769	765423	180899
1994	1340090	1123076	824998	217014
1995	1491687	1239195	900550	252492
1996	1607619	1321780	948271	285839
1997	1700635	1399021	987404	301614
1998	1893271	1546097	1066325	347174
1999	2056799	1684648	1155344	372151
2000	2363174	1945091	1351669	418083

5-6 续表 continued

单位：万千瓦·时　　　　(10000 kWh)

年 份 Year	用电总量 Consumption	各行业用电 Total Electricity Consumption of Industry	#工 业 Industry	生活用电 Power Consumed by Urbanites
2001	2540201	2072950	1428461	467251
2002	2849015	2373574	1607851	475441
2003	3349712	2804357	1943780	545355
2004	3846375	3228990	2239481	617385
2005	4256677	3537004	2531916	719673
2006	4694234	3898916	2740256	795318
2007	5271258	4372014	3063610	899244
2008	5459185	4472140	3098761	987045
2009	5670810	4559439	3098871	1111371
2010	6258983	5075414	3497243	1183569
2011	6635544	5349058	3614532	1286486
2012	6941253	5519444	3589545	1421809
2013	7106910	5692959	3656433	1413951
2014	7658542	6052408	3860372	1606134
2015	7793233	6179721	3937448	1613512
2016	8235701	6533151	4164565	1702550
2017	9024753	7137209	4344911	1887544
2018	9369013	7407839	4368114	1961174
2019	10055838	7987146	4537710	2068692

注：1．本表数据由广东电网有限责任公司广州供电局提供，用电量包括法人单位自发自用电量。
2．1987年起行业用电分类调整，之前无各行业用电和生活用电分类。
3．2018年开始广东电网有限责任公司广州供电局统计全市用电量包含抽水蓄能用电量。2017年同口径调整，原口径用电总量为8695865万千瓦·时。

Note: I. The data in this table is provided by Guangzhou Power Supply Bureau of Guangdong Power Grid Co., Ltd and the data includes Spontaneous electricity consumption of legal entity.

II. Since 1987, the classification of electricity consumption in different industries has been adjusted. Before that, there was no classification of electricity consumption in different industries and in daily life.

III. Total Electricity Consumption includes the electricity consumption of pumped storage since 2018. The data of 2017 has been adjusted according to this new coverage. The original data is 8695865(10000kWh).

5-7 全市分行业用电量

Electricity Consumption by Industrial Sector

单位:万千瓦•时 (10000 kWh)

项　　目	Item	2018	2019
用电总量	**Total Consumption of Electricity**	**9369013**	**10055838**
各行业用电	**Total Electricity Consumption of Industry**	**7407839**	**7987146**
按产业分	**Grouped By Industry**		
第一产业	Primary Industry	58894	56335
第二产业	Secondary Industry	4391356	4589542
第三产业	Tertiary Industry	2957589	3341269
按行业分	**Grouped By Sector**		
农、林、牧、渔业	Agriculture, Forestry, Animal Husbandry and Fishery	72315	69472
工　业	Industry	4368114	4537710
按工业行业分	By Sector		
采矿业	Mining	12873	7211
制造业	Manufacturing	3293638	3385761
农副食品加工业	Processing of Food from Agricultural Products	37684	41639
食品制造业	Manufacture of Foods	71036	72742
酒、饮料和精制茶制造业	Manufacture of wine,Beverages and Refined Tea	50862	47693
烟草制品业	Manufacture of Tobacco	7183	8264
纺织业	Manufacture of Textile	120390	113249
纺织服装、服饰业	Manufacture of Textile Wearing Apparel,Clothing	80318	79829
皮革、毛皮、羽毛及其制品和制鞋业	Manufacture of Leather,Fur,Feather and Related Products and Footwear	178942	165960
木材加工和木、竹、藤、棕、草制品业	Processing of Timber,Manufacture of Wood, Bamboo, Rattan, Plam and Straw Products	60443	56509
家具制造业	Manufacture of Furniture	10840	13611
造纸和纸制品业	Manufacture of Paper and Paper Products	91851	88721
印刷和记录媒介复制业	Printing, Reproduction of Recording Media	25163	26434
文教、工美、体育和娱乐用品制造业	Manufacture of Culture and Education ,Arts and Crafts, Sports and Entertainment Supplies	142333	140000
石油、煤炭及其他燃料加工业	Petroleum ,Coal and Other Fuel Proccesing	155514	154016
化学原料和化学制品制造业	Manufacture of Raw Chemical Materials and Chemical Products	127888	140000
医药制造业	Manufacture of Medicines	47449	53753
化学纤维制造业	Manufacture of Chemical Fibers	18060	20187

5-7 续表 continued

单位:万千瓦·时 (10000 kWh)

项　　目	Item	2018	2019
橡胶和塑料制品业	Manufacture of Rubber	180220	187232
非金属矿物制品业	Manufacture of Non-metallic Mineral Products	119287	111723
黑色金属冶炼和压延加工业	Smelting and Pressing of Ferrous Metals	158815	155780
有色金属冶炼和压延加工业	Smelting and Pressing of Non-Ferrous Metals	60278	55869
金属制品业	Manufacture of Metal Products	197461	196011
通用设备制造业	Manufacture of General Purpose Machinery	300475	213451
专用设备制造业	Manufacture of Special Purpose Machinery	17375	18541
汽车制造业	Manufacture of Automobile	253170	279693
铁路、船舶、航空航天和其他运输设备制造业	Manufacture of Railway, Ship, Aerospace and Other Transportation Equipment	112466	85236
电气机械和器材制造业	Manufacture of Electrical Machinery and Equipment	63179	70125
计算机、通信和其他电子设备制造业	Manufacture of Computers, Communications and Other Electronic Equipment	241864	469169
仪器仪表制造业	Manufacture of Instrument	2106	2111
其他制造业	Other Manufacturing	271121	244650
废弃资源综合利用业	Comprehensive Utilization of Waste Resources	6384	6227
金属制品、机械和设备修理业	Metal Products, Machinery and Equipment Repair	83481	67336
电力、热力、燃气及水生产和供应业	Production and Supply of Electricity,Heat,Gas and Water	1061603	1144738
电力、热力生产和供应业	Production and Supply of Electric Power and Heat Power	915753	993394
燃气生产和供应业	Production and Supply of Gas	46768	51841
水的生产和供应业	Production and Supply of Water	99082	99503
建筑业	Construction	106724	119168
批发和零售业	Wholesale and Retail Trade	311442	404612
交通运输、仓储和邮政业	Transport, Storage and Post	359235	428857
住宿和餐饮业	Hotels and Catering Services	164349	187203
信息传输、软件和信息技术服务业	Information Transmission, Software and Information Technology	198126	219604
金融业	Financial Intermediation	37777	39743
房地产业	Real Estate	143999	173831
租赁和商务服务业	Leasing and Business Services	910460	987906
公共服务及管理组织	Public Service and Management Organization	735298	819040
生活用电	**Electricity Consumption by Urban and Rural Households**	**1961174**	**2068692**
城镇居民	Urban Residents	1206993	1262698
乡村居民	Rural Residents	754181	805994

5-8 主要年份环境保护基本情况

项 目	Item	1995
市区二氧化硫年日平均值 （毫克/立方米）	**Daily Mean Value of SO_2 in Urban Area (mg/m^3)**	**0.059**
市区二氧化氮年日平均值 （毫克/立方米）	Daily Mean Value of NO_2 in Urban Area (mg/m^3)	
市区可吸入颗粒平均浓度 （毫克/立方米）	Annual Concentration of Breathable Particular Matter (mg/m^3)	
市区PM2.5平均浓度 （毫克/立方米）	PM2.5 Average Concentrations in Urban Area (mg/m^3)	
降水PH值	The PH Value of the Precipitation	3.65
酸雨频率 (%)	Frequency of Acid Rain (%)	73.40
环境空气质量优良天数 （天）	The Number of Days of Good Air Quality (day)	
环境空气质量优良率 (%)	The Rate of Good Air Quality (%)	
废水排放总量 （万吨）	**Volume of Waste Water Discharged (10000 tons)**	**91267**
工业废水排放量	Volume of Industrial Waste Water Discharged	30930
生活污水排放量	Volume of Living Waste Water Discharged	60337
工业废水排放达标量 （万吨）	Volume of Industrial Waste Water up to the Discharge Standards (10000 tons)	19685
工业废水排放达标率 (%)	Percentage of Industrial Waste Water up to the Discharge Standards (%)	63.64
工业废气排放总量 （亿立方米）	**Volume of Industrial Waste Gas Emission (100 million cu.m)**	**1871.61**
二氧化硫排放量 （万吨）	Volume of Sulphur Dioxide Emission (10000 tons)	14.09
工 业	Industry	14.09
生 活	Living	
工业烟粉尘排放量 （万吨）	Volume of Industrial Soot and Dust Emission (10000 tons)	3.09
建成烟尘控制区数 （个）	**Number of Soot Control Zones Established (unit)**	
建成烟尘控制区面积 （平方公里）	Area of Soot Control Zones Established (sq.km)	
一般工业固体废物产生量 （万吨）	**Volume of General Industrial Solid Wastes Produced (10000 tons)**	**313.00**
一般工业固体废物综合利用量	Volume of Comprehensive Utilization of General Industrial Solid Wastes	224.00
一般工业固体废物综合利用率 (%)	Comprehensive Utilization Rate of General Industrial Solid Wastes (%)	71.30
危险废物产生量 （万吨）	**Volume of Hazardous Wastes Produced (10000 tons)**	
道路交通噪声昼间平均等效声级 （分贝）	**Day-time Average Equivalent Sound Level of Road Traffic Noise (decibel)**	**72.60**

注：1. 从2012年起市环保局不再统计工业废水排放达标量、工业废水排放达标率、建成烟尘控制区数、建成烟尘控制区面积4个指标。
2. 从2013年起广州市全面实施新的环境空气质量标准(GB3095—2012)，环境空气质量优良天数和环境空气质量优良率依据二氧化硫、二氧化氮、可吸入颗粒物、细颗粒物、一氧化碳和臭氧等6项指标进行评价。
3. 废水排放总量从2013年起统计口径调整为包含工业废水排放量、城镇生活污水排放量和集中式治理设施废水排放量(不包括污水处理厂)。
4. 二氧化硫排放量从2013年起统计口径调整为包含工业二氧化硫排放量、生活二氧化硫排放量和集中式治理设施二氧化硫排放量。
5. 根据《环境噪声监测技术规范 城市声环境常规监测》(HJ 640—2012)关于道路交通噪声评价要求，从2014年起将“交通干线噪声平均值”指标修改为“道路交通噪声昼间平均等效声级”，指标内容不变。
6. 根据《环境空气质量标准》(GB3095—2012)等有关环境空气质量评价要求，增加指标“市区PM2.5平均浓度”。
7. 2010年(含)之前，“工业烟粉尘排放量”为“烟尘排放量”。
8. 2015年“一般工业固体废物综合利用量”包括了综合利用往年贮存量0.46万吨。

Fundamental State of Environment Protection in Main Year

2000	2005	2006	2007	2008	2009	2010	2011	2012	2013	2014	2015
0.045	**0.053**	**0.054**	**0.051**	**0.046**	**0.039**	**0.030**	**0.028**	**0.022**	**0.020**	**0.017**	**0.013**
0.061	0.068	0.067	0.065	0.056	0.056	0.050	0.049	0.049	0.052	0.048	0.047
	0.088	0.076	0.077	0.071	0.070	0.070	0.069	0.069	0.072	0.067	0.059
									0.053	0.049	0.039
4.71	4.34	4.41	4.42	4.47	4.74	5.06	5.20	5.24	5.34	5.21	5.24
62.30	81.40	75.40	82.60	77.80	60.50	50.70	42.00	40.60	23.70	40.50	38.40
	332	334	333	345	347	357	360	360	260	282	312
98.57	91.00	91.51	91.20	94.50	95.07	97.81	98.63	98.36	71.23	77.50	85.50
95434	**125837**	**128302**	**111491**	**126156**	**119317**	**125662**	**141521**	**152747**	**157843**	**161484**	**161905**
24123	20249	20445	21103	34475	26023	23604	24580	22716	22558	19181	18608
71311	105588	107858	90388	91681	93294	102059	116941	130031	135179	142149	143112
21732	19449	19629	20102	33045	25116	22828	23916				
90.09	96.05	96.01	95.25	95.85	96.51	96.72	97.30				
1959.16	**2342.16**	**2126.49**	**1994.63**	**2435.84**	**2539.47**	**3155.59**	**4120.19**	**3646.58**	**3753.74**	**3737.21**	**3550.92**
19.58	14.94	12.92	10.53	9.99	9.05	7.85	6.83	6.66	6.57	5.89	5.02
19.21	14.50	12.48	10.09	9.55	8.61	7.41	6.59	6.42	6.33	5.65	4.78
0.37	0.44	0.44	0.44	0.44	0.44	0.44	0.24	0.24	0.24	0.24	0.24
4.69	1.79	1.80	1.79	1.86	1.38	1.13	1.53	1.26	1.10	1.00	0.92
	14	**14**	**13**	**13**	**15**	**15**	**15**				
284.60	441.61	470.82	779.86	908.62	895.00	927.10	952.03				
346.80	**540.36**	**632.30**	**609.03**	**661.56**	**641.84**	**691.79**	**659.34**	**614.85**	**555.56**	**495.88**	**463.38**
285.30	520.25	605.46	592.13	605.65	597.95	621.91	625.53	588.98	528.89	468.47	441.35
83.48	91.23	91.13	100.00	91.24	92.35	89.75	94.87	95.70	95.17	94.47	95.15
18.30	**22.48**	**18.43**	**20.39**	**16.38**	**22.59**	**24.54**	**30.30**	**29.78**	**38.55**	**46.50**	**50.52**
69.10	**69.30**	**69.40**	**69.20**	**69.10**	**69.20**	**69.10**	**68.90**	**68.90**	**68.80**	**68.90**	**69.00**

Note: Ⅰ. Since 2012,Guangzhou Municipal Bureau of Environmental Protection has canceled the following items:Volume of Industrial Waste Water Discharged, Percentage of Industrial Waste Water up to the Discharge Standards, Number of Soot Control Zones Established and Area of Soot Control Zones Established.

Ⅱ. Since 2013, new environment air quality standard (GB3095-2012) has been implemented in Guangzhou. The Number of Days of Good Air Quality and The Rate of Good Air Quality are tested on the basis of the following items : Sulfur dioxide, Nitrogen dioxide, TSP, PM, carbon monoxide,ozone.

Ⅲ. Since 2013,Volume of Waste Water Discharged statistic scope has been adjusted.The scope includes Volume of Industrial Waste Water Discharged, Volume of Living Waste Water Discharged and Volume of Waste Water Discharged of centralized facilities.

Ⅳ. Since 2013, Volume of Sulphur Dioxide Emission statistic scope has been adjusted. The scope includes Volume of Industry Sulphur Dioxide Emission, Volume of Living Sulphur Dioxide Emission and Volume of Sulphur Dioxide Emission of centralized facilities.

Ⅴ. Since 2014,the index "Average of Main Road Noise" has been renamed as "Day-time Average Equivalent Sound Level of Road Traffic Noise according to "Technical Specifications for Environmental Noise Monitoring Routine Monitoring for Urban Environmental Noise"(HJ 640-2012).

Ⅵ. There adds an index of " PM2.5 Average Concentrations in Urban area" according to "Ambient Air Quality Standards "(GB3095-2012).

Ⅶ. The statistical coverage of data of "Volume of Industrial Soot and Dust Emission" of year 2010 and before is "Soot and Dust Emission".

Ⅷ. The data of "Volume of Comprehensive Utilization of General Industrial Solid Wastes" of year 2015 includes utilizing the stocks of industrial solid wastes of the previous year .

5-9 环境保护基本情况

Fundamental State of Environment Protection

项　　目	Item	2016	2017	2018	2019
水环境	**Water Environment**				
降水量 (毫米)	Precipitation (mm)	2448.6	1846.9	1820.7	2306.2
水资源总量 (亿立方米)	Total Amount of Water Resource (100 million cu.m)	105.35	77.32	74.76	99.30
人均水资源量 (立方米/人)	Per Capita Water Resources (cu.m/person)	750.17	533.30	501.57	648.76
用水总量 (亿立方米)	Water Use (100 million cu.m)	64.53	65.39	64.39	62.25
# 农业用水	Agriculture	10.55	11.06	10.95	10.69
工业用水	Industry	36.46	36.49	34.79	32.78
生活用水	Consumption	16.62	16.89	17.70	17.80
生态环境补水	Ecological Protection	0.90	0.95	0.95	0.98
废水排放总量 (万吨)	Total Waste Water Discharged (10000 tons)	161111	172658	155630	163593
# 工业废水排放量	Industrial Waste Water Discharged	19326	20605	14031	14019
城镇生活污水排放量	Urban Living Waste Discharged	141562	151795	141414	149426
大气环境	**Atomospheric Environment**				
二氧化硫平均浓度 (微克/立方米)	Average Concentration of Sulfur Dioxide (micrograms/m^3)	12	12	10	7
二氧化氮平均浓度 (微克/立方米)	Average Concentration of Nitrogen Dioxide (micrograms/m^3)	46	52	50	45
可吸入颗粒物平均浓度(微克/立方米)	Average Concentration of Inhalable Particles (micrograms/m^3)	56	56	54	53
PM2.5平均浓度 (微克/立方米)	Mean Concentration of PM2.5 (micrograms/m^3)	36	35	35	30
降水PH值	The PH Value of the Precipitation	5.42	5.96	5.84	5.79
酸雨频率 (%)	Frequency of Acid Rain (%)	29.4	12.7	9.1	15.4
环境空气质量达标天数 (天)	Up to Standard Days of the Environment Air Quality (day)	310	294	294	293
环境空气质量达标率 (%)	Up to Standard Rate of Air Environmental Quality (%)	84.7	80.5	80.5	80.3
工业废气排放总量 (亿立方米)	Volume of Industrial Waste Gas Emission (100 million cu.m)	4075.23	4131.49	4132.17	4710.44
二氧化硫排放量 (万吨)	Volume of Sulphur Dioxide Emission (10000 tons)	2.08	1.54	0.52	0.40
# 工业二氧化硫排放量	Industry	2.07	1.53	0.51	0.39
氮氧化物排放量 (万吨)	Volume of Nitrogen Dioxide Emission (10000 tons)	7.23	1.92	1.72	1.67
# 工业氮氧化物排放量	Industry	2.09	1.89	1.66	1.60
烟(粉)尘排放量 (万吨)	Volume of Soot and Dust Emission (10000 tons)	1.29	0.87	0.81	1.07
# 工业烟粉尘排放量	Volume of Industrial Soot and Dust Emission	0.90	0.86	0.81	1.06
固体废物	**Solid Wastes**				
一般工业固体废物产生量 (万吨)	Volume of General Industrial Solid Wastes Produced (10000 tons)	509.92	535.21	598.26	623.11
一般工业固体废物综合利用量 (万吨)	Volume of Comprehensive Utilization of General Industrial Solid Wastes (10000 tons)	492.06	511.28	485.54	596.05
一般工业固体废物综合利用率 (%)	Comprehensive Utilization Rate of General Industrial Solid Wastes (%)	96.48	95.10	81.10	95.37
危险废物产生量 (万吨)	Volume of Hazardous Wastes Produced (10000 tons)	57.22	55.89	59.79	60.61

5-9 续表 continued

项　　目	Item	2016	2017	2018	2019
生态环境	**Ecological Environment**				
人均耕地面积 (亩/人)	Per Capita Area of Cultivated land (mu)	0.09	0.08	0.08	/
累计水土流失治理面积 (千公顷)	Accumulated Area of Soil Erosion Control (1000 hectares)	5.5	11.3	18.1	23.9
自然保护区数 (个)	Number of Natural Reserves (unit)	5	5	6	6
自然保护区面积 (万公顷)	Area of Natural Reserves (1000 hectares)	0.96	0.96	0.97	0.97
自然灾害	**Natural Disasters**				
地质灾害次数 (次)	Geological Disasters (unit)	21	58	37	46
地质灾害直接经济损失 (万元)	Direct Economic Losses (unit)	97	574	206	133
森林火灾次数 (次)	Forest Fires (unit)	7	17	67	32
城市环境	**City Environment**				
城区面积 (平方公里)	Urban Area (sq.km)	2099.20	2099.20	2099.20	2202.03
城市建设用地面积 (平方公里)	Urban Construction Area (sq.km)	728.54	733.00	741.08	/
城市供水总量 (亿立方米)	Urban Water Supply (10000 cu.m)	22.89	23.81	24.81	25.46
#生活用水量	Consumption	15.46	16.04	16.65	17.20
污水处理厂集中处理率 (%)	Centralized Treatment Rate of Sewage Treatment Plant (%)	94.2	95.0	95.5	97.0
道路交通噪声昼间平均等效声级(分贝)	Average Diurnal Equivalent Sound Level of Road Traffic Noise (decibels)	69.0	69.0	68.9	69.3
农村环境	**Rural Environment**				
农村自来水普及率 (%)	Rural Water Supply Popularizing Rate (%)	100.00	100.00	100.00	100.00
农村卫生户厕普及率 (%)	Rural Sanitary Latrine per Unit Popularizing Rate (%)	99.52	99.76	99.80	100.00

注：1. 从2016年起根据《环境空气质量标准》(GB3095—2012)等有关环境空气质量评价要求：

1) 市区二氧化硫年日平均值、市区二氧化氮年日平均值、市区可吸入颗粒平均浓度、市区PM2.5平均浓度4个指标分别修改为二氧化硫平均浓度、二氧化氮平均浓度、可吸入颗粒物平均浓度、PM2.5平均浓度；且单位毫克/立方米均修改为微克/立方米。

2) 环境空气质量优良天数修改为环境空气质量达标天数。

3) 环境空气质量优良率修改为环境空气质量达标率。

2. 从2018年起危险废物产生量为工业源数据。

3. 2019年环境保护中废水、废气、固体废物等指标为快报数。

4. 森林火灾次数指标从2018年起统计范围为发生森林火灾的情况均统计。

5. 人均耕地面积和城市建设用地面积因第三次全国土地调查尚未全面完成，数据暂缺。

Note: I. According to the Environmental Air quality Standards (GB3095-2012) and other relevant environmental air quality evaluation requirements:

I) The annual daily average of sulfur dioxide in urban area,the annual daily average of nitrogen dioxide in urban area,the average concentration of inhalable particles in urban area and the average concentration of PM2.5 in urban area were revised to mean concentration of sulfur dioxide and nitrogen dioxide, respectively. The mean concentration of inhalable particulate matter and PM2.5; And unit milligram/cubic meter is revised to microgram /cubic meter.

II) The number of good days of ambient air quality has been revised to the number of days when the quality of ambient air has reached the standard.

III) The ambient air quality rate is modified to the ambient air quality standard rate.

II. The data of Forest Fires in 2018 includes all the forest fires.

III. The data of Waste Water ,Waste Gas and Solid Wastes in 2019 is from quick statistics data.

IV. The statistical coverage of Forest Fires has included all kinds of forest fires since 2018.

V. The per capita arable land area and urban construction land area are temporarily missing because the Third National Land Survey has not been fully completed.

【能源消费总量】是指一定地域内，全国（地区）国民经济各行业和居民家庭在一定时间消费的各种能源的总和。包括：原煤、原油、天然气、水能、核能、风能、太阳能、地热能、生物质能等一次能源；一次能源通过加工转换产生的洗煤、焦炭、煤气、电力、热力、成品油等二次能源和同时产生的其它产品；其他化石能源、可再生能源和新能源。其中水能、风能、太阳能、地热能、生物质能等可再生能源，是指人们通过一定技术手段获得的，并作为商品能源使用的部分。在核算过程中，一次能源、二次能源消费不能重复计算。能源消费总量分为终端能源消费量、能源加工转换损失量和能源损失量三部分。

（1）终端能源消费量：指一定时期内，全国（地区）生产和生活消费的各种能源在扣除了用于加工转换二次能源消费量和损失量以后的数量。

（2）能源加工转换损失量：指一定时期内，全国（地区）投入加工转换的各种能源数量之和与产出各种能源产品之和的差额。该指标是观察能源在加工转换过程中损失量变化的指标。

（3）能源损失量：指在一定时期内，能源在输送、分配、储存过程中发生的损失和由客观原因造成的各种损失量，不包括各种气体能源放空、放散量。

【废水排放总量】为工业废水排放量、城镇生活污水排放量和集中式治理设施污水排放量之和。

【工业废水排放量】指报告期内经过企业厂区所有排放口排到企业外部的工业废水量。包括生产废水、外排的直接冷却水、超标排放的矿井地下水和与工业废水混排的厂区生活污水，不包括外排的间接冷却水（清污不分流的间接冷却水应计算在废水排放量内）。

【一般工业固体废物产生量】指未被列入《国家危险废物名录》或者根据国家规定的危险废物鉴别标准（GB5085）、固体废物浸出毒性浸出方法（GB5086)及固体废物浸出毒性测定方法（GB/T 15555）鉴定方法判定不具有危险特性的工业固体废物。

【一般工业固体废物综合利用量】报告期内企业通过回收、加工、循环、交换等方式，从固体废物中提取或者使其转化为可以利用的资源、能源和其他原材料的固体废物量（包括当年利用的往年工业固体废物累计贮存量）。如用作农业肥料、生产建筑材料、筑路等。

【Total Energy Consumption】refers to the total consumption of energy of various kinds by the production sectors of the economy and the households in a given period of time. It includes the primary kinds of energy such as coal, crude oil, natural gas, hydro-power, nuclear power, wind power, solar power, geothermal power and bio-energy; the secondary kinds of energy and their products which are transformed from the primary energy such as washed coal, coke, coal gas, electricity, heating, and petroleum products; and other kinds of fossil energy, renewable energy and new energy. The renewable energy, including hydro-power, wind power, solar power, geothermal power and bio-energy, refers to the part attained with some given technical means and used for commercial purposes. Total energy consumption can be divided into three parts: end-use energy consumption; loss during the process of energy conversion; and energy loss.

(1) End-use Energy Consumption: It refers to the total energy consumption by the production sectors and the households in the country (region) in a given period of time. It does not include the consumption during the conversion of primary energy into secondary energy and the loss in the process of energy conversion.

(2) Loss During the Process of Energy Conversion: It refers to the total input of various kinds of energy for conversion, minus the total output of various kinds of energy in the country in a given period of time. It is an indicator to show the loss that occurs during the process of energy conversion.

(3) Energy Loss: It refers to the total of the loss of energy during the course of energy transport, distribution and storage and the loss caused by any objective reason in a given period of time. The loss of various kinds of gas due to gas discharges and stocktaking is not included.

【Total Volume of Waste Water Discharged】includes the total volume of industrial wastewater emissions, urban sewage and centralized sewage treatment facilities emissions.

【Volume of Industrial Waste Water Discharged】refers to the volume of industrial waste water discharged ,through all outlets to the outside of industrial enterprises in the reference period, including waste water produced, direct cooling water, underground water from mines that does not meet the standard of discharge, and the domestic sewage mixed up with industrial waste water when discharged, but excluding discharged indirect cooling water. (the indirect cooling water that clear water and turbid water is not divided should be included in total volume of waste water discharged)

【Volume of General Industrial Solid Wastes Produced】refers not included in the “National List of Hazardous Waste”or in accordance with state hazardous waste identification standard(GB5085),solid waste leaching toxicity method(GB5086)and solid waste leaching toxicity determination method(GB/T 15555)identification of characteristics is determined not to be hazardous industrial solid waste.

【Volume of General Industrial Solid Wastes Utilized in a Comprehensive Way】refers to the volume of solid wastes from which useful materials can be extracted or which can be converted into usable resources, energy or other materials by means of reclamation, processing, recycling and exchange(including utilizing in the year the stocks of industrial solid wastes of the previous year). Examples of such utilizations include fertilizers, building materials and road materials.

第六篇 CHAPTER 6

财政和金融

GOVERNMENT FINANCE AND BANKING

第六篇　财政和金融

一、本篇资料的主要内容

本篇反映广州市财政、金融方面的基本情况。包括以下五个部分：1.财政收支情况；2.金融机构的存贷款情况；3.资本市场的业务情况；4.保险业务情况；5.外资金融机构及代表处一览表等。

二、本篇各部分的资料来源

1．财政收支资料根据广州市财政局财政总决算报表等统计报表的有关项目加工整理；

2．金融机构存贷款资料由中国人民银行广州分行营业管理部提供；

3．保险业务、外资保险公司及外资银行代表处资料由中国银行保险监督管理委员会广东监管局提供；

4．资本市场资料由中国证券业监督管理委员会广东监管局提供；

三、本篇资料由广州市统计局国民经济核算处负责整理

6 Government Finance and Banking

Ⅰ. The main contents of this chapter reflect the basic financial and financial situation of Guangzhou. Including the following five parts: FIinancial revenue and expenditure; The deposit and loan situation of financial institutions; Capital market operations;Insurance business List of foreign financial institutions and representative offices.

Ⅱ. Data sources of each part of this chapter

1. The data of financial revenue and expenditure is processed according to the statistical statements of Guangzhou Municipal Bureau of Finance General accounts of Finance and other statistical statements;

2. The data on deposits and loans of financial institutions is provided by the Business Administration Department of the Guangzhou Branch of the Bank of China;

3. The information of insurance business, foreign insurance companies and representative offices of foreign banks is provided by the China Banking and Insurance Regulatory Commission;

4. The capital market information is provided by Guangdong Supervision Bureau of China Securities Regulatory Commission.

Ⅲ.The data of this chapter are collated by the Department of National accounts of Guangzhou Bureau of Statistics.

6-1 财政和金融业主要经济指标

Main Indicators of Government Finance and Financial Intermediation

项　　目	Item	2018	2019	2019年比2018年增长(%) Growth Rate in 2019 over 2018 (%)
地方财政收入 (万元)	Revenue of Local Government (10000 yuan)	31737500	33678876	6.1
一般公共预算收入	General Budgetary Revenue	16342242	16990383	4.0
# 增值税	Value-added Tax	4383714	4299666	-1.9
企业所得税	Corporate Income Tax	2064211	2126665	3.0
个人所得税	Individual Income Tax	1044782	742215	-29.0
政府性基金收入	Governmental Funds Revenue	15395258	16688493	8.4
地方财政支出 (万元)	Expenditure of Local Government (10000 yuan)	39488632	44564819	12.9
一般公共预算支出	General Budgetary Expenditure	25061818	28653263	14.3
# 一般公共服务支出	General Public Expenditure	2378855	2874620	20.8
教育支出	Operating Expenses for Education	4408209	5239743	18.9
科学技术支出	Operating Expenses for Science and Technology	1636655	2439456	49.1
卫生健康支出	Operating Expenses for Medical and Health	2243298	2461764	9.7
政府性基金支出	Governmental Fund Expenditure	14426814	15911556	10.3
金融机构本外币各项存款余额 (亿元)	Balance of Savings Deposit in Standard and Foreign Currencies in Financial Institutions (100 million yuan)	54788.09	59131.20	7.9
# 人民币	RMB	52647.47	56701.75	7.7
# 住户存款余额	Deposits of Households	16042.06	17980.56	12.1
金融机构本外币各项贷款余额 (亿元)	Balance of Loan in Standard and Foreign Currencies in Financial Institutions (100 million yuan)	40749.32	47103.31	15.6
# 人民币	RMB	39764.44	46155.78	16.1
国内财产保险公司业务	Domestic Property Insurance Companies			
保险金额 (亿元)	Amount Insured (100 million yuan)	6431689	9774110	52.0
原保险保费收入 (万元)	Premium of Primary Insurance (10000 yuan)	3177356	3847323	21.1
赔款支出 (万元)	Indemnity Expenditure (10000 yuan)	1732398	1883838	8.7
国内人身保险公司业务	Domestic Life Insurance Companies			
原保险保费收入 (万元)	Premium of Primary Insurance (10000 yuan)	8451258	10401014	23.1
期满给付 (万元)	Mature Payment (10000 yuan)	694042	913722	31.7
死伤医疗给付 (万元)	Payment for Death, Injury and Medical Treatment (10000 yuan)	183909	241909	31.5

注：2019年起一般公共预算支出中的“医疗卫生与计划生育支出”改为“卫生健康支出”。

Note: Since 2019, the term "Expenditure for Medical and Health and Family Planning" is replaced by "Operating Expenses for Medical and Health" in the General Budgetary Expenditure.

6-2 主要年份地方财政收支

Local Government Revenue and Expenditure in Main Years

单位:亿元 (100 million yuan)

年份 year	地方财政收入 Revenue of Local Government	#一般公共预算收入 General Budgetary Revenue	地方财政支出 Expenditure of Local Government	#一般公共预算支出 General Budgetary Expenditure
1978	14.01	13.65	4.40	3.87
1979	13.64	13.12	4.47	4.16
1980	16.29	15.43	4.98	4.35
1985	30.18	28.85	11.82	10.75
1986	32.44	31.15	16.27	15.23
1987	35.24	34.18	16.45	15.13
1988	41.37	39.71	21.52	19.95
1989	47.23	46.51	25.41	24.66
1990	37.82	36.94	25.12	24.31
1991	49.62	48.49	32.16	30.71
1992	52.92	51.35	33.79	32.25
1993	79.27	77.37	55.19	53.82
1994	64.87	62.87	75.77	73.74
1995	99.75	97.08	112.78	111.24
1996	88.11	85.24	125.12	121.91
1997	106.07	97.72	146.92	138.99
1998	137.32	132.19	179.61	175.11
1999	188.14	176.15	231.09	222.37
2000	219.91	200.55	258.60	240.72
2001	271.91	246.19	314.98	292.63
2002	269.10	245.87	350.19	326.67
2003	300.55	274.77	395.52	370.09
2004	338.45	302.87	447.06	408.34
2005	408.85	371.26	476.28	438.41
2006	476.72	427.08	559.42	506.79
2007	838.99	523.79	850.01	623.69
2008	843.14	621.84	997.94	713.35
2009	1107.66	702.65	1059.50	789.92
2010	1399.16	872.65	1487.16	977.32
2011	1535.14	979.48	1793.35	1181.25
2012	1579.68	1102.40	1796.91	1343.65
2013	2088.14	1141.80	2283.51	1386.13
2014	2318.84	1243.10	2525.38	1436.22
2015	2391.33	1349.47	2641.02	1727.72
2016	2218.48	1393.64	2845.66	1943.75
2017	2844.83	1536.74	3484.70	2186.01
2018	3173.75	1634.22	3948.86	2506.18
2019	3367.89	1699.04	4456.48	2865.33

6-3 地方财政收入

Revenue of Local Government

单位:万元 (10000 yuan)

项　　目	Item	2018	2019
地方财政收入合计	Total Revenue of Local Government	31737500	33678876
一般公共预算收入	General Budgetary Revenue	16342242	16990383
# 增值税	Value-added Tax	4383714	4299666
企业所得税	Corporate Income Tax	2064211	2126665
个人所得税	Individual Income Tax	1044782	742215
城市维护建设税	City Maintenance and Construction Tax	1428792	1382988
房产税	House Property Tax	1022161	1145324
印花税	Stamp Tax	396767	420593
城镇土地使用税	Urban Land Use Tax	215632	143936
车船税	Tax on Vehicles and Boat Operation	140915	149301
契　税	Deed Tax	1337934	1500769
国有资本经营收入	Operation Income of State-owned Assets		
行政事业性收费收入	Charge of Administrative and Institutional Units	258806	301669
罚没收入	Penalty Receipts	331751	405374
专项收入	Special Revenue	1332088	1399324
其他收入	Others	840156	904292
政府性基金收入	Revenue from Government-controlled Funds	15395258	16688493
附:上级补助收入	Subsidies from Higher Levels Taxed Tax Return	4890804	5245636
# 消费税和增值税税收返还收入	Consumption Tax and Value-added	406982	406982
所得税基数返还收入	Tax Base Return	404972	406258

6-4 地方财政支出

Expenditure of Local Government

单位:万元 (10000 yuan)

项　　目	Item	2018	2019
地方财政支出合计	Total Expenditure of Local Government	39488632	44564819
一般公共预算支出	General Budgetary Expenditure	25061818	28653263
# 一般公共服务支出	Expenditure for General Public Services	2378855	2874620
国防支出	Expenditure for National Defense	10863	11293
公共安全支出	Expenditure for Public Security	2334170	2404690
教育支出	Expenditure for Education	4408209	5239743
科学技术支出	Expenditure for Science and Technology	1636655	2439456
文化旅游体育与传媒支出	Expenditure for Culture, Tourism, Sports and Media	471352	526666
社会保障和就业支出	Expenditure for Social Safety Net and Employment Effort	2654619	2959326
卫生健康支出	Expenditure for Medical and Health	2243298	2461764
城乡社区支出	Expenditure for Urban and Rural Community Affairs	4152934	4552926
农林水支出	Expenditure for Agriculture, Forestry and Water Conservancy	856899	940700
交通运输支出	Expenditure for Transportation	502772	393201
资源勘探信息等支出	Expenditure for Affairs of Exploration, Power and Information	735772	459833
商业服务业等支出	Expenditure for Affairs of Commerce and Services	149796	157418
金融支出	Expenditure for Affairs of Financial Supervision	90297	99846
援助其他地区支出	Expenditure for Post-earthquake Recovery and Reconstruction	235617	140384
住房保障支出	Expenditure for Affairs of Housing Security	1319017	1313858
其他支出	Other Expenditures	57346	80689
政府性基金支出	Expenditure for Government-controlled Funds	14426814	15911556
附:上解上级支出	Expenditure for Cental and Provincial Governments	498085	1235903

6-5 主要年份金融机构(含外资)存贷款余额

Deposits and Loans in All Financial Institutions (Foreign Currencies)in Main Years

单位：亿元 (100 million yuan)

年 份 year	金融机构 本 外 币 存款余额 Deposits in Renminbi and Foreign Currencies in All Financial Institutions	#人民币 存款余额 Deposits in Renminbi Currencies in Financial Institutions	金融机构 本 外 币 贷款余额 Loans Institutions in Renminbi and Foreign Currencies in Financial Institutions	#人民币 贷款余额 Loans in Renminbi Currencies in Financial Institutions
1978		25.56		26.04
1979		31.02		26.97
1980		43.73		40.25
1981		49.19		47.04
1982		56.22		53.50
1983		64.31		59.11
1984		87.91		93.60
1985		100.72		105.19
1986		141.49		142.95
1987		203.74		211.58
1988		260.54		265.08
1989		325.47		359.28
1990		440.47		420.38
1991		601.91		491.13
1992		871.44		651.21
1993		1085.96		835.60
1994		1439.01		984.48
1995		2001.96		1312.15
1996		2712.98		1605.22
1997		3497.65		2166.01
1998		4103.45		2502.12
1999		4823.87		3435.71
2000		5545.19		3895.49
2001		6228.04		4336.50
2002		7498.35		5257.21
2003		8676.72		6127.27
2004		9613.57		6535.39
2005		11085.30		6908.03
2006		12731.23		7931.78
2007	14783.46	14309.71	9661.38	8737.05
2008	16929.47	16421.05	11079.55	10304.73
2009	20944.19	20401.72	13851.83	12598.16
2010	23953.96	23384.50	16284.31	14987.73
2011	26460.80	25791.70	17732.88	16333.43
2012	30186.57	29006.99	19936.52	18023.02
2013	33838.20	32850.57	22016.18	20172.97
2014	35469.29	34170.66	24231.71	22688.33
2015	42843.67	41574.49	27296.16	26136.95
2016	47530.20	45937.34	29669.82	28885.54
2017	51369.03	49332.53	34137.05	33312.73
2018	54788.09	52647.47	40749.32	39764.44
2019	59131.20	56701.75	47103.31	46155.78

6-6 中外资金融机构本外币存贷款年末余额

Deposits and Loans in Renminbi and Foreign Currencies of All Financial Institutions at Year-end

单位:亿元 (100 million yuan)

项目	Item	2018	2019
各项存款余额	**Total Deposits**	**54788.09**	**59131.20**
一、境内存款	Domestic Deposits	52977.89	57050.34
(一) 住户存款	Deposits of Households	16456.56	18383.44
(二) 非金融企业存款	Deposits of Non-financial Enterprises	19100.21	20258.63
(三) 机关团体存款	Deposits of Government Departments & Organizations	8304.53	9643.85
(四) 财政性存款	Fiscal Deposits	1342.23	805.72
(五) 非银行业金融机构存款	Deposits of Non-banking Financial Institutions	7774.35	7958.70
二、境外存款	Overseas Deposits	1810.21	2080.86
各项贷款余额	**Total Loans**	**40749.32**	**47103.31**
一、境内贷款	Domestic Loans	40192.94	46372.77
(一) 住户贷款	Loans to Households	16776.46	19107.25
(二) 非金融企业存款及机关团体贷款	Loans to Non-financial Enterprises and Government Departments & Organizations	23361.69	27008.73
1. 短期贷款	Short-term loans	5854.01	6132.64
2. 中长期贷款	Medium & Long-term Loans	15978.46	18748.26
3. 票据融资	Paper Financing	1367.91	1943.00
4. 融资租赁	Financial Leasing	155.43	176.00
5. 各项垫款	Total Advances	5.87	8.83
(三) 非银行业金融机构贷款	Loans to Non-banking Financial Institutions	54.79	256.79
二、境外贷款	Overseas Loans	556.37	730.54

6-7 中外资金融机构外币存贷款年末余额

Deposits and Loans in Foreign Currencies of All Financial Institutions at Year-end

单位:亿美元 (100 million USD)

项　目	Item	2018	2019
各项存款余额	**Total Deposits**	**311.90**	**348.25**
一、境内存款	Domestic Deposits	137.78	132.31
(一) 住户存款	Deposits of Households	60.39	57.75
(二) 非金融企业存款	Deposits of Non-financial Enterprises	69.43	64.01
(四) 机关团体存款	Deposits of Government Departments & Organizations	1.22	1.47
(四) 财政性存款	Fiscal Deposits		
(五) 非银行业金融机构存款	Deposits of Non-banking Financial Institutions	6.74	9.07
二、境外存款	Overseas Deposits	174.12	215.94
各项贷款余额	**Total Loans**	**143.50**	**135.82**
一、境内贷款	Domestic Loans	87.78	59.14
(一) 住户贷款	Loans to Households	0.35	0.60
(二) 非金融企业存款及机关团体贷款	Loans to Non-financial Enterprises and Government Departments & Organizations	87.44	58.53
1. 短期贷款	Short-term loans	51.78	28.79
2. 中长期贷款	Medium & Long-term Loans	35.66	29.74
3. 票据融资	Paper Financing	…	…
4. 融资租赁	Financial Leasing		
5. 各项垫款	Total Advances	…	…
(三) 非银行业金融机构贷款	Loans to Non-banking Financial Institutions		
二、境外贷款	Overseas Loans	55.72	76.69

6-8 中外资金融机构存贷款年末余额(折人民币，2008-2019年)

Deposits and Loans of All Financial Institutions at Year-end (converted into RMB, at the end of year from 2008 to 2019)

单位：亿元 (100 million yuan)

项目	Item	2008	2009	2010	2011	2012
存款余额（折人民币）	Saving Deposits Balance (as RMB)	16929.47	20944.19	23953.96	26460.80	30186.57
中资金融机构	Chinese Financial Institutions					
人民币	RMB	16219.23	20081.46	22775.50	25048.61	28270.68
外汇（亿美元）	Foreign Exchange (USD 100 million)	63.11	63.67	68.09	86.82	166.36
外资金融机构	Foreign-funded Financial Institutions					
人民币	RMB	201.82	320.26	609.00	743.08	736.31
外汇（亿美元）	Foreign Exchange (USD 100 million)	11.27	15.77	17.90	19.38	21.31
贷款余额（折人民币）	Loans Balance (as RMB)	11079.55	13851.83	16284.31	17732.88	19936.52
中资金融机构	Chinese Financial Institutions					
人民币	RMB	10042.19	12316.01	14597.74	15904.65	17554.90
外汇（亿美元）	Foreign Exchange (USD 100 million)	88.10	153.88	160.92	187.33	271.91
外资金融机构	Foreign-funded Financial Institutions					
人民币	RMB	262.54	282.15	389.99	428.79	468.12
外汇（亿美元）	Foreign Exchange (USD 100 million)	26.15	29.72	34.86	34.78	32.52

6-8 续表 continued

单位:亿元 (100 million yuan)

项目	Item	2013	2014	2015	2016	2017	2018	2019
存款余额（折人民币）	Saving Deposits Balance (as RMB)	33838.20	35469.29	42843.67	47530.20	51369.03	54788.09	59131.20
中资金融机构	Chinese Financial Institutions							
人民币	RMB	31884.74	33215.35	40732.02	44978.42	48290.54	51336.03	55275.71
外汇（亿美元）	Foreign Exchange (USD 100 million)	143.82	193.55	175.25	206.65	285.24	286.24	318.92
外资金融机构	Foreign-funded Financial Institutions							
人民币	RMB	965.83	955.31	844.97	963.91	1044.08	1319.81	1442.32
外汇（亿美元）	Foreign Exchange (USD 100 million)	18.17	18.68	20.20	22.97	26.43	25.66	29.33
贷款余额（折人民币）	Loans Balance (as RMB)	22016.18	24231.71	27296.16	29669.82	34137.05	40749.32	47103.31
中资金融机构	Chinese Financial Institutions							
人民币	RMB	19652.37	22154.37	25540.40	28283.46	32571.07	38871.63	45122.08
外汇（亿美元）	Foreign Exchange (USD 100 million)	260.66	214.50	156.47	96.85	104.99	120.66	111.37
外资金融机构	Foreign-funded Financial Institutions							
人民币	RMB	520.60	533.95	622.85	651.60	787.53	959.68	1085.73
外汇（亿美元）	Foreign Exchange (USD 100 million)	41.66	37.73	22.75	16.26	21.27	22.98	24.79

6-9 中外资金融机构人民币信贷资金平衡表
Credit Funds Balance Sheet of Financial Institutions

单位:亿元 (100 million yuan)

项　　目	Item	2018	2019
资金来源项目	**Sources of Funds**		
合　计	Total	59798.38	63904.09
一、各项存款	Total Deposits	52647.47	56701.75
(一) 境内存款	Domestic Deposits	52032.28	56127.35
1. 住户存款	Deposits of Households	16042.06	17980.56
2. 非金融企业存款	Deposits of Non-financial Enterprises	18623.73	19812.10
3. 机关团体存款	Deposits of Government Departments & Organizations	8296.14	9633.58
4. 财政性存款	Fiscal Deposits	1342.23	805.72
5. 非银行业金融机构存款	Deposits of Non-banking Financial Institutions	7728.12	7895.40
(二) 境外存款	Overseas Deposits	615.19	574.40
二、金融债券	Financial Bonds	800.31	764.58
三、卖出回购资产	Repo	73.65	61.62
四、借款及非银行业金融机构拆入	Borrowings & Placements from Non-depository Financial Institutions	67.73	116.12
五、联行往来(净)	Inter-bank Transaction		
六、应付及暂收款	Payable and Suspense Credit	1405.27	1377.65
七、各项准备	All Reserves	975.81	1169.69
八、所有者权益	Creditors' Equity	3201.28	4084.12
九、其　他	Others	626.86	-371.44
资金运用项目	**Uses of Funds**		
合　计	Total	59798.38	63904.09
一、各项贷款	Total Loans	39764.44	46155.78
(一) 境内贷款	Domestic Loans	39590.47	45960.22
1. 住户贷款	Loans to Households	16774.07	19103.03
2. 非金融企业及机关团体贷款	Loans to Non-financial Enterprises andGovernment Departments & Organizations	22761.60	26600.39
3. 非银行业金融机构贷款	Loans to Non-banking Financial Institutions	54.79	256.79
(二) 境外贷款	Overseas Loans	173.97	195.56
二、债券投资	Portfolio Investments	6594.63	7182.59
三、股权及其他投资	Shares and Other Investments	4076.21	3811.74
四、买入返售资产	Reverse Repo	829.29	554.16
五、存放非银行业金融机构款项	Due From Non-depository Financial Institutions	56.80	49.88
六、联行往来(净)	Inter-bank Transaction	7346.52	5040.74
七、金银占款	Purchase of Gold & Silver		
八、中央银行外汇占款	Foreign Exchange		
九、应收及预付款	Receivables and Prepayments	787.15	767.12
十、投资性房地产	Investment Real Estate	19.43	20.25
十一、 固定资产	Fixed Asset	323.91	321.82

6-10 中资金融机构人民币各项存贷款年末余额
Deposits and Loans in Renminbi of Chinese Financial Institutions at Year-end

单位:亿元 (100 million yuan)

项目	Item	2018	2019
各项存款余额	**Total Deposits**	**51336.03**	**55275.71**
一、境内存款	Domestic Deposits	50759.37	54740.89
（一）住户存款	Deposits of Households	15965.46	17903.24
（二）非金融企业存款	Deposits of Non-financial Enterprises	17576.16	18695.90
（三）机关团体存款	Deposits of Government Departments & Organizations	8233.65	9549.82
（四）财政性存款	Fiscal Deposits	1341.93	805.72
（五）非银行业金融机构存款	Deposits of Non-banking Financial Institutions	7642.17	7786.20
二、境外存款	Overseas Deposits	576.66	534.83
各项贷款余额	**Total Loans**	**38871.65**	**45122.08**
一、境内贷款	Domestic Loans	38701.06	44929.82
（一）住户贷款	Loans to Households	16686.57	19002.76
（二）非金融企业存款及机关团体贷款	Loans to Non-financial Enterprises and Government Departments & Organizations	21959.70	25670.27
1. 短期贷款	Short-term loans	5091.26	5478.47
2. 中长期贷款	Medium & Long-term Loans	15390.36	18105.84
3. 票据融资	Paper Financing	1316.98	1901.32
4. 融资租赁	Financial Leases	155.43	176.00
5. 各项垫款	Total Advances	5.67	8.64
（三）非银行业金融机构贷款	Loans to Non-banking Financial Institutions	54.79	256.79
二、境外贷款	Overseas Loans	170.59	192.26

6-11 上市公司及新三板概况（2011-2019年）
Listed Companies and NEEQ-listed Companies (2011-2019)

单位:家 (unit)

年份 Year	境内上市公司数量 Numbers of Domestic Listed Companies	主板上市公司 Main Board-Listed Companies	中小企业板上市公司 SME-Listed Companies	创业板上市公司 GEM-Listed Companies	科创板上市公司 TIB-Listed Companies	新三板公司 NEEQ-listed Companies
2011	53	26	20	7		
2012	61	27	24	10		
2013	60	26	24	10		
2014	62	26	26	10		35
2015	68	27	26	15		138
2016	78	31	28	19		347
2017	97	39	34	24		429
2018	98	39	33	26		393
2019	107	41	34	30	2	322

注：2019年起，境内上市公司新增科创板上市公司。
Note: From 2019, the domestic listed companies add new companies listed on the science and technology innovation board.

6-12 证券市场股票筹资概况(2011-2019年)
Equity Financing of Securities Market (2011-2019)

单位:亿元 (100 million yuan)

年 份 Year	股票筹资额 Equity Financing	IPO筹资 IPO financing	股票再筹资 Equity Re-financing
2011	213.59	40.18	173.41
2012	244.55	50.58	193.97
2013	57.30	…	57.30
2014	42.92	6.93	35.99
2015	616.40	24.48	591.92
2016	676.72	43.01	633.71
2017	508.72	137.45	371.27
2018	182.43	2.96	179.47
2019	70.15	67.43	2.72

6-13 证券市场交易额概况(2011-2019年)
Turnover of Securities Market (2011-2019)

单位：亿元 (100 million yuan)

年 份 Year	证券市场交易额 Turnover of Securities Market	# 股票交易 Turnover of Stock Trading
2011	38170.94	31393.64
2012	31558.13	21898.72
2013	48320.55	30858.05
2014	74196.95	49514.63
2015	217238.20	171139.46
2016	141833.54	81611.10
2017	153625.46	71038.98
2018	131665.66	53231.50
2019	150687.72	76241.97

6-14 主要年份原保险保费收入和赔款及给付支出

Premium of Primary Insurance and Payment in Main Years

年 份 Year	原保险保费收入 (万元) Premium of Primary Insurance (10000 yuan)	赔款及给付支出 (万元) Claim and Payment (10000 yuan)	赔款率 (%) Indemnity and Payment Ratio (%)
1980	197		
1985	5043	1153	22.86
1986	8654	3117	36.02
1987	14855	3784	25.47
1988	17985	4052	22.53
1989	28017	7742	27.63
1990	46963	45207	96.26
1991	58771	19762	33.63
1992	94839	32846	34.63
1993	204267	89930	44.03
1994	244017	96299	39.46
1995	313528	113052	36.06
1996	411021	168637	41.03
1997	579787	200828	34.64
1998	559618	195177	34.88
1999	555424	201673	36.31
2000	574506	133011	23.15
2001	810415	180525	22.28
2002	998741	230440	23.07
2003	1172755	242972	20.72
2004	1329411	278910	20.98
2005	1586302	312074	19.67
2006	1754637	399586	22.77
2007	2275036	542852	23.86
2008	3106047	675962	21.76
2009	3273766	785375	23.98
2010	4204166	880790	20.95
2011	3972972	1083773	27.28
2012	4208014	1258986	29.92
2013	4748884	1482555	31.22
2014	6018083	1710441	28.42
2015	7100726	2259963	31.83
2016	11661901	2458547	21.08
2017	11272520	2697222	23.93
2018	11628614	3219983	27.69
2019	14248337	3624694	25.44

注：1．本表数据2008年前来源于广东省保险行业协会；

2．自2011年起，保险行业数据按照执行“企业会计准则解释第2号”的新口径统计(下同)。

Note: I. The data before 2008 were provided by the Guangdong Association of Insurance Industry.

II. Since 2011 figures of insurance industry are calculated according to new standards (The same as in the following tables).

6-15 保险公司主要业务指标（2019年）
Major Business Indicators of Insurance Companies (2019)

单位：万元 (10000 yuan)

指　　标	Indicators	保险金额（亿元）Amount Insured (100 million yuan)	原保险保费收入 Premium of Primary Insurance	赔款及给付支出 Claim and Payment
总　计	**Total**	**9988565**	**14248337**	**3624694**
财产保险公司	Property Insurance Companies	9774110	3847323	1883838
人身保险公司	Personal Insurance Companies	214455	10401014	1740856

6-16 财产保险公司主要指标
Main Indicators of Property Insurance Companies

单位：万元 (10000 yuan)

项　　目	Item	2018		2019	
		原保险保费收入 Premium of Primary Insurance	赔款支出 Claim and Payment	原保险保费收入 Premium of Primary Insurance	赔款支出 Claim and Payment
合　计	**Total**	**3177356**	**1732398**	**3847323**	**1883838**
企业财产保险	Enterprise Property Insurance	196140	174979	216056	105249
家庭财产保险	Family Property Insurance	15829	5381	19486	4155
# 投资型家财险	Investment Family Property Insurance	160	48	151	21
机动车辆保险	Motor Vehicle Insurance	1736926	1016762	1851853	1000561
工程保险	Enginerring Insurance	107794	36109	107590	61306
责任保险	Liability Insurance	236597	105503	282153	125042
信用保险	Export Credit Insurance	185457	135957	206902	107959
保证保险	Guarantee Insurance	264198	73528	504043	161547
# 机动车辆消费贷款保证保险	Vehicle Loan Guarantee Insurance	891	3507	131	1944
个人贷款抵押房屋保证保险	Personal Loan Mortgage Housing Guarantee Insurance	-174	1	-105	60
船舶保险	Ship Insurance	25493	18095	27810	16211
货物运输保险	Freight Transport Insurance	52474	31636	53263	38831
特殊风险保险	Special Risk Insurance	55579	16153	66780	35233
农业保险	Agricultural Insurance	10110	10253	13133	12114
健康险	Health Insurance	98786	52709	209127	108914
意外伤害保险	Accident Injury Insurance	159994	37529	199510	49851
其他险	Other Insurance	31979	17804	89616	56865

6-17 人身保险公司主要指标
Main Indicators of Personal Insurance Companies

单位：万元 (10000 yuan)

项　　目	Item	2018	2019
原保险保费收入	Premium of Primary Insurance	8451258	10401014
按险种分	**Classify by Insurance Code**		
寿　险	Life Insurance	6577166	8141646
个人业务	Individual Insurance	6549788	8105805
新单保费	Initial Premiums	2871617	3854219
续期保费	Renewable Premiums	3678171	4251585
团体业务	Group Isurance	27378	35841
新单保费	Initial Premiums	17122	25633
续期保费	Renewable Premiums	10256	10208
意外伤害险	Personal Accidental Death and Injury Insurance	287615	274909
一年期以内业务	Within One-year Product	14771	41742
一年期业务	One-year Product	157495	115597
一年以上业务	Over One-year Product	115349	117571
健康险	Health Insurance	1586477	1984459
一年期以内及一年期业务	Winthin One Year and One-Year Product	306444	373263
个人业务	Individual Insurance	172864	194370
团体业务	Group Isurance	133580	178893
一年期以上业务	Over One-year Period Product	1280033	1611196
个人业务	Individual Insurance	1255582	1545764
团体业务	Group Isurance	24451	65431
按新型产品分	**Classify by New Insurance Products**		
寿险保费收入合计	Total Life Insurance Premiums	6577166	8141646
普通寿险	Ordinary Life Insurance	3255040	4130760
新单保费	Initial Premiums	1293547	1755880
续期保费	Renewable Premiums	1961493	2374880
分红寿险	Participating Insurance	3298795	3986292
新单保费	Initial Premiums	1593399	2121396
续期保费	Renewable Premiums	1705396	1864896
投资连结保险	Unit-linked Insurance	5728	5964
万能寿险	Universal Life Insurance	17603	18630

6-17 续表 continued

单位:万元 (10000 yuan)

项　　目	Item	2018	2019
赔付支出	Claims Paid	1487585	1740856
赔款支出	Compensation Expenses	208890	250336
意外伤害险	Personal Accidental And Injury Insurance	32049	33446
一年期以内业务	Within One-year Product	1508	6508
一年期业务	One-year	30541	26938
一年期以内及一年期健康险	Winthin One Year and One-Year Health Insurance	176841	216890
个人业务	Individual Insurance	49933	68090
团体业务	Group Insurance	126907	148801
死伤医疗给付合计	Total Casualty Medical Payments	183909	241909
寿　险	Life Insurance	59557	66683
个人业务	Individual Insurance	50527	55285
团体业务	Group Insurance	9030	11397
一年期以上健康险	Over One-year Period Health Insurance	124352	175226
个人业务	Individual Insurance	121010	170507
团体业务	Group Insurance	3342	4719
满期给付合计	Total Mature Payment	694042	913722
寿　险	Life Insurance	693056	912180
个人业务	Individual Insurance	672482	896153
团体业务	Group Insurance	20574	16027
一年期以上健康险	Over One-year Period Health Insurance	986	1542
个人业务	Individual Insurance	986	1542
团体业务	Group Insurance		
年金给付合计	Total Pension Payments	400744	334889
个人业务	Individual Insurance	374456	319069
团体业务	Group Insurance	26288	15820
退保金	Cash Surrender Value	3596224	2067067
寿　险	Life Insurance	2632111	1853260
个人业务	Individual Insurance	2629165	1842299
团体业务	Group Insurance	2946	10961
一年期以上健康险	Over One-year Period Health Insurance	964113	213807

6-18 主要外资金融机构及代表处一览表
List of Main Foreign Financial Institutions and Representative Offices

机构(代表处)名称及所属国家(地区)	Name of Institutions (Representative Offices)	批准日期 Date of Approval
法国兴业银行(中国)有限公司广州分行(法国)	Societe Generale,(China)Ltd., Guangzhou Branch (France)	1992.08
三井住友银行(中国)有限公司广州分行(日本)	Sumitomo Mitsui Banking Corporation (China), Ltd, Guangzhou Branch (Japan)	1992.12
东亚银行(中国)有限公司广州分行(中国香港)	The Bank of East Asia (China)Ltd., Guangzhou Branch (Hong Kong, China)	1992.10
南洋商业银行(中国)有限公司广州分行(中国香港)	Nanyang Commercial Bank (China), Ltd., Guangzhou Branch (Hong Kong, China)	1992.11
美国银行广州分行(美国)	Bank of Amercia N.A., Guangzhou Branch (USA)	1993.01
法国巴黎银行(中国)有限公司广州分行(法国)	BNP Paribas(China)Ltd., Guangzhou Branch (France)	1995.06
大华银行(中国)有限公司广州分行(新加坡)	United Overseas Bank Ltd., Guangzhou Branch (Singapore)	1993.12
德意志银行(中国)有限公司广州分行(德国)	Deutsche Bank (China)Ltd.AG, Guangzhou Branch (Germany)	1994.11
东方汇理银行(中国)有限公司广州分行(法国)	Credit Agricole Corparate And Investment Bank (China)Ltd. Guangzhou Branch (France)	1994.11
加拿大丰业银行广州分行(加拿大)	The Bank of Nova Scotia, Guangzhou Branch (Canada)	1994.11
蒙特利尔银行(中国)有限公司广州分行(加拿大)	Bank of Montreal (China), Co, Ltd, Guangzhou Branch (Canada)	1995.01
恒生银行(中国)有限公司广州分行(中国香港)	Hang Seng Bank Ltd., Guangzhou Branch (Hong Kong, China)	1995.12
花旗银行(中国)有限公司广州分行(美国)	Citibank, N.A.(China)Ltd., Guangzhou Branch (USA)	1997.12
汇丰银行(中国)有限公司广州分行(中国香港)	The Hong Kong and Shanghai Banking Corporation Ltd., Guangzhou Branch (Hong Kong, China)	1999.08
星展银行(中国)有限公司广州分行(新加坡)	DBS Bank Ltd., Guangzhou Branch (Singapore)	2004.04
韩国产业银行广州分行(韩国)	The Korea Development Bank Ltd., Guangzhou Branch (Republic of Korea)	2005.05
渣打银行(中国)有限公司广州分行(中国香港)	Standard Charted Bank Ltd. Guangzhou Branch (Hong Kong, China)	2005.06
华侨永亨银行(中国)有限公司广州分行(中国香港)	OCBC Wing Hang Bank Ltd., Guangzhou Branch (Hong Kong, China)	2006.09
国民银行(中国)有限公司广州分行(韩国)	Kookmin Bank Ltd., Guangzhou Branch (Republic of Korea)	2007.06

6-18 续表 continued

机构（代表处）名称及所属国家（地区）	Name of Institutions (Representative Offices)	批准日期 Date of Approval
三菱日联银行（中国）有限公司广州分行（日本）	Bank of Mitsubishi UFJ (China), Ltd., Guangzhou Branch (Japan)	2008.02
瑞穗银行（中国）有限公司广州分行（日本）	Mizuho Bank (China), Ltd. Guangzhou Branch (Japan)	2008.08
华商银行广州分行（中国香港）	Chinese Mercantile Bank Guangzhou Branch (Hong Kong, China)	2008.11
摩根大通银行（中国）有限公司广州分行（美国）	JPMorgan Chase Bank (China) Company Limited Guangzhou Branch (USA)	2009.03
澳大利亚和新西兰银行（中国）有限公司广州分行（澳大利亚）	Australia and New Zealand Banking (China) Ltd. Guangzhou Branch (Australia)	2009.05
大新银行（中国）有限公司广州分行（中国香港）	DahSing Bank (China) Limited Guangzhou Branch (Hong Kong, China)	2011.04
韩亚银行（中国）有限公司广州分行（韩国）	Hana Bank (China) Company Limited ,Guangzhou Branch (Republic of Korea)	2012.07
中国信托商业银行股份有限公司广州分行（中国台湾）	CTBC Bank Co. Ltd., Guangzhou Branch (Taiwan, China)	2015.07
台湾银行股份有限公司广州分行（中国台湾）	Bank of Taiwan Co., Ltd. Guangzhou Branch (Taiwan, China)	2015.08
招商永隆银行有限公司广州分行（中国香港）	CMB Wing Lung Bank Ltd., Guangzhou Branch (Hong Kong, China)	2015.09
创兴银行有限公司广州分行（中国香港）	Chong Hing Bank Limited Guangzhou Branch (Hong Kong, China)	2016.05
澳门国际银行股份有限公司广州分行（中国澳门）	Luso International Banking Limited Guangzhou Branch(Macao, China)	2017.03
永丰银行（中国）有限公司广州分行（中国台湾）	Bank SinoPac(China)Ltd.,Guangzhou Branch(Taiwan, China)	2017.07
玉山银行（中国）有限公司广州分行（中国台湾）	E.SUN Bank (China) Company，Ltd. Guangzhou Branch(Taiwan, China)	2018.09
富邦华一银行有限公司广州分行（中国台湾）	Fubon Bank (China) Co. , Ltd. Guangzhou Branch(Taiwan, China)	2019.04
美国华美银行股份有限公司广州代表处（美国）	East West Bbank Guangzhou Representative Office (USA)	1996.01
葡萄牙商业银行股份有限公司广州代表处（葡萄牙）	Banco Commercial Portugues, Guangzhou Representative Office (Portugal)	1997.03
瑞士信贷银行有限公司广州代表处（瑞士）	Credit Suisse Guangzhou Representative Office (Swiss)	2005.04
意大利西雅那银行股份有限公司广州代表处（意大利）	Banca Monte Dei Paschi Di Siena S.P.A Guangzhou Representative Office (Italy)	2005.08
埃及银行广州代表处（埃及）	Banque Misr Guangzhou Representative Office(Egypt)	2016.07
孟加拉东方银行广州代表处（孟加拉）	Eastern Bank Limited Guangzhou Representative Office(Bangladesh)	2018.09
澳门华人银行股份有限公司广州代表处（中国澳门）	The Macau Chinese Bank Limited Guangzhou Representative Office (Macao, China)	2019.06

6-19 外资保险公司及代表处一览表

List of Foreign Insurance Companies and Representative Offices

机构(代表处)名称及所属国家(地区)	Name of Institutions (Representative Offices)	批准日期 Date of Approval
美亚财产保险有限公司广东分公司(美国)	AIG Insurance Company China Limited Guangdong Branch (USA)	1995.10
友邦保险有限公司广东分公司(中国香港)	AIA Company Limited Guangdong Provincial Branch(Hong Kong, China)	1995.10
中意人寿保险有限公司广东分公司(意大利)	Generali China Life Insurance Co., Ltd., Guangdong Branch (Italy)	2002.01
中宏人寿保险公司广州分公司(加拿大)	Manulife-Sinochem Life Insurance Co., LTD, Guangzhou Branch (Canada)	2003.01
京东安联财产保险(中国)有限公司(德国)	Allianz Jingdong General Insurance Company (Germany)	2003.01
工银安盛人寿保险有限公司广东分公司(法国)	ICBC-AXA Assurance Co., Ltd., Guangdong Branch (France)	2003.04
中德安联人寿保险公司广东分公司(德国)	Allianz China Life Insurance Company Limited Guangdong Branch (Germany)	2004.12
中英人寿保险公司广东分公司(英国)	Aviva-Cofco Life Insurance Co., Ltd., Guangdong Branch (UK)	2005.11
中美联泰大都会人寿保险有限公司广东分公司(美国)	Sino-US United MetLife Insurance Co., Ltd., Guangdong Branch (USA)	2006.02
安盛天平财产保险股份有限公司广东分公司(法国)	Tian Ping Auto Insurance Co., Ltd., Guangdong Branch (France)	2006.08
平安健康保险股份有限公司广东分公司(南非)	Ping An Health Insurance Company Of China,Ltd. Guangdong Branch (South Africa)	2007.09
瑞泰人寿保险有限公司广东分公司(南非)	Oldmutual-guodian life insurance company limited guangdong branch (South Africa)	2008.01
同方全球人寿保险有限公司广东分公司(荷兰)	AEGON THTF Life Insurance Co.,Ltd. Guangdong Branch(Holland)	2008.02
信诚人寿保险有限公司广东省分公司(英国)	CITIC-Prudential Life Insurance Company Limited Guangdong Branch (UK)	2008.06
三井住友海上火灾保险(中国)有限公司广东分公司(日本)	Mitsui Sumitomo Insurance (China) Company, Ltd, Guangdong Branch (Japan)	2008.08
陆家嘴国泰人寿保险有限责任公司广东分公司(中国台湾)	Cathay Lujiazui Life Insurance Co., Ltd, Guangdong Branch (Taiwan, China)	2008.09
日本财产保险(中国)有限公司广东分公司(日本)	Sompo Japan Insurance (China) Company, Ltd, Guangdong Branch(Japan)	2009.02
恒安标准人寿保险有限公司广东分公司(英国)	Heng An Standard Life Insurance Co., Ltd., Guangdong Branch (UK)	2009.05
东京海上日动火灾保险(中国)有限公司广东分公司(日本)	The Tokio Marine & Nichido Fire Insurance Company (China) Limited Guangdong Branch (Japan)	2010.06
国泰财产保险有限责任公司广东分公司(中国台湾)	Cathay Insurance Co., Ltd., Guangdong Branch (Taiwan,China)	2010.10
招商信诺人寿保险有限公司广东分公司(美国)	CIGNA & CMC Life Insurance Co., Ltd., Guangdong Branch (USA)	2010.12
华泰人寿保险股份有限公司广东分公司(美国)	Huatai Life Insurance Co.,Ltd..Guangdong Branch (USA)	2011.05
利宝保险有限公司广东省分公司(美国)	Liberty Insurance Co., Ltd., Guangdong Branch (USA)	2011.11
中意财产保险有限公司广东分公司(意大利)	Generali China Insurance Co., Ltd., Guangdong Branch (Italy)	2012.07
中银三星人寿保险有限公司广东分公司(韩国)	BOC SAMSUNG Life Insurance Company Limited Guangdong Branch (Korea)	2013.06
交银康联人寿保险有限公司广东省分公司(澳大利亚)	BoCommLife Insurance Company Limited Guangdong Branch (Australia)	2014.05
乐爱金财产保险(中国)有限公司广东分公司(韩国)	LIG Insurance (China) Co.,Ltd. Guangdong Branch (Korea)	2014.05
京东安联财产保险(中国)有限公司广东分公司(德国)	Allianz China General Insurance Company Ltd Guangdong Branch(Germany)	2015.10
汇丰人寿保险有限公司广东分公司(中国香港)	HSBC Life Insurance Company Limited Guangdong Branch (Hong Kong, China)	2015.10
史带财产保险股份有限公司广东分公司(美国)	Starr Property & Casualty Insurance (China) Company Limited, Guangdong branch(USA)	2016.01
安达保险有限公司广东分公司(美国)	Chubb Insurance Company Limited Guangdong Branch(USA)	2016.07
恒大人寿保险有限公司广东分公司(新加坡)	Evergrande Life Assurance Co.,Ltd., Guangdong Branch (Singapore)	2016.09
北大方正人寿保险有限公司广东分公司(日本)	Founder Life Insurance Co., Ltd. Guangdong Branch(Japan)	2016.12
苏黎世财产保险(中国)有限公司广东分公司(瑞士)	Zurich General Insurance Company(China)Ltd Guangdong Branch(Switzerland)	2016.12
澳大利亚昆士兰保险集团股份有限公司广州代表处(澳大利亚)	QBE Insurance Group Limited, Guangzhou Representative Office (Australia)	1997.11
日本爱和谊日生同和保险公司广州代表处(日本)	Aioi Nissay Dowa Insurance Co.,Ltd. Guangzhou Representative Office(Japan)	2004.06

6-20 金融机构人民币法定存款利率

Official Interest Rates of Deposits of Financial Institutions

单位:年利率 %　　　　(% p.a.)

调整时间 Adjustment time	活期存款 Demand Deposit	定期存款 Time Deposit					
		三个月 3 Months	半年 6 Months	一年 1 Year	二年 2 Years	三年 3 Years	五年 5 Years
1996. 05. 01	2.97	4.86	7.20	9.18	9.90	10.80	12.06
1996. 08. 23	1.98	3.33	5.40	7.47	7.92	8.28	9.00
1997. 10. 23	1.71	2.88	4.14	5.67	5.94	6.21	6.66
1998. 03. 25	1.71	2.88	4.14	5.22	5.58	6.21	6.66
1998. 07. 01	1.44	2.79	3.96	4.77	4.86	4.95	5.22
1998. 12. 07	1.44	2.79	3.33	3.78	3.96	4.14	4.50
1999. 06. 10	0.99	1.98	2.16	2.25	2.43	2.70	2.88
2002. 02. 21	0.72	1.71	1.89	1.98	2.25	2.52	2.79
2004. 10. 29	0.72	1.71	2.07	2.25	2.70	3.24	3.60
2006. 08. 19	0.72	1.80	2.25	2.52	3.06	3.69	4.14
2007. 03. 18	0.72	1.98	2.43	2.79	3.33	3.96	4.41
2007. 05. 19	0.72	2.07	2.61	3.06	3.69	4.41	4.95
2007. 07. 21	0.81	2.34	2.88	3.33	3.96	4.68	5.22
2007. 08. 22	0.81	2.61	3.15	3.60	4.23	4.95	5.49
2007. 09. 15	0.81	2.88	3.42	3.87	4.50	5.22	5.76
2007. 12. 21	0.72	3.33	3.78	4.14	4.68	5.40	5.85
2008. 10. 09	0.72	3.15	3.51	3.87	4.41	5.13	5.58
2008. 10. 30	0.72	2.88	3.24	3.60	4.14	4.77	5.13
2008. 11. 27	0.36	1.98	2.25	2.52	3.06	3.60	3.87
2008. 12. 23	0.36	1.71	1.98	2.25	2.79	3.33	3.60
2010. 10. 20	0.36	1.91	2.20	2.50	3.25	3.85	4.20
2010. 12. 26	0.36	2.25	2.50	2.75	3.55	4.15	4.55
2011. 02. 09	0.40	2.60	2.80	3.00	3.90	4.50	5.00
2011. 04. 06	0.50	2.85	3.05	3.25	4.15	4.75	5.25
2011. 07. 07	0.50	3.10	3.30	3.50	4.40	5.00	5.50
2012. 06. 08	0.40	2.85	3.05	3.25	4.10	4.65	5.10
2012. 07. 06	0.35	2.60	2.80	3.00	3.75	4.25	4.75
2014. 11. 22	0.35	2.35	2.55	2.75	3.35	4.00	--
2015. 03. 01	0.35	2.10	2.30	2.50	3.10	3.75	--
2015. 05. 11	0.35	1.85	2.05	2.25	2.85	3.50	--
2015. 06. 28	0.35	1.60	1.80	2.00	2.60	3.25	--
2015. 08. 26	0.35	1.35	1.55	1.75	2.35	3.00	--
2015. 10. 24	0.35	1.10	1.30	1.50	2.10	2.75	--

注：自2014年11月22日起，人民银行不再公布金融机构人民币五年期定期存款基准利率。

Note: Since November 22,2014,the central bank will not announce the official interest rate of time deposits for 5 years of financial institutions.

6-21 金融机构人民币法定贷款利率

Official Interest Rates of Loans of Financial Institutions

单位:年利率 % (% p.a.)

调整时间 Adjustment time	6个月以内（含六个月） within 6 months (include 6 months)	六个月至一年（含一年） 6 months–1 year (include 1 year)	一至三年（含三年） 1–3years (include 3 years)	三至五年（含五年） 3–5years (include 5 years)	五年以上 above 5 years
1996. 05. 01	9.72	10.98	13.14	14.94	15.12
1996. 08. 23	9.18	10.08	10.98	11.70	12.42
1997. 10. 23	7.65	8.64	9.36	9.90	10.53
1998. 03. 25	7.02	7.92	9.00	9.72	10.35
1998. 07. 01	6.57	6.93	7.11	7.65	8.01
1998. 12. 07	6.12	6.39	6.66	7.20	7.56
1999. 06. 10	5.58	5.85	5.94	6.03	6.21
2002. 02. 21	5.04	5.31	5.49	5.58	5.76
2004. 10. 29	5.22	5.58	5.76	5.85	6.12
2006. 04. 28	5.40	5.85	6.03	6.12	6.39
2006. 08. 19	5.58	6.12	6.30	6.48	6.84
2007. 03. 18	5.67	6.39	6.57	6.75	7.11
2007. 05. 19	5.85	6.57	6.75	6.93	7.20
2007. 07. 21	6.03	6.84	7.02	7.20	7.38
2007. 08. 22	6.21	7.02	7.20	7.38	7.56
2007. 09. 15	6.48	7.29	7.47	7.65	7.83
2007. 12. 21	6.57	7.47	7.56	7.74	7.83
2008. 09. 16	6.21	7.20	7.29	7.56	7.74
2008. 10. 09	6.12	6.93	7.02	7.29	7.47
2008. 10. 30	6.03	6.66	6.75	7.02	7.20
2008. 11. 27	5.04	5.58	5.67	5.94	6.12
2008. 12. 23	4.86	5.31	5.40	5.76	5.94
2010. 10. 20	5.10	5.56	5.60	5.96	6.14
2010. 12. 26	5.35	5.81	5.85	6.22	6.40
2011. 02. 09	5.60	6.06	6.10	6.45	6.60
2011. 04. 06	5.85	6.31	6.40	6.65	6.80
2011. 07. 07	6.10	6.56	6.65	6.90	7.05
2012. 06. 08	5.85	6.31	6.40	6.65	6.80
2012. 07. 06	5.60	6.00	6.15	6.40	6.55
2014. 11. 22		5.60		6.00	6.15
2015. 03. 01		5.35		5.75	5.90
2015. 05. 11		5.10		5.50	5.65
2015. 06. 28		4.85		5.25	5.40
2015. 08. 26		4.60		5.00	5.15
2015. 10. 24		4.35		4.75	4.90

注：自2014年11月22日起，金融机构人民币贷款基准利率期限档次简并为一年以内(含一年)、一至五年(含五年)和五年以上三个档次。

Note: Since Novemeber 22, 2014, the brackets of official interest rates of loans of financial institutions have changed into three brackets: one year (include one year), one to five years(include five years) and five years above.

【一般公共预算收入】 指国家财政参与社会产品分配所取得的收入，是实现国家职能的财力保证。主要包括：（1）各项税收：包括国内增值税、国内消费税、进口货物增值税及消费税、出口货物退增值税和消费税、营业税、企业所得税、个人所得税、资源税、城市维护建设税、房产税、印花税、城镇土地使用税、土地增值税、车船税、船舶吨税、车辆购置税、关税、耕地占用税、契税、烟叶税等。（2）非税收入：包括专项收入、行政事业性收费、罚没收入和其他收入。财政收入按现行分税制财政体制划分为中央本级收入和地方本级收入。

【一般公共预算支出】 指国家财政将筹集起来的资金进行分配使用，以满足经济建设和各项事业的需要。主要包括：一般公共服务、外交、国防、公共安全、教育、科学技术、文化体育与传媒、社会保障和就业、医疗卫生与计划生育、节能环保、城乡社区、农林水、交通运输、资源勘探信息等、商业服务业等、金融、援助其他地区、国土海洋气象等、住房保障、粮油物资储备、政府债务付息等方面的支出。财政支出根据政府在经济和社会活动中的不同职权，划分为中央财政支出和地方财政支出。

【存款】 指企业、机关、团体或居民根据资金必须收回的原则，把货币资金存入银行或其他信贷机构保管并取得一定利息的一种信用活动形式。根据存款对象或性质的不同可划分为住户存款、非金融企业存款、政府存款、非银行业金融机构存款等科目。它是银行信贷资金的主要来源。

【贷款】 指银行或其他信贷机构根据资金必须归还的原则，按一定利率，为企业、个人等提供资金的一种信用活动形式。我国银行贷款分为短期贷款、中长期贷款、融资租赁、票据融资、各项贷款、境外贷款等。

【保险公司】 在中国境内的、经过保险监督管理部门批准设立，并依法登记注册的各类商业保险公司。

【保险金额】 指保险人承担赔偿或者给付保险金责任的最高限额。

【保费】 指投保人为取得保险人在约定范围内所承担赔偿责任而支付给保险人的费用。

【赔款】 指保险人根据保险合同的规定，向被保险人支付的赔偿保险责任损失的金额。

【给付】 包括死伤医疗给付和期满给付。死伤医疗给付是指保险人根据人寿保险及长期健康保险合同的规定，因被保险人在保险期内发生保险责任范围内的保险事故支付给被保险人（或受益人）的金额。期满给付是指被保险人生存期满，保险人按人寿保险合同规定支付给被保险人的期满保险金额。

【General Public Budget Revenue】 refers to income for the government finance through participating in the distribution of social products. It is the financial guarantee to ensure government functioning. The government revenue includes the following main items: (1) Various tax revenues including domestic value added tax (VAT), domestic consumption tax, VAT and consumption tax from imports, VAT and consumption tax rebate for exports, corporate income tax, individual income tax, resource tax, city maintenance and construction tax, house property tax, stamp tax, urban land use tax, land appreciation tax, tax on vehicles and boat operation, ship tonnage tax, vehicle purchase tax, tariffs, farm land occupation tax, deed tax, and tobacco tax, etc. (2) Non-tax revenue, including special program receipts, charge of administrative and institutional units, penalty receipts and others non-tax receipts. Fiscal revenues are divided into central revenues and local revenues according to the current tax-sharing fiscal system.

【General Public Budget Expenditure】 refers to the distribution and use of the funds which the government finance has raised, so as to meet the needs of economic construction and various undertakings. It includes the following main items: expenditure for general public services, expenditure for foreign affairs, expenditure for national defence expenditure for public security, expenditure for education, expenditure for science and technology, expenditure for culture, sport and media, expenditure for social safety net and employment effort, expenditure for medical and health care and family planning, expenditure for energy conservation and environment protection, expenditure for urban and rural community affairs, expenditure for agriculture, forestry and water conservancy, expenditure for transportation, expenditure for resource exploration and information, expenditure for affairs of commerce and services, expenditure for finance, aid to other regions, expenditure for land, ocean and weather, expenditure for housing security, expenditure for grain & oil reserves, interest payment for public debts. General public budget expenditure is divided into general public budget expenditure of central government and general public budget expenditure of local government according to the different functions of the governments played in economic and social activities,

【Deposit】 is a form of credit by which enterprises, institutions, organizations or households can put money into banks and other credit institutions for safekeeping and interest earning and can withdraw anytime or at appointed time.l. According to different depositors, deposits are divided into household deposits, non financial enterprise deposits, government deposits, non banking financial institutions deposits. Deposits are major sources of the credit funds of banks.

【Loan】 is a form of credit by which banks and other credit institutions provide funds at certain interest rate to enterprises and individuals in the light of the principle of unconditional repayment. Loans from Chinese banks include short-term loan, medium-term and long-term loans, financial lease, bill financing, various money advanced, foreign loans.

【Insurance Companies】 refer to commercial insurance companies of various forms registered by law and established in China with the approval of insurance regulatory agencies.

【Amount Insured】 refers to the maximum that the insurant will get for the claim of the case insured.

【Premium】 is the fee paid by the insurant to the insurer to obtain the obligation of compensation from the insurance within the agreed terms.

【Settled Claim】 is the compensation paid by the insurer to the insurant in accordance with the insurance contract.

【Payment】 includes payment for death, injury or medical treatment and payment at maturity. Payment for death, injury or medical treatment refers to the money paid to the insurant (or the beneficiary) in accordance with the life or health insurance contract when the insurant encounters accidents within the insured period covered in the contract. Payment at maturity refers to the payment to the insurant in accordance with the life insurance contract at the end of the insured period.

第七篇 CHAPTER 7

价格指数

PRICE INDICES

第七篇　价格指数

一、本篇资料反映生产、消费等环节的价格变动情况。

二、本篇资料由国家统计局广州调查队提供。

三、居民消费价格指数采用抽样调查方法编制，按照大中小兼顾以及地区分布合理的原则，采用划类选择法抽选价格调查点以及消费量较大，价格变动有代表性的商品和服务项目作为样本，对市场价格进行经常性调查，以样本推断总体。

四、工业生产者出厂价格指数和工业生产者购进价格指数均采用重点调查与典型调查相结合的调查方法，采用主观选择和随机抽样的方法选择调查企业。

五、固定资产投资价格指数采用重点调查与典型调查相结合的方法，数据采集使用企业报表与调查员实地采价相结合的方式。

六、新建商品住宅销售价格统计的采集渠道为部门统计，数据取自市住房和城乡建设委员会的房地产交易管理平台网签成交情况；二手住宅销售价格调查为非全面调查，采用重点调查与典型调查相结合的方法，数据来源于房地产经纪机构。

7 Price Indices

I. The data on the price indices in this chapter show the changing trend and the changing rates in production and consumption.

II. The data in this chapter are prepared and provided by Guangzhou Survey Team of National Bureau of Statistics.

Ⅲ. The data for the calculation of the consumer price indices of resident are collected with the stratified sampling method. Areas distributed in different economic regions in the districts and counties of Guangzhou are selected as the sample areas and the commodities with more consumption and the representative commodities and service item are selected as the samples. Regular surveys are conducted to collect the data on the market prices. The data on the population are estimated on the basis of the sample.

IV. The data for the calculation of the industrial producer price indices and industrial producers purchasing price indices are collected by key unit's survey and typical unit's survey under subjective choice and random sample.

V. The data for the calculation of price indices of fixed assets investment and price indices of real estate are collected by key unit's survey and typical unit's survey through enterprises reporting forms and investigators collecting prices on the spot.

Ⅵ. The data for sales prices of newly built residential buildings are department statistics, which are collected from the internet signed transaction situation on the Real Estate Transaction Management Platform of the Guangzhou Housing and Urban-Rural Construction Committee.The data for sales prices of second-hand residential buildings are collected from non-all round investigation by key unit's survey and typical unit's survey through real estate brokerage agencies.

7-1 主要年份城市居民消费价格指数
Urban Residents Consumer Price Indices in Main Years

年 份 Year	以上年价格为100 (preceding year=100)	以1978年价格为100 (1978=100)	以1952年价格为100 (1952=100)
1978	100.3		134.1
1979	104.0	104.0	172.7
1980	107.2	112.9	240.5
1985	121.5	168.1	370.8
1986	103.9	177.4	398.1
1987	113.7	212.2	465.6
1988	127.7	274.0	599.8
1989	121.6	339.6	729.3
1990	97.3	322.2	709.6
1991	103.0	329.2	711.9
1992	111.7	374.6	795.2
1993	125.0	472.4	1020.5
1994	120.0	575.4	1224.6
1995	113.5	653.1	1389.9
1996	108.2	706.7	1503.9
1997	102.2	722.2	1537.0
1998	97.7	705.6	1501.6
1999	98.5	695.0	1479.1
2000	102.8	714.5	1520.5
2001	98.9	706.6	1503.8
2002	97.6	689.6	1467.7
2003	100.1	690.3	1469.2
2004	101.7	702.0	1494.2
2005	101.5	712.5	1516.6
2006	102.3	728.9	1551.5
2007	103.4	753.7	1604.2
2008	105.9	798.2	1698.8
2009	97.5	778.2	1656.3
2010	103.2	803.1	1709.3
2011	105.5	847.3	1803.3
2012	103.0	872.7	1857.4
2013	102.6	895.4	1905.7
2014	102.3	916.0	1949.5
2015	101.7	931.6	1982.6
2016	102.7	956.8	2036.1
2017	102.3	978.8	2082.9
2018	102.4	1002.3	2132.9
2019	103.0	1032.4	2196.9

7-2 城市居民消费价格分类指数(上年=100)

Urban Residents Consumer Price Indices by Category (Preceding Year=100)

项　　目	Item	2018	2019
居民消费价格总指数	**Consumer Price Index**	**102.4**	**103.0**
消费品价格指数	Consumer Goods Price Index	102.2	103.4
服务价格指数	Service Price Index	102.6	102.6
一、食品烟酒	I. Food，Tobacoo and Liquor	102.5	107.5
#食　品	Food	102.4	108.8
#粮　食	Grain	105.4	99.9
食用油	Cooking Oil	101.0	98.4
菜	Vegetables	104.9	103.9
#鲜　菜	Fresh Vegetables	105.4	104.5
畜肉类	Meat Products	96.8	125.8
禽肉类	Poultry Products	104.0	108.2
水产品	Aquatic Products	104.6	102.8
蛋　类	Eggs	114.2	105.8
烟　酒	Tobacoo and Liquors	101.7	102.6
二、衣　着	II. Clothing	104.2	101.1
三、居　住	III.Residence	101.3	100.4
四、生活用品及服务	IV. Household Articles and Services	101.9	100.5
#家用器具	Household Appliances	101.4	94.9
五、交通和通信	V. Transportation and Communication	101.7	98.4
六、教育文化和娱乐	VI.Education, Culture and Recreation	102.4	102.5
七、医疗保健	VII. Health Care	106.1	103.8
#医疗服务	Health Care Services	107.7	106.1
八、其他用品和服务	VIII.Other Articles and Services	101.2	104.6

7-3 主要年份城市商品零售价格指数

Urban Retail Price Indices in Main Years

年 份 Year	以上年价格为100 (preceding year=100)	以1978年价格为100 (1978=100)	以1952年价格为100 (1952=100)
1978	100.3		
1979	104.5	104.5	184.6
1980	107.6	113.8	252.8
1985	122.5	171.4	400.4
1986	103.3	179.8	426.0
1987	114.3	218.0	507.6
1988	129.6	284.9	656.5
1989	121.6	351.7	798.2
1990	96.3	331.4	768.7
1991	102.0	338.2	784.1
1992	108.9	379.3	853.9
1993	125.1	480.0	1068.2
1994	116.6	559.7	1245.5
1995	109.7	614.0	1366.3
1996	104.3	640.4	1425.1
1997	99.4	636.6	1416.5
1998	96.3	613.0	1364.1
1999	96.8	593.4	1320.4
2000	99.4	589.8	1312.5
2001	97.4	574.5	1278.4
2002	97.4	559.6	1245.2
2003	99.1	554.5	1234.0
2004	102.1	566.1	1259.9
2005	101.6	575.2	1280.1
2006	101.2	582.1	1295.5
2007	102.9	599.0	1333.0
2008	105.7	633.1	1409.0
2009	96.8	612.8	1363.9
2010	103.2	632.4	1407.5
2011	105.1	664.7	1479.3
2012	101.9	677.3	1507.4
2013	100.5	680.7	1514.9
2014	101.5	690.9	1537.6
2015	99.1	684.7	1523.8
2016	101.2	692.9	1542.1
2017	102.0	706.8	1572.9
2018	102.2	722.3	1607.5
2019	100.6	726.6	1617.1

7-4 城市商品零售价格指数（上年=100）

Urban Retail Price Indices by Category (Preceding Year=100)

项　目	Item	2018	2019
商品零售价格指数	**Retail Price Index**	**102.2**	**100.6**
食　品	Food	102.8	107.4
饮料、烟酒	Beverages, Tobacco and Liquor	101.6	102.0
服装、鞋帽	Garments, Shoes and Hats	104.2	101.0
纺织品	Textiles	99.4	98.5
家用电器及音像器材	Household Appliances, Music and Video Equipment	102.3	94.3
文化办公用品	Cultural and Office Appliances	96.2	94.8
日用品	Articles for Daily Use	99.1	99.7
体育娱乐用品	Sports and Recreation Articles	100.0	97.9
交通、通信用品	Transportation and Communication Appliances	99.3	98.0
家　具	Furniture	103.1	99.1
化妆品	Cosmetics	100.4	101.1
金银饰品	Gold, Silver and Jewelry	96.8	109.8
中西药品及医疗保健用品	Traditional Chinese and Western Medicines & Health Care Articles	104.6	101.2
书报杂志及电子出版物	Books, Newspapers, Magazines and Electronic Publications	101.1	101.8
燃　料	Fuels	107.5	94.8
建筑材料及五金电料	Building Materials and Hardware	101.7	100.4

7-5 主要食品平均价格

Average Price of Major Food

单位:元/千克　　(yuan/kg)

商品名称	Item	规格描述	Standard and Rate	2018	2019
东北大米	Rice	散装一级	Northeast Rice	5.36	5.25
油粘米	High Quality Rice	散装一级	Glutinous Rice	6.62	6.97
黄　豆	Soybean	一级	First Rate	8.00	8.20
绿　豆	Mung Bean	一级	First Rate	15.25	15.14
花生油	Peanut Oil	瓶装纯净	Pure First Rate	26.09	26.59
大白菜	Cabbage	一级绍菜	First Rate nappa cabbage	4.93	5.22
西兰花	Broccoli	一级	First Rate	11.56	11.71
青　瓜	Green Cucumber	一级	First Rate	7.88	8.11
冬　瓜	Wax gourd	一级青皮冬瓜	First Rate	4.26	4.52
西红柿	Tomato	一级番茄	First Rate	9.23	9.36
萝　卜	Radish	一级白萝卜	First Rate	3.87	3.91
空心菜	Water spinach	一级	First Rate	7.94	8.49
菜　心	Chinese flowering cabbage	一级	First Rate	9.50	10.08
豇　豆	Cowpea	一级白豆角	First Rate asparagus bean	11.74	12.84
生　菜	Lettuce	一级	First Rate	7.28	7.46
节　瓜	Zucchini	一级	First Rate	8.36	7.77
西洋菜	Watercress	一级	First Rate	8.13	8.67
猪　肉	Pork	上肉一级	Fresh High Quality Pork	28.33	39.24
牛　肉	Beef	净肉	Net Beef	80.46	89.92
鸡	Chicken	白条鸡(杂交开刀)	Pulled Chicken	36.47	38.49
鸡　蛋	Eggs	新鲜褐壳	Fresh Brown Eggs	10.98	11.67
带　鱼	Hairtail	冰鲜中等原条	Middling Iced Whole Hairtail	57.40	58.26
鳙　鱼	Variegated Carp	一级	First Rate	19.45	20.76
鲫　鱼	Crucian	一级	First Rate	24.36	24.46
草　鱼	Grass Carp	一级	First Rate	27.09	27.53
苹　果	Apple	红富士一级	First Rate of Red Fuji	12.83	15.18
雪　梨	Pear	一级	First Rate	9.07	11.01
香　蕉	Banana	黄熟一级	Ripe First Rate	6.62	6.66
葡　萄	Grape	加州红提	American Red Grape	28.28	27.56
西　瓜	Watermelon	黑美人一级	Ordinary First Rate	4.15	5.84

7-6 主要年份工业生产者价格指数（上年=100）

Price Indices for Industrial Products in Main Years (Preceding Year=100)

年 份 Year	工业生产者出厂价格指数 Producer Price Index for Industrial Products	工业生产者购进价格指数 Purchasing Price Index for Industrial Products
1994	126.0	121.1
1995	112.3	118.7
1996	101.4	104.5
1997	100.2	96.9
1998	95.2	91.1
1999	98.3	99.7
2000	103.2	113.6
2001	98.6	99.5
2002	96.8	96.5
2003	99.6	105.7
2004	102.1	111.7
2005	101.7	107.9
2006	101.2	104.9
2007	101.4	104.7
2008	103.7	109.4
2009	96.5	91.8
2010	102.4	110.9
2011	103.1	109.1
2012	99.7	98.4
2013	98.0	98.2
2014	98.2	98.0
2015	96.8	93.7
2016	98.8	98.5
2017	102.3	108.8
2018	101.0	104.6
2019	99.0	98.6

7-7 工业生产者出厂价格指数（上年＝100）
Producer Price Index for Industrial Products (Preceding Year=100)

项　　目	Item	2018	2019
工业生产者出厂价格指数	**Producer Price Index for Industrial Products**	**101.0**	**99.0**
轻工业	Light Industry	100.5	99.1
以农产品为原材料	Using Farm Produce as Raw Materials	102.3	101.1
以非农产品为原材料	Using Nonfarm Produce as Raw Materials	99.0	97.5
重工业	Heavy Industry	101.2	99.0
采掘工业	Mining and Quarrying Industry		
原料工业	Raw Materials Industry	103.4	97.4
加工工业	Manufacturing Industry	100.5	99.6
生产资料	Means of Production	101.5	98.9
采掘工业	Mining and Quarrying Industry		
原料工业	Raw Materials Industry	103.5	97.5
加工工业	Processing Industry	100.6	99.5
生活资料	Consumer Goods	100.4	99.2
食品类	Food	100.8	103.7
衣着类	Clothing	103.9	97.3
一般日用品类	Articles for Daily Use	100.8	97.9
耐用消费品类	Durable Consumer Goods	99.3	98.5

7-8 按工业行业分工业生产者出厂价格指数
Producer Price Indices for Industrial Products by Sector

(上年=100) (preceding year=100)

行业	Sector	2018	2019
总指数	Producer Price Indices for Industrial Products	101.0	99.0
农副食品加工业	Processing of Food from Agricultural Products	99.8	98.3
食品制造业	Manufacture of Foods	101.6	101.3
酒、饮料及精制茶制造业	Manufacture of Liquor,Beverages and Refined Tea	101.1	109.4
烟草制品业	Manufacture of Tobacco	100.0	103.4
纺织业	Manufacture of Textile	102.1	104.6
纺织服装、服饰业	Manufacture of Textile,Wearing Apparel and Accessories	100.5	97.4
皮革、毛皮、羽毛及其制品和制鞋业	Manufacture of Leather,Fur,Feather and Related Products and Footware	110.6	97.0
木材加工和木、竹、藤、棕、草制品业	Processing of Timber,Manufacture of Wood,Bamboo,Rattan,Palm and Straw Products	103.0	100.1
家具制造业	Manufacture of Furniture	103.6	108.6
造纸和纸制品业	Manufacture of Paper and Paper Products	109.7	90.7
印刷和记录媒介复制业	Printing and Reproduction of Recording Media	104.5	101.7
文教、工美、体育和娱乐用品制造业	Manufacture of Articles for Culture,Education,Arts and Crafts, Sport and Entertainment Activities	97.9	100.1
石油、煤炭及其他燃料加工业	Processing of Petroleum,Coking and Processing of Nuclear Fuel	115.8	96.0
化学原料和化学制品制造业	Manufacture of Raw Chemical Materials and Chemical Products	102.4	95.1
医药制造业	Manufacture of Medicines	103.9	103.4
化学纤维制造业	Manufacture of Chemical Fibres	103.7	98.4
橡胶和塑料制品业	Manufacture of Rubber and Plastics Products	101.3	98.9
非金属矿物制品业	Manufacture of Non-metallic Mineral Products	106.4	103.8
黑色金属冶炼和压延加工业	Smelting and Pressing of Ferrous Metals	105.8	97.1
有色金属冶炼和压延加工业	Smelting and Pressing of Non-ferrous Metals	105.9	95.5
金属制品业	Manufacture of Metal Products	103.9	100.0
通用设备制造业	Manufacture of General Purpose Machinery	99.9	101.6
专用设备制造业	Manufacture of Special Purpose Machinery	100.8	101.1
汽车制造业	Manufacture of Automobiles	99.9	99.5
铁路、船舶、航空航天和其他运输设备制造业	Manufacture of Railway,Ship,Aerospace and Other Transport Equipments	96.7	101.8
电气机械和器材制造业	Manufacture of Electrical Machinery and Apparatus	101.7	100.7
计算机、通信和其他电子设备制造业	Manufacture of Computers,Communication and Other Electronic Equipments	96.3	97.3
仪器仪表制造业	Manufacture of Measuring Instruments and Machinery	99.7	102.8
其他制造业	Other Manufacture	106.0	102.1
废弃资源综合利用业	Utilization of Waste Resources	159.4	119.5
金属制品、机械和设备修理业	Repair Service of Metal Products,Machinery and Equipment	100.0	100.0
电力、热力生产和供应业	Production and Supply of Electric Power and Heat Power	93.1	100.1
燃气生产和供应业	Production and Supply of Gas	104.4	96.7
水的生产和供应业	Production and Supply of Water	100.0	100.0

7-9 工业生产者购进价格指数(上年=100)

Purchasing Price Index for Industrial Producers (Preceding Year=100)

项　　目	Item	2018	2019
工业生产者购进价格指数	**Purchasing Price Index for Industrial Producers**	**104.6**	**98.6**
燃料、动力类	Fuels and Power	108.7	96.9
黑色金属材料类	Ferrous Metals	105.6	98.5
#钢　材	Steel	106.5	98.1
其　他	Others	102.0	100.1
有色金属材料和电线类	Nonferrous Metals and Wires	104.6	95.1
化工原料类	Raw Chemical Materials	104.8	99.1
木材及纸浆类	Timber and Paper Pulp	102.9	95.0
建筑材料及非金属类	Building Materials and Nonmetal Minerals	114.2	105.9
其他工业原料及半成品类	Raw Materials and Semi-finished Products of Other Industries	99.9	100.2
农副产品类	Agricultural Products	98.2	97.7
纺织原料类	Textile Raw Materials	102.4	100.4

7-10 固定资产投资价格指数（上年=100）

Prices Indices of Investment in Fixed Assets (Preceding Year=100)

项　　目	Item	2018	2019
固定资产投资价格指数	**Prices Indices of Investment in Fixed Assets**	**104.7**	**104.8**
建筑安装、装饰工程	Construction and Installation	106.2	105.1
人工费	Manpower	105.0	103.6
材料费	Materials	106.9	105.9
金属材料	Metal material		100.2
非金属材料	Nonmetallic materials		110.6
化工材料	Chemical Materials		99.3
木、竹材及其制品	Wood, bamboo and others		100.1
装饰材料及配件	Decoration materials and accessories		103.5
水暖及厨卫洁具	Water heating and sanitary ware		100.1
电气电料	Electical Materials and Appliances		100.6
仪表及其他	Instruments and others		101.0
机械使用费	Machinery	103.1	102.7
设备、工器具购置	Purchase of Equipment, Tools and Installation	100.6	100.9
其他费用	Others	100.0	106.3

注：2019年固定资产投资价格指数进行了方法制度改革，其他费用由土地使用费和银行贷款利率组成，其中土地使用费由国家统一发布。材料费由7大类改为8大类，并重新划分了内容，材料费之下的类与2018年的数据不具对比性。

Note: In 2019, the method and system reform of fixed assets investment price index is carried out. Other expenses consist of land use fee and bank loan interest rate, and land use fee is uniformly issued by the state. The material cost has been changed from 7 categories to 8 categories, and the contents have been re divided. Therefore, the data under material cost is not comparable with the data of 2018 years.

7-11 各月住宅销售价格指数（2019年，上年同期=100）
Sales Prices Indices of Residence Buildings (2019, Preceding Year=100)

项　　目	Item	1月	2月	3月	4月	5月	6月
新建住宅销售价格指数	**Newly Built Residential Buildings**						
新建商品住宅	Newly Built Commodity Residential Buildings	**109.7**	**111.3**	**111.9**	**113.3**	**112.2**	**110.5**
90平方米及以下	90 square meters and below	109.0	110.6	111.8	113.1	111.9	110.8
90-144平方米	90 - 144 square meters	109.4	110.2	111.0	112.6	111.2	109.8
144平方米以上	144 square meters and above	110.5	113.2	113.4	114.4	113.5	111.2
二手住宅销售价格指数	**Second-hand Residential Buildings**	**102.1**	**101.6**	**100.9**	**100.0**	**98.7**	**98.5**
90平方米及以下	90 square meters and below	100.7	100.3	99.7	98.7	97.8	97.8
90-144平方米	90 - 144 square meters	103.2	102.5	102.1	101.4	99.8	99.1
144平方米以上	144 square meters and above	104.0	104.2	101.5	100.4	98.8	99.2

注：2018年后国家统计局无公布新建住宅销售价格指数。
Note: After 2018, the National Bureau of Statistics did not publish the sales price index of newly built residential buildings.

7-11 续表 continued

项　　目	Item	7月	8月	9月	10月	11月	12月
新建住宅销售价格指数	**Newly Built Residential Buildings**						
新建商品住宅	Newly Built Commodity Residential Buildings	**110.2**	**109.4**	**109.0**	**108.7**	**108.1**	**104.7**
90平方米及以下	90 square meters and below	111.8	110.7	110.8	110.2	109.1	106.2
90-144平方米	90 - 144 square meters	110.0	109.3	108.2	107.8	107.7	104.1
144平方米以上	144 square meters and above	109.8	109.1	109.3	109.1	108.3	104.9
二手住宅销售价格指数	**Second-hand Residential Buildings**	**98.6**	**98.0**	**97.6**	**97.6**	**97.7**	**98.1**
90平方米及以下	90 square meters and below	97.9	97.3	96.6	96.8	96.9	97.4
90-144平方米	90 - 144 square meters	99.3	99.0	98.6	98.8	99.0	99.3
144平方米以上	144 square meters and above	99.1	98.2	98.0	97.0	97.0	96.9

注：2018年后国家统计局无公布新建住宅销售价格指数。
Note: After 2018, the National Bureau of Statistics did not publish the sales price index of newly built residential buildings.

【商品零售价格指数】商品零售价格是商品在流通过程中最后一个环节的价格，主要包括：工业、商业、餐饮业和其他零售企业向城乡居民、机关团体出售生活消费品和办公用品的价格。商品零售价格调查任务是系统地调查、搜集和整理市场商品零售价格资料，编制商品零售价格指数，以反映市场商品零售价格的变动趋势和变动程度，为国家宏观调控和国民经济核算提供参考依据。

【城市居民消费价格指数】是度量消费商品及服务项目价格水平随着时间而变动的相对数，它反映城市居民家庭购买的生活消费品及服务价格水平的变动情况，是宏观经济调控、价格总水平监测以及国民经济核算的重要指标，其变动率在一定程度上反映了通货膨胀(或紧缩)的程度。

【工业生产者购进价格指数】是反映工业企业作为生产投入，从物资交易市场和能源、原材料生产企业购买原材料、燃料和动力产品时，所支付的价格水平变动趋势和程度的统计指标，是扣除工业企业物质消耗成本中的价格变动影响的重要依据。

【工业生产者出厂价格指数】是反映一定时期内全部工业产品出厂价格总水平的变动趋势和程度的相对数，包括工业企业售给本企业以外所有单位的各种产品和直接售给居民用于生活消费的产品。该指数可以观察出厂价格变动对工业总产值及增加值的影响。

【固定资产投资价格指数】是反映固定资产投资活动中所涉及的建筑安装工程、设备工器具购置和其他费用这三部分投资价格水平变动趋势和幅度的相对数。

【住宅销售价格指数】住宅销售价格指数分为新建住宅销售价格指数和二手住宅销售价格指数两部分。其中，新建住宅销售价格指数的统计范围是所有进入房地产市场第一次进行产权交易及网上签约的住宅交易价格，分为保障性住房和新建商品住宅两部分。二手住宅销售价格指数的统计范围是进入房屋市场进行交易，第二次及以上进行产权登记的住宅。

【Retail Price Index】 measures the relative trend and degree of changes in retail prices of commodities,reflecting the trend of changes in prices in the last link of circulation,i.e. prices of consumer goods and office appliances sold to households or organizations by enterprises of industry,commerce,catering services and other retail trades. It reflects the changing trend and degree of retail prices of commodities.

It provides a reference for macroeconomic adjustment and control as well as national economic accounting.

【Urban Consumer Price Index】 reflects the trend and degree of changes in prices of consumer goods and services purchased by urban residents. It is an important indicator for macroeconomic analysis decision-making,regularization and control, supervision of general price level and national economic accounting.The rates of change are generally considered as an indicator of inflation or deflation.

【Purchasing Price Index for Industrial Producers】reflects changes in the level and degree of prices paid by industrial enterprises when they purchase production input such as raw materials, fuels and power from the market or from other energy or raw materials producing enterprises. These indices provide important basis for measuring the material consumption of industrial enterprises after removing influence of price changes.

【Producer Price Index for Manufactured Goods】Producer Price Index for Manufactured Goods reflects the trend and degree of changes in general ex-factory prices of all industrial products during a given period, including sales of industrial products by an industrial enterprise to all units outside the enterprise, as well as sales of consumer goods to residents. It can be used to analyze the impact of ex-factory prices on gross output value and value-added of the industrial sector.

【Prices Indices of Investment in Fixed Assets】reflects the trend and extent of changes in the price level in the investment activities in fixed asset, which involve three parts: the construction and installation project, purchase of engineering equipment and instrument and other expenses.

【Sales Prices Indices of Residence Buildings】Sales Prices Indices of Residence Buildings consists of Sales Prices Indices of Newly Built Residential Buildings and Sales Prices Indices of Second-hand Residential Buildings. The statistical range of Sales Prices Indices of Newly Built Residential Buildings covers the first-time transaction of real estates in the market and the internet signed price. The newly built residential buildings include the indemnificatory buildings and the newly built commercial buildings. The statistical range of Sales Prices Indices of Second-hand Residential Buildings covers the registration of residential buildings for the second time and above in the real estate market.

第八篇 CHAPTER 8

人民生活
PEOPLE'S LIVELIHOOD

第八篇　人民生活

一、本篇资料反映广州城乡居民生活状况，包括家庭基本情况、居民收支、消费水平、住房及主要消费品消费量和拥有量等基本情况。

二、本篇资料由广州市统计局和国家统计局广州调查队共同提供。

三、根据国家统计局广东调查总队要求，2014年起，城乡一体化住户调查收支数据绝对值以新口径公布使用。新口径是指不论户口性质和户口登记地、不论以家庭形式居住还是集体形式居住、不论居住在城市、农村还是城乡结合部，只要是常住地为广州的住户均纳入调查范围；旧口径是指以城市区域有固定居所的常住户籍居民家庭为调查范围。

四、由于新旧调查方案在调查范围和对象、城乡划分标准、样本抽选方法、计算和汇总方式、指标名称和口径等方面变化较大，新旧口径指标数据不可以直接对比使用。其中，新口径“消费支出”比旧口径“消费性支出”增加了自有住房虚拟租金折算，8-2表删除了部分指标，8-8表部分指标删除常住二字。

五、8-4表中“净收入”是指在相关获得收入中扣除投入成本、折旧和税费后得到净收入，因此部分指标为负。

8 People's Livelihood

I. The data in this chapter show the basic conditions of the people's livelihood in the urban and rural areas of Guangzhou Municipality, including basic conditions of families, income and expenditure of the residents, level of consumption, housing condition, consumption possession of the major Consumer goods, etc.

II. The data in this chapter are prepared and provided by Guangzhou Municipal Bureau of Statistics and Guangzhou Survey Team of National Bureau of Statistics.

III. According to the requirement of Guangdong Survey Team of National Bureau of Statistics, the value of income and expenditures of urban and rural integrated households are published with new statistical standard. No matter what kind of the household register is or register place is, whether living as a family or collective form in urban, rural or rural-urban continuum, as long as it is for local residents in Guangzhou, is classified into the new statistical standard. The old statistical standard covers the families which have permanent household register and resident in urban areas.

IV. The investigation field and respondent, the standard of classifying urban and rural, the sample selection rule, the calculating and summarizing method, the name of index and the statistical standard are different between the new survey method and the old one. As a result, the data of old and new statistical standard are incomparable. the "Consumption Expenditures" in new standard includes the virtue rent of private housing.

V. In table 8-4, "Net Income" refers to the related revenue deducts the input costs, depreciation and tax fees. As a result, some parts of "Net Income" can be negative.

8-1 城乡居民人均全年可支配收入和消费支出情况
Per Capita Annual Disposable Income and Expenditure for Consumption of Urban and Rural Residents

单位：元 (yuan)

项　目	Item	城市居民 Urban Residents	
		2018	2019
可支配收入	Disposable Income	59982	65052
消费支出	Total Living Expenditures for Consumption	42181	45049
食品烟酒	Food,Tobacco and Liquor	13549	14402
衣着	Clothing	2277	2314
居住	Residence	9459	10026
生活用品及服务	Articles for Daily Use and Services	2690	2843
交通通信	Transportation and Communication	5244	5701
教育文化娱乐	Education, Cultural and Recreation	5640	6149
医疗保健	Health Care and Medical Services	1875	2146
其他用品和服务	Miscellaneous Articles for Use and Services	1447	1468

8-1 续表 continued

单位：元 (yuan)

项　目	Item	农村居民 Rural Residents	
		2018	2019
可支配收入	Disposable Income	26020	28868
消费支出	Total Living Expenditures for Consumption	20634	22522
食品烟酒	Food,Tobacco and Liquor	7903	8607
衣着	Clothing	797	852
居住	Residence	4342	4781
生活用品及服务	Articles for Daily Use and Services	1228	1297
交通通信	Transportation and Communication	2962	3222
教育文化娱乐	Education, Cultural and Recreation	2030	2258
医疗保健	Health Care and Medical Services	1017	1121
其他用品和服务	Miscellaneous Articles for Use and Services	355	384

注：本表“消费支出”数据为新口径，新口径在原有消费支出中增加了“自有住房折算租金”。

Note: The data for "Total Living Expenditures for Consumption" in this table are the new caliber, which adds "the Owner Occupied Housing Discount Rent" to the orginal consumption expenditure.

8-2 城乡居民家庭平均每百户年末耐用消费品拥有量

Ownership of Major Durable Consumer Goods per 100 Urban and Rural Households at Year-end

项　目		Item		城市居民 Urban Households		农村居民 Rural Households	
				2018	2019	2018	2019
家用汽车	(辆)	Automobile	(unit)	48	50	46	49
摩托车	(辆)	Motorcycle	(unit)	20	19	106	97
助力车	(辆)	Moped	(unit)	25	24	56	57
洗衣机	(台)	Washing Machine	(set)	102	103	105	107
电冰箱(柜)	(台)	Refrigerator	(set)	103	104	109	110
微波炉	(台)	Microwave Oven	(set)	58	59	34	38
彩色电视机	(台)	Color TV Set	(set)	131	128	145	146
空调	(台)	Air Conditioner	(set)	239	244	221	237
热水器	(台)	Water Heater	(unit)	106	108	115	116
洗碗机	(台)	Dish-washing Machine	(unit)	4	4	5	6
排油烟机	(台)	Vacuum Cleaner	(unit)	90	93	78	84
固定电话	(部)	Telephone	(set)	56	50	30	27
移动电话	(台)	Mobile Telephone	(set)	263	269	318	319
# 接入互联网	(台)	Connected to the Internet	(set)	196	213	237	268
计算机	(台)	Computer	(set)	122	123	87	88
# 接入互联网	(台)	Connected to the Internet	(set)	111	118	75	78
照相机	(架)	Camera	(set)	66	58	20	22
中高档乐器	(台)	Medium and High Grade Musical Instruments	(set)	14	16	7	7
健身器材	(台)	Fitness Equipment	(set)	21	21	11	12

8-3 城市居民家庭基本情况（2019年）

Basic Conditions of Urban Households (2019)

单位：人 (person)

项　目	Item	合　计 Total	低收入户 Low Income Households	中等偏下收入户 Lower Middle Income Households
一、调查户数(户)	Number of Households Surveyed (household)	1200	240	240
二、家庭人口数	Number of Family Members	3701	857	775
平均每户人口数	Average Household Size	3.08	3.57	3.23
1. 就业者人数	Number of Employed Persons	2164	490	472
平均每户就业人数	Average Number of Employed Persons per Household	1.80	2.04	1.97
平均每一就业者负担人数	Number of Dependents per Employee	1.71	1.75	1.64
2. 离退休人数	Number of Retired Veterans and Persons	603	85	119

8-3 续表 continued

单位：人 (person)

项　目	Item	中等收入户 Middle Income Households	中等偏上收入户 Upper Middle Income Households	高收入户 High Income Households
一、调查户数(户)	Number of Households Surveyed (household)	240	240	240
二、家庭人口数	Number of Family Members	737	691	641
平均每户人口数	Average Household Size	3.07	2.88	2.67
1. 就业者人数	Number of Employed Persons	427	396	379
平均每户就业人数	Average Number of Employed Persons per Household	1.78	1.65	1.58
平均每一就业者负担人数	Number of Dependents per Employee	1.72	1.75	1.69
2. 离退休人数	Number of Retired Veterans and Persons	147	133	119

8-4　按收入五等份分组的城市居民人均收支及构成（2019年）

单位：元

项　　目	Item	总平均 Average
人均可支配收入	**Disposable Income**	**65052.10**
工资性收入	Income from Wages and Salaries	42334.68
经营净收入	Net Business Income	3855.84
财产净收入	Net Income from Property	12804.27
转移净收入	Net Income from Transfers	6057.31
可支配收入构成　(%)	**Composition of Disposable Income　(%)**	**100.00**
工资性收入	Income of Wages and Salaries	65.08
经营净收入	Net Business Income	5.93
财产净收入	Net Income from Properties	19.68
转移净收入	Net Income from Transfers	9.31
人均消费支出	**Total Consumption Expenditures**	**45049.28**
食品烟酒	Food,Tobacco and Liquor	14401.78
衣着	Clothing	2313.88
居住	Residence	10026.41
生活用品及服务	Articles for Daily Use and Services	2842.99
交通通信	Transport and Communications	5700.82
教育文化娱乐	Education, Cultural and Recreation	6149.34
医疗保健	Health Care and Medical Services	2146.33
其他用品和服务	Miscellaneous Articles for Use	1467.73
消费支出构成　(%)	**Composition of Consumption Expenditure　(%)**	**100.00**
食品烟酒	Food,Tobacco and Liquor	31.97
衣着	Clothing	5.14
居住	Living	22.26
生活用品及服务	Daily Necessities and Services	6.31
交通通信	Transportation and Telecommunication	12.65
教育文化娱乐	Education,Culture and Entertainment	13.65
医疗保健	Health Service	4.76
其他用品和服务	Other Necessities and Services	3.26

Per Capita Income and Expenditure of Urban Residents Grouped by Five Income Parts and Their Composition(2019)

(yuan)

低收入户 Low Income Households	中等偏下收入户 Lower Middle Income Households	中等收入户 Middle Income Households	中等偏上收入户 Upper Middle Income Households	高收入户 High Income Households
34134.10	**51194.99**	**65781.68**	**80842.00**	**113488.54**
24657.55	33998.13	43666.78	52058.81	68753.80
1379.19	3083.59	1445.62	3445.66	10858.75
5835.31	9646.54	15256.20	16116.29	22070.81
2262.05	4466.73	5413.08	9221.24	11805.18
100.00	**100.00**	**100.00**	**100.00**	**100.00**
72.24	66.41	66.38	64.40	60.58
4.04	6.02	2.20	4.26	9.57
17.10	18.84	23.19	19.94	19.45
6.62	8.73	8.23	11.40	10.40
28365.44	**35874.94**	**45534.08**	**54122.39**	**69228.01**
10582.54	13178.70	14966.81	16116.87	18648.52
1326.07	1617.91	2407.66	2743.73	3742.37
5954.45	7830.21	10264.42	12519.28	15902.31
1839.33	2007.03	2725.35	3540.10	5183.38
3231.20	4178.77	5451.90	7315.90	9674.62
3563.66	4303.53	6312.75	7345.65	8955.94
1258.01	1593.97	2100.22	2602.89	4294.37
610.18	1164.82	1304.97	1937.97	2826.50
100.00	**100.00**	**100.00**	**100.00**	**100.00**
37.31	36.74	32.87	29.78	26.94
4.67	4.51	5.29	5.07	5.41
20.99	21.83	22.54	23.13	22.97
6.48	5.59	5.99	6.54	7.49
11.39	11.65	11.97	13.52	13.98
12.56	12.00	13.86	13.57	12.94
4.44	4.44	4.61	4.81	6.20
2.16	3.24	2.87	3.58	4.07

8-5 城市居民人均可支配收入、恩格尔系数及人均住房建筑面积
Per Capita Annual Disposable Income, Engel's Coefficient and Per Capita Housing Construction Area of Urban Households

年 份 Year	人均可支配收入 Disposable Income		恩格尔系数 (%) Engel's Coefficient of Urban Households (%)	人均住房建筑面积 (平方米) Per Capita housing construction area (sq.m)
	绝对数（元） Value (yuan)	指 数（上年=100） Index (preceding year=100)		
1980	606.12		70.4	4.0
1985	1099.77	125.2	62.5	6.6
1986	1299.64	118.2	61.3	6.9
1987	1500.99	115.5	60.7	7.1
1988	1857.30	123.7	61.8	7.3
1989	2492.63	134.2	60.4	7.6
1990	2748.95	110.3	60.6	8.0
1991	3124.07	113.6	58.9	8.2
1992	3966.76	127.0	56.1	8.5
1993	5260.00	132.6	51.5	8.9
1994	7571.00	143.9	50.1	9.3
1995	9038.16	119.4	50.2	9.6
1996	9905.31	109.6	50.4	10.1
1997	10444.60	105.4	49.1	10.8
1998	11255.70	107.8	44.7	11.6
1999	12018.52	106.8	44.0	12.4
2000	13966.53	116.2	42.6	13.1
2001	14694.00	105.2	40.0	13.9
2002	13380.47	104.9	41.0	15.7
2003	15002.59	112.1	38.9	17.2
2004	16884.16	112.5	38.3	18.2
2005	18287.24	108.3	37.3	18.9
2006	19850.66	108.5	37.0	19.5
2007	22469.22	113.2	32.8	20.0
2008	25316.72	112.7	33.7	20.5
2009	27609.59	109.1	33.2	21.0
2010	30658.49	111.0	33.3	21.4
2011	34438.08	112.3	34.0	21.9
2012	38053.52	111.4	34.0	22.5
2013	42049.14	110.5	33.9	22.7
2014(旧口径)(Old Standard)	45791.51	108.9	33.6	33.5
2014(新口径)(New Standard)	42954.60	108.9	32.9	
2015	46734.60	108.8	32.8	32.17
2016	50940.70	109.0	32.8	33.98
2017	55400.49	108.8	32.1	33.07
2018	59982.10	108.3	32.1	34.22
2019	65052.10	108.5	32.0	34.37

8-6　城市居民家庭年末居住情况（2019年）

Housing Conditions of Urban Households at Year-end (2019)

项　　目	Item	调查户（户）Households Surveyed (household)
按居住空间样式分	**Grouped by Design of Residential Buildings**	**1200**
单栋楼房	Separate Residential Buildings	281
单栋平房	Separate Residential Terraces	29
四居室及以上单元房	Four-room and Above Apartments	72
三居室单元房	Three-room Apartments	367
二居室单元房	Two-room Apartments	379
一居室单元房	One-room Apartments	72
筒子楼或连片平房	Tube-shaped Apartments or Bungalows	
其他	Others	
按主要建筑材料分	**Grouped by Main Building Materials**	**1200**
钢筋混凝土	Reinforced Concrete	1152
砖混材料	Brick and Reinforced Concrete	48
砖瓦砖木	Brick-tile and Brick-wood	
竹草土坯	Bamboo Grass and Adobe	
其他	Others	
按房屋来源分	**Grouped by Source of Buildings**	**1200**
租赁公房	Public Apartments for Lease	36
租赁私房	Private Apartments for Lease	91
自建住房	Self-built	368
购买商品房	Purchase Commercial Residential Apartment	456
购买房改住房	Purchase Housing-reformation Apartment	156
购买保障性住房	Purchase Indemnificatory Apartment	24
拆迁安置房	Settlement Apartment for House Removal	45
继承或获赠住房	Inherited or Gifted	12
免费借用房	Borrow for Free	12
雇主提供免费住房	Employer-provided for Free	
其他来源	Others	
按主要炊用能源状况分	**Grouped by Fuel for Cooking**	**1200**
柴草	Firewood	
煤炭	Coal	
罐装液化石油气	Tanked LPG	470
管道液化石油气	Pipeline LPG Gas	22
管道煤气	Pipeline Gas	48
管道天然气	Pipeline Natural Gas	588
电	Electricity	72
燃料用油	Oil for Fuel	
沼气	Methane	
其他	Others	
无炊用行为	Without Cooking Behavior	

8-7 主要年份农村居民人均可支配收入、恩格尔系数及人均住房建筑面积

Per Capita Annual Disposable Income, Engel's Coefficient and Per Capita Housing Construction Area of Rural Households in Main Years

单位：元 (yuan)

年 份 Year	人均可支配收入 Disposable Income		恩格尔系数 (%)	人均住房建筑面积 (平方米)
	绝对数（元） Value (yuan)	指 数（上年=100) Index (preceding year=100)	Engel's Coefficient of Rural Households (%)	Per Capita housing construction area (sq.m)
1978	249.80		67.13	6.84
1979	250.95	100.46	65.13	7.26
1980	322.66	128.58	54.68	10.43
1985	732.70	106.53	55.49	20.29
1986	857.17	116.99	51.76	21.32
1987	1074.92	125.40	52.70	23.51
1988	1324.48	123.22	50.06	24.24
1989	1524.80	115.12	50.06	24.07
1990	1538.93	100.93	49.05	24.36
1991	1735.57	112.78	51.59	25.59
1992	2152.28	124.01	54.94	25.87
1993	2661.34	123.65	48.72	26.54
1994	3670.24	137.91	49.55	27.67
1995	4482.51	122.13	46.33	29.35
1996	5164.67	115.22	44.96	31.63
1997	5545.91	107.38	47.37	32.21
1998	5628.95	101.50	42.62	35.73
1999	5833.92	103.64	48.54	36.66
2000	6085.97	104.32	38.21	30.60
2001	6445.72	105.91	43.77	30.43
2002(旧口径)	6856.62	106.37	43.27	31.42
2002(新口径)	5831.34			
2003	6129.95	105.12	43.88	36.01
2004	6625.16	108.08	43.75	36.59
2005	7080.19	106.87	43.22	35.66
2006	7788.27	110.00	42.60	36.44
2007	8612.84	110.59	42.82	38.54
2008	9828.12	114.11	42.33	38.73
2009	11066.69	112.60	43.95	40.59
2010	12675.55	114.54	45.91	43.67
2011	14817.72	116.90	44.71	44.70
2012	16788.48	113.30	44.50	45.27
2013	18887.04	112.50	44.21	45.32
2014	17662.80	110.30	42.89	49.87
2015	19323.10	109.40	39.42	49.58
2016	21448.60	111.00	39.50	49.74
2017	23483.88	109.50	38.80	49.86
2018	26020.10	110.80	38.30	50.33
2019	28867.90	110.94	38.22	50.41

注：1.自2014年起广州实施城乡一体化分市县住户调查制度，农村家庭居民收入数据以新口径公布，"人均可支配收入"指标代替"人均纯收入"指标，不再公布"人均纯收入"数据。本表收入指标2014年以前数据为"人均纯收入"数据，2014年指数按可支配收入同口径计算。

2.2015年起"消费支出"和"恩格尔系数"为新口径数据，本表2014年以前该两项指标数据为旧口径。

Note: I.Guangzhou started an integrated household income and expenditure survey in 2014 and the income of rural households is published with new statistical standard.The "Per Capita Net Income" is no longer used and the "Per Capita Disposable Income" takes the place of it. In this table, the "Per Capita Net Income" is preserved before 2014. The index in 2014 is calculated in the same standard of disposable income.

II.Since 2015, "Consumer expenditure" and "Engel's coefficient" for the new caliber data, this table in 2014 before the two indicators of data for the old caliber.

8-8 农村居民家庭基本情况（2019年）

Basic Conditions of Rural Households (2019)

项目	Item	总平均 Average	低收入户 Low Income Households	中等偏下收入户 Lower Middle Income Households
调查户数（户）	Number of Households Surveyed (household)	450	90	90
各组比重（%）	Proportion (%)	100	20	20
调查户人口（人）	Number of Residents in Households Surveyed (person)	1812	406	403
平均每户人口（人）	Average Number of Residents per Household (person)	4.03	4.51	4.47
# 整半劳动力（人）	Average Number of Full/Semi Labor Force per Household (person)	2.98	2.84	3.29
从业人员数（人）	Number of Employees (person)	2.65	2.52	2.83
平均每个从业人员负担人口数（人）	Average Number of Residents per Employee (person)	1.52	1.79	1.58

8-8 续表 continued

项目	Item	中等收入户 Middle Income Households	中等偏上收入户 Upper Middle Income Households	高收入户 High Income Households
调查户数（户）	Number of Households Surveyed (household)	90	90	90
各组比重（%）	Proportion (%)	20	20	20
调查户人口（人）	Number of Residents in Households Surveyed (person)	374	341	288
平均每户人口（人）	Average Number of Residents per Household (person)	4.15	3.79	3.20
# 整半劳动力（人）	Average Number of Full/Semi Labor Force per Household (person)	3.29	3.01	2.46
从业人员数（人）	Number of Employees (person)	2.83	2.84	2.24
平均每个从业人员负担人口数（人）	Average Number of Residents per Employee (person)	1.47	1.33	1.43

8-9 按收入五等份分组的农村居民人均收支及构成（2019年）

单位：元

项目	Item	总平均 Average
人均可支配收入	**Disposable Income**	**28867.90**
工资性收入	Income from Wages and Salaries	21254.27
经营净收入	Net Business Income	3163.73
财产净收入	Net Income from Property	2856.41
转移净收入	Net Income from Transfers	1593.49
可支配收入构成 (%)	**Composition of Disposable Income (%)**	**100.00**
工资性收入	Income of Wages and Salaries	73.63
经营净收入	Net Business Income	10.96
财产净收入	Net Income from Properties	9.89
转移净收入	Net Income from Transfers	5.52
人均消费支出	**Total Consumption Expenditures**	**22521.88**
食品烟酒	Food,Tobacco and Liquor	8607.15
衣着	Clothing	851.75
居住	Residence	4780.72
生活用品及服务	Articles for Daily Use and Services	1297.02
交通通信	Transport and Communications	3222.14
教育文化娱乐	Education, Cultural and Recreation	2258.33
医疗保健	Health Care and Medical Services	1121.32
其他用品和服务	Miscellaneous Articles for Use	383.45
消费支出构成 (%)	**Composition of Consumption Expenditure (%)**	**100.00**
食品烟酒	Food,Tobacco and Liquor	38.22
衣着	Clothing	3.78
居住	Living	21.23
生活用品及服务	Daily Necessities and Services	5.76
交通通信	Transportation and Telecommunication	14.30
教育文化娱乐	Education,Culture and Entertainment	10.03
医疗保健	Health Service	4.98
其他用品和服务	Other Necessities and Services	1.70

Per Capita Income and Expenditure of Rural Residents Grouped by Five Income Parts and Their Composition(2019)

(yuan)

低收入户 Low Income Households	中等偏下收入户 Lower Middle Income Households	中等收入户 Middle Income Households	中等偏上收入户 Upper Middle Income Households	高收入户 High Income Households
16507.37	**23182.61**	**28709.15**	**35965.44**	**50795.56**
14316.11	18968.60	22248.93	25833.78	32960.51
1079.26	1955.32	2930.01	5281.60	5738.57
432.22	1792.44	2107.00	3295.52	8617.87
679.78	466.25	1423.21	1554.54	3478.61
100.00	**100.00**	**100.00**	**100.00**	**100.00**
86.72	81.83	77.49	71.83	64.89
6.54	8.43	10.21	14.69	11.30
2.62	7.73	7.34	9.16	16.97
4.12	2.01	4.96	4.32	6.84
15394.60	**19405.45**	**21418.91**	**25642.13**	**34181.07**
5998.64	7785.96	8066.15	9875.79	11991.76
521.36	720.74	708.96	1006.45	1285.26
3212.81	4217.92	4678.03	5054.64	7206.08
914.25	1018.63	1261.84	1366.01	2283.09
1776.02	2543.57	3138.87	4474.28	5041.18
1881.69	1771.85	2155.70	2380.02	3907.94
884.06	1004.19	1103.74	1094.60	1681.85
205.77	342.59	305.62	390.34	783.91
100.00	**100.00**	**100.00**	**100.00**	**100.00**
38.96	40.12	37.66	38.51	35.09
3.39	3.71	3.31	3.93	3.76
20.87	21.74	21.84	19.71	21.08
5.94	5.25	5.89	5.33	6.68
11.54	13.11	14.66	17.45	14.75
12.22	9.13	10.06	9.28	11.43
5.74	5.17	5.15	4.27	4.92
1.34	1.77	1.43	1.52	2.29

【可支配收入】指住户在调查期内获得的、可用于最终消费支出和储蓄的总和，即调查户可以用来自由支配的收入。按照收入的来源，可支配收入包含四项，分别为：工资性收入、经营净收入、财产净收入和转移净收入。

【工资性收入】指就业人员通过各种途径得到的全部劳动报酬和各种福利，包括受雇于单位或个人、从事各种自由职业、兼职和零星劳动得到的全部劳动报酬和福利。

【经营净收入】指住户或住户成员从事生产经营活动所获得的净收入，是全部经营收入中扣除经营费用、生产性固定资产折旧和生产税之后得到的净收入。计算公式具体为：

经营净收入=经营收入-经营费用-生产性固定资产折旧-生产税

【财产净收入】指住户或住户成员将其所拥有的金融资产、住房等非金融资产和自然资源交由其他机构单位、住户或个人支配而获得的回报并扣除相关的费用之后得到的净收入。财产净收入包括利息净收入、红利收入、储蓄性保险净收益、转让承包土地经营权租金净收入、出租房屋净收入、出租其他资产净收入和自有住房折算租金等。财产净收入不包括转让资产所有权的溢价所得，这应该计入“非收入所得”。计算公式具体为：

财产净收入=财产性收入-财产性支出

【转移净收入】指国家、单位、社会团体对住户的各种经常性转移支付和住户之间的经常性收入转移扣除调查户对国家、单位、住户或个人的经常性或义务性转移支付之后得到的净收入。包括国家、单位、社会团体对住户转移的养老金或退休金、社会救济和补助、政策性生活补贴、救灾款、经常性捐赠和赔偿、政策性生产补贴以及报销医疗费等，住户之间的赡养收入、住户非常住成员寄回带回的收入等，在扣除缴纳的税款、各项社会保障支出、赡养支出、经常性捐赠和赔偿支出以及其他经常转移支出等的净收入。计算公式具体为：

转移净收入=转移性收入-转移性支出

【消费支出】指住户用于满足家庭日常生活消费需要的全部支出，包括用于消费品的支出和用于服务性消费的支出。根据用途不同，消费支出可划分为食品烟酒、衣着、居住、生活用品及服务、交通通信、教育文化娱乐、医疗保健、其他用品及服务八大类。根据来源不同，消费支出可划分为现金消费支出、实物消费支出（含自产自用、来自单位和个人、来自政府和其他社会组织）。

【Disposable Income】 refers to the sum of the household income gained during the period of investigation that can be used as final consumption expenditure and deposit. It means the discretionary income of the households. According to the source of income, disposable income contains four parts: income from wages and salaries, net business income, net income from property and net income from transfers.

【Income from Wages and Salaries】 refers to the labor remuneration and benefits obtained by the employments through various means, including all the labor remuneration and benefits in the employ of enterprises or individual, self-employed and part-time jobs.

【Net Business Income】 refers to the net income of residents or resident members obtained in the production and business operation activities. It means the operating income deducts operating costs, productive fixed assets depreciation and production taxes. Calculation:

Net business income = operating income – operating costs – productive fixed assets depreciation – production taxes

【Net Income from Property】 means that the residents or resident members give the financial assets,Non-financial assets(such as housing)and natural resources they owned to other enterprises, residents or individual to manage, then they receive the net income after deducting the related expenses of the return. Net income from property includes net income from interest, income from bonus, net income from savings insurance, net income from the rent of transferring the right of management of contracted land, income from rental, income from renting other assets and virtual rent. Net income from property does not include the premium income of transferring the ownership of assets, and this premium income should be accounted into gain. Calculation:

Net income from property = Income from property – Expenditure of property

【Net Income from Transfers】 refers the transfer income from country, institutions and social organizations to the residents minus the transfer expenditures from investigated residents to country, institutions ,residents or personal. Income from transfers includes pension or retirement pay, social relief and assistance, policy allowance, relief, regular donations, policy production subsidies and medical reimbursement that country, institutions, social organizations transfer to residents. It also includes alimony, the revenue sent back by the non-permanent residents. Net income means that all the income mentioned above should deduct the payment of taxes, the social security expenditure, alimony expenditure, regular donations, compensation expenditure and other regular expenditure on transfers. Calculation:

Net income from transfers = Income from transfers – Expenditure on transfers

【Expenditure for Consumption】 refers to all the expenditures paid by urban households for consumption in daily life, including expenditure for customer goods and services. According to the different purposes, expenditure for consumption can be divided into eight categories: Food, tobacco and liquor, Clothing, Residence, Household facilities, articles and services, Transportation and communication services, Education, cultural and recreation services, Health care and medical services, Miscellaneous commodities and services. According to the different sources, expenditure for consumption divided into monetary expenditure for consumption and material expenditure for consumption (including self-produced and self-used, from institutions and person, from government and other social organizations).

第九篇 CHAPTER 9

城市建设

CITY CONSTRUCTION

第九篇　城市建设

一、本篇资料反映广州市城市建设和公用事业的规模、速度、效益及综合水平等基本情况。

二、本篇资料由广州市统计局固定资产投资统计处整理提供。

三、本篇资料依据国家住房和城乡建设部制定的《城市（县城）建设统计报表制度》编制。统计数据由广州市住房和城乡建设局、广州市交通运输局、广州市水务局、广州市城市管理和综合执法局以及广州市林业和园林局等单位提供。

9 City Construction

I.The data in this chapter show the basic conditions of scale, speed, mileage and comprehensive level of the city construction and utilities in Guangzhou.

II.The data in this chapter are prepared and provided by the Division of Investment and Construction Statistics of Guangzhou Municipal Bureau of Statistics.

III. The data in this chapter are collected and tabulated in accordance with the statistical survey scheme of Construction of cities and Counties stipulated by Ministry of Housing and Urban-Rural Development of the People's Republic of China, all of which are provided by Guangzhou Municipal Housing and Urban-Rural Development Bureau, Guangzhou Municipal Transportation Bureau, Guangzhou Water Authority, Guangzhou Municipal City Administration and Law Enforcement Bureau, Guangzhou Municipal Forestry and Landscaping Bureau.

9-1 城市市政设施
Public Facilities in Urban Districts

项　　目		Item		2018	2019
道路长度	(公里)	Length of Roads	(1000 m)	14007.14	14083.44
# 快速路		Expressways		196.48	196.48
主干路		Main Roads		1208.97	1245.77
道路面积	(万平方米)	Area of Roads	(10000 sq.m)	18742.99	18792.69
# 人行道		Pavement		2388.03	2438.43
人均城市道路面积	(平方米)	Per Capita Area of Roads	(sq.m)	12.61	12.46
桥梁座数	(座)	Number of Bridges	(unit)	1363	1356
# 立交桥		Crossroads		245	248
道路照明灯盏数	(千盏)	Number of Street Lights	(1000 units)	556.06	585.11
排水管道长度	(公里)	Length of Sewer Pipelines	(1000 m)	24239	28793
污水排放量	(万立方米)	Sewage Discharge Quantity	(10000 cubic metres)	188622	203641
污水处理厂	(座)	Sewage Treatment Plant	(unit)	50	53
污水处理厂处理能力	(万立方米/日)	Sewage Treatment Capacity	(10000 cubic metres/day)	544	572
污水处理厂处理量	(万立方米)	Quantity of Sewage Treatment	(10000 cubic metres)	180195	197533
污水处理率	(%)	Sewage Treatment Rate	(%)	95.5	97.0
# 污水处理厂集中处理率	(%)	Concentrated Sewage Treatment Rate	(%)	95.5	97.0

注：1．本表数据为全市(11区)口径；

2.2018年、2019年道路长度、道路面积等指标数据包括高速公路和国省道路、市政道路和县乡村道路；

3．本表数据由广州市住房和城乡建设局汇总相关单位数据后提供，具体数据由相关单位负责解释。

Note: I. The coverage in this table includes 11 districts.

II.The index data of road length and road area include expressways, national and provincial roads, municipal roads and county and rural roads in 2018 and 2019.

III.The data in this table are collected by Housing and Urban-Rural Construction Bureau of Guangzhou Municipality from the related sectors. The responsibility to interpret the data shall be remained with the related sectors.

9-2 城市供水
Water Supply in Urban Districts

项　　目	Item	2018	2019
综合生产能力（万立方米/日）	Overall Production Capacity (10000 cu.m/day)	786.90	845.35
供水管道长度 (公里)	Length of Water Supply Pipelines (1000 m)	22801.68	35293.20
供水总量 (万立方米)	Total Volume of Water Supply (10000 cu.m)	248128.75	256155.03
# 售水量	Sales Volume of Tap Water	202558.70	207190.14
生产运营用水	For Production Use	36060.25	35219.33
公共服务用水	For Public Services	46888.95	49656.40
居民家庭用水	For Household Use	112360.70	117104.61
其他用水	Others	7248.80	5209.81
用水户数 (户)	Number of Households with Access to Tap Water (unit)	3019053	3118277
# 家庭用户	Number of Families with Access to Tap Water	2744141	2852512
用水人口 (万人)	Number of Residents with Access to Tap Water (10000 persons)	1745.38	1785.65
人均日生活用水量 (升)	Per Capita Daily Consumption of Tap Water for Residential Use (liter)	261.36	263.86
用水普及率 (%)	Coverage Rate of Urban Population with Access to Tap Water (%)	100.00	100.00

注：1.本表数据为全市(11区)口径；

2.本表资料不包企业自建设施供水；

3.本表数据由广州市水务局提供。

Note: I. The coverage in this table includes 11 districts.

II. The data in this table exclude the water supply by self-built facilities of corporations.

III. The data in this table are collected by Water Affairs Bureau of Guangzhou Municipality.

9-3 城市燃气供应
Gas Supply in Urban Districts

项　　目	Item	2018	2019
液化石油气	**Liquefied Petroleum Gas**		
储气能力　(吨)	Storage Capacity (ton)	36888.49	6824.10
供气管道长度（公里）	Length of Gas Supply Pipelines (1000 m)	6.44	10.05
供气总量　(吨)	Total Supply of Gas (ton)	656206.00	758758.86
销售气量	Sales Volume of Gas	656018.35	758653.54
# 居民家庭	Households	346088.23	312878.56
用气户数　(户)	Number of Households (unit)	2517163	2297965
# 家庭用户	Families	2408926	2177772
用气人口　(万人)	Number of Residents with Access to Gas (10000 persons)	622.87	563.10
天然气	**Natural Gas**		
储气能力（万立方米）	Storage Capacity (10000 cu.m)	669.45	594.34
供气管道长度（公里）	Length of Gas Supply Pipelines (1000 m)	7758.76	9439.47
供气总量（万立方米）	Total Supply of Gas (10000 cu.m)	210419.07	235420.91
# 销售气量	Sales Volume of Gas	192897.43	219498.78
# 居民家庭	Households	36991.20	39553.64
用气户数　(户)	Number of Households (unit)	2509059	2602984
# 家庭用户	Families	2496643	2586183
用气人口　(万人)	Number of Residents with Access to Gas (10000 persons)	680.72	778.44
燃气普及率　(%)	Coverage Rate of Urban Population with Access to Gas (%)	99.10	99.20

注：1.本表数据为全市(11区)口径；
2.本表数据由广州市城市管理和综合执法局提供。
Note: I. The coverage in this table includes 11 districts.
II. The data in this table are provided by City Management and Comprehensive Law Enforcement Bureau of Guangzhou Municipality.

9-4 城市市政公用设施建设固定资产投资额
Investment in Fixed Assets in Public Facilities in Urban Districts

单位:万元 (10000 yuan)

项　　目	Item	2018	2019
本年完成投资	Investment Completed in Current Year	6485652	6946208
供　水	Water Supply	152055	206368
燃　气	Gas Supply	119433	64656
轨道交通	Rail Traffic	3084483	2968153
道路桥梁	Roads and Bridges	1587246	1533994
排　水	Drainage	877421	87239
园林绿化	Parks and Green Areas	63844	49086
市容环境卫生	Environmental sanitation	225977	190056
其　他	Others	375193	1846657

注：1.本表数据为全市(11区)口径；
2.本表数据由广州市住房和城乡建设局汇总相关单位数据后提供，具体数据由相关单位负责解释。
Note: I. The coverage in this table includes 11 districts.
II.The data in this table are collected by Housing & Urban-Rural Construction Commission of Guangzhou Municipality from the related sectors. The responsibility to interpret the data shall be remained with the related sectors.

9-5 城市园林绿化
Parks, Gardens and Green Areas in Urban Districts

项目	Item	2018	2019
绿化覆盖面积 （公顷）	Coverage Area of Afforestation (hectare)	156698	156831
# 建成区	Developed Areas	58669	60250
建成区绿化覆盖率 （%）	Green Coverage Rate in Developed Areas (%)	45.13	45.50
绿地面积 （公顷）	Area of Green Areas (hectare)	147048	147720
# 建成区	Developed Areas	50986	52848
建成区绿地率 （%）	Rate of Green Areas in Developed Areas (%)	39.22	39.91
公园绿地面积 （公顷）	Area of Gardens (hectare)	30189	32081
人均公园绿地面积 （平方米）	Per Capita Garden (sq.m)	17.30	17.96
公园个数 （个）	Number of Parks (unit)	247	247
公园面积 （公顷）	Area of Parks (hectare)	5198	5198
建成区面积 （平方公里）	Developed Areas (sq.km)	1300.01	1324.17

注：1.本表数据为全市(11区)口径；
2.本表数据由广州市林业和园林局提供。
Note: I. The coverage in this table includes 11 districts.
II. The data in this table are provided by Forestry & Landscape Gardens Bureau of Guangzhou Municipality.

9-6 城市市容环境卫生
City Appearance and Environmental Sanitation

项目	Item	2018	2019
道路清扫保洁面积 （万平方米）	Area of Roads under Cleaning Program (10000 sq.m)	22414	23223
# 机械化	By Mechanization	9533	10217
城镇生活垃圾清运量 （万吨）	Volume of Living Garbage Disposal (10000 tons)	557.56	668.04
城镇生活垃圾处理量 （万吨）	Garbage Treatment (10000 tons)	557.56	668.04
城镇生活垃圾无害化处理厂(场)数 （座）	Number of Garbage Harmless Disposal Factories (unit)	13	15
城镇生活垃圾无害化处理量 （万吨）	Volume of Garbage Harmless Disposal (10000 tons)	557.56	668.04
城镇生活垃圾无害化处理率 （%）	Rate of Garbage Harmless Disposal (%)	100.00	100.00
公共厕所 （座）	Number of Public Lavatories (unit)	1457	1622
市容环卫专用车辆设备总数 （辆）	Number of Special Vehicles for Environmental Sanitation (unit)	5645	5558

注：1.本表数据为全市(11区)口径；
2.本表数据由广州市城市管理和综合执法局提供。
Note: I. The coverage in this table includes 11 districts.
II. The data in this table are provided by City Management and Comprehensive Law Enforcement Bureau of Guangzhou Municipality.

【道路长度】指道路长度和与道路相通的桥梁、隧道的长度，按车行道中心线计算。

【快速路】城市道路中设有中央分隔带，具有四条以上的车道，全部或部分采用立体交叉与控制出入，供车辆以较高的速度行驶的道路。

【主干路】在城市道路网中起骨架作用的道路。

【供水总量】指报告期供水企业（单位）供出的全部水量，包括有效供水量和漏损水量。有效供水量指水厂将水供出厂外后，各类用户实际使用到的水量，包括售水量和免费供水量。漏损水量指在供水过程中由于管道及附属设施破损而造成的漏水量、失窃水量以及水表失灵少计算的水量。

【售水量】指报告期供水企业(单位)收费供应的水量，只包括本地售水量，不包括销往本区域外的售水量。

【生产运营用水】指在城市范围内生产、运营的农、林、牧、渔业、工业、建筑业、交通运输业等单位在生产、运营过程中的用水。

【公共服务用水】指为城市社会公共生活服务的用水。包括行政事业单位、部队营区和公共设施服务、社会服务业、批发零售贸易业、旅馆饮食业以及社会服务业等单位的用水。

【居民家庭用水】指城市范围内所有居民家庭的日常生活用水。包括城市居民、农民家庭、公共供水站用水。

【污水处理厂】指在城市或工业区的城市污水通过排水管道集中于一个或几个处所，并利用由各种处理单元组成的污水处理系统进行净化处理，最终使处理后的污水和污泥达到规定要求后排放水体或再利用的生产场所。不包括渗水井、化粪池（含改良化粪池）和污水处理装置。

【污水处理能力】指污水处理厂（或处理装置）每昼夜处理污水量的设计能力。

【污水处理量】指污水处理厂（或污水处理装置）实际处理的污水量。包括物理处理量、生物处理量和化学处理量。

【生活垃圾清运量】指报告期内收集和运送到各垃圾处理场（厂）的垃圾的数量。

【生活垃圾无害化处理量】指报告期内简易处理场和各种垃圾无害化处理场（厂）处理垃圾的总量。垃圾简易处理量指垃圾简易填埋场所处理的垃圾总量。垃圾无害化处理量指垃圾无害化处理场（厂）所处理的垃圾总量。

【绿地面积】指报告期末用作园林和绿化的各种绿地面积。包括公园绿地、生产绿地、防护绿地、附属绿地和其他绿地的面积。

【公园绿地面积】指城市中向公众开放的、以游憩为主要功能，有一定的游憩设施和服务设施，同时兼有健全生态、美化景观、防灾灭灾等综合作用的绿化用地。它是城市建设用地、城市绿地系统和城市市政公用设施的重要组成部分。

【Length of Roads】 refers to the length of roads and of the bridges and tunnels connected to the roads, calculated by the center line of the roads.

【Annual Volume of Water Supply】 refers to the total volume of water supplied by water-works(units) during the reference period, including both the effective water supply and loss during the water supply.

【Expressway】 refers to the road which there is a central separation zone in, with more than four lanes, all or part of which adopts three-dimensional intersection and control access for vehicles to drive at high speed.

【Main Road】 refers to the road that acts as a leading part in urban road network.

【Volume of Sold Water】 refers to the total volume of paid water supplied by water-works(units) during the reference period, only including the volume of paid water sold to local region, not including the volume of paid water sold to other regions.

【Volume of Water for Production】 refers to water consumption for urban production of enterprises of farming, forestry, animal husbandry and fishery, industry, construction, transport, and so on.

【Water Consumption of Public Service】 refers to water consumption for urban public services, including the consumption of government agencies and public institutions. Military barracks, public facilities, wholesale and retail outlets, restaurants, hotels, and other units providing public services.

【Household Water Consumption】 refers to consumption of water for daily life of all households within the boundary of cities, including water consumption of urban residents and farmers, and public water supply stations.

【Wastewater Treatment Plant】 refers to place where wastewater in urban or industrial areas is concentrated in one or several spaces through drainage pipes, and purified by wastewater treatment system composed of various treatment units, and finally the treated wastewater and sludge are discharged after meeting the specified requirements. Seepage wells, septic tanks (including improved septic tanks) and sewage treatment plants are not included.

【Wastewater Treated Capability】 refers to design capacity of wastewater treatment plant (or treatment system) to dispose wastewater day and night.

【Wastewater Treatment Volume】 refers to the amount of wastewater actually disposed by wastewater treatment sites (or wastewater treatment plants), including physical processing volume, biological processing volume and chemical processing capacity.

【Consumption Wastes Disposed Volume】 refers to the volume of consumption wastes collected and transported to disposal factories or sites during the reference period.

【Consumption Wastes Harmlessly Disposed Volume】 refers to the total amount of garbage handled by simply disposed sites and innocuously disposed sites (or plants). The amount of garbage simply disposed refers to the total amount of garbage disposed in a simple landfill. The amount of garbage innocuous disposed refers to the total amount of garbage handled by the garbage innocuous treatment sites (or plants).

【Area of Urban Greenbelt】 refers to the total area occupied for green projects at the end of the reference period, including park green land, production green land, protection green land, green land attached to institutions, and other greenbelt.

【Park Green Areas】 refers to green areas open to the public for amusement and rest with the facilities of amusement, rest and services, Its function includes perfecting ecology, beautifying landscape, and preventing and reducing disaster. It is an important component of urban construction sites, urban green area system and public facilities in urban districts.

第十篇 CHAPTER 10

农 业

AGRICULTURE

简要说明
Brief Introduction

第十篇　农　业

一、本篇资料反映广州市农业生产和农村社会经济的基本情况。

二、本篇资料由广州市统计局农村统计处整理提供。

三、本篇资料主要来源于广州市农村统计报表制度。农村统计报表制度的统计范围包括各区、镇街（涉农）、村居（涉农）基本情况以及各种经济类型的全部农林牧渔生产单位和农户进行的农业生产经营情况。

10 Agriculture

I. The data in this chapter show the basic conditions of agricultural production and rural economy in Guangzhou.

II. The data in this chapter are prepared and provided by the Division of Rural Statistics of Guangzhou Municipal Bureau of Statistics.

III. The data in this chapter mainly come from the statistical reporting summary on rural area of Guangzhou. The statistical coverage of the statistical reporting summary includes the basic information of all districts, towns and streets (agriculture), villages (agriculture), and the agricultural production and operation of all agricultural, forestry, animal husbandry and fishery production units and farmers of various economic types.

10-1 农业主要指标

Major Indicators of Agriculture

项　　目	Item	2018	2019
乡镇户数 (户)	Number of Rural Households (household)	1839391	2016260
乡镇人口 (人)	Rural Population (person)	6038660	6461028
乡镇从业人员 (人)	Number of Rural Employed Persons (person)	3707365	3908707
农、林、牧、渔业从业人员 (人)	Number of Rural Employed Persons in Agriculture, Forestry, Animal Husbandry and Fishery (person)	639114	653999
森林覆盖率 (%)	Forest Coverage (%)	42.31	42.31
常用耕地面积 (公顷)	Area of Cultivated Land (hectare)	90486	90696
有效灌溉面积 (公顷)	Irrigated Area (hectare)	75180	75294
耕地水利化程度 (%)	Irrigation Degree of Cultivated Land (%)	80.87	81.49
农业机械总动力 (万瓦)	Total Power of Agricultural Machinery (10000 w)	127524	122812
农、林、牧、渔业劳动机械化程度 (%)	Labor Mechanization Degree of Agriculture, Forestry, Animal Husbandry and Fishery (%)	7.23	6.93
化肥施用量(折纯) (吨)	Consumption of Chemical Fertilizers (100 percent effective content equivalent) (ton)	105922	102875
农药使用量 (吨)	Consumption of Pesticides (ton)	3100	2863
农村用电量 (万千瓦·时)	Electricity Consumed in Rural Area (10000 kwh)	1504095	1478089
农、林、牧、渔业总产值 (万元)	Gross Output Value of Agriculture, Forestry, Animal Husbandry and Fishery (10000 yuan)	4166916	4462804
农、林、牧、渔业增加值 (万元)	Value-added of Agriculture, Forestry, Animal Husbandry and Fishery (10000 yuan)	2530891	2718021
农、林、牧、渔业商品产值率 (%)	Rate of Commodity Output Value of Agriculture, Forestry, Animal Husbandry and Fishery (%)	98.9	98.8
主要农产品产量	Output of Major Agricultural Products		
粮　食 (吨)	Grain (ton)	130056	131988
花　生 (吨)	Peanuts (ton)	15541	14542
蔬　菜 (吨)	Vegetables (ton)	3687937	3853154
园林水果 (吨)	Fruits (ton)	605697	642578
肉　类 (吨)	Meat (ton)	135233	114935
水产品 (吨)	Aquatic Products (ton)	454214	465236
都市农业从业人员 (万人)	Employed Persons in Urban Agriculture (10000 person)	140	151
都市农业总收入 (万元)	Total Income of Urban Agriculture (10000 yuan)	21675653	23838601
农村居民人均可支配收入 (元)	Per Capita Disposable Income of Rural Residents (yuan)	26020	28868

注：1.自2014年起广州实施城乡一体化分市县住户调查制度，农村家庭居民收入数据以新口径公布，"人均可支配收入"指标代替"人均纯收入"指标，不再公布"人均纯收入"数据。

2.本表森林覆盖率数据由广州市林业和园林局提供，农、林、渔业劳动机械化程度、化肥施用量和农药使用量数据由广州市农村和农业局提供并计算得出。

Note: I. Guangzhou started an integrated household income and expenditure survey in 2014 and the income of rural households is published with new statistical standard. The "Per Capita Net Income" is no longer used and the "Per Capita Disposable Income" takes the place of it.

II. The data of forest coverage rate in this table is provided by Guangzhou Municipal Bureau of forestry and landscape architecture,and the data of labor mechanization degree, fertilizer application amount and pesticide use amount of agriculture, forestry, animal husbandry and fishery are provided and calculated by Guangzhou agricultural and rural Bureau.

10-2　主要年份年末耕地面积

Area of Cultivated Land at Year-end in Main Years

单位：公顷　　　　(hectare)

年 份 Year	常用耕地面积 Area of Cultivated Land	水(旱)田 Paddy Fields	旱 地 Dry Fields	平均每个农业人口拥有耕地 Cultivated Area Per Rural Person	平均每个农业从业人员拥有耕地 Cultivated Area Per Rural Employee
1978	249479	221451	28028	0.09	0.21
1980	248260	220258	28002	0.11	0.23
1985	234171	207431	26740	0.09	0.24
1990	221138	196266	24872	0.09	0.24
1995	177892	158849	19043	0.07	0.20
1996	172179	153332	18847	0.07	0.19
1997	169700	151631	18069	0.07	0.19
1998	168491	150843	17648	0.07	0.19
1999	164816	147455	17361	0.07	0.19
2000	159115	142220	16895	0.05	0.17
2001	154941	137628	17313	0.05	0.17
2002	146311	128888	17423	0.05	0.16
2003	134934	115565	19369	0.06	0.15
2004	131954	116943	15011	0.06	0.16
2005	130094	111700	18394	0.06	0.15
2006	106579	88971	17608	0.05	0.13
2007	104500	84747	19753	0.05	0.13
2008	102155	85064	17091	0.04	0.13
2009	100784	84992	15792	0.03	0.13
2010	100647	87516	13131	0.03	0.13
2011	99552	85267	14285	0.03	0.15
2012	99086	85522	13564	0.03	0.15
2013	98148	84495	13653	0.03	0.14
2014	96398	82719	13679	0.03	0.15
2015	95411	81742	13669	0.03	0.15
2016	95188	80820	14368	0.03	0.15
2017	92108	77907	14201	0.03	0.14
2018	90486	76492	13994	0.03	0.14
2019	90696	72617	18079	0.03	0.14

注：2002年及以前年份的常用耕地面积数按国家新口径进行了换算。

Note: The data of the area of cultivated land in 2002 and before have been converted to the new statistical standard.

10-3 耕地面积及变动情况（2019年）

Statistics on Area of Cultivated Land and Its Changes (2019)

单位:公顷 (hectare)

项　目	Item	全 市 Total	荔湾区 Liwan	海珠区 Haizhu	天河区 Tianhe	白云区 Baiyun	黄埔区 Huangpu
年初耕地总资源	Total Resources of Cultivated Land at Year-beginning	93003	615	96	196	8926	2394
年末耕地总资源	Total Resources of Cultivated Land at Year-end	92396	612	96	194	9252	2351
# 常用耕地面积	Area of Cultivated Land	90696	611	93	195	8807	2165
# 水　田	Paddy Fields	72617	48		94	7436	1418
当年增加耕地面积	Area of Increased Cultivated Land in Current Year	1114				605	3
# 园地改为耕地	Area of Cultivated Land Adapted from Garden Land	114					3
当年减少耕地面积	Area of Decreased Cultivated Land in Current Year	1721	3		2	279	46
# 国家基建占用	Occupied by Capital Construction	752				203	36
其他基建占用	Occupied by Other Construction	281	3		1	72	9
粮食占用耕地面积	Area of Cultivated Land Occupied by Grain	13224				207	286
蔬菜占用耕地面积	Area of Cultivated Land Occupied by Vegetables	27519	43	93	90	5547	657

10-3　续表 continued

单位：公顷 (hectare)

项　目	Item	番禺区 Panyu	花都区 Huadu	南沙区 Nansha	从化区 Conghua	增城区 Zengcheng
年初耕地总资源	Total Resources of Cultivated Land at Year-beginning	6350	10418	17202	20507	26299
年末耕地总资源	Total Resources of Cultivated Land at Year-end	6308	10278	16636	20488	26181
# 常用耕地面积	Area of Cultivated Land	6252	10277	16223	20046	26027
# 水　田	Paddy Fields	4482	8976	12045	16818	21300
当年增加耕地面积	Area of Increased Cultivated Land in Current Year	110	50	346		
# 园地改为耕地	Area of Cultivated Land Adapted from Garden Land		40	71		
当年减少耕地面积	Area of Decreased Cultivated Land in Current Year	152	190	912	19	118
# 国家基建占用	Occupied by Capital Construction	35	62	308	19	89
其他基建占用	Occupied by Other Construction	61	9	126		
粮食占用耕地面积	Area of Cultivated Land Occupied by Grain	64	1050	621	6479	4517
蔬菜占用耕地面积	Area of Cultivated Land Occupied by Vegetables	1415	3848	3347	2147	10332

10-4 农村基层基本情况（2019年）

项目	Item	全市 Total
农村基层组织（个）	Rural Grassroots Units (unit)	
镇政府	Number of Town Governments	35
村(居)民委员会	Number of Villagers' Committees	1256
农村人口状况	Statistics on Rural Population	
乡镇户数（户）	Number of Rural Households (household)	2016260
乡镇人口（人）	Rural Population (person)	6461028
农村社会基础设施（个）	Number of Rural Infrastructure (unit)	
自来水受益村	Number of Villages Benefiting from Tap Water	1237
通有线电视村	Number of Villages Available for Cable Television	1244
通宽带村	Number of Villages Available for Broadband Internet	1244
农村劳动力资源总数（人）	Total Number of Rural Labor Force (person)	4409919
# 本地劳动力	Local Labor Force	2143862
# 劳动年龄内的人口数	Number of Population within Labor Age	4306652
农村从业人员合计（人）	Total Number of Rural Employed Persons (person)	3908707
# 劳动年龄内	Within Labor Age	3771145
农、林、牧、渔业从业人员	Number of Rural Employed Persons in Agriculture, Forestry, Animal Husbandry and Fishery	623062
农业	Agriculture	521382
林业	Forestry	7477
畜牧业	Animal Husbandry	27261
渔业	Fishery	40337
农、林、牧、渔服务业	Service Industry for Agriculture	26605
工 业	Industry	1749230
建筑业	Construction	245930
批发和零售业	Wholesale and Retail Trade	330313
交通运输、仓储和邮电业	Transport, Storage and Post	190569
住宿和餐饮业	Hotels and Catering Services	279644
信息传输、软件和信息技术服务业	Information Transmission, Software and Information Technology Services	127334
其他行业	Others	362579

Basic Statistics on Rural Grassroots Units (2019)

白云区 Baiyun	黄埔区 Huangpu	番禺区 Panyu	花都区 Huadu	南沙区 Nansha	从化区 Conghua	增城区 Zengcheng
4	1	6	6	6	5	7
137	29	197	202	141	236	314
269266	24713	621359	279243	290450	142284	388945
1097919	113017	1749287	1019108	733385	550706	1197606
136	28	198	202	145	214	314
136	29	198	202	145	220	314
136	29	198	202	145	220	314
724567	72864	1273645	669083	522437	369019	778304
301010	58806	373564	327054	247184	337139	499105
710179	70586	1252333	659513	514076	344957	755008
628261	69596	1113380	624553	485363	319133	668421
610585	66587	1085713	611160	472960	288772	635368
68619	20918	51722	96259	81289	137144	167111
61639	16266	37362	86017	69540	115711	134847
22	1212	229	800	119	2332	2763
438	165	2545	1880	430	11435	10368
3163	1323	9525	6525	8292	3015	8494
3357	1952	2061	1037	2908	4651	10639
305458	14910	492224	353211	234123	85731	263573
33040	6210	82982	29798	31295	21877	40728
51330	5903	141096	43762	30699	20162	37361
39958	4223	61690	29123	22386	9420	23769
55987	5207	106905	29845	25727	21690	34283
18699	1453	64900	12436	12994	5699	11153
55170	10772	111861	30119	46850	17364	90443

10-5 农林牧渔业生产经营户及从业人员情况(2019年)

项　　目	Item
从事农、林、牧、渔业生产经营户(户)	Number of Households Engaging in Agriculture, Forestry, Animal Husbandry and Fishery (household)
农、林、牧、渔业从业人员数　(人)	Number of Rural Employed Persons in Agriculture, Forestry, Animal Husbandry and Fishery (person)
农业	Agriculture
林业	Forestry
畜牧业	Animal Husbandry
渔业	Fishery
农、林、牧、渔服务业	Service Industry for Agriculture

10-5　续表

项　　目	Item
从事农、林、牧、渔业生产经营户(户)	Number of Households Engaging in Agriculture, Forestry, Animal Husbandry and Fishery (household)
农、林、牧、渔业从业人员数　(人)	Number of Rural Employed Persons in Agriculture, Forestry, Animal Husbandry and Fishery (person)
农业	Agriculture
林业	Forestry
畜牧业	Animal Husbandry
渔业	Fishery
农、林、牧、渔服务业	Service Industry for Agriculture

Number of Households and Laborers Engaging in Agriculture, Forestry, Animal Husbandry and Fishery (2019)

全 市 Total	荔湾区 Liwan	海珠区 Haizhu	天河区 Tianhe	白云区 Baiyun	黄埔区 Huangpu
411825	2795	444	460	40472	18924
653999	6838	929	966	72293	34483
548784	6577	929	916	65146	28702
7800			6	22	1521
27584				438	223
42017	245		7	3165	2033
27814	16		37	3522	2004

continued

番禺区 Panyu	花都区 Huadu	南沙区 Nansha	从化区 Conghua	增城区 Zengcheng
27195	70174	37913	104917	108531
51722	96259	85979	167111	137419
37362	86017	72325	115963	134847
229	800	119	2340	2763
2545	1880	695	11435	10368
9525	6525	9002	3021	8494
2061	1037	3838	4660	10639

10-6 主要年份农林牧渔业总产值

Gross Output Value of Agriculture, Forestry, Animal Husbandry and Fishery in Main Years

单位：万元　　　　(10000 yuan)

年份 Year	合计 Total	农业 Agriculture	林业 Forestry	畜牧业 Animal Husbandry	渔业 Fishery
1978	79940	62212	1367	11018	3551
1980	89465	69534	2316	11730	3650
1985	180163	117429	2312	43583	9530
1986	207553	133272	2921	48420	12630
1987	259437	171381	3534	58134	15286
1988	374875	235199	4210	100127	22571
1989	410575	258918	5325	105375	25131
1990	439322	280156	5011	110313	28142
1991	489080	311918	4809	124979	32183
1992	590289	359850	8004	165373	42635
1993	773560	415462	9442	220827	108282
1994	1034215	562429	8198	315842	125140
1995	1268076	673678	10672	369589	185396
1996	1429078	701636	11152	429758	247883
1997	1508110	748281	12706	449656	254502
1998	1540244	770438	12643	439267	265520
1999	1600738	818349	12683	433928	280155
2000	1630468	823477	13224	430589	296503
2001	1670518	878086	13344	406407	304442
2002	1750598	942935	11577	404566	321379
2003	1806678	978410	12823	388590	332774
2004	2014423	1055554	36602	401247	358246
2005	2208105	1126688	38424	477025	376560
2006	2178394	1140576	18192	421336	406265
2007	2544675	1349965	18284	519306	432804
2008	2913008	1445324	19898	639605	526876
2009	2956200	1500816	21683	612002	536132
2010	3221258	1662415	26613	641581	583252
2011	3506065	1783512	34286	721893	627707
2012	3667902	1872361	32169	766839	637314
2013	3899763	2027062	39615	758607	677539
2014	3983015	2141475	40369	648663	732958
2015	4134562	2260493	42178	618008	751349
2016	4366530	2407531	38691	657981	767014
2017	4329167	2401771	36563	565886	794899
2018	4166916	2316909	25355	419744	819757
2019	4462804	2504592	24176	440968	888886

10-7 主要年份农林牧渔业总产值指数

Indices of Gross Output Value of Agriculture, Forestry, Animal Husbandry and Fishery in Main Years

上年=100 (preceding year=100)

年 份 Year	合 计 Total	农业 Agriculture	林业 Forestry	畜牧业 Animal Husbandry	渔业 Fishery
1978	103.2	101.5	124.9	113.4	102.4
1980	108.2	107.1	230.1	98.1	127.9
1985	108.1	103.8	110.8	125.1	112.9
1986	105.2	101.9	113.1	110.4	113.0
1987	104.4	104.8	120.6	103.0	103.2
1988	105.7	101.0	86.2	120.1	114.6
1989	101.4	100.5	138.3	98.7	101.2
1990	106.3	106.1	62.3	109.3	109.5
1991	111.1	111.8	98.5	113.0	106.3
1992	114.0	109.4	182.1	123.3	121.7
1993	99.1	81.2	75.2	119.3	160.8
1994	117.4	118.6	83.9	114.8	122.3
1995	109.3	106.0	106.1	104.5	126.9
1996	106.6	97.1	107.2	106.9	128.0
1997	106.6	107.4	97.5	105.3	106.3
1998	104.6	100.1	97.2	103.7	112.1
1999	109.5	118.0	110.5	99.9	106.3
2000	102.0	98.9	108.4	101.8	104.8
2001	101.6	103.6	92.9	95.2	107.1
2002	109.1	123.5	96.1	97.4	101.7
2003	100.7	94.5	75.4	98.5	108.5
2004	105.1	112.6	120.5	97.5	101.9
2005	104.1	102.3	103.7	108.4	101.2
2006	98.1	100.7	47.1	87.9	107.3
2007	103.1	102.2	90.2	103.1	101.3
2008	103.4	97.3	104.0	110.0	109.1
2009	103.9	103.0	109.0	104.9	105.2
2010	103.1	103.3	96.6	102.1	102.9
2011	102.6	103.6	122.0	98.3	102.5
2012	102.8	103.5	93.1	100.3	104.4
2013	102.9	102.4	120.7	98.2	106.5
2014	100.1	104.7	98.0	84.0	102.4
2015	102.2	103.8	104.2	91.8	103.1
2016	100.7	101.1	100.4	96.1	101.1
2017	100.7	102.6	94.3	91.1	99.9
2018	103.9	102.8	70.6	103.5	106.6
2019	103.2	105.0	95.3	91.0	106.7

注：农林牧渔业总产值指数按可比价计算。
Note: The indices of gross output value of farming, forestry, animal husbandry and fishery are calculated by comparable price.

10-8 农林牧渔业总产值、增加值和商品产值（2019年）

单位:万元

项　　目	Item	全　市 Total
农、林、牧、渔业总产值(当年价格)	**Gross Output Value of Agriculture, Forestry, Animal Husbandry and Fishery (at current prices)**	**4462804**
农业	Agriculture	2504592
林业	Forestry	24176
畜牧业	Animal Husbandry	440968
渔业	Fishery	888886
农、林、牧、渔服务业	Service Industry for Agriculture	604182
农、林、牧、渔业总产值构成　(%)	**Composition of Gross Output Value of Agriculture, Forestry, Animal Husbandry and Fishery (%)**	**100.00**
农业	Agriculture	56.12
林业	Forestry	0.54
畜牧业	Animal Husbandry	9.88
渔业	Fishery	19.92
农、林、牧、渔服务业	Service Industry for Agriculture	13.54
农、林、牧、渔业增加值	**Value-added of Agriculture, Forestry, Animal Husbandry and Fishery**	**2718021**
农业	Agriculture	1744451
林业	Forestry	17455
畜牧业	Animal Husbandry	179778
渔业	Fishery	526931
农、林、牧、渔服务业	Service Industry for Agriculture	249406
农、林、牧、渔业增加值构成　(%)	**Composition of Value-added of Agriculture, Forestry, Animal Husbandry and Fishery (%)**	**100.00**
农业	Agriculture	64.18
林业	Forestry	0.64
畜牧业	Animal Husbandry	6.61
渔业	Fishery	19.39
农、林、牧、渔服务业	Service Industry for Agriculture	9.18
农、林、牧、渔业商品产值	**Commodity Output Value of Agriculture, Forestry, Animal Husbandry and Fishery**	**4407350**
农业	Agriculture	2496988
林业	Forestry	24112
畜牧业	Animal Husbandry	409810
渔业	Fishery	872258
农、林、牧、渔服务业	Service Industry for Agriculture	604182
农、林、牧、渔业商品率　(%)	**Rate of Commodity Output Value of Agriculture, Forestry, Animal Husbandry and Fishery (%)**	**98.76**
农业	Agriculture	99.70
林业	Forestry	99.74
畜牧业	Animal Husbandry	92.93
渔业	Fishery	98.13
农、林、牧、渔服务业	Service Industry for Agriculture	100.00

Gross Output Value, Value-added and Commodity Output Value of Agriculture, Forestry, Animal Husbandry and Fishery (2019)

(10000 yuan)

荔湾区 Liwan	海珠区 Haizhu	天河区 Tianhe	白云区 Baiyun	黄埔区 Huangpu	番禺区 Panyu	花都区 Huadu	南沙区 Nansha	从化区 Conghua	增城区 Zengcheng
68758	**24002**	**79317**	**640997**	**78139**	**539587**	**654360**	**939402**	**477266**	**960976**
61617	7782	3283	391683	37683	164347	417746	489222	291490	639739
			734	1209	122	1654		7744	12713
			104960	7178	46565	73477	40412	79055	89321
2421	16084	30047	32393	6359	297617	84120	354369	11263	54213
4720	136	45987	111227	25710	30936	77363	55399	87714	164990
100.00	**100.00**	**100.00**	**100.00**	**100.00**	**100.00**	**100.00**	**100.00**	**100.00**	**100.00**
89.62	32.42	4.14	61.12	48.22	30.46	63.84	52.08	61.08	66.58
			0.11	1.55	0.02	0.25		1.62	1.32
			16.37	9.19	8.63	11.23	4.30	16.56	9.29
3.52	67.01	37.88	5.05	8.14	55.16	12.86	37.72	2.36	5.64
6.86	0.57	57.98	17.35	32.90	5.73	11.82	5.90	18.38	17.17
46231	**17272**	**44150**	**380678**	**39558**	**340330**	**400836**	**582182**	**267173**	**599611**
42936	5772	2381	273133	21087	132858	283181	333578	195256	454269
			487	938	84	1237		4915	9794
			42809	3681	19413	30455	15445	31916	36059
1348	11440	19963	18367	3246	175214	49672	210634	5616	31431
1947	60	21806	45882	10606	12761	36291	22525	29470	68058
100.00	**100.00**	**100.00**	**100.00**	**100.00**	**100.00**	**100.00**	**100.00**	**100.00**	**100.00**
92.87	33.42	5.39	71.75	53.3	39.05	70.65	57.3	73.08	75.77
			0.13	2.37	0.02	0.31		1.84	1.63
			11.25	9.31	5.70	7.60	2.65	11.95	6.01
2.92	66.23	45.22	4.82	8.21	51.48	12.39	36.18	2.10	5.24
4.21	0.35	49.39	12.05	26.81	3.75	9.05	3.87	11.03	11.35
68758	**22680**	**78969**	**640462**	**76399**	**537019**	**653375**	**922006**	**460080**	**947602**
61617	7743	3281	391660	36701	162321	417630	486958	289810	639267
			734	1209	122	1590		7744	12713
			104825	6420	46439	73021	37641	63951	77513
2421	14801	29701	32016	6359	297201	83771	342008	10861	53119
4720	136	45987	111227	25710	30936	77363	55399	87714	164990
100.00	**94.49**	**99.56**	**99.92**	**97.77**	**99.52**	**99.85**	**98.15**	**96.40**	**98.61**
100.00	99.50	99.94	99.99	97.39	98.77	99.97	99.54	99.42	99.93
			100.00	100.00	100.00	96.13		100.00	100.00
			99.87	89.44	99.73	99.38	93.14	80.89	86.78
100.00	92.02	98.85	98.84	100.00	99.86	99.59	96.51	96.43	97.98
100.00	100.00	100.00	100.00	100.00	100.00	100.00	100.00	100.00	100.00

10-9 按历史时期分农林牧渔业总产值

Gross Output Value of Agriculture, Forestry, Animal Husbandry and Fishery by History Period

时　　期	Period	合计 Total	农业 Agriculture	林业 Forestry	畜牧业 Animal Husbandry	渔业 Fishery
按现行价格计算(万元)	**Current Price (10000 yuan)**					
"六五" 时期	6th Five-year Plan Period	658543	455112	8949	135454	34854
"七五" 时期	7th Five-year Plan Period	1691762	1078926	21001	422369	103760
"八五" 时期	8th Five-year Plan Period	4155220	2323337	41125	1196610	493636
"九五" 时期	9th Five-year Plan Period	7708638	3862181	62408	2183198	1344563
"十五" 时期	10th Five-year Plan Period	9450322	4981673	112770	2077835	1693401
"十一五" 时期	11th Five-year Plan Period	13813535	7099096	104670	2833830	2485329
"十二五" 时期	12th Five-year Plan Period	19191307	10084903	188617	3514011	3426867
1979-2019	1979-2019	74165962	39649747	667642	14471422	12859472
1991-2019	1991-2019	71644439	37981992	634375	13890063	12714353
2001-2019	2001-2019	59780581	31796474	530842	10510255	10876154
平均增长速度 (%)	**Average Speed of Growth (%)**					
"六五" 时期	6th Five-year Plan Period	6.2	3.3	-5.8	17.9	15.5
"七五" 时期	7th Five-year Plan Period	4.6	2.8	0.3	8.1	8.2
"八五" 时期	8th Five-year Plan Period	10.0	4.6	3.7	14.8	26.4
"九五" 时期	9th Five-year Plan Period	5.9	4.0	4.0	3.5	11.2
"十五" 时期	10th Five-year Plan Period	5.8	7.8	-3.2	1.2	4.8
"十一五" 时期	11th Five-year Plan Period	2.3	1.3	-14.2	1.3	5.1
"十二五" 时期	12th Five-year Plan Period	2.1	3.6	6.9	-5.7	3.8
1979-2019	1979-2019	4.7	3.7	-1.1	4.1	9.2
1991-2019	1991-2019	4.4	3.9	-2.3	1.4	8.9
2001-2019	2001-2019	2.7	3.7	-5.4	-2.4	4.1

10-10 渔业生产情况（2019年）
Statistics on Fishery Production (2019)

项　目	Item	全　市 Total	荔湾区 Liwan	海珠区 Haizhu	天河区 Tianhe	白云区 Baiyun	黄埔区 Huangpu
水产品养殖总面积（公顷）	**Total Cultured Area of Aquatic Products (hectare)**	**22230**	**25**		**19**	**1650**	**372**
# 淡水养殖	Freshwater Artificially Cultured	17896	25		19	1650	372
# 鱼　塘	Fish Pond	16970	22		8	1650	372
水产品总产量（吨）	**Total Aquatic Products (ton)**	**465236**	**30**	**4934**	**10047**	**26786**	**5798**
按作业分	Grouped by Production						
海洋捕捞	Marine Fishing	28572		4934	9882		146
海水养殖	Mariculture	77730					
淡水捕捞	Freshwater Fishing	35407				225	
淡水养殖	Freshwater Aquaculture	323527	30		165	26561	5652
按种类分	Grouped by Species						
鱼　类	Fish	424304		4879	8845	25582	5770
甲壳类	Shrimps, Prawns and Crabs	23393				127	22
贝　类	Shell-fish	14416					6
其他水产类	Other Aquatic Products	3123	30	55	1202	1077	

10-10 续表 continued

项　目	Item	番禺区 Panyu	花都区 Huadu	南沙区 Nansha	从化区 Conghua	增城区 Zengcheng
水产品养殖总面积（公顷）	**Total Cultured Area of Aquatic Products (hectare)**	**3573**	**5055**	**6886**	**1539**	**3111**
# 淡水养殖	Freshwater Artificially Cultured	2113	5055	4012	1539	3111
# 鱼　塘	Fish Pond	2113	4727	4011	956	3111
水产品总产量(吨)	**Total Aquatic Products (ton)**	**150300**	**72178**	**134026**	**8149**	**52988**
按作业分	Grouped by Production					
海洋捕捞	Marine Fishing	12780		810		20
海水养殖	Mariculture	34474		43256		
淡水捕捞	Freshwater Fishing	31520	44	3450		168
淡水养殖	Freshwater Aquaculture	71526	72133	86511	8149	52800
按种类分	Grouped by Species					
鱼　类	Fish	129218	72155	117422	8125	52308
甲壳类	Shrimps, Prawns and Crabs	6750	23	16464		7
贝　类	Shell-fish	14288		117		5
其他水产类	Other Aquatic Products	44		23	24	668

10-11 畜牧业生产情况（2019年）

项　　目		Item		全　市 Total
年末牛存栏量	（头）	Number of Farm Cattle on Hand at Year-end	(head)	13157
役用牛		Draft Cattle		
肉用牛		Beef Cattle		4392
奶　牛		Cow		8765
牛奶产量	（吨）	Output of Milk	(ton)	32154
牛出栏量	（头）	Number of Slaughtered Cattle	(head)	4569
牛肉产量	（吨）	Output of Beef	(ton)	611
生猪饲养量	（头）	Total Number of Hogs Raised	(head)	578769
年末生猪存栏量	（头）	Number of Hogs on Hand at Year-end	(head)	166746
# 能繁殖的母猪		Female Hogs		16341
生猪出栏量	（头）	Number of Slaughtered Fattened Hogs	(head)	412023
猪肉产量	（吨）	Output of Pork	(ton)	31610
年末羊存栏量	（头）	Number of Sheep and Goats on Hand at Year-end	(head)	4845
羊出栏量	（头）	Number of Slaughtered Sheep and Goats	(head)	6536
羊肉产量	（吨）	Output of Mutton	(ton)	112
年末兔存栏量	（只）	Number of Rabbits on Hand at Year-end	(unit)	3167
兔出栏量	（只）	Number of Slaughtered Rabbits	(unit)	7172
兔肉产量	（吨）	Output of Rabbit Meat	(ton)	2
年末家禽存栏量	（万只）	Number of Poultry on Hand at Year-end	(10000 units)	1378
#三　鸟		Chickens, Ducks and Gooses		993
#鸡		Chickens		782
家禽出栏量	（万只）	Number of Slaughtered Poultry	(10000 units)	6829
#三　鸟		Chickens, Ducks and Gooses		4637
#鸡		Chickens		4074
禽肉产量	（吨）	Output of Poultry Meat	(ton)	81945
禽蛋产量	（吨）	Output of Poultry Eggs	(ton)	23017
肉类总产量	（吨）	Output of Meat	(ton)	114935
蜂蜜产量	（吨）	Output of Honey	(ton)	2742

Statistics on Animal Husbandry Production (2019)

白云区 Baiyun	黄埔区 Huangpu	番禺区 Panyu	花都区 Huadu	南沙区 Nansha	从化区 Conghua	增城区 Zengcheng
1228		737	120	67	4836	6169
		125		56	295	3916
1228		612	120	11	4541	2253
4344		1635	362	10	17462	8341
143	40	149	160	7	975	3095
18	5	20	22	1	125	420
10377	8600		193077	102509	179666	84540
2877			37543	41524	58222	26580
291			3967	3105	4815	4163
7500	8600		155534	60985	121444	57960
562	644		11666	4568	8777	5393
		220	518	102	468	3537
165	563	17	937		878	3976
3	10		16		16	67
		300	2867			
		350	6822			
		2				
268		156	112	67	229	546
244		147	78	65	196	263
244		35	60	24	182	237
2319	189	608	659	462	508	2084
1109	118	572	606	461	374	1397
1108	115	323	546	348	308	1326
23471	1643	13087	11400	9099	5605	17640
134	46	4265	608	164	13366	4434
24210	2302	13109	23280	13671	14713	23650
124		11	702	2	1319	584

10-12 农村电力、化肥用量和农田水利建设情况（2019年）

项　　目		Item		全　市 Total
农村电气化		**Rural Electrification**		
农村用电量	（万千瓦·时）	Electricity Consumed in Rural Areas	(10000 kilowatt/hour)	1478089
农村小水电站个数	（个）	Number of Small Hydropower Stations in Rural Areas	(unit)	152
农村小水电站装机容量	（千瓦）	Installed Capacity of Small Hydropower Stations in Rural Areas	(kilowatt)	143137
农村小水电站发电量	（万千瓦·时）	Generated Energy of Small Hydropower Stations in Rural Areas	(10000 kilowatts/hour)	32641
农村化学化		**Rural Chemicalizing**		
化肥施用量	（实物量、吨）	Consumption of Chemical Fertilizers (gross weight)	(ton)	261396
化肥施用量	（折纯量、吨）	Consumption of Chemical Fertilizers (effective weight)	(ton)	102875
农用薄膜使用量	（吨）	Consumption of Plastic Film in Agriculture	(ton)	2635
农药施用量	（吨）	Consumption of Agricultural Pesticide	(ton)	2863
农用柴油使用量	（吨）	Consumption of Diesel Oil in Agriculture	(ton)	37177
农田水利建设		**Construction of Water Conservancy Works**		
有效灌溉面积	（公顷）	Irrigated Area	(hectare)	75294
有效灌溉面积占耕地比重	(%)	As Percentage of Total Cultivated Land	(%)	83.02
旱涝保收面积	（公顷）	Drought and Flooded Area under Control and Ensuring Stable Yields	(hectare)	65147
旱涝保收面积占耕地比重	(%)	As Percentage of Total Cultivated Land	(%)	71.83
机电排灌面积	（公顷）	Area with Motorized Drainage and Irrigation Facilities	(hectare)	48339
机电排灌面积占耕地比重	(%)	As Percentage of Total Cultivated Land	(%)	53.30

Statistics on Electricity, Chemical Fertilizer Consumption and Construction of Water Conservancy Works in Rural Areas (2019)

荔湾区 Liwan	海珠区 Haizhu	天河区 Tianhe	白云区 Baiyun	黄埔区 Huangpu	番禺区 Panyu	花都区 Huadu	南沙区 Nansha	从化区 Conghua	增城区 Zengcheng
24000	41340	25091	265111	63027	405074	238617	334475	21689	59665
						17		120	15
						6510		109357	27270
								24043	8598
47		41	35716	6788	11792	29800	40226	53508	83478
47	72	41	15237	2376	4300	10547	18124	18701	33430
203	4	3	101	30	231	510	585	288	680
6	7	5	244	218	305	476	442	469	691
	1208	11	991	122	2002	5005	9098	13900	4840
243	81	195	7438	2020	4422	10277	16223	16848	17547
39.77	87.10	100.00	84.46	93.30	70.73	100.00	100.00	84.05	67.42
243		195	7410	2020	3518	9977	16223	11360	14201
39.77		100.00	84.14	93.30	56.27	97.08	100.00	56.67	54.56
184	88	101	5898	2020	3342	7013	14638	3188	11867
30.11	94.62	51.79	66.97	93.30	53.45	68.24	90.23	15.90	45.59

10-13 农业机械总动力和拥有量（2019年）

项　目		Item		全　市 Total
农业机械总动力	**（千瓦）**	**Total Power of Agricultural Machinery**	**(kilowatt)**	**1247210**
其中：柴油发动机动力		Power of Diesel Engines		624976
汽油发动机动力		Power of Gasoline Engines		192751
电动机动力		Power of Electric Motors		429483
主要农业机械拥有量		**Possession of Major Agricultural Machinery**		
大中型拖拉机	（台）	Number of Large and Medium Tractors	(unit)	317
小型拖拉机	（台）	Number of Mini-Tractors	(unit)	2623
大中型拖拉机配套农具	（台）	Number of Large and Medium Tractor Accessory Farm Machinery	(unit)	535
小型拖拉机配套农具	（台）	Number of Mini-Tractor Towing Farm Machinery	(unit)	3251
农用排灌柴油机	（台）	Diesel Engines for Agricultural Use	(unit)	25447
农用排灌电动机	（台）	Electric Motors for Agricultural Use	(unit)	23057
农用水泵	（台）	Water Pumps for Agricultural Use	(unit)	44821
节水灌溉机械	（套）	Irrigation Machinery of Saving Water	(set)	26212
联合收割机	（台）	Combine Harvesters	(unit)	200
机动脱粒机	（台）	Motorized Threshers	(unit)	6587
渔用机动船	（艘）	Motorized Fishing Boats	(unit)	1450

Total Power and Possession of Major Agricultural Machinery (2019)

荔湾区 Liwan	海珠区 Haizhu	天河区 Tianhe	白云区 Baiyun	黄埔区 Huangpu	番禺区 Panyu	花都区 Huadu	南沙区 Nansha	从化区 Conghua	增城区 Zengcheng
1150	**2773**	**1569**	**60917**	**2745**	**174315**	**169821**	**413000**	**180320**	**240600**
	2734	1115	10188	1809	71324	84416	248000	122890	82500
	14		23460	45	21219	23803	64000	15210	45000
1150	25	454	27269	891	81772	61602	101000	42220	113100
			17	6	27	42	50	103	72
			31		264	252	222	1034	820
			14	4	27	59	120	14	297
			3		264	479	96	180	2229
					1853	2977	18500	592	1525
		7	2589	300	4542	5528	7500	316	2275
		6	2589	300	6395	8505	23000	3612	414
	2512		942	5	2677	427	16000	3612	37
				1		18	38	84	59
					35	656		5070	826
				29	704		694		23

10-14 主要农作物及水果种植面积和产量（2019年）

项目	Item	全市 Total	荔湾区 Liwan	海珠区 Haizhu
农作物总播种面积（公顷）	**Total Sown Area of Farm Crops (hectare)**	**210433**	**1937**	**642**
粮食作物	Grain Crops	26447		
#稻谷	Rice	20352		
大豆	Soybeans	507		
经济作物	Economic Crops	35259	1712	
#甘蔗	Sugarcane	5422		
花生	Peanuts	5205		
木薯	Cassava	40		
花卉	Flowers	22440	1712	
其他作物	Other Farm Crops	148727	226	642
#蔬菜	Vegetables	148064	226	642
果用瓜	Melon-fruits	199		
园林水果年末面积（公顷）	**Planting Area of Fruits at Year-end (hectare)**	**63796**		**208**
#柑桔橙	Citrus	3667		
香(大)蕉	Bananas and Plantains	6051		31
荔枝	Lychees	30336		2
龙眼	Longans	7966		2
番石榴	Guavas	2086		4
主要农作物产量（吨）	**Yield of Major Farm Crops (ton)**			
粮食作物	Grain Crops	131988		
#稻谷	Rice	106341		
大豆	Soybeans	1756		
经济作物	Economic Crops			
#甘蔗	Sugarcane	656216		
花生	Peanuts	14542		
木薯	Cassava	1006		
花卉（万元）	Flowers (10000 yuan)	510634	60134	
其他作物	Other Farm Crops			
#蔬菜	Vegetables	3853154	3234	13853
果用瓜	Melon-fruits	3582		
园林水果总产量（吨）	**Gross Output of Fruits (ton)**	**642578**		**4079**
#柑桔橙	Citrus	63532		
香(大)蕉	Bananas and Plantains	272788		1324
荔枝	Lychees	39762		
龙眼	Longans	32916		6
番石榴	Guavas	103175		166

Sown Area and Output of Major Farm Crops and Fruits (2019)

天河区 Tianhe	白云区 Baiyun	黄埔区 Huangpu	番禺区 Panyu	花都区 Huadu	南沙区 Nansha	从化区 Conghua	增城区 Zengcheng
504	**40921**	**4410**	**16655**	**27948**	**29912**	**31412**	**56092**
	413	571	127	2100	1241	12960	9035
	75	295	45	428	531	11539	7439
	7		…	143	79	72	206
	1795	449	8083	6443	7796	4650	4331
	8	27	4	81	4912	74	316
	186	137	3	470	11	1804	2594
						22	18
	1222	285	7373	5829	2844	1867	1308
504	38712	3390	8445	19406	20874	13802	42726
497	38684	3372	8411	19208	20862	13798	42364
7	28	18	34	15	12	4	81
69	**1603**	**2646**	**371**	**3877**	**6399**	**26932**	**21691**
	41	47		19	27	2357	1176
…	34	257	95	82	3765	287	1500
24	733	1415	13	1585	932	14159	11473
19	495	587	79	1760	181	2247	2596
…	15	14	99	51	1270	72	561
	2895	3687	617	9453	5781	66596	42959
	361	2031	201	2528	2781	60656	37783
	31		1	475	491	171	587
	268	2400	393	8161	617077	3883	24034
	413	576	21	1322	47	4966	7197
						404	602
	26878	5688	78434	196240	37136	78294	27830
7024	845693	54091	179301	484284	656961	306474	1302239
55	460	384	382	279	292	28	1702
344	**4230**	**9142**	**10818**	**20241**	**250299**	**112561**	**230864**
	213	580		60	1155	27884	33640
3	1186	2812	3726	1871	166601	2264	93001
138	490	2884	58	5398	2690	16116	11988
96	374	1120	1108	7748	936	11938	9590
2	76	281	3018	1557	71459	1523	25093

10-15 主要农产品产量与建国以来最高年份比较（2019年）

Output of Major Farm Products in Comparison with that of Peak Year since 1949 (2019)

项　目	Item	2019	建国以来最高年份（不含当年）Peak Year since 1949 (excluding current year)		2019年为建国以来最高年(%) 2019 as Percentage of Peak Year (%)
			年　份 Year	产　量 Output	
农产品总产量　（吨）	**Total Yield of Farm Products　(ton)**				
粮　食	Grain	131988	1984	1259928	10.48
#稻　谷	Rice	106341	1984	1242982	8.56
花　生	Peanuts	14542	1982	56397	25.79
糖　蔗	Sugarcane		1985	2395941	
蔬　菜	Vegetables	3853154	2017	3837712	100.40
水　果(含果用瓜)	Fruits　(Containing fruit melon)	646160	2018	613045	105.40
单位播种面积产量（千克/公顷）	**Yield per Unit Sowed Area (kilogram/hectare)**				
粮　食	Grain	4991	2000	5758	86.68
#稻　谷	Rice	5225	2000	5952	87.79
花　生	Peanuts	2794	2017	2728	102.42
蔬　菜	Vegetables	26023	2016	25644	101.48
水　果	Fruits	10072	2018	9704	103.79
禽畜产品产量　（吨）	**Total Output of Poultry and Animal Husbandry Products　(ton)**				
肉类总产量	Output of Meat	114935	2000	327702	35.07
#猪　肉	Pork	31610	2010	174778	18.09
牛羊肉	Beef and Mutton	723	2003	1973	36.64
家禽肉	Poultry Meat	81945	2002	184134	44.50
牛　奶	Milk	32154	2010	61530	52.26
鲜　蛋	Eggs	23017	1994	37321	61.67
水产品总产量　（吨）	**Total Output of Aquatic Products(ton)**				
海水产品	Seawater Aquatic Products	106302	2017	98559	107.86
淡水产品	Freshwater Aquatic Products	358934	2016	400639	89.59

10-16 农业生产水平

Production Level of Agriculture, Animal Husbandry and Fishery

单位：千克 (kg)

项目	Item	2018	2019
平均每个农业户生产	**Average Production per Household**		
粮 食	Grain	326	320
#稻 谷	Rice	280	258
花 生	Peanuts	39	35
甘 蔗	Sugarcane	2003	1593
蔬 菜	Vegetables	9240	9356
水 果（含果用瓜）	Fruits (Containing fruit melon)	1536	1569
花 卉 （元）	Flowers (yuan)	12210	12399
生 猪 （头）	Hogs (unit)	1	1
家 禽 （只）	Poultry (unit)	168	166
#鸡	Chickens	100	99
禽 蛋	Eggs of Poultry	59	56
水产品	Aquatic Products	1138	1130
#鱼 类	Fish	1031	1030
平均每个农业从业人员生产	**Average Production per Employed Person Engaging in Farming**		
粮 食	Grain	245	241
#稻 谷	Rice	211	194
花 生	Peanuts	29	26
甘 蔗	Sugarcane	1508	1196
蔬 菜	Vegetables	6956	7021
水 果（含果用瓜）	Fruits (Containing fruit melon)	1156	1177
花 卉 （元）	Flowers (yuan)	9191	9305
平均每个畜牧业从业人员生产	**Average Production per Employed Person Engaging in Animal Husbandry**		
肉类总产量	Output of Meat	4497	4167
#猪 肉	Pork	1482	1146
牛羊肉	Beef and Mutton	35	26
禽 肉	Meat of Poultry	2960	2971
禽 蛋	Eggs of Poultry	784	834
平均每个渔业从业人员生产	**Average Production per Employed Person Engaging in Fishery**		
水产品	Aquatic Products	10046	11073
#鱼 类	Fish	9105	10098
农、林、牧、渔业劳动生产率（元/人）	Labor Productivity of Agriculture, Forestry, Animal Husbandry and Fishery (yuan/person)	39600	41560
农业	Agriculture	30439	31788
林业	Forestry	20698	22378
畜牧业	Animal Husbandry	56917	65175
渔业	Fishery	107483	125409

10-17　建制镇社会经济发展基本情况（2019年）

乡镇名称	Name of Towns	乡镇行政区域面积（公顷）Area of Administrative Division (hectare)	户籍户数（户）Registered Households (household)	户籍人口（人）Registered Population (Person)	一般公共预算收入（万元）Public Budget Revenue (10000 yuan)	一般公共预算支出（万元）Public Budget Expenditure (10000 yuan)	耕地面积（公顷）Area of Cultivated Land (hectare)
白云区	**Baiyun**						
人和镇	Renhe Town	7440	32397	105569	46513	54216	2062
太和镇	Taihe Town	15537	30360	112029	72251	78461	1224
钟落潭镇	Zhongluotan Town	16900	39633	151068	71934	72521	3038
江高镇	Jianggao Town	10228	41140	133927	67956	61526	2183
黄埔区	**Huangpu**						
新龙镇	Xinlong Town	7539	7258	40675	22637	34684	1114
番禺区	**Panyu**						
南村镇	Nancun Town	4689	39097	102794	76157	75731	429
新造镇	Xinzao Town	1400	7750	17623	16166	16017	142
化龙镇	Hualong Town	5373	14053	36418	35000	30000	1222
石楼镇	Shilou Town	12600	40964	97268	77623	77615	1669
沙湾镇	Shawan Town	3745	24737	64572	49279	49979	383
石基镇	Shiji Town	4703	21495	53894	66206	64263	1634
花都区	**Huadu**						
梯面镇	Timian Town	9127	2929	10492	8213	8213	321
花山镇	Huashan Town	11640	27798	90954	13600	13609	2221
花东镇	Huadong Town	20844	39385	132092	120223	120223	1804
炭步镇	Tanbu Town	11330	19360	55787	26676	26281	2091
赤坭镇	Chini Town	16040	19634	58783	17622	16300	1875
狮岭镇	Shiling Town	13631	16559	65726	19959	19959	828
南沙区	**Nansha**						
万顷沙镇	Wanqingsha Town	14285	11339	36286	34484	32826	3142
横沥镇	Hengli Town	5400	11750	32310	27432	22315	1427
黄阁镇	Huangge Town	7650	20476	55287	38826	39877	294
东涌镇	Dongyong Town	9153	35479	85564	97824	95151	4024
大岗镇	Dagang Town	9007	30786	83773	96961	94858	3239
榄核镇	Lanhe Town	7450	21771	58436	106141	90798	3118
从化区	**Conghua**						
温泉镇	Wenquan Town	21244	13758	54076	11134	11134	2518
良口镇	Liangkou Town	53080	12127	49142	10834	7996	1144
吕田镇	Liangtian Town	39300	9134	32416	6474	5994	2186
太平镇	Taiping Town	21033	24753	99178	22026	22026	2770
鳌头镇	Aotou Town	41000	36854	151125	17718	17718	7208
增城区	**Zengcheng**						
新塘镇	Xintang Town	8632	43925	156606	155073	183260	1207
石滩镇	Shitan Town	17097	45292	123836	42240	29143	5550
中新镇	Zhongxin Town	23237	35247	93455	24975	10995	3387
正果镇	Zhengguo Town	23941	21747	65548	13766	16655	2285
派潭镇	Paitan Town	28965	28055	88889	15000	15987	4131
小楼镇	Xiaolou Town	13667	19486	54590	9500	8639	2635
仙村镇	Xiancun Town	5665	15619	48631	17031	18578	1449

Basic Statistics on Social and Economic Development of Towns(2019)

农业企业数（个） Number of Agricultural Enterprises (unit)	规模以上工业企业数（个） Number of Industrial Enterprises above Designated Size(unit)	商品交易市场个数（个） Number of Commodity Markets (unit)	小学在校学生数（人） Number of Enolled Primary School Students (person)	幼儿园托儿所数（个） Number of Kindergartens (unit)	医疗卫生机构床位数（床） Hospital Beds (bed)	城乡居民基本医疗保险参保人数(人) Number of Persons Participating in Basic Medical Care Insurance for Urban and Rural Residents(person)	城乡居民基本养老保险参保人数(人) Number of Persons Participating in Basic Pension Insurance for Urban and Rural Residents(person)
10	119	13	10981	24	550	57665	32825
29	117	27	18554	42	372	85761	2263
28	182		14139	32	520	85127	6035
6	165	5	11637	28	1308	52972	2592
77	14	2	3361	6	440	19000	8080
1	113	11	12706	41	1128	59083	16952
6	17	3	1584	5	81	8912	3628
3	54	9	3681	10	100	28181	11564
28	119	3	10476	24	597	49504	19283
7	77	6	10305	25	120	43272	3256
40	128	1	14501	21	300	46277	34951
5	5		868	2	36	6433	3930
16	104	1	11348	17	91	59788	34425
28	102	10	12084	22	238	85244	45590
2	79	1	11139	5	72	38110	22975
49	26	2	3126	3	65	38332	24083
5	189	16	24521	51	330	52780	20884
10	15	3	3118	8	112	25802	7545
	22	5	1825	14	253	19706	9201
	64		4051	11	125	27656	11988
9	194	6	10270	19	260	51615	10608
4	79	4	7518	30	359	39895	20326
3	100	2	7842	19	91	35433	14870
7	20	2	3516	7	317	34914	26681
9	1	1	3538	4	50	32833	5346
17	1	1	1585	4	34	22791	14644
31	90	1	10812	25	115	63034	39203
51	16	3	12150	14	293	105880	98790
5	357	12	29115	82	1168	75386	41595
27	64	5	13062	19	162	84300	40601
120	40	4	8031	17	120	61500	27577
14	6	2	1944	2	75	43799	25154
27	3	1	4263	5	95	67463	28285
30	2	4	2050	4	108	39216	18417
3	43	1	3000	5	38	30500	10304

10-18 全市村委会社会经济基本情况(2019年)

项　　目		Item		全市 Total
一、基本情况		**Basic Information**		
村委会数	(个)	Number of Village Committees	(unit)	1142
行政区域面积	(公顷)	Area of Administrative Region	(hectare)	564764
通公共交通村数	(个)	Number of Villages Available for Public Transport	(unit)	1094
有公共厕所数	(个)	Number of public toilets available	(unit)	1006
垃圾集中处理村数	(个)	Number of Villages with Centralized Garbage Disposal	(unit)	1136
污水集中处理村数	(个)	Number of Villages with Centralized Sewage Treatment	(unit)	1113
有电子商务配送站点村数	(个)	Number of Villages with E-Commerce Distribution Centre	(unit)	678
二、人口情况		**Population**		
户籍户数	(户)	Registered Households	(household)	980848
户籍人口	(人)	Registered Population	(person)	3104090
# 全家外出半年以上人口	(人)	The Whole Family Has Been Away for More Than Half a Year	(person)	191794
常住户数	(户)	Permanent Households	(household)	1711774
常住人口	(人)	Permanent Population	(person)	5450728
三、社会保障及社会服务情况		**Social Insurance and Social Service**		
农村特困救助供养人数	(人)	Number of Rural Special Poverty Relief Providers	(Persons)	5811
体育健身场所数	(个)	Number of Gymnasia and Stadium	(unit)	3092
图书室(馆)、文化站数	(个)	Number of Liberaries and Cultural Stations	(unit)	1132

注：本表村委会是指全市所有挂牌的村委会，不包括空壳村。村集体经济情况指标是指由村委会(村集体)支配的收入和支出情况。

Social and Economic Information of Village Committees (2019)

白云区 Baiyun	黄埔区 Huangpu	番禺区 Panyu	花都区 Huadu	南沙区 Nansha	从化区 Conghua	增城区 Zengcheng
118	28	177	188	128	221	282
44459	17138	40786	86693	43216	181230	151242
117	28	177	160	128	210	274
118	28	173	184	127	125	251
118	28	177	188	128	221	276
103	22	177	186	124	220	281
70	11	151	115	118	92	121
130127	18162	178451	161893	122727	115249	254239
468638	93208	453219	533327	324199	488708	742791
14438	2879	23975	44463	9369	24004	72666
256250	20989	543343	238196	251246	111359	290391
960143	98342	1514927	896794	617511	471840	891171
317	161	246	1376	591	1111	2009
462	57	371	521	172	575	934
124	16	191	179	108	229	285

Note: The whole family has been away for more than half a year. the village committee in this table refers to all the village committees listed in the city, excluding empty shell villages. The indicators of village collective economy refer to the income and expenditure controlled by the village committee (village collective).

10-18 续表

项目	Item	全市 Total
卫生室数 (个)	Number of Health Rooms (unit)	1057
执业(助理)医师数 (个)	Number of Practicing (Assistant) Doctors (person)	1292
四、产业发展情况	**Industrial Development**	
种植规模户 (户)	Planting Scale Households (household)	1283
畜禽养殖规模户 (户)	Livestock and Poultry Breeding Scale Households (household)	283
家庭农场 (个)	Family Farm (unit)	398
农民专业合作社 (个)	Farmers' Professional Cooperatives (unit)	1061
农民专业合作社成员 (户)	Members of Farmers' Professional Cooperatives (household)	21849
营业面积50平米以上的综合商店或超市 (个)	Number of Comprehensive Stores or Supermarkets with Business Area over 50 Square Meters (unit)	5724
五、农田水利情况	**Situation of farmland and water conservancy**	
能正常使用的机电井 (个)	Mechanical and Electrical Wells That Can be Used Normally (unit)	1198
能正常使用的排灌站 (个)	Drainage and Irrigation Stations That Can be Used Normally (unit)	1613
本村能够使用的灌溉用水塘和水库 (个)	Irrigation Ponds and Reservoirs That Can Be Used in the Village (unit)	1710
六、村务情况	**Village Administrative Affairs**	
全年村集体收入 (万元)	Annual Income of Village Collectives (10000 yuan)	692995
# 经营收入 (万元)	Operating Income (10000 yuan)	421520
村级办公支出 (万元)	Village Level Office Expenditure (10000 yuan)	90529
村干部人数 (人)	Number of Village Cadres (person)	8066

continued

白云区 Baiyun	黄埔区 Huangpu	番禺区 Panyu	花都区 Huadu	南沙区 Nansha	从化区 Conghua	增城区 Zengcheng
113	27	129	195	110	216	267
137	21	221	242	131	251	289
14	25	105	216	152	202	569
13		35	31	24	54	126
63		24	54	67	56	134
79	9	36	55	119	276	487
2880	141	889	1069	1586	6568	8716
768	74	2112	1090	496	261	923
241		207	179	12	139	420
179	2	102	103	952	50	225
78	40	303	297	225	303	464
41261	14831	372654	79855	99259	6414	78721
23239	629	277064	53851	39693	3116	23928
25868	1739	22610	10599	11817	3511	14385
794	239	1205	1271	776	1698	2083

10-19 都市农业主要指标

Main Economic Indicators of Urban Agriculture

指标	Item	2018	2019
都市农业总收入 (万元)	Total Income of Urban Agriculture (10000 yuan)	21675653	23838601
#农林牧渔业收入 (万元)	Income of Agriculture, Forestry, Animal Husbandry and Fishery (10000 yuan)	4119607	4519896
加工本地农产品总收入 (万元)	Total Income of Processing of Local Agriculture Products (10000 yuan)	11672653	12236788
运输本地农产品总收入 (万元)	Total Income of Transpot of Local Agriculture Products (10000 yuan)	1387497	1567872
批发零售本地农产品总收入 (万元)	Total Income of Wholesale and Retail Trade of Local Agriculture Products (10000 yuan)	4398487	4539239
观光休闲旅游农业企业总收入(万元)	Total Income of Agricultural sightseeing Tourism Enterpises (10000 yuan)	974090	974806
都市农业增加值 (万元)	Value-added of Urban Agriculture (10000 yuan)	8482594	9327360
#农林牧渔业增加值 (万元)	Value-added of Agriculture, Forestry, Animal Husbandry and Fishery (10000 yuan)	2530891	2763118
加工本地农产品增加值 (万元)	Value-added of Processing of Local Agriculture Products (10000 yuan)	2622270	2973658
运输本地农产品增加值 (万元)	Value-added of Transpot of Local Agriculture Products (10000 yuan)	769500	869535
批发零售本地农产品增加值 (万元)	Value-added of Wholesale and Retail Trade of Local Agriculture Products (10000 yuan)	2551109	2632745
观光休闲旅游农业增加值 (万元)	Value-added of Agricultural Sightseeing Tourism (10000 yuan)	88240	88304
都市农业实现利润 (万元)	Total Profit of Urban Agriculture (10000 yuan)	1411636	1552613
都市农业实现税金 (万元)	Total Pre-tax Profit of Urban Agriculture (10000 yuan)	855308	940726
种子、种苗销售额 (万元)	Sales value of Seeds and Seedlings (10000 yuan)	197271	222916
接待观光休闲游客人次 (万人次)	Total Number of Agricultural Sightseeing Tourist (10000 Person-times)	5808	6679
都市农业从业人员 (万人)	Employed Persons in Urban Agriculture (10000 Person)	140	151
都市农业劳动生产率 (元/人)	Urban Agriculture Labor Productivity (yuan/person)	60541	61771
农业产业化规模比重 (%)	Proportion of Industrialization of Agriculture (%)	17.3	17.1
农业产业化企业(组织)幅射能力 (%)	Radiation Ability of Industrialization of Agriculture Enterprises (Organizations) (%)	34.2	39.3
带动本地农户数 (户)	Numbers of Local Farmers Drived by Industrialization of Agriculture Enterprises (unit)	136527	152577
绿色农产品个数 (个)	Numbers of Green Agricultural Products (unit)	43	34
绿色农产品产值 (万元)	Output Value of Green Agricultural Products (10000 yuan)	24611	12841
高新科技农产品个数 (个)	Numbers of High-tech Agricultural Products (unit)	69	-
高新科技农产品产值 (万元)	Output Value of High-tech Agricultural Products (10000 yuan)	109827	-
农业产业化生产单位 (个)	Industrialization of Agriculture Enterprises (unit)	2064	2013
#农业龙头企业 (个)	Agriculture Leading Enterprises (unit)	206	233
#国家级 (个)	National (unit)	7	11
省　级 (个)	Provincial (unit)	35	73
市　级 (个)	Municipal (unit)	93	172
农业生产基地(示范区) (个)	Agricultural Production Bases (Demonstration Area) (unit)	54	52
规模以上农业生产单位 (个)	Agricultural Enterprises above the Designcoted Size (unit)	675	693
农产品交易市场 (个)	Trade Markets of Agricultural Products (unit)	65	65

注：1．从2019年起，“观光休闲旅游农业企业总收入”改为“农业观光休闲旅游总收入”，统计范围由农业龙头企业扩展为全社会涉农观光休闲单位。

2．“绿色农产品个数”不含“有机农产品个数”。

3．从2019年起，“高新科技农产品个数”、“高新科技农产品产值”不再进行统计。

Note: I. Since 2019，the "total income of agricultural enterprises in sightseeing and leisure tourism" will be changed to "total income of agricultural sightseeing and leisure tourism", and the statistical scope will be expanded from leading agricultural enterprises to agriculture-related sightseeing and leisure units in the whole society.

II. The number of green agricultural products does not contain the number of organic agricultural products.

III. Since 2019, the "number of high-tech agricultural products" and "output value of high-tech agricultural products" will no longer be counted.

【**农林牧渔业总产值**】是以货币表现的农林牧渔业的全部产品总量和对农林牧渔业生产活动进行的各种支持性服务活动的价值。它反映一定时期内农林牧渔业生产总规模和总成果，是观察农林牧渔业生产水平和发展速度，研究农林牧渔业内部比例关系、农林牧渔业与工业、农林牧渔业与国家建设、人民生活比例关系的重要指标，同时也是计算农林牧渔业劳动生产率和农林牧渔业增加值的基础资料。

农林牧渔业总产值的计算，一般采用"产品法"，即凡有产品产量的，都按单位产品价格乘产量的办法求得每种产品产量的产值，然后相加求得各业的产值，最后各业相加求出农林牧渔业总产值。

【**常用耕地面积**】是指可以用来种植各种农作物，经常进行耕锄的田地，包括熟地、当年新开荒地、连续撂荒未满三年的耕地和当年的休闲地(轮歇地)，还包括以种植农作物为主，并附带种植桑、茶、果树和其他林木的土地，以及沿海、沿湖地区已围垦利用的"海涂"、"湖田"等面积。但不包括专业性的桑园、茶园、果园、果木苗圃、林地、芦苇地、天然或人工草地面积。

【**农作物播种面积**】是指一定生产季节结束时实际播种或移植有农作物的面积。播种面积的统计年度，凡是能在本日历年度内(自1月1日至12月31日)收获的农作物(包括上年秋冬播和本年春播、夏播在本年收获的全部作物)播种面积，都包括在内。

【**农业机械总动力**】是指主要用于农、林、牧、渔业的各种动力机械的动力总和。包括耕作机械、农用排灌机械、收获机械、植保机械、林业机械、畜牧机械、渔业机械、农产品加工机械、农用运输机械、其他农业机械。

【**都市农业**】是指在城市化地区，利用田园景观、自然生态及环境资源，通过农林牧渔业生产、农业经营活动、农村文化及农家生活，为人们休闲旅游、体验农业、了解农村提供场所，集农业的生产、生活、生态等功能于一体的产业。

【**绿色农业**】是指以获得国家认证的绿色农产品生产基地为场所，实施绿色农业工程，开发无污染、安全、优质的绿色农产品、有机农产品的综合高效产业。

【**都市农业总收入**】是指都市农业统计地理区域内各生产经营单位当年农业生产、加工本地农产品的价值量以及运输、批发零售本地农产品和观光休闲旅游农业的总收入。它是由农业生产产值、加工本地农产品产值、运输本地农产品总收入、批发零售本地农产品总收入和观光休闲旅游农业企业总收入组成。

【**农业产业化**】农业产业化是以国内外市场为导向，以经济效益为中心，通过自身的组织形式和运行机制，把分散的农户与某组织联成一体，众多的农户在该组织的带动下按同一标准进行统一生产，使一种或一类产品的生产在一个较大的区域内连成一片，形成较大规模，实现了农业由家庭分工向区域分工和社会分工的转变，形成了农户生产的专业化、农业布局的区域化、农产品生产的标准化和农业经营的规模化，将农业的产前、产中、产后诸环节有机地联为一体的经济运行方式。

【**农业龙头企业**】是指由区级或县级以上政府部门认定的，以农副产品生产、加工或流通企业为龙头，用合同契约关系或产权联结等多种形式，带动当地农户从事专业生产的经营组织。

【**自然村**】是指在农村地域内由居民自然聚居而形成的村落，自然村一般都应该有自己的名称。自然村与行政村在地域上往往会相互重叠，如果一个自然村包括多个行政村，按一个自然村计算；如果一个行政村包括多个自然村的，按实际自然村个数计算。如果一个行政村的村民居住过于分散，没有明显的聚居现象，可将邻近的20户左右的住户组合成一个自然村。自然村的划分遵从当地的习惯划分方法。

【Gross Output Value of Agriculture】 refers to the total volume of products of farming,forestry,animal husbandry,and fishery and the value of various services supporting the production of farming,forestry,animal husbandry and fishery in monetary terms, which reflects the total scale and total results of farming, forestry, animal husbandry, and fishery production during a given period of time.It is an important indicator to observe the production level and development speed of farming,forestry, animal husbandry,and fishery,to study the internal structure of farming, forestry,animal husbandry,and fishery,and to review the relationship among farming, forestry, animal husbandry,and fishery and industry, national construction and people's life.It is also the basic data to calculate the labor productivity and value-added of farming,forestry, animal husbandry,and fishery.

Generally,the gross output value of farming,forestry,animal husbandry, and fishery is calculated with the production approach, i.e.the gross output value of each single product is obtained by multiplying the output of each product by its price.Then the output value of each sector is obtained.Finally,the sum of output value of all sectors is equal to the gross output value of farming, forestry, animal husbandry,and fishery.

【Area of Regularly Cultivated Land】 refers to farmland among the total land resources which is exclusively used for farming and is under regular cultivation with harvest in normal years. Included are currently cultivated land ,land that has been abandoned or put in idle for less than 3 years and could be re-used for cultivation at any time,and new-claimed land that has been put into cultivation for more than 3 years,Excluded are the land under temporary cultivation,land (large or small plots)that is claimed along river bends,lake sides or banks of reservoirs,as well as land that has been designated under the reen for Grainprograms of the state and provincial governments but is still temporarily under cultivation.

【Sown Area of Crops】 refers to area of land sown or transplanted crops at the end of a production season.

The statistical year of sown area refers to area of land sown during the year (from Jan.1 to Dec.31)with a harvest of crops (including all those sown in the autumn and winter of the preceding year).

【Total Power of Agricultural Machinery】 refers to total mechanical power of machinery used in agriculture, forestry, animal,husbandry and fishery,including machinery for ploughing,irrigation and darinage,harvesting,farm products process,transport,plant protection,animal husbandry,forestry and fishery and other agricultural machineries.

【Urban Agriculture】 refers to industry that integrates agricultural production, life and ecology in urbanized area. This industry utilizes countryside landscape, natural ecology and environmental resources to provide places for leisure traveling, agricultural experience and understanding through production of agriculture, forestry, animal husbandry and fishery, agricultural operating activities, rural culture and life experience.

【Green Agriculture】 refers to comprehensive efficient industry that implements green agriculture engineering and develops non-polluting, safe and high quality green agricultural products in the green agricultural production base that obtained national certification.

【Total Income of Urban Agriculture】 refers to the total income of production and business enterprises in the statistical geographic area of urban agriculture. The income includes agricultural production of the year, magnitude of value of processing local agriculture products, transporting, wholesaling and retailing local agriculture products and the income of agricultural sightseeing and tourism.

【Industrialization of Agriculture】 refers to an economical operation method that oriented by domestic and international market, and takes economic benefits as centre. This method unites the scattered farmer households to the organizations through its organizational forms and operating mechanism. The organizations lead numerous farmer households to product unified productions under the unified standard. The production of the same species can extend within a large region and have a large scale. This method achieves the agriculture transition from family division to regional division and social division. It forms a specialization of agricultural production, regionalization of agricultural distribution, standardization of agricultural products and scaled agricultural operation. This economical operation method dynamically links the agricultural pre-production, in-production and post-production to integration.

【Agriculture Leading Enterprises】 refers to the enterprises that recognized by governments above district-level or country-level. The enterprises producing, processing and circulating agricultural and sideline products are the leading enterprises, and they can encourage local farmer households to work on professional production through contract, agreement or property right connection.

【Village】 refers to a clustered human settlement in rural area, which normally owns its name. The area of village and administrative village often overlaps. If a village is divided into many administrative villages, it should be taken as a village. If an administrative village contains many villages, it should be taken as many villages. If the villagers of an administrative village live far from each other, 20 households nearby would be taken as a village. The division of a village should follow local customs.

工 业

INDUSTRY

第十一篇　工　业

一、本篇资料反映广州市工业基本情况。

二、规模以上工业指年主营业务收入2000万元以上的工业企业。

三、本篇资料中工业行业分类按2017年《国民经济行业分类》（GB/T4754-2017）标准划分；企业规模按国家统计局《统计上大中小微企业划分办法》（国统字〔2011〕75号）标准执行。

四、本篇资料由广州市统计局工业处整理提供。

11 Industry

I. The data in this chapter reflect the statistics on industrial enterprises of Guangzhou.

II. The industrial enterprises above designated size refer to the industrial enterprises with an annual sales income of 20 million yuan and above.

III. The industrial sectors in this chapter are grouped in accordance with the National Economic Sector Grouping Standard of 2017 (GB/T4754-2017) , the industrial scale is grouped In accordance with the Grouping Way of Large, Medium, Small size and Micro-enterprise Standards (State Statistics [2011] No. 75).

IV. The data in this chapter are prepared and provided by Industry Department of Guangzhou Municipal Statistics Bureau.

11-1 工业总产值

Gross Output Value of Industry

项　　目	Item	工业总产值（万元）Gross Output Value of Industry (10000 yuan) 2018	2019	工业总产值指数(%) Indices of Gross Output Value of Industry (%)
总　计	**Total**	**203142272**	**213664922**	**106.0**
规模以上工业企业	**Industrial Enterprises above Designated Size**	**185951072**	**195549063**	**106.2**
按登记注册类型分	Grouped by Registration Status			
内资企业	Domestic Funded Enterprises	83158046	90001941	109.3
国有企业	State-owned Enterprises	522072	513053	99.2
集体企业	Collective-owned Enterprises	232077	205060	89.2
股份合作企业	Cooperative Enterprises	151658	134448	89.5
联营企业	Joint Ownership Enterprises			
国有联营企业	State Joint Ownership Enterprises			
集体联营企业	Collective Joint Ownership Enterprises			
国有与集体联营企业	Joint State-collective Enterprises			
其他联营企业	Other Joint Ownership Enterprise			
有限责任公司	Limited Liability Corporations	38714819	41383462	107.9
国有独资有限责任公司	Sole State Funded Corporations	20973532	21164556	101.9
其他有限责任公司	Other Limited Liability Corporations	17741287	20218906	115.1
股份有限公司	Share-holding Corporations Ltd.	18193876	17870577	99.2
私营企业	Private Enterprises	25343544	29895341	119.1
私营独资企业	Private-funded Enterprises	302430	302867	101.1
私营合伙企业	Private Partnership Enterprises	34920	26932	77.9
私营有限责任公司	Private Limited Liability Corporations	21520079	25707680	120.6
私营股份有限公司	Private Share Holding Corporations	3486116	3857862	111.7
其他企业	Other Enterprises			
港、澳、台商投资企业	Enterprises with Funds from Hong Kong, Macao and Taiwan	21664857	21829507	101.7
与港、澳、台商合资经营企业	Joint-venture Enterprises	6553548	6342256	97.7
与港、澳、台商合作经营企业	Cooperative Enterprises	537369	531858	99.9
港、澳、台商独资经营企业	Enterprises with Sole Funds	14275724	14589956	103.2
港、澳、台商投资股份有限公司	Share-holding Corporations Ltd.	288648	334493	117.0
其他港澳台投资	Other Enterprises with Funds from Hong Kong, Macao and Taiwan	9569	30944	326.5
外商投资企业	Foreign Funded Enterprises	81128168	83717615	104.2
中外合资经营企业	Joint-venture Enterprises	53006917	54406083	103.6
中外合作经营企业	Cooperative Enterprises	334552	261984	79.1
外资企业	Enterprises with Sole Foreign Funds	26822578	28233331	106.3
外商投资股份有限公司	Share-holding Corporations Ltd.	589301	448112	76.8
其他外商投资	Other Foreign Funded Enterprises	374821	368105	99.2
按隶属关系分	Grouped by Administrative Relationship			
中央企业	Central Governments	26209813	25920094	99.8
地方企业	Local Governments	159741258	169628969	107.2
按轻重工业分	Grouped by Light & Heavy Industries			
轻工业	Light Industry	50623617	52651644	104.9
重工业	Heavy Industry	135327455	142897419	106.7
按生产规模分	Grouped by Size of Enterprises			
大型企业	Large Enterprises	108149695	110245452	102.9
中型企业	Medium Enterprises	30750293	30602410	100.5
小微型企业	Small and Micro Industrial Enterprises	47051084	54701201	117.4

11-1 续表 continue

项 目	Item	工业总产值(万元) Gross Output Value of Industry (10000 yuan)		工业总产值指数(%) Indices of Gross Output Value of Industry (%)
		2018	2019	
按工业行业分	Grouped by Sector			
煤炭开采和洗选业	Mining and Washing of Coal			
石油和天然气开采业	Extraction of Petroleum and Natural Gas			
黑色金属矿采选业	Mining and Processing of Ferrous Metal Ores			
有色金属矿采选业	Mining and Processing of Non-Ferrous Metal Ores			
非金属矿采选业	Mining and Processing of Nonmetal Ores	12830	6820	53.2
开采专业及辅助性活动	Mining Professional and Auxiliary Activities			
其他采矿业	Mining of Other Ores			
农副食品加工业	Processing of Food from Agricultural Products	3129702	3342748	108.7
食品制造业	Manufacture of Foods	4974911	6083145	120.7
酒、饮料和精制茶制造业	Manufacture of Wine ,Beverages and Refined Tea	2280239	2336258	93.7
烟草制品业	Manufacture of Tobacco	2061937	2185327	102.5
纺织业	Manufacture of Textile	1631407	1410943	82.7
纺织服装、服饰业	Manufacture of Textile Wearing Apparel,Clothing	2751084	2940788	109.8
皮革、毛皮、羽毛及其制品和制鞋业	Manufacture of Leather, Fur, Feather and Related Products and Footwear	1646862	1770497	110.9
木材加工和木、竹、藤、棕、草制品业	Processing of Timber, Manufacture of Wood, Bamboo,Rattan, Palm and Straw Products	331685	361847	109.0
家具制造业	Manufacture of Furniture	2616944	2973890	104.6
造纸和纸制品业	Manufacture of Paper and Paper Products	1552536	1566592	111.2
印刷业和记录媒介复制业	Printing, Reproduction of Recording Media	1068319	1119440	103.0
文教、工美、体育和娱乐用品制造业	Manufacture of Culture and Education ,Arts and Crafts, Sports and Entertainment Supplies	1691550	1716285	101.4
石油、煤炭及其他燃料加工业	Petroleum, Coal and Other Fuel Processing Industries	6655945	6464019	101.1
化学原料和化学制品制造业	Manufacture of Raw Chemical Materials and Chemical Products	13386186	11683351	91.8
医药制造业	Manufacture of Medicines	2971388	3482990	113.3
化学纤维制造业	Manufacture of Chemical Fibers	60418	69956	117.7
橡胶和塑料制品业	Manufacture of Rubber	3991313	5089041	128.9
非金属矿物制品业	Manufacture of Non-metallic Mineral Products	3172302	4637570	140.9
黑色金属冶炼和压延加工业	Smelting and Pressing of Ferrous Metals	3431947	3335723	100.1
有色金属冶炼和压延加工业	Smelting and Pressing of Non-Ferrous Metals	3633689	3834182	110.5
金属制品业	Manufacture of Metal Products	3230821	3481000	107.8
通用设备制造业	Manufacture of General Purpose Machinery	6529331	7676956	115.7
专用设备制造业	Manufacture of Special Purpose Machinery	2893856	3480572	118.9
汽车制造业	Manufacture of Automobile	54652429	54122696	99.6
铁路、船舶、航空航天和其他运输设备制造业	Manufacture of Railway, Ship, Aerospace and Other Transportation Equipment	3359338	3890914	113.8
电气机械及器材制造业	Manufacture of Electrical Machinery and Equipment	8680980	9430266	107.9
计算机、通信和其他电子设备制造业	Manufacture of Computers, Communications and Other Electronic Equipment	21410310	20916472	100.4
仪器仪表制造业	Manufacture of Instrument	1134120	2396275	205.6
其他制造业	Other Manufacturing	178756	242387	132.8
废弃资源综合利用业	Comprehensive Utilization of Waste Resources	168360	215190	106.9
金属制品、机械和设备修理业	Metal Products, Machinery and Equipment Repair	733133	796471	108.6
电力、热力生产和供应业	Production and Supply of Electric Power and Heat Power	14453760	15644648	108.1
燃气生产和供应业	Production and Supply of Gas	4629855	5929245	132.5
水的生产和供应业	Production and Supply of Water	842830	914559	108.5

11-2 主要年份工业总产值及工业总产值指数
Gross Output Value and Indices of Industry in Main Years

年 份 Year	工业总产值（万元） Gross Output Value of Industry (10000 yuan)	轻工业 Light Industry	重工业 Heavy Industry	工业总产值指数（%） Indices of Gross Output Value of Industry (%)	轻工业 Light Industry	重工业 Heavy Industry
1978	753873	476737	277136	104.4	102.9	106.8
1980	881242	574239	307003	111.7	118.0	103.0
1985	1779333	1163704	615629	122.1	122.9	120.9
1986	1921490	1206778	714712	104.3	106.1	101.3
1987	2421760	1551033	870727	120.7	122.7	117.2
1988	3413107	2251117	1161990	125.6	128.4	120.4
1989	4071472	2598755	1472717	106.2	103.4	111.7
1990	4424437	2830366	1594071	110.1	113.6	103.7
1991	5794842	3588318	2206524	123.6	122.7	125.4
1992	7905237	4753211	3152026	132.2	129.9	136.7
1993	11422184	6595134	4827050	132.5	129.8	137.5
1994	14921455	8784293	6137162	122.4	126.0	116.2
1995（原规定） 1995 (original stipulation)	19353440	11263263	8090177	120.2	115.6	128.9
1995（新规定） 1995 (new stipulation)	17224948	10263515	6961433	120.2	115.6	128.9
1996	20685796	12641264	8044532	119.1	126.1	106.8
1997	23753915	14395602	9358313	117.9	116.8	120.2
1998	25127025	15661603	9465422	114.0	112.8	116.3
1999	27793652	16797164	10996488	114.3	111.3	120.1
2000	31000188	17622183	13378005	113.6	107.9	123.9
2001	33931904	18855507	15076397	114.9	110.6	121.9
2002	37889079	20185702	17703377	115.0	109.6	122.8
2003	47059104	23752778	23306326	126.5	119.5	135.5
2004	57666925	25977971	31688954	120.0	108.9	130.1
2005	67679563	28714137	38965426	115.4	110.1	118.8
2006	81123964	31875454	49248510	116.9	111.0	120.2
2007	98757886	37208718	61549168	120.1	114.8	124.3
2008	114684010	43536797	71147213	112.0	114.2	111.0
2009	123554645	46730599	76824046	111.7	109.8	112.8
2010	144389877	51073851	93316026	118.5	115.2	120.4
2011	150817300	53145376	97671924	111.6	116.8	108.8
2012	158814499	55926385	102888114	111.2	114.5	109.7
2013	165578552	57522821	108055731	113.0	112.6	113.1
2014	174792999	58981934	115811065	107.5	105.4	108.7
2015	179351607	59696082	119655525	106.0	102.7	107.8
2016	187458032	59963215	127494817	105.8	100.2	109.0
2017	196199756	60041726	136158030	104.5	99.1	107.1
2018	203142256	60507017	142635239	103.7	100.1	105.3
2019	213664922	64793517	148871405	106.0	104.7	106.6

11-3 按历史时期分工业总产值
Gross Output Value of Industry by History Periods

时 期 Period	工业总产值（万元） Gross Output Value of Industry (10000 yuan)	轻工业 Light Industry	重工业 Heavy Industry	工业总产值年平均增长（%） Annual Average Growth Speed of Gross Output Value of Industry (%)	轻工业 Light Industry	重工业 Heavy Industry
"六五"时期 6th Five-year Plan Period	6447893	4209237	2238656	12.8	13.1	12.4
"七五"时期 7th Five-year Plan Period	16252266	10438049	5814217	13.1	14.5	10.6
"八五"时期 8th Five-year Plan Period	59397158	34984219	24412939	26.1	24.7	28.7
"九五"时期 9th Five-year Plan Period	128360576	77117816	51242760	15.7	14.8	17.3
"十五"时期 10th Five-year Plan Period	244226575	117486095	126740480	18.3	12.0	26.1
"十一五"时期 11th Five-year Plan Period	562510382	210425419	352084963	15.8	13.2	17.9
"十二五"时期 12th Five-year Plan Period	829354957	285272598	544082359	9.8	10.2	9.5
1979-2019	2488260429	878543477	1609716952	14.5	13.0	15.8
1991-2019	2467162068	865068385	1602093683	15.3	12.8	17.9
2001-2019	2344755359	796247801	1548507558	12.5	9.4	15.3
2011-2019	1629819923	530578073	1099241850	7.7	6.0	8.4

11-4 规模以上工业企业单位数

Number of Industrial Enterprises above the Designated Size

单位：个 (unit)

项　　目	Item	2018	2019
总　　计	**Total**	**4809**	**5804**
按登记注册类型分	Grouped by Registration Status		
内资企业	Domestic Funded Enterprises	3512	4476
国有企业	State-owned Enterprises	15	13
集体企业	Collective-owned Enterprises	17	17
股份合作企业	Cooperative Enterprises	13	13
联营企业	Joint Ownership Enterprises		
国有联营企业	State Joint Ownership Enterprises		
集体联营企业	Collective Joint Ownership Enterprises		
国有与集体联营企业	Joint State-collective Enterprises		
其他联营	Other Joint Ownership Enterprise		
有限责任公司	Limited Liability Corporations	600	713
国有独资有限责任公司	State Sole Funded Corporations	58	63
其他有限责任公司	Other Limited Liability Corporations	542	650
股份有限公司	Share-holding Corporations Ltd.	165	177
私营企业	Private Enterprises	2702	3543
私营独资企业	Private-funded Enterprises	62	57
私营合伙企业	Private Partnership Enterprises	10	9
私营有限责任公司	Private Limited Liability Corporations	2538	3373
私营股份有限公司	Private Share Holding Corporations	92	104
其他企业	Other Enterprises		

11-4 续表 continued

单位:个 (unit)

项　　目	Item	2018	2019
港、澳、台商投资企业	Enterprises with Funds from Hong Kong, Macao and Taiwan	663	679
与港、澳、台商合资经营企业	Joint-venture Enterprises	125	128
与港、澳、台商合作经营企业	Cooperative Enterprises	25	28
港、澳、台商独资经营企业	Enterprises with Sole Funds	502	509
港、澳、台商投资股份有限公司	Share-holding Corporations Ltd.	9	11
其他港澳台投资	Other Enterprises with Funds from Hong Kong, Macao and Taiwan	2	3
外商投资企业	Foreign Funded Enterprises	634	649
中外合资经营企业	Joint-venture Enterprises	182	191
中外合作经营企业	Cooperative Enterprises	11	10
外资企业	Enterprises with Sole Foreign Funds	422	426
外商投资股份有限公司	Share-holding Corporations Ltd.	10	12
其他外商投资	Other Foreign Funded Enterprises	9	10
按隶属关系分	Grouped by Administrative Relationship		
中央企业	Central Government	55	46
地方企业	Provincial Government	4754	5758
按轻重工业分	Grouped by Light & Heavy Industries		
轻工业	Light Industry	2481	3032
重工业	Heavy Industry	2328	2772
按生产规模分	Grouped by Size of Enterprises		
大型企业	Large Enterprises	168	168
中型企业	Medium Enterprises	642	603
小微型企业	Small and Micro Industrial Enterprises	3999	5033

11-5 规模以上工业销售产值

Sales Value of Industrial Enterprises above the Designated Size

单位：万元 (10000 yuan)

项　目	Item	2018	2019
总　计	**Total**	**185723217**	**190765499**
按登记注册类型分	**Grouped by Registration Status**		
国有企业	State-owned Industry	511300	551483
集体企业	Collective-owned Industry	231647	216493
私营企业	Private Entreprises	26717162	26669029
港、澳、台商投资企业	Enterprises with Funds from Hong Kong, Macao and Taiwan	21071205	21396797
外商投资企业	Foreign Funded Enterprises	80426448	86805876
其他企业	Other Enterprises	56765455	55125821
按隶属关系分	**Grouped by Administrative Relationship**		
中央企业	Central Governments	25778577	24587742
地方企业	Local Governments	159944640	166177757
按轻重工业分	**Grouped by Light & Heavy Industries**		
轻工业	Light Industry	50241681	48363941
重工业	Heavy Industry	135481536	142401558
按生产规模分	**Grouped by Size of Enterprises**		
大中型企业	Large and Medium Industrial Enterprises	137105109	140339526
小微型企业	Small and Micro Industrial Enterprises	48618108	50425973

11-6 主要年份规模以上工业企业出口交货值及比重

Delivery Value of Exports and Proportion of Industrial Enterprises above the Designated Size in Main Years

单位：万元 (10000 yuan)

年 份 Year	工业销售产值 Sale Output Value of Industry	出口交货值 Delivery Value of Exports	出口交货值比重(%) Proportion of Exports Delivery Value (%)
2001	27171297	6502235	23.93
2002	31156870	7881230	25.30
2003	39241536	9599697	24.46
2004	50207200	12824023	25.54
2005	59120813	14945688	25.28
2006	71756225	17218091	24.00
2007	87657013	19543878	22.30
2008	103134403	22092456	21.42
2009	111566225	22173771	19.87
2010	133127027	27046367	20.32
2011	138247622	28060074	20.30
2012	146583202	26330137	17.96
2013	152817401	27672722	18.11
2014	158400387	28273891	17.85
2015	162062563	27444560	16.93
2016	168376153	26394955	15.68
2017	177607921	22999291	15.18
2018	185723217	27199454	14.65
2019	190765499	27696705	14.52

11-7 规模以上工业企业出口交货值（2019年）

Delivery Value of Exports of Industrial Enterprises above the Designated Size (2019)

单位：万元 (10000 yuan)

项　目	Item	出口产品交货值 Delivery Value of Exports
总　计	**Total**	**27696705**
按登记注册类型分	Grouped by Registration Status	
国有企业	State-owned Industry	3680
集体企业	Collective-owned Industry	135169
其他企业	Others	27557856
按隶属关系分	Grouped by Administrative Relationship	
中央企业	Central Governments	1131245
地方企业	Local Governments	26565460
按轻重工业分	Grouped by Light & Heavy Industries	
轻工业	Light Industry	9058730
重工业	Heavy Industry	18637975
按生产规模分	Grouped by Size of Enterprises	
大中型企业	Large and Medium Enterprises	22339059
小微型企业	Small and Micro Industrial Enterprises	5357646
按工业行业分	Grouped by Sector	
煤炭开采和洗选业	Mining and Washing of Coal	
石油和天然气开采业	Extraction of Petroleum and Natural Gas	
黑色金属矿采选业	Mining and Processing of Ferrous Metal Ores	
有色金属矿采选业	Mining and Processing of Non-Ferrous Metal Ores	
非金属矿采选业	Mining and Processing of Nonmetal Ores	
开采专业及辅助性活动	Mining Professional and Auxiliary Activities	
其他采矿业	Mining of Other Ores	
农副食品加工业	Processing of Food from Agricultural Products	54475
食品制造业	Manufacture of Foods	230925
酒、饮料和精制茶制造业	Manufacture of wine,Beverages and Refined Tea	1853
烟草制品业	Manufacture of Tobacco	5724
纺织业	Manufacture of Textile	648015
纺织服装、服饰业	Manufacture of Textile Wearing Apparel,Clothing	570763
皮革、毛皮、羽毛及其制品和制鞋业	Manufacture of Leather,Fur,Feather and Related Products and Footwear	770164

11-7 续表 continued

单位：万元 (10000 yuan)

项　目	Item	出口产品交货值 Delivery Value of Exports
木材加工和木、竹、藤、棕、草制品业	Processing of Timber,Manufacture of Wood, Bamboo, Rattan, Plam and Straw Products	5418
家具制造业	Manufacture of Furniture	191063
造纸和纸制品业	Manufacture of Paper and Paper Products	62878
印刷业和记录媒介复制业	Printing, Reproduction of Recording Media	450935
文教、工美、体育和娱乐用品制造业	Manufacture of Culture and Education ,Arts and Crafts, Sports and Entertainment Supplies	495001
石油、煤炭及其他燃料加工业	Petroleum, Coal and Other Fuel Processing Industries	375110
化学原料和化学制品制造业	Manufacture of Raw Chemical Materials and Chemical Products	867943
医药制造业	Manufacture of Medicines	167937
化学纤维制造业	Manufacture of Chemical Fibers	4829
橡胶和塑料制品业	Manufacture of Rubber	1069550
非金属矿物制品业	Manufacture of Non-metallic Mineral Products	368986
黑色金属冶炼和压延加工业	Smelting and Pressing of Ferrous Metals	212858
有色金属冶炼和压延加工业	Smelting and Pressing of Non-Ferrous Metals	67923
金属制品业	Manufacture of Metal Products	806419
通用设备制造业	Manufacture of General Purpose Machinery	1225117
专用设备制造业	Manufacture of Special Purpose Machinery	615510
汽车制造业	Manufacture of Automobile	1390859
铁路、船舶、航空航天和其他运输设备制造业	Manufacture of Railway, Ship, Aerospace and Other Transportation Equipment	775094
电气机械及器材制造业	Manufacture of Electrical Machinery and Equipment	2620744
计算机、通信和其他电子设备制造业	Manufacture of Computers, Communications and Other Electronic Equipment	12389598
仪器仪表制造业	Manufacture of Instrument	781715
其他制造业	Other Manufacturing	42002
废弃资源综合利用业	Comprehensive Utilization of Waste Resources	
金属制品、机械和设备修理业	Metal Products, Machinery and Equipment Repair	96202
电力、热力生产和供应业	Production and Supply of Electric Power and Heat Power	331095
燃气生产和供应业	Production and Supply of Gas	
水的生产和供应业	Production and Supply of Water	

11-8 工业三大支柱产业主要指标(2019年)

Major Indicators of Three Pillar Industrial Industries (2019)

行业	Sector	单位数(个) Number of Units (unit)	从业人员(万人) Employed Persons (10000 persons)	工业总产值(亿元) Gross Output Value of Industry (100 million yuan)
合计	**Total**	**1677**	**46.07**	**9870.02**
汽车制造业	Automobile Manufacturing	328	16.04	5412.27
#汽车零部件制造业	Auto Parts Manufacturing	304	9.86	1427.60
电子产品制造业	Electronic Appliance Manufacturing	777	22.67	2657.40
石油化工制造业	Petrochemical Manufacturing	572	7.36	1800.35
三大支柱产业占全市比重 (%)	Three Pillar Industries Proportion of All Industrial Enterprises (%)	28.89	36.69	50.47

注：本表统计范围为规模以上工业企业。

Note:The data in this table cover the industrial enterprises above designated size.

11-8 续表 continued

行业	Sector	营业收入(亿元) Business Revenue	利润总额(亿元) Total Profits (100 million yuan)	税金总额(亿元) Total Pre-tax Profits (100 million yuan)
合计	**Total**	**10209.37**	**644.90**	**516.96**
汽车制造业	Automobile Manufacturing	5609.36	386.13	307.56
#汽车零部件制造业	Auto Parts Manufacturing	1487.05	137.63	42.86
电子产品制造业	Electronic Appliance Manufacturing	2661.40	115.29	32.83
石油化工制造业	Petrochemical Manufacturing	1938.61	143.48	176.57
三大支柱产业占全市比重(%)	Three Pillar Industries Proportion of All Industrial Enterprises (%)	49.88	48.38	57.37

11-9 主要工业产品产量(2019年)
Output of Major Industrial Products(2019)

产品名称		Name of Products		2018	2019
食用植物油	(吨)	Edible Vegetable Oil	(ton)	1695103	1861695
乳制品	(吨)	Dairy Products	(ton)	383763	406475
罐　头	(吨)	Canned Food	(ton)	7897	8278
饮料酒(混合量)	(千升)	Alcoholic Beverages (mixed)	(1000 litre)	928587	972015
#啤　酒	(千升)	Beer	(1000 litre)	928587	972015
饲　料	(吨)	Fodder	(ton)	2939650	2538814
卷　烟	(万支)	Cigarettes	(10000 piece)	6048094	5947600
纱	(吨)	Yarn	(ton)	10942	1889
布	(万米)	Cloth	(10000 meters)	39225	59089
印染布	(万米)	Dyeing cloth	(10000 meters)	46113	35780
服　装	(万件)	Garments	(10000 units)	55143	35371
皮革鞋靴	(万双)	Leather Shoes	(10000 pairs)	3938	2606
手提包(袋)、背包	(万个)	Handbag, Backpack	(10000units)	13432	12732
人造板	(立方米)	Artificial Boards	(cu.m)	944357	831615
家　具	(万件)	Furniture	(10000 units)	1194	1047
机制纸及纸板	(吨)	Machine-made Paper and Paperboards	(ton)	653702	604811
#新闻纸		Newsprint		372628	329999
纸制品	(吨)	Paper Products	(ton)	1001713	875866
化学试剂	(吨)	Chemical Reagent	(ton)	104621	197243
涂　料	(吨)	Coating	(ton)	912091	915203
初级形态的塑料	(吨)	Plastics	(ton)	1472879	1436677
橡胶轮胎外胎	(条)	Tires	(unit)	12776590	11655420
塑料制品	(吨)	Plastic Products	(ton)	1276557	1214280
合成洗涤剂	(吨)	Synthetic Detergents	(ton)	1978953	1970571
化学药品原药	(吨)	Chemical Medicines	(ton)	20443	19336
中成药	(吨)	Traditional Chinese Medicine	(ton)	60404	87116
发电量	(亿千瓦·时)	Electricity	(100 million kWh)	333	-
原油加工量	(吨)	Crude Oil Processing	(ton)	12613704	11860095
汽　油	(吨)	Gasoline	(ton)	3035566	3134578
煤　油	(吨)	Kerosene	(ton)	1973192	2052341
柴　油	(吨)	Diesel Oil	(ton)	3635982	3459992
燃料油	(吨)	Fuel Oil	(ton)	1144	1434
粗　钢	(吨)	Steel	(ton)	1604330	1596310
钢　材	(吨)	Steel Products	(ton)	8663835	6431144
交流电动机	(千瓦)	AC Motors	(kw)	225108	224217
发动机生产量	(万千瓦)	Internal Combustion Engines	(10000 kw)	26089	22454

11-9 续表 continued

产品名称		Name of Products		2018	2019
自动柜员机(ATM机)	(台)	Automated Teller Machines	(set)	31932	30403
工业机器人	(套)	Industrial Robots	(set)	4188	4200
工业自动调节仪表与控制系统	(套)	Industrial Automatic Regulating Instrument and Control System	(set)	1826693	1668037
电　梯	(台)	Elevators & Escalators	(unit)	98699	128003
医疗仪器设备及器械	(台)	Medical Equipment and Instruments	(set)	144933	203514
钟	(只)	Clocks	(unit)	1186112	901621
自行车	(辆)	Bicycles	(unit)	1490036	1188715
摩托车整车	(辆)	Motorcycles	(unit)	2307828	2184125
汽　车	(辆)	Motor Vehicles	(unit)	2965156	2922609
其中：乘用车	(辆)	Sedans	(unit)	2956020	2898402
其中：运动型多用途乘用车(SUV)	(辆)	Sports Utility Vehicle	(unit)	1142267	986172
新能源汽车	(辆)	New Energy Vehicle	(unit)	28228	60606
变压器	(千伏安)	Transformers	(1000 volt-amperes)	45718036	41107274
原电池及原电池组(非扣式)	(万只)	Batteries	(10000 units)	8859	9512
家用电冰箱	(台)	Household Refrigerators	(set)	3298399	3094958
家用电风扇	(台)	Electric Fans	(set)	421486	332983
房间空气调节器	(台)	Air Conditioners	(set)	7323214	8132004
电饭锅	(个)	Electric Rice Cooker	(unit)	968224	813858
家用吸排油烟机	(台)	Extractor Hoods	(set)	65006	45146
家用燃气灶具	(台)	Gas Appliances	(unit)	2170565	2502958
电光源	(万只)	Bulbs	(10000 units)	10681	9787
电话单机	(部)	Telephone Sets	(unit)	1034380	1150095
移动通信手持机	(台)	Mobile Telecommunication Handset	(unit)	1931179	4033275
微型电子计算机	(台)	Micro-computers	(unit)	136918	240417
其中：平板电脑	(台)	Tablet Personal Computer	(unit)	109083	203290
彩色电视机	(台)	Color TV Sets	(set)	10747196	9673218
其中：智能电视	(台)	Smart TV	(set)	6099134	5367838
移动通信基站设备	(信道)	Mobile Communication Base Station Equipmen	(channel)	1534011	1343940
光缆	(芯千米)	Optical Cable	(km)	9851	7963
锂离子电池	(万只)	Li-ion Battery	(10000units)	18092	25633
光电子器件	(万只)	Optoelectronic Device	(10000units)	858032	798693
其中：液晶显示屏	(万片)	Liquid Crystal Display	(10000units)	9530	9599
数字激光音、视盘机	(台)	Digital Video Player	(set)	42562	50867
显示器	(台)	Displayer	(set)	381440	447452
其中：平板显示器	(台)	Flat-panel Displayer	(set)	311047	388172

11-10 主要年份规模以上工业企业全员劳动生产率

Overall Labor Productivity of Industrial Enterprises above the Designated Size in Main Years

单位：元/人 (yuan/person)

年　份 Year	合　计 Total	国有企业 State-owned Enterprises	集体企业 Collective-owned Enterprises	“三资”企业 Foreign Funded Enterprises	其他企业 Other Enterprises
1998	53499	64347	27238	56952	46688
1999	60087	81519	30910	58846	47523
2000	60342	108088	32429	61748	48220
2001	69917	89566	40058	72400	67034
2002	76324	103186	40514	76773	79963
2003	89991	126215	36475	97733	83382
2004	96845	168409	30129	107890	70332
2005	115051	231185	31305	125912	86735
2006	132200	300403	31106	145278	97882
2007	156811	392930	32447	170755	116857
2008	175472	242679	25413	193910	153715
2009	181874	170356	31688	213960	142523
2010	189103	197233	38990	223761	145249
2011	213069	216681	45536	239725	179971
2012	229692	231914	40209	240817	191849
2013	234556	186829	75529	256619	212647
2014	255517	205164	74531	287356	231897
2015	270906	179132	101921	305602	262179
2016	292630	240810	110977	334070	279395
2017	322118	228782	62375	352981	293469
2018	339734	277878	84997	376995	308216
2019	346318	304116	90347	394729	305378

注：本表数据按工业增加值计算，以下劳动生产率表同。

Note: The data in this table are calculated on basis of the value-added of industry. The same as in the following tables.

11-11 规模以上工业企业全员劳动生产率(2019年，按行业分)

单位：元/人

行　　业	Sector
合　计	**Total**
煤炭开采和洗选业	Mining and Washing of Coal
石油和天然气开采业	Extraction of Petroleum and Natural Gas
黑色金属矿采选业	Mining and Processing of Ferrous Metal Ores
有色金属矿采选业	Mining and Processing of Non-Ferrous Metal Ores
非金属矿采选业	Mining and Processing of Nonmetal Ores
开采专业及辅助性活动	Mining Professional and Auxiliary Activities
其他采矿业	Mining of Other Ores
农副食品加工业	Processing of Food from Agricultural Products
食品制造业	Manufacture of Foods
酒、饮料和精制茶制造业	Manufacture of Wine ,Beverages and Refined Tea
烟草制品业	Manufacture of Tobacco
纺织业	Manufacture of Textile
纺织服装、服饰业	Manufacture of Textile Wearing Apparel,Clothing
皮革、毛皮、羽毛及其制品和制鞋业	Manufacture of Leather, Fur, Feather and Related Products and Footwear
木材加工和木、竹、藤、棕、草制品业	Processing of Timber, Manufacture of Wood, Bamboo,Rattan,Palm and Straw Products
家具制造业	Manufacture of Furniture
造纸和纸制品业	Manufacture of Paper and Paper Products
印刷业和记录媒介复制业	Printing, Reproduction of Recording Media
文教、工美、体育和娱乐用品制造业	Manufacture of Culture and Education ,Arts and Crafts, Sports and Entertainment Supplies
石油、煤炭及其他燃料加工业	Petroleum, Coal and Other Fuel Processing Industries
化学原料和化学制品制造业	Manufacture of Raw Chemical Materials and Chemical Products
医药制造业	Manufacture of Medicines
化学纤维制造业	Manufacture of Chemical Fibers
橡胶和塑料制品业	Manufacture of Rubber
非金属矿物制品业	Manufacture of Non-metallic Mineral Products
黑色金属冶炼和压延加工业	Smelting and Pressing of Ferrous Metals
有色金属冶炼和压延加工业	Smelting and Pressing of Non-Ferrous Metals
金属制品业	Manufacture of Metal Products
通用设备制造业	Manufacture of General Purpose Machinery
专用设备制造业	Manufacture of Special Purpose Machinery
汽车制造业	Manufacture of Automobile
铁路、船舶、航空航天和其他运输设备制造业	Manufacture of Railway, Ship, Aerospace and Other Transportation Equipment
电气机械及器材制造业	Manufacture of Electrical Machinery and Equipment
计算机、通信和其他电子设备制造业	Manufacture of Computers, Communications and Other Electronic Equipment
仪器仪表制造业	Manufacture of Instrument
其他制造业	Other Manufacturing
废弃资源综合利用业	Comprehensive Utilization of Waste Resources
金属制品、机械和设备修理业	Metal Products, Machinery and Equipment Repair
电力、热力生产和供应业	Production and Supply of Electric Power and Heat Power
燃气生产和供应业	Production and Supply of Gas
水的生产和供应业	Production and Supply of Water

Overall Labor Productivity of Industrial Enterprises above the Designated Size(2019, by Sector)

(yuan/person)

全　市 Total	国有企业 State-owned Enterprises	集体企业 Collective-owned Enterprises	“三资”企业 Foreign Funded Enterprises	其他企业 Other Enterprises
346318	**304116**	**90347**	**394729**	**305378**
210642				210642
301237		121620	549376	266448
387022	133578		441286	240559
567257			440639	858500
6323073				6323073
163815			162590	165301
145093		232765	130279	152417
86552		24609	66892	101047
287628			185156	330624
200826			188648	204888
244183		213422	439697	127399
166218			152661	188267
123071			114688	136328
3346416			2388507	3412089
405915	50159	340553	644661	224392
377756	151362		414862	369695
225608			285486	187799
186971			201181	175898
289162		343598	363267	255035
228879	49475		227937	272375
132385			65048	183744
149358	148641		148557	150017
199960		88149	227882	178269
236489	149876		308861	199434
764175	151627		979817	219691
188015			167202	193403
181420	173331		193471	173494
201120		77185	196287	227607
303067			308890	295355
166011			127138	176092
291529			350390	233972
248226	153916		337363	178122
1188542			1134050	1190721
2191064			966073	2663577
469316	398345	318688	553212	530806

11-12 主要年份规模以上工业企业主要经济指标

单位：万元

项目	Item	2000	2006	2007
企业单位数 （个）	Number of Enterprises (unit)	4531	5188	4988
#亏损企业	Number of Loss-making Enterprises	954	1032	886
营业收入	Business Revenue			
主营业务收入	Revenue from Principal Business	25342544	72493321	88630531
营业成本	Cost of Business			
税金及附加	Taxes and Other Charges			
盈利企业的盈利总额	Total Profits of Profitable Enterprises	1577983	6008538	8044372
亏损企业的亏损总额	Total Losses of Loss-making Enterprises	393740	620087	513225
利润总额	Total Profits of All Enterprises	1184243	5388451	7531147
所得税费用	Income Tax Payable	160118	676932	861833
应交增值税	Value-added Tax Payable	919339	2643027	3199893
流动资产合计	Total Working Capitals at the Year-end	15082653	31365356	37716223
#存　货	Inventory	4301980	8145761	9334080
#产成品存货	Inventory of Finished Goods	1528452	2478717	2960730
固定资产原价	Original Value of Fixed Assets at the Year-end	17672981	33587396	37780990
资产总计	Total Assets at the Year-end	30861594	69036123	80412681
负债合计	Total Liabilities at the Year-end	18249287	33474848	40571015
年末所有者权益合计	Total Owners' Equity at the Year-end	12612307	35561275	39841666
#实收资本	Capital Hold	8458358	20776240	22730283
#国家资本	State Capital	1375635	6936604	7035569
外商资本	Foreign Capital	3578053	7759689	8286574
应付职工薪酬	Wages Payable	1623490	4184674	5216279
平均用工人数 （人）	Annual Average Number of Staff and Workers (person)	1173960	1490877	1540930
工业总产值 （当年价格）	Gross Industrial Output Value (at current prices)	25685694	72820564	89104386
工业增加值 （当年价格）	Value-added of Industry (at current prices)	7083953	19709445	24163424

Main Indicators of Industrial Enterprises above the Designated Size in Main Years

(10000 yuan)

2008	2009	2010	2011	2012	2013	2014	2015	2016	2017	2018	2019
7442	7023	6969	4437	4373	4812	4774	4650	4662	4664	4809	5804
1725	1407	1060	689	744	652	676	757	628	583	755	808
			145086461	150822672	158167813	167023591	171224204	175237274	181888742	193203157	204661205
104244867	112140930	136246497	142702405	147964380	155067607	163773477	168050610	171355762	177824134	188940859	200789709
			121561470	125267159	130014079	137662449	141345831	145312089	149153580	159289442	168977900
			3225061	3342312	3456332	3528065	3830470	3683607	4042079	4996688	4862051
8003202	8584412	10910868	10629334	9666882	11721003	11707720	11919417	12885022	14183445	15140201	15255302
1072933	793247	598124	1044071	1410834	667252	827867	933685	568663	694547	1080421	1924833
6930269	7791165	10312744	9585263	8256048	11053751	10879853	10985732	12316359	13488898	14059780	13330468
983288	1138346	1440506	1616771	1473553	1902197	2005738	2190998	2232541	2387294	2351971	2162005
4520708	3843777	4696284	4545000	4354268	5125516	4882891	5386846	5177392	5228958	5091789	4149001
43871519	50733991	60871184	65179319	64593607	74129378	74764969	80408497	88188186	96779199	101717230	110643480
11054940	11529881	14111012	15232168	14522684	16005082	17037284	17158817	18033526	18627915	19570116	19723127
3751238	3761104	4694208	5213396	5427243	5540642	5958356	5632484	6056731	6892340	7314025	7498511
45244307	47978199	52094111	53921739	55980684	62689307	68562811	76523257	78525615	83420835	81127100	87101336
91648730	99655278	112655080	118306012	121573804	135540623	140934954	155333696	167377121	179076236	186667654	209952476
49694345	55020064	63320448	66428322	64458098	73585807	76229825	82261928	86779985	90880623	91685081	104542418
41954385	44635214	49334632	51877690	57115706	61954816	64705129	73071768	80597136	88195613	94982573	105410058
26272164	27564197	28796044	29125022	30434735	32278772	33859432	36002643	39035369	38744839	40175303	45186190
7510952	4533428	4529442	3763637	1692610	4011019	4419667	11612683	12734788	13956470	15644310	13219619
5586787	5940516	5915409	6476297	6874272	7019315	7711786	6920908	7226057	6725689	6828975	7592051
8089617	8159771	8634171	7650769	8148319	9441451	10920005	11495875	11694022	12648031	15371683	15656641
1719873	1615692	1662226	1547037	1499914	1534434	1462674	1418883	1355635	1276030	1239051	1255434
105149110	113767645	135312498	141702680	148577082	155323091	162829719	167268662	171911624	178585638	185951072	195549063
27875000	29385200	31433200	32962618	34451765	35991105	37373803	38438366	39669962	41103222	42094777	43477896

11-13　规模以上工业企业主要经济指标（2019年）

单位：万元

项　　目		Item	
企业单位数	（个）	Number of Enterprises	(unit)
# 亏损企业		Number of Loss-making Enterprises	
营业收入		Business Revenue	
营业成本		Cost of Business	
税金及附加		Taxes and Other Charges	
盈利企业的盈利总额		Total Profits of Profitable Enterprises	
亏损企业的亏损总额		Total Losses of Loss-making Enterprises	
利润总额		Total Profits of All Enterprises	
所得税费用		Income Tax Payable	
应交增值税		Value-added Tax Payable	
流动资产合计		Total Working Capitals at the Year-end	
# 应收账款		Accounts Receivable	
# 存　货		Inventory	
# 产成品存货		Inventory of Finished Goods	
固定资产原价		Original Value of Fixed Assets at the Year-end	
累计折旧		Accumulated Depreciation	
固定资产净额		Net Fixed Assets	
资产总计		Total Assets at the Year-end	
负债合计		Total Liabilities at the Year-end	
所有者权益合计		Total Owners' Equity at the Year-end	
# 实收资本		Capital Hold	
# 国家资本		State Capital	
外商资本		Foreign Capital	
应付职工薪酬		Wages Payable	
平均用工人数	（人）	Annual Average Number of Staff and Workers	(person)
工业总产值	（当年价格）	Gross Industrial Output Value	(at current prices)
工业增加值	（当年价格）	Value-added of Industry	(at current prices)

Main Indicators of Industrial Enterprises above the Designated Size (2019)

(10000 yuan)

全 市 Total	# 中央企业 Central Enterprises	# 地方企业 Local Enterprises
5804	46	5758
808	9	799
204661205	26703693	177957512
168977900	22664418	146313482
4862051	2330006	2532045
15255302	2941247	12314055
1924833	176424	1748409
13330468	2764822	10565646
2162005	245425	1916580
4149001	501194	3647807
110643480	13003198	97640282
28190915	1314869	26876046
19723127	2611079	17112048
7498511	211218	7287293
87101336	16814488	70286848
46318604	9409576	36909028
39934058	7333736	32600322
209952476	46041288	163911188
104542418	15210069	89332349
105410058	30831219	74578839
45186190	9170868	36015322
13219619	7448093	5771526
7592051	60686	7531365
15656641	1252434	14404207
1255434	43889	1211545
195549063	25920094	169628969
43477896	6171961	37305935

11-14 规模以上工业企业主要经济指标(2019年，按轻重工业分)

单位：万元

项 目	Item
企业单位数 (个)	Number of Enterprises (unit)
#亏损企业	Number of Loss-making Enterprises
营业收入	Business Revenue
营业成本	Cost of Business
税金及附加	Taxes and Other Charges
盈利企业的盈利总额	Total Profits of Profitable Enterprises
亏损企业的亏损总额	Total Losses of Loss-making Enterprises
利润总额	Total Profits of All Enterprises
所得税费用	Income Tax Payable
应交增值税	Value-added Tax Payable
流动资产合计	Total Working Capitals at the Year-end
#应收账款	Accounts Receivable
#存　货	Inventory
#产成品存货	Inventory of Finished Goods
固定资产原价	Original Value of Fixed Assets at the Year-end
累计折旧	Accumulated Depreciation
固定资产净额	Net Fixed Assets
资产总计	Total Assets at the Year-end
负债合计	Total Liabilities at the Year-end
所有者权益合计	Total Owners' Equity at the Year-end
#实收资本	Capital Hold
#国家资本	State Capital
外商资本	Foreign Capital
应付职工薪酬	Wages Payable
平均用工人数 (人)	Annual Average Number of Staff and Workers (person)
工业总产值 (当年价格)	Gross Industrial Output Value (at current prices)
工业增加值 (当年价格)	Value-added of Industry (at current prices)

Main Indicators of Industrial Enterprises above the Designated Size
(2019 by Light and Heavy Industry)

(10000 yuan)

全　市 Total		# 中央企业 Central Enterprises		# 地方企业 Local Enterprises	
轻工业 Light Industry	重工业 Heavy Industry	轻工业 Light Industry	重工业 Heavy Industry	轻工业 Light Industry	重工业 Heavy Industry
3032	2772	5	41	3027	2731
428	380		9	428	371
56866422	147794783	2522007	24181686	54344415	123613097
40715610	128262290	980569	21683849	39735041	106578441
1437565	3424486	1104012	1225994	333553	2198492
4775394	10479908	144119	2797128	4631275	7682780
231507	1693326		176424	231507	1516902
4543886	8786582	144118	2620704	4399768	6165878
832078	1329927	68563	176862	763515	1153065
1721202	2427799	236165	265029	1485037	2162770
36083576	74559904	1717995	11285203	34365581	63274701
8163343	20027572	61479	1253390	8101864	18774182
7563082	12160045	1248586	1362493	6314496	10797552
2794924	4703587	15888	195330	2779036	4508257
18604541	68496795	768107	16046381	17836434	52450414
9524364	36794240	489599	8919977	9034765	27874263
8903227	31030831	278509	7055227	8624718	23975604
56435403	153517073	2380636	43660652	54054767	109856421
27813622	76728796	427734	14782335	27385888	61946461
28621781	76788277	1952902	28878317	26668879	47909960
13029625	32156565	846258	8324610	12183367	23831955
2957553	10262066	4865	7443228	2952688	2818838
1874485	5717566		60686	1874485	5656880
6193737	9462904	152661	1099773	6041076	8363131
603826	651608	3122	40767	600704	610841
52651644	142897419	2322923	23597171	50328721	119300248
15377592	28100304	1829516	4342445	13548076	23757859

11-15 规模以上工业企业主要经济指标(2019年，按经济类型分)

单位:万元

项　　目		Item	
企业单位数	(个)	Number of Enterprises	(unit)
#亏损企业		Number of Loss-making Enterprises	
营业收入		Business Revenue	
营业成本		Cost of Business	
税金及附加		Taxes and Other Charges	
盈利企业的盈利总额		Total Profits of Profitable Enterprises	
亏损企业的亏损总额		Total Losses of Loss-making Enterprises	
利润总额		Total Profits of All Enterprises	
所得税费用		Income Tax Payable	
应交增值税		Value-added Tax Payable	
流动资产合计		Total Working Capitals at the Year-end	
#应收账款		Accounts Receivable	
#存　货		Inventory	
#产成品存货		Inventory of Finished Goods	
固定资产原价		Original Value of Fixed Assets at the Year-end	
累计折旧		Accumulated Depreciation	
固定资产净额		Net Fixed Assets	
资产总计		Total Assets at the Year-end	
负债合计		Total Liabilities at the Year-end	
所有者权益合计		Total Owners' Equity at the Year-end	
#实收资本		Capital Hold	
#国家资本		State Capital	
外商资本		Foreign Capital	
应付职工薪酬		Wages Payable	
平均用工人数	(人)	Annual Average Number of Staff and Workers	(person)
工业总产值	(当年价格)	Gross Industrial Output Value	(at current prices)
工业增加值	(当年价格)	Value-added of Industry	(at current prices)

Main Indicators of Industrial Enterprises above the Designated Size
(2019, by Type of Ownership)

(10000 yuan)

全 市 Total	国有企业 State-owned Enterprises	集体企业 Collective-owned Enterprises	“三资”企业 Foreign Funded Enterprises	其他企业 Other Enterprises	# 国有及国有控股工业企业 State-owned and State-holding Enterprises
5804	13	17	1328	4446	291
808	2	2	272	532	53
204661205	492753	208439	110323824	93636189	78125427
168977900	401252	159105	89482315	78935228	67421327
4862051	4421	846	2139210	2717574	3501376
15255302	36534	7588	8497247	6713933	6289946
1924833	16494	47	727185	1181107	1095866
13330468	20040	7541	7770062	5532825	5194080
2162005	150	1758	1541016	619081	634385
4149001	11680	2682	2396983	1737656	1425389
110643480	451757	81496	55552365	54557862	35327730
28190915	77027	13254	14944465	13156169	5773819
19723127	90471	13203	8900345	10719108	6337428
7498511	55936	6330	3725897	3710348	1938408
87101336	2586739	82483	38246745	46185369	47210221
46318604	921355	67878	22432683	22896688	23864217
39934058	1664937	13880	15314650	22940591	22956656
209952476	2661393	121212	83958572	123211299	96459453
104542418	1589629	63021	47119943	55769825	43318506
105410058	1071764	58191	36838629	67441474	53140947
45186190	156847	6560	19044216	25978567	21494579
13219619	20265	150	1756682	11442522	12937530
7592051			7504663	87388	1135728
15656641	144655	84352	8303300	7124334	4416209
1255434	7576	11020	601852	634986	196085
195549063	513053	205060	105547122	89283828	72407266
43477896	230398	99562	23756834	19391102	15516686

11-16 规模以上工业企业主要经济指标(2019年，按企业规模分)

单位：万元

项　　目	Item
企业单位数 (个)	Number of Enterprises (unit)
# 亏损企业	Number of Loss-making Enterprises
营业收入	Business Revenue
营业成本	Cost of Business
税金及附加	Taxes and Other Charges
盈利企业的盈利总额	Total Profits of Profitable Enterprises
亏损企业的亏损总额	Total Losses of Loss-making Enterprises
利润总额	Total Profits of All Enterprises
所得税费用	Income Tax Payable
应交增值税	Value-added Tax Payable
流动资产合计	Total Working Capitals at the Year-end
# 应收账款	Accounts Receivable
# 存　货	Inventory
# 产成品存货	Inventory of Finished Goods
固定资产原价	Original Value of Fixed Assets at the Year-end
累计折旧	Accumulated Depreciation
固定资产净额	Net Fixed Assets
资产总计	Total Assets at the Year-end
负债合计	Total Liabilities at the Year-end
所有者权益合计	Total Owners' Equity at the Year-end
# 实收资本	Capital Hold
# 国家资本	State Capital
外商资本	Foreign Capital
应付职工薪酬	Wages Payable
平均用工人数 (人)	Annual Average Number of Staff and Workers (person)
工业总产值 (当年价格)	Gross Industrial Output Value (at current prices)
工业增加值 (当年价格)	Value-added of Industry (at current prices)

Main Indicators of Industrial Enterprises above the Designated Size (2019, by Size of Enterprises)

(10000 yuan)

全市 Total			# 国有及国有控股工业企业 State-owned and State-holding Enterprises		
大型 Large Enterprises	中型 Medium Enterprises	小微型 Small and Micro Enterprises	大型 Large Enterprises	中型 Medium Enterprises	小微型 Small and Micro Enterprises
168	603	5033	41	64	186
19	81	708	10	10	33
115046285	30987171	58627749	56659343	5150925	16315159
94158255	23985264	50834380	47437783	4091487	15892057
4417790	209029	235231	3410329	60792	30255
9529964	2743810	2981528	5489108	331937	468900
867490	236650	820693	547679	94436	453751
8662475	2507158	2160835	4941430	237501	15149
1249402	479236	433367	512304	47581	74500
2484024	726551	938426	1223217	129943	72229
54862821	23118197	32662462	24683608	4655135	5988986
11359881	6719569	10111466	2994530	1231609	1547680
8795950	4464587	6462590	4422679	892927	1021821
3249897	1767593	2481022	1174062	330987	433359
54996681	14077633	18027022	36847231	3706886	6656104
30050022	7244474	9024108	19074233	1636725	3153259
24673515	6610973	8649570	17618483	2025793	3312380
123119106	37578905	49254465	76764614	8231862	11462977
58862979	18694581	26984858	31965112	4798082	6555312
64256127	18884324	22269607	44799502	3433780	4907665
23635879	8921129	12629182	15992238	2361544	3140798
9962430	1348134	1909055	9822124	1258471	1856935
2654571	2537004	2400476	730801	372159	32768
7948973	3798078	3909591	3450781	593518	371909
453637	347072	454725	134598	37978	23509
110245452	30602410	54701201	54700511	4923364	12783391
25466373	7967042	10044481	12700087	1208654	1607944

11-17　规模以上工业企业主要经济指标(2019年，按行业分)

单位:万元

行　　业	Sector
合　计	**Total**
煤炭开采和洗选业	Mining and Washing of Coal
石油和天然气开采业	Extraction of Petroleum and Natural Gas
黑色金属矿采选业	Mining and Processing of Ferrous Metal Ores
有色金属矿采选业	Mining and Processing of Nonferrous Metal Ores
非金属矿采选业	Mining and Processing of Nonmetal Ores
开采专业及辅助性活动	Mining Professional and Auxiliary Activities
其他矿采选业	Mining of Other Ores
农副食品加工业	Processing of Food from Agricultural Products
食品制造业	Manufacturing of Foods
酒、饮料和精制茶制造业	Manufacture of Wine ,Beverages and Refined Tea
烟草制品业	Manufacturing of Tobacco
纺织业	Textile Industry
纺织服装、服饰业	Manufacture of Textile Wearing Apparel,Clothing
皮革、毛皮、羽毛及其制品和制鞋业	Manufacture of Leather, Fur, Feather and Related Products and Footwear
木材加工及木、竹、藤、棕、草制品业	Processing of Timber, Manufacture of Wood, Bamboo,Rattan,Palm and Straw Products
家具制造业	Manufacturing of Furniture
造纸及纸制品业	Manufacturing of Paper and Paper Products
印刷和记录媒介复制业	Printing and Record Media Duplication Industry
文教、工美、体育和娱乐用品制造业	Manufacture of Culture and Education ,Arts and Crafts, Sports and Entertainment Supplies
石油、煤炭及其他燃料加工业	Petroleum, Coal and Other Fuel Processing Industries
化学原料及化学制品制造业	Manufacturing of Raw Chemical Material and Chemical Products
医药制造业	Manufacturing of Medical and Pharmaceutical Products
化学纤维制造业	Manufacturing of Chemical Fiber
橡胶和塑料制品业	Manufacture of Rubber and Plastic
非金属矿物制品业	Manufacturing of Non-metallic Mineral Products
黑色金属冶炼和压延加工业	Smelting and Pressing of Ferrous Metals
有色金属冶炼和压延加工业	Smelting and Pressing of Non-ferrous Metals
金属制品业	Manufacturing of Metal Products
通用设备制造业	Manufacturing of General Purpose Equipment
专用设备制造业	Manufacturing of Special Purpose Equipment
汽车制造业	Manufacture of Automobile
铁路、船舶、航空航天和其他运输设备制造业	Manufacture of Railway, Ship, Aerospace and Other Transportation Equipment
电气机械及器材制造业	Manufacturing of Electric Machinery and Equipment
计算机、通信和其他电子设备制造业	Manufacture of Computers, Communications and Other Electronic Equipment
仪器仪表制造业	Manufacture of Instrument
其他制造业	Other Manufacturing
废弃资源综合利用业	Comprehensive Utilization of Waste Resources
金属制品、机械和设备修理业	Metal Products, Machinery and Equipment Repair
电力、热力生产和供应业	Production and Supply of Electric Power and Heat Power
燃气生产和供应业	Production and Supply of Gas
水的生产和供应业	Production and Supply of Water

Main Indicators of Industrial Enterprises above the Designated Size (2019, by Sector)

(10000 yuan)

单位数（个）Number of Enterprises (unit)	# 亏损企业 Loss-making Enterprises	工业总产值 Gross Output Value of Industry	工业增加值 Value-added of Industry	工业销售产值 Sales Value of Industry	营业收入 Business Revenue	营业成本 Cost of Business	税金及附加 Taxes and Other Charges
5804	**808**	**195549063**	**43477896**	**190765499**	**204661205**	**168977900**	**4862051**
2	1	6820	1706	4740	6827	4975	408
119	24	3342748	399922	3122251	3455957	3026328	7016
153	21	6083145	2220772	6030801	7949373	4167332	66420
30	2	2336258	920488	2239124	2680925	1751754	40233
1		2185327	1781210	2465563	2485117	954706	1103687
119	19	1410943	330579	1342635	1440073	1257573	6901
489	67	2940788	1065608	2481729	2961181	2422440	15679
335	46	1770497	466006	1464108	1814920	1575423	9419
57	4	361847	172145	320247	391705	328375	4447
147	19	2973890	716970	2687193	2951946	2243458	14827
121	15	1566592	284596	1527033	1600769	1388971	6280
94	9	1119440	357418	1079615	1124175	909872	5336
165	33	1716285	587269	1561301	1789900	1377380	11067
16	1	6464019	1851572	6281332	6350631	4778655	1197381
558	66	11683351	2780275	11252395	13179345	9623504	71142
107	14	3482990	1255776	3303306	3477921	1818492	29513
10	3	69956	14281	62840	62823	53758	328
382	51	5089041	1062690	4750773	5283703	4296887	26769
252	24	4637570	801239	4457474	4635214	3881614	24629
30	7	3335723	129660	3328030	3512566	3340596	8852
54	10	3834182	76611	3753885	5773611	5673522	2905
318	30	3481000	653665	3280880	3773054	3215099	17269
357	46	7676956	1483800	7296896	7395415	5993839	35569
315	46	3480572	921623	3227771	3415535	2561524	18245
328	51	54122696	12254763	55174337	56093609	47615312	1931480
86	22	3890914	574105	2340002	4540458	4209163	12246
421	57	9430266	1665523	9112610	9388129	7760556	44954
512	95	20916472	3561145	20535687	21048874	18230787	76718
72	6	2396275	582981	2267153	2379767	2086872	5479
28	4	242387	50383	214764	218780	175868	1042
7		215190	46877	187047	199030	152179	1361
19	4	796471	357743	781181	824894	708663	7536
46	3	15644648	2615744	16051625	15590226	14514346	43370
23	6	5929245	944568	5881391	5962261	6209418	4041
31	2	914559	488183	897780	902491	668659	9502

11-17 续表 1

单位:万元

行　　业	Sector	
合　计	**Total**	
煤炭开采和洗选业	Mining and Washing of Coal	
石油和天然气开采业	Extraction of Petroleum and Natural Gas	
黑色金属矿采选业	Mining and Processing of Ferrous Metal Ores	
有色金属矿采选业	Mining and Processing of Nonferrous Metal Ores	
非金属矿采选业	Mining and Processing of Nonmetal Ores	
开采专业及辅助性活动	Mining Professional and Auxiliary Activities	
其他矿采选业	Mining of Other Ores	
农副食品加工业	Processing of Food from Agricultural Products	
食品制造业	Manufacturing of Foods	
酒、饮料和精制茶制造业	Manufacture of Wine ,Beverages and Refined Tea	
烟草制品业	Manufacturing of Tobacco	
纺织业	Textile Industry	
纺织服装、服饰业	Manufacture of Textile Wearing Apparel,Clothing	
皮革、毛皮、羽毛及其制品和制鞋业	Manufacture of Leather, Fur, Feather and Related Products and Footwear	
木材加工及木、竹、藤、棕、草制品业	Processing of Timber, Manufacture of Wood, Bamboo,Rattan,Palm and Straw Products	
家具制造业	Manufacturing of Furniture	
造纸和纸制品业	Manufacture of Paper and Paper Products	
印刷和记录媒介复制业	Printing and Record Media Duplication Industry	
文教、工美、体育和娱乐用品制造业	Manufacture of Culture and Education ,Arts and Crafts, Sports and Entertainment Supplies	
石油、煤炭及其他燃料加工业	Petroleum, Coal and Other Fuel Processing Industries	
化学原料及化学制品制造业	Manufacturing of Raw Chemical Material and Chemical Products	
医药制造业	Manufacturing of Medical and Pharmaceutical Products	
化学纤维制造业	Manufacturing of Chemical Fiber	
橡胶和塑料制品业	Manufacture of Rubber and Plastic	
非金属矿物制品业	Manufacturing of Non-metallic Mineral Products	
黑色金属冶炼和压延加工业	Smelting and Pressing of Ferrous Metals	
有色金属冶炼和压延加工业	Smelting and Pressing of Non-ferrous Metals	
金属制品业	Manufacturing of Metal Products	
通用设备制造业	Manufacturing of General Purpose Equipment	
专用设备制造业	Manufacturing of Special Purpose Equipment	
汽车制造业	Manufacture of Automobile	
铁路、船舶、航空航天和其他运输设备制造业	Manufacture of Railway, Ship, Aerospace and Other Transportation Equipment	
电气机械及器材制造业	Manufacturing of Electric Machinery and Equipment	
计算机、通信和其他电子设备制造业	Manufacture of Computers, Communications and Other Electronic Equipment	
仪器仪表制造业	Manufacture of Instrument	
其他制造业	Other Manufacturing	
废弃资源综合利用业	Comprehensive Utilization of Waste Resources	
金属制品、机械和设备修理业	Metal Products, Machinery and Equipment Repair	
电力、热力生产和供应业	Production and Supply of Electric Power and Heat Power	
燃气生产和供应业	Production and Supply of Gas	
水的生产和供应业	Production and Supply of Water	

continued

(10000 yuan)

利润总额 Total Profits	利税总额 Total Pre-tax Profits	所得税费用 Income Tax Payable	应交增值税 Value-added Tax Payable	流动资产合计 Total Working Capitals at the Year-end	# 应收账款 Accounts Receivable	# 存 货 Inventory	# 产成品存货 Inventory of Finished Goods
13330468	**22341520**	**2162005**	**4149001**	**110643480**	**28190915**	**19723127**	**7498511**
413	1135	246	314	2557			
222572	251181	31168	21593	1689711	287038	347590	148222
741503	1262125	189213	454202	3311436	563939	610982	382068
424599	578240	68485	113408	2081527	410678	246881	154991
138230	1476731	67943	234815	1700421	55806	1245630	15649
58588	83252	11247	17763	911041	220989	264088	68415
157095	256652	30871	83879	1505848	367610	455353	241514
4713	42839	3903	28708	820493	280042	218921	86906
27383	48343	1742	16512	413586	75386	60731	27458
275299	372927	30111	82801	2243392	334629	192496	61176
70344	101843	16524	25220	1597724	438714	130568	55848
63361	83865	9542	15167	523716	203137	128673	44908
96504	138292	17104	30720	1242638	249237	479767	191503
202971	1525393	50688	125041	1253899	190043	463725	90120
1220233	1641276	246623	349901	8335046	2601726	1255734	476948
545147	749180	70104	174520	3567024	513983	653703	261209
-390	1153	229	1214	37230	10848	9465	4535
272393	386261	43418	87099	3412991	961726	642111	265821
265074	419782	51327	130079	2574928	1178306	298923	124698
-31720	-2768	12082	20100	1185109	144244	462863	172822
13381	25167	2855	8882	1513985	246359	340289	96642
140298	211221	26026	53654	2281485	772804	561031	223426
379319	572407	46880	157518	6879754	1886622	1880412	990713
313185	419264	42203	87835	3000219	1030076	770757	270821
3861338	6936906	716880	1144088	21449470	5429740	3151151	1251474
163764	198277	21694	22268	4808837	780821	632833	82392
563433	729278	72931	120891	6679393	2388449	1322953	627556
847124	1089942	139604	166101	14829814	4261813	2157798	828524
103669	238903	11344	129755	1461187	755034	283659	135937
18013	22688	4207	3630	110943	15688	31090	13595
18343	27879	3784	8174	215361	6038	26405	15674
10368	45921	2678	28017	706028	317341	169130	41387
2395144	2632274	99898	193760	6420671	850694	128750	3244
-305931	-313811	10648	-11921	944120	213412	75199	41558
54708	87502	7803	23293	931896	147943	23466	757

11-17 续表 2

单位：万元

行　　　业	Sector
合　　计	**Total**
煤炭开采和洗选业	Mining and Washing of Coal
石油和天然气开采业	Extraction of Petroleum and Natural Gas
黑色金属矿采选业	Mining and Processing of Ferrous Metal Ores
有色金属矿采选业	Mining and Processing of Nonferrous Metal Ores
非金属矿采选业	Mining and Processing of Nonmetal Ores
开采专业及辅助性活动	Mining Professional and Auxiliary Activities
其他矿采选业	Mining of Other Ores
农副食品加工业	Processing of Food from Agricultural Products
食品制造业	Manufacturing of Foods
酒、饮料和精制茶制造业	Manufacture of Wine ,Beverages and Refined Tea
烟草制品业	Manufacturing of Tobacco
纺织业	Textile Industry
纺织服装、服饰业	Manufacture of Textile Wearing Apparel,Clothing
皮革、毛皮、羽毛及其制品和制鞋业	Manufacture of Leather, Fur, Feather and Related Products and Footwear
木材加工及木、竹、藤、棕、草制品业	Processing of Timber, Manufacture of Wood, Bamboo,Rattan,Palm and Straw Products
家具制造业	Manufacturing of Furniture
造纸及纸制品业	Manufacturing of Paper and Paper Products
印刷和记录媒介复制业	Manufacture of Leather, Fur, Feather and Related Products and Footwear
文教、工美、体育和娱乐用品制造业	Manufacture of Culture and Education ,Arts and Crafts, Sports and Entertainment Supplies
石油、煤炭及其他燃料加工业	Petroleum, Coal and Other Fuel Processing Industries
化学原料及化学制品制造业	Manufacturing of Raw Chemical Material and Chemical Products
医药制造业	Manufacturing of Medical and Pharmaceutical Products
化学纤维制造业	Manufacturing of Chemical Fiber
橡胶和塑料制品业	Manufacture of Rubber and Plastic
非金属矿物制品业	Manufacturing of Non-metallic Mineral Products
黑色金属冶炼和压延加工业	Smelting and Pressing of Ferrous Metals
有色金属冶炼和压延加工业	Smelting and Pressing of Non-ferrous Metals
金属制品业	Manufacturing of Metal Products
通用设备制造业	Manufacturing of General Purpose Equipment
专用设备制造业	Manufacturing of Special Purpose Equipment
汽车制造业	Manufacture of Automobile
铁路、船舶、航空航天和其他运输设备制造业	Manufacture of Railway, Ship, Aerospace and Other Transportation Equipment
电气机械及器材制造业	Manufacturing of Electric Machinery and Equipment
计算机、通信和其他电子设备制造业	Manufacture of Computers, Communications and Other Electronic Equipment
仪器仪表制造业	Manufacture of Instrument
其他制造业	Other Manufacturing
废弃资源综合利用业	Comprehensive Utilization of Waste Resources
金属制品、机械和设备修理业	Metal Products, Machinery and Equipment Repair
电力、热力生产和供应业	Production and Supply of Electric Power and Heat Power
燃气生产和供应业	Production and Supply of Gas
水的生产和供应业	Production and Supply of Water

continued

(10000 yuan)

固定资产原价 Original Value of Fixed Assets at the Year-end	累计折旧 Accumulated Depreciation	固定资产净额 Net Fixed Assets	资产总计 Total Assets at the Year-end	负债合计 Total Liabilities at the Year-end	所有者权益合计 Total Owners' Equity at the Year-end	平均用工人数(人) Average Number of Employed Persons (person)
87101336	**46318604**	**39934058**	**209952476**	**104542418**	**105410058**	**1255434**
320	131	188	3560	830	2730	81
676525	336988	337637	2377411	1294869	1082542	13276
2095230	1246601	840997	4886490	2630688	2255802	57381
1162351	608094	547434	2847316	1284468	1562848	16227
703570	476706	226864	2305579	397197	1908382	2817
797098	499777	297558	1269748	495128	774620	20180
344416	175103	164703	1822924	980434	842490	73443
303029	180379	117146	1140731	673033	467698	53841
102888	57783	41246	752384	207803	544581	5985
471380	199048	267771	3281947	1498416	1783531	35701
597830	218432	348485	2263896	1368670	895226	11655
576758	324434	235377	820614	443174	377440	21503
724766	407402	316019	1733371	826065	907306	47718
2327626	1774147	553479	2404460	1406970	997490	5533
3760894	2069189	1680668	12044238	6256824	5787414	68494
1544948	765689	752706	6747008	2270252	4476756	33243
71413	44257	27156	87864	24336	63528	633
2159971	1139903	994603	5947111	3205082	2742029	56837
1331553	721206	593541	4528310	2838519	1689791	27709
2052134	1089167	962732	2371993	1520635	851358	5665
259493	136547	104596	1896719	1430932	465787	5787
1136041	584049	539861	3206562	1706582	1499980	43765
2216416	1266197	914647	9149405	4899132	4250273	74205
999281	466268	518352	4285459	2309983	1975476	38971
15311274	8429282	6640129	32590456	19252027	13338429	160366
1823295	781727	1041569	7015846	4922787	2093059	30535
1939272	984671	922832	9359289	4563455	4795834	91805
8300590	4723076	3488989	25785227	13815546	11969681	177066
589489	350848	227023	1808261	1135193	673068	19236
52997	26868	25982	145976	89464	56512	3035
78741	37151	41592	318031	180657	137374	1608
748020	304145	442957	1252685	704981	547704	14412
25866716	13603602	12178517	44528615	13805575	30723040	22008
1093108	463772	487245	2102387	1426586	675801	4311
4881903	1825965	3053457	6870603	4676125	2194478	10402

11-18 规模以上大中型工业企业主要经济指标（2019年，按轻重工业分）

单位：万元

项目	Item
企业单位数（个）	Number of Enterprises (unit)
#亏损企业	Number of Loss-making Enterprises
营业收入	Business Revenue
营业成本	Cost of Business
税金及附加	Taxes and Other Charges
盈利企业的盈利总额	Total Profits of Profitable Enterprises
亏损企业的亏损总额	Total Losses of Loss-making Enterprises
利润总额	Total Profits of All Enterprises
所得税费用	Income Tax Payable
应交增值税	Value-added Tax Payable
流动资产合计	Total Working Capitals at the Year-end
#应收账款	Accounts Receivable
#存　货	Inventory
#产成品存货	Inventory of Finished Goods
固定资产原价	Original Value of Fixed Assets at the Year-end
累计折旧	Accumulated Depreciation
固定资产净额	Net Fixed Assets
资产总计	Total Assets at the Year-end
负债合计	Total Liabilities at the Year-end
所有者权益合计	Total Owners' Equity at the Year-end
#实收资本	Capital Hold
#国家资本	State Capital
外商资本	Foreign Capital
应付职工薪酬	Wages Payable
平均用工人数（人）	Annual Average Number of Staff and Workers (person)
工业总产值（当年价格）	Gross Industrial Output Value (at current prices)
工业增加值（当年价格）	Value-added of Industry (at current prices)

Major Indicators of Large and Medium-sized Industrial Enterprises above the Designated Size (2019，by Light and Heavy Industry)

(10000 yuan)

全 市 Total		# 中央企业 Central Enterprises		# 地方企业 Local Enterprises	
轻工业 Light Industry	重工业 Heavy Industry	轻工业 Light Industry	重工业 Heavy Industry	轻工业 Light Industry	重工业 Heavy Industry
390	381	1	17	389	364
48	52		3	48	49
37516166	108517290	2485117	20421611	35031049	88095679
24785937	93357582	954706	17886528	23831231	75471054
1343850	3282969	1103687	1222622	240163	2060347
3649504	8624270	138230	2723138	3511274	5901132
53459	1050681		29220	53459	1021461
3596044	7573589	138230	2693918	3457814	4879671
677012	1051626	67943	159877	609069	891749
1358483	1852092	234815	256799	1123668	1595293
24246651	53734367	1700421	10589513	22546230	43144854
4946863	13132587	55806	1088614	4891057	12043973
4940796	8319741	1245630	1171171	3695166	7148570
1817234	3200256	15649	86799	1801585	3113457
12968718	56105596	703570	15718355	12265148	40387241
6764353	30530143	476706	8808963	6287647	21721180
6096675	25187813	226864	6841525	5869811	18346288
38793914	121904097	2305579	42390725	36488335	79513372
18239492	59318068	397197	14097176	17842295	45220892
20554422	62586029	1908382	28293549	18646040	34292480
8395915	24161093	812049	7998973	7583866	16162120
2501746	8808818		7324371	2501746	1484447
1209250	3982325		53931	1209250	3928394
4399009	7348042	148751	1048341	4250258	6299701
360431	440278	2817	38160	357614	402118
34341732	106506130	2185327	20204806	32156405	86301324
10942211	22491204	1781210	3776970	9161001	18714234

11-19 规模以上大中型工业企业主要经济指标（2019年，按经济类型分）

单位:万元

项　　目		Item	
企业单位数	(个)	Number of Enterprises	(unit)
#亏损企业		Number of Loss-making Enterprises	
营业收入		Business Revenue	
营业成本		Cost of Business	
税金及附加		Taxes and Other Charges	
盈利企业的盈利总额		Total Profits of Profitable Enterprises	
亏损企业的亏损总额		Total Losses of Loss-making Enterprises	
利润总额		Total Profits of All Enterprises	
所得税费用		Income Tax Payable	
应交增值税		Value-added Tax Payable	
流动资产合计		Total Working Capitals at the Year-end	
#应收账款		Accounts Receivable	
#存　货		Inventory	
#产成品存货		Inventory of Finished Goods	
固定资产原价		Original Value of Fixed Assets at the Year-end	
累计折旧		Accumulated Depreciation	
固定资产净额		Net Fixed Assets	
资产总计		Total Assets at the Year-end	
负债合计		Total Liabilities at the Year-end	
所有者权益合计		Total Owners' Equity at the Year-end	
#实收资本		Capital Hold	
#国家资本		State Capital	
外商资本		Foreign Capital	
应付职工薪酬		Wages Payable	
平均用工人数	(人)	Annual Average Number of Staff and Workers	(person)
工业总产值	(当年价格)	Gross Industrial Output Value	(at current prices)
工业增加值	(当年价格)	Value-added of Industry	(at current prices)

Major Indicators of Large and Medium-sized Industrial Enterprises above the Designated Size (2019, by Type of Ownership)

(10000 yuan)

合 计 Total	国有企业 State-owned Enterprises	集体企业 Collective-owned Enterprises	"三资"企业 Foreign Funded Enterprises	其他企业 Other Enterprises
771	3	5	413	350
100	1		56	43
146033456	381910	115014	93662861	51873671
118143519	311412	79552	75520142	42232413
4626819	3599	308	2053868	2569044
12273774	2054	2070	7295971	4973679
1104140	16096		512962	575082
11169633	-14042	2070	6783009	4398596
1728638	-413	518	1327920	400613
3210575	9193	2	2115828	1085552
77981018	329657	19950	43808172	33823239
18079450	55906	2716	11469340	6551488
13260537	63238		6792549	6404750
5017490	37603		2956901	2022986
69074314	2520226	28899	30268526	36256663
37294496	890658	21886	17892514	18489438
31284488	1629568	7013	12105072	17542835
160698011	2379368	29761	67033472	91255410
77557560	1470218	4061	38632667	37450614
83140451	909150	25700	28400805	53804796
32557008	51051	590	13648778	18856589
11310564	8905		1335393	9966266
5191575			5132642	58933
11747051	128609	75782	7085932	4456728
800709	6219	10053	490745	293692
140847862	412326	114948	89575247	50745341
33433415	211661	79168	20780305	12362281

11-20　规模以上工业企业主要经济效益指标

项　　目		Item	
工业经济效益综合指数	(%)	Industrial Economic Benefit Synthetic	(%)
总资产贡献率	(%)	Ratio of Total Assets to Industrial Output Value	(%)
资本保值增值率	(%)	Ratio of Capital Maintenance and Appreciation	(%)
资产负债率	(%)	Assets-Liability Ratio	(%)
流动资产周转率	(次)	Number of Times of Annual of Turnover Working Capitals	(times)
工业成本费用利润率	(%)	Ratio of Profits to Industrial Cost	(%)
工业全员劳动生产率	(元/人)	Overall Labor Productivity	(yuan/person)
工业产品销售率	(%)	Proportion of Products Sold	(%)
工业资金利税率	(%)	Ratio of Pre-tax Profits to Total Capital	(%)
营业收入利润率	(%)	Ratio of Business Revenue	(%)
每百元营业收入中的成本	(元)	Cost of Business Per 100 Yuan	(yuan)
工业增加值率	(%)	Ratio of Value-added to Gross Industrial Output Value	(%)
企业亏损面	(%)	Ratio of Loss-making Enterprises to Total Industrial Enterprises	(%)
工业产成品存货可供销售天数	(天)	Days for Sale of Inventory of Finished Products	(day)
每百元资金提供的总产值	(元)	Output Value Created by per 100 yuan	(yuan)
每百元资金提供的利税	(元)	Pre-tax Profits Created by per 100 Yuan	(yuan)
每百元固定资产原价提供利税	(元)	Pre-tax Profits Created by per 100 yuan Original Value of Fixed Assets	(yuan)
每百元固定资产原价提供总产值	(元)	Output Value Created by per 100 yuan Original Value of Fixed Assets	(yuan)
每百元固定资产净值提供利税	(元)	Pre-tax Profits Created by per 100 yuan Net Value of Fixed Assets	(yuan)
每百元固定资产净值提供总产值	(元)	Output Value Created by per 100 yuan Net Value of Fixed Assets	(yuan)
每百元总产值实现利税	(元)	Pre-tax Profits Created by per 100 yuan Output Value	(yuan)
每百元总产值占用全部资产	(元)	Total Assets Used by per 100 yuan Output Value	(yuan)
平均每个职工拥有全部资产	(元)	Average Assets Owned by per Staff and Worker	(yuan)
平均每个职工提供利税	(元)	Average Pre-tax Profits Created by per Staff and Worker	(yuan)

Main Indicators on Economic Benefit of Industrial Enterprises above the Designated Size

2018			2019		
全　市 Total	# 中央企业 Central Enterprises	# 地方企业 Local Enterprises	全　市 Total	# 中央企业 Central Enterprises	# 地方企业 Local Enterprises
320.07	944.64	291.53	316.65	978.95	290.56
13.79	13.93	13.74	11.81	12.65	11.56
107.70	122.54	102.15	110.98	104.92	113.69
49.12	36.16	53.36	49.79	33.04	54.50
1.90	2.01	1.88	1.85	2.05	1.82
7.89	10.13	7.54	7.00	11.64	6.34
339734	1350516	296480	346318	1406266	307920
99.88	101.27	99.65	97.55	94.86	97.97
17.21	25.24	15.65	14.75	27.42	12.78
7.28	8.95	7.00	6.51	10.35	5.94
82.45	84.51	82.11	82.56	84.87	82.22
22.64	26.20	22.05	22.23	23.81	21.99
15.70	25.45	15.59	13.92	19.57	13.88
13.63	3.97	15.20	13.19	2.85	14.74
132.55	114.85	135.98	129.14	127.01	129.47
17.21	25.24	15.65	14.75	27.42	12.78
29.77	29.74	29.77	25.65	33.28	23.82
229.21	135.32	258.65	224.51	154.15	241.34
62.60	61.76	62.87	54.78	75.57	50.17
482.05	280.98	546.18	479.49	350.04	508.21
12.99	21.98	11.51	11.43	21.59	9.87
100.39	175.60	88.04	107.37	177.63	96.63
1506537	9051802	1183658	1672350	10490394	1352910
194893	1132964	154751	177959	1275040	138216

11-21 规模以上工业企业主要经济效益指标（2019年，按轻重工业分）

项目		Item	
工业经济效益综合指数	(%)	Industrial Economic Benefit Synthetic	(%)
总资产贡献率	(%)	Ratio of Total Assets to Industrial Output Value	(%)
资本保值增值率	(%)	Ratio of Capital Maintenance and Appreciation	(%)
资产负债率	(%)	Assets-Liability Ratio	(%)
流动资产周转率	(次)	Number of Times of Annual of Turnover Working Capitals	(times)
工业成本费用利润率	(%)	Ratio of Profits to Industrial Cost	(%)
工业全员劳动生产率	(元/人)	Overall Labor Productivity	(yuan/person)
工业产品销售率	(%)	Proportion of Products Sold	(%)
工业资金利税率	(%)	Ratio of Pre-tax Profits to Total Capital	(%)
营业收入利润率	(%)	Ratio of Business Revenue	(%)
每百元营业收入中的成本	(元)	Cost of Business Per 100 Yuan	(yuan)
工业增加值率	(%)	Ratio of Value-added to Gross Industrial Output Value	(%)
企业亏损面	(%)	Ratio of Loss-making Enterprises to Total Industrial Enterprises	(%)
工业产成品存货可供销售天数	(天)	Days for Sale of Inventory of Finished Products	(day)
每百元资金提供的总产值	(元)	Output Value Created by per 100 yuan	(yuan)
每百元资金提供的利税	(元)	Pre-tax Profits Created by per 100 Yuan	(yuan)
每百元固定资产原价提供利税	(元)	Pre-tax Profits Created by per 100 yuan Original Value of Fixed Assets	(yuan)
每百元固定资产原价提供总产值	(元)	Output Value Created by per 100 yuan Original Value of Fixed Assets	(yuan)
每百元固定资产净值提供利税	(元)	Pre-tax Profits Created by per 100 yuan Net Value of Fixed Assets	(yuan)
每百元固定资产净值提供总产值	(元)	Output Value Created by per 100 yuan Net Value of Fixed Assets	(yuan)
每百元总产值实现利税	(元)	Pre-tax Profits Created by per 100 yuan Output Value	(yuan)
每百元总产值占用全部资产	(元)	Total Assets Used by per 100 yuan Output Value	(yuan)
平均每个职工拥有全部资产	(元)	Average Assets Owned by per Staff and Worker	(yuan)
平均每个职工提供利税	(元)	Average Pre-tax Profits Created by per Staff and Worker	(yuan)

Main Indicators on Economic Benefit of Industrial Enterprises above the Designated Size (2019, by Light and Heavy Industry)

全 市 Total		# 中央企业 Central Enterprises		# 地方企业 Local Enterprises	
轻工业 Light Industry	重工业 Heavy Industry	轻工业 Light Industry	重工业 Heavy Industry	轻工业 Light Industry	重工业 Heavy Industry
270.13	365.08	3730.39	768.60	249.11	336.05
14.92	10.66	43.18	10.17	12.97	10.86
110.30	111.23	69.45	108.68	115.27	112.83
49.28	49.98	17.97	33.86	50.66	56.39
1.58	1.98	1.47	2.14	1.58	1.95
8.80	6.34	12.51	11.60	8.71	5.31
254669	431246	5860078	1065186	225537	388937
91.86	99.65	112.09	93.16	90.92	100.94
17.05	13.78	74.34	22.33	14.41	11.98
7.99	5.95	5.71	10.84	8.10	4.99
71.60	86.78	38.88	89.67	73.12	86.22
29.21	19.66	78.76	18.40	26.92	19.91
14.12	13.71		21.95	14.14	13.58
17.69	11.46	2.27	2.91	18.41	13.13
116.58	134.48	116.35	128.16	116.59	135.80
17.05	13.78	74.34	22.33	14.41	11.98
41.40	21.37	193.24	25.62	34.86	20.07
283.00	208.62	302.42	147.06	282.17	227.45
84.83	46.18	532.94	57.70	70.65	42.83
579.85	450.74	834.06	331.12	571.81	485.43
14.63	10.24	63.90	17.42	12.36	8.82
107.19	107.43	102.48	185.02	107.40	92.08
934630	2355973	7625356	10709803	899857	1798445
127564	224658	4754309	1008592	103518	172338

11-22 规模以上工业企业主要经济效益指标（2019年，按经济类型分）

项　　目		Item	
工业经济效益综合指数	(%)	Industrial Economic Benefit Synthetic	(%)
总资产贡献率	(%)	Ratio of Total Assets to Industrial Output Value	(%)
资本保值增值率	(%)	Ratio of Capital Maintenance and Appreciation	(%)
资产负债率	(%)	Assets-Liability Ratio	(%)
流动资产周转率	(次)	Number of Times of Annual of Turnover Working Capitals	(times)
工业成本费用利润率	(%)	Ratio of Profits to Industrial Cost	(%)
工业全员劳动生产率	(元/人)	Overall Labor Productivity	(yuan/person)
工业产品销售率	(%)	Proportion of Products Sold	(%)
工业资金利税率	(%)	Ratio of Pre-tax Profits to Total Capital	(%)
营业收入利润率	(%)	Ratio of Business Revenue	(%)
每百元营业收入中的成本	(元)	Cost of Business Per 100 Yuan	(yuan)
工业增加值率	(%)	Ratio of Value-added to Gross Industrial Output Value	(%)
企业亏损面	(%)	Ratio of Loss-making Enterprises to Total Industrial Enterprises	(%)
工业产成品存货可供销售天数	(天)	Days for Sale of Inventory of Finished Products	(day)
每百元资金提供的总产值	(元)	Output Value Created by per 100 yuan	(yuan)
每百元资金提供的利税	(元)	Pre-tax Profits Created by per 100 Yuan	(yuan)
每百元固定资产原价提供利税	(元)	Pre-tax Profits Created by per 100 yuan Original Value of Fixed Assets	(yuan)
每百元固定资产原价提供总产值	(元)	Output Value Created by per 100 yuan Original Value of Fixed Assets	(yuan)
每百元固定资产净值提供利税	(元)	Pre-tax Profits Created by per 100 yuan Net Value of Fixed Assets	(yuan)
每百元固定资产净值提供总产值	(元)	Output Value Created by per 100 yuan Net Value of Fixed Assets	(yuan)
每百元总产值实现利税	(元)	Pre-tax Profits Created by per 100 yuan Output Value	(yuan)
每百元总产值占用全部资产	(元)	Total Assets Used by per 100 yuan Output Value	(yuan)
平均每个职工拥有全部资产	(元)	Average Assets Owned by per Staff and Worker	(yuan)
平均每个职工提供利税	(元)	Average Pre-tax Profits Created by per Staff and Worker	(yuan)

Main Indicators on Economic Benefit of Industrial Enterprises above the Designated Size (2019, by Type of Ownership)

全 市 Total	国有企业 State-owned Enterprises	集体企业 Collective-owned Enterprises	"三资"企业 Foreign Funded Enterprises	其他企业 Other Enterprises	# 国有及国有控股工业企业 State-owned and State-holding Enterprises
316.65	255.37	154.90	358.15	282.13	590.29
11.81	2.79	10.47	15.91	9.22	11.69
110.98	106.29	111.19	110.68	111.22	110.47
49.79	59.73	51.99	56.12	45.26	44.91
1.85	1.09	2.56	1.99	1.72	2.21
7.00	3.80	3.77	7.67	6.26	7.18
346318	304116	90347	394729	305378	791325
97.55	107.49	105.58	102.52	91.61	97.38
14.75	1.71	11.52	17.24	12.83	17.25
6.51	4.07	3.62	7.04	5.91	6.65
82.56	81.43	76.33	81.11	84.30	86.30
22.23	44.91	48.55	22.51	21.72	21.43
13.92	15.38	11.76	20.48	11.97	18.21
13.19	40.87	10.93	12.16	14.27	8.93
129.14	24.23	213.38	147.89	114.69	123.41
14.75	1.71	11.52	17.24	12.83	17.25
25.65	1.40	13.42	32.18	21.63	21.44
224.51	19.83	248.61	275.96	193.32	153.37
54.78	2.17	75.79	77.82	42.89	43.35
479.49	30.81	1404.02	667.43	383.38	310.15
11.43	7.04	5.40	11.66	11.19	13.98
107.37	518.74	59.11	79.55	138.00	133.22
1672350	3512927	109993	1395004	1940378	4919267
177959	47705	10045	204473	157296	516146

11-23 规模以上工业企业主要经济效益指标（2019年，按企业规模分）

项 目		Item	
工业经济效益综合指数	(%)	Industrial Economic Benefit Synthetic	(%)
总资产贡献率	(%)	Ratio of Total Assets to Industrial Output Value	(%)
资本保值增值率	(%)	Ratio of Capital Maintenance and Appreciation	(%)
资产负债率	(%)	Assets-Liability Ratio	(%)
流动资产周转率	(次)	Number of Times of Annual of Turnover Working Capitals	(times)
工业成本费用利润率	(%)	Ratio of Profits to Industrial Cost	(%)
工业全员劳动生产率	(元/人)	Overall Labor Productivity	(yuan/person)
工业产品销售率	(%)	Proportion of Products Sold	(%)
工业资金利税率	(%)	Ratio of Pre-tax Profits to Total Capital	(%)
营业收入利润率	(%)	Ratio of Business Revenue	(%)
每百元营业收入中的成本	(元)	Cost of Business Per 100 Yuan	(yuan)
工业增加值率	(%)	Ratio of Value-added to Gross Industrial Output Value	(%)
企业亏损面	(%)	Ratio of Loss-making Enterprises to Total Industrial Enterprises	(%)
工业产成品存货可供销售天数	(天)	Days for Sale of Inventory of Finished Products	(day)
每百元资金提供的总产值	(元)	Output Value Created by per 100 yuan	(yuan)
每百元资金提供的利税	(元)	Pre-tax Profits Created by per 100 Yuan	(yuan)
每百元固定资产原价提供利税	(元)	Pre-tax Profits Created by per 100 yuan Original Value of Fixed Assets	(yuan)
每百元固定资产原价提供总产值	(元)	Output Value Created by per 100 yuan Original Value of Fixed Assets	(yuan)
每百元固定资产净值提供利税	(元)	Pre-tax Profits Created by per 100 yuan Net Value of Fixed Assets	(yuan)
每百元固定资产净值提供总产值	(元)	Output Value Created by per 100 yuan Net Value of Fixed Assets	(yuan)
每百元总产值实现利税	(元)	Pre-tax Profits Created by per 100 yuan Output Value	(yuan)
每百元总产值占用全部资产	(元)	Total Assets Used by per 100 yuan Output Value	(yuan)
平均每个职工拥有全部资产	(元)	Average Assets Owned by per Staff and Worker	(yuan)
平均每个职工提供利税	(元)	Average Pre-tax Profits Created by per Staff and Worker	(yuan)

Main Indicators on Economic Benefit of Industrial Enterprises above the Designated Size (2019, by Size of Enterprises)

全市 Total			# 国有及国有控股工业企业 State-owned and State-holding Enterprises		
大型 Large Enterprises	中型 Medium Enterprises	小微型 Small and Micro Enterprises	大型 Large Enterprises	中型 Medium Enterprises	小微型 Small and Micro Enterprises
458.01	243.85	221.36	696.99	268.91	487.37
13.81	9.99	8.10	13.74	5.34	2.25
110.19	105.79	118.33	112.84	76.43	125.47
47.81	49.75	54.79	41.64	58.29	57.19
2.10	1.34	1.79	2.30	1.11	2.72
8.24	8.80	3.81	9.69	4.84	0.09
561382	229550	220891	943557	318251	683969
99.57	99.88	92.18	97.28	108.21	93.64
19.50	11.49	8.00	22.55	6.37	1.24
7.53	8.09	3.69	8.72	4.61	0.09
81.84	77.40	86.71	83.72	79.43	97.41
23.10	26.03	18.36	23.22	24.55	12.58
11.31	13.43	14.07	24.39	15.63	17.74
10.17	20.54	15.23	7.46	23.13	9.56
138.14	102.17	131.29	128.84	73.21	134.68
19.50	11.49	8.00	22.55	6.37	1.24
28.30	24.46	18.50	25.99	11.55	1.77
200.46	217.38	303.44	148.45	132.82	192.06
62.39	50.38	37.04	53.87	20.69	3.36
441.92	447.85	607.59	307.77	237.83	364.94
14.12	11.25	6.10	17.50	8.70	0.92
111.68	122.80	90.04	140.34	167.20	89.67
2714045	1082741	1083170	5703251	2167534	4875995
343100	99194	73330	711376	112759	50038

11-24 规模以上工业企业分组主要指标（2019年）

Major Indicators of Industrial Enterprises above the Designated Size by Group (2019)

单位：万元 (10000 yuan)

项 目	Item	企业单位数（个） Number of Enterprises (unit)	利润总额 Total Profits of All Enterprises	固定资产原价 Original Value of Fixed Assets at the Year-end	工业增加值 Value-added of Industry	工业总产值 Gross Industrial Output Value	平均用工人数（人） Annual Average Employed Persons (person)
总 计	**Total**	**5804**	**13330468**	**87101336**	**43477896**	**195549063**	**1255434**
按总产值分组	Grouped by Gross Output Value						
1亿元及以上	100 million yuan and above	1708	12883071	81865036	39018613	178371425	915589
5000万元-9999万元	50-99.99 million yuan	1243	282252	2517225	2196234	8516114	149275
4999万元及以下	49.99 million yuan and below	2853	165146	2719075	2263049	8661524	190570
按固定资产原价分组	Grouped by Original Value of Fixed Assets						
1亿元及以上	100 million yuan and above	739	11268820	79966320	32678072	145925850	651433
5000万元-9999万元	50-99.99 million yuan	422	768613	2971906	2473328	10438703	129009
4999万元及以下	49.99 million yuan and below	4643	1293035	4163110	8326496	39184510	474992
按利税总额分组	Grouped by Pre-tax Profits						
1亿元及以上	100 million yuan and above	258	12396129	56107037	28566444	114932325	400498
5000万元-9999万元	50-99.99 million yuan	192	1045501	5250535	2842702	13683465	104559
4999万元及以下	49.99 million yuan and below	5354	-111162	25743764	12068750	66933273	750377
按从业人员人数分组	Grouped by Staff and Workers						
2000人及以上	2000 Persons and above	87	7055921	47614206	21190212	92301379	346322
500人-1999人	500-1999 Persons	364	3220640	16347063	9456875	36813568	334587
499人及以下	499 Persons and below	5353	3053907	23140068	12830810	66434116	574525

【工业】 指从事自然资源的开采，对采掘品和农产品进行加工和再加工的物质生产部门。具体包括：

(1)对自然资源的开采，如采矿、晒盐等(但不包括禽兽捕猎和水产捕捞)；

(2)对农副产品的加工、再加工，如粮油加工、食品加工、轧花、缫丝、纺织、制革等;

(3)对采掘品的加工、再加工，如炼铁、炼钢、化工生产、石油加工、机器制造、木材加工等，以及电力、燃气及水的生产和供应等;

(4)对工业品的修理、翻新，如机器设备的修理等。

工业统计调查单位为工业法人单位。

工业法人单位指从事工业生产经营活动的法人单位。工业法人单位应同时具备以下条件：①依法成立，有自己的名称、组织机构和场所，能够独立承担民事责任；②独立拥有（或授权）使用资产，承担负债，有权与其他单位签订合同；③具有包括资产负债表在内的账户，或者能够根据需要编制账户。

【工业法人单位】 指从事工业生产经营活动的法人单位。工业法人单位应同时具备以下条件：①依法成立，有自己的名称、组织机构和场所，能够独立承担民事责任；②独立拥有（或授权）使用资产，承担负债，有权与其他单位签订合同；③具有包括资产负债表在内的账户，或者能够根据需要编制账户。

【轻工业】 指主要提供生活消费品和制作手工工具的工业。按其所使用的原料不同，可分为两大类：

(1)以农产品为原料的轻工业，是指直接或间接以农产品为基本原料的轻工业。主要包括食品制造、饮料制造、烟草加工、纺织、缝纫、皮革和毛皮制作、造纸以及印刷等工业;

(2)以非农产品为原料的轻工业，是指以工业品为原料的轻工业。主要包括文教体育用品、化学药品制造、合成纤维制造、日用化学制品、日用玻璃制品、日用金属制品、手工工具制造、医疗器械制造、文化和办公用机械制造等工业。

【重工业】 是指为国民经济各部门提供物质技术基础的主要生产资料的工业。按其生产性质和产品用途，可分为下列三类:

(1)采掘(伐)工业，是指对自然资源的开采，包括石油开采、煤炭开采、金属矿开采、非金属矿开采和木材采伐等工业;

(2)原材料工业，指向国民经济各部门提供基本材料、动力和燃料的工业。包括金属冶炼及加工、炼焦及焦炭化学、化工原料、水泥、人造板以及电力、石油和煤炭加工等工业;

(3)加工工业，是指对工业原材料进行再加工制造的工业。包括装备国民经济各部门的机械设备制造工业、金属结构、水泥制品等工业，以及为农业提供的生产资料如化肥、农药等工业。

根据上述划分原则，修理业中以重工业产品为修理作业对象的划为重工业，反之划为轻工业。

【资产总计】 指企业过去的交易或者事项形成的、由企业拥有或者控制的、预期会给企业带来经济利益的资源。资产一般按流动性（资产的变现或耗用时间长短）分为流动资产和非流动资产。其中流动资产可分为货币资金、交易性金融资产、应收票据、应收账款、预付款项、其他应收款、存货等；非流动资产可分为长期股权投资、固定资产、无形资产及其他非流动资产等。

【负债合计】 指企业过去的交易或者事项形成的，预期会导致经济利益流出企业的现时义务。负债一般按偿还期长短分为流动负债和非流动负债。

【所有者权益】 指企业资产扣除负债后由所有者享有的剩余权益。公司的所有者权益又称股东权益。包括实收资本、资本公积、盈余公积、未分配利润等。

【固定资产原价】 指固定资产的成本，包括企业在购置、自行建造、安装、改建、扩建、技术改造某项固定资产时所发生的全部支出总额。

【利润总额】 指企业在一定会计期间的经营成果，是生产经营过程中各种收入扣除各种耗费后的盈余，反映企业在报告期内实现的盈亏总额。根据会计“利润表”中“利润总额”项目的本年累计数填报。

【应交增值税】 指按照税法规定，以销售货物、服务、无形资产、不动产或提供加工、修理修配劳务的增值额和货物进口金额为计税依据而课征的一种流转税。填报本指标时，应按权责发生制核算企业本期应负担的增值税。

【Industry】 refers to the material production sector which is engaged in the extraction of natural resources and processing and reprocessing of minerals and agricultural products, including

I.Extraction of natural resources, such as mining, salt production (but not including hunting and fishing);

II.Processing and reprocessing of farm and sideline produces, such as grain and oil processing, food processing, silk reeling, spinning and weaving and leather making;

III. Processing and reprocessing of mineral products, such as steel making, iron smelting, chemicals manufacturing, petroleum processing, machine building, timber processing, and production and supply of electricity, gas and water;

IV. repairing and renovating of industrial products such as the machinery.

In industrial surveys, the units of enquiry are industrial corporate units.

Industrial corporate units refer to corporate units engaging in industrial production and operation activities, which meet the following requirements:

I.They are established legally, having their own names, organizations, location, and are able to take civil liability independently;

II.They possess (or are authorized to use) assets independently, assume liabilities and are entitled to sign contracts with other units;

III. They have accounts including the balance sheets or can compile the accounts according to the need.

【Industrial corporate units】 refer to corporate units engaging in industrial production and operation activities, which meet the following requirements:

I.They are established legally, having their own names, organizations, location, and are able to take civil liability independently;

II.They possess (or are authorized to use) assets independently, assume liabilities and are entitled to sign contracts with other units;

III. They have accounts including the balance sheets or can compile the accounts according to the need.

【Light Industry】 refers to industry which produces consumer goods and hand tools.It consists of two categories depending on the materiais used:

(1)Industries using farm products as raw materials.These are branches of light industry which directly or indirectly use farm products as basic raw materials,including the manufacture of food and beverages,tobacco processing,textile,clothing,fur and leather manufacturing ,paper making, printing,etc.

(2)Industries using nonfarm products as raw materials.These are branches of light industry which use manufactured goods as raw materials, including the manufacture of cultural,educational articles and sports goods,chemicals,synthetic fiber,chemical products for daily use,glass products for daily use,metal products machinery,etc.

【Heavy Industry】 refers to the industry which produces capital goods,and provides various sectors of the national economy with necesary material and technical basis.It consists of the following three branches according to the purpose of production or the use of products:

(1)Mining,quarrying and logging industry refers to the industry that extracts natural resources,including extraction of petroleum, coal,metal and nonmetalores and logging.

(2)Raw materials industry refers to the industry that provides various sectors of the national economy with raw materials,fuels and power.It inc1udes smelting and processing of metals,coking and coke chemistry, chemical materials and building materials such as cement,plywood,and power,petroleum refining and coal dressing.

(3)Manufacturing industry refers to the industry that processes raw materials.It includes machine building industry which equips sectors of the national economy,industry of metal structure and cement products, industries producing means of agricultural production,such as chemical fertilizers and pesticides.

According to the above principle of classification,the repairing trades which are engaged primarily in repairing products of heavy industry are classified into heavy industry while these engaged in repairing products of light industry are classified into light industry.

【Total Assets】 refer to all resources that are owned or controlled by enterprises through previous trades or transactions with expectation of making economic profits. Classified by the degree of liquidity, total assets include current assets and non-current assets. Current assets can be classified into monetary capital, trading financial assets, notes receivable, accounts receivable, advanced payments, other receivables and inventories. Non-current assets can be divided into long-term equity investment, fixed assets, intangible assets and other non-current assets. Data on this indicator can be obtained from the year-end figures of total assets in the Balance Sheet of accounting records.

【Total Liabilities】 refer to payable liabilities of enterprises that accumulated from previous trades or transactions with expectation of economic profits leaking out. In terms of payment, it can be divided into liquid liabilities and long-term liabilities. Data on this indicator can be obtained from the year-end figures of total liabilities in the Balance Sheet of accounting records.

【Owner undefined equity】 refers to the residual equity enjoyed by the owner after deducting liabilities from the assets of the enterprise. The owner undefined equity of the company is also known as the shareholder undefined equity. Including paid-in capital, capital reserves, surplus reserves, undistributed profits and so on.

【The Cost of fixed Assets】 including the total amount of expenditure incurred by an enterprise in purchasing, building, installing, rebuilding, expanding, and technically transforming a fixed asset.

【Total Profits】 refers to the operation results in a certain accounting period, and it is the balance of various incomes minus various spendings in the course of operation, reflecting the total profits and losses of enterprises in reference period. Data are obtained from the amount of total profits in the profit statement of the accounting record of enterprise.

【Value added tax (VAT)】 refers to a turnover tax levied on the basis of taxation to sell goods, services, intangible assets, immovable property or provide processing, repair and repair services and import goods. When completing this index, the value-added tax that enterprises should bear in the current period should be accounted for on the accrual basis.

第十二篇 CHAPTER 12

建筑业

CONSTRUCTION

简要说明

Brief Introduction

第十二篇 建筑业

一、本篇资料反映广州市建筑业概况和发展情况。主要包括资质以上施工总承包、专业承包建筑业企业生产经营和资质以上劳务分包建筑企业经营资料。

二、本篇资料由广州市统计局固定资产投资统计处整理提供。

三、本篇资料是依据国家统计局和广东省统计局制定的“建筑业统计报表制度”规定收集的年报资料，其统计范围包括：广州市境内各种登记注册类型（个体户除外）的具有建筑业资质的所有独立核算建筑业企业（包括没有工作量的建筑业企业）及所属产业活动单位。

12 Construction

I.The data in this chapter show the general situation and the development of the construction industry of Guangzhou Municipality. It mainly includes the operation materials of the general contracting, specialized contracting and labor subcontracting construction enterprises with above qualifications.

II.The data in this chapter are prepared and provided by the Division of Investment and Construction Statistics of Guangzhou Municipal Bureau of Statistics.

III.The data in this chapter are collected in accordance with the Reporting Scheme of Construction Statistics stipulated by the National Bureau of Statistics and Guangdong Provincia1 Bureau of Statistics. The coverage of construction statistics includes the various registration types (except the self-employed) with the construction industry qualified independent accounting construction enterprises (including the workload of construction enterprises) and their respective industrial units of Guangzhou Municipality.

12-1 资质以上建筑业企业主要经济指标

Major Indicators of Grade Construction Enterprises

项目		Item		2018	2019
建筑企业个数	(个)	Number of Construction Enterprises	(unit)	1088	1316
年末从业人员	(人)	Number of Employed Persons at Year-end	(person)	626321	847027
固定资产原价	(亿元)	Original Value of Fixed Assets	(100 million yuan)	480	454
固定资产净值	(亿元)	Net Value of Fixed Assets	(100 million yuan)	252	
建筑业总产值	(万元)	Gross Output Value of Construction	(10000 yuan)	40192380	53043655
#建筑工程		Output Value of Construction		35221002	46742169
安装工程		Output Value of Installation		3872850	4333551
房屋建筑施工面积	(万平方米)	Floor Space of Buildings under Construction	(10000 sq.m)	27755.15	32043.52
#新开工		Floor Space Started in Current Year		8572.92	7929.47
房屋建筑竣工面积	(万平方米)	Floor Space of Buildings Completed	(10000 sq.m)	4648.09	6536.75
#住宅		Residential Buildings		3526.47	5446.76
主营业务收入	(万元)	Income on Projects Settlement Account	(10000 yuan)	46033501	59413560
主营业务成本	(万元)	Cost on Projects Settlement Account	(10000 yuan)	42786677	55283615
利润总额	(万元)	Total Profits	(10000 yuan)	1295382	1227019

注：本表统计范围为施工总承包、专业承包法人建筑业企业。

Note: The statistical scope of this table covers legal construction enterprises with general contracting and professional contracting.

12-2 主要年份建筑业主要指标

Major Indicators of Construction Sector in Main Years

年 份 Year	建筑业总产值（万元） Gross Output Value (10000 yuan)	房屋建筑施工面积（万平方米） Floor Space of Buildings under Construction (10000 sq.m)	房屋建筑竣工面积（万平方米） Floor Space of Buildings Completed (10000 sq.m)
1978	30673	247.42	138.52
1985	153489	674.77	285.22
1986	176960	773.88	300.17
1987	184390	772.38	330.14
1988	287655	1076.05	408.85
1989	368755	1094.90	489.88
1990	355333	876.08	439.08
1991	425798	909.09	377.71
1992	668171	1257.61	487.95
1993	1031846	1680.21	605.50
1994	1516519	2268.99	734.75
1995	1816133	2708.58	890.81
1996	1893478	2983.56	1043.26
1997	1965269	2764.64	941.10
1998	2287004	3086.95	1054.71
1999	2470523	3136.47	1187.02
2000	2561326	3161.25	1150.36
2001	3403870	3490.22	1205.79
2002	3733922	3522.67	1334.43
2003	4785787	4291.55	1398.91
2004	5459314	4727.78	1596.21
2005	6331382	5311.14	1598.79
2006	6870406	5502.47	1520.25
2007	7507109	5951.92	1623.36
2008	8754491	6156.62	1719.79
2009	10134050	6190.86	1500.35
2010	12805288	7135.48	1509.20
2011	15613171	8439.12	1596.98
2012	17417072	9119.66	2859.31
2013	21828895	15055.70	2556.74
2014	23339417	16398.88	2674.22
2015	24898087	15159.70	2861.93
2016	27653341	16289.56	2805.16
2017	31874585	19323.31	3167.27
2018	40192380	27755.15	4648.09
2019	53043655	32043.52	6536.75

注：1.2004年及以后年份统计数据口径为资质以上建筑业企业；
2.本表统计范围为施工总承包、专业承包法人建筑业企业。

Note: I. Since 2004 the statistical coverage of all data in this table is all grade construction enterprises.
II.The statistical scope of this table covers legal construction enterprises with general contracting and professional contracting.

12-3 资质以上建筑业企业签订合同情况(2019年)

Statistics on Construction Contracts of Grade Construction Enterprises (2019)

单位：万元 (10000 yuan)

项　目	Item	签订合同额 Value of Signed Contracts	上年结转合同额 Value of Contracts Balanced from Preceding Year	本年新签合同额 Value of Contracts Newly Signed in Current Year
总　计	**Total**	**189561934**	**107562462**	**81999472**
按地区分	**Grouped by District**			
荔湾区	Liwan	5789129	2641474	3147655
越秀区	Yuexiu	35044442	20506964	14537478
海珠区	Haizhu	31477294	17288336	14188958
天河区	Tianhe	37033432	22513665	14519767
白云区	Baiyun	5762732	2315512	3447220
黄埔区	Huangpu	12895143	6366804	6528339
番禺区	Panyu	4446494	1739891	2706603
花都区	Huadu	7032057	4590384	2441673
南沙区	Nansha	41032044	24932988	16099056
从化区	Conghua	1403442	447302	956140
增城区	Zengcheng	7645725	4219142	3426583
按隶属关系分	**Grouped by Administrative Relationship**			
中央属企业	Central Government	99761270	58824077	40937193
地方企业	Provincial Government	51139860	28495651	22644209
其他企业	Others	38660804	20242734	18418070
按登记注册类型分	**Grouped by Registration Status**			
内资企业	Domestic Funded Enterprises	189192413	107402340	81790073
国有企业	State-owned Enterprises	1523731	752345	771386
集体企业	Collective-owned Enterprises	1340247	890856	449391
股份合作企业	Share-holding Cooperative Enterprises	155154	20240	134914
联营企业	Joint Ownership Enterprises	89638	39949	49689
#国有联营企业	State Joint Ownership Enterprises			
集体联营企业	Collective Joint Ownership Enterprises	7558	5358	2200
国有与集体联营企业	Joint State-collective Enterprises	82080	34591	47489
有限责任公司	Limited Liability Corporations	155855055	89914995	65940060
#国有独资公司	State Sole Funded Corporations	53944889	30356274	23588615
股份有限公司	Share-holding Corporations Ltd.	12606019	8213367	4392652
私营企业	Private Enterprises	17622569	7570588	10051981
其他企业	Other Enterprises			
港、澳、台商投资企业	Enterprises with Funds from Hong Kong, Macao and Taiwan	249953	105753	144200
#与港、澳、台商合资经营企业	Joint-venture Enterprises	222943	86284	136659
与港、澳、台商合作经营企业	Cooperative Enterprises	26521	19469	7052
港、澳、台商独资经营企业	Enterprises with Sole Funds	489		489
港、澳、台商投资股份有限公司	Share-holding Corporations Ltd.			
外商投资企业	Foreign Funded Enterprises	119568	54369	65199
#中外合资经营企业	Joint-venture Enterprises	12733	1328	11405
中外合作经营企业	Cooperative Enterprises			
外资企业	Enterprises with Sole Foreign Funds	106835	53041	53794
外商投资股份有限公司	Share-holding Corporations Ltd.			

注：本表统计范围为施工总承包、专业承包法人建筑业企业。

Note: The statistical scope of this table covers legal construction enterprises with general contracting and professional contracting.

12-4 资质以上建筑业企业生产情况(2019年)

项 目	Item	企业数(个) Number of Construction Enterprises (unit)
总 计	**Total**	**1316**
按地区分	**Grouped by District**	
荔湾区	Liwan	51
越秀区	Yuexiu	167
海珠区	Haizhu	217
天河区	Tianhe	309
白云区	Baiyun	137
黄埔区	Huangpu	75
番禺区	Panyu	163
花都区	Huadu	36
南沙区	Nansha	65
从化区	Conghua	46
增城区	Zengcheng	50
按隶属关系分	**Grouped by Administrative Relationship**	
中央属企业	Central Government	47
地方企业	Provincial Government	173
其他企业	Others	1096
按登记注册类型分	**Grouped by Registration Status**	
内资企业	Domestic Funded Enterprises	1304
国有企业	State-owned Enterprises	29
集体企业	Collective-owned Enterprises	16
股份合作企业	Share-holding Cooperative Enterprises	3
联营企业	Joint Ownership Enterprises	2
#国有联营企业	State Joint Ownership Enterprises	
集体联营企业	Collective Joint Ownership Enterprises	1
国有与集体联营企业	Joint State-collective Enterprises	1
有限责任公司	Limited Liability Corporations	326
#国有独资公司	State Sole Funded Corporations	57
股份有限公司	Share-holding Corporations Ltd.	26
私营企业	Private Enterprises	902
其他企业	Other Enterprises	
港、澳、台商投资企业	Enterprises with Funds from Hong Kong, Macao and Taiwan	8
与港、澳、台商合资经营企业	Joint-venture Enterprises	5
与港、澳、台商合作经营企业	Cooperative Enterprises	2
港、澳、台商独资经营企业	Enterprises with Sole Funds	1
港、澳、台商投资股份有限公司	Share-holding Corporations Ltd.	
外商投资企业	Foreign Funded Enterprises	4
中外合资经营企业	Joint-venture Enterprises	2
中外合作经营企业	Cooperative Enterprises	
外资企业	Enterprises with Sole Foreign Funds	2
外商投资股份有限公司	Share-holding Corporations Ltd.	

注：本表统计范围为施工总承包、专业承包法人建筑业企业。

Statistics on Production of Grade Construction Enterprises (2019)

建筑业总产值（万元）Gross Output Value of Construction (10000 yuan)	建筑工程 Output Value of Construction	安装工程 Output Value of Installation	其　他 Others	竣工产值（万元）Output Value of Completed Projects (10000 yuan)	竣工率（%）Ratio of Floor Space of Buildings Completed (%)
53043655	**46742169**	**4333551**	**1967935**	**19002829**	**35.82**
1496051	1055229	418643	22179	894116	59.77
9201547	7713941	1320382	167224	5222894	56.76
6530280	5620596	318305	591379	1548820	23.72
12566792	11625153	569873	371766	5012511	39.89
2530968	2086152	125326	319490	563609	22.27
5754322	4577702	876044	300576	1102929	19.17
1576799	1160776	357778	58245	368314	23.36
2447511	2410909	14406	22196	514269	21.01
8730352	8628020	95754	6578	2782830	31.88
699215	585921	86932	26362	273936	39.18
1509818	1277770	150108	81940	718601	47.60
23882421	21888519	1338793	655109	7106824	29.76
13426113	11970478	931477	524158	5138952	38.28
15735121	12883172	2063281	788668	6757053	42.94
52895684	46633590	4294375	1967719	18985167	35.89
914049	787563	11720	114766	88559	9.69
439866	437023	621	2222	221840	50.43
137514	90748	1939	44827	78569	57.14
38480	38155		325	14231	36.98
2280	2280			1034	45.35
36200	35875		325	13197	36.46
40920261	36755868	2778407	1385986	14504871	35.45
12861324	11817361	658391	385572	5223265	40.61
2342508	2184312	102756	55440	742931	31.72
8103006	6339921	1398932	364153	3334166	41.15
122081	83641	38440		5434	4.45
111141	72701	38440		70	0.06
10451	10451			4875	46.65
489	489			489	100.00
25890	24938	736	216	12228	47.23
6840	6625		215	12228	178.77
19050	18313	736	1		

Note: The statistical scope of this table covers legal construction enterprises with general contracting and professional contracting.

12-4 续表

项 目	Item	房屋建筑施工面积（平方米）Floor Space of Buildings under Construction (sq.m)
总 计	**Total**	**320435183**
按地区分	**Grouped by District**	
荔湾区	Liwan	9133260
越秀区	Yuexiu	71823559
海珠区	Haizhu	84513200
天河区	Tianhe	92756415
白云区	Baiyun	6775025
黄埔区	Huangpu	16518238
番禺区	Panyu	4064686
花都区	Huadu	13243569
南沙区	Nansha	11352613
从化区	Conghua	1512070
增城区	Zengcheng	8742548
按隶属关系分	**Grouped by Administrative Relationship**	
中央属企业	Central Government	170367031
地方企业	Provincial Government	66992808
其他企业	Others	83075344
按登记注册类型分	**Grouped by Registration Status**	
内资企业	Domestic Funded Enterprises	320275142
国有企业	State-owned Enterprises	317741
集体企业	Collective-owned Enterprises	1488527
股份合作企业	Share-holding Cooperative Enterprises	592231
联营企业	Joint Ownership Enterprises	57470
#国有联营企业	State Joint Ownership Enterprises	
集体联营企业	Collective Joint Ownership Enterprises	57470
国有与集体联营企业	Joint State-collective Enterprises	
有限责任公司	Limited Liability Corporations	270819672
#国有独资公司	State Sole Funded Corporations	112981732
股份有限公司	Share-holding Corporations Ltd.	12249697
私营企业	Private Enterprises	34749804
其他企业	Other Enterprises	
港、澳、台商投资企业	Enterprises with Funds from Hong Kong, Macao and Taiwan	160041
与港、澳、台商合资经营企业	Joint-venture Enterprises	
与港、澳、台商合作经营企业	Cooperative Enterprises	158401
港、澳、台商独资经营企业	Enterprises with Sole Funds	1640
港、澳、台商投资股份有限公司	Share-holding Corporations Ltd.	
外商投资企业	Foreign Funded Enterprises	
中外合资经营企业	Joint-venture Enterprises	
中外合作经营企业	Cooperative Enterprises	
外资企业	Enterprises with Sole Foreign Funds	
外商投资股份有限公司	Share-holding Corporations Ltd.	

continued

# 本年新开工 Floor Space Started in Current Year	房屋建筑竣工面积（平方米） Floor Space of Buildings Completed (sq.m)	# 住 宅 Residential Buildings	年平均人数（人） Average Annual Employed Persons (person)
79294655	**65367486**	**54467602**	**922686**
1076962	2744972	1116426	27893
20088435	15883433	13098817	165317
27204576	18743116	18167100	163139
12479297	19652024	17622444	210301
2895308	375641	45145	55634
4807050	2638872	1629172	69151
2027789	1121376	400535	33266
2776338	2044157	1528356	19606
1859307	1377236	413070	130005
549902	288100	166651	21614
3529691	498559	279886	26760
37783580	31843424	31073568	367991
15052547	10722751	5024185	204352
26458528	22801311	18369849	350343
79246844	65346626	54467602	919363
139			10527
267612	268322	74900	7092
86865	232009	38653	2260
13749	8620		1454
13749	8620		209
			1245
61903874	54394984	47892177	662319
16922738	17856877	15372848	227174
2379319	1462319	1034985	22661
14595286	8980372	5426887	213050
47811	20860		2599
			2030
47811	19220		559
	1640		10
			724
			86
			638

12-5 资质以上建筑业企业承包工程完成情况(2019年)

单位：万元

项　　目	Item
总　　计	**Total**
按地区分	**Grouped by District**
荔湾区	Liwan
越秀区	Yuexiu
海珠区	Haizhu
天河区	Tianhe
白云区	Baiyun
黄埔区	Huangpu
番禺区	Panyu
花都区	Huadu
南沙区	Nansha
从化区	Conghua
增城区	Zengcheng
按隶属关系分	**Grouped by Administrative Relationship**
中央属企业	Central Government
地方企业	Provincial Government
其他企业	Others
按登记注册类型分	**Grouped by Registration Status**
内资企业	Domestic Funded Enterprises
国有企业	State-owned Enterprises
集体企业	Collective-owned Enterprises
股份合作企业	Share-holding Cooperative Enterprises
联营企业	Joint Ownership Enterprises
#国有联营企业	State Joint Ownership Enterprises
集体联营企业	Collective Joint Ownership Enterprises
国有与集体联营企业	Joint State-collective Enterprises
有限责任公司	Limited Liability Corporations
#国有独资公司	State Sole Funded Corporations
股份有限公司	Share-holding Corporations Ltd.
私营企业	Private Enterprises
其他企业	Other Enterprises
港、澳、台商投资企业	Enterprises with Funds from Hong Kong, Macao and Taiwan
与港、澳、台商合资经营企业	Joint-venture Enterprises
与港、澳、台商合作经营企业	Cooperative Enterprises
港、澳、台商独资经营企业	Enterprises with Sole Funds
港、澳、台商投资股份有限公司	Share-holding Corporations Ltd.
外商投资企业	Foreign Funded Enterprises
中外合资经营企业	Joint-venture Enterprises
中外合作经营企业	Cooperative Enterprises
外资企业	Enterprises with Sole Foreign Funds
外商投资股份有限公司	Share-holding Corporations Ltd.

注：本表统计范围为施工总承包、专业承包法人建筑业企业。

Statistics on Contracted Projects of Grade Construction Enterprises (2019)

(10000 yuan)

直接从建设单位承揽工程完成的产值 Output Value of Completed Projects Directly Contracted with Construction Units	自行完成施工产值 Output Value of Projects Completed by Oneself	分包出去工程产值 Output Value of Projects Subcontracted	从建设单位以外承揽工程完成的产值 Output Value of Completed Projects Contracted with Other Units
59726834	**49025722**	**10701112**	**4017933**
1773446	1294425	479021	201626
12933654	8809864	4123790	391683
9702180	6328885	3373295	201395
13425258	12158839	1266419	407953
1719612	1545815	173797	985153
4670556	4445824	224732	1308498
1551504	1459900	91604	116899
2416675	2402218	14457	45293
8562063	8402363	159700	327989
705144	695486	9658	3729
2266742	1482103	784639	27715
25198371	22075405	3122966	1807016
18512099	12175806	6336293	1250307
16016364	14774511	1241853	960610
59561756	48877751	10684005	4017933
904945	866834	38111	47215
435746	435746		4120
135705	135625	80	1889
38480	38480		
2280	2280		
36200	36200		
46440632	37628939	8811693	3291322
15109861	11705961	3403900	1155363
3367240	2305312	1061928	37196
8239008	7466815	772193	636191
133800	122081	11719	
122860	111141	11719	
10451	10451		
489	489		
31278	25890	5388	
12228	6840	5388	
19050	19050		

Note: The statistical scope of this table covers legal construction enterprises with general contracting and professional contracting.

12-6 资质以上建筑业企业财务指标(2019年)

单位：万元

项　　目	Item	资产总计 Total Assets
总　　计	**Total**	**73886964**
按地区分	**Grouped by District**	
荔湾区	Liwan	4288863
越秀区	Yuexiu	15988748
海珠区	Haizhu	12209991
天河区	Tianhe	16559880
白云区	Baiyun	2396810
黄埔区	Huangpu	5180468
番禺区	Panyu	1332795
花都区	Huadu	2284750
南沙区	Nansha	7976560
从化区	Conghua	1305491
增城区	Zengcheng	4362608
按隶属关系分	**Grouped by Administrative Relationship**	
中央属企业	Central Government	30973670
地方企业	Provincial Government	20728587
其他企业	Others	22184707
按登记注册类型分	**Grouped by Registration Status**	
内资企业	Domestic Funded Enterprises	72303571
国有企业	State-owned Enterprises	951789
集体企业	Collective-owned Enterprises	323012
股份合作企业	Share-holding Cooperative Enterprises	65410
联营企业	Joint Ownership Enterprises	17465
#国有联营企业	State Joint Ownership Enterprises	
集体联营企业	Collective Joint Ownership Enterprises	4283
国有与集体联营企业	Joint State-collective Enterprises	13182
有限责任公司	Limited Liability Corporations	54331274
#国有独资公司	State Sole Funded Corporations	18390500
股份有限公司	Share-holding Corporations Ltd.	6217938
私营企业	Private Enterprises	10396683
其他企业	Other Enterprises	
港、澳、台商投资企业	Enterprises with Funds from Hong Kong, Macao and Taiwan	1514010
与港、澳、台商合资经营企业	Joint-venture Enterprises	275841
与港、澳、台商合作经营企业	Cooperative Enterprises	1237116
港、澳、台商独资经营企业	Enterprises with Sole Funds	1053
港、澳、台商投资股份有限公司	Share-holding Corporations Ltd.	
外商投资企业	Foreign Funded Enterprises	69383
中外合资经营企业	Joint-venture Enterprises	16833
中外合作经营企业	Cooperative Enterprises	
外资企业	Enterprises with Sole Foreign Funds	52550
外商投资股份有限公司	Share-holding Corporations Ltd.	

注：本表统计范围为施工总承包、专业承包法人建筑业企业。

Financial Indicators of Grade Construction Enterprises (2019)

(10000 yuan)

负债合计 Total Liabilities	所有者权益 Owners' Equity	# 实收资本 Paid-in Capitals
56171336	**17715628**	**9196026**
2594817	1694046	1141108
13075683	2913065	1354827
8508212	3701779	1593757
13278652	3281228	2123355
1745243	651567	437249
4011495	1168973	569541
888545	444250	284509
1892463	392287	268692
6708122	1268438	928304
1000004	305487	83883
2468100	1894508	410801
24616755	6356915	3276436
15829624	4898963	2792634
15724957	6459750	3126956
55901425	16402146	9084864
756389	195400	119120
241675	81337	45584
44487	20923	14784
9457	8008	5028
255	4028	4028
9202	3980	1000
42876670	11454604	6336759
14553726	3836774	2533099
4681004	1536934	549552
7291743	3104940	2014037
225234	1288776	102294
202066	73775	64310
23161	1213955	36949
7	1046	1035
44677	24706	8868
8749	8084	2600
35928	16622	6268

Note: The statistical scope of this table covers legal construction enterprises with general contracting and professional contracting.

12-6 续表 1

单位:万元

项　　目	Item	营业收入 Income of Business
总　计	**Total**	**59956240**
按地区分	**Grouped by District**	
荔湾区	Liwan	2205272
越秀区	Yuexiu	12070022
海珠区	Haizhu	9552882
天河区	Tianhe	13532986
白云区	Baiyun	2256754
黄埔区	Huangpu	5286192
番禺区	Panyu	1611887
花都区	Huadu	2114553
南沙区	Nansha	8464448
从化区	Conghua	710306
增城区	Zengcheng	2150938
按隶属关系分	**Grouped by Administrative Relationship**	
中央属企业	Central Government	24554034
地方企业	Provincial Government	17899560
其他企业	Others	17502646
按登记注册类型分	**Grouped by Registration Status**	
内资企业	Domestic Funded Enterprises	59755098
国有企业	State-owned Enterprises	999839
集体企业	Collective-owned Enterprises	476470
股份合作企业	Share-holding Cooperative Enterprises	82627
联营企业	Joint Ownership Enterprises	46917
# 国有联营企业	State Joint Ownership Enterprises	
集体联营企业	Collective Joint Ownership Enterprises	10107
国有与集体联营企业	Joint State-collective Enterprises	36810
有限责任公司	Limited Liability Corporations	45499794
# 国有独资公司	State Sole Funded Corporations	14113559
股份有限公司	Share-holding Corporations Ltd.	3224028
私营企业	Private Enterprises	9425423
其他企业	Other Enterprises	
港、澳、台商投资企业	Enterprises with Funds from Hong Kong, Macao and Taiwan	157280
与港、澳、台商合资经营企业	Joint-venture Enterprises	125089
与港、澳、台商合作经营企业	Cooperative Enterprises	30721
港、澳、台商独资经营企业	Enterprises with Sole Funds	1470
港、澳、台商投资股份有限公司	Share-holding Corporations Ltd.	
外商投资企业	Foreign Funded Enterprises	43862
中外合资经营企业	Joint-venture Enterprises	11917
中外合作经营企业	Cooperative Enterprises	
外资企业	Enterprises with Sole Foreign Funds	31945
外商投资股份有限公司	Share-holding Corporations Ltd.	

continued

(10000 yuan)

#主营业务收入 Revenue from Principal Business	主营业务成本 Cost of Principal Business	其他业务利润 Other Operational Profit
59413560	**55283615**	**60405**
2172327	1952147	3418
12027296	11369200	16890
9511591	8749435	15605
13495727	12462977	11470
2232850	2050671	4830
5254762	4864379	2743
1592734	1410096	2442
2086887	1961728	1221
8181238	7861282	1044
710060	606437	211
2148088	1995263	531
24160982	22652349	21660
17804658	16841181	29569
17447920	15790085	9176
59214141	55114738	60382
996969	910036	1816
474719	454027	394
82086	75114	
46917	44834	
10107	9587	
36810	35247	
45004542	42208605	53498
14013850	13265849	15523
3220180	3028015	865
9388728	8394107	3809
156624	142814	1
124433	111943	1
30721	29516	
1470	1355	
42795	26063	22
11917	8123	
30878	17940	22

12-6 续表 2

单位：万元

项 目	Item	管理费用 Management Cost
总 计	**Total**	**1503756**
按地区分	**Grouped by District**	
荔湾区	Liwan	75356
越秀区	Yuexiu	339889
海珠区	Haizhu	202314
天河区	Tianhe	310793
白云区	Baiyun	84973
黄埔区	Huangpu	138632
番禺区	Panyu	91160
花都区	Huadu	44061
南沙区	Nansha	146324
从化区	Conghua	25012
增城区	Zengcheng	45242
按隶属关系分	**Grouped by Administrative Relationship**	
中央属企业	Central Government	400679
地方企业	Provincial Government	402594
其他企业	Others	700483
按登记注册类型分	**Grouped by Registration Status**	
内资企业	Domestic Funded Enterprises	1491246
国有企业	State-owned Enterprises	40624
集体企业	Collective-owned Enterprises	12646
股份合作企业	Share-holding Cooperative Enterprises	2617
联营企业	Joint Ownership Enterprises	1383
# 国有联营企业	State Joint Ownership Enterprises	
集体联营企业	Collective Joint Ownership Enterprises	464
国有与集体联营企业	Joint State-collective Enterprises	919
有限责任公司	Limited Liability Corporations	893540
# 国有独资公司	State Sole Funded Corporations	274287
股份有限公司	Share-holding Corporations Ltd.	68084
私营企业	Private Enterprises	472352
其他企业	Other Enterprises	
港、澳、台商投资企业	Enterprises with Funds from Hong Kong, Macao and Taiwan	8124
与港、澳、台商合资经营企业	Joint-venture Enterprises	7290
与港、澳、台商合作经营企业	Cooperative Enterprises	727
港、澳、台商独资经营企业	Enterprises with Sole Funds	107
港、澳、台商投资股份有限公司	Share-holding Corporations Ltd.	
外商投资企业	Foreign Funded Enterprises	4386
中外合资经营企业	Joint-venture Enterprises	1416
中外合作经营企业	Cooperative Enterprises	
外资企业	Enterprises with Sole Foreign Funds	2970
外商投资股份有限公司	Share-holding Corporations Ltd.	

continued

(10000 yuan)

财务费用 Financial Cost	营业利润 Business Profits	利润总额 Total Profits	产值利润率(%) Rate of Profits to Output (%)
300922	**1213699**	**1227019**	**2.31**
-7264	122034	119784	8.01
55967	130226	135246	1.47
36126	360854	362727	5.55
123407	87508	94705	0.75
17307	53743	53513	2.11
9836	145200	143628	2.50
7646	52833	51783	3.28
11106	35359	36142	1.48
18468	107169	108538	1.24
4399	66642	67281	9.62
23924	52131	53672	3.55
123338	555634	570352	2.39
36415	325222	322618	2.40
141169	332843	334049	2.12
299494	1199002	1212283	2.29
1209	29596	30325	3.32
234	5366	4500	1.02
79	831	831	0.60
-37	442	411	1.07
	1	1	
-13	-6	-6	
-24	447	416	1.15
171162	1016451	1030148	2.52
74313	220773	227964	1.77
34725	45860	46842	2.00
92122	100456	99226	1.22
144	4935	4820	3.95
175	4538	4438	3.99
-31	394	379	3.63
	3	3	0.61
1284	9762	9916	38.30
-8	2333	2397	35.04
1292	7429	7519	39.47

12-7　资质以上建筑业企业盈亏情况(2019年)

单位:个、万元

项　　目	Item
总　计	**Total**
按地区分	**Grouped by District**
荔湾区	Liwan
越秀区	Yuexiu
海珠区	Haizhu
天河区	Tianhe
白云区	Baiyun
黄埔区	Huangpu
番禺区	Panyu
花都区	Huadu
南沙区	Nansha
从化区	Conghua
增城区	Zengcheng
按隶属关系分	**Grouped by Administrative Relationship**
中央属企业	Central Government
地方企业	Provincial Government
其他企业	Others
按登记注册类型分	**Grouped by Registration Status**
内资企业	Domestic Funded Enterprises
国有企业	Stateowned Enterprises
集体企业	Collectiveowned Enterprises
股份合作企业	Shareholding Cooperative Enterprises
联营企业	Joint Ownership Enterprises
#国有联营企业	State Joint Ownership Enterprises
集体联营企业	Collective Joint Ownership Enterprises
国有与集体联营企业	Joint Statecollective Enterprises
有限责任公司	Limited Liability Corporations
#国有独资公司	State Sole Funded Corporations
股份有限公司	Shareholding Corporations Ltd.
私营企业	Private Enterprises
其他企业	Other Enterprises
港、澳、台商投资企业	Enterprises with Funds from Hong Kong, Macao and Taiwan
与港、澳、台商合资经营企业	Jointventure Enterprises
与港、澳、台商合作经营企业	Cooperative Enterprises
港、澳、台商独资经营企业	Enterprises with Sole Funds
港、澳、台商投资股份有限公司	Shareholding Corporations Ltd.
外商投资企业	Foreign Funded Enterprises
中外合资经营企业	Jointventure Enterprises
中外合作经营企业	Cooperative Enterprises
外资企业	Enterprises with Sole Foreign Funds
外商投资股份有限公司	Shareholding Corporations Ltd.

注：本表统计范围为施工总承包、专业承包法人建筑业企业。

Statistics on Profits and Losses of Grade Construction Enterprises (2019)

(unit, 10000 yuan)

企业数 Number of Construction Enterprises	盈 余 Profits		亏 损 Losses	
	企业数 Number of Enterprises	金 额 Value	企业数 Number of Enterprises	金 额 Value
1316	**1085**	**1530668**	**231**	**303649**
51	41	120517	10	733
167	137	158328	30	23081
217	165	366975	52	4248
309	250	337743	59	243038
137	116	56197	21	2684
75	69	156805	6	13177
163	141	57120	22	5337
36	29	42719	7	6577
65	57	110431	8	1893
46	34	68277	12	998
50	46	55556	4	1883
47	44	576447	3	6095
173	149	355838	24	33220
1096	892	598383	204	264334
1304	1074	1515893	230	303610
29	26	30628	3	304
16	9	6723	7	2223
3	2	856	1	25
2	1	416	1	6
1			1	6
1	1	416		
326	278	1077077	48	46929
57	55	233564	2	5599
26	21	58614	5	11772
902	737	341579	165	242351
8	7	4859	1	39
5	4	4477	1	39
2	2	379		
1	1	3		
4	4	9916		
2	2	2397		
2	2	7519		

Note: The statistical scope of this table covers legal construction enterprises with general contracting and professional contracting.

【建筑业总产值】指以货币表现的建筑业企业在一定时期内生产的建筑业产品和服务的总和。建筑业总产值包括三部分内容:

(1)建筑工程产值:指列入建筑工程预算内的各种工程价值。

(2)设备安装工程产值:指设备安装工程价值，以及将预制部品部件安装成建筑工程产品的价值。

(3)其他产值:建筑业总产值中除建筑工程、安装工程以外的产值。包括房屋构筑物修理产值、非标准设备制造产值、总包企业向分包企业收取的管理费以及不能明确划分的施工活动所完成的产值。

a. 房屋构筑物修理产值：指房屋和构筑物的修理所完成的产值，但不包括被修理房屋、构筑物的本身价值和生产设备的本身的价值。

b. 非标准设备制造产值：指加工制造没有定型的非标准生产设备的加工费和原材料价值以及附属加工厂为本企业承建工程制作的非标准设备的价值。

【房屋建筑面积】指房屋全部平面面积的总和。它从房屋的外墙线算起，包括可供使用的有效面积和墙柱等结构占用面积。多层房屋按各层(包括地下室)面积总和计算。旧房加层或改造，只计算增加的建筑面积；旧房拆除重建，计算其全部面积；临时房屋不计算建筑面积。

【主营业务收入】指企业确认的销售商品、提供劳务等主营业务的收入。根据会计“主营业务收入”科目的本年各月贷方余额（结转前）之和填报。如未设置该科目，以“营业收入”代替填报。

【营业收入】指企业经营主要业务和其他业务所确认的收入总额。营业收入合计包括“主营业务收入”和“其他业务收入”。根据会计“利润表”中“营业收入”项目的本年累计数填报，即：

营业收入 =主营业务收入 +其他业务收入

【Gross Output Value of Construction】refers to total Volume of construction products and services, expressed in monetary terms, completed by construction and installation enterprises during a given period of time. It includes:

(1)Output value of construction projects, that is the value of projects covered by the project budgets；

(2)Output value of installation projects, those are the value of the installation of equipment and the value of installing prefabricated parts into construction engineering products.

(3)Other output values, that is the values excluding output value of construction projects and output value of installation projects, including output value of repair of buildings and structures, output value of manufactured non-standard equipment, management expenses received by head enterprises from subcontract enterprises and output value of construction activities completed but unclassified.

a.Output value of repair of buildings and structures, that is the value created through the repairs of buildings or structures, but does not include the value of buildings or structures being repaired and the value of the repair of production equipment.

b.Output value of manufactured non-standard equipment, that is the value of non-standard production equipment (including raw materials and manufacturing cost) made for the construction project, and equipment manufactured by subsidiary workshops.

【Floor Space of Buildings under Construction】refers to the sum of all of the surface area of the housing. Counting from the housing exterior lines, including the availability of effective area and wall and column structure occupied the area. The floor space of multi-storey housing is the sum of area of all layers (including basement). The additional layer or transformation of existing homes, only the increase in construction area; old house demolition and reconstruction, to calculate the total area; temporary housing does not calculate the building area.

【Main business income】refers to the enterprise recognizes sales of goods and services, and other main business income. According to the sum of the credit balance (before carry-over) of each month of this year in the accounting subject of "main business income". If without a set of the subjects, operating income instead.

【Operating income】refers to the total income of the business recognized by business and other business. Total operating revenue includes the main business income and other operating income. Fill in the number of business income project accounting income statement for accumulated data in the year, .its calculating formula is:

Operating income = the main business income + other operating income

第十三篇 CHAPTER 13

运输和邮电

TRANSPORT, POSTAL AND TELECOMMUNICATION SERVICES

简要说明

Brief Introduction

第十三篇　运输和邮电

一、本篇资料反映广州市运输、邮电通信业发展的基本状况。交通运输业资料主要包括：五种运输方式的线路里程、运输设备拥有量、各种运输方式完成的货物运输量和旅客运输量、港口设备拥有量、港口货物吞吐量等。

邮电通信业资料主要包括：邮电业务量、邮电通信工具、邮电通信网、邮电通信水平等。

二、本篇资料由广州市统计局服务业统计处整理提供。

三、资料分别来源于民航、铁路、公路、水运、港口、公安、邮电等部门。管道运输资料由有关管道运输企业提供。

13 Transport,Postal and Telecommunication Services

I.The data in this chapter cover mainly the basis conditions of the development of transport, posts and telecommunications in Guangzhou. The data on transport cover mainly the length of the routes of five means of transportation, the owner-ship of the transport equipment, the freight traffic and passenger traffic accomplished by various means of transportation, the ownership of the port equipment and the cargo handled at ports, etc. The data on posts and telecommunications cover mainly the postal and telecommunication services, means of post and telecommunications, network of post and telecommunications, main financial of indicators of postal and telecommunication enterprises and the level of the development of the postal and telecommunication services, etc.

II.The data in this chapter are prepared and provided by the Division of Service Industries Statistics of Guangzhou Municipal Bureau of Statistics.

III.The data in this chapter come respectively from Guangzhou municipal departments of railways, transportation, post and telecommunications, etc. The data on the pipeline transport are provided by related pipeline enterprises.

13-1 运输邮电主要指标

Basic Statistics of Transport and Post

项目	Item	2018	2019
民用车辆拥有量 (辆)	Civilian Vehicle (unit)	2660191	2882296
#汽车	Automobile	2573308	2789056
货运量 (万吨)	Freight Traffic (10000 tons)	127752	136165
#铁路	Railways	1989	2105
公路	Highways	82032	88352
水路	Waterways	42608	44571
民航	Civil Aviation	137	140
货物周转量 (万吨公里)	Freight Ton-kilometers (10000 ton-km)	214871658	218291463
#铁路	Railways	208617	239874
公路	Highways	9521612	10264110
水路	Waterways	204462938	207107575
民航	Civil Aviation	673332	674954
客运量 (万人次)	Passenger Traffic (10000 person-times)	48048	49819
铁路	Railways	13355	14530
公路	Highways	25725	25625
水路	Waterways	55	33
民航	Civil Aviation	8913	9630
旅客周转量 (万人公里)	Passenger-kilometers (10000 passenger-km)	21950302	23760253
铁路	Railways	1269676	1322899
公路	Highways	2649145	2628568
水路	Waterways	5344	3242
民航	Civil Aviation	18026137	19805544
港口货物吞吐量 (万吨)	Volume of Freight Handled in Coastal Ports (10000 tons)	55669	62687
进港	Import	32415	36151
出港	Export	23254	26536
白云国际机场货邮行吞吐量 (万吨)	Volume of Freight and Post Handled in Baiyun International Airport (10000 tons)	249	255
白云国际机场旅客吞吐量 (万人次)	Volume of Passengers Handled in Baiyun International Airport (10000 person-times)	6974	7339
邮电业务收入 (万元)	Revenue of Postal and Telecommunication Services (10000 yuan)	8778953	10450611
电话交换机总容量 (万门)	Total Capacity of Telephone Exchanges (10000 gates)	81	81
报纸发行量 (万份)	Newspapers Issued (10000 copies)	108327	90427
杂志发行量 (万份)	Magazines Issued (10000 copies)	5133	4934
固定电话用户 (万户)	Number of Telephone Sets at Year-end (10000 subscribes)	371	331
移动电话用户 (万户)	Number of Mobile Telephone Subscribers (10000 subscribes)	4008	3645
互联网宽带接入用户数(万户)	Number of Internet Subscribers (10000 subscribes)	544	566
城市电话普及率(含移动电话) (部/百人)	Popularity Rate of Urban Telephones (Including Mobile Telephones) (set/100 persons)	472.00	265.01
#移动电话	Mobile Telephones	432.01	242.97

注：交通运输部自2019年1月起调整了港口统计口径和部分货类吞吐量的计算方法，同时对2018年同期数作同口径调整。

Note:The Ministry of Transport has adjusted the calculation method of port statistical caliber and throughput of some cargo classes since January 2019 while making the same caliber adjustment for the corresponding period in 2018.

13-2 公路和航道线路基本情况

Basic Statisics on Highways and Waterways

项　目	Item	2018	2019
公路里程　（公里）	**Length of Highways　(kilometer)**	**8975**	**8984**
# 晴雨通车里程	Length of Highways in Any Weathers	8975	8984
等级公路	Expressway and Class I to IV Highways	8914	8984
高　速	Expressway	1022	1030
一　级	First Class	1058	1068
二　级	Second Class	871	872
三　级	Third Class	1458	1452
四　级	Fourth Class	4505	4562
等外公路	Highways below Class IV	61	
有路面里程	Paved Highways	8952	8972
沥青混凝土	High Class	2277	2297
水泥混凝土	Second High Class	6675	6675
简易铺路面	Medium Class	23	12
未铺装路面	Low Class		
桥　梁	**Bridges**		
座　（座）	Number　(unit)	3324	3377
长　度　（米）	Length　(meter)	582561	612095
永久式桥梁	**Permanent Bridges**		
座　（座）	Number　(unit)	3714	3377
长　度　（米）	Length　(meter)	549332	612095
渡　口　（个）	**Ferries　(unit)**	**2**	**2**
内河航道里程　（公里）	**Length of Navigable Inland Waterways　(kilometer)**	**1303**	**1301**
# 等级航道里程	Standand Waterways　(kilometer)	473	579

注：1.广州市交通运输局2019年底对桥梁数量进行校核，修订2017年和2018年桥梁座数和长度，分别更新为3167座、56.46万米；3324座58.26万米。

2.本表数据由广州市交通运输局等单位提供。

Note: I. Guangzhou Municipal Transportation Bureau has checked the number of Bridges at the end of 2019, and revised the number and length of Bridges in 2017 and 2018 to 3167 units, 564600 meters and 3324 units, 582.6 thousand meters respectively.

II. The data in this table are provided by Guangzhou Municipal Transportation Bureau, etc.

13-3 民用车辆拥有量（2019年）

Possession of Civil Vehicles (2019)

单位：辆 (unit)

项 目	Item	全市 Total	#私人 Private
合 计	**Total**	**2882296**	**2234790**
汽 车	Civil Automobile	2789056	2169343
载客汽车	Passenger Vehicles	2373629	1993129
大 型	Large	38794	566
中 型	Medium	9886	3049
小 型	Small	2311190	1983055
微 型	Minicar	13759	6459
载货汽车	Trucks	399888	170971
重 型	Heavy	78454	3266
中 型	Medium	21648	3968
轻 型	Light	296113	160434
微 型	Mini	3673	3303
其他汽车	Others	15539	5243
电 车	Trolleybuses and Trams	236	
无 轨	Trolleybuses	236	
有 轨	Trams		
摩托车	Motorcycle	66449	65229
普 通	Ordinary	66449	65229
轻 便	Light		
挂 车	Trailers	26555	218
其他类型车	Other Kinds of Vehicles		

注：本表资料由广州市公安局交警支队提供。
Note: The data in this table are provided by the transportation policy branch of Guangzhou Policy Bureau.

13-4 营业性民用运输轮驳船拥有量
Possession of Business Civil Transport Vessels

项　　目		Item		2018	2019
机动船		**Motor Vessels**			
艘数	(艘)	Number of Motor Vessels	(unit)	1663	1622
#客船	(艘)	Passenger Vessels	(unit)	91	85
货船	(艘)	Cargo Vessels	(unit)	1566	1531
载客量	(客位)	Passenger Capacity	(seat)	23710	19540
净载重量	(吨位)	Dead Weight Tonnage	(ton)	33476631	37240523
总功率	(千瓦)	Total Power	(kw)	5180378	5485246
驳　船		**Barges**			
艘数	(艘)	Number of Barges	(unit)	2	1
净载重量	(吨位)	Dead Weight Tonnage	(ton)	8411	4206

注：本表资料由广州港务局等单位提供。
Note:The data in this table are provided by Guangzhou Port Authority.

13-5 主要年份客货运输(吞吐量)和邮电业务收入
Total Passenger and Freight Traffic and Revenue of Postal and Telecommunication Services in Main Years

年 份 Year	客运量 (万人次) Passenger Traffic (10000 persontimes)	旅客周转量 (万人公里) Passenger-kilometers (10000 passengerkm)	货运量 (万吨) Freight Traffic (10000 tons)	货物周转量 (万吨公里) Freight Tonkilometers (10000 ton-km)	港口旅客吞吐量 (万人次) Volume of Passenger Handled in Coastal Ports (10000 persontimes)
1978					433
1980					489
1985	11653	1017045	18233	15653824	514
1986	10985	1090054	15439	16584196	788
1987	9152	1158152	18947	17143674	742
1988	10290	1340611	21390	18968882	765
1989	9051	1269994	18397	20193670	610
1990	9461	1340608	17842	21417482	531
1991	9996	1574625	19535	26703071	485
1992	12459	1897547	22562	28156518	484
1993	15988	2198885	24818	29564344	447
1994	17307	2202816	26461	35696673	406
1995	16107	2227019	26992	39618131	343
1996	15638	2066438	23315	30739572	233
1997	17725	2417966	23768	30573646	134
1998	19587	2563072	24443	26210641	91
1999	22007	2799796	24238	20924658	153
2000	26097	4533805	27972	22660161	134
2001	27461	4986901	28248	23370862	135
2002	30084	5570611	28496	22346711	135
2003	30546	5408605	29309	25104134	112
2004	36941	8557982	35700	27833246	119
2005	40524	9750755	38153	27240509	99
2006	43777	10915614	42759	27954630	98
2007	51180	12906006	45852	24706845	111
2008	55385	13752318	49586	24620645	90
2009	57053	14538626	52525	21762287	78
2010	62595	16936472	57369	24508491	79
2011	67756	18790926	64929	28611908	80
2012	76070	20746062	76100	49383911	75
2013	89269	22776307	89099	68224384	77
2014	98062	24996168	96553	86335522	71
2015	106082	26681268	100124	90504153	61
2016	45823	21698556	107992	153864229	87
2017	45279	19990354	117429	212596804	92
2018	48048	21950302	127752	214871658	101
2019	49819	23760253	136165	218291463	78

注：交通运输部自2019年1月起调整了港口统计口径和部分货类吞吐量的计算方法，同时对2018年同期数作同口径调整。

Note:The Ministry of Transport has adjusted the calculation method of port statistical caliber and throughput of some cargo classes since January 2019 while making the same caliber adjustment for the corresponding period in 2018.

13-5 续表 continued

年 份 Year	港口货物吞吐量 (万吨) Volume of Freight Handled (10000 tons)	#集装箱 Container	机场旅客吞吐量 (万人次) Volume of Passenger Handled in Airport (10000 persontimes)	机场货邮行吞吐量 (万吨) Volume of Freight Mail and Luggage Handled in Airport (10000 tons)	邮电业务收入 (万元) Revenue of Postal and Telecommun-ication Services (10000 yuan)
1978	1950		66		2357
1980	2107		131	3	3631
1985	3700		290	6	9927
1986	3954		389	7	12744
1987	4561		505	10	19822
1988	5115	115	542	11	28482
1989	5106	103	485	11	38605
1990	5099	107	605	12	55960
1991	5657	161	745	15	79642
1992	6477	168	902	17	121473
1993	7610	177	927	19	180606
1994	8121	231	1070	23	270330
1995	8340	440	1257	28	380323
1996	8510	485	1264	32	528343
1997	8390	599	1251	35	687781
1998	8716	789	1241	41	841107
1999	11336	1355	1190	45	981527
2000	12455	1699	1279	49	1384846
2001	13539	2633	1384	53	1515282
2002	16772	3255	1601	59	1751392
2003	19200	4161	1501	54	1851326
2004	23887	4734	2033	63	2108788
2005	27283	6672	2340	75	2220589
2006	32816	9493	2622	82	2307436
2007	37053	13298	3096	90	2478199
2008	36954	15172	3344	93	2663183
2009	37549	15383	3705	122	2680007
2010	42526	18070	4098	145	2900942
2011	44770	20682	4504	153	3123440
2012	45125	21338	4831	163	3373039
2013	47267	23053	5246	173	4585063
2014	50097	24297	5479	190	5052592
2015	52096	26026	5521	200	5400082
2016	54437	27799	5974	216	6352822
2017	59012	30002	6584	234	7560250
2018	55669	32829	6974	249	8778953
2019	62687	33980	7339	255	10450611

注：交通运输部自2019年1月起调整了港口统计口径和部分货类吞吐量的计算方法，同时对2018年同期数作同口径调整。

Note:The Ministry of Transport has adjusted the calculation method of port statistical caliber and throughput of some cargo classes since January 2019 while making the same caliber adjustment for the corresponding period in 2018.

13-6 民航运输主要指标
Main Indicators on Civil Aviation

项　　目	Item	2018	2019
客运量（万人次）	Passenger Traffic (10000 person-times)	8913	9630
国际航线	International Routes	1752	1644
国内航线	Domestic Routes	7161	7986
# 地区航线	Regional Routes	118	114
旅客周转量（万人公里）	Passenger-kilometers (10000 person-km)	18026137	19805544
国际航线	International Routes	6133646	7101487
国内航线	Domestic Routes	11892491	12704057
# 地区航线	Regional Routes	183046	176100
货邮运量（吨）	Freight Traffic (ton)	1370791	1397951
国际航线	International Routes	622204	667100
国内航线	Domestic Routes	748587	730851
# 地区航线	Regional Routes	14801	16250
货邮周转量（万吨公里）	Freight Ton-kilometers (10000 ton-km)	673332	674994
国际航线	International Routes	549957	551179
国内航线	Domestic Routes	123375	123815
# 地区航线	Regional Routes	1763	1852
总周转量（万吨公里）	Total Air Traffic Ton-kilometers(10000 ton-km)	2258564	2415017
国际航线	International Routes	1088018	1173479
国内航线	Domestic Routes	1170546	1241538
# 地区航线	Regional Routes	17808	17318
飞行班次（班次）	Flying Times of General Aviation (time)	667382	695472
国际航线	International Routes	96425	107560
国内航线	Domestic Routes	570957	587912
# 地区航线	Regional Routes	7974	7723
飞行时间（小时）	Flying Time of General Aviation (hr)	1880921	1994190
运输飞行	Transportation Flying	1858979	1978929
专业飞行	Flying for Special Purpose	21942	15261

13-7 民航航线及飞机年末数

Number of Civil Aviation Routes and Civil Aircraft at Year-end

指标名称	Item	2018	2019
定期航班航线条数　(条)	Number of Civil Aviation Routes (line)	845	978
国际航线	International Routes	175	194
国内航线	Domestic Routes	670	784
# 地区航线	Regional Routes	18	20
定期航班航线里程(公里)	Length of Civil Aviation Routes (km)	2056444	1953574
国际航线	International Routes	639757	657709
国内航线	Domestic Routes	1416687	1295865
# 地区航线	Regional Routes	32336	32474
民航飞机期末架数　(架)	Number of Civil Aircraft (unit)	555	708
运输飞机	Aero Transport	524	687
大中型飞机	Air Bus	504	673
小型飞机	Puddle-jumper	20	14
通用航空飞机	General Aircraft	31	21
教学校验飞机	Others		
国外通航国家和地区(个)	Foreign Countries and Regions Linked with Civil Aviation Routes(unit)	44	48
通航城市　(个)	Cities Linked with Civil Aviation Routes (unit)	246	325
# 国外通航城市	Foreign Cities Linked with Civil Aviation Routes	82	131

13-8 白云国际机场吞吐量

Volume Handled in Baiyun International Airport

项　　目	Item	2018	2019
飞机起降架次　（万次）	Number of Aircrafts Taking off and Landing (10000 times)	47.74	49.12
进　港	Landing	23.87	24.56
出　港	Taking off	23.87	24.56
旅客吞吐量　（万人次）	Volume of Passengers Handled (10000 person-times)	6974	7339
进　港	Landing	3466	3639
出　港	Taking off	3509	3699
货邮行吞吐量　（万吨）	Volume of Freight Handled (10000 ton)	249.33	254.85
进　港	Landing	113.56	113.12
出　港	Taking off	135.77	141.73
航线条数　（条）	Number of Civil Aviation Routes (line)	256	327
国际航线	International Routes	92	115
国内航线	Domestic Routes	164	212
# 地区航线	Regional Routes	4	4
国外通航国家和地区　（个）	Foreign Countries and Regions Linked with Civil Aviation Routes (unit)	41	48
通航城市	Cities Linked with Civil Aviation Routes	207	240
# 国外通航城市	Foreign Cities Linked with Civil Aviation Routes	74	91

注：本表数据由白云国际机场提供。

Note:The data in this table are provided by Baiyun International Airport.

13-9 输油(气)管道基本情况(2019年)
Basic Statistics on Pipelines (2019)

项目	Item	合计 Total	#输成品油管道 Refined Oil Pipelines	#输其他气体管道 Others Gas Pipelines
条数 (条)	Number Of Pipelines (unit)	31	18	11
输油(气)里程 (公里)	Length Of Pipelines (km)	121.89	57.07	61.42
延展长度 (公里)	Extension Length of Pipelines (km)	121.89	57.07	61.42
输油(气)能力	Capacity of Pipeline Traffic	5030.76	4023.28	987.48
(万吨/年、千万立方米/年)	(10000 ton/year, 10 million cu.m/year)			
输油(气)量 (万吨)	Pipeline Traffic (10000 tons)	997.84	820.60	169.62
输油(气)周转量 (万吨公里)	Ton-kilometers (10000 ton-km)	4949.67	4335.11	588.66

注：本表数据由中石化广州分公司提供。
Note:The data in this table are provided by Sinopec Guangzhou Branch.

13-10 港口码头泊位数
Number of Berths in Ports

项目	Item	2018	2019
总计	**Total**		
码头长度 (米)	Length of Quay Line (m)	70229	70999
泊位 (个)	Number of Berths (unit)	807	809
#万吨级	10000 Ton Class	76	78
泊位年通过能力	Berths Capacity		
#货物 (万吨)	Cargo (10000 tons)	37445	37445
集装箱 (万TEU)	Containers (10000 TEU)	1576	1576
旅客 (万人)	Passengers (10000 persons)	2862	2937
汽车 (万辆)	Automobile (10000 units)	1034	1034
生产用	**For Productive Use**		
码头长度 (米)	Length of Quay Line (m)	58535	59305
泊位 (个)	Number of Berths (unit)	631	633
#万吨级	10000 Ton Class	73	75

注：本表数据由广州市港务局提供。
Note:The data in this table are provided by Guangzhou Port Bureau.

13-11 港口吞吐量及货物分类（2019年）

Volume Handled in Ports and Type of Freight (2019)

单位：万吨 (10000 tons)

项　目	Item	合　计 Total	出 港 Out-port	进 港 In-port	#沿海港口 Coastal Harbour	出 港 Out-port	进 港 In-port
货物吞吐量	**Volume of Freight Handled**	**62687.30**	**26536.03**	**36151.27**	**60615.83**	**25997.58**	**34618.25**
外　贸	Foreign Trade	14401.01	5258.79	9142.22	14229.10	5184.73	9044.37
内　贸	Inland Trade	48286.29	21277.24	27009.05	46386.73	20812.85	25573.88
货物分类	**Type of Freight**						
煤炭及制品	Coal and Related Products	7297.91	2325.36	4972.55	7038.54	2325.36	4713.18
石油、天然气及制品	Petroleum, Natural Gas and Related Products	2206.11	928.48	1277.63	2151.31	914.69	1236.62
#原　油	Crude Oil	12.68	6.34	6.34	12.68	6.34	6.34
金属矿石	Metal Ores	535.66	12.04	523.62	535.66	12.04	523.62
钢　铁	Steel and Iron	3487.91	921.17	2566.74	3424.05	906.06	2517.99
矿建材料	Mineral Building Materials	10017.97	4541.09	5476.88	9702.99	4523.73	5179.26
水　泥	Cement	215.97	162.25	53.72	48.95	22.68	26.27
木　材	Timber	375.76	81.02	294.74	375.76	81.02	294.74
非金属矿石	Nonmetal Ores	377.22	131.10	246.12	278.29	131.10	147.19
化肥及农药	Chemical Fertilizers and Pesticides	32.93	6.16	26.77	19.67	6.16	13.51
盐	Salt	12.42	0.15	12.27	12.06	0.15	11.91
粮　食	Grain	2611.97	707.80	1904.17	2484.67	706.88	1777.79
机械、设备、电器	Machinery, Equipment and Electric Appliance	3837.58	1900.63	1936.95	3792.52	1876.78	1915.74
化工原料及制品	Chemical Raw Materials and Related Products	1065.94	160.24	905.70	802.24	157.76	644.48
有色金属	Nonferrous Metals	55.09	9.02	46.07	55.09	9.02	46.07
轻工、医药产品	Light Industry, Medical and Pharmacestical Products	1002.13	324.99	677.14	866.12	260.23	605.89
农林牧渔业产品	Agricultural, Forestry, Animal Husbandry and Fishery Products	414.18	45.26	368.92	333.83	29.29	304.54
其　他	Others	29140.55	14279.27	14861.28	28694.08	14034.63	14659.45

注：本表数据由广州市港务局提供。

Note:The data in this table are provided by Guangzhou Port Bureau.

13-12 港口标准集装箱吞吐量(2019年)

Cargo Handled in International Standard Containers (2019)

项目	Item	合计 Total	出港 Out-port	进港 In-port
箱数合计 (万箱)	Total Containers (10000 units)	2323.62	1172.14	1151.48
重量合计 (万吨)	Total Weight (10000 tons)	33980.28	16004.70	17975.58
国内小计	National Total			
箱数 (万箱)	Number of Containers(10000 units)	1450.05	739.79	710.26
重量 (万吨)	Weight (10000 tons)	24536.73	11067.37	13469.36
国际小计	International Total			
箱数 (万箱)	Number of Containers(10000 units)	873.57	432.35	441.22
# 中国香港	Hong Kong, China	290.57	147.07	143.50
新加坡	Singapore	31.29	17.19	14.10
马来西亚	Malaysia	34.49	27.10	7.40
韩国	Korea, Rep.	15.49	4.11	11.38
印尼	Indonesia	8.26	7.63	0.63
日本	Japan	4.76	1.18	3.58
泰国	Thailand	3.69	2.91	0.78
意大利	Italia	1.12	0.83	0.29
重量 (万吨)	Weight (10000 tons)	9443.54	4937.32	4506.22
# 中国香港	Hong Kong, China	4038.96	1772.34	2266.62
新加坡	Singapore	360.52	228.86	131.66
马来西亚	Malaysia	423.55	364.22	59.33
韩国	Korea, Rep.	181.60	25.90	155.70
印尼	Indonesia	113.27	110.99	2.28
日本	Japan	49.01	15.87	33.14
泰国	Thailand	47.56	37.02	10.54
意大利	Italia	14.75	11.30	3.45

注：本表数据由广州市港务局提供。

Note:The data in this table are provided by Guangzhou Port Bureau.

13-13 邮政电信网

Network of Postal and Telecommunication Services

项　　目	Item	2018	2019
邮政网　（个）	Post Network (unit)	243	243
自办邮政网点	Post Office Owned by Itself	183	184
代办网点	Commission Office	60	59
邮政储蓄所　（个）	Postal Savings Office (unit)	131	131
信箱、信筒　（个）	Mail Box (unit)	963	944
电信网　（个）	Telecommunication Office (unit)	11577	10927
自办电信网点	Telecommunication Office Owned by Itself	422	409
代办网点	Commission Office	11155	10518
邮政网络　（公里）	Postal Service Network (km)		
邮路总长度	Total Length of Mail Routes	54719	54719
农村投递线路总长度	Length of Rural Delivery Routes	32461	27854

13-14 邮政业务主要指标
Main Indicators on Post

项 目	Item	2018	2019
国内分类业务总量	Category of Domestic Services		
函 件 （万件）	Number of Letters (10000 pcs)	11641	11174
包 裹 （万件）	Packages (10000 pcs)	45	42
汇 兑 （万笔）	Remittance (10000 transactions)	52	31
订销报纸累计数 （万份）	Number of Newspapers Circulation (10000 copies)	14193	13504
订销杂志累计数 （万份）	Number of Magazines Circulation (10000 copies)	1161	1294
快 递 （万件）	Pieces of Express Mail Services (10000 pcs)	506448	634680
同 城	City Express	105661	105013
异 地	Long-distance Express	393272	518793
国际及港澳台	International and Hong Kong, Macao and Taiwan Express	7514	10874
邮政储蓄年末收储余额 （万元）	Postal Savings Deposits at Year-end (10000 yuan)	3579217	3983986

13-15 电信业务主要指标

Main Indicators on Telecommunication Services

项　　目	Item	2018	2019
通信业务量	Business Volume of Telecommunications		
移动电话用户　（万户）	Number of Mobile Telephone Subscribers (10000 subscribers)	4007.73	3644.56
# 3G移动电话用户	3G Mobile Telephone Subscribers	98.60	86.12
4G移动电话用户	4G Mobile Telephone Subscribers	2509.66	2671.77
5G移动电话用户	5G Mobile Telephone Subscribers		23.11
移动短信通信量　（亿条）	Short Message Services (100 million)	40.37	33.62
固定电话用户　（万户）	Landline Users (10000 subscribers)	370.98	330.57
公用电话　（万户）	Number of Public Telephones (10000 subscribers)	43.42	40.59
互联网宽带接入用户	Broadband Users	544.17	565.83
移动互联网用户	Mobile Internet Users	3129.16	3256.43
电信主要通信能力	Main Communication Capacity of Telecommunications		
长途电话交换机容量（万路端）	Capacity of Long-distance Telephone Exchanges (10000 circuits)	50.20	50.20
电话交换机总容量　（万门）	Capacity of Telephone Exchanges (10000 gates)	80.68	81.17
局用交换机容量	Capacity of Office Exchanges	40.37	39.91
接入网交换机容量	Capacity of Exchanges Linked-out	40.31	41.27
移动电话交换机容量　（万户）	Capacity of Mobile Telephone Exchanges (10000 subscribers)	4985	4985
移动电话基站数　（个）	Number of Mobile Phone Base Station (unit)	114236	134284
互联网宽带接入端口　（个）	Broad Band Subscribers Post Of Internet (unit)	12143146	13759938

13-16 邮电业务收入

Revenue of Postal and Telecommunication Services

单位：万元 (10000 yuan)

项　　目	Item	2018	2019
总　　计	**Total**	**8778953**	**10450611**
#港澳及国际	Hong Kong, Macao and International	553327	724081
邮政收入	**Revenue of Posts**	**5181081**	**6861781**
#港澳及国际	Hong Kong, Macao and International	538418	686968
函　　件	Letters	79369	96359
快　　递	Express Mail Services	4797456	6354932
汇　　兑	Postal Orders	2999	2061
包　　裹	Package	7662	6196
报　　刊	Newspapers and Magazines	8341	8508
其　　他	Others	285254	393724
电信收入	**Revenue of Telecommunications**	**3597872**	**3588830**
#港澳及国际	Hong Kong, Macao and International	14909	37113
固定电话收入	Fixed-line Telephone	130422	105407
移动电话收入	Mobile Telephone	2250361	2219930
宽带收入	Broadband Network	472049	452981
其他收入	Other Revenue	745040	810512

13-17 城市公共交通（2019年）

Public Traffic in City (2019)

项　目	Item	合计 Total	汽车 Buses	电车 Trolleys
营运车、船数 （辆、艘）	Number of Vehicles and Vessels (unit)	38510	15105	283
营运车船客位数 （个）	Seat for Vehicles and Vessels for Business Transportation (seat)	1862113	1014406	24339
营运线路条数 （条）	Lines Used by Public Traffic for Business Transportation (line)	1296	1254	14
营运线路长度 （公里）	Length of Public Traffic (km)	24944	24188	180
客运量 （万人次）	Number of Passenger Traffic (10000 person-times)	609935	219026	5064
客运收入 （万元）	Revenue of Passenger Transport (10000 yuan)	1102108	402454	5725
每辆汽、电车负担人数（人）	Number of Passengers per Bus and Trolley (person)	620		

13-17 续表 continued

项　目	Item	轮渡 Ferries	出租汽车 Cabs	轨道交通 Track Traffic
营运车、船数 （辆、艘）	Number of Vehicles and Vessels (unit)	46	20222	2854
营运车船客位数 （个）	Seat for Vehicles and Vessels for Business Transportation (seat)	9157	80666	733545
营运线路条数 （条）	Lines Used by Public Traffic for Business Transportation (line)	13		15
营运线路长度 （公里）	Length of Public Traffic (km)	53		523
客运量 （万人次）	Number of Passenger Traffic (10000 person-times)	1354	53497	330994
客运收入 （万元）	Revenue of Passenger Transport (10000 yuan)	1191	109680	583058
每辆汽、电车负担人数（人）	Number of Passengers per Bus and Trolley (person)			

注：1.本表数据由广州市交通运输局等单位提供。
　　2.营运车船客位数按行驶证上核定载人数计算。

Note: I. The data in this table are provided by Guangzhou Municipal Transportation Burea,etc.
　　II. Seats of vehicles and vessels for business tran-sportation are caculated by the number of passengers authorized on the driving license.

13-18 规模以上运输邮电企业财务指标（2019年）

单位：万元

项目	Item	企业单位数（个）Number of Enterprises (unit)	# 亏损企业 Loss-making Enterprises	营业收入 Business Revenue	营业成本 Business Costs	营业税金及附加 Tax and Extra Charges on Business
合计	**Total**	**774**	**167**	**36022636**	**30122762**	**189748**
按经济类型分	**Grouped by Economic Type**					
1. 内资	Domestic Funded	715	159	31687826	27371726	175295
2. 港、澳、台商投资	Enterprises with Funds from Hong Kong, Macao and Taiwan Investors	24	4	2751723	1768199	5866
3. 外商投资	Foreign Funded Enterprises	35	4	1583087	982837	8587
按行业类型分	Grouped by Sector Type					
1. 公路运输	Highway Transport	575	117	10049693	7687058	111139
2. 水上运输	Waterway Transport	73	15	4205528	3482875	14009
# 港 口	Port	20	1	943025	699527	7104
3. 民 航	Civil Aviation	12	3	12500297	11088265	32527
4. 邮 电	Postal and Telecom-munication Services	108	28	7757384	6387448	26014
5. 其 它	Others	6	4	1509734	1477118	6060

Finance Indicators of Transport, Postal and Telecommunication Services Enterprises above the Designated Size (2019)

(10000 yuan)

销售费用 Selling Expenses	管理费用 Management Expenses	财务费用 Financial Expenses	营业利润 Business Profits	利润总额 Total Profits	所得税费用 Income Tax Expenses	应付职工薪酬 Total Wages Payable	应交增值税 Value-added Tax Payable	平均用工人数(人) Average Number of Employed Persons (person)
1177046	**1977550**	**2283603**	**2994074**	**3073268**	**828737**	**6035765**	**527354**	**341064**
1019063	1761829	2084223	1896098	1932258	652268	5475158	407687	305269
129190	152855	78785	726317	756957	107241	334567	79498	19455
28793	62866	120595	371660	384053	69229	226040	40169	16340
101457	680751	1287458	1378069	1450731	263756	2096899	216343	157621
13536	323582	228292	189693	141570	78271	586328	24840	17908
9314	108860	37417	301618	242449	53341	194476	11689	7831
564767	337050	577915	206326	276516	75956	1858520	77586	84878
497175	612163	-101599	1285988	1274315	407703	1226729	188451	66095
111	24004	291537	-66001	-69864	3052	267289	20135	14562

【货(客)运量】 指在一定时期内，各种运输工具实际运送的货物重量（旅客数量）。货运按吨计算,客运按人计算。货物不论运输距离长短、货物类别,均按实际重量统计；旅客不论行程远近或票价多少,均按一人一次作为客运量统计；半价票、小孩票也按一人统计。

【货物(旅客)周转量】 指在一定时期内，由各种运输工具运送的货物（旅客）数量与其相应运输距离的乘积之总和。该指标反映可以运输业生产总成果，也是编制和检查运输生产计划,计算运输效率、劳动生产率以及核算运输单位成本的主要基础资料。计算货物周转量通常按发出站与到达站之间的最短距离，也就是计费距离计算。计算公式为：

货物（(旅客)周转量=Σ（货物（旅客）运输量×运输距离）

【移动电话用户】 指在电信运营企业营业网点办理开户登记手续，通过移动电话交换机进入移动电话网、占用移动电话号码的各类电话用户。包括各类签约用户、智能网预付费用户、无线上网卡用户。

【Freight (Passenger) Traffic】 refers to the weight of freight (number of passenger) transported with various means within a specific period of time. Freight transport is calculated in tons and passenger traffic is calculated in terms of number of persons. Freight transport is calculated in terms of the actual weight of the goods and takes no account of the type of freight and distance of travel. Passenger traffic is calculated by the principle that one person can be counted only once in one trip and takes no account of the travelling distance and ticket price. The passengers who travel with a half price ticket or a child's ticket is also calculated as one person.

【Freight Ton-kilometres (Passenger-kilometres)】 refers to the sum of the product of the volume of transported cargo (passengers) multiplied by the transport distance. It is an important indicator to reflect the achievement of the transportation industry. This is an important indicator to show the total results of the transport industry; to prepare and examine the transport plan; and to serve as the main basic data for calculating the efficiency, labour productivity and unit cost of transport. Normally, the shortest distance between the departure station and the destination station (i.e., the payable distance) is the basis in calculating the freight ton-kilometres. The formula is as follows:

Freight ton-kilometres (passenger-kilometres)=∑freight (passenger) traffic×distance of transportation

【Mobile Telephone Subscribers】 refer to persons who have gone through registration procedures in the operation points of enterprises engaged in telecommunications and are hence connected with the mobile telephone communication network through the mobile telephone switchboards and occupy mobile phone numbers. Included are various types of subscriber, prepaid users for intelligent network and wireless network card users.

第十四篇 CHAPTER 14

国内贸易

DOMESTIC TRADE

第十四篇　国内贸易

一、本篇资料反映广州市国内市场发展的基本情况。

二、本篇资料由广州市统计局贸易外经统计处整理提供。

三、本篇资料主要根据国家统计局制定的批发和零售业、住宿和餐饮业统计报表制度，通过采取全面调查、抽样调查等方法，对基层数据汇总取得。

四、各表的调查范围：

社会消费品零售总额表的调查范围是各种经济类型的批发和零售业、住宿和餐饮业法人单位、产业活动单位及个体户。

批发和零售业商品购、销、存总额表的调查范围是各种经济类型的批发和零售业法人单位及个体户。

商品购、销、存类值表的调查范围是各种经济类型的限额以上批发和零售业的法人单位及个体户。

财务状况表的调查范围是各种经济类型的限额以上批发和零售业、住宿和餐饮法人单位。

五、关于历史数据调整问题

根据2018年第四次经济普查结果，对1992年-2018年社会消费品零售总额进行了调整。

14 Domestic Trade

I.The data in this chapter show the development of Guangzhou's domestic markets.

II.The data in this chapter are prepared and provided by the Division of Trade and External Economic Relations Statistics of Guangzhou Municipal Bureau of Statistics.

III.The data are obtained mainly in accordance with the Statistical Reporting Scheme on Wholesale and Retail Trade and Catering Services stipulated by the National Bureau of Statistics. The Methods used in data collection for enterprises (units) are complete enumeration and sample surveys, under which data are reported from lower to higher level statistical offices.

IV. The statistical coverage comes as follows:

The total retail sales of social consumer goods covered the retail value of the corporation units, economic active units and individual operators of all economic types of wholesale and retail trade, accommodation and catering industry.

The investigated objects of total purchases and sales and inventory of wholesale and retail trade come from corporation units and individual operators.

The investigated objects of commodity purchases, sales and inventory covered the corporation units and individual operators of wholesale and retail trade enterprises above the designated size.

The investigated objects of financial situation covered the corporation units of wholesale and retail trade, catering and accommodation above the designated size.

V. Based on results from the Fourth National Economic Census in 2018, the total retail sales consumer goods from year 1992 to 2018 are revised. The data of year 2008 are from the census in 2008.

14-1 主要年份社会消费品零售总额

Total Retail Sales of Consumer Goods in Main Years

单位：万元 (10000 yuan)

年 份 Year	总 计 Total	按行业分 By Sector			
		批发和零售业 Wholesale and Retail Trades	住宿和餐饮业 Hotels and Catering Services	其他行业 Others	#制造业 Manufacturing
1978	176300	148378	16242	11680	7327
1980	287127	224457	23307	39363	24261
1985	749841	499571	115750	134520	64827
1986	802044	536172	107943	157929	69972
1987	952332	622077	134437	195818	67362
1988	1303688	833448	175891	294349	86936
1989	1442483	910670	234931	296882	90114
1990	1477826	945047	239607	293172	74574
1991	1701215	1062833	286924	351458	83978
1992	2149240	1396818	317912	434510	108827
1993	3114295	2095692	401053	617550	167954
1994	4499972	3028655	570592	900725	275664
1995	5712275	3864311	706234	1141730	344573
1996	6590603	4700098	813954	1076551	355871
1997	7693181	5493784	944091	1255306	488769
1998	8848523	6327972	1100940	1419611	549565
1999	9727415	6984432	1261213	1481770	588325
2000	10795918	8128043	1425322	1242553	567860
2001	11894799	9046636	1628785	1219378	544127
2002	12934476	9906249	1788390	1239837	449640
2003	14004188	11864803	1867179	272206	
2004	15654635	13575131	1976852	102652	
2005	17650089	15498368	2104240	47481	
2006	20085340	17842916	2242424		
2007	23459002	21032527	2426475		
2008	28363730	25583434	2780296		
2009	31708764	28630223	3078541		
2010	38090381	34227990	3862391		
2011	43672840	39217193	4455647		
2012	48996900	43912294	5084606		
2013	55667741	50110919	5556822		
2014	62527057	56554832	5972225		
2015	69944246	63339740	6604506		
2016	75620262	68568734	7051528		
2017	81906273	74428793	7477480		
2018	88109103	80207859	7901244		
2019	95515699	86921314	8594385		

注：2019年，根据第四次全国经济普查结果，对1992—2018年社零数据进行了修订。
Note:According to the results of the fourth national economic census, the total retail sales of consumer goods from 1992 to 2018 are revised In 2019.

14-2 主要年份社会消费品零售总额指数

Indices of Total Retail Sales of Consumer Goods in Main Years

上年=100 (preceding year=100)

年份 Year	总计 Total	按行业分 By Sector			
		批发和零售业 Wholesale and Retail Trades	住宿和餐饮业 Hotels and Catering Services	其他行业 Others	# 制造业 Manufacturing
1978	106.6	105.6	118.2	104.3	95.4
1980	136.1	130.5	121.6	198.2	181.8
1985	138.1	124.7	224.2	147.9	133.1
1986	107.0	107.3	93.3	117.4	107.9
1987	118.7	116.0	124.5	124.0	96.3
1988	136.9	134.0	130.8	150.3	129.1
1989	110.6	109.3	133.6	100.9	103.7
1990	102.4	103.8	102.0	98.8	82.8
1991	115.1	112.5	119.8	119.9	112.6
1992	126.3	131.4	110.8	123.6	129.6
1993	144.9	150.0	126.2	142.1	154.3
1994	144.5	144.5	142.3	145.9	164.1
1995	126.9	127.6	123.8	126.8	125.0
1996	115.4	121.6	115.3	94.3	103.3
1997	116.7	116.9	116.0	116.6	137.3
1998	115.0	115.2	116.6	113.1	112.4
1999	109.9	110.4	114.6	104.4	107.1
2000	111.0	116.4	113.0	83.9	96.5
2001	110.2	111.3	114.3	98.1	95.8
2002	108.7	109.5	109.8	101.7	82.6
2003	108.3	119.8	104.4	22.0	
2004	111.8	114.4	105.9	37.7	
2005	112.7	114.2	106.4	46.3	
2006	113.8	115.1	106.6		
2007	116.8	117.9	108.2		
2008	120.9	121.6	114.6		
2009	111.8	111.9	110.7		
2010	120.1	119.6	125.5		
2011	114.7	114.6	115.4		
2012	112.2	112.0	114.1		
2013	113.6	114.1	109.3		
2014	112.3	112.9	107.5		
2015	111.9	112.0	110.6		
2016	108.1	108.3	106.8		
2017	108.3	108.5	106.0		
2018	107.6	107.8	105.7		
2019	108.4	108.4	108.8		

注：1.当年指数按可比口径计算。

2.2019年，根据第四次全国经济普查结果，对1992—2018年社零数据进行了修订。

Note: I. The indices are calculated at the comparable coverage.

II. According to the results of the fourth national economic census,the total retail sales of consumer goods from 1992 to 2018 are revised In 2019.

14-3 各时期社会消费品零售总额

Total Retail Sales of Consumer Goods in Different Periods

单位：万元 (10000 yuan)

时　期	Period	总　计 Total	按行业分 By Sector 批发和零售业 Wholesale and Retail Trades	住宿和餐饮业 Hotels and Catering Services	其他行业 Others	# 制造业 Manufacturing
“六五”时期	6th Five-year Plan Period	2459903	1775024	260620	424259	222331
“七五”时期	7th Five-year Plan Period	5978373	3847414	892809	1238150	388958
“八五”时期	8th Five-year Plan Period	17176997	11448309	2282715	3445973	980996
“九五”时期	9th Five-year Plan Period	43655640	31634329	5545520	6475791	2550390
“十五”时期	10th Five-year Plan Period	72138187	59891187	9365446	2881554	993767
“十一五”时期	11th Five-year Plan Period	141707217	127317090	14390127		
“十二五”时期	12th Five-year Plan Period	280808784	253134978	27673806		
1979-2019	1979-2019	905574555	799571455	91478154		

注：2019年，根据第四次全国经济普查结果，对1992—2018年社零数据进行了修订。
Note:According to the results of the fourth national economic census, the total retail sales of consumer goods from 1992 to 2018 are revised In 2019.

14-4 社会消费品零售总额

Total Retail Sales of Consumer Goods

单位:万元 (10000 yuan)

项　　目	Item	2018	2019
社会消费品零售总额	**Total**	**88109103**	**95515699**
按行业分	**By Sector**		
批发和零售业	Wholesale and Retail Trades	80207859	86921314
限额以上	Enterprises above Designated Size	38998530	39696055
限额以下	Enterprises (Units) below Designated Size and Individuals	41209329	47225259
住宿和餐饮业	Hotels and Catering Services	7901244	8594385
限额以上	Enterprises above Designated Size	3735857	3741295
限额以下	Enterprises (Units) below Designated Size and Individuals	4165387	4853090

注：根据第四次全国经济普查结果，对2018年社零数据进行了修订。

Note:According to the results of the fourth national economic census, the total retail sales of consumer goods in 2018 are revised.

14-5 限额以上批发和零售业法人企业商品分类销售总额(2019年)

Total Sales Value of Enterprises above Designated Size in Wholesale and Retail Trade by Category of Commodities (2019)

单位:万元 (10000 yuan)

项目	Item	销售总额 Total Sales Value	批发额 Wholesale Value	零售额 Retail Value
合计	**Total**	**387105751**	**341224451**	**45881300**
粮油、食品类	Grain and Oil	14198501	9940373	4258128
# 肉禽蛋类	Meat, Poultry and Eggs	1841857	1480059	361798
饮料类	Beverages	3227580	2486618	740962
烟酒类	Tobacco and Liquor	4019533	3185836	833697
服装鞋帽、针、纺织品类	Garments, Footwear, Headgear, Knitwear and Textiles	14648447	10436195	4212252
服装类	Clothing	9606706	6656520	2950186
鞋帽类	Footwear and Headgear	2964458	1971533	992925
针、纺织品类	Knitwear and Textiles	2077284	1808143	269141
化妆品类	Cosmetics	5731951	3187446	2544505
金银珠宝类	Gold, Silver and Jewelry	3582677	2473696	1108981
日用品类	Daily-Use Articles	10669665	7759225	2910440
# 可穿戴智能设备类	Wearable intelligent device	23287	22134	1153
五金、电料类	Hardware and Electrical Materials	2109264	1963412	145852
体育、娱乐用品类	Sports and Recreation Articles	1338113	610761	727352
书报杂志类	Newspapers and Magazines	1034854	836433	198421
电子出版物及音像制品类	E-journal and Video Products	31998	28096	3902
家用电器和音像器材类	Household Appliances and Video Appliances	6972723	4211636	2761087
中西药品类	Traditional Chinese and Western Medicines	20873707	18484922	2388785
# 西药	Western Medicines	15845024	13767952	2077072
中草药及中成药	Traditional Chinese Medicines	3518248	3345365	172883
文化办公用品类	Cultural and Office Goods	5667459	4223267	1444192
家具类	Furniture	1450139	1177699	272440
通讯器材类	Communication Appliances	5884347	1836861	4047486
煤炭及制品类	Coal and Related Products	8715968	8715968	
木材及制品类	Wood and Wooden Products	689275	689275	
石油及制品类	Petroleum and Related Products	59804233	55494119	4310114
化工材料及制品类	Chemical Materials and Related Products	22891948	22891948	
# 化肥类	Chemical Fertilizers	876650	876650	
金属材料类	Metal Materials	102171157	102171157	
建筑及装潢材料类	Building and Decoration Materials	5416117	5347337	68780
机电产品及设备类	Mechanical and Electrical Products	8313728	8247093	66635
# 农机类	Agricultural Machinery	16849	16849	
汽车类	Motor Vehicles	66119554	53585375	12534179
种子饲料类	Seeds and Feedstuff	2637752	2637752	
棉麻类	Cotton and Hemp	710565	710565	
其他类	Others	8194496	7891386	303110

14-6 限额以上批发业法人企业商品购、销、存总额(2019年)

单位：万元

项　　目	Item
合　计	**Wholesale Trade**
#国有及国有控股	State-owned and State-controlled Enterprises
按登记注册类型分	**By Status of Registration**
内资企业	Domestic-funded Enterprises
国有企业	State-owned Enterprises
集体企业	Collective-owned Enterprises
股份合作企业	Cooperative Enterprises
联营企业	Joint Ownership Enterprises
国有联营企业	State Joint Ownership Enterprises
集体联营企业	Collective Joint Ownership Enterprises
国有与集体联营企业	Joint State-collective Enterprises
其他联营企业	Other Joint Ownership Enterprise
有限责任公司	Limited Liability Corporations
国有独资企业	State Sole Funded Corporations
其他有限责任公司	Other Limited Liability Corporations
股份有限公司	Share-holding Corporations Ltd.
私营企业	Private Enterprises
私营独资企业	Private-funded Enterprises
私营合伙企业	Private Partnership Enterprises
私营有限责任公司	Private Limited Liability Corporations
私营股份有限公司	Private Share-holding Corporations Ltd.
其他企业	Other Enterprises
港、澳、台商投资企业	Enterprises with Funds from Hong Kong, Macao and Taiwan
与港、澳、台商合资经营企业	Joint-venture Enterprises
与港、澳、台商合作经营企业	Cooperative Enterprises
港、澳、台商独资经营企业	Enterprises with Sole Funds
港、澳、台商投资股份有限公司	Share-holding Corporations Ltd.
其他港、澳、台投资企业	Other Enterprises with Funds from Hong Kong, Macao and Taiwan
外商投资企业	Foreign Funded Enterprises
中外合资经营企业	Joint-venture Enterprises
中外合作经营企业	Cooperative Enterprises
外资企业	Enterprises with Sole Foreign Funds
外商投资股份有限公司	Share-holding Corporations Ltd.
其他外商投资企业	Other Foreign Funded Enterprises
按国民经济行业分组	**By Economic Sector**
农、林、牧产品批发	Wholesale of Farming, Forestry, Animal Husbandry Products
食品、饮料及烟草制品批发	Wholesale of Food, Beverages and Tobacco Products
#米、面制品及食用油批发	Wholesale of Rice, Flour and Edible Oil
烟草制品批发	Wholesale of Tobacco
纺织、服装及家庭用品批发	Wholesale of Textile, Clothing and Household Goods
#服装批发	Wholesale of Garments
家用视听设备批发	Wholesale of Household Electrical Appliances
文化、体育用品及器材批发	Wholesale of Cultural, Sports Appliances and Equipment
医药及医疗器材批发	Wholesale of Medicine and Medical Appliances
矿产品、建材及化工产品批发	Wholesale of Mineral Products, Building Materials and Chemical Products
#煤炭及制品批发	Wholesale of Coal and Related Products
石油及制品批发	Wholesale of Petroleum and Related Products
金属及金属矿批发	Wholesale of Metal Minerals
建材批发	Wholesale of Building Materials
化肥批发	Wholesale of Chemical Fertilizers
机械设备、五金产品及电子产品批发	Wholesale of Mechanical Equipment, Metal Products and Electronic Products
#汽车及零配件批发	Wholesale of Automobile and Automobile Accessories
摩托车及零配件批发	Wholesale of Motorcycles and Accessories
计算机、软件及辅助设备批发	Wholesale of Computers, Software and Assistant Equipments
贸易经纪与代理	Trade Broker and Agency
其他批发业	Wholesale of Other Trades

Total Purchases, Sales and Stock of Enterprises above Designated Size in Wholesale Trade (2019)

(10000 yuan)

购进总额 Total Purchase Value	# 进口 Imports Value	销售总额 Total Sales Value	批发额 Wholesale Value	零售额 Retail Value	年末库存 Stock at Year-end
330562486	**14518581**	**342337012**	**336977949**	**5359063**	**15471710**
22537503	1357551	23939850	23866151	73699	1281716
271837541	9579294	276378887	273100856	3278031	12041312
1001017	97532	1339581	1319769	19812	391285
95410		105698	103874	1824	4416
118388	1738	134265	129458	4807	7312
1450		2317	2317		
1450		2317	2317		
129226510	4734797	137268254	136179822	1088432	4171409
21535036	1260019	22597952	22544065	53887	890431
107691474	3474778	114670302	113635757	1034545	3280978
48359529	683037	35931779	35621331	310448	1924340
93035237	4062190	101596993	99744285	1852708	5542550
22160		23643	22135	1508	2739
4755		5332	5332		438
91728427	3958831	100247535	98418792	1828743	5430715
1279895	103359	1320483	1298026	22457	108658
13895244	1805136	17110377	16850975	259402	2050101
5096006	907374	5451756	5445256	6500	498069
8679579	889930	11495169	11243516	251653	1521936
57414	7600	92687	92522	165	26063
62245	232	70765	69681	1084	4033
44829701	3134151	48847748	47026118	1821630	1380297
31764772	1052667	34418075	32701844	1716231	564217
107271	107271	107271	107271		
12448256	1966186	13732904	13653529	79375	797277
32725	7738	34720	34720		134
476677	289	554778	528754	26024	18669
4579896	919128	4813019	4759606	53413	487177
13230653	1137703	16459864	16224983	234881	1917498
2260035	178664	2373162	2363371	9791	535219
1266838		1778716	1767882	10834	67511
18625962	925456	22511522	21379720	1131802	2169414
2607350	78670	3176787	2945822	230965	455611
1386553	27479	1546975	1513678	33297	126332
11071391	179551	12879872	12640869	239003	1200862
19946529	1651308	22399546	21926907	472639	2106797
201117267	6604554	194767769	192632184	2135585	5769029
8312409	802326	8665896	8664095	1801	250236
66844986	2318934	55415407	53512270	1903137	2178248
92447205	889669	94228729	94105403	123326	1698965
10968883	228197	11973106	11938466	34640	430257
1020369	155497	1097517	1097466	51	83819
59843713	2851338	65611252	64620340	990912	1684089
45601003	861471	49584126	49007905	576221	565916
140779	4985	171881	162450	9431	9131
3325193	760348	3631472	3510326	121146	204694
335503	26698	386846	386845	1	12113
1811572	222845	2507322	2406495	100827	124731

14-7 限额以上零售业法人企业商品购、销、存总额(2019年)

单位：万元

项目	Item
合　计	**Retail Trade**
# 国有及国有控股	State-owned and State-controlled Enterprises
按登记注册类型分	**By Status of Registration**
内资企业	Domestic-funded Enterprises
国有企业	State-owned Enterprises
集体企业	Collective-owned Enterprises
股份合作企业	Cooperative Enterprises
联营企业	Joint Ownership Enterprises
国有联营企业	State Joint Ownership Enterprises
集体联营企业	Collective Joint Ownership Enterprises
国有与集体联营企业	Joint State-collective Enterprises
其他联营企业	Other Joint Ownership Enterprise
有限责任公司	Limited Liability Corporations
国有独资企业	State Sole Funded Corporations
其他有限责任公司	Other Limited Liability Corporations
股份有限公司	Share-holding Corporations Ltd.
私营企业	Private Enterprises
私营独资企业	Private-funded Enterprises
私营合伙企业	Private Partnership Enterprises
私营有限责任公司	Private Limited Liability Corporations
私营股份有限公司	Private Share-holding Corporations Ltd.
其他企业	Other Enterprises
港、澳、台商投资企业	Enterprises with Funds from Hong Kong, Macao and Taiwan
与港、澳、台商合资经营企业	Joint-venture Enterprises
与港、澳、台商合作经营企业	Cooperative Enterprises
港、澳、台商独资经营企业	Enterprises with Sole Funds
港、澳、台商投资股份有限公司	Share-holding Corporations Ltd.
其他港、澳、台投资企业	Other Enterprises with Funds from Hong Kong, Macao and Taiwan
外商投资企业	Foreign Funded Enterprises
中外合资经营企业	Joint-venture Enterprises
中外合作经营企业	Cooperative Enterprises
外资企业	Enterprises with Sole Foreign Funds
外商投资股份有限公司	Share-holding Corporations Ltd.
其他外商投资企业	Other Foreign Funded Enterprises
按国民经济行业分组	**By Economic Sector**
综合零售	Comprehensive Retail Trade
# 百货零售	Retail of General Merchandise
超级市场零售	Retail of Supermarket
食品、饮料及烟草制品专门零售	Retail of Food, Beverage and Tobacco
纺织、服装及日用品专门零售	Retail of Textile, Garments and Daily Articles Consumer
# 服装零售	Retail of Garments
文化、体育用品及器材专门零售	Retail of Cultural, Sports Appliances and Equipment
# 体育用品及器材零售	Retail of Sports Goods
图书、报刊零售	Retail of Books and Newspapers
医药及医疗器材专门零售	Retail of Medicine and Medical Appliances
# 西药零售	Retail of Medicine
中药零售	Retail of Chinese Medicine
汽车、摩托车、零配件和燃料及其他动力设备零售	Retail of Motor Vehicles, Motorcycles, Fuels and Parts
# 汽车新车零售	Retail of Motor Vehicles
机动车燃油零售	Retail of Motor Vehicle Fuels
家用电器及电子产品专门零售	Retail of Household Electrical Appliances and Electronic Products
# 家用视听设备零售	Retail of Household Audio and Video Equipment
日用家电零售	Retail of Household Electrical Appliances
计算机、软件及辅助设备零售	Retail of Computers, Software and Assistant Equipments
通信设备零售	Retail of Communication Equipments
五金、家具及室内装饰材料专门零售	Retail of Hardware, Furniture and Decoration Materials
货摊、无店铺及其他零售业	Retail of Booth and Others
# 互联网零售	E-Retail

Total Purchases, Sales and Stock of Enterprises above Designated Size in Retail Trade (2019)

(10000 yuan)

购进总额 Total Purchase Value	#进口 Imports Value	销售总额 Total Sales	批发额 Wholesale Trade	零售额 Retail Trade	年末库存 Stock at Year-end
36909638	**1407059**	**44768739**	**4246502**	**40522237**	**3346549**
636318		779844	139675	640169	96955
28180316	1119467	34054572	3161920	30892652	2238351
69369		126005	12622	113383	19823
218354		266518	10163	256355	17481
30634		37445	6909	30536	2947
47910		60225	3278	56947	2114
25667		31538	2054	29484	1518
7406		9733	1224	8509	195
14837		18954		18954	401
15356676	746068	16605745	1147831	15457914	883077
526445		603347	124999	478348	75213
14830231	746068	16002398	1022832	14979566	807864
1558557	1247	3749158	664275	3084883	139013
10898816	372152	13209476	1316842	11892634	1173896
19777		25901	1569	24332	2829
12445		14550	919	13631	383
10649143	372152	12922135	1303139	11618996	1137450
217451		246890	11215	235675	33234
4861607	115390	6116922	435351	5681571	503799
1326983	22358	1729189	56425	1672764	117492
30707		38182	121	38061	3031
3497195	93032	4342464	378805	3963659	382856
6722		7087		7087	420
3867715	172202	4597245	649231	3948014	604399
1345406	66647	1677787	78056	1599731	337637
723906		733574	544284	189290	24373
1644892	71010	2033338	26628	2006710	225663
35710		39226		39226	3309
117801	34545	113320	263	113057	13417
5618953	6123	6481448	771207	5710241	415537
2835402	8	3495270	92946	3402324	196666
2292513	6115	2377442	678262	1699180	197471
532246	10915	735724	150073	585651	84406
1598410	120410	2482553	355625	2126928	749464
709420	6044	1400447	235934	1164513	559426
631841	21862	931458	238591	692867	130680
36938		58871	3423	55448	3767
170705		186183	59445	126738	37446
1124160	491	1445063	122357	1322706	152362
1059321		1348783	89671	1259112	138561
29385	396	44896	9554	35342	6130
13633288	1104070	16428134	2008849	14419285	1232495
11650733	1103010	12021197	1241613	10779584	1098776
1659796		4036671	662616	3374055	106698
3007891	2786	3298240	229375	3068865	130099
1438469		1485409	23647	1461762	6236
853599		967601	20770	946831	56734
281514		348499	47450	301049	22997
369445	1384	417731	112040	305691	25422
203085	717	280120	59554	220566	28505
10559764	139685	12685999	310871	12375128	423001
10375759	42381	12379008	256551	12122457	390634

14-8 限额以上批发业法人企业财务状况(2019年)

单位：万元

项目	Item
总计	**Total**
按登记注册类型分	**Grouped by Registration Status**
内资企业	Domestic-funded Enterprises
国有企业	State-owned Enterprises
集体企业	Collective-owned Enterprises
股份合作企业	Share-holding Cooperative Enterprises
联营企业	Joint-opeartion Enterprises
国有联营企业	State-owned Joint-opeartion Enterprises
集体联营企业	Collective Joint-opeartion Enterprises
国有与集体联营企业	Joint State-collective Enterprises
其他联营企业	Other Joint Ownership Enterprises
有限责任公司	Limited Liability Corporations
国有独资公司	State Sole Investment Corporations
其他有限责任公司	Other Limited Liability Corporations
股份有限公司	Share-holding Corporations Ltd.
私营企业	Private Enterprises
私营独资企业	Private Sole Investment Enterprises
私营合伙企业	Private Partnership Enterprises
私营有限责任公司	Private Limited Liability Corporations
私营股份有限公司	Private Share-holding Corporations Ltd.
其他企业	Other Enterprises
港、澳、台商投资企业	Enterprises with Funds from Hong Kong, Macao and Taiwan
与港、澳、台商合资经营企业	Joint-venture Enterprises
与港、澳、台商合作经营企业	Cooperative Enterprises
港、澳、台商独资经营企业	Enterprises with Sole Funds
港、澳、台商投资股份有限公司	Share-holding Corporations Ltd.
其他港、澳、台投资企业	Other Enterprises with Funds from Hong Kong, Macao and Taiwan
外商投资企业	Foreign Funded Enterprises
中外合资经营企业	Joint-venture Enterprises
中外合作经营企业	Cooperative Enterprises
外资企业	Enterprises with Sole Foreign Funds
外商投资股份有限公司	Share-holding Corporations Ltd.
其他外商投资企业	Other Foreign Funded Enterprises
按行业分	**Grouped by Sector**
农、林、牧产品批发	Wholesale of Farming, Forestry, Animal Husbandry Products
食品、饮料及烟草制品批发	Wholesale of Food, Beverages and Tobacco Products
#米、面制品及食用油批发	Wholesale of Rice, Flour and Edible Oil
烟草制品批发	Wholesale of Tobacco
纺织、服装及家庭用品批发	Wholesale of Textile, Garments and Daily Articles Consumer
#服装批发	Wholesale of Garments
家用视听设备批发	Wholesale of Household Electrical Appliances
文化、体育用品及器材批发	Wholesale of Cultural, Sports Appliances and Equipment
医药及医疗器材批发	Wholesale of Medicine and Medical Appliances
矿产品、建材及化工产品批发	Wholesale of Mineral Products, Building Materials and Chemical Products
#煤炭及制品批发	Wholesale of Coal and Related Products
石油及制品批发	Wholesale of Petroleum and Related Products
金属及金属矿批发	Wholesale of Metal Minerals
建材批发	Wholesale of Building Materials
化肥批发	Wholesale of Chemical Fertilizers
机械设备、五金产品及电子产品批发	Wholesale of Mechanical Equipment, Metal Products and Electronic Products
#汽车及零配件批发	Wholesale of Automobile
摩托车及零配件批发	Wholesale of Motorcycles and Accessories
计算机、软件及辅助设备批发	Wholesale of Computers, Software and Assistant Appliances
贸易经纪与代理	Trade Broker and Agency
其他批发业	Other Wholesales Trades

Financial Situation of Enterprises above Designated Size in Wholesale Trade (2019)

(10000 yuan)

资产总计 Total Assets	固定资产原价 Original Value of Fixed Assets	负债合计 Total Liabilities	所有者权益 Owners' Equity	营业收入 Revenue from Principal Business
123801333	**8826654**	**91516340**	**32284993**	**317674155**
97933233	7832836	73071113	24862120	260328343
1030194	39932	869092	161102	1259480
54239	8735	17115	37124	96004
62707	10330	39767	22940	124204
154	2	-21	175	2030
154	2	-21	175	2030
45342694	1154785	34040982	11301712	122332713
8358245	412867	6139884	2218361	20123295
36984449	741918	27901098	9083351	102209418
15242367	3838673	9307808	5934559	45402966
36200878	2780379	28796370	7404508	91110946
8304	157	7778	526	21061
968	79	447	521	4731
35457886	2008797	28401232	7056654	89870943
733720	771346	386913	346807	1214211
9311539	338120	6165547	3145992	15319868
3734292	129991	2572274	1162018	4834129
5486168	206388	3548721	1937447	10342609
70565	1430	23021	47544	79830
20514	311	21531	-1017	63300
16556561	655698	12279680	4276881	42025944
10099928	469305	8027983	2071945	28840697
32262	460	27569	4693	96757
6336391	182900	4084522	2251869	12568589
7344	31	3292	4052	30671
80636	3002	136314	-55678	489230
3846332	98552	2045957	1800375	4556724
10191364	620493	6669278	3522086	15091408
1959695	153070	1443152	516543	2235065
499792	72670	87137	412655	1569511
14202594	683003	10264434	3938160	20389639
2510034	86737	1744847	765187	2915125
508566	22354	337440	171126	1385192
5112116	229048	3019543	2092573	11643804
11615323	385384	8560293	3055030	20058867
58483129	5379849	44240272	14242857	184638767
2473567	64037	1467057	1006510	7670638
15944447	4195751	10954767	4989680	61108591
26224877	272709	20734802	5490075	83362951
6556247	117626	5813653	742594	10640634
493228	12254	420481	72747	1009289
18879219	1349755	15586534	3292685	58618528
11936459	115886	10449766	1486693	43915736
57486	8164	40404	17082	164428
1320121	58273	1016888	303233	3319602
216239	21844	131419	84820	369112
1255017	58726	998610	256407	2307306

14-8 续表 1

单位：万元

项　　目	Item
总　计	**Total**
按登记注册类型分	**Grouped by Registration Status**
内资企业	Domestic-funded Enterprises
国有企业	State-owned Enterprises
集体企业	Collective-owned Enterprises
股份合作企业	Share-holding Cooperative Enterprises
联营企业	Joint-opeartion Enterprises
国有联营企业	State-owned Joint-opeartion Enterprises
集体联营企业	Collective Joint-opeartion Enterprises
国有与集体联营企业	Joint State-collective Enterprises
其他联营企业	Other Joint Ownership Enterprises
有限责任公司	Limited Liability Corporations
国有独资公司	State Sole Investment Corporations
其他有限责任公司	Other Limited Liability Corporations
股份有限公司	Share-holding Corporations Ltd.
私营企业	Private Enterprises
私营独资企业	Private Sole Investment Enterprises
私营合伙企业	Private Partnership Enterprises
私营有限责任公司	Private Limited Liability Corporations
私营股份有限公司	Private Share-holding Corporations Ltd.
其他企业	Other Enterprises
港、澳、台商投资企业	Enterprises with Funds from Hong Kong, Macao and Taiwan
与港、澳、台商合资经营企业	Joint-venture Enterprises
与港、澳、台商合作经营企业	Cooperative Enterprises
港、澳、台商独资经营企业	Enterprises with Sole Funds
港、澳、台商投资股份有限公司	Share-holding Corporations Ltd.
其他港、澳、台投资企业	Other Enterprises with Funds from Hong Kong, Macao and Taiwan
外商投资企业	Foreign Funded Enterprises
中外合资经营企业	Joint-venture Enterprises
中外合作经营企业	Cooperative Enterprises
外资企业	Enterprises with Sole Foreign Funds
外商投资股份有限公司	Share-holding Corporations Ltd.
其他外商投资企业	Other Foreign Funded Enterprises
按行业分	**Grouped by Sector**
农、林、牧产品批发	Wholesale of Farming, Forestry, Animal Husbandry Products
食品、饮料及烟草制品批发	Wholesale of Food, Beverages and Tobacco Products
# 米、面制品及食用油批发	Wholesale of Rice, Flour and Edible Oil
烟草制品批发	Wholesale of Tobacco
纺织、服装及家庭用品批发	Wholesale of Textile, Garments and Daily Articles Consumer
# 服装批发	Wholesale of Garments
家用视听设备批发	Wholesale of Household Electrical Appliances
文化、体育用品及器材批发	Wholesale of Cultural, Sports Appliances and Equipment
医药及医疗器材批发	Wholesale of Medicine and Medical Appliances
矿产品、建材及化工产品批发	Wholesale of Mineral Products, Building Materials and Chemical Products
# 煤炭及制品批发	Wholesale of Coal and Related Products
石油及制品批发	Wholesale of Petroleum and Related Products
金属及金属矿批发	Wholesale of Metal Minerals
建材批发	Wholesale of Building Materials
化肥批发	Wholesale of Chemical Fertilizers
机械设备、五金产品及电子产品批发	Wholesale of Mechanical Equipment, Metal Products and Electronic Products
# 汽车及零配件批发	Wholesale of Automobile
摩托车及零配件批发	Wholesale of Motorcycles and Accessories
计算机、软件及辅助设备批发	Wholesale of Computers, Software and Assistant Appliances
贸易经纪与代理	Trade Broker and Agency
其他批发业	Other Wholesales Trades

continued

(10000 yuan)

主营业务收入 Revenue from Principal Business	营业成本 Cost of Business	税金及附加 Taxes and Other Charges	其他业务利润 Profit from Other Business	销售费用 Operating Expenses
315968673	**297851498**	**637299**	**426370**	**9897481**
259032586	245682777	528312	355929	7035069
1249743	1207128	2359	5671	31087
95297	92089	184	541	1755
122577	112891	440	880	3921
2031	2010	1		9
2031	2010	1		9
121918648	116019304	346462	135929	3173032
20047428	19105538	229100	23205	483117
101871220	96913766	117362	112724	2689915
44820165	43003247	47516	108666	1279962
90824125	85246108	131350	104242	2545303
21061	19561	33	485	426
4731	4226	9		
89587863	84126213	129601	101630	2500357
1210470	1096108	1707	2127	44520
15195672	13236000	51972	38914	1080006
4800201	4532773	11428	28317	165701
10253651	8590430	40155	10592	898934
78520	59882	256	5	6240
63300	52915	133		9131
41740415	38932721	57015	31527	1782406
28762723	26813440	40110	2459	1256123
96757	94377	36		1693
12361184	11535995	16417	29055	476612
30671	28863	34		547
489080	460046	418	13	47431
4544486	4255863	2667	2903	70486
14958987	12861850	247880	45028	1061737
2225318	2120491	3162	19311	104134
1568168	1110391	217575	1175	20398
20118939	16917349	49387	98551	1902770
2859668	2361469	6950	11369	281638
1375607	1281772	1909	1634	54511
11502303	10718974	29152	6993	482609
19893495	17901322	44385	66823	1051166
183903779	179308304	152962	173907	2446984
7668232	7444060	9504	3002	103952
60508250	58582870	55855	115153	1353389
83305469	82462026	52051	25898	232945
10614707	10064538	14365	8786	275414
1006869	970129	537	2178	18182
58407340	53505286	105610	30171	2744035
43836919	40113873	68904	12467	2241164
164121	145492	921	53	5147
3309538	3142884	3534	681	57480
367995	335003	763	1159	12607
2271349	2047547	4493	835	125087

14-8 续表 2

单位：万元

项　　目	Item
总　计	**Total**
按登记注册类型分	**Grouped by Registration Status**
内资企业	Domestic-funded Enterprises
国有企业	State-owned Enterprises
集体企业	Collective-owned Enterprises
股份合作企业	Share-holding Cooperative Enterprises
联营企业	Joint-opeartion Enterprises
国有联营企业	State-owned Joint-opeartion Enterprises
集体联营企业	Collective Joint-opeartion Enterprises
国有与集体联营企业	Joint State-collective Enterprises
其他联营企业	Other Joint Ownership Enterprises
有限责任公司	Limited Liability Corporations
国有独资公司	State Sole Investment Corporations
其他有限责任公司	Other Limited Liability Corporations
股份有限公司	Share-holding Corporations Ltd.
私营企业	Private Enterprises
私营独资企业	Private Sole Investment Enterprises
私营合伙企业	Private Partnership Enterprises
私营有限责任公司	Private Limited Liability Corporations
私营股份有限公司	Private Share-holding Corporations Ltd.
其他企业	Other Enterprises
港、澳、台商投资企业	Enterprises with Funds from Hong Kong, Macao and Taiwan
与港、澳、台商合资经营企业	Joint-venture Enterprises
与港、澳、台商合作经营企业	Cooperative Enterprises
港、澳、台商独资经营企业	Enterprises with Sole Funds
港、澳、台商投资股份有限公司	Share-holding Corporations Ltd.
其他港、澳、台投资企业	Other Enterprises with Funds from Hong Kong, Macao and Taiwan
外商投资企业	Foreign Funded Enterprises
中外合资经营企业	Joint-venture Enterprises
中外合作经营企业	Cooperative Enterprises
外资企业	Enterprises with Sole Foreign Funds
外商投资股份有限公司	Share-holding Corporations Ltd.
其他外商投资企业	Other Foreign Funded Enterprises
按行业分	**Grouped by Sector**
农、林、牧产品批发	Wholesale of Farming, Forestry, Animal Husbandry Products
食品、饮料及烟草制品批发	Wholesale of Food, Beverages and Tobacco Products
#米、面制品及食用油批发	Wholesale of Rice, Flour and Edible Oil
烟草制品批发	Wholesale of Tobacco
纺织、服装及家庭用品批发	Wholesale of Textile, Garments and Daily Articles Consumer
#服装批发	Wholesale of Garments
家用视听设备批发	Wholesale of Household Electrical Appliances
文化、体育用品及器材批发	Wholesale of Cultural, Sports Appliances and Equipment
医药及医疗器材批发	Wholesale of Medicine and Medical Appliances
矿产品、建材及化工产品批发	Wholesale of Mineral Products, Building Materials and Chemical Products
#煤炭及制品批发	Wholesale of Coal and Related Products
石油及制品批发	Wholesale of Petroleum and Related Products
金属及金属矿批发	Wholesale of Metal Minerals
建材批发	Wholesale of Building Materials
化肥批发	Wholesale of Chemical Fertilizers
机械设备、五金产品及电子产品批发	Wholesale of Mechanical Equipment, Metal Products and Electronic Products
#汽车及零配件批发	Wholesale of Automobile
摩托车及零配件批发	Wholesale of Motorcycles and Accessories
计算机、软件及辅助设备批发	Wholesale of Computers, Software and Assistant Appliances
贸易经纪与代理	Trade Broker and Agency
其他批发业	Other Wholesales Trades

continued

(10000 yuan)

管理费用 Management Cost	营业利润 Business Profit	利润总额 Total Profits	本年应付职工薪酬 Total Wages Payable	本年应交增值税 Total Value-added Payable Tax
4041660	**5703104**	**5823629**	**4221045**	**2094720**
3187367	3651412	3742937	3072147	1569139
23290	3916	15957	22397	6778
1782	3	468	1636	299
4115	2263	2971	4662	1130
1	9	8	22	2
1	9	8	22	2
952830	1981142	2021746	1234372	676924
171712	288291	317277	259457	103282
781118	1692851	1704469	974915	573642
284727	732751	757485	394067	223693
1920622	931328	944302	1414991	660313
713	328	326	393	171
194	310	311	126	68
1884468	885516	896266	1380935	650928
35247	45174	47399	33537	9146
436129	521001	535868	573307	237380
71998	55943	54842	90429	50967
358594	457542	473518	475963	184820
3164	8841	8835	3235	990
2373	-1325	-1327	3680	603
418164	1530691	1544824	575591	288201
103458	618015	623140	195971	191365
433	272	276	873	66
305860	938391	947466	350204	94151
311	1005	895	405	195
8102	-26992	-26953	28138	2424
91455	117268	120401	92244	11651
523321	555976	590776	599557	250115
40827	6361	29753	42023	11185
45173	199223	200089	50030	61271
991535	427432	448528	979513	328703
222984	41057	50045	199641	44672
38637	2147	2014	30956	10936
227169	861607	862417	352756	75488
539428	480402	481328	515048	292461
930436	1509868	1548648	909129	596479
41947	97094	98720	29579	33480
220281	768139	796469	369206	256190
229603	307317	307067	149494	111907
115504	136770	140004	124570	70461
11000	6960	7623	11708	1640
666617	1673934	1692282	708259	511819
181049	1418381	1429298	245291	353177
6942	1969	2663	5463	3514
67680	32644	34018	62782	27447
10403	11157	12148	7547	3582
61296	65460	67101	56992	24422

14-9 限额以上零售业法人企业财务状况(2019年)

单位：万元

项　　目	Item
总　计	**Total**
按登记注册类型分	**Grouped by Registration Status**
内资企业	Domestic-funded Enterprises
国有企业	State-owned Enterprises
集体企业	Collective-owned Enterprises
股份合作企业	Share-holding Cooperative Enterprises
联营企业	Joint-opeartion Enterprises
国有联营企业	State-owned Joint-opeartion Enterprises
集体联营企业	Collective Joint-opeartion Enterprises
国有与集体联营企业	Joint State-collective Enterprises
其他联营企业	Other Joint Ownership Enterprises
有限责任公司	Limited Liability Corporations
国有独资公司	State Sole Investment Corporations
其他有限责任公司	Other Limited Liability Corporations
股份有限公司	Share-holding Corporations Ltd.
私营企业	Private Enterprises
私营独资企业	Private Sole Investment Enterprises
私营合伙企业	Private Partnership Enterprises
私营有限责任公司	Private Limited Liability Corporations
私营股份有限公司	Private Share-holding Corporations Ltd.
其他企业	Other Enterprises
港、澳、台商投资企业	Enterprises with Funds from Hong Kong, Macao and Taiwan
与港、澳、台商合资经营企业	Joint-venture Enterprises
与港、澳、台商合作经营企业	Cooperative Enterprises
港、澳、台商独资经营企业	Enterprises with Sole Funds
港、澳、台商投资股份有限公司	Share-holding Corporations Ltd.
其他港、澳、台投资企业	Other Enterprises with Funds from Hong Kong, Macao and Taiwan
外商投资企业	Foreign Funded Enterprises
中外合资经营企业	Joint-venture Enterprises
中外合作经营企业	Cooperative Enterprises
外资企业	Enterprises with Sole Foreign Funds
外商投资股份有限公司	Share-holding Corporations Ltd.
其他外商投资企业	Other Foreign Funded Enterprises
按行业分	**Grouped by Sector**
综合零售	Integrated Retail
#百货零售	Retail of General Merchandise
超级市场零售	Retail of Supermarket
食品、饮料及烟草制品专门零售	Retail of Food, Beverage and Tobacco
纺织、服装及日用品专门零售	Retail of Textile, Garments and Daily Articles Consumer
#服装零售	Retail of Garments
文化、体育用品及器材专门零售	Retail of Cultural, Sports Appliances and Equipment
#体育用品及器材零售	Retail of Sporting Goods and Equipment
图书、报刊零售	Retail of Books and Newspapers
医药及医疗器材专门零售	Retail of Medicine and Medical Appliances
#西药零售	Retail of Medicine
中药零售	Retail of Chinese Medicine
汽车、摩托车、零配件和燃料及其他动力设备零售	Retail of Motor Vehicles, Motorcycles, Fuels and Parts
#汽车新车零售	Retail of Motor Vehicles
机动车燃油零售	Retail of Fuels for Motor Vehicles
家用电器及电子产品专门零售	Retail of Household Electrical Appliances and Electronic Products
#家用视听设备零售	Retail of Household Audio and Video Equipment
日用家电零售	Retail of Household Electrical Appliances
计算机、软件及辅助设备零售	Retail of Computers, Software and Assistant Equipment
通信设备零售	Retail of Communication Equipment
五金、家具及室内装饰材料专门零售	Retail of Hardware, Furniture and Decoration Materials
货摊、无店铺及其他零售业	Retail of Booth and Others
#互联网零售	E-Retail

Financial Situation of Enterprises above Designated Size in Retail Trade (2019)

(10000 yuan)

资产总计 Total Assets	# 固定资产原价 Original Value of Fixed Assets	负债合计 Total Liabilities	所有者权益 Owners' Equity	营业收入 Revenue from Principal Business
22506226	**2052841**	**16701814**	**5804412**	**40830432**
18062590	1204371	13377519	4685071	31066241
58119	6183	30543	27576	118049
126226	15184	72648	53578	241981
15405	2763	5672	9733	33439
13184	5046	6134	7050	54214
4863	2568	967	3896	28628
2376	1077	699	1677	8627
5945	1401	4468	1477	16959
6405697	412652	4744930	1660767	15185865
235753	13862	140260	95493	559544
6169944	398790	4604670	1565274	14626321
6184155	376163	4096092	2088063	3338009
5259804	386380	4421500	838304	12094684
5623	427	3137	2486	23224
5166	605	2162	3004	13002
5071394	368264	4280968	790426	11815910
177621	17084	135233	42388	242548
2406095	392684	1819416	586679	5584267
591724	209498	425342	166382	1587579
21953	4699	24897	-2944	36754
1789121	174523	1366367	422754	3952805
3297	3964	2810	487	7129
2037541	455786	1504879	532662	4179924
827716	194020	494341	333375	1475053
299580	44488	259615	39965	702314
848556	209001	718966	129590	1861820
26591	1872	9747	16844	35615
35098	6405	22210	12888	105122
2919021	791161	2070426	848595	6004993
1852428	460401	1047288	805140	3205348
868619	274595	782624	85995	2232223
358233	28514	340392	17841	668308
2041148	172446	1430588	610560	2233096
1270848	100966	767560	503288	1219438
571801	72288	349531	222270	874425
43482	14429	12942	30540	54833
199068	34750	96736	102332	190678
578379	37840	443829	134550	1317794
522955	35251	405680	117275	1231779
22098	1715	13907	8191	40180
10272383	734147	7347792	2924591	15139348
4042469	410901	3214490	827979	11232389
6115334	300962	4039003	2076331	3564784
1915916	38694	1565446	350470	3007019
396711	5478	270928	125783	1319266
937750	23303	907836	29914	894059
128451	4498	83763	44688	339752
398209	1748	271826	126383	381358
199364	80492	151593	47771	253777
3649981	97259	3002217	647764	11331672
3547113	90945	2944869	602244	11031240

14-9 续表 1

单位：万元

项　　目	Item
总　　计	Total
按登记注册类型分	**Grouped by Registration Status**
内资企业	Domestic-funded Enterprises
国有企业	State-owned Enterprises
集体企业	Collective-owned Enterprises
股份合作企业	Share-holding Cooperative Enterprises
联营企业	Joint-opeartion Enterprises
国有联营企业	State-owned Joint-opeartion Enterprises
集体联营企业	Collective Joint-opeartion Enterprises
国有与集体联营企业	Joint State-collective Enterprises
其他联营企业	Other Joint Ownership Enterprises
有限责任公司	Limited Liability Corporations
国有独资公司	State Sole Investment Corporations
其他有限责任公司	Other Limited Liability Corporations
股份有限公司	Share-holding Corporations Ltd.
私营企业	Private Enterprises
私营独资企业	Private Sole Investment Enterprises
私营合伙企业	Private Partnership Enterprises
私营有限责任公司	Private Limited Liability Corporations
私营股份有限公司	Private Share-holding Corporations Ltd.
其他企业	Other Enterprises
港、澳、台商投资企业	Enterprises with Funds from Hong Kong, Macao and Taiwan
与港、澳、台商合资经营企业	Joint-venture Enterprises
与港、澳、台商合作经营企业	Cooperative Enterprises
港、澳、台商独资经营企业	Enterprises with Sole Funds
港、澳、台商投资股份有限公司	Share-holding Corporations Ltd.
其他港、澳、台投资企业	Other Enterprises with Funds from Hong Kong, Macao and Taiwan
外商投资企业	Foreign Funded Enterprises
中外合资经营企业	Joint-venture Enterprises
中外合作经营企业	Cooperative Enterprises
外资企业	Enterprises with Sole Foreign Funds
外商投资股份有限公司	Share-holding Corporations Ltd.
其他外商投资企业	Other Foreign Funded Enterprises
按行业分	**Grouped by Sector**
综合零售	Integrated Retail
#百货零售	Retail of General Merchandise
超级市场零售	Retail of Supermarket
食品、饮料及烟草制品专门零售	Retail of Food, Beverage and Tobacco
纺织、服装及日用品专门零售	Retail of Textile, Garments and Daily Articles Consumer
#服装零售	Retail of Garments
文化、体育用品及器材专门零售	Retail of Cultural, Sports Appliances and Equipment
#体育用品及器材零售	Retail of Sporting Goods and Equipment
图书、报刊零售	Retail of Books and Newspapers
医药及医疗器材专门零售	Retail of Medicine and Medical Appliances
#西药零售	Retail of Medicine
中药零售	Retail of Chinese Medicine
汽车、摩托车、零配件和燃料及其他动力设备零售	Retail of Motor Vehicles, Motorcycles, Fuels and Parts
#汽车新车零售	Retail of Motor Vehicles
机动车燃油零售	Retail of Fuels for Motor Vehicles
家用电器及电子产品专门零售	Retail of Household Electrical Appliances and Electronic Products
#家用视听设备零售	Retail of Household Audio and Video Equipment
日用家电零售	Retail of Household Electrical Appliances
计算机、软件及辅助设备零售	Retail of Computers, Software and Assistant Equipment
通信设备零售	Retail of Communication Equipment
五金、家具及室内装饰材料专门零售	Retail of Hardware, Furniture and Decoration Materials
货摊、无店铺及其他零售业	Retail of Booth and Others
#互联网零售	E-Retail

continued

(10000 yuan)

主营业务收入 Revenue from Principal Business	营业成本 Cost of Business	税金及附加 Taxes and Other Charges	其他业务利润 Profit from Other Business	销售费用 Operating Expenses
40015792	**34857450**	**136945**	**470588**	**4074228**
30559354	27255261	89320	186088	2523411
115375	95852	632	2643	11242
240921	193693	843	216	17470
33426	28560	83	215	2436
54178	42250	203	14	2788
28616	22205	109		1436
8627	6933	31	15	556
16935	13112	63		796
14973833	13595339	38286	74124	1171897
549014	496620	1613	3979	40028
14424819	13098719	36673	70145	1131869
3243865	2872740	11446	30370	254023
11897756	10426827	37827	78506	1063555
23093	19030	94	131	1884
12999	11173	34	599	884
11625023	10191609	36714	72856	1041648
236641	205015	985	4920	19139
5415611	4357740	34628	128010	862290
1532148	1184929	5781	53063	276329
36148	23603	177	681	4132
3841045	3142569	28657	74111	581266
6270	6639	13	155	563
4040827	3244449	12997	156490	688527
1441463	1177355	5370	62322	243295
660877	613515	902	41437	60974
1800890	1333159	6067	49670	374313
34563	27436	77	1052	4673
103034	92984	581	2009	5272
5773638	4825677	26444	231691	927493
3097618	2556118	19872	109827	459687
2135427	1911013	4283	110631	294647
662679	525754	1806	1452	111142
2132365	1468830	9885	73466	558540
1177004	710242	6534	17090	373099
848501	652092	19104	16803	121998
53616	37185	215	118	12617
176903	141515	1030	8703	29567
1291782	1072996	3552	6981	171280
1206114	1007050	3191	6924	161483
39834	29811	192	57	6711
14805634	13694073	43214	120988	695818
10968578	10343557	35701	115522	444184
3500439	3041555	6799	2718	233547
2963613	2727469	4832	9677	173500
1306170	1255580	1990	2154	38495
874712	796077	1322	2220	70945
336146	275732	799	3335	45096
375086	342272	514	1110	14923
249003	189770	1204	5022	40501
11288577	9700789	26904	4508	1273956
10991419	9524036	24665	4444	1182777

14-9 续表 2

单位：万元

项目	Item
总计	**Total**
按登记注册类型分	**Grouped by Registration Status**
内资企业	Domestic-funded Enterprises
国有企业	State-owned Enterprises
集体企业	Collective-owned Enterprises
股份合作企业	Share-holding Cooperative Enterprises
联营企业	Joint-opeartion Enterprises
国有联营企业	State-owned Joint-opeartion Enterprises
集体联营企业	Collective Joint-opeartion Enterprises
国有与集体联营企业	Joint State-collective Enterprises
其他联营企业	Other Joint Ownership Enterprises
有限责任公司	Limited Liability Corporations
国有独资公司	State Sole Investment Corporations
其他有限责任公司	Other Limited Liability Corporations
股份有限公司	Share-holding Corporations Ltd.
私营企业	Private Enterprises
私营独资企业	Private Sole Investment Enterprises
私营合伙企业	Private Partnership Enterprises
私营有限责任公司	Private Limited Liability Corporations
私营股份有限公司	Private Share-holding Corporations Ltd.
其他企业	Other Enterprises
港、澳、台商投资企业	Enterprises with Funds from Hong Kong, Macao and Taiwan
与港、澳、台商合资经营企业	Joint-venture Enterprises
与港、澳、台商合作经营企业	Cooperative Enterprises
港、澳、台商独资经营企业	Enterprises with Sole Funds
港、澳、台商投资股份有限公司	Share-holding Corporations Ltd.
其他港、澳、台投资企业	Other Enterprises with Funds from Hong Kong, Macao and Taiwan
外商投资企业	Foreign Funded Enterprises
中外合资经营企业	Joint-venture Enterprises
中外合作经营企业	Cooperative Enterprises
外资企业	Enterprises with Sole Foreign Funds
外商投资股份有限公司	Share-holding Corporations Ltd.
其他外商投资企业	Other Foreign Funded Enterprises
按行业分	**Grouped by Sector**
综合零售	Integrated Retail
# 百货零售	Retail of General Merchandise
超级市场零售	Retail of Supermarket
食品、饮料及烟草制品专门零售	Retail of Food, Beverage and Tobacco
纺织、服装及日用品专门零售	Retail of Textile, Garments and Daily Articles Consumer
# 服装零售	Retail of Garments
文化、体育用品及器材专门零售	Retail of Cultural, Sports Appliances and Equipment
# 体育用品及器材零售	Retail of Sporting Goods and Equipment
图书、报刊零售	Retail of Books and Newspapers
医药及医疗器材专门零售	Retail of Medicine and Medical Appliances
# 西药零售	Retail of Medicine
中药零售	Retail of Chinese Medicine
汽车、摩托车、零配件和燃料及其他动力设备零售	Retail of Motor Vehicles, Motorcycles, Fuels and Parts
# 汽车新车零售	Retail of Motor Vehicles
机动车燃油零售	Retail of Fuels for Motor Vehicles
家用电器及电子产品专门零售	Retail of Household Electrical Appliances and Electronic Products
# 家用视听设备零售	Retail of Household Audio and Video Equipment
日用家电零售	Retail of Household Electrical Appliances
计算机、软件及辅助设备零售	Retail of Computers, Software and Assistant Equipment
通信设备零售	Retail of Communication Equipment
五金、家具及室内装饰材料专门零售	Retail of Hardware, Furniture and Decoration Materials
货摊、无店铺及其他零售业	Retail of Booth and Others
# 互联网零售	E-Retail

continued

(10000 yuan)

管理费用 Management Cost	营业利润 Business Profit	利润总额 Total Profits	本年应付职工薪酬 Total Wages Payable	本年应交增值税 Total Value-added Payable Tax
1205364	**572280**	**619085**	**1595105**	**563043**
782504	341241	379537	1023301	391450
7515	4320	5958	12144	2340
7090	23155	23274	12285	6205
1052	1362	1369	1694	607
247	8643	8709	1762	1352
55	4776	4819	914	732
161	949	978	274	156
31	2918	2912	574	464
257556	190243	234341	416198	180637
9355	10999	17007	23935	7667
248201	179244	217334	392263	172970
46115	137428	133382	102214	27689
462929	-23910	-27496	477004	172620
1592	602	652	2354	683
352	522	522	520	266
447697	-27548	-31250	461072	168497
13288	2514	2580	13058	3174
281891	107102	114223	365231	103917
106390	38025	36663	151515	31645
7003	1896	1748	4159	1069
168016	67599	76229	209263	71136
482	-418	-417	294	67
140969	123937	125325	206573	67676
30635	51673	51753	89174	22678
15611	8617	8865	15815	6231
92381	56183	57215	97271	37237
823	2493	2520	1491	573
1519	4971	4972	2822	957
239257	66958	71114	403170	90790
114369	96478	103304	207863	48753
64840	-10347	-11415	134396	25577
32578	-3870	2167	58623	10673
222723	-13848	-14614	244837	54226
128909	-16915	-23819	149857	32669
53281	32030	34228	84278	15453
3304	1470	1509	3567	1404
19826	1830	3540	22764	1453
61252	11085	11777	93995	23946
51407	11503	11915	83065	21730
3609	-233	-52	6754	1297
293984	338261	347669	449875	165316
240565	103943	106082	351102	124197
41901	232488	239284	86407	37640
65936	18367	19224	85462	33225
7003	5050	4477	14267	13121
23101	-2324	-1573	22668	6344
12066	3049	3370	33230	9587
17569	10581	10782	11173	2790
30094	-9750	-10184	19326	3460
206259	133047	157704	155539	165954
195493	115410	139967	138880	164064

14-10 限额以上住宿业法人企业基本情况(2019年)

项 目	Item
合 计	**Accommodation Trade**
#国有及国有控股	State-owned and State-controlled Enterprises
按登记注册类型分组	**Grouped by Registration Status**
内资企业	Domestic Funded Enterprises
国有企业	State-owned Enterprises
集体企业	Collective-owned Enterprises
股份合作企业	Share-holding Cooperative Enterprises
联营企业	Joint Ownership Enterprises
国有联营企业	State Joint Ownership Enterprises
集体联营企业	Collective Joint Ownership Enterprises
国有与集体联营企业	Joint State-collective Enterprises
其他联营企业	Other Joint Ownership Enterprise
有限责任公司	Limited Liability Corporations
国有独资公司	State Sole Investment Corporations
其他有限责任公司	Other Limited Liability Corporations
股份有限公司	Share-holding Corporations Ltd.
私营企业	Private Enterprises
私营独资企业	Private Sole Investment Enterprises
私营合伙企业	Private Partnership Enterprises
私营有限责任公司	Private Limited Liability Corporations
私营股份有限公司	Private Share-holding Corporations Ltd.
其他企业	Other Enterprises
港、澳、台商投资企业	Enterprises with Funds from Hong Kong, Macao and Taiwan
与港、澳、台商合资经营企业	Joint-venture Enterprises
与港、澳、台商合作经营企业	Cooperative Enterprises
港、澳、台商独资经营企业	Enterprises with Sole Funds
港、澳、台商投资股份有限公司	Share-holding Corporations Ltd.
其他港、澳、台投资企业	Other Enterprises with Funds from Hong Kong, Macao and Taiwan
外商投资企业	Foreign Funded Enterprises
中外合资经营企业	Joint-venture Enterprises
中外合作经营企业	Cooperative Enterprises
外资企业	Enterprises with Sole Foreign Funds
外商投资股份有限公司	Share-holding Corporations Ltd.
其他外商投资企业	Other Foreign Funded Enterprises
按住宿行业中类分组	**Grouped by Accomodation Middle Sector**
旅游饭店	Travel Hotel
一般旅馆	Common Hotel
民宿服务	Minshuku
其它住宿服务业	Others

Basic Statistics of Enterprises above Designated Size of Hotels (2019)

法人企业 (个) Number of Corporation Units (unit)	营业额 (万元) Business Revenue (10000 yuan)			
		# 客房收入 Lodging Revenue	# 餐费收入 Dinner Revenue	# 商品销售收入 Sale Revenue of Commodities
731	**1659835**	**932674**	**429774**	**18744**
107	585158	252466	190483	11305
684	1357360	782696	332002	15223
55	197578	84358	63408	5703
8	6429	2779	280	20
2	586	260		
167	580917	309882	161928	6234
21	174407	80107	63288	3417
146	406510	229775	98640	2817
5	36412	11434	15139	
447	535438	373983	91247	3266
27	14192	13628	294	5
5	1321	920		
412	518690	358291	90953	3261
3	1235	1144		
31	149169	83125	43779	1219
9	45332	27260	11902	367
6	26710	14769	6207	
16	77127	41096	25670	852
16	153307	66856	53995	2303
3	68180	22927	19329	170
1	2789	678	1409	
9	71245	36448	29376	1989
3	11093	6803	3881	144
294	1192484	582032	365903	13643
397	420810	317347	58737	5084
2	1741	1487	237	
38	44799	31808	4898	17

14-11 限额以上餐饮业法人企业基本情况(2019年)

项　　目	Item
合　计	**Catering Trade**
# 国有及国有控股	State-owned and State-controlled Enterprises
按登记注册类型分组	**Grouped by Registration Status**
内资企业	Domestic Funded Enterprises
国有企业	State-owned Enterprises
集体企业	Collective-owned Enterprises
股份合作企业	Share-holding Cooperative Enterprises
联营企业	Joint Ownership Enterprises
国有联营企业	State Joint Ownership Enterprises
集体联营企业	Collective Joint Ownership Enterprises
国有与集体联营企业	Joint State-collective Enterprises
其他联营企业	Other Joint Ownership Enterprise
有限责任公司	Limited Liability Corporations
国有独资公司	State Sole Investment Corporations
其他有限责任公司	Other Limited Liability Corporations
股份有限公司	Share-holding Corporations Ltd.
私营企业	Private Enterprises
私营独资企业	Private Sole Investment Enterprises
私营合伙企业	Private Partnership Enterprises
私营有限责任公司	Private Limited Liability Corporations
私营股份有限公司	Private Share-holding Corporations Ltd.
其他企业	Other Enterprises
港、澳、台商投资企业	Enterprises with Funds from Hong Kong, Macao and Taiwan
与港、澳、台商合资经营企业	Joint-venture Enterprises
与港、澳、台商合作经营企业	Cooperative Enterprises
港、澳、台商独资经营企业	Enterprises with Sole Funds
港、澳、台商投资股份有限公司	Share-holding Corporations Ltd.
其他港、澳、台投资企业	Other Enterprises with Funds from Hong Kong, Macao and Taiwan
外商投资企业	Foreign Funded Enterprises
中外合资经营企业	Joint-venture Enterprises
中外合作经营企业	Cooperative Enterprises
外资企业	Enterprises with Sole Foreign Funds
外商投资股份有限公司	Share-holding Corporations Ltd.
其他外商投资企业	Other Foreign Funded Enterprises
按餐饮行业中类分组	**Grouped by Catering Middle Sector**
正餐服务	Dinner
快餐服务	Snack
饮料及冷饮服务	Baverage and cold drinks
餐饮配送及外卖送餐服务	Restaurants distribution and take-away service
其他餐饮服务	Others

Basic Statistics of Enterprises above Designated Size of Catering Sevices (2019)

法人企业（个） Number of Corporation Units (unit)	营业额（万元） Business Revenue (10000 yuan)	# 客房收入 Lodging Revenue	# 餐费收入 Dinner Revenue	# 商品销售收入 Sale Revenue of Commodities
1317	**3894395**	**41928**	**3620871**	**172344**
22	180941	22664	122701	17940
1211	2139255	39033	1907205	141992
7	32417	6825	21730	314
6	14754	376	10661	
30	38040		37976	59
195	709841	17431	609484	63812
195	709841	17431	609484	63812
5	85010		65675	15137
968	1259193	14401	1161679	62670
93	60758	77	60403	152
33	43113	408	42461	33
834	1142702	13916	1051096	57584
8	12620		7719	4901
68	594683	295	561400	29672
9	24776		24550	186
5	45516		43295	1268
53	524391	295	493555	28218
1				
38	1160457	2599	1152265	682
9	448253	1751	442586	34
1				
27	711767	848	709243	648
1	437		436	
1136	1973811	41092	1822880	66851
73	1290787	20	1273545	8030
26	389555		356328	29921
52	197531	816	128349	66691
30	42712		39769	852

14-12 限额以上住宿业法人企业财务状况(2019年)

单位:万元

项　　目	Item
合　计	**Accommodation Trade**
# 国有及国有控股	State-owned and State-controlled Enterprises
按登记注册类型分组	**Grouped by Registration Status**
内资企业	Domestic Funded Enterprises
国有企业	State-owned Enterprises
集体企业	Collective-owned Enterprises
股份合作企业	Share-holding Cooperative Enterprises
联营企业	Joint Ownership Enterprises
国有联营企业	State Joint Ownership Enterprises
集体联营企业	Collective Joint Ownership Enterprises
国有与集体联营企业	Joint State-collective Enterprises
其他联营企业	Other Joint Ownership Enterprise
有限责任公司	Limited Liability Corporations
国有独资公司	State Sole Investment Corporations
其他有限责任公司	Other Limited Liability Corporations
股份有限公司	Share-holding Corporations Ltd.
私营企业	Private Enterprises
私营独资企业	Private Sole Investment Enterprises
私营合伙企业	Private Partnership Enterprises
私营有限责任公司	Private Limited Liability Corporations
私营股份有限公司	Private Share-holding Corporations Ltd.
其他企业	Other Enterprises
港、澳、台商投资企业	Enterprises with Funds from Hong Kong, Macao and Taiwan
与港、澳、台商合资经营企业	Joint-venture Enterprises
与港、澳、台商合作经营企业	Cooperative Enterprises
港、澳、台商独资经营企业	Enterprises with Sole Funds
港、澳、台商投资股份有限公司	Share-holding Corporations Ltd.
其他港、澳、台投资企业	Other Enterprises with Funds from Hong Kong, Macao and Taiwan
外商投资企业	Foreign Funded Enterprises
中外合资经营企业	Joint-venture Enterprises
中外合作经营企业	Cooperative Enterprises
外资企业	Enterprises with Sole Foreign Funds
外商投资股份有限公司	Share-holding Corporations Ltd.
其他外商投资企业	Other Foreign Funded Enterprises
按住宿行业中类分组	**Grouped by Accomodation Middle Sector**
旅游饭店	Travel Hotel
一般旅馆	Common Hotel
民宿服务	Minshuku
其它住宿服务业	Others

Financial Situation of Enterprises above Designated Size of Hotels (2019)

(10000 yuan)

资产总计 Total Assets	固定资产原价 Original Value of Fixed Assets	负债合计 Total Liabilities	所有者权益 Owners' Equity	营业收入 Revenue from Business	#主营业务收入 Revenue from Principal Business
8318240	**2513750**	**6786577**	**1531663**	**1609567**	**1585788**
1670789	1144852	682683	988105	558827	558827
4308986	1878470	3093367	1215622	1320635	1302566
435771	335594	192051	243720	192769	189034
10424	11343	5370	5055	6047	5830
407	1154	753	-346	565	565
2240681	1123062	1556906	683776	577223	568810
525136	350271	196104	329033	164189	161286
1715545	772791	1360802	354743	413034	407524
308154	89918	23786	284368	34432	34432
1313549	317399	1314501	-951	509599	503895
13181	4571	9685	3497	13531	13531
334	21	1256	-922	1259	1259
1298754	312789	1302906	-4152	493623	487919
1280	18	654	626	1186	1186
794972	335612	719547	75425	142835	137369
198683	66627	190850	7833	42920	41859
103496	98431	77552	25944	25347	25262
492793	170554	451145	41648	74568	70248
3214281	299669	2973664	240618	146096	145854
447438	131900	291188	156250	65380	65321
9182	5875	7148	2034	2736	2736
2747128	161487	2664880	82249	67412	67229
10533	407	10448	85	10568	10568
7212416	2205388	5849853	1362563	1165936	1146281
1060946	289594	896210	164736	399359	395619
386	22	1057	-671	1666	1666
44492	18746	39456	5036	42605	42223

14-12 续表 1

单位：万元

项 目	Item
合 计	**Accommodation Trade**
# 国有及国有控股	State-owned and State-controlled Enterprises
按登记注册类型分组	**Grouped by Registration Status**
内资企业	Domestic Funded Enterprises
国有企业	State-owned Enterprises
集体企业	Collective-owned Enterprises
股份合作企业	Share-holding Cooperative Enterprises
联营企业	Joint Ownership Enterprises
国有联营企业	State Joint Ownership Enterprises
集体联营企业	Collective Joint Ownership Enterprises
国有与集体联营企业	Joint State-collective Enterprises
其他联营企业	Other Joint Ownership Enterprise
有限责任公司	Limited Liability Corporations
国有独资公司	State Sole Investment Corporations
其他有限责任公司	Other Limited Liability Corporations
股份有限公司	Share-holding Corporations Ltd.
私营企业	Private Enterprises
私营独资企业	Private Sole Investment Enterprises
私营合伙企业	Private Partnership Enterprises
私营有限责任公司	Private Limited Liability Corporations
私营股份有限公司	Private Share-holding Corporations Ltd.
其他企业	Other Enterprises
港、澳、台商投资企业	Enterprises with Funds from Hong Kong, Macao and Taiwan
与港、澳、台商合资经营企业	Joint-venture Enterprises
与港、澳、台商合作经营企业	Cooperative Enterprises
港、澳、台商独资经营企业	Enterprises with Sole Funds
港、澳、台商投资股份有限公司	Share-holding Corporations Ltd.
其他港、澳、台投资企业	Other Enterprises with Funds from Hong Kong, Macao and Taiwan
外商投资企业	Foreign Funded Enterprises
中外合资经营企业	Joint-venture Enterprises
中外合作经营企业	Cooperative Enterprises
外资企业	Enterprises with Sole Foreign Funds
外商投资股份有限公司	Share-holding Corporations Ltd.
其他外商投资企业	Other Foreign Funded Enterprises
按住宿行业中类分组	**Grouped by Accomodation Middle Sector**
旅游饭店	Travel Hotel
一般旅馆	Common Hotel
民宿服务	Minshuku
其它住宿服务业	Others

continued

(10000 yuan)

营业成本 Cost of Business	税金及附加 Taxes and Other Charges on Business	其他业务利润 Profit from Other Business	销售费用 Operating Expenses
583929	**24058**	**5252**	**450098**
200143	12099	1535	148364
481997	19306	4513	385001
54431	3489	1033	66198
3199	213		461
61	2		342
205048	10958	2162	181769
56921	2814	176	41342
148127	8144	1986	140427
15228	1563	23	4273
204030	3081	1295	131958
6123	55		2611
880	23		106
196346	3000	1295	129073
681	3		168
37025	2563	683	45894
9269	615		18266
3908	921		7556
23848	1027	683	20072
64907	2189	56	19204
21123	633		12505
624	45		799
38320	1466	56	4014
4840	45		1886
416905	20759	5037	327604
145112	3037	166	111191
244	2		748
21668	260	48	10555

14-12 续表 2

单位:万元

项 目	Item
合 计	**Accommodation Trade**
# 国有及国有控股	State-owned and State-controlled Enterprises
按登记注册类型分组	**Grouped by Registration Status**
内资企业	Domestic Funded Enterprises
国有企业	State-owned Enterprises
集体企业	Collective-owned Enterprises
股份合作企业	Share-holding Cooperative Enterprises
联营企业	Joint Ownership Enterprises
国有联营企业	State Joint Ownership Enterprises
集体联营企业	Collective Joint Ownership Enterprises
国有与集体联营企业	Joint State-collective Enterprises
其他联营企业	Other Joint Ownership Enterprise
有限责任公司	Limited Liability Corporations
国有独资公司	State Sole Investment Corporations
其他有限责任公司	Other Limited Liability Corporations
股份有限公司	Share-holding Corporations Ltd.
私营企业	Private Enterprises
私营独资企业	Private Sole Investment Enterprises
私营合伙企业	Private Partnership Enterprises
私营有限责任公司	Private Limited Liability Corporations
私营股份有限公司	Private Share-holding Corporations Ltd.
其他企业	Other Enterprises
港、澳、台商投资企业	Enterprises with Funds from Hong Kong, Macao and Taiwan
与港、澳、台商合资经营企业	Joint-venture Enterprises
与港、澳、台商合作经营企业	Cooperative Enterprises
港、澳、台商独资经营企业	Enterprises with Sole Funds
港、澳、台商投资股份有限公司	Share-holding Corporations Ltd.
其他港、澳、台投资企业	Other Enterprises with Funds from Hong Kong, Macao and Taiwan
外商投资企业	Foreign Funded Enterprises
中外合资经营企业	Joint-venture Enterprises
中外合作经营企业	Cooperative Enterprises
外资企业	Enterprises with Sole Foreign Funds
外商投资股份有限公司	Share-holding Corporations Ltd.
其他外商投资企业	Other Foreign Funded Enterprises
按住宿行业中类分组	**Grouped by Accomodation Middle Sector**
旅游饭店	Travel Hotel
一般旅馆	Common Hotel
民宿服务	Minshuku
其它住宿服务业	Others

continued

(10000 yuan)

管理费用 Management Cost	营业利润 Business Profit	利润总额 Total Profits	本年应付职工薪酬 Total Wages Payable	应交增值税 Value Added Tax Payable
495588	**-21820**	**-12522**	**471765**	**40269**
155383	20552	25989	200590	16451
400726	-20863	-12359	391316	34395
54623	14714	19554	81429	5428
1228	1004	929	2213	191
162	-3	-3	191	20
162295	-45458	-42365	174976	16331
48970	-23152	-21925	61875	6921
113325	-22306	-20440	113101	9410
10842	21882	21884	12077	605
171576	-13002	-12358	120430	11820
5726	-1060	-1053	2431	333
358	-172	-171	238	22
165140	-11753	-11117	117566	11442
352	-17	-17	195	23
63513	-21819	-21374	48459	2369
15891	-5709	-5655	12030	674
13403	-1372	-1012	9967	933
34219	-14738	-14707	26462	762
31348	20862	21210	31990	3506
18529	6390	6391	10485	1499
1160	108	130	885	117
9587	12650	12964	17273	1672
2072	1714	1725	3347	218
349735	-23995	-16780	359656	30180
135261	1800	3602	100152	9321
762	-94	-79	397	25
9830	468	736	11560	743

14-13 限额以上餐饮业法人企业财务状况(2019年)

单位：万元

项　　目	Item
合　计	**Catering Trade**
# 国有及国有控股	State-owned and State-controlled Enterprises
按登记注册类型分组	**Grouped by Registration Status**
内资企业	Domestic Funded Enterprises
国有企业	State-owned Enterprises
集体企业	Collective-owned Enterprises
股份合作企业	Share-holding Cooperative Enterprises
联营企业	Joint Ownership Enterprises
国有联营企业	State Joint Ownership Enterprises
集体联营企业	Collective Joint Ownership Enterprises
国有与集体联营企业	Joint State-collective Enterprises
其他联营企业	Other Joint Ownership Enterprise
有限责任公司	Limited Liability Corporations
国有独资公司	State Sole Investment Corporations
其他有限责任公司	Other Limited Liability Corporations
股份有限公司	Share-holding Corporations Ltd.
私营企业	Private Enterprises
私营独资企业	Private Sole Investment Enterprises
私营合伙企业	Private Partnership Enterprises
私营有限责任公司	Private Limited Liability Corporations
私营股份有限公司	Private Share-holding Corporations Ltd.
其他企业	Other Enterprises
港、澳、台商投资企业	Enterprises with Funds from Hong Kong, Macao and Taiwan
与港、澳、台商合资经营企业	Joint-venture Enterprises
与港、澳、台商合作经营企业	Cooperative Enterprises
港、澳、台商独资经营企业	Enterprises with Sole Funds
港、澳、台商投资股份有限公司	Share-holding Corporations Ltd.
其他港、澳、台投资企业	Other Enterprises with Funds from Hong Kong, Macao and Taiwan
外商投资企业	Foreign Funded Enterprises
中外合资经营企业	Joint-venture Enterprises
中外合作经营企业	Cooperative Enterprises
外资企业	Enterprises with Sole Foreign Funds
外商投资股份有限公司	Share-holding Corporations Ltd.
其他外商投资企业	Other Foreign Funded Enterprises
按行业分	**Grouped by Catering Middle Sector**
正餐服务	Dinner
快餐服务	Snack
饮料及冷饮服务	Beverage and Cold Drinks
餐饮配送及外卖送餐服务	Restaurants distribution and take-away service
其他餐饮服务	Others

Financial Situation of Enterprises above Designated Size of Catering Services (2019)

(10000 yuan)

资产总计 Total Assets	# 固定资产原价 Original Value of Fixed Assets	负债合计 Total Liabilities	所有者权益 Owners' Equity	营业收入 Revenue from Business	# 主营业务收入 Revenue from Principal Business
2256168	**809332**	**1384635**	**871284**	**3681449**	**3668158**
388962	189089	214569	174394	168330	168330
1248423	425091	947629	300547	2026719	2015505
38682	49397	14920	23762	30588	30588
16717	4295	2815	13903	13882	13833
10780	3308	9779	1001	36024	35967
466839	218883	420067	46773	667603	662078
466839	218883	420067	46773	667603	662078
214486	14502	32137	182349	77758	74154
500919	134706	467911	32759	1200864	1198885
12846	5326	10152	2694	58103	57962
11498	5599	8708	2790	40867	40735
473217	123570	446865	26103	1089747	1088041
3358	211	2186	1172	12147	12147
513096	122064	238758	274337	560245	558317
15207	7521	9037	6170	23439	22795
43176	25035	51230	-8055	42794	42786
454713	89508	178491	276222	494012	492736
494652	262178	198251	296401	1094486	1094335
300079	140523	124493	175586	422897	422875
194303	121592	73690	120613	671176	671049
270	63	68	202	413	411
1305779	500131	985288	320241	1871110	1861440
566545	245122	238206	328339	1218316	1216095
294765	47338	97322	197441	365603	365019
68065	14412	49135	18929	186140	186019
21015	2330	14683	6332	40281	39584

14-13 续表 1

单位：万元

项　　目	Item
合　计	**Catering Trade**
# 国有及国有控股	State-owned and State-controlled Enterprises
按登记注册类型分组	**Grouped by Registration Status**
内资企业	Domestic Funded Enterprises
国有企业	State-owned Enterprises
集体企业	Collective-owned Enterprises
股份合作企业	Share-holding Cooperative Enterprises
联营企业	Joint Ownership Enterprises
国有联营企业	State Joint Ownership Enterprises
集体联营企业	Collective Joint Ownership Enterprises
国有与集体联营企业	Joint State-collective Enterprises
其他联营企业	Other Joint Ownership Enterprise
有限责任公司	Limited Liability Corporations
国有独资公司	State Sole Investment Corporations
其他有限责任公司	Other Limited Liability Corporations
股份有限公司	Share-holding Corporations Ltd.
私营企业	Private Enterprises
私营独资企业	Private Sole Investment Enterprises
私营合伙企业	Private Partnership Enterprises
私营有限责任公司	Private Limited Liability Corporations
私营股份有限公司	Private Share-holding Corporations Ltd.
其他企业	Other Enterprises
港、澳、台商投资企业	Enterprises with Funds from Hong Kong, Macao and Taiwan
与港、澳、台商合资经营企业	Joint-venture Enterprises
与港、澳、台商合作经营企业	Cooperative Enterprises
港、澳、台商独资经营企业	Enterprises with Sole Funds
港、澳、台商投资股份有限公司	Share-holding Corporations Ltd.
其他港、澳、台投资企业	Other Enterprises with Funds from Hong Kong, Macao and Taiwan
外商投资企业	Foreign Funded Enterprises
中外合资经营企业	Joint-venture Enterprises
中外合作经营企业	Cooperative Enterprises
外资企业	Enterprises with Sole Foreign Funds
外商投资股份有限公司	Share-holding Corporations Ltd.
其他外商投资企业	Other Foreign Funded Enterprises
按行业分	**Grouped by Catering Middle Sector**
正餐服务	Dinner
快餐服务	Snack
饮料及冷饮服务	Beverage and Cold Drinks
餐饮配送及外卖送餐服务	Restaurants distribution and take-away service
其他餐饮服务	Others

continued

(10000 yuan)

营业成本 Cost of Business	税金及附加 Taxes and Other Charges on Business	其他业务利润 Profit from Other Business	销售费用 Operating Expenses
1693133	**7517**	**10676**	**1353158**
73875	1335	3479	49852
1025647	6416	10774	657334
19230	576		2515
10551	127		1664
17489	102	25	12236
325147	1395	2013	239648
325147	1395	2013	239648
34145	499	3694	28644
619085	3717	5042	372627
32814	380	33	13454
20377	199	103	13305
557599	3115	4906	344299
8295	23		1569
176091	594	10	261914
8136	23	22	10639
21698	134	17	17375
146257	437	-29	233900
491394	508	-107	433911
139134	168	21	221789
352139	339	-129	211826
121	1	1	296
861512	6221	9873	663487
556624	621	763	471819
131075	186	20	159243
119729	425	18	50283
24193	65	2	8326

14-13 续表 2

单位：万元

项 目	Item
合 计	**Catering Trade**
# 国有及国有控股	State-owned and State-controlled Enterprises
按登记注册类型分组	**Grouped by Registration Status**
内资企业	Domestic Funded Enterprises
国有企业	State-owned Enterprises
集体企业	Collective-owned Enterprises
股份合作企业	Share-holding Cooperative Enterprises
联营企业	Joint Ownership Enterprises
国有联营企业	State Joint Ownership Enterprises
集体联营企业	Collective Joint Ownership Enterprises
国有与集体联营企业	Joint State-collective Enterprises
其他联营企业	Other Joint Ownership Enterprise
有限责任公司	Limited Liability Corporations
国有独资公司	State Sole Investment Corporations
其他有限责任公司	Other Limited Liability Corporations
股份有限公司	Share-holding Corporations Ltd.
私营企业	Private Enterprises
私营独资企业	Private Sole Investment Enterprises
私营合伙企业	Private Partnership Enterprises
私营有限责任公司	Private Limited Liability Corporations
私营股份有限公司	Private Share-holding Corporations Ltd.
其他企业	Other Enterprises
港、澳、台商投资企业	Enterprises with Funds from Hong Kong, Macao and Taiwan
与港、澳、台商合资经营企业	Joint-venture Enterprises
与港、澳、台商合作经营企业	Cooperative Enterprises
港、澳、台商独资经营企业	Enterprises with Sole Funds
港、澳、台商投资股份有限公司	Share-holding Corporations Ltd.
其他港、澳、台投资企业	Other Enterprises with Funds from Hong Kong, Macao and Taiwan
外商投资企业	Foreign Funded Enterprises
中外合资经营企业	Joint-venture Enterprises
中外合作经营企业	Cooperative Enterprises
外资企业	Enterprises with Sole Foreign Funds
外商投资股份有限公司	Share-holding Corporations Ltd.
其他外商投资企业	Other Foreign Funded Enterprises
按行业分	**Grouped by Catering Middle Sector**
正餐服务	Dinner
快餐服务	Snack
饮料及冷饮服务	Beverage and Cold Drinks
餐饮配送及外卖送餐服务	Restaurants distribution and take-away service
其他餐饮服务	Others

continued

(10000 yuan)

管理费用 Management Cost	营业利润 Business Profit	利润总额 Total Profits	本年应付职工薪酬 Total Wages Payable	应交增值税 Value Added Tax Payable
446472	**201063**	**197039**	**860641**	**40461**
34599	43410	43243	56047	1945
298823	65599	65374	458469	33224
6450	2020	2098	10931	1178
945	679	733	3571	405
4652	1317	1681	8834	825
85906	9969	10588	162116	8523
85906	9969	10588	162116	8523
13614	38442	38441	23069	257
187256	13172	11833	249948	22036
9575	1561	1432	14607	1457
5103	1766	1864	7754	979
170402	9784	8564	225945	19463
2176	61	-27	1642	137
47630	73827	74992	121102	6109
3725	785	915	5318	597
4165	-583	-580	8737	931
39740	73625	74657	107047	4581
100021	61637	56675	281068	1129
16663	38996	37860	116455	-698
83345	22662	18836	164486	1821
13	-21	-21	127	6
290784	73808	72935	450077	34699
115621	67453	63416	292415	1332
17837	58572	58514	73871	1294
15488	485	1027	35616	2664
6741	746	1147	8662	473

14-14 连锁店(公司)基本情况(2019年)
Statistics on Chain Stores (Companies) (2019)

单位：个 (unit)

项 目	Item	连锁总店 General Chain Stores	连锁门店 Branch Chain Stores	直营店 Direct Stores	加盟店 League Stores
总 计	**Total**	**135**	**10158**	**8834**	**1324**
批发业	Wholesale Trade	10	571	230	341
零售业	Retail Trade	95	6688	5738	950
按注册类型分	Grouped by Registration Status				
内资	Domestic Funded Enterprises	73	2968	2439	529
外商及港澳台投资	Enterprises with Funds from Foreign Countries, Hong Kong, Macao and Taiwan	22	3720	3299	421
按零售业态分	By Retail Format				
百货商店	Department Stores	8	719	719	
超级市场	Supermarkets	11	480	458	22
专业店	Specialized Stores	50	1875	1688	187
专卖店	Franchised Stores	15	1024	1019	5
其 他	Others	11	2590	1854	736
住宿业	Accommodation Services	6	39	39	
餐饮业	Catering Services	24	2860	2827	33
# 外商及港澳台投资	Enterprises with Funds from Foreign Countries, Hong Kong, Macao and Taiwan	9	2078	2078	
正 餐	Dinner	10	275	267	8
快 餐	Snack	9	1648	1648	
其 他	Others	5	937	912	25

14-14 续表 continued

单位：万元 (10000 yuan)

项 目	Item	营业面积（平方米）Business Area (sq.m)	从业人数（人）Employed Persons (person)	商品销售额（营业额）Commodity Sales (turnover)	# 零售额 Retail Sales
总 计	**Total**	**5703964**	**161121**	**16671029**	**14269519**
批发业	Wholesale Trade	76257	2522	251514	39886
零售业	Retail Trade	4668558	76349	14563665	12402422
按注册类型分	Grouped by Registration Status				
内资	Domestic Funded Enterprises	2675901	40634	10147128	8687452
外商及港澳台投资	Enterprises with Funds from Foreign Countries, Hong Kong, Macao and Taiwan	1992657	35715	4416537	3714970
按零售业态分	By Retail Format				
百货商店	Department Stores	1274940	10057	2566092	2445685
超级市场	Supermarkets	1319683	21904	2249483	1700075
专业店	Specialized Stores	1328748	25411	5785220	4739979
专卖店	Franchised Stores	92287	5535	473677	473622
其 他	Others	652900	13442	3489193	3043061
住宿业	Accommodation Services	1956	988	27339	401
餐饮业	Catering Services	957193	81262	1828511	1826810
# 外商及港澳台投资	Enterprises with Funds from Foreign Countries, Hong Kong, Macao and Taiwan	787176	63616	1431533	1430788
正 餐	Dinner	179428	12680	289846	288890
快 餐	Snack	612661	60181	1189349	1189349
其 他	Others	165104	8401	349316	348571

注：“营业面积”指标，批发业和零售业反映年末零售营业面积数据，住宿业和餐饮业反映年末餐饮营业面积数据。“商品销售额(营业额)”指标，批发业和零售业反映商品销售额数据，住宿业和餐饮业反映营业额数据。

Note: "Business area" indicator reflects data on retail business area at the end of the year for wholesale and retail trade,and it reflects data on catering business area at the end of the year for accommodation and catering services. "Commodity sales (turnover)" indicator reflects the sales data of commodities for wholesale and retail trade, and it reflects the turnover data for accommodation and catering services.

14-15 亿元以上商品交易市场成交情况(2019年)

Statistics on Commodity Exchange Markets with Total Sale over 100 Million Yuan (2019)

项　　目	Item	出租摊位数 (个) Number of Booths (unit)	总成交额 (万元) Total Transaction Values (10000 yuan)
合　计	**Total**	**76627**	**20028791**
粮油、食品类	Grain and Oil	9111	4887823
饮料类	Beverages	491	115734
烟酒类	Tobacco and Liquor	178	33477
服装鞋帽、针、纺织品类	Garments, Shoes, Hats, Knitwear and Textiles	40076	9685411
化妆品类	Cosmetics	2000	103086
金银珠宝类	Gold, Silver and Jewelry	572	36197
日用品类	Articles for Daily Use	10944	1138632
五金电料类	Hardware and Electrical Appliances	3268	900354
体育、娱乐用品类	Sports and Recreation Articles	402	53180
书报杂志类	Books, Newspapers and Magazines	90	19023
电子出版物及音像制品类	E-journal and Video Products		
家用电器和音像器材类	Household Appliances and Video Appliances	680	103200
中西药品类	Traditional Chinese and Western Medicines	421	12101
文化办公用品类	Cultural and Office Goods	632	129334
家具类	Furniture	733	87235
通讯器材类	Communication Equipments	61	3690
煤炭及制品类	Coal and Coal Products		
木材及制品类	Wood and Wooden Products	188	32369
石油及制品类	Petroleum and Related Products		
化工材料及制品类	Chemical Materials and Related Products	16	3515
金属材料类	Metal Materials	660	514265
建筑及装潢材料类	Building and Decoration Materials	1753	206763
机电产品及设备类	Mechanical and Electrical Products	24	3738
汽车类	Automobiles	2668	1825196
种子饲料类	Seed and Feedstuff	12	327
棉麻类	Cotton and Hemp		
其他类	Others	1647	134141

【社会消费品零售总额】 指企业（单位、个体户）通过交易直接售给个人、社会集团非生产、非经营用的实物商品金额，以及提供餐饮服务所取得的收入金额。个人包括城乡居民和入境人员，社会集团包括机关、社会团体、部队、学校、企事业单位、居委会或村委会等。

【商品购进总额】 指从本企业以外的单位和个人购进（包括从国外直接进口）作为转卖或加工后转卖的商品金额（含增值税）。本指标反映批发和零售业从国内外市场上购进商品的总价。

商品购进包括：（1）从工农业生产者、批发和零售业、住宿和餐饮业、出版社或报社的出版发行部门和其他服务业等企事业单位和个体经营户购进的商品；（2）从机关、社会团体购进的商品；（3）从海关、市场管理部门购进的缉私和没收的商品；（4）从居民收购的废旧商品等。

不包括：（1）企业为本单位自身经营用，不是作为转卖而购进的商品，如材料物资、包装物、低值易耗品、办公用品等；（2）未通过买卖行为而收入的商品，如接受其他部门移交的商品、借入的商品、收入代其他单位保管的商品、其他单位赠送的样品、加工回收的成品等；（3）经本单位介绍，由买卖双方直接结算，本单位只收取手续费的业务；（4）销售退回和买方拒付货款的商品；（5）商品溢余；（6）期货交易商品。

【商品销售总额】 指对本单位以外的单位和个人出售的商品金额（包括售给本单位消费用的商品，含增值税），在批发和零售业中，本指标反映在国内市场上销售商品以及出口商品的总价。

商品销售包括：（1）售给个人和社会集团消费用的商品；（2）售给农业、工业、建筑业、服务业等国民经济各行业用于生产、经营用的商品，包括售予批发和零售业作为转卖或加工后转卖的商品；（3）对国（境）外直接出口的商品。

商品销售不包括：（1）未通过买卖行为付出的商品，如因机构变动移交给其他企业单位的商品、借出的商品、归还受其他单位委托代保管的商品、付出的加工原料和赠送给其他单位的样品等；（2）促销返券所销售的、不计入营业收入的商品；（3）经本单位介绍，由买卖双方直接结算，本单位只收取手续费的业务；（4）未发生所有权转移的商品预付卡销售，如加油卡；（5）汽车维修、电话卡销售等服务性经济活动；（6）购货退回的商品；（7）商品损耗和损失；（8）出售本单位自用的废旧物资；（9）期货交易商品；（10）自来水供应企业、电力企业、天然气供应企业提供的水、电、气。

【住宿餐饮业营业额】 指住宿和餐饮业单位在经营活动中因提供服务或销售商品等取得的全部收入（含销项税），收入主要来源于提供客房、餐费服务、商品销售和其他服务，如商务服务。不包括多产业法人企业附营的其他行业产业活动单位的餐费收入、商品销售收入等各项收入。

【Total Retail Sales of Consumer Goods】 refer to the amount obtained by enterprises (units, self-employed individuals) through direct sales of non-production and non-business physical commodity to individuals, social institutions, and revenue from providing catering services. Individuals include rural and urban households, population from abroad, social institutions include government agencies, social organizations, military units, schools, institutions, neighbourhood (village) committees.

【Total Purchases of Commodities】 refer to the total value of purchases of commodities by enterprises (establishments) from other establishments or individuals (including direct import from abroad) for the purpose of re-selling, either with or without further processing of the commodities purchased. The commodities include: (1) commodities purchased from agricultural and industrial producer, wholesaler, retailer, publishing house and other service business; (2) commodities purchased from institutions and government departments; (3) confiscated goods purchased from the customs authorities or market management agencies; (4) second-hand goods and wastes purchased from residents; The commodities exclude (1) commodities purchased by enterprises (establishments) for use in their own business operation, commodities obtained without buying or selling procedures such as materials, consumable goods of low value, office appliance, etc. (2) received goods without trading, such as goods handed over from others, borrowed goods, preserved goods for others, donated goods from others, processed and retrieved goods, etc. (3) goods of direct settlement between buyer and seller with handling fees introduced by others, (4) goods returned or refused to pay by the buyer, (5) excessive goods.

【Total Sales of Commodities】 refer to value of commodities sold by the establishments to other establishments and individuals (including goods sold for self consumption, including the value-added tax). The commodities include: (1) commodities sold to urban and rural residents and social groups for their consumption; (2) commodities sold to establishments in all industries for their production and operation, including ?agriculture, industry, construction, and catering services including commodities sold to wholesale and retail establishments for re-selling, with or without further processing; and (3) commodities for direct export to abroad. Excluded are (1) extended commodities without trading, such as goods handed over to other enterprises and institutions because of the change of organizations, lent goods, returned goods preserved for others, extended processing materials and samples donated to others, (2)? goods of direct settlement between buyer and seller with handling fees introduced by others, (3) goods returned after purchase, (4) damaged and spoiled goods, (5) waste and used goods of self use.

【Hotel Services and Catering Services Business Revenue】 refers to total revenue (including VAT) of hotels and catering services received from providing services or selling commodities through business activities, income comes mainly from providing hotels, catering services, selling of commodities and other services, such as commodity services. It does not include revenue such as meal fees, selling of commodities of other industrial units affiliated with multi industrial legal entities. Income from hotels refers to income (including VAT) of hotels and catering services by providing lodging services through business activities. Income from catering services refers to income (including VAT) from providing catering services, including selling of cooked or prepared foods, such as staple food, cooked dishes, or cold dishes. It does not include meal fees of other industrial units affiliated with multi industrial legal entities.

第十五篇 CHAPTER 15

对外经济贸易和旅游

FOREIGN ECONOMY AND TOURISM

简要说明

2020 Brief Introduction

第十五篇　对外经济贸易和旅游

一、本篇资料反映广州市对外贸易、利用外资、对外承包工程和劳务合作、境外投资、外商投资企业工商注册登记以及旅游业概况及发展情况。

二、本篇资料由广州市统计局贸易外经统计处整理提供。

三、资料来源及统计范围：

1. 广州进出口贸易的规模、结构情况资料主要来源于广州海关和黄埔海关，统计范围为广州地区进出口经营单位（广州地区口岸进出口资料除外）。

2. 广州利用外资规模及结构、对外承包工程及劳务合作状况、境外投资情况、软件出口和技术进口情况的资料来源于广州市商务局。

3. 广州外商投资企业注册登记情况的资料由广州市市场监督管理局提供，但不包括在广东省市场监督管理局注册登记的在穗外商投资企业。

4. 广州旅游业发展情况的资料由广州市文化广电旅游局提供。

5. 广州与国外城市交流情况，广州与国外结成友好城市情况及各国驻广州领事馆情况的资料由广州市政府外事办公室提供。

6. 外商投资企业包括国外及港澳台投资企业。

15 Foreign Economy and Tourism

I.The data in this chapter show the Summary data of Guangzhou's foreign trade, utilization of foreign capital, contracted projects and labor cooperation with the foreign countries or territories, external investment, basic indicators of three kinds of registered foreign-funded enterprises and international tourism.

II.The data in this chapter are prepared and provided by the Division of Trade and External Economic Relations Statistics of Guangzhou Municipal Bureau of Statistics.

III. Data sources and statistical coverage:

(1) The data on the size and composition of Guangzhou's imports and exports come from Guangzhou and Huangpu Customs Office; the statistical coverage covers the imports and exports operating units in Guangzhou, excluding the data of imports and exports through ports in Guangzhou.

(2)The data on the scale and composition of the utilization of foreign capitals and the contracted projects and labor cooperation with the foreign countries or territories, external investment, software exports and technical imports of Guangzhou come from Guangzhou Municipal Commerce Bureau.

(3)The basic indicators of the registered foreign-funded enterprises come from the Guangzhou Municipal Market Regulatory Administration but exclude those registered by the Administration for Market Regulation of Guangdong Province.

(4)The data on the development of international tourism are provided by Guangzhou Municipal Culture,Radio,Televison and Tourism Bureau.

(5) The data on exchange between Guangzhou and foreign friendly cities, consulate generals in Guangzhou are provided by Foreign Affair Office of Guangzhou Municipal People's Government.

(6) The foreign-funded enterprises cover the enterprises whose fund come from Hong Kong, Macao, Taiwan and foreign countries.

15-1 主要年份商品进出口总值和商品进出口总值指数
Total Value and Indices of Import and Export Commodities in Main Years

年份 Year	进出口总值（亿美元）Total Value of Imports and Exports (USD 100 million)	进口总值 Imports	出口总值 Exports	进出口差额（亿美元）Balance (USD 100 million)	进出口总值指数（上年=100）Indices of Total Imports and Exports (preceding year=100)	进口总值 Imports	出口总值 Exports
1988	32.25	17.66	14.59	-3.07	148.5	154.0	142.4
1989	35.32	17.62	17.70	0.08	109.5	99.8	121.3
1990	41.79	18.24	23.55	5.31	118.3	103.5	133.0
1991	53.82	24.40	29.42	5.02	128.8	133.8	125.0
1992	70.75	33.88	36.87	2.99	131.5	138.8	125.3
1993	134.33	69.84	64.49	-5.35	189.9	206.2	174.9
1994	161.36	74.67	86.69	12.02	120.1	106.9	134.4
1995	166.99	71.32	95.67	24.35	103.5	95.5	110.4
1996	166.89	75.53	91.36	15.83	99.9	105.9	95.5
1997	187.46	81.51	105.95	24.44	112.3	107.9	116.0
1998	178.77	75.39	103.38	27.99	95.4	92.5	97.6
1999	191.85	93.18	98.67	5.49	107.3	123.6	95.4
2000	233.51	115.60	117.91	2.31	121.7	124.1	119.5
2001	230.37	114.13	116.24	2.11	98.7	98.7	98.6
2002	279.27	141.49	137.78	-3.71	121.2	124.0	118.5
2003	349.41	180.52	168.89	-11.63	125.1	127.6	122.6
2004	447.88	233.14	214.74	-18.40	128.2	129.2	127.2
2005	534.75	268.07	266.68	-1.39	119.4	115.0	124.2
2006	637.62	313.85	323.77	9.92	119.2	117.1	121.4
2007	734.94	355.91	379.03	23.12	115.3	113.4	117.1
2008	818.73	389.47	429.26	39.79	111.4	109.4	113.3
2009	766.85	392.82	374.03	-18.79	93.7	100.9	87.1
2010	1037.68	553.89	483.79	-70.10	135.3	141.0	129.3
2011	1161.68	596.94	564.74	-32.20	112.0	107.8	116.7
2012	1171.67	582.52	589.15	6.63	100.9	97.6	104.3
2013	1188.96	560.89	628.07	67.18	101.5	96.3	106.6
2014	1305.90	578.77	727.13	148.36	109.8	103.2	115.8
2015	1338.68	527.01	811.67	284.66	102.5	91.1	111.6
2016	1293.09	511.32	781.77	270.45	96.6	97.0	96.3
2017	1432.50	579.30	853.20	273.90	110.8	113.3	109.1
2018	1485.05	636.55	848.50	211.95	103.7	109.9	99.4
2019	1450.19	687.96	762.23	74.27	97.7	108.1	89.8

15-1 续表 continue

年份 Year	进出口总值（亿元）Total Value of Imports and Exports (RMB 100 million)	进口总值 Imports	出口总值 Exports	进出口差额（亿元）Balance (RMB 100 million)	进出口总值指数（上年=100）Indices of Total Imports and Exports (preceding year=100)	进口总值 Imports	出口总值 Exports
2014	8022.80	3555.15	4467.65	912.50	108.7	102.2	114.6
2015	8306.28	3271.71	5034.57	1762.86	103.5	92.0	112.7
2016	8541.02	3382.26	5158.76	1776.50	102.8	103.4	102.5
2017	9715.52	3923.09	5792.43	1869.34	113.8	116.0	112.3
2018	9811.59	4204.09	5607.50	1403.41	101.0	107.2	96.8
2019	10001.04	4742.68	5258.36	515.68	101.9	112.8	93.8

注：为进一步完善海关统计数据公布制度，从2014年开始海关总署全面公布以人民币计价的各类海关统计数据。

Note:In order to improve the customs statistical data publication system, since 2014 the General Administration of Customs has announced all kinds of Customs Statistics in RMB.

15-2 商品进出口总值(人民币计价)

单位：万元

项 目	Item
总 计	**Total**
按贸易方式分	**By Trade Form**
一般贸易	Ordinary Trade
国家间国际组织无偿援助和捐赠的物资	Donation and Gratis Aid of International Organizations
华侨港澳同胞外籍华人捐赠的物资	Donation of Overseas Chinese
补偿贸易	Compensation Trade
来料加工装配贸易	Trade of Processing and Assembling Supplied Materials
进料加工贸易	Trade of Processing Imported Materials
寄售代销贸易	Sale by Consignment
边境小额贸易	Small Trade on Border
来料加工装配进口的设备	Equipment for Processing and Assembling by Import
对外承包工程货物	Goods for Contracted Foreign Projects
租赁贸易	Leasing Trade
外商投资企业作为投资进口的设备物品	Imported Equipment Used as Investment by Foreign Funded Enterprises
出料加工贸易	Trade of Processing Exported Materials
保税监管场所进出境货物	Inbound and Outbound Goods in Bonded Warehouses
海关特殊监管区域物流货物	Storage of Transit Goods in Bonded Warehouses
易货贸易	Barter Trade
海关特殊监管区域进口设备	Facility of Export Manufacturing District
其他贸易	Others
按登记注册类型分	**Grouped by Registration Status**
国有企业	State-owned Enterprises
集体企业	Collective-owned Enterprises
外商及港澳台投资企业	Enterprises with Funds from Foreign Countries, Hong Kong, Macao and Taiwan
合资企业	Joint-venture Enterprises
合作企业	Cooperative Enterprises
外资企业	Enterprises with Sole Foreign Funds
私营企业	Private Enterprises
其他企业	Others
个体工商户	Individual Operating Households

Total Value of Import and Export Commodities through Customs (Renminbi-denominated)

(10000 yuan)

2018			2019		
合 计 Total (by RMB)	进 口 Imports	出 口 Exports	合 计 Total (by RMB)	进 口 Imports	出 口 Exports
98115885	**42040898**	**56074987**	**100010429**	**47426778**	**52583651**
45888167	25224072	20664095	48944418	26869337	22075081
4007	6	4001	4308		4308
7229639	3181237	4048402	6433063	2814810	3618253
19313928	7404195	11909733	18487236	7294449	11192787
8714	8714		8494	8494	
156847		156847	188353		188353
42647	42605	42	70963	69809	1154
185218	185218		1695961	1695961	
8665	4447	4218	24210	13364	10846
3643215	2164117	1479098	4669035	2858202	1810833
5335358	3669946	1665412	6535987	5071604	1464383
			1		1
1880	1880		1996	1996	
16297600	154461	16143139	12946404	728752	12217652
12735897	6858525	5877372	13671092	8265680	5405412
374257	220762	153495	355296	223296	132000
41981137	21579673	20401464	42201169	22779602	19421567
15337417	8339297	6998120	15273920	9333924	5939996
590224	163325	426899	533665	153679	379986
26053496	13077051	12976445	26393584	13291999	13101585
42157594	12581140	29576454	42341959	14779395	27562564
857262	800572	56690	1431301	1377533	53768
9738	226	9512	9612	1272	8340

15-2 续表

单位:万元

项　　目	Item	
按国别(地区)分	**By Country (Territory)**	
亚洲小计	Asia	
# 中国香港	Hong Kong, China	
中国澳门	Macao, China	
印度尼西亚	Indonesia	
日　本	Japan	
马来西亚	Malaysia	
新加坡	Singapore	
韩　国	Republic of Korea	
泰　国	Thailand	
中国台湾	Taiwan, China	
阿拉伯联合酋长国	United Arab Emirates	
印　度	India	
非洲小计	Africa	
# 南　非	South Africa	
欧洲小计	Europe	
# 英　国	United Kingdom	
德　国	Germany	
法　国	France	
意大利	Italy	
荷　兰	Netherlands	
西班牙	Spain	
比利时	Belgium	
瑞　士	Switzerland	
俄罗斯	Russia	
拉丁美洲小计	Latin America	
# 墨西哥	Mexico	
巴拿马	Panama	
北美洲小计	North America	
# 加拿大	Canada	
美　国	United States	
大洋洲小计	Oceania	
# 澳大利亚	Australia	
其　他	Others	

continued

(10000 yuan)

2018			2019		
合 计 Total (by RMB)	进 口 Imports	出 口 Exports	合 计 Total (by RMB)	进 口 Imports	出 口 Exports
52334393	25246848	27087545	53124650	28054600	25070050
8412843	325621	8087222	7667210	388137	7279073
316613	7638	308975	350567	5766	344801
2368982	1207872	1161110	2491394	1286609	1204785
10388272	7895838	2492434	11953902	9609752	2344150
2876084	1084725	1791359	2912575	1262593	1649982
1568614	560440	1008174	1630449	711531	918918
6496070	5305071	1190999	6973949	5885532	1088417
2188326	994997	1193329	2232253	1136277	1095976
2876855	2165567	711288	3247915	2585355	662560
1502043	512393	989650	1244672	418240	826432
2551003	907178	1643825	1796894	347400	1449494
7950149	2327112	5623037	7752868	2052382	5700486
2331793	1898098	433695	1974995	1628574	346421
16063725	6989496	9074229	18993901	9659851	9334050
1984145	358977	1625168	2073285	446016	1627269
3915843	2520701	1395142	4230345	2995172	1235173
1686304	1012651	673653	2462348	1766099	696249
1079157	498360	580797	1144224	509998	634226
1673894	679277	994617	1846734	744299	1102435
712143	214188	497955	795134	281569	513565
577926	182833	395093	886616	443282	443334
435035	391934	43101	1134941	1080479	54462
935740	142492	793248	974222	123631	850591
4939485	1023939	3915546	4978765	1143471	3835294
1952702	316938	1635764	2042985	352969	1690016
228730	11025	217705	224352	6265	218087
14444207	5324662	9119545	12038670	4472132	7566538
1299443	419825	879618	1083554	442304	641250
13119868	4904827	8215041	10952641	4029827	6922814
2380141	1125056	1255085	2744271	1667038	1077233
1760457	701764	1058693	1963921	1086809	877112
3785	3785		377304	377304	

15-3 商品进出口总值(美元计价)

单位：万美元

项　　目	Item
总　　计	**Total**
按贸易方式分	**By Trade Form**
一般贸易	Ordinary Trade
国家间国际组织无偿援助和捐赠的物资	Donation and Gratis Aid of International Organizations
华侨港澳同胞外籍华人捐赠的物资	Donation of Overseas Chinese
补偿贸易	Compensation Trade
来料加工装配贸易	Trade of Processing and Assembling Supplied Materials
进料加工贸易	Trade of Processing Imported Materials
寄售代销贸易	Sale by Consignment
边境小额贸易	Small Trade on Border
来料加工装配进口的设备	Equipment for Processing and Assembling by Import
对外承包工程货物	Goods for Contracted Foreign Projects
租赁贸易	Leasing Trade
外商投资企业作为投资进口的设备物品	Imported Equipment Used as Investment by Foreign Funded Enterprises
出料加工贸易	Trade of Processing Exported Materials
保税监管场所进出境货物	Inbound and Outbound Goods in Bonded Warehouses
海关特殊监管区域物流货物	Storage of Transit Goods in Bonded Warehouses
易货贸易	Barter Trade
海关特殊监管区域进口设备	Facility of Export Manufacturing District
其他贸易	Others
按登记注册类型分	**Grouped by Registration Status**
国有企业	State-owned Enterprises
集体企业	Collective-owned Enterprises
外商及港澳台投资企业	Enterprises with Funds from Foreign Countries, Hong Kong, Macao and Taiwan
合资企业	Joint-venture Enterprises
合作企业	Cooperative Enterprises
外资企业	Enterprises with Sole Foreign Funds
私营企业	Private Enterprises
其他企业	Others
个体工商户	Individual Operating Households

Total Value of Import and Export Commodities through Customs (U.S.dollar-denominated)

(USD10000)

2018			2019		
合 计 Total (by USD)	进 口 Imports	出 口 Exports	合 计 Total (by USD)	进 口 Imports	出 口 Exports
14850529	**6365507**	**8485022**	**14501947**	**6879666**	**7622281**
6955660	3820004	3135656	7100041	3897951	3202090
610	1	609	622		622
1094443	481973	612470	933879	408848	525031
2926253	1121256	1804997	2683816	1059144	1624672
1324	1324		1233	1233	
23683		23683	27447		27447
6494	6488	6	10363	10197	166
27248	27248		248124	248124	
1261	645	616	3520	1941	1579
550636	327088	223548	676384	413464	262920
810651	555825	254826	947594	734551	213043
281	281		286	286	
2451985	23374	2428611	1868638	103927	1764711
1934882	1041299	893583	1979360	1196434	782926
56705	33392	23313	51633	32471	19162
6361625	3267439	3094186	6129377	3309086	2820291
2322754	1260236	1062518	2220483	1356988	863495
89551	24784	64767	77473	22306	55167
3949320	1982419	1966901	3831421	1929792	1901629
6370588	1906699	4463889	6134202	2143329	3990873
125244	116644	8600	205983	198163	7820
1485	34	1451	1392	183	1209

15-3 续表

单位:万美元

项　　目	Item	
按国别(地区)分	**By Country (Territory)**	
亚洲小计	Asia	
# 中国香港	Hong Kong, China	
中国澳门	Macao, China	
印度尼西亚	Indonesia	
日　本	Japan	
马来西亚	Malaysia	
新加坡	Singapore	
韩　国	Republic of Korea	
泰　国	Thailand	
中国台湾	Taiwan, China	
阿拉伯联合酋长国	United Arab Emirates	
印　度	India	
非洲小计	Africa	
# 南　非	South Africa	
欧洲小计	Europe	
# 英　国	United Kingdom	
德　国	Germany	
法　国	France	
意大利	Italy	
荷　兰	Netherlands	
西班牙	Spain	
比利时	Belgium	
瑞　士	Switzerland	
俄罗斯	Russia	
拉丁美洲小计	Latin America	
# 墨西哥	Mexico	
巴拿马	Panama	
北美洲小计	North America	
# 加拿大	Canada	
美　国	United States	
大洋洲小计	Oceania	
# 澳大利亚	Australia	
其　他	Others	

continued

(USD10000)

2018			2019		
合 计 Total (by USD)	进 口 Imports	出 口 Exports	合 计 Total (by USD)	进 口 Imports	出 口 Exports
7920162	3822240	4097922	7707988	4072056	3635932
1272318	48782	1223536	1112804	56295	1056509
48502	1164	47338	51362	837	50525
359271	183592	175679	360779	186265	174514
1574204	1195853	378351	1736510	1395670	340840
434157	164176	269981	421547	182959	238588
238132	85083	153049	236137	102999	133138
982691	801202	181489	1012909	855041	157868
331265	150924	180341	323575	164691	158884
435898	328199	107699	471601	375416	96185
225541	77334	148207	180379	60750	119629
386151	137575	248576	260662	50403	210259
1199667	352669	846998	1122465	298869	823596
353054	287269	65785	287592	237323	50269
2431821	1057041	1374780	2752003	1398785	1353218
300692	54108	246584	300853	64765	236088
592272	381474	210798	614823	435779	179044
254608	152825	101783	355153	254174	100979
163512	75400	88112	166011	73937	92074
253436	102660	150776	267913	108189	159724
107954	32415	75539	115378	40880	74498
87502	27576	59926	128159	64010	64149
66264	59711	6553	163016	155129	7887
141523	21227	120296	141166	17916	123250
748420	155098	593322	722160	165964	556196
295957	48033	247924	296419	51179	245240
34591	1682	32909	32457	906	31551
2189768	807402	1382366	1746561	649307	1097254
195649	63130	132519	157097	64231	92866
1990249	744270	1245979	1589113	585076	1004037
360105	170471	189634	397942	241857	156085
266465	106473	159992	284816	157665	127151
586	586		52828	52828	

15-4 商品进出口总值(2019年，按地区分)

Total Value of Import and Export Commodities through Customs (2019, by Region)

地　区	District	按美元计价 (By USD) 商品进出口总值(万美元) Total Value of Imports and Exports (USD 10000)	进口总值 Imports	出口总值 Exports
全　市	**Total**	**14501947**	**6879666**	**7622281**
#荔湾区	Liwan	247869	117203	130666
越秀区	Yuexiu	1131544	477689	653855
海珠区	Haizhu	456908	169277	287631
天河区	Tianhe	840585	478609	361976
白云区	Baiyun	743611	224903	518708
黄埔区	Huangpu	4129325	2326963	1802362
番禺区	Panyu	1760747	602474	1158273
花都区	Huadu	1287984	471201	816783
南沙区	Nansha	3096493	1673470	1423023
从化区	Conghua	172621	33496	139125
增城区	Zengcheng	634260	304381	329879

15-4 续表 continued

地 区	District	按人民币计价 (By RMB) 商品进出口总值 (万元) Total Value of Imports and Exports (10000 yuan)	进口总值 Imports	出口总值 Exports
全 市	**Total**	**100010429**	**47426778**	**52583651**
# 荔湾区	Liwan	1710252	809835	900417
越秀区	Yuexiu	7821306	3300934	4520372
海珠区	Haizhu	3158459	1174110	1984349
天河区	Tianhe	5797438	3298889	2498549
白云区	Baiyun	5117802	1548547	3569255
黄埔区	Huangpu	28446727	16025697	12421030
番禺区	Panyu	12137454	4148586	7988868
花都区	Huadu	8891084	3250744	5640340
南沙区	Nansha	21380127	11553182	9826945
从化区	Conghua	1190956	230763	960193
增城区	Zengcheng	4358824	2085491	2273333

15-5 主要进口商品数量和金额

商品名称		Name of Commodities	
鲜干水果及坚果	(吨)	Fresh or Dried Fruits and Nuts	(ton)
乳　品	(吨)	Dairy	(ton)
谷物及谷物粉	(吨)	Cereals and Cereal Flour	(ton)
大　豆	(吨)	Soybean	(ton)
食用植物油	(吨)	Edible Vegetable Oil	(ton)
合成橡胶	(吨)	Synthetic Rubber	(ton)
原　木	(立方米/吨)	Logs	(cu.m/ton)
铁矿砂及其精矿	(吨)	Iron Ore	(ton)
煤及褐煤	(吨)	Coal and Brown Coal	(ton)
成品油	(吨)	Petroleum Products Refined	(ton)
医药品	(吨)	Pharmaceutical Products	(ton)
初级形状的塑料	(吨)	Primary Plastics	(ton)
牛皮革及马皮革	(吨)	Bovine or Equine Leather	(ton)
纸及纸板	(吨)	Paper and Paperboards	(ton)
棉纱线	(吨)	Cotton Yarn	(ton)
合成纤维纱线	(吨)	Yarn of Synthetic Fibers	(ton)
针织或钩编织物	(万米)	Knitted or Crocheted Fabrics	(10000 meters)
钻　石	(千克)	Diamonds	(kg)
钢　材	(吨)	Rolled Steel	(ton)
未锻造的铜及铜材	(吨)	Unwrought Copper and Copper Products	(ton)
未锻造的铝及铝材	(吨)	Unwrought Aluminum and Aluminum Products	(ton)
活塞式内燃机的零件	(吨)	Parts of Piston Combustion Engines	(ton)
涡轮喷气发动机	(台)	Gas Turbine Engine	(set)
机械提升搬运装卸设备及零件		Mechanical Handling Equipment and Parts	
印刷、装订机械及零件		Printing or Book-binding Machinery and Parts	
金属加工机床	(台)	Machine Tools	(set)
自动数据处理设备及其部件	(万台)	Automatic Data Processing Machines and Components	(10000 sets)
制造平板显示器用的机器及装置	(台)	Machines and Devices for the Manufacture of Flat Display	(set)
变压、整流、电感器及零件		Transformers, Rectifiers and Inductance Suppliers and Parts	
电视、收音机及无线电讯设备的零附件	(吨)	Parts of Television, Radio, Telecommunications Apparatus	(ton)
电容器	(吨)	Capacitors and Parts	(ton)
印刷电路	(百万块)	Printed Circuit	(10 000 units)
通断及保护电路装置及零件		Electrical Apparatus and Parts for Switching or Protecting Electrical Circuits	
二极管及类似半导体器件	(百万个)	Diode and Semi-conductors	(million units)
集成电路	(百万个)	IC	(1 million pcs)
电线和电缆	(吨)	Electric Wires and Cables	(ton)
汽车零配件		Parts of Motor Vehicles	
飞机及其他航空器	(架)	Aircraft	(unit)
液晶显示板	(万个)	LCD Panel	(10 000 units)
医疗仪器及器械		Medical Instruments and Appliances	
计量检测分析自控仪器及器具		Measuring or Checking Instruments and Apparatus	
塑料制品	(吨)	Plastic Articles	(ton)

注：“原木”统计计量单位2019年为吨。

Main Import Commodities in Volume and Value

2018			2019		
数　量 Volume	金　额（万美元） Value (USD 10000)	金　额（万元） Value (10000 yuan)	数　量 Volume	金　额（万美元） Value (USD 10000)	金　额（万元） Value (10000 yuan)
60073	13016	86250	67558	20857	143864
206604	181857	1201105	224064	200745	1382831
2629063	72851	473844	1697036	49203	338150
136553	5766	36951			
159869	12692	84198	329144	20173	138329
79041	17357	114214	79283	15380	105877
677863	26510	173343	826274	21584	148527
3505616	28012	184329	4838042	46374	320519
13671968	89414	586716	15057443	83796	575827
756343	51467	339821	929448	56392	388175
10474	127450	843673	10874	185890	1282051
2341604	422703	2784290	2478549	387492	2668544
37532	22125	144726	27569	14869	102152
276216	24259	159687	292445	21622	149031
118084	35993	236987	82868	24872	170906
23188	16238	106714	16894	12291	84690
3462	10149	66501	2633	6932	47660
816	271768	1796627	716	228331	1570704
1887832	159413	1050602	1833440	142290	981517
157638	117158	768891	141721	99563	686112
35099	10490	70964	24760	8996	62026
22805	44280	291193	16856	36462	251083
40	43226	282566	47	52810	364096
	15655	103079		21389	146621
	71229	469697		66839	460245
3027	36771	242209	2546	28281	194398
265	21687	143133	319	20155	138995
224	50801	349486	887	209810	1434188
	38325	253948		59363	410948
1880	26265	174952	1983	38401	266036
2075	23856	157417	2391	22594	155905
751	37860	250377	685	37203	256657
	74252	490433		78744	541571
13123	96214	633759	10066	50422	347393
6113	281159	1858849	5872	321397	2216203
9003	17309	114275	15864	27677	190886
	399208	2629176		332605	2293255
57	371012	2450279	84	384178	2655912
6509	301897	1993386	10864	294903	2027586
	52077	343258		49447	341337
	186055	1230699		223752	1539907
18482	24207	160007	19809	26494	182730

Note: The statistical measurement unit of "log" is ton in 2019.

15-6 主要出口商品数量和金额

商品名称		Name of Commodities	
印刷品	(吨)	Presswork	(ton)
成品油	(吨)	Refined Petroleum Products	(ton)
医药品	(吨)	Medical and Pharmaceutical Products	(ton)
新的充气橡胶轮胎	(万条/吨)	New Pneumatic Rubber Tires	(10000 units/ton)
纺织纱线、织物及制品		Textile Yarn, Fabrics and Related Products	
玻璃制品	(吨)	Glasswork	(ton)
陶瓷产品	(吨)	Ceramic	(ton)
珍珠、钻石、宝石及半宝石		Pearls, Diamonds, Jewelry and Semi-jewelry	
钢　材	(吨)	Rolled Steel	(ton)
不锈钢厨具、餐具等家用器具	(吨)	Household Stainless Steel Cookware and Tableware	(ton)
电　扇	(万台)	Electric Fans	(10000 sets)
空气调节器	(万台)	Air conditioner	(10000 sets)
冰　箱	(万台)	Fridge	(10000 sets)
自动数据处理设备及其部件	(万台)	Automatic Data Processing Machines and Components	(10000 sets)
自动数据处理设备的零件	(吨)	Parts of Automatic Data Processing Machines	(ton)
打印机(包括多功能一体机)	(万台)	Printer(Multi Function Printer)	(10000 sets)
液晶显示板	(万个)	LCD Panel	(10000 sets)
静止式变流器	(百万个)	Static Converter	(million units)
原电池	(百万个)	Primary Cells and Batteries	(million units)
蓄电池	(万个)	Electric Accumulators	(10000 units)
电话机	(万台)	Telephone	(10000 units)
扬声器	(万个)	Loudspeakers	(10000 units)
录、放像机	(万台)	Video Tape Recorders	(10000 sets)
电视机	(万台)	TV	(10000 sets)
电视、收音机及无线电讯设备的零附件	(吨)	Parts of TV,radio,wireless telecommunication device	(ton)
印刷电路	(百万块)	Printed Circuits	(million units)
电线和电缆	(吨)	Electronic Wires and Cables	(ton)
集装箱	(个)	Containers	(unit)
汽车零配件		Parts of Motor Vehicles	
摩托车	(辆)	Motorcycles	(unit)
自行车	(万辆)	Bicycles	(10000 units)
摩托车及自行车的零配件		Parts of Motorcycles and Bicycles	
船　舶	(艘)	Ships	(unit)
照相机	(万架)	Cameras	(10000 sets)
手　表	(万只)	Wrist Watches	(10000 units)
家具及其零件		Furniture and Parts	
灯具、照明装置及类似品		Lamps and Lighting Fittings	
箱包及类似容器	(吨)	Package Bags and Similar Containers	(ton)
服装及衣着附件		Garments and Clothing Accessories	
鞋	(万双/吨)	Footwear	(10000 pairs/ton)
塑料制品	(吨)	Plastic Articles	(ton)
玩　具		Toys	
贵金属或包贵金属的首饰	(千克)	Jewelry of Precious Metals or Rolled Precious Metals	(kilogramme)

注："新的充气橡胶轮胎"、"鞋"2019年计量单位为吨。

Main Export Commodities in Volume and Value

2018			2019		
数 量 Volume	金 额（万美元） Value (USD 10000)	金 额（万元） Value (10000 yuan)	数 量 Volume	金 额（万美元） Value (USD 10000)	金 额（万元） Value (10000 yuan)
39675	17233	113767	46155	18263	125954
1840968	120447	796184	2290211	142196	979427
21689	11872	78434	22297	13689	94240
1425	22107	145897	96519	23282	160538
	294213	1939456		263693	1820210
188878	29151	192484	201400	31589	218429
1020375	140873	933204	709841	101088	697178
	17882	118501		17837	122701
524984	77889	512879	473250	66335	457064
66917	34581	228427	53514	28093	194222
3314	19423	127240	3271	18608	128058
391	82568	534248	457	91260	623459
336	51300	337795	348	51758	356450
6830	145114	955267	4794	117806	811421
19651	38056	252756	24898	59630	412230
547	110549	727375	409	82514	568026
2684	396637	2610714	3179	382574	2631481
290	95795	631511	227	92732	640329
6765	29112	191918	7144	29527	203259
8696	33988	225210	8467	36700	252984
376	20667	135958	280	17194	119338
9593	78649	520843	7770	72305	499457
1223	20768	137858	299	5776	39891
643	75647	498723	600	58966	406407
18281	94203	617277	18120	69722	482652
1473	115664	763715	1376	96321	665245
72469	54521	359906	62099	45181	311764
94508	32037	210474	67691	19417	133668
	274395	1810789		216050	1488078
1422026	73970	486733	1386362	64991	447614
183	13024	85630	130	8780	60503
	45708	303216		58349	403756
84	150674	999185	66	111607	769113
514	56455	377237	575	47644	327696
7071	16421	108909	6188	17655	121734
	268154	1778273		223988	1547983
	249196	1653332		205941	1423669
355149	317542	2097156	284908	251279	1734877
	964294	6399881		740465	5124056
53232	205582	1360582	219365	174618	1206642
399416	185073	1224737	364749	161359	1113604
	219164	1451780		147926	1020431
167737	401040	2654665	156553	337787	2328317

Note: The unit of measurement of "new pneumatic rubber tire" and "shoe" is ton in 2019.

15-7 进出口商品分类金额(按人民币计价)

单位:万元

项目	Item
合计	**Total**
第一类 活动物、动物产品	Live Animals & Animal Products
活动物	Live Animals
肉及食用杂碎	Meat and Edible Haslets
水产品	Aquatic Products
乳品、蛋品、天然蜂蜜、其他食用动物产品	Dairy Products, Eggs, Natural Honey and Other Edible Animal Products
其他动物产品	Other Animal Products
第二类 植物产品	Vegetables Products
树苗及花草	Saplings, Flowers and Herbs
蔬菜	Edible Vegetables
水果及坚果	Fruits and Nuts
咖啡、茶叶及调味香料	Coffee, Tea and Spices
谷物	Cereals
制粉工业产品	Flour,Starch and Related Prouducts
植物油籽、果实、种子、药材及饲料	Oil Seeds and Kernels and Oleaginous Fruits, Seeds, Plants for Medicinal Use and Forge
虫胶、树胶、树脂	Shellacs, Gums and Resins
编结植物材料、其他植物产品	Vegetable Plaiting Materials and Other Vegetable Products
第三类 动、植物油脂及蜡	Animal Fat ,Vegetable Oils and Waxes
动、植物油脂及蜡	Animal and Vegetable Oils, Fats and Waxes
第四类 食品、烟草及制品	Food, Tobacco and Related Products
动物产品制品	Animal Products
糖及糖食	Sugar and Sugar Confectionery
可可及可可制品	Cocoa and Cocoa Products
粮食及乳制品、糕饼点心	Grain, Milk and Pastry Products
蔬菜、水果等植物制品	Vegetable and Fruit Products
杂项食品	Miscellaneous Edible Preparation
饮料、酒及醋	Beverages, Liquor and Vinegar
食品的残渣、动物饲料	Residues and Waste from Food and Animal Fodder
烟草及烟草制品	Tobacco and Tobacco Products
第五类 矿产品	Mineral
盐、硫磺、建筑材料	Salt, Sulfur and Building Materials
矿砂、矿渣及矿灰	Ore, Slag and Mortar
矿物燃料、矿物油及产品	Mineral Fuels, Mineral Oils and Related Products
第六类 化工产品	Chemicals
无机化学品	Inorganic Chemicals
有机化学品	Organic Chemicals
药品	Medicinal and Pharmaceuticaland Products
肥料	Fertilizers
鞣料、染料浸膏、染料、颜料、油漆、油墨	Tanning and Dyeing Extracts, Coloring and Dyeing Materials, Paint and Printing Ink

Value of Imports and Exports by Category of Commodities (Renminbi-denominated)

(10000 yuan)

2018		2019	
进 口 Imports	出 口 Exports	进 口 Imports	出 口 Exports
42040900	**56074988**	**47426778**	**52583651**
690815	68529	737589	87988
3466	41967	3564	59029
205725	15593	173606	20039
262113	4938	283089	3586
211642	4883	266998	5053
7869	1148	10332	281
884481	118781	762190	132736
4769	925	7142	1179
89884	34876	51265	42512
91281	5655	159661	4035
11815	15655	25389	16063
470357		326296	
24400	29514	32161	36082
157015	10002	121974	13777
21670	13548	25016	10023
13290	8606	13286	9065
184056	46195	266510	17780
184056	46195	266510	17780
2011628	366183	2321071	409051
5453	13433	8311	16208
30391	47483	44518	57451
16202	3382	15732	3537
1103134	112977	1282255	129441
58081	10655	86055	12634
331911	82606	408875	79108
271404	16119	267702	22588
192245	64606	202464	72191
2807	14922	5159	15893
3144303	1378030	3424278	1652081
76723	20530	74413	14602
381931	1889	457803	7039
2685649	1355611	2892062	1630440
3750671	1394110	4645331	1542284
146956	124346	161752	130115
934555	244132	852299	250961
818701	58222	1259892	74528
1622	11134	2142	21417
214070	98730	244671	121871

15-7 续表 1

单位:万元

项　　目	Item
化妆品及其原料、芳香料制品	Cosmetics and Related Products, Perfumed Materials
洗涤用品	Detergents
蛋白类物质、改性淀粉、胶、酶	Protein Materials, Modified Starches, Glues and Enzymes
炸药、烟火制品、易燃材料制品	Explosives, Pyrotechnic Products and Combustible Products
照相及电影用品	Photographic and Cinematographic Goods
杂项化学产品	Miscellaneous Chemical Products
第七类 塑料、橡胶及其制品	Plastics, Rubber and Related Products
塑料及其制品	Plastics and Related Products
橡胶及其制品	Rubber and Related Products
第八类 皮革、毛皮及其制品、旅行用品、手提包	Leather, Furs Skins and Related Products, Travel Articles and Handbags
生皮及皮革	Raw Hides and Leather
皮革制品、旅行用品及手提包	Leather Products, Travel Articles and Handbags
毛皮、人造毛皮及制品	Furs Shins, Artificial Furs Manufactures Thereof
第九类 木及木制品、草柳编结品	Wood and Wooden Products, Straw and Wicker Plaited Products
木及木制品、木炭	Wood and Wooden Products, Charcoal
软木及软木制品	Cork and Related Products
草柳编结品	Straw and Wicker Plaited Products
第十类 木浆、纸、纸板及制品	Wood Paper Pulp, Paper, Paperboard and Related Products
木浆及其他纤维素浆、废碎纸板	Paper Pulp and Cellulose, Waste Paperboard
纸及纸板、纸浆、纸制品	Paper and Paperboard, Articles of Paper Pulp and Paper Products
书籍、印刷品、设计图纸	Books, Printed Matter and Design Drawings
第十一类 纺织原料及纺织制品	Textile Materials and Products
蚕　丝	Natural Silk
羊毛、动物毛、毛纱线及制品	Wool, Animal Hair and Woolen Woven Fabrics
棉花及制品	Cotton and Related Products
其他纺织纤维、纸纱线及机织物	Other Textile Fiber, Yarn and Related Woven Fabrics
化学纤维长丝	Chemical Fiber, Continuous Filament
化学纤维短丝	Chemical Fiber, Staple Fiber
絮胎、毡尼及无纺物、特种纱线、线绳索缆	Wadding, Felt and Adhesive-Bond Fabrics, Special Yarn, Thread, Rope and Cable
地毯及纺织铺地制品	Carpets and Related Products
特种机织物、纺织装饰品、刺绣品	Special Woven Fabrics, Textile Trimmings and Embroidery
浸渍、涂布、包覆或层压的纺织物	Soaked, Coated or Overlapping Textiles
针织物及钩编织物	Knitwear and Crocheted Fabrics
针织或钩编的服装及衣着附件	Knitted or Crocheted Garments and Clothing Accessories
非针织或非钩编的服装及衣着附件	Garments and Clothing Accessories Not Knitted or Crocheted
其他纺织制成品、成套物品	Other Textile Products
第十二类 鞋帽伞杖、加工羽毛、人造花、人发制品	Footwear, Headgear, Umbrellas, Canes, Processed Feather, Artificial Flowers and Wigs
鞋类及零件	Footwear and Accessories
帽类及零件	Headgear and Accessories

continued

(10000 yuan)

2018		2019	
进　口 Imports	出　口 Exports	进　口 Imports	出　口 Exports
758286	343369	1105318	397495
253299	176306	268685	197518
105431	111872	119295	122391
195	25554	17	19905
31546	12711	43312	14662
486010	187734	587948	191421
3483027	2725612	3406291	2596077
3171221	2413448	3075861	2286023
311806	312164	330430	310054
254447	2185131	268181	1810710
178125	1471	130350	1621
52530	2174482	97412	1803281
23792	9178	40419	5808
358493	115548	279661	96536
357962	106898	279372	90357
40	105	135	120
491	8545	154	6059
470877	638437	533169	618552
255735	3909	302104	3261
176602	520761	162450	489337
38540	113767	68615	125954
844357	8197566	744236	6824381
1477	32743	2138	74327
10300	2893	10150	21071
268600	314284	193116	178786
29082	1488	14430	1437
134479	90532	121820	108698
104605	52579	72774	58060
49974	98561	46947	110707
2808	43393	2175	41780
15832	165252	15115	146325
35565	202672	34720	191017
66501	709775	47660	650643
64435	1664530	88578	1324769
48199	4579908	81573	3669282
12500	238956	13040	247479
140584	1702374	192205	1589229
136361	1454965	184112	1304188
2858	60014	5260	52120

15-7 续表 2

单位:万元

项　　目	Item
伞、杖、鞭及零件	Umbrellas, Canes, Whips and Accessories
加工羽毛、羽绒及制品、人造花、人发制品	Processed Feathers and Related Products, Artificial Flowers and Wigs
第十三类 石材制品、陶瓷产品、玻璃及其制品	Stone Products,Leramics,Glass and Glossware
石材制品	Stone and Related Products
陶瓷产品	Ceramics
玻璃及其制品	Glass and Glassware
第十四类 珠宝首饰、硬币	Jewellery and Coins
珠宝首饰	Jewellery
第十五类 贱金属及其制品	Base Metals and Related Products
钢　铁	Iron and Steel
钢铁制品	Iron and Steel Products
铜及其制品	Copper and Related Products
镍及其制品	Nickel and Related Products
铝及其制品	Aluminum and Related Products
铅及其制品	Lead and Related Products
锌及其制品	Zinc and Related Products
锡及其制品	Tin and Related Products
其他贱金属、金属陶瓷及其制品	Other Base Metals, Metal Ceramics and Related Products
贱金属工具、器具、利口器、餐具及零件	Base Metal Tools, Implements, Cutlery, Tableware and Related Parts
贱金属杂项制品	Miscellaneous Products of Base Metals
第十六类 机械、电气设备、电视机及音响设备	Machinery, Electric Equipment, Television Sets and Sound Appliances
核反应堆、锅炉、机械设备及零件	Nuclear Reactors, Boilers, Mechanical Equipment and Accessories
机电、电气设备、电视机及音响设备	Machinery and Electric Equipment, Television Sets and Sound Appliances
第十七类 车辆、航空器、船舶及有关运输设备	Locomotives, Vehicles, Aircraft, Ships and Related Transportation Equipment
铁道及电车机车、车辆及零件	Railway Locomotives, Tramcars and Accessories
车辆及零附件(铁道车辆除外)	Vehicles and Related Parts and Accessories (excluding railway locomotives)
航空器、航天器及零件	Aircraft, Spacecraft and Related Parts
船舶及浮动结构体	Ships and Related Products
第十八类 仪器、医疗器械、钟表及乐器	Instruments, Medical Instruments and Equipment, Clocks and Musical Instruments
光学、照相电影、计量检验、医疗仪器设备	Optical, Photographic, Film, Measuring and Checking, Medical Instruments and Equipments
钟表及零件	Clocks and Related Parts
乐器及零附件	Musical Instruments and Related Parts and Accessories
第十九类 武器、弹药及其零件、附件	Arms and Ammunition, Parts and Accessories thereof
第二十类 杂项制品	Miscellaneous Products
家具、床上用品、照明装置、活动房	Furniture, Bed Articles, Lighting Apparatus and Luminous Signs
玩具、游戏、运动用品及零附件	Toys, Games and Sports Goods and Related Parts and Accessories
杂项制品	Miscellaneous Manufactured Articles
第二十一类 艺术品、收藏品及古物	Works of Art, Collector's Pieces and Antiques
第二十二类 特殊交易品及未分类商品	Special Commodities and Unclassified Commodities

continued

(10000 yuan)

2018		2019	
进口 Imports	出口 Exports	进口 Imports	出口 Exports
515	29682	994	21697
850	157713	1839	211224
294237	1616612	314205	1395692
44235	326697	41349	306091
15275	933204	29432	697178
234727	356711	243424	392423
2091187	2925242	3088844	2600723
2091187	2925242	3088844	2600723
2657264	3703367	2740409	3330877
1154799	324805	1191459	291889
300746	1455651	315952	1338253
789710	90571	707072	115218
83184	371	196168	9307
105440	508218	101129	443041
4479	22	4752	140
19973	4137	13524	2886
10150	1286	8726	27028
14363	19704	25620	16802
113780	361385	110542	329017
60640	937217	65465	757296
10121758	15270400	12648647	14945474
4740605	6085341	6713077	6015661
5381153	9185059	5935570	8929813
4812818	3395814	4891002	3231009
1987	215130	657	135759
2221141	2115934	2102487	2237070
2586042	40811	2783668	65122
3648	1023939	4190	793058
4264555	3885701	4858322	3954841
4110527	3587876	4622902	3663311
133043	209382	216657	222034
20985	88443	18763	69496
458	38	742	90
470126	5986166	582932	4987002
134416	3595404	120227	3129374
86296	2023502	164859	1539275
249414	367260	297846	318353
2574	127	4349	791
1108184	355025	716614	759747

15-8 进出口商品分类金额(按美元计价)

单位:万美元

项　　目	Item
合　　计	**Total**
第一类 活动物、动物产品	Live Animals & Animal Products
活动物	Live Animals
肉及食用杂碎	Meat and Edible Haslets
水产品	Aquatic Products
乳品、蛋品、天然蜂蜜、其他食用动物产品	Dairy Products, Eggs, Natural Honey and Other Edible Animal Products
其他动物产品	Other Animal Products
第二类 植物产品	Vegetables Products
树苗及花草	Saplings, Flowers and Herbs
蔬　菜	Edible Vegetables
水果及坚果	Fruits and Nuts
咖啡、茶叶及调味香料	Coffee, Tea and Spices
谷　物	Cereals
制粉工业产品	Flour,Starch and Related Prouducts
植物油籽、果实、种子、药材及饲料	Oil Seeds and Kernels and Oleaginous Fruits, Seeds, Plants for Medicinal Use and Forge
虫胶、树胶、树脂	Shellacs, Gums and Resins
编结植物材料、其他植物产品	Vegetable Plaiting Materials and Other Vegetable Products
第三类 动、植物油脂及蜡	Animal Fat ,Vegetable Oils and Waxes
动、植物油脂及蜡	Animal and Vegetable Oils, Fats and Waxes
第四类 食品、烟草及制品	Food, Tobacco and Related Products
动物产品制品	Animal Products
糖及糖食	Sugar and Sugar Confectionery
可可及可可制品	Cocoa and Cocoa Products
粮食及乳制品、糕饼点心	Grain, Milk and Pastry Products
蔬菜、水果等植物制品	Vegetable and Fruit Products
杂项食品	Miscellaneous Edible Preparation
饮料、酒及醋	Beverages, Liquor and Vinegar
食品的残渣、动物饲料	Residues and Waste from Food and Animal Fodder
烟草及烟草制品	Tobacco and Tobacco Products
第五类 矿产品	Mineral
盐、硫磺、建筑材料	Salt, Sulfur and Building Materials
矿砂、矿渣及矿灰	Ore, Slag and Mortar
矿物燃料、矿物油及产品	Mineral Fuels, Mineral Oils and Related Products
第六类 化工产品	Chemicals
无机化学品	Inorganic Chemicals
有机化学品	Organic Chemicals
药　品	Medicinal and Pharmaceuticaland Products
肥　料	Fertilizers
鞣料、染料浸膏、染料、颜料、油漆、油墨	Tanning and Dyeing Extracts, Coloring and Dyeing Materials, Paint and Printing Ink

Value of Imports and Exports by Category of Commodities (U.S.dollar-denominated)

(USD 10000)

2018		2019	
进 口 Imports	出 口 Exports	进 口 Imports	出 口 Exports
6365508	**8485022**	**6879666**	**7622281**
105278	10354	106934	12746
517	6323	517	8542
31654	2360	25185	2907
39788	755	41030	524
32113	741	38704	732
1206	175	1498	41
134745	17949	110670	19247
721	139	1032	170
13304	5234	7396	6163
13777	841	23144	585
1752	2377	3684	2328
72345		47484	
3655	4474	4686	5236
23884	1514	17681	1990
3282	2062	3624	1456
2025	1308	1939	1319
27902	7057	38764	2584
27902	7057	38764	2584
303940	55345	336761	59388
818	2029	1201	2350
4637	7178	6400	8325
2431	512	2278	512
166864	17004	186102	18830
8731	1622	12467	1830
49922	12511	59258	11481
41237	2443	38844	3275
28873	9775	29466	10480
427	2271	745	2305
477303	209412	495385	239996
11678	3131	10780	2117
58136	296	66288	1038
407489	205985	418317	236841
566913	210979	674011	223911
22280	18877	23460	18926
141794	36918	123736	36529
123673	8796	182675	10828
252	1684	317	3115
32515	14935	35515	17685

15-8 续表 1

单位:万美元

项目	Item
化妆品及其原料、芳香料制品	Cosmetics and Related Products, Perfumed Materials
洗涤用品	Detergents
蛋白类物质、改性淀粉、胶、酶	Protein Materials, Modified Starches, Glues and Enzymes
炸药、烟火制品、易燃材料制品	Explosives, Pyrotechnic Products and Combustible Products
照相及电影用品	Photographic and Cinematographic Goods
杂项化学产品	Miscellaneous Chemical Products
第七类 塑料、橡胶及其制品	Plastics, Rubber and Related Products
塑料及其制品	Plastics and Related Products
橡胶及其制品	Rubber and Related Products
第八类 皮革、毛皮及其制品、旅行用品、手提包	Leather, Furs Skins and Related Products, Travel Articles and Handbags
生皮及皮革	Raw Hides and Leather
皮革制品、旅行用品及手提包	Leather Products, Travel Articles and Handbags
毛皮、人造毛皮及制品	Furs Shins, Artificial Furs Manufactures Thereof
第九类 木及木制品、草柳编结品	Wood and Wooden Products, Straw and Wicker Plaited Products
木及木制品、木炭	Wood and Wooden Products, Charcoal
软木及软木制品	Cork and Related Products
草柳编结品	Straw and Wicker Plaited Products
第十类 木浆、纸、纸板及制品	Wood Paper Pulp, Paper, Paperboard and Related Products
木浆及其他纤维素浆、废碎纸板	Paper Pulp and Cellulose, Waste Paperboard
纸及纸板、纸浆、纸制品	Paper and Paperboard, Articles of Paper Pulp and Paper Products
书籍、印刷品、设计图纸	Books, Printed Matter and Design Drawings
第十一类 纺织原料及纺织制品	Textile Materials and Products
蚕 丝	Natural Silk
羊毛、动物毛、毛纱线及制品	Wool, Animal Hair and Woolen Woven Fabrics
棉花及制品	Cotton and Related Products
其他纺织纤维、纸纱线及机织物	Other Textile Fiber, Yarn and Related Woven Fabrics
化学纤维长丝	Chemical Fiber, Continuous Filament
化学纤维短丝	Chemical Fiber, Staple Fiber
絮胎、毡尼及无纺物、特种纱线、线绳索缆	Wadding, Felt and Adhesive-Bond Fabrics, Special Yarn, Thread, Rope and Cable
地毯及纺织铺地制品	Carpets and Related Products
特种机织物、纺织装饰品、刺绣品	Special Woven Fabrics, Textile Trimmings and Embroidery
浸渍、涂布、包覆或层压的纺织物	Soaked, Coated or Overlapping Textiles
针织物及钩编织物	Knitwear and Crocheted Fabrics
针织或钩编的服装及衣着附件	Knitted or Crocheted Garments and Clothing Accessories
非针织或非钩编的服装及衣着附件	Garments and Clothing Accessories Not Knitted or Crocheted
其他纺织制成品、成套物品	Other Textile Products
第十二类 鞋帽伞杖、加工羽毛、人造花、人发制品	Footwear, Headgear, Umbrellas, Canes, Processed Feather, Artificial Flowers and Wigs
鞋类及零件	Footwear and Accessories
帽类及零件	Headgear and Accessories

continued

(USD 10000)

2018		2019	
进 口 Imports	出 口 Exports	进 口 Imports	出 口 Exports
113424	51894	160398	57681
38408	26622	38998	28626
15948	16943	17354	17745
30	3881	2	2906
4795	1929	6251	2125
73794	28500	85305	27745
528648	412495	494510	376450
481342	365324	446565	331495
47306	47171	47945	44955
38653	330837	38922	262266
27203	223	18964	236
7793	329224	14119	261190
3657	1390	5839	840
54714	17507	40588	14003
54634	16196	40547	13107
6	16	19	17
74	1295	22	879
71243	96495	77386	89670
38576	580	43887	475
26820	78681	23574	70932
5847	17234	9925	18263
128004	1237095	108118	986810
223	5068	308	10634
1574	448	1485	2994
40801	48015	28107	25911
4450	226	2098	209
20376	13622	17670	15778
15962	7952	10559	8410
7588	14912	6819	16028
431	6556	317	6056
2407	25075	2195	21216
5387	30711	5045	27700
10149	107672	6932	94383
9603	250904	12854	191840
7168	689906	11833	529803
1885	36028	1896	35848
21175	257210	27872	229878
20538	219848	26698	188746
427	9049	764	7541

15-8 续表 2

单位:万美元

项　　　目	Item
伞、杖、鞭及零件	Umbrellas, Canes, Whips and Accessories
加工羽毛、羽绒及制品、人造花、人发制品	Processed Feathers and Related Products, Artificial Flowers and Wigs
第十三类 石材制品、陶瓷产品、玻璃及其制品	Stone Products,Leramics,Glass and Glossware
石材制品	Stone and Related Products
陶瓷产品	Ceramics
玻璃及其制品	Glass and Glassware
第十四类 珠宝首饰、硬币	Jewellery and Coins
珠宝首饰	Jewellery
第十五类 贱金属及其制品	Base Metals and Related Products
钢　铁	Iron and Steel
钢铁制品	Iron and Steel Products
铜及其制品	Copper and Related Products
镍及其制品	Nickel and Related Products
铝及其制品	Aluminum and Related Products
铅及其制品	Lead and Related Products
锌及其制品	Zinc and Related Products
锡及其制品	Tin and Related Products
其他贱金属、金属陶瓷及其制品	Other Base Metals, Metal Ceramics and Related Products
贱金属工具、器具、利口器、餐具及零件	Base Metal Tools, Implements, Cutlery, Tableware and Related Parts
贱金属杂项制品	Miscellaneous Products of Base Metals
第十六类 机械、电气设备、电视机及音响设备	Machinery, Electric Equipment, Television Sets and Sound Appliances
核反应堆、锅炉、机械设备及零件	Nuclear Reactors, Boilers, Mechanical Equipment and Accessories
机电、电气设备、电视机及音响设备	Machinery and Electric Equipment, Television Sets and Sound Appliances
第十七类 车辆、航空器、船舶及有关运输设备	Locomotives, Vehicles, Aircraft, Ships and Related Transportation Equipment
铁道及电车机车、车辆及零件	Railway Locomotives, Tramcars and Accessories
车辆及零附件(铁道车辆除外)	Vehicles and Related Parts and Accessories (excluding railway locomotives)
航空器、航天器及零件	Aircraft, Spacecraft and Related Parts
船舶及浮动结构体	Ships and Related Products
第十八类 仪器、医疗器械、钟表及乐器	Instruments, Medical Instruments and Equipment, Clocks and Musical Instruments
光学、照相电影、计量检验、医疗仪器设备	Optical, Photographic, Film, Measuring and Checking, Medical Instruments and Equipments
钟表及零件	Clocks and Related Parts
乐器及零附件	Musical Instruments and Related Parts and Accessories
第十九类 武器、弹药及其零件、附件	Arms and Ammunition, Parts and Accessories thereof
第二十类 杂项制品	Miscellaneous Products
家具、床上用品、照明装置、活动房	Furniture, Bed Articles, Lighting Apparatus and Luminous Signs
玩具、游戏、运动用品及零附件	Toys, Games and Sports Goods and Related Parts and Accessories
杂项制品	Miscellaneous Manufactured Articles
第二十一类 艺术品、收藏品及古物	Works of Art, Collector's Pieces and Antiques
第二十二类 特殊交易品及未分类商品	Special Commodities and Unclassified Commodities

continued

(USD 10000)

2018		2019	
进　口 Imports	出　口 Exports	进　口 Imports	出　口 Exports
78	4500	144	3149
132	23813	266	30442
44693	244158	45656	202023
6718	49301	6000	44179
2331	140873	4273	101088
35644	53984	35383	56756
316245	441940	447390	377326
316245	441940	447390	377326
403232	560121	397136	483001
175407	49434	172402	42385
45456	220211	45824	193994
120309	13765	102603	16689
12523	58	28401	1321
15682	76878	14688	64307
661	3	697	20
3044	622	1963	418
1540	193	1279	3935
2181	2984	3732	2433
17206	54759	16066	47707
9223	141214	9481	109792
1529680	2316437	1838020	2167571
715561	925458	977345	873894
814119	1390979	860675	1293677
729839	513848	708608	468433
301	32755	97	19723
337541	320555	305218	324353
391449	6242	402687	9345
548	154296	606	115012
645306	589659	705544	574437
622039	544680	671459	532206
20081	31607	31359	32171
3186	13372	2726	10060
68	6	108	13
70845	902658	84491	722029
20230	542090	17419	452726
13006	304948	23890	223163
37609	55620	43182	46140
372	19	621	117
166710	53441	102171	110382

15-9 广州地区口岸进出口商品总值

Commodity Value of Imports and Exports through Ports in Guangzhou Area

项　目	Item	2018 万美元 (USD 10000)	2018 万元 (10000 yuan)	2019 万美元 (USD 10000)	2019 万元 (10000 yuan)
进出口商品货物总值	**Total**	**20624130**	**136226828**	**20144648**	**138952214**
进口商品货物总值	Imports	9865925	65138406	10427960	71873188
出口商品货物总值	Exports	10758205	71088422	9716688	67079027

15-10 软件出口和技术进口情况

Software Export and Technology Import

项　目	Item	2019 项　目 (个) Number (unit)	2019 金　额 (万美元) Amount (USD 10000)
软件出口	Software Export		
软件产品	Software Products		
软件服务	Software Services	864	103392
技术进口	Technology Import	55	176425
其中：制造业	Manufacturing	45	173883
房地产业	Real Estate	4	322
计算机应用业	Computer Applied Software Industry	5	3125
租赁和商务服务业	Leasing and BusinessServices	1	52

注：技术进口是指办理了合同登记手续的，通过贸易、投资或经济技术合作等方式转移技术到境内的行为。

Notes:Technology import refers to the action of transferring technology into China in forms of trade,investment or economic technological cooperation after the contracts registrations formalities have been gone through.

15-11 历年利用外资情况

Statistics on Utilization of Foreign Capital in Main Years

年 份 Year	项目(企业)个数(个) Number of Contracts (unit)	# 外商直接投资 Foreign Direct Investment	合同外资金额(万美元) Amount of Contracted Foreign Capital (USD 10000)	# 外商直接投资 Foreign Direct Investment	实际使用外资金额(万美元) Amount of Foreign Capital Actually Used (USD 10000)	# 外商直接投资 Foreign Direct Investment
1978	2		53			
1980	1379	21	24905	24794	3013	1287
1985	4394	290	70175	51575	15782	10389
1986	2062	104	33668	29569	17966	9316
1987	2271	126	28510	20374	8574	5562
1988	2120	289	52650	39338	27119	14521
1989	2121	292	57778	40101	43892	27481
1990	2711	389	55426	47183	27263	18613
1991	2678	571	87517	70635	40519	25938
1992	2925	1193	471080	449654	74595	57135
1993	2620	1275	704764	683634	147028	128464
1994	2907	1906	709683	685763	204816	181403
1995	2564	1774	685657	673101	225298	214444
1996	1793	865	510301	447393	260002	233153
1997	3066	661	219922	169824	289379	248003
1998	986	643	245058	193178	304467	271608
1999	1053	537	172808	141377	317600	298687
2000	1445	647	163454	152759	311541	298923
2001	1087	678	200604	196229	332746	300119
2002	1177	776	316579	302322	265299	228386
2003	1204	870	402176	351117	306409	258076
2004	1506	1046	334767	320494	247696	240062
2005	1599	1061	366155	340205	284128	264882
2006	1465	1025	463987	439124	305477	292339
2007	1460	959	715269	703506	341138	328579
2008	1378	991	604536	591864	377413	362277
2009	1022	844	388633	378401	387476	377339
2010	1170	980	505928	497384	408121	397862
2011	1273	1134	683809	674734	437626	427009
2012	1204	1095	693071	680188	474312	457485
2013	1258	1092	734009	711428	507853	480385
2014	1324	1155	827560	803975	543905	510707
2015		1429		836335		541634
2016		1757		990123		570120
2017		2459		1339133		628947
2018		5376		3995880		661108
2019		3446		3952881		714349

注：1.合同外资金额、实际使用外资金额按当年口径统计。

2.由于制度变化，2015年开始不再统计外商其他投资，仅统计外商直接投资。

Note: I. The amount of contracted foreign capital and foreign capital actually used are calculated at current coverage.

II. Recording to the statistical system,the only statistical indicator is foreign direct investment instead of other foreign invest since 2015.

15-12 历年利用外资项目(企业)个数、合同外资金额、实际使用外资金额指数(上年=100)

Indices of Contracts Number, Contracted Foreign Capital and Foreign Capital Actually Used in Main Years (Preceding Year=100)

年 份 Year	项目(企业)个数 Number of Contracts	# 外商直接投资 Foreign Direct Investment	合同外资金额 Amount of Contracted Foreign Capital	# 外商直接投资 Foreign Direct Investment	实际使用外资金额 Amount of Foreign Capital Actually Used	# 外商直接投资 Foreign Direct Investment
1980	250.3	300.0	1080.5	1258.6	306.2	780.0
1985	97.2	163.8	344.8	272.3	101.3	79.7
1986	46.9	35.9	48.0	57.3	113.8	89.7
1987	110.1	121.2	84.7	68.9	47.7	59.7
1988	93.4	229.4	184.7	193.1	316.3	261.1
1989	100.1	101.0	109.7	101.9	161.9	189.3
1990	127.8	133.2	95.9	117.7	62.1	67.7
1991	98.8	146.8	157.9	149.7	148.6	139.4
1992	109.2	208.9	538.3	636.6	184.1	220.3
1993	89.6	106.9	149.6	152.0	197.1	224.8
1994	111.0	149.5	100.7	100.3	139.3	141.2
1995	88.2	93.1	96.6	98.2	110.0	118.2
1996	69.9	48.8	74.4	66.5	115.4	108.7
1997	171.0	76.4	43.1	38.0	111.3	106.4
1998	32.2	97.3	111.4	113.8	105.2	109.5
1999	106.8	83.5	70.5	73.2	104.3	110.0
2000	137.2	120.5	94.6	108.1	98.1	100.1
2001	75.2	104.8	122.7	128.5	106.8	100.4
2002	108.3	114.5	174.1	170.4	110.6	110.2
2003	102.3	112.1	127.0	116.1	115.5	113.0
2004	125.1	120.2	127.7	125.6	164.8	164.4
2005	106.2	101.4	109.4	106.2	114.7	110.3
2006	91.6	96.6	126.7	129.1	107.5	110.4
2007	99.7	93.6	154.2	160.2	111.7	112.4
2008	94.4	103.3	84.5	84.1	110.6	110.3
2009	74.2	85.2	64.3	63.9	102.7	104.2
2010	114.5	116.1	130.2	131.4	105.3	105.4
2011	108.8	115.7	135.2	135.7	107.2	107.3
2012	94.6	96.6	101.4	100.8	108.4	107.1
2013	104.5	99.7	105.9	104.6	107.1	105.0
2014	105.2	105.8	112.7	113.0	107.1	106.3
2015		123.7		104.0		106.1
2016		123.0		118.4		105.3
2017		140.0		135.3		110.3
2018		218.6		298.4		105.1
2019		64.1		98.9		108.1

注：2002年和2004年合同外资金额、实际使用外资金额统计口径调整，当年指数按可比口径计算。

Note: The coverage of amount of contracted foreign capital and foreign capital actually used were adjusted in 2002 and 2004, the indices of which being calculated on the same coverage.

15-13 外商直接投资情况
Statistics on Foreign Direct Investment

单位：万美元 (USD 10000)

项　　目	Item	2018	2019	1978-2019
项目(企业)个数　(个)	**Number of Contracts　(unit)**			
外商直接投资	Foreign Direct Investment	5376	3446	40007
合资企业	Joint-venture Enterprises	1007	684	7814
合作企业	Cooperative Enterprises	10	5	5734
外资企业	Enterprises with Sole Foreign Funds	4353	2751	26430
外商投资股份制企业	Share-holding Corporations	6	5	28
合伙企业	Partnership Enterprises		1	
合同外资金额	**Contracted Foreign Capital**			
外商直接投资	Foreign Direct Investment	3995880	3952881	22065108
合资企业	Joint-venture Enterprises	977994	518200	4049961
合作企业	Cooperative Enterprises	18604	1078	3242360
外资企业	Enterprises with Sole Foreign Funds	2946806	3422141	14120479
外商投资股份制企业	Share-holding Corporations	52476	4397	645243
合伙企业	Partnership Enterprises		7065	
实际使用外资金额	**Amount of Foreign Capital Actually Used**			
外商直接投资	Foreign Direct Investment	661108	714349	10111140
合资企业	Joint-venture Enterprises	312640	246581	2603311
合作企业	Cooperative Enterprises	4293	796	1803256
外资企业	Enterprises with Sole Foreign Funds	288332	443717	5027735
外商投资股份制企业	Share-holding Corporations	55843	20344	673927
合伙企业	Partnership Enterprises		2911	

15-14 外商直接投资情况(按地区分)

Statistics on Utilization of Foreign Direct Investment Capital (by Region)

单位：万美元　　　　(USD 10000)

项　目	Item	2018			2019		
		项目(企业)个数(个) Number of Contracts (unit)	合同外资金　额 Contracted Foreign Capital	实际使用外资金额 Amount of Foreign Capital Actually Used	项目(企业)个数(个) Number of Contracts (unit)	合同外资金　额 Contracted Foreign Capital	实际使用外资金额 Amount of Foreign Capital Actually Used
全　市	**Total**	**5376**	**3995880**	**661108**	**3446**	**3952881**	**714349**
# 荔湾区	Liwan	284	36093	17898	244	31270	17032
越秀区	Yuexiu	691	87903	32299	491	72339	24636
海珠区	Haizhu	229	48956	40034	154	127708	51115
天河区	Tianhe	1348	373392	37402	736	273836	62636
白云区	Baiyun	302	55413	14817	230	55009	31348
黄埔区	Huangpu	173	414501	224705	166	200884	228097
番禺区	Panyu	294	44508	21260	245	70906	50128
花都区	Huadu	81	87772	83038	66	21208	2448
南沙区	Nansha	1582	2769621	97424	979	3003331	186311
从化区	Conghua	296	26684	12045	41	12045	10449
增城区	Zengcheng	94	49118	71643	83	64626	47310
广州空港经济区	Guangzhou Airport Economic Zone	2	1919	8543	11	19719	2839

15-15　外商直接投资项目分类(2019年)

Amount of Foreign Direct Investment Capital Actually Used by Category (2019)

单位：万美元　　(USD 10000)

项　　目	Item	项目(企业)个数(个) Number of Contracts (unit)	合同外资金　额 Contracted Foreign Capital	实际使用外资金额 Amount of Foreign Capital Actually Used
总　　计	**Total**	**3446**	**3952881**	**714349**
# 投资额1000万美元以上项目	Projects with Investment above 10 million USD	660	3795324	685293
按国民经济行业分	**By Sector**			
农、林、牧、渔业	Agriculture, Forestry, Animal Husbandry and Fishing	13	1720	
采矿业	Mining			
制造业	Manufacturing	118	195309	188373
电力、热力、燃气及水生产和供应业	Production and Supply of Electricity, Heat,Gas and Water	5	18694	
建筑业	Construction	31	20690	223
交通运输、仓储和邮政业	Transport, Storage and Post	54	57823	48720
信息传输、计算机服务和软件业	Information Transmission, Software and Information Technology Services	241	144313	33457
批发和零售业	Wholesale and Retail Trade	1498	185887	48172
住宿和餐饮业	Hotels and Catering Services	42	10690	445
金融业	Financial Intermediation	363	856514	15918
房地产业	Real Estate	89	1199065	136519
租赁和商务服务业	Leasing and Business Services	544	781828	202660
科学研究和技术服务业	Scientific Research and Technical Services	347	470286	39317
水利、环境和公共设施管理业	Management of Water Conservancy,Environment and Public Facilities	2	56	
居民服务、修理和其他服务业	Service to Households, Repair and Other Services	11	-1472	11
教育	Education	14	462	
卫生和社会工作	Health and Social Service	3	3632	29
文化、体育和娱乐业	Culture, Sports and Entertainment	70	7235	505
公共管理、社会保障和社会组织	Public Management, Social Security and Social Organization	1	149	
国际组织	International Organizations			

15-15 续表 continued

单位：万美元 (USD 10000)

项　　目	Item	项目(企业)个数(个) Number of Contracts (unit)	合同外资金　额 Contracted Foreign Capital	实际使用外资金额 Amount of Foreign Capital Actually Used
按国别(地区)分	**By Country (Territory)**			
中国香港	Hong Kong, China	1788	3441730	462216
韩 国	Republic of Korea	98	17991	110124
日 本	Japan	27	45830	44794
新加坡	Singapore	67	65618	31613
英属维尔京群岛	Virgin Islands	16	42935	19223
荷 兰	Netherlands	6	2719	456
英 国	United Kingdom	34	5144	1573
萨摩亚	Samoa	6	656	328
美 国	United States	70	-105	714
中国台湾	Taiwan, China	152	57344	567
德 国	Germany	15	4420	1154
瑞 士	Switzerland	2	357	335
澳大利亚	Australia	28	1849	81
泰 国	Thailand	14	4153	632
开曼群岛	Cayman Islands	3	3392	500
加拿大	Canada	27	3031	7
法 国	France	18	7473	10320
中国澳门	Macao, China	66	34317	44
意大利	Italy	8	457	263
马来西亚	Malaysia	61	13707	40
塞舌尔	Seychelles	5	639	34
印 度	India	85	2006	10
马 里	Mali	18	333	5
亚美尼亚	Armenia	3	15	2
以色列	Israel	17	1008	371
毛里求斯	Mauritius		8557	6457
奥地利	Austria	2	2537	116
孟加拉国	The People's Republic of Bangladesh	40	1495	50
新西兰	New Zealand	6	276	25
巴拿马	Panama			9
沙特阿拉伯	Saudi Arabia	25	632	6
喀麦隆	Cameroon	17	598	5
印度尼西亚	Indonesia	20	1868	2
西班牙	Spain	15	460	2
利比里亚	Liberia			2
其 他	Others	687	179439	22269

15-16　境外企业情况(2019年)

Statistics on Overseas Enterprises Funded by Domestic Capital (2019)

单位：万美元　　(USD 10000)

项　目	Item	当年新增 Newly Increased in Current Year	
		企业数(个) Number of Enterprises (unit)	中方投资额 Volume of Investment from China
总　计	**Total**	**190**	**183224**
按投资企业类型分	**By Status of Investment**		
国有企业	State-owned enterprises	11	52412
私营企业	Private-owned enterprises	170	114787
外资企业	Foreign-owned enterprises	9	16025
按国民经济行业分	**By Sector**		
农、林、牧、渔业	Agriculture, Forestry, Animal Husbandry and Fishing	5	16995
采矿业	Mining		
制造业	Manufacturing	32	48016
电力、热力、燃气及水生产和供应业	Production and Supply of Electricity, Heat,Gas and Water		
建筑业	Construction	4	644
批发和零售业	Wholesale and Retail Trade	58	29103
交通运输、仓储和邮政业	Transport, Storage and Post	6	858
住宿和餐饮业	Hotels and Catering Services		
信息传输、软件和信息技术服务业	Information Transmission, Software and Information Technology Services	40	54395
金融业	Financial Intermediation		
房地产业	Real Estate	2	-4880
租赁和商务服务业	Leasing and Business Services	18	33829
科学研究和技术服务业	Scientific Research and Technical Services	21	3903
水利、环境和公共设施管理业	Management of Water Conservancy,Environment and Public Facilities	1	100
居民服务、修理和其他服务业	Service to Households, Repair and Other Services	2	6
教育	Education		
卫生和社会工作	Health and Social Service	1	255
文化、体育和娱乐业	Culture, Sports and Entertainment		
其他	Others		

15-16 续表 continued

单位：万美元 (USD 10000)

项目	Item	当年新增 Newly Increased in Current Year 企业数(个) Number of Enterprises (unit)	中方投资额 Volume of Investment from China
按投资国家(地区)分	**By Investment Destination**		
中国香港	Hong Kong, China	87	57870
中国澳门	Macao，China	1	18335
中国台湾	Taiwan,China	1	22
日本	Japan	8	1663
韩国	Republic of Korea	3	50
柬埔寨	Cambodia	3	800
泰国	Thailand	7	2496
新加坡	Singapore	6	1560
印度	India	3	411
越南	Vietnam	5	15105
缅甸	Burma	1	
印度尼西亚	Indonesia	3	1488
马来西亚	Malaysia	3	228
沙特阿拉伯	Saudi Arabia	1	27
土耳其	Turkey	1	300
英国	Britain	1	200
德国	Germany	2	162
爱尔兰	Ireland	1	214
意大利	Italy	2	544
荷兰	Holland		4392
瑞士	Switzerland	2	3407
爱沙尼亚	Esthonia		961
拉脱维亚	Latvia	1	27
俄罗斯	Russia	2	235
加拿大	Canada	1	
美国	United States of America	22	4934
澳大利亚	Australia	4	207
新西兰	New Zealand	1	500
加纳	Ghana		100
肯尼亚	Kenya		-500
莫桑比克	Mozambique	1	282
塞舌尔	Republic of Seychelles	1	50
乌干达	Uganda	1	100
以色列	Israel	1	28
老挝	Laos	1	16240
尼泊尔	Nepal	1	90
巴基斯坦	Pakistan	1	148
菲律宾	Filipino	2	3040
埃及	Egypt	1	1540
尼日利亚	Nigeria	2	210
丹麦	Denmark	1	169
法国	France	1	66
芬兰	Finland	1	17500
波兰	Poland	1	335
瑞典	Sweden	1	11
开曼群岛	Cayman Islands	1	27277
秘鲁	Peru		400

15-17 对外劳务合作业务情况(2019年)

Statistics on Labor Cooperation with Foreign Countries or Territories (2019)

项　目	Item	合同额(万美元) Contracted Value (USD 10000)	完成营业额(万美元) Turnover (USD 10000)
合　计	**Total**	**58946**	**38138**
中国香港	Hong Kong, China	547	2500
中国澳门	Macao, China	57621	34195
中国台湾	Taiwan,China	5	19
日本	Japan	28	28
印度尼西亚	Indonesia	25	25
马来西亚	Malaysia	178	178
新加坡	Singapore	10	66
越南	Vietnam	68	160
利比里亚	Liberia	24	130
刚果(布)	The Republic of Congo	179	179
德国	Germany	2	7
马耳他	The Republic of Malta	12	67
巴拿马	The Republic of Panama	18	136
科威特	Kuwait		174
沙特阿拉伯	Saudi Arabia		45
泰国	Thailand	9	9
伊拉克	Iraq	141	141
阿拉伯联合酋长国	The United Arab Emirates	7	7
柬埔寨	Cambodia	63	63
马达加斯加	Madagascar	9	9

15-18 主要年份对外经济合作业务情况

Contracted Projects and Labor Cooperation with Foreign Countries or Territories in Main Years

年 份 Year	新签合同数（个） Number of Contracts Newly Signed (unit)	合同额（万美元） Contracted Value (USD 10000)	完成营业额（万美元） Turnover (USD 10000)	派出人数（人次） Persons Sent Abroad (person-times)	年末在外人数（人） Persons Abroad at Year-end (person)
1985	201	189	189	113	113
1990	1005	1887	1072	994	1201
1995	806	6632	5810	1473	2893
2000	4989	10588	7288	684	1833
2001	6317	8186	7487	1088	2247
2002	6577	7837	9115	2390	3378
2003	9089	10737	10919	3237	4080
2004	9728	13047	13247	3530	4456
2005	11815	16490	16237	3556	5001
2006	13611	19691	18093	3784	5011
2007	13615	23174	21365	4503	5962
2008	19872	30362	32037	4844	7912
2009	20457	40527	38827	5187	8142
2010	47416	81878	47187	6685	8970
2011		43928	24765	8795	11790
2012		44553	28856	9867	13770
2013		51373	36696	11282	16617
2014		62866	57141	15292	24368
2015		90214	85491	16117	24375
2016		53840	45606	17887	25014
2017		59285	39262	20493	39496
2018		49532	36814	26326	37848
2019		58946	38138	21432	38026

注：1.2011年开始取消新签合同数统计。
　　2.本表中2017年—2019年的数据为对外劳务合作业务数据。

Note: 1.Since 2011, the indicator number of contracts newly signed has been canceled.
　　2.The data of year 2017 and 2019 is about the foreign labour cooperation.

15-19 旅游业总收入、外汇收入情况(2019年)

Total Income from Tourism and Foreign Exchange Earnings (2019)

项 目	Item	旅游业总收入（万元） Total Income (10000 yuan)	国内旅游收入 Domestic Travel Income	旅游外汇收入 Foreign Exchange Income	旅游外汇收入（万美元） Foreign Exchange Income (USD 10000)
合　计	**Total**	**44545875**	**40033735**	**4512140**	**653025**
商品销售	Commodity Sales	14006049	12887489	1118560	161885
餐　饮	Catering Services	5954804	5417408	537396	77775
长途交通	Long Distance Transport	10756365	9267810	1488555	215433
住　宿	Accommodation	8302659	7599668	702991	101742
邮电通讯	Post and Telecommunications	86221	60051	26170	3787
市内交通	Local Transport	799408	692921	106487	15412
游　览	Tours	1284569	1197936	86633	12538
娱　乐	Recreation	1630821	1497262	133559	19329
其　他	Others	1724979	1413190	311789	45124

15-20 城市接待过夜旅游者情况

Tourists Staying Overnight in Guangzhou

项　　目	Item	2018	2019
人次数合计　（万人次）	**Total Number of Tourists (10000 person-times)**	**6532.55**	**6773.15**
入境旅游者	Overseas Tourists	900.63	899.43
外国人	Foreigners	340.13	346.28
亚　洲	Asia	165.83	163.97
#日　本	Japan	19.08	21.21
韩　国	Republic of Korea	16.21	13.91
蒙　古	Mongolia	0.15	0.32
印度尼西亚	Indonesia	5.90	6.28
马来西亚	Malaysia	12.56	12.31
菲律宾	Philippines	3.44	3.58
新加坡	Singapore	8.68	9.18
泰　国	Thailand	7.22	7.64
印　度	India	10.34	10.56
越　南	Vietnam	3.84	3.15
沙特阿拉伯	Saudi Arabia	4.62	4.46
欧　洲	Europe	62.32	66.75
#英　国	United Kingdom	6.32	6.32
法　国	France	5.81	5.60
德　国	Germany	5.50	5.14
意大利	Italy	3.90	3.95
瑞　士	Switzerland	0.93	0.99
瑞　典	Sweden	0.96	0.90
荷　兰	Netherlands	2.40	2.12
俄罗斯	Russia	5.65	6.41
西班牙	Spain	2.40	2.30
美　洲	America	45.13	44.85
#美　国	United States	24.28	23.28
加拿大	Canada	4.77	4.41
大洋洲	Oceania	9.58	9.20
#澳大利亚	Australia	6.54	6.08
新西兰	New Zealand	1.16	1.02
非　洲	Africa	57.27	61.51
香港同胞	Compatriots from Hong Kong	441.90	427.58
澳门同胞	Compatriots from Macao	54.96	57.41
台湾同胞	Compatriots from Taiwan	63.64	68.16
境内旅游者	Domestic Tourists	5631.92	5873.72
人天数合计　（万人天）	**Total Number of Tourists and Days (10000 person-days)**	**15202.23**	**15898.85**
入境旅游者	Overseas Tourists	2100.61	2116.22
外国人	Foreigners	886.04	897.02
香港同胞	Compatriots from Hong Kong	932.33	911.47
澳门同胞	Compatriots from Macao	116.48	122.45
台湾同胞	Compatriots from Taiwan	165.76	185.28
境内旅游者	Domestic Tourists	13101.62	13782.63

15-21 主要宾馆(酒店)基本情况

Statistics on Main Hotels

项　　目		Item		2018	2019
企业情况		**Statistics of Enterprises**			
宾馆酒店数	(家)	Number of Hotels	(unit)	344	337
#星　级		Star-rated		170	160
五星级		Five-star		22	22
四星级		Four-star		35	29
三星级		Three-star		96	93
二星级		Two-star		17	16
一星级		One-star			
客房总数	(间)	Number of Guest Rooms	(unit)	91962	91004
床位总数	(张)	Number of Beds	(unit)	137943	133805
接待情况		**Reception Capacity**			
过夜旅游者	(万人次)	Tourists Staying Overnight	(10000 person-times)	1876.70	1935.76
海外旅游者		Overseas Tourists		215.50	214.87
国内旅游者		Domestic Tourists		1661.20	1720.89
过夜旅游者	(万人天)	Tourists Staying Overnight	(10000 person-days)	2792.30	2871.15
经营情况		**Statistics of Operation**			
营业收入	(万元)	Operating Income	(10000 yuan)	1606342	1614450
营业成本	(万元)	Operating Cost	(10000 yuan)	513812	517438
税金及附加	(万元)	Taxes and Extra Charges	(10000 yuan)	23723	21587
销售费用	(万元)	Selling expenses	(10000 yuan)	146434	166426
管理费用	(万元)	Management Expense	(10000 yuan)	378414	376100
财务费用	(万元)	Financial Expense	(10000 yuan)	53494	50473
营业利润	(万元)	Operating Profit	(10000 yuan)	203947	210830
投资收益	(万元)	Investment Revenue	(10000 yuan)	5051	5740
营业外收支净额	(万元)	Net Non-operating Income and Expenditure	(10000 yuan)	10945	8426
利润总额	(万元)	Total Profits	(10000 yuan)	214892	219254
年末从业人员	(人)	Employed Person at Year-end	(person)	53611	51466
开房率	(%)	Room Occupancy	(%)	66.21	67.42

15-22 旅行社基本情况
Statistics on Travel Agencies

单位：万元 (10000 yuan)

项　　目	Item	2018	2019
企业情况	**Statistics of Enterprises**		
企业数 （个）	Number of Enterprises (unit)	701	799
年末从业人员 （人）	Employed Persons at Year-end (person)	16311	16619
组团(外联)旅游情况	**Organized (Overseas) Tourism Contracted**		
组团(外联)人数 （万人次）	Organized (Overseas) Persons Contracted (10000 person-times)	1261.44	1332.93
入境旅游者	Overseas Tourists	13.28	12.62
国内旅游者	Domestic Tourists	1248.16	1320.31
# 出境游	Local Residents Going Overseas	307.53	359.57
经营情况	**Statistics of Operation**		
营业收入	Operating Income	3264876	3637230
营业成本	Operating Cost	3009159	3325560
税金及附加	Taxes and Extra Charges	3053	2866
销售费用	Selling expenses	42234	38104
管理费用	Management Expense	103469	120454
财务费用	Financial Expense	3604	7166
营业利润	Operating Profit	1623	27493
营业外收支净额	Net Income of Non-business	6914	21374
利润总额	Total Profits	10072	51571

注：组团(外联)人数包括旅行社外联入境旅游者人数和组团境内旅游者人数，包括过夜人数和不过夜人数，不包括接待人数。

Note: The organized (overseas) persons contracted includes both international and domestic tourists contracted by travel agencies and the data includes tourists staying overnight or not, except reception persons.

15-23 主要年份人民币对主要外币年平均汇价
Average Exchange Rates of RMB Against Main Convertible in Main Years

单位:人民币，元 (RMB/yuan)

年 份 year	100美元 100 US Dollars	100日元 100 Japanese Yen	100港元 100 Hong Kong Dollars	100欧元 100 Euros
1987	372.21	2.5799	47.74	
1988	372.21	2.9082	47.70	
1989	376.59	2.7360	48.28	
1990	478.38	3.3233	61.39	
1991	532.27	3.9602	68.45	
1992	551.49	4.3608	71.24	
1993	576.19	5.2020	74.41	
1994	861.87	8.4370	111.53	
1995	835.07	8.9225	107.96	
1996	830.57	7.6238	107.40	
1997	828.97	6.8623	107.09	
1998	827.90	6.3487	106.88	
1999	827.83	7.2913	106.66	
2000	827.84	7.6950	106.17	
2001	827.71	6.8098	106.07	
2002	827.70	6.6651	106.08	801.45
2003	827.70	7.1347	106.24	937.77
2004	827.70	7.6552	106.23	1029.00
2005	819.17	7.4484	105.00	1019.53
2006	797.18	6.8570	102.62	1001.90
2007	760.40	6.4632	97.46	1041.75
2008	694.51	6.7427	89.19	1022.27
2009	683.25	7.3244	88.15	955.25
2010	678.89	7.7122	87.39	906.86
2011	649.43	8.1309	83.39	902.34
2012	631.71	7.9343	81.43	814.64
2013	621.35	6.4682	80.11	824.47
2014	615.16	5.7456	79.34	803.45
2015	623.71	5.1643	80.46	690.12
2016	664.98	6.1178	85.68	734.12
2017	673.98	6.0254	86.47	766.10
2018	662.34	6.0074	84.51	780.72
2019	689.85	6.3347	88.05	772.55

15-24 外商投资企业及分支机构工商登记情况（2019）

Statistics on Foreign Funded Enterprises Registered by Departments of Industry and Commerce (2019)

单位：万美元 (USD 10000)

项　　目	Item	年末户数（个）Number of Enterprises at Year-end (unit)	注册资本 Registered Capital	#外方 Capital from Foreign Partners
总　计	**Total**	**33706**	**21476725**	**15133566**
按国民经济行业分	By Sector			
农、林、牧、渔业	Agriculture, Forestry, Animal Husbandry and Fishing	119	108935	103959
采矿业	Mining	4		
制造业	Manufacturing	3754	3742202	2303812
电力、热力、燃气及水生产和供应业	Production and Supply of Electricity,Heat,Gas and Water	64	116144	76160
建筑业	Construction	296	247818	70473
批发和零售业	Wholesale and Retail Trade	13134	1043824	895295
交通运输、仓储和邮政业	Transport, Storage and Post	891	265218	164796
住宿和餐饮业	Hotels and Catering Services	1740	96738	84127
信息传输、软件和信息技术服务业	Information Transmission, Software and Information Technology	1540	763289	553983
金融业	Financial Intermediation	539	1330663	670591
房地产业	Real Estate	1430	3542463	2950981
租赁和商务服务业	Leasing and Business Services	7000	8708761	5988147
科学研究和技术服务业	Scientific Research and Technical Services	2503	1212124	1059523
水利、环境和公共设施管理业	Management of Water Conservancy,Environment and Public Facilities	23	38158	28710
居民服务、修理和其他服务业	Service to Households, Repair and Other Services	210	54016	51163
教育	Education	38	423	363
卫生和社会工作	Health and Social Service	28	74316	10606
文化、体育和娱乐业	Culture, Sports and Entertainment	393	131632	120877
其他	Others			

注：本表不包括在省市场监督管理局注册登记的在穗企业数。

Note: The number of enterprises loctated in Guangzhou but registered in Guangdong Provincial Administration for Market Regulation is excluded.

15-25 广州市与国外结成友好城市一览(2019年末)

List of Foreign Friendly Cities with Guangzhou (Year-end of 2019)

国 别	Country	城 市	City	缔结日期（年、月、日）	Date of Signing
日 本	Japan	福 冈	Fukuoka	1979.05.02	May 2,1979
美 国	United States	洛杉矶	Los Angeles	1981.12.08	December 8,1981
菲律宾	Philippines	马尼拉	Manila	1982.11.05	November 05,1982
加拿大	Canada	温哥华	Vancouver	1985.03.27	March 27,1985
澳大利亚	Australia	悉 尼	Sydney	1986.05.12	May 12,1986
意大利	Italy	巴 里	Bari	1986.11.12	November 12,1986
法 国	France	里 昂	Lyon	1988.01.19	January 19,1988
德 国	Germany	法兰克福	Frankfurt	1988.04.11	April 11,1988
新西兰	New Zealand	奥克兰	Auckland	1989.02.17	February 17,1989
韩 国	Republic of Korea	光 州	Gwangju	1996.10.25	October 25,1996
瑞 典	Sweden	林雪平	Linkoping	1997.11.24	November 24,1997
南 非	South Africa	德 班	Durban	2000.07.17	July 17,2000
英 国	United Kingdom	布里斯托尔	Bristol	2001.05.23	May 23,2001
俄罗斯	Russia	叶卡捷琳堡	Ekaterinburg	2002.07.10	July 10,2002
秘 鲁	Peru	阿雷基帕	Arequipa	2004.10.27	October 27,2004
印度尼西亚	Indonesia	泗 水	Surabaya	2005.12.21	December 21,2005
立陶宛	Litawen	维尔纽斯	Vilnius	2006.10.12	October 12,2006
英 国	United Kingdom	伯明翰	Birmingham	2006.12.04	December 4,2006
斯里兰卡	Sri lanka	汉班托塔	Hambantota	2007.02.27	February 27,2007
巴 西	Brazil	累西腓	Recife	2007.10.22	October 22,2007
芬 兰	Finland	坦佩雷	Tampere	2008.12.02	December 2,2008
泰 国	Thailand	曼 谷	Bangkok	2009.11.13	November 13,2009
阿根廷	Agentine Republic	布宜诺斯艾利斯	Buenos Aires	2012.04.16	April 16,2012
阿联酋	United Arab Emirates	迪 拜	Dubai	2012.04.18	April 18,2012
科威特	State of Kuwait	科威特城	Kuwait City	2012.04.25	April 25,2012
俄罗斯	Russian Federation	喀 山	Kazan	2012.07.06	July 6,2012
土耳其	Republic of Turkey	伊斯坦布尔	Istanbul	2012.07.18	July 18,2012
津巴布韦	Repulic of Zimbabwe	哈拉雷	Harare	2012.09.03	September 3,2012
哥斯达黎加	Republic of Costa Rica	圣何塞	San Jose	2012.09.11	September 11,2012
日 本	Japan	登 别	Noboribetsu	2012.11.15	November 15,2012
西班牙	Kingdom of Spain	巴伦西亚	Valencia	2012.12.29	December 29,2012
摩洛哥	Kingdom of Morocco	拉巴特	Rabat	2013.10.03	October 3,2013
波 兰	The Republic Of Poland	罗 兹	Lodz	2014.08.20	August 20,2014
印 度	India	艾哈迈达巴德	Ahmedabad	2014.09.17	September 17,2014
尼泊尔	Federal Democratic Republic of Nepal	博克拉	Pokhara	2014.11.29	November 29,2014
厄瓜多尔	The Republic of Ecuador	基 多	Quito	2014.11.29	November 29,2014
智 利	Chile	圣地亚哥	San Diego	2017.06.20	June 20,2017
肯尼亚	Kenya	蒙巴萨郡	Mombasa County	2018.11.27	November 27，2018

15-26 各国驻广州总领事馆一览(2019年末)
List of Consulate General in Guangzhou (Year-end of 2019)

馆　务	Consulates	设立时间 Date of Setting up	领区范围	Consular Region
美　国	United States	1979.08.31	广东、广西、福建、海南	Guangdong Guangxi Fujian Hainan
日　本	Japan	1980.03.01	广东、广西、福建、海南	Guangdong Guangxi Fujian Hainan
泰　国	Thailand	1989.02.12	广东、海南	Guangdong Hainan
波　兰	Poland	1989.07.22	广东、广西、海南	Guangdong Guangxi Hainan
澳大利亚	Australia	1992.12.09	广东、广西、福建、海南、湖南	Guangdong Guangxi Fujian Hainan Hunan
越　南	Viet Nam	1993.01.18	广东	Guangdong (Interim)
马来西亚	Malaysia	1993.10.24	广东、福建、海南、江西、湖南	Guangdong Fujian Hainan Jiangxi Hunan
德　国	Germany	1995.11.07	广东、广西、福建、海南	Guangdong Guangxi Fujian Hainan
英　国	United Kingdom	1997.01.14	广东、广西、湖南、福建、海南、江西	Guangdong Guangxi Hunan Fujian Hainan Jiangxi
法　国	France	1997.04.24	广东、广西、福建、海南	Guangdong Guangxi Fujian Hainan
菲律宾	Philippines	1997.05.23	广东、广西、湖南、海南	Guangdong Guangxi Hunan Hainan
荷　兰	Netherlands	1997.09.15	广东、广西、福建、海南	Guangdong Guangxi Fujian Hainan
加拿大	Canada	1997.11.20	广东、广西、福建、海南、湖南、江西	Guangdong Guangxi Fujian Hainan Hunan Jiangxi
柬埔寨	Cambodia	1998.07.01	广东、福建、海南	Guangdong Fujian Hainan
丹　麦	Denmark	1998.09.23	广东、广西、福建、海南	Guangdong Guangxi Fujian Hainan
意大利	Italy	1998.11.04	广东、广西、福建、海南、湖南、江西	Guangdong Guangxi Fujian Hainan Hunan Jiangxi
韩　国	Republic of Korea	2001.08.28	广东、广西、福建、海南	Guangdong Guangxi Fujian Hainan
印度尼西亚	Indonesia	2002.12.12	广东、广西、福建、海南	Guangdong Guangxi Fujian Hainan
瑞　士	Switzerland	2005.10.10	广东、广西、福建、海南、湖南、江西	Guangdong Guangxi Fujian Hainan Hunan Jiangxi
比利时	belgium	2005.12.10	广东、福建、海南、云南、广西	Guangdong Fujian Hainan Yunnan Guangxi
新加坡	Singapore	2006.04.13	广东、海南、湖南、广西、云南、贵州	Guangdong Hainan Hunan Guangxi Yunnan Guizhou
古　巴	Cuba	2006.11.08	广东、广西、海南	Guangdong Guangxi Hainan
俄罗斯	Russia	2007.04.05	广东、福建、海南、云南、江西、广西	Guangdong Fujian Hainan Yunnan Jiangxi Guangxi
新西兰	New Zealand	2007.04.26	广东、广西、湖南、福建、海南	Guangdong Guangxi Hunan Fujian Hainan
希　腊	Greece	2007.05.15	广东、福建、海南、广西、湖南、云南、贵州	Guangdong Fujian Hainan Guangxi Hunan Yunnan Guizhou
印　度	India	2007.10.18	广东、福建、湖南、海南、云南、四川、广西	Guangdong Fujian Hunan Hainan Yunnan Sichuan Guangxi
奥地利	Austria	2007.11.25	广东、海南、湖南、广西	Guangdong Hainan Hunan Guangxi
挪　威	Norway	2008.02.18	广东、福建、海南、广西	Guangdong Fujian Hainan Guangxi
科威特	Kuwait	2008.02.21	广东、福建、海南、广西	Guangdong Fujian Hainan Guangxi
墨西哥	Mexico	2008.04.25	广东、海南、福建、湖南、江西、广西	Guangdong Hainan Fujian Hunan Jiangxi Guangxi
巴基斯坦	Pakistan	2008.06.27	广东、福建、湖南、海南、广西	Guangdong Fujian Hunan Hainan Guangxi

注：瑞典总领事馆2009年已撤馆，墨西哥领事馆已于2008年升级为总领事馆。

Note: The Consulate General of Sweden in Guangzhou was withdrawn in 2009. And the Mexican Consulate has upgraded to the Consulate General of Mexico since 2008.

15-26 续表 conitnued

馆　务	Consulates	设立时间 Date of Setting up	领区范围	Consular Region
以色列	Israel	2009.03.22	广东、福建、海南、广西	Guangdong Fujian Hainan Guangxi
西班牙	Spain	2009.06.14	广东、福建、湖南、广西、海南、贵州、云南	Guangdong Fujian Hunan Guangxi Hainan Guizhou Yunnan
埃塞俄比亚	Ethiopia	2009.06.14	广东、湖南、福建、江西、海南、广西	Guangdong Hunan Fujian Jiangxi Hainan Guangxi
阿根廷	Argentina	2009.07.21	广东、福建、海南、广西	Guangdong Fujian Hainan Guangxi
厄瓜多尔	Ecuador	2009.09.08	广东	Guangdong
巴　西	Brazil	2010.04.15	广东、海南、广西、福建、湖南、贵州、云南	Guangdong Hainan Guangxi Fujian Hunan Guizhou Yunnan
智　利	Chile	2010.12.29	广东、海南、广西、福建	Guangdong Hainan Guangxi Fujian
马　里	Mali	2011.07.18	广东、福建、海南、广西	Guangdong Fujian Hainan Guangxi
乌干达	Uganda	2011.08.15	广东、福建、海南、广西	Guangdong Fujian Hainan Guangxi
伊　朗	Iran	2011.12.23	广东、福建、湖南、广西	Guangdong Fujian Hunan Guangxi
土耳其	Turkey	2012.01.12	广东、福建、海南、广西	Guangdong Fujian Hainan Guangxi
斯里兰卡	Sri Lanka	2012.03.27	广东、福建、海南、广西、江西	Guangdong Fujian Hainan Guangxi Jiangxi
乌克兰	Ukraine	2012.05.30	广东、贵州、海南、湖南、广西	Guangdong Guizhou Hainan Hunan Guangxi
老　挝	Lao	2013.09.23	广东、海南、江西、福建	Guangdong Hainan Jiangxi Fujian
秘　鲁	Peru	2013.10.02	广东、广西、贵州、海南、云南、湖南	Guangdong Guangxi Guizhou Hainan Yunnan Hunan
吉尔吉斯斯坦	Kyrgyzstan	2014.04.08	广东、福建、江西、湖南、海南、广西	Guangdong Fujian Jiangxi Hunan Hainan Guangxi
尼日利亚	Nigeria	2014.07.09	广东、广西、海南	Guangdong Guangxi Hainan
科特迪瓦	Cote d Ivoire	2014.07.12	广东、福建、海南、江西、广西	Guangdong Fujian Hainan Jiangxi Guangxi
刚　果	Coga	2014.08.15	广东、海南、福建、广西	Guangdong Hainan Fujian Guangxi
哥伦比亚	Colombia	2014.12.12	广东、广西、贵州、云南、海南	Guangdong Guangxi Guizhou Yunnan Hainan
安哥拉	Angola	2015.11.06	广东、福建、海南、广西	Guangdong Fujian Hainan Guangxi
卡塔尔	Qatar	2015.11.10	广东、广西、福建、海南	Guangdong Guangxi Fujian Hainan
阿联酋	Emirates	2016.06.15	广东、广西、海南	Guangdong Guangxi Hainan
赞比亚	Zambia	2016.06.28	广东、福建、海南、广西	Guangdong Fujian Hainan Guangxi
沙特阿拉伯	Saudi Arab	2017.01.01	广东、福建、广西、海南	Guangdong Fujian Guangxi Hainan
塞内加尔	Senegal	2017.03.06	广东、广西、福建、海南	Guangdong Guangxi Fujian Hainan
尼泊尔	Nepal	2017.04.25	广东、广西、福建、海南	Guangdong Guangxi Fujian Hainan
苏　丹	Sudan	2017.05.15	广东、江西、福建、湖南、贵州、海南、浙江、广西	Guangdong Jiangxi Fujian Hunan Guizhou Hainan Zhejiang Guangxi
葡萄牙	Portugal	2017.07.17	广东、湖南、海南、福建、广西	Guangdong Hunan Hainan Fujian Guangxi
白俄罗斯	Belarus	2017.12.28	广东、湖南、贵州、海南、云南广西	Guangdong Hunan Guizhou Hainan Yunnan Guangxi
乌拉圭	Uruguay	2018.03.26	广东、福建、贵州、海南、广西	Guangdong Fujian Guizhou Hainan Guangxi
委内瑞拉	Venezuela	2018.10.26	广东、福建、湖南、贵州、海南广西	Guangdong Fujian Hunan Guizhou Hainan Guangxi
加　纳	Ghana	2019.03.04	广东、福建、海南、广西	Guangdong Fujian Hainan Guangxi
巴拿马	Panama	2019.04.01	广东、福建、海南、贵州、湖南广西	Guangdong Fujian Hainan Guizhou Hunan Guangxi

【外商直接投资】 是指外国投资者在我国境内通过设立外商投资企业、合伙企业、与中方投资者共同进行石油资源的合作勘探开发以及设立外国公司分支机构等方式进行投资。外国投资者可以用现金、实物、无形资产、股权等投资，还可以用从外商投资企业获得的利润进行再投资。

【对外劳务合作】 指组织劳务人员赴其他国家或地区为国外的企业或机构工作的经营性活动。

【国际旅游（外汇）收入】 指入境游客在中国（大陆）境内旅行、游览过程中用于交通、参观游览、住宿、餐饮、购物、娱乐等全部花费。

【国内旅游收入（旅游总花费）】 指国内游客在国内旅行、游览过程中用于交通、参观游览、住宿、餐饮、购物、娱乐等全部花费。

【Foreign Direct Investment】 refers to foreign investment in China through the establishment of foreign invested enterprises, cooperative exploration and development of petroleum resources with domestic investors and the establishment of branch organizations of foreign enterprises. Foreign investment can be made in forms of cash, physical investment, intangible assets and equity, in addition with reinvestment of the foreign enterprises with the profits gained from the investment.

【Overseas Labour Services】 refer to operational activities of organizing labour force to go abroad providing services to foreign enterprises or agencies.

【Foreign Exchange Earnings from International Tourism】 refer to the total expenditure of foreigners, overseas Chinese, Chinese compatriots from Hong Kong, Macao and Taiwan during their stay in the mainland of China on transportation, sighting, accommodation, food, shopping and entertainment.

【Income from Domestic Tourism】 refer to expenditure of domestic tourists on transportation, sighting, accommodation, food, shopping and entertainment while they travel.

第十六篇 CHAPTER 16

规模以上服务业

SERVICE ENTERPRISES ABOVE THE THE DESIGNATED SIZE

第十六篇 规模以上服务业

一、本篇资料反映广州市规模以上服务业基本情况。

二、统计范围：辖区内规模以上服务业法人单位。

三、规模以上服务业涉及行业包括：交通运输、仓储和邮政业，信息传输、软件和信息技术服务业，租赁和商务服务业，科学研究和技术服务业，水利、环境和公共设施管理业，居民服务、修理和其他服务业，教育，卫生和社会工作，文化、体育和娱乐业；以及房地产业中除房地产开发经营外等行业。

四、规模以上服务业法人单位的介定标准为：居民服务、修理和其他服务业，文化、体育和娱乐业年营业收入合计大于等于500万或从业人数大于等于50人的法人单位，上述其他行业年营业收入合计大于等于1000万或从业人数大于等于50人的法人单位。

五、调查方法：执行国家统计局制定的《规模以上服务业一套表制度》，调查方法为符合上述行业条件法人单位的全面调查。

六、本篇资料由广州市统计局服务业处整理提供。

16 Service Enterprises Above Designated Size

I.This data in this chapter reflect the basic information of some service enterprises above designated size of Guangzhou.

II. The statistical coverage of service enterprises above designated size includes relative sectors enterprises in every district in Guangzhou Municipality.

III. The sectors of service enterprises above designated size includes: Transport Storage and Postal Services Information Transmission Software and Information Technology Services Leasing and Business Services Scientific Research and Technical Services Management of Water Conservancy,Environment and Public Facilities Households' Service,Repair and Other Services Education Health and Social Work Culture,Sports and Entertainment and Real Estate (Not including Real Estate Development and Management).

IV. The service enterprises above designated size refer to the enterprises with over 50 employees by the end of the year or with annual business revenue of over 5 million yuan, of sectors including households' service, repair and other services, culture, sports and entertainment services. Besides, it covers services sectors as above III involved with over 50 employees by the end of the year or with annual business revenue of over 10 million yuan.

V. Survey method:implement the "a set of table system for Service Enterprises Above Designated Size" formulated by the National Bureau of Statistics, and is a comprehensive survey of legal entities meeting the above IV conditions..

VI. The data in this chapter are prepared and edited by the Division of Service Statistics of Guangzhou Statistics Bureau.

16-1 规模以上服务业企业主要财务指标

Main Financial Indicators of Service Enterprises above the Designated Size

单位：万元 (10000 yuan)

项　目	Item	2019	同比增速(%) Year-on-year Growth Rate (%)
一、损益及分配	Profits and Loss		
营业收入	Business Revenue	136308072	17.5
营业成本	Business Costs	102255631	17.1
税金及附加	Tax and Extra Charges on Business	838693	9.6
销售费用	Sales Expenses	7049069	11.6
管理费用	Management Expenses	13575797	-4.8
财务费用	Financial Expenses	3877484	9.9
投资收益(损失以"-"号记)	Investment Income(loss with "-"mark)	7995834	4.4
营业利润	Business Profits	14759461	22.4
利润总额	Total Profits	15147133	18.9
所得税费用	Income Taxes Payable	2590143	14.4
二、成本费用及增值税	Labor Cost and Value-added Tax		
应付职工薪酬(本年贷方累计发生额)	Total Wages Payable(Credit Accumulated Amount in this year)	27857120	13.4
其中：社会保险和住房公积金	Social insurance and Housing Fund	3820450	15.3
应交增值税	Value-added Tax Payable	2962502	0.1
三、平均用工人数(人)	Average number of employed persons(person)	2004759	8.3

注：同比增速按本年数和上年同口径数计算得出，下同。

Note: The year-on-year growth rate is calculated based on the number of this year and the same caliber number of last year, the same below.

16-2 规模以上服务业企业主要财务指标(2019年，按行业分)

单位：万元

项　　目	Item	企业单位数(个) Number of Enterprises (unit)
合　计	**Total**	**10546**
按行业分	**Grouped by Sector**	
交通运输、仓储和邮政业	Transport, Storage and Postal Services	1382
铁路运输业	Railway Transport Service	7
道路运输业	Road Transport Services	575
水上运输业	Waterway Transport Service	73
航空运输业	Air Transport Service	12
管道运输业	Pipeline Transportation	1
装卸搬运和运输代理业	Handling and Transportation Agency	492
仓储业	Warehousing Service	160
邮政业	Postal Service	62
信息传输、软件和信息技术服务业	Information Transmission, Software and Information Technology Services	1965
电信、广播电视和卫星传输服务	Telecommunications, Broadcasting Television and Satellite Transmission Services	56
互联网和相关服务	Internet and Related Services	282
软件和信息技术服务业	Software and Information Technology Services	1627
房地产业(不含房地产开发)	Real Estate (Not including Real Estate Development and Management)	1539
租赁和商务服务业	Leasing and Business Services	2934
租赁业	Leasing	177
商务服务业	Business Services	2757
科学研究和技术服务业	Scientific Research and Technical Services	1343
研究和试验发展	Research and Experimental Development	220
专业技术服务业	Professional Technical Services	935
科技推广和应用服务业	Services of Science and Technology Exchanges and Promotion	188
水利、环境和公共设施管理业	Management of Water Conservancy,Environment and Public Facilities	102
水利管理业	Management of Water Conservancy	3
生态保护和环境治理业	Ecological Protection and Environmental Treatment	28
公共设施管理业	Management of Public Facilities	69
土地管理业	Land Management	2
居民服务、修理和其他服务业	Households' service,Repair and Other Services	377
居民服务业	Services to Households	91
机动车、电子产品和日用产品修理业	Motor Vehicle,Electronic Products and Consumer Products Repair	136
其他服务业	Other Services	150
教育	Education	271
卫生和社会工作	Health and Social Work	178
卫生	Health	141
社会工作	Social Work	37
文化、体育和娱乐业	Culture,Sports and Entertainment	455
新闻和出版业	News and Publication	64
广播、电视、电影和影视录音制作业	Production of Radio,Television,Film and Video Recording	155
文化艺术业	Culture and Arts	74
体育	Sports	58
娱乐业	Entertainment	104

Main Financial Indicators of Service Enterprises above the Designated Size (2019,by Sector)

(10000 yuan)

营业收入 Business Revenue	营业成本 Business Costs	营业税金及附加 Tax and Extra Charges on Business	销售费用 Selling Expenses	管理费用 Management Expenses	财务费用 Financial Expenses
136308072	**102255631**	**838693**	**7049069**	**13575797**	**3877484**
44640777	38394542	192476	838551	2225554	2400140
7367257	6642760	8707	111	232397	255010
10049693	7687058	111139	101457	680751	1287458
4205528	3482875	14009	13536	323582	228292
12500297	11088265	32527	564767	337050	577915
92056	40231	450	229	1380	12068
5686049	5214512	9168	78973	300434	12785
1124282	926319	9584	43562	108958	23447
3615615	3312523	6893	35916	241002	3165
36034703	23950856	133213	3154985	3350720	-59873
4860834	3570407	20121	509768	497366	-95398
10772463	6843862	26065	1033572	1021699	-13126
20401406	13536586	87027	1611645	1831655	48652
9003400	5594654	204474	488716	1647931	354391
25356357	19132914	204381	1301977	3242663	1040597
889046	648846	3657	48696	111957	36205
24467311	18484067	200724	1253281	3130706	1004392
12782999	9205370	58909	460668	1739402	74405
2002577	1489276	8890	122290	242898	6611
9585000	6975172	44346	257594	1267040	14880
1195423	740922	5672	80784	229465	52914
1411635	1128777	6141	19178	152751	1895
18076	15138	54		2255	-1
239570	175328	1172	6199	33309	1754
1145169	933802	4869	12939	113551	147
8820	4509	46	40	3636	-6
1094497	716556	5878	142799	182121	8016
325407	180157	1448	58714	60957	5999
340097	224890	1656	58777	52432	1025
428993	311509	2774	25308	68732	992
1484057	892572	3912	129815	382003	18259
1353250	849834	1348	221001	242724	18955
1269940	796893	1285	213416	218623	18293
83310	52942	63	7585	24101	662
3146396	2389555	27961	291379	409927	20699
644187	486888	8235	44565	97484	-2940
1073392	818123	7869	86218	73414	364
248427	200259	1399	12623	42650	675
401588	513621	6420	45527	54363	911
778803	370666	4039	102447	142017	21690

16-2 续表

单位：万元

项 目	Item	营业利润 Business Profits
合 计	**Total**	**14759461**
按行业分	**Grouped by Sector**	
交通运输、仓储和邮政业	Transport, Storage and Postal Services	2452292
铁路运输业	Railway Transport Service	528267
道路运输业	Road Transport Services	1378069
水上运输业	Waterway Transport Service	189693
航空运输业	Air Transport Service	206326
管道运输业	Pipeline Transportation	39206
装卸搬运和运输代理业	Handling and Transportation Agency	92872
仓储业	Warehousing Service	5614
邮政业	Postal Service	12246
信息传输、软件和信息技术服务业	Information Transmission, Software and Information Technology Services	5098521
电信、广播电视和卫星传输服务	Telecommunications, Broadcasting Television and Satellite Transmission	1366878
互联网和相关服务	Internet and Related Services	1213476
软件和信息技术服务业	Software and Information Technology Services	2518167
房地产业(不含房地产开发)	Real Estate (Not including Real Estate Development and Management)	1150503
租赁和商务服务业	Leasing and Business Services	4784804
租赁业	Leasing	29888
商务服务业	Business Services	4754916
科学研究和技术服务业	Scientific Research and Technical Services	746883
研究和试验发展	Research and Experimental Development	-108431
专业技术服务业	Professional Technical Services	710763
科技推广和应用服务业	Services of Science and Technology Exchanges and Promotion	144550
水利、环境和公共设施管理业	Management of Water Conservancy,Environment and Public Facilities	120568
水利管理业	Management of Water Conservancy	630
生态保护和环境治理业	Ecological Protection and Environmental Treatment	28249
公共设施管理业	Management of Public Facilities	91629
土地管理业	Land Management	60
居民服务、修理和其他服务业	Households' service,Repair and Other Services	47130
居民服务业	Services to Households	28925
机动车、电子产品和日用产品修理业	Motor Vehicle,Electronic Products and Consumer Products Repair	1767
其他服务业	Other Services	16437
教育	Education	65468
卫生和社会工作	Health and Social Work	7416
卫生	Health	9154
社会工作	Social Work	-1738
文化、体育和娱乐业	Culture, Sports and Entertainment	285879
新闻和出版业	News and Publication	94280
广播、电视、电影和影视录音制作业	Production of Radio,Television,Film and Video Recording	97852
文化艺术业	Culture and Arts	5581
体育	Sports	-214683
娱乐业	Entertainment	302850

continued

(10000 yuan)

利润总额 Total Profits	所得税费用 Income Tax Expenses	应付职工薪酬 Total Wages Payable	应交增值税 Value-added Tax Payable	平均用工人数（人） Average Number of Employed Persons (person)
15147133	**2590143**	**27857120**	**2962502**	**2004759**
2563023	631141	7808659	918474	483711
506202	135797	1957363	487779	102163
1450731	263756	2096899	216343	157621
141570	78271	586328	24840	17908
276516	75956	1858520	77586	84878
39173	9686	10235	1420	464
102981	25990	644398	41380	57872
35781	11680	191151	19366	18749
10071	30007	463764	49761	44056
5201813	772090	6439021	750380	306864
1367385	374715	971010	139924	33900
1238040	144981	1267110	165158	52108
2596388	252394	4200902	445299	220856
1220535	258686	2476384	301845	288559
4827602	630769	5313536	507481	514644
33242	14909	105285	-591	10767
4794360	615860	5208251	508073	503877
789579	162701	3184959	321387	182338
-89251	28565	434343	34755	22275
728321	114125	2530517	265780	145392
150509	20011	220100	20852	14671
111727	17962	278786	35919	37105
632	105	1576	567	110
28919	4828	36293	4340	2430
82114	12961	237964	30939	34436
63	67	2953	74	129
47222	10500	381682	36130	64399
27061	5130	88005	8708	9923
3392	3012	75208	11570	8800
16769	2359	218469	15852	45676
70166	17100	666730	25939	51084
7264	13171	425429	853	33914
6812	11416	385845	231	27795
451	1755	39584	622	6119
308202	76023	881935	64094	42141
96484	572	192237	17157	8028
99112	10613	92875	17262	8587
11856	1858	47204	5073	3974
-199902	16250	364152	10328	6502
300652	46731	185467	14276	15050

16-3 规模以上服务业企业主要财务指标(2019年，按地区分)

单位：万元

地 区	District	企业单位数（个）Number of Enterprises (unit)	营业收入 Business Revenue	营业成本 Business Costs	营业税金及附加 Tax and Extra Charges on Business	销售费用 Selling Expenses	管理费用 Management Expenses
合 计	**Total**	**10546**	**136308072**	**102255631**	**838693**	**7049069**	**13575797**
按地区分	**By District**						
荔湾区	Liwan	396	3240587	1724016	31799	512219	570141
越秀区	Yuexiu	1802	26317743	21551743	152530	851583	2412592
海珠区	Haizhu	1642	11366356	7316987	154364	695267	1434912
天河区	Tianhe	2740	42883195	30891505	236690	2665638	4767918
白云区	Baiyun	1068	19058694	15859148	92219	840977	1225376
黄埔区	Huangpu	1153	12802142	9695213	58301	683432	1007097
番禺区	Panyu	765	8872303	6077088	55501	445690	810690
花都区	Huadu	273	2322366	1830018	12687	93519	246666
南沙区	Nansha	399	7818460	6217659	28787	167358	878898
从化区	Conghua	104	619129	438517	4503	13310	70718
增城区	Zengcheng	204	1007098	653737	11313	80076	150789

Main Financial Indicators of Service Enterprises above the Designated Size (2019,by Region)

(10000 yuan)

财务费用 Financial Expenses	营业利润 Business Profits	利润总额 Total Profits	所得税费用 Income Tax Expenses	应付职工薪酬 Total Wages Payable	应交增值税 Value-added Tax Payable	平均用工人数(人) Average Number of Employed Persons (person)
3877484	**14759461**	**15147133**	**2590143**	**27857120**	**2962502**	**2004759**
46386	523840	538959	77174	631340	96960	49433
736536	1983819	2037555	739422	5874434	879098	409830
590993	1809476	1828219	289416	2672622	251022	182841
983546	6323869	6240015	495118	8631393	942240	573035
682300	983243	1190273	435833	3234578	220394	227269
193131	1789130	1845333	211172	2527586	211896	187433
124468	1228088	1301014	185504	1496858	183661	129314
31412	172661	194255	40572	378821	19322	38245
362389	34928	47125	91002	2018595	119623	166648
106751	-143795	-136191	14748	153262	13016	16964
19573	54204	60576	10184	237631	25272	23747

16-4 规模以上服务业企业主要财务指标(2019年，按登记注册类型分)

单位：万元

项　　目	Item	企业单位数（个）Number of Enterprises (unit)
合　计	**Total**	**10546**
按登记注册类型分	**Grouped by Registration Status**	
内资企业	Domestic Funded	9710
国有企业	State-owned	182
集体企业	Collective-owned	414
股份合作企业	Cooperative	21
联营企业	Joint Ownership Enterprises	8
国有联营企业	State Joint Ownership Enterprises	3
集体联营企业	Collective Joint Ownership Enterprises	3
其他联营企业	Joint State-collective Enterprises	2
有限责任公司	Limited Liability Corporations	3014
国有独资公司	State Sole Funded Corporations	372
其他有限责任公司	Other Limited Liability Corporations	2642
股份有限公司	Share-holding Corporations Ltd.	275
私营企业	Private Enterprises	5599
私营独资企业	Private-funded Enterprises	27
私营合伙企业	Private Partnership Enterprises	148
私营有限责任公司	Private Limited Liability Corporations	5259
私营股份有限公司	Private Share Holding Corporations	165
其他企业	Others	197
港、澳、台商投资企业	Enterprises with Funds from Hong Kong, Macao and Taiwan Investors	494
与港澳台商合资经营企业	Joint-venture Enterprises	97
与港澳台商合作经营企业	Cooperative Enterprises	42
港澳台商独资经营企业	Enterprises with Sole Funds	344
港澳台商投资股份有限公司	Share-holding Corporations Ltd.	4
其他港澳台投资企业	Other Enterprises with Funds from Hong Kong, Macao and Taiwan	7
外商投资企业	Foreign Funded Enterprises	342
中外合资经营企业	Joint-venture Enterprises	120
中外合作经营企业	Cooperative Enterprises	15
外资企业	Enterprises with Sole Foreign Funds	177
外商投资股份有限公司	Share-holding Corporations Ltd.	10
其他外商投资企业	Other Foreign Funded Enterprises	20

Main Financial Indicators of Service Enterprises above the Designated Size (2019,by Registration Status)

(10000 yuan)

营业收入 Business Revenue	营业成本 Business Costs	营业税金及附加 Tax and Extra Charges on Business	销售费用 Selling Expenses	管理费用 Management Expenses	财务费用 Financial Expenses
136308072	**102255631**	**838693**	**7049069**	**13575797**	**3877484**
120331085	92612881	715608	6015530	11688213	3551699
3768168	3104470	35144	111065	471546	-52105
1027945	362861	39582	21887	300718	-3141
73050	47217	1149	2488	16076	482
48679	12602	2199	5071	16078	2843
20881	2945	1400	1499	9398	-762
11451	6237	53	590	2383	-193
16348	3420	746	2982	4297	3798
55887834	42646900	400707	2458355	4970847	2567215
18219697	15443313	166077	172285	1450698	1385189
37668137	27203587	234630	2286070	3520149	1182027
21211253	17964978	93174	1090485	1248873	666191
37343803	27851577	142027	2285708	4412959	357493
79065	44240	177	3550	23638	-26
793184	175647	5219	86282	350758	-1369
34657711	26351870	128752	2081814	3864529	347280
1813844	1279820	7878	114062	174035	11609
970353	622277	1627	40471	251117	12720
9992726	5999830	70074	661960	1120893	102754
963120	742246	8662	65542	116204	9874
1855967	813155	13843	153289	83686	78508
7017689	4338164	45993	436472	908915	14134
56125	39772	1205	1682	5962	140
99824	66493	372	4975	6126	98
5984261	3642920	53011	371580	766692	223032
2180626	1500534	26174	78524	204869	153197
496542	134756	3205	92771	63562	26844
2872508	1608275	19952	165928	476233	40723
154346	122601	1876	24476	9525	1627
280238	276753	1804	9880	12503	642

16-4 续表

单位：万元

项　　目	Item	营业利润 Business Profits
合　计	**Total**	**14759461**
按登记注册类型分	**Grouped by Registration Status**	
内资企业	Domestic Funded	11387841
国有企业	State-owned	897223
集体企业	Collective-owned	329554
股份合作企业	Cooperative	4529
联营企业	Joint Ownership Enterprises	10288
国有联营企业	State Joint Ownership Enterprises	6629
集体联营企业	Collective Joint Ownership Enterprises	2552
其他联营企业	Joint State-collective Enterprises	1108
有限责任公司	Limited Liability Corporations	5800609
国有独资公司	State Sole Funded Corporations	2508779
其他有限责任公司	Other Limited Liability Corporations	3291829
股份有限公司	Share-holding Corporations Ltd.	2649260
私营企业	Private Enterprises	1650948
私营独资企业	Private-funded Enterprises	5707
私营合伙企业	Private Partnership Enterprises	260646
私营有限责任公司	Private Limited Liability Corporations	1214304
私营股份有限公司	Private Share Holding Corporations	170292
其他企业	Others	45430
港、澳、台商投资企业	Enterprises with Funds from Hong Kong, Macao and Taiwan Investors	2358250
与港澳台商合资经营企业	Joint-venture Enterprises	48102
与港澳台商合作经营企业	Cooperative Enterprises	717800
港澳台商独资经营企业	Enterprises with Sole Funds	937043
港澳台商投资股份有限公司	Share-holding Corporations Ltd.	635227
其他港澳台投资企业	Other Enterprises with Funds from Hong Kong, Macao and Taiwan	20079
外商投资企业	Foreign Funded Enterprises	1013370
中外合资经营企业	Joint-venture Enterprises	264268
中外合作经营企业	Cooperative Enterprises	169706
外资企业	Enterprises with Sole Foreign Funds	557154
外商投资股份有限公司	Share-holding Corporations Ltd.	-6293
其他外商投资企业	Other Foreign Funded Enterprises	28535

continued

(10000 yuan)

利润总额 Total Profits	所得税费用 Income Tax Expenses	应付职工薪酬 Total Wages Payable	应交增值税 Value-added Tax Payable	平均用工人数（人） Average Number of Employed Persons (person)
15147133	**2590143**	**27857120**	**2962502**	**2004759**
11669137	2180318	23508683	2550093	1739820
920228	93511	1065057	77766	58618
427764	17790	168915	35702	24294
4901	1004	10162	1283	974
10503	2383	10418	2234	872
6615	1876	5662	1045	466
2788	265	2817	386	202
1101	242	1938	803	204
5682166	1639966	12017973	1501186	832496
2364509	852960	4475495	677223	227650
3317657	787006	7542478	823963	604846
2785009	76665	3999624	223089	205486
1789237	341573	5827744	698173	584658
3331	502	27194	1041	2786
262685	27120	152084	39786	14798
1347691	297677	5253215	611445	535006
175530	16274	395250	45901	32068
49328	7427	408789	10661	32422
2420716	239914	2588340	267146	156482
90503	12286	289391	22837	24086
718287	111973	193983	83640	11519
956429	104528	2087679	156996	119241
635082	7425	9602	1687	865
20415	3702	7685	1986	771
1057280	169911	1760097	145262	108457
292838	58558	466359	55988	44584
174731	24643	141079	12733	6349
567488	76898	1015043	64246	48580
-6011	2229	112258	7933	7288
28233	7583	25359	4363	1656

16-5 规模以上服务业企业主要财务指标(2019年，按控股情况分)

单位：万元

项 目	Item	合计 Total
按控股情况分	**Group by Type of Ownership**	
单位数(个)	Number of Enterprises(unit)	10546
一、损益及分配	Profits and Loss	
营业收入	Business Revenue	136308072
营业成本	Business Costs	102255631
税金及附加	Tax and Extra Charges on Business	838693
销售费用	Sales Expenses	7049069
管理费用	Management Expenses	13575797
财务费用	Financial Expenses	3877484
投资收益(损失以“-”号记)	Investment Income(loss with “-”mark)	7995834
营业利润	Business Profits	14759461
利润总额	Total Profits	15147133
所得税费用	Income Taxes Payable	2590143
二、成本费用及增值税	Labor Cost and Value-added Tax	
应付职工薪酬(本年贷方累计发生额)	Total Wages Payable(Credit Accumulated Amount in this year)	27857120
其中：社会保险和住房公积金	Social Insurance and Housing Fund	3820450
应交增值税	Value-added Tax Payable	2962502
三、平均用工人数(人)	Average number of employed persons(person)	2004759

Main Financial Indicators of Service Enterprises above the Designated Size (2019,by Type of Ownership)

(10000 yuan)

国有控股 State-owned	集体控股 Collective-owned	私人控股 Private Holdings	港澳台商控股 Hong Kong, Macao and Taiwan Holdings	外商控股 Foreign Holdings	其他 Other Holdings
1188	345	7035	453	274	1251
55788771	2024097	50989119	8333885	4507545	14664656
45730185	1105133	37393587	5140368	2777602	10108756
378920	42039	221263	69135	36606	90731
1597665	82241	3718965	586104	273998	790096
3782716	367229	6024162	1066336	611776	1723579
2980019	38477	523549	84237	82052	169150
6091349	39824	691039	794249	99895	279478
8330984	268422	2165687	1733920	682784	1577664
8338068	290098	2291763	1793240	713035	1720928
1541067	35268	463701	149341	112336	288431
11529294	312270	8437945	2457813	1561510	3558289
1915073	43617	871082	312494	273550	404635
1331368	60453	975911	192418	113484	288869
593742	33561	819682	146751	110994	300029

16-6 规模以上服务业企业营业收入(2019年，按行业分)

单位：万元

项 目	Item
合 计	**Total**
按行业划分	**Grouped by Sector**
交通运输、仓储和邮政业	Transport, Storage and Postal Services
铁路运输业	Railway Transport Service
道路运输业	Road Transport Services
水上运输业	Waterway Transport Service
航空运输业	Air Transport Service
管道运输业	Pipeline Transportation
装卸搬运和运输代理业	Handling and Transportation Agency
仓储业	Warehousing Service
邮政业	Postal Service
信息传输、软件和信息技术服务业	Information Transmission, Software and Information Technology Services
电信、广播电视和卫星传输服务	Telecommunications, Broadcasting Television and Satellite Transmission Services
互联网和相关服务	Internet and Related Services
软件和信息技术服务业	Software and Information Technology Services
房地产业(不含房地产开发)	Real Estate (Not including Real Estate Development and Management)
租赁和商务服务业	Leasing and Business Services
租赁业	Leasing
商务服务业	Business Services
科学研究和技术服务业	Scientific Research and Technical Services
研究和试验发展	Research and Experimental Development
专业技术服务业	Professional Technical Services
科技推广和应用服务业	Services of Science and Technology Exchanges and Promotion
水利、环境和公共设施管理业	Management of Water Conservancy,Environment and Public Facilities
水利管理业	Management of Water Conservancy
生态保护和环境治理业	Ecological Protection and Environmental Treatment
公共设施管理业	Management of Public Facilities
土地管理业	Land Management
居民服务、修理和其他服务业	Households' service,Repair and Other Services
居民服务业	Services to Households
机动车、电子产品和日用产品修理业	Motor Vehicle,Electronic Products and Consumer Products Repair
其他服务业	Other Services
教育	Education
卫生和社会工作	Health and Social Work
卫生	Health
社会工作	Social Work
文化、体育和娱乐业	Culture,Sports and Entertainment
新闻和出版业	News and Publication
广播、电视、电影和影视录音制作业	Production of Radio,Television,Film and Video Recording
文化艺术业	Culture and Arts
体育	Sports
娱乐业	Entertainment

Business Revenue of Service Enterprises above the Designated Size (2019, by Sector)

(10000 yuan)

企业单位数 (个) Number of Enterprises (unit)	营业收入 (万元) Business Revenue (10000 yuan)	2019年比2018年增长 (%) Growth Rate in 2019 Over 2018 (%)
10546	**136308072**	**17.5**
1382	44640777	14.0
7	7367257	16.5
575	10049693	13.5
73	4205528	9.7
12	12500297	14.2
1	92056	15.2
492	5686049	18.2
160	1124282	6.5
62	3615615	11.0
1965	36034703	20.7
56	4860834	0.2
282	10772463	33.7
1627	20401406	20.4
1539	9003400	17.0
2934	25356357	17.5
177	889046	33.5
2757	24467311	17.0
1343	12782999	22.1
220	2002577	40.0
935	9585000	18.6
188	1195423	25.5
102	1411635	13.9
3	18076	98.1
28	239570	19.6
69	1145169	11.8
2	8820	49.1
377	1094497	18.2
91	325407	18.8
136	340097	14.6
150	428993	20.9
271	1484057	16.3
178	1353250	23.8
141	1269940	22.9
37	83310	39.1
455	3146396	17.2
64	644187	7.7
155	1073392	15.2
74	248427	27.0
58	401588	29.2
104	778803	20.2

16-7　规模以上服务业企业营业收入(2019年，按地区分)

Business Revenue of Service Enterprises above the Designated Size (2019,by District)

地　区	District	企业单位数 (个) Number of Enterprises (unit)	营业收入 (万元) Business Revenue (10000 yuan)	同比增速 (%) Year-on-year Growth Rate (%)
合　计	**Total**	**10546**	**136308072**	**17.5**
按地区分	**By District**			
荔湾区	Liwan	396	3240587	18.2
越秀区	Yuexiu	1802	26317743	10.8
海珠区	Haizhu	1642	11366356	27.4
天河区	Tianhe	2740	42883195	16.2
白云区	Baiyun	1068	19058694	10.7
黄埔区	Huangpu	1153	12802142	32.3
番禺区	Panyu	765	8872303	19.2
花都区	Huadu	273	2322366	23.9
南沙区	Nansha	399	7818460	28.0
从化区	Conghua	104	619129	19.6
增城区	Zengcheng	204	1007098	21.0

16-8 规模以上服务业企业营业收入(2019年，按登记注册类型和控股情况分)

Business Revenue of Service Enterprises above the Designated Size (2019，by Registration Status and Type of Ownership)

项目	Item	企业单位数(个) Number of Enterprises (unit)	营业收入(万元) Business Revenue (10000 yuan)	同比增速(%) Year-on-year Growth Rate (%)
合 计	**Total**	**10546**	**136308072**	**17.5**
按登记注册类型分	**Grouped by Registration Status**			
内资企业	Domestic Funded	9710	120331085	18.3
国有企业	State-owned	182	3768168	14.6
集体企业	Collective-owned	414	1027945	15.0
股份合作企业	Cooperative	21	73050	5.4
联营企业	Joint Ownership Enterprises	8	48679	4.1
国有联营企业	State Joint Ownership Enterprises	3	20881	-1.6
集体联营企业	Collective Joint Ownership Enterprises	3	11451	-9.9
其他联营企业	Joint State-collective Enterprises	2	16348	27.7
有限责任公司	Limited Liability Corporations	3014	55887834	20.0
国有独资公司	State Sole Funded Corporations	372	18219697	21.0
其他有限责任公司	Other Limited Liability Corporations	2642	37668137	19.5
股份有限公司	Share-holding Corporations Ltd.	275	21211253	4.6
私营企业	Private Enterprises	5599	37343803	26.0
私营独资企业	Private-funded Enterprises	27	79065	21.4
私营合伙企业	Private Partnership Enterprises	148	793184	18.9
私营有限责任公司	Private Limited Liability Corporations	5259	34657711	27.0
私营股份有限公司	Private Share Holding Corporations	165	1813844	12.3
其他企业	Others	197	970353	9.5
港、澳、台商投资企业	Enterprises with Funds from Hong Kong, Macao and Taiwan Investors	494	9992726	13.3
与港澳台商合资经营企业	Joint-venture Enterprises	97	963120	10.2
与港澳台商合作经营企业	Cooperative Enterprises	42	1855967	1.9
港澳台商独资经营企业	Enterprises with Sole Funds	344	7017689	17.6
港澳台商投资股份有限公司	Share-holding Corporations Ltd.	4	56125	17.3
其他港澳台投资企业	Other Enterprises with Funds from Hong Kong, Macao and Taiwan	7	99824	-10.5
外商投资企业	Foreign Funded Enterprises	342	5984261	9.2
中外合资经营企业	Joint-venture Enterprises	120	2180626	3.0
中外合作经营企业	Cooperative Enterprises	15	496542	5.1
外资企业	Enterprises with Sole Foreign Funds	177	2872508	11.4
外商投资股份有限公司	Share-holding Corporations Ltd.	10	154346	79.0
其他外商投资企业	Other Foreign Funded Enterprises	20	280238	24.6
按控股情况分	**Group by Type of Ownership**			
国有控股	State-owned	1188	55788771	12.8
集体控股	Collective-owned	345	2024097	5.7
私人控股	Private Holdings	7035	50989119	24.3
港澳台商控股	Hong Kong, Macao and Taiwan Holdings	453	8333885	15.7
外商控股	Foreign Holdings	274	4507545	13.3
其他	Other Holdings	1251	14664656	18.3

【营业收入】指企业经营主要业务和其他业务所确认的收入总额。营业收入合计包括“主营业务收入”和“其他业务收入”。

【营业成本】指企业经营主要业务和其他业务所发生的成本总额。包括企业（单位）在报告期内从事销售商品、提供劳务等日常活动发生的各种耗费。

【营业利润】指企业从事生产经营活动所取得的利润。执行《企业会计准则》的企业，营业利润为营业收入减去营业成本、税金及附加、销售费用、管理费用、财务费用、资产减值损失，再加上公允价值变动收益、投资收益和其他收益。执行《小企业会计准则》的企业，营业利润为营业收入减去营业成本、税金及附加、销售费用、管理费用、财务费用，再加上投资收益和其他收益后的金额；执行其他企业会计制度的企业，营业利润为主营业务收入减去主营业务成本、主营业务税金及附加，加上其他业务利润后，再减去销售费用、管理费用、财务费用后的金额，应符合以下逻辑关系：营业利润等于营业收入减去营业成本、税金及附加、销售费用、管理费用、财务费用。根据会计“利润表”中“营业利润”项目的本年累计数填报。

【利润总额】指企业在一定会计期间的经营成果，是生产经营过程中各种收入扣除各种耗费后的盈余，反映企业在报告期内实现的盈亏总额。

【应付职工薪酬】指企业为获得职工提供的服务而给予各种形式的报酬以及其他相关支出。包括职工工资、奖金、津贴和补贴，职工福利费，医疗保险费、养老保险费、失业保险费、工伤保险费和生育保险费等社会保险费，住房公积金，工会经费和职工教育经费，非货币性福利，因解除与职工的劳动关系给予的补偿，其他与获得职工提供的服务相关的支出。

【平均用工人数】指报告期内(年度、月度)平均拥有的从事服务业活动的人员数。按“谁用工，谁统计”的原则实施统计，包括参加企业服务业活动的正式人员，劳务派遣人员和临时聘用人员。不包括在本企业领取工资、股息、红利未参加服务业活动的人员。

【Business Revenue】 refers to the total income of the business recognized by business and other business. Total operating revenue includes the main business income and other operating income.

【Business Costs】 is defined as indirect business costs that cannot be assigned to a particular product or operation.

【Business Profits】 refers to the profit gained by an enterprise in its production and operation activities. For an enterprise performing the accounting standards for enterprises, the operating profit shall be the operating income minus the business cost, taxes and extra charges, selling expenses,management expenses, financial expenses, and impairment losses of assets, plus the fair value variation income, investment income and other income. For enterprises that implement the accounting standards for small enterprises, the operating profit shall be the amount of the operating income after deducting operating costs, taxes and surcharges, sales expenses, administrative expenses and financial expenses, plus the investment income and other earnings. Perform other enterprises accounting system of enterprises, operating profit of main business income minus the advocate business wu cost, advocate business wu taxes and add, and other business profits, after subtracting the cost of sales, management fees, the amount after financial expenses, shall meet the following logic: operating profit is equal to revenue minus the operating cost, additional, sales tax and fees, management fees, financial costs. According to the "business profit" item in the accounting "income statement".

【Total Profits】 refers to all kinds of income surplus of enterprises after the deduction of the various cost in the process of production, to reflect the realized total profit and loss of the enterprise in the reporting period.

【Total Wages Payable】 refers to various forms of compensation and other related expenses paid by an enterprise to obtain the services provided by employees. Including workers' wages, bonuses, allowances and subsidies, employee welfare, health insurance, endowment insurance, unemployment insurance, industrial injury insurance and birth insurance premium of social insurance premiums and housing accumulation fund, union funds and employee education funds, non-monetary benefits, for lifting and worker labor relations of compensation, other expenses related to for services rendered by employees.

【Average number of employed persons】 refers to the average number of persons engaged in the service industry activities within the reporting period, according to the statistics principle of "who labor, who statistics", including the formal staff, labor dispatch personnel and temporary staff who participate in the activities of the service industry enterprises. And the people receiving wages, dividends, bonus from the enterprise but not participating in the service industry activities are not included.

第十七篇 CHAPTER 17

科 技

SCIENCE AND TECHNOLOGY

简要说明 Brief Introduction

第十七篇　科　技

一、本篇资料反映广州市科学技术活动的基本情况。

二、资料来源：

17-1至17-5表根据广州市科学技术局、广州市市场监督管理局（知识产权局）、广州市科协等部门提供的统计数据加工整理。17-6至17-11由广州市统计局人口和社会科技统计处根据国家统计局企业研发活动情况年报表数据整理。17-12至17-14表分别由广州市统计局综合处、工业处和服务业处提供。

17 Science and Technology

I.The data in this chapter show the basic conditions of Guangzhou's activities of science and technology.

II. Data resources:

Tables 17-1 to 17-5 is provided by Guangzhou Municipal Science and Technology Bureau,Guangzhou Administration for Market Regulation(Intellectual Property Office), Guangzhou Association of Science and Technology.Tables 17-6 to 17-11 are organized by the population and Social Science and Technology Statistics Department of the Bureau of Statistics of Guangzhou, according to the annual report on enterprise R&D activities in the National Bureau of Statistics. Tables 17-12 to 17-14 is provided by Guangzhou Bureau of Statistics, Integrated Branch, Industry Branch and Service Branch, respectively.

17-1 科技监测主要指标

Main Indicators of Scientific and Technological Monitoring

项　　目	Item	2018	2019
科研机构人均固定资产原价　（千元/人）	Per Capita Original Value of Fixed Assets of Scientific Research Institutions (1000 yuan/person)	690.00	830.00
科学研究和技术服务业新增固定资产占全社会新增固定资产比重　（%）	Proportion of Newly-increasing Fixed Assets in Science Research and Technology Services to Newly-increasing Fixed Assets of the Whole Society (%)	0.23	0.38
每万人口专利申请量　（件/万人）	Number of Patent Applications per 1 Million Persons (piece/10000 persons)	189.67	188.39
每万人口专利授权量　（件/万人）	Number of Patent Applications Granted per 1 Million Persons (piece/10000 persons)	98.41	111.42
每万人口发明专利授权量　（件/万人）	Number of Invention & Patent Applications Granted per Million Persons (piece/10000 persons)	11.83	12.99
专业技术人才数　（万人）	Number of professional and technical personnel (10000 persons)	176.70	
其中：高级职称	Senior title of professional	20.30	
中级职称	Middle title of professional	77.10	
初级职称	Junior title of professional	79.30	
技术市场合同成交金额年增长率　（%）	Annual Growth Rates of Contracted Transaction Value in Technical Market (%)	101.20	77.01

注：因2019年职称评审现未完成，“专业技术人才”指标数据无法提供。

Note: Because the 2019 professional title review has not been completed, "Number of professional and technical personnel" indicator data can not be provided.

17-2 各类科学研究与开发机构基本情况

Basic Statistics of Scientific Research and Development Institutions

项　　目	Item	2018 全市 Total	# 市属 Managed by Municipal Government
机构数 (个)	Number of Institutions (unit)	166	51
# 自然科学	Natural Science	156	47
从业人员 (人)	Employed Persons (person)	29400	6262
# 自然科学	Natural Science	28667	5947
在从业人员中的科研人员（人）	Scientific Researchers of Employed Persons (person)	23137	4280
# 自然科学	Natural Science	22443	3972

17-2 续表 continue

项　　目	Item	2019 全市 Total	# 市属 Managed by Municipal Government
机构数 (个)	Number of Institutions (unit)	185	61
# 自然科学	Natural Science	175	57
从业人员 (人)	Employed Persons (person)	31947	7221
# 自然科学	Natural Science	31174	6878
在从业人员中的科研人员（人）	Scientific Researchers of Employed Persons (person)	25547	5320
# 自然科学	Natural Science	24847	5013

17-3 获得省级以上科技成果奖励情况

Statistics on Provincial Prizes and Above for Scientific and Technological Research Achievements

单位：项 (item)

指　　标	Indicators	2018	2019
国家级科技奖励成果	**National Prizes for Scientific and Technological Research Achievements**	**21**	**26**
国家发明奖	Number of National Invention Prizes Awarded	3	2
国家自然科学奖	Number of National Natural Sciences Prizes Awarded	2	2
国家科技进步奖	Number of National Scientific and Technological Progress Prizes Awarded	16	22
省级科技奖励成果	**Provincial Prizes for Scientific and Technological Research Achievements**	**140**	**136**
省科技进步奖	Number of Provincial Scientific and Technological Progress Prizes Awarded	106	100

17-4　科协基本情况（2019年）

项　　目		Item	
机构数	（个）	Number of Associations for Science & Technology	(unit)
机关人数	（人）	Number of Agency Personnel	(person)
在册学会、协会、研究会	（个）	Number of Registered Societies, Associations and Research Societies	(unit)
企业科协	（个）	Associations in Enterprises	(unit)
乡镇/街道科协个数	（个）	Associations in County-level cities/Communities	(unit)
农技协个数	（个）	Specialized Rural Technological Societies	(unit)
举行国内外学术交流活动	（次）	Number of Domestic and International Academic Meetings	(times)
参加人数	（人）	Number of Participants	(person-times)
举办科普宣讲活动	（次）	Number of Lectures on Popular Science	(times)
# 举办专题展览	（次）	Number of Special Subject Exhibitions	(times)
开展科技咨询	（次）	Number of Scientific and Technological Consulting	(times)
科普宣讲活动受众人数	（人次）	Number of Participants in Lectures on Popular Science	(person-time)
举办实用技术培训	（次）	Number of Practical and Technical Training Courses	(times)
实用技术培训人数	（人）	Number of Participants to Practical and Technical Training Courses	(person)
推广新技术、新品种	（项）	Popularizing New Technologies and New Species	(items)
科普宣讲活动覆盖村(社区)个数	（个）	Number of Villages covered (Communities covered) by Lectures on Popular Science	(unit)
举办青少年科普活动	（次）	Number of Lectures on Popular Science for Teenagers	(times)
青少年科普活动受众人数	（人次）	Number of Participants to Lectures on Popular Science for Teenagers	(person-time)
举办青少年科技竞赛	（项）	Number of Teenagers Science and Technology Competitions	(times)
青少年科技竞赛参加人数	（人）	Number of Persons Engaged in Teenagers Science and Technology Competitions	(person)
青少年科技竞赛获奖人数	（人）	Number of Winners in Teenagers Science and Technology Competitions	(person)
科技馆(科普活动中心)	（个）	Number of Science Centers	(unit)
科普活动站(室)	（个）	Number of Popular Science labs	(unit)
科普画廊建筑面积(宣传栏、科普橱窗)	（平方米）	Construction Area of Popular Science Galleries	(Square meter)
科普画廊展示面积	（平方米）	Demonstration Area of Popular Science Galleries	(Square meter)
制作科普挂图种数	（种）	Types of Popular Science Charts	(type)
科普挂图总印数	（张）	Total Amount of Printed Popular Science Charts	(piece)
接待国外专家学者	（人）	Foreign Experts and Scholars	(person)
接待港澳台地区专家学者	（人）	Experts and Scholars from Hong Kong, Macao and Taiwan	(person)
参与“创交会”人数	（人）	Number of Persons Engaged in China Innovation and Entrepreneurship Fair	(person)

Basic Statistics on Associations for Science and Technology (2019)

合 计 Total	# 市科协 City-level Associations	区科协 District-level Associations
12	1	11
107	42	65
205	98	107
102	34	68
174		174
5		5
6	5	1
1509	1009	500
569	230	339
23		23
49		49
2169875	2066596	103279
30		30
2231		2231
9		9
606		606
288	209	79
109403	65024	44379
33	6	27
26465	8026	18439
9300	4746	4554
3	1	2
343		343
14138	300	13838
25294	970	24324
372	362	10
8865	7475	1390
180	180	
74000	74000	

17-5 专利申请量和专利授权量

Patent Applications and Patent Certified

单位：件 (item)

指　　标	Indicators	专利申请量 Patent Applications 2018	2019	专利授权量 Patent Certified 2018	2019
总　　计	**Total**	**173124**	**177223**	**89826**	**104813**
按种类分	**By Sort**				
发　　明	Creations and Inventions	50169	46643	10797	12222
实用新型	Utility Models	79598	81728	51307	54746
外观设计	Appearance Designs	43357	48852	27722	37845
按对象分	**By Applicant**				
非职务发明创造	Non-position Creations and Inventions	24734	43276	10452	14885
职务发明创造	Position Creations and Inventions	148390	133947	79374	89928
大专院校	Universities and Colleges	16523	16012	7414	7956
科研单位	Research Institutions	3401	3332	1763	2010
工矿企业	Industrial Enterprises	125880	111471	69542	78384
机关团体	Govermment Agencies and Organizations	2586	3132	655	1578

17-6 主要年份研究与试验发展(R&D)投入情况

Research and Experimental Development (R&D) in Main Years

年份 Year	R&D经费内部支出(亿元) Internal Expenditure on R&D (100 million yuan)	R&D人员(万人) Number of R&D Personnel (10000 persons)	R&D人员折合全时当量(万人年) Number of R&D Personnel (10 000 man-year)	研发强度(%) Percentage of R&D Expenditure in Provincial GDP (%)
2000	29.06		2.58	1.17
2001	32.66		2.72	1.15
2002	34.86		2.82	1.09
2003	37.27		2.89	0.99
2004	44.51		2.99	1.00
2005	47.29		3.05	0.92
2006	51.38		3.07	0.84
2007	100.40		4.36	1.41
2008	129.19		4.80	1.56
2009	171.01	9.07	6.58	1.87
2010	192.43	9.91	6.60	1.79
2011	238.06	11.58	8.41	1.92
2012	262.87	12.87	9.04	1.94
2013	292.07	14.38	10.02	1.90
2014	334.01	15.34	10.28	2.00
2015	380.13	16.57	10.96	2.10
2016	457.46	16.27	11.02	2.31
2017	532.41	19.57	11.80	2.48
2018	600.17	20.36	13.42	2.63
2019	677.74	22.90	15.06	2.87

注：1．本表研发强度数据按当年地区生产总值计算，未对过往年份数据进行调整。
　　2．2009年以前未对R&D人员进行统计。

Note: I. The Percentage of R&D Expenditure in Provincial GDP data in this table is calculated based on the current year's Provincial GDP, and the previous year's data is not adjusted.

II. No statistics on Number of R&D Personnel before 2009.

17-7 研究与试验发展(R&D)投入基本情况

Basic situation of Research and Experimental Development (R&D)

指 标	Item	2018	2019
R&D人员 （万人）	Number of R&D Personnel (10 000 persons)	20.36	22.90
# 企业	Enterprises	13.22	14.33
科研机构	R&D Institutions	1.88	2.13
高校	Institutions of Higher Education	4.74	5.94
其他	others	0.52	0.50
R&D人员折合全时当量 （万人年）	Number of R&D Personnel (10 000 person-years)	13.42	15.06
# 企业	Enterprises	9.52	10.34
科研机构	R&D Institutions	1.52	1.64
高校	Institutions of Higher Education	2.01	2.74
其他	others	0.37	0.35
R&D经费内部支出 （亿元）	Internal Expenditure on R&D (100 million yuan)	600.17	677.74
# 企业	Enterprises	389.93	432.54
科研机构	R&D Institutions	91.64	131.48
高校	Institutions of Higher Education	109.25	103.30
其他	others	9.35	10.42
全社会R&D经费内部支出占GDP比例 （%）	Percentage of Research and Development Expenditure in Provincial GDP (%)	2.63	2.87

17-8 规模以上工业企业研发情况

Research and Experimental Development (R&D) of Industrial Enterprises above the Designated Size

项　　目	Item	2018	2019
规模以上工业企业数　（个）	Number of Industrial Enterprises above Designated Size (unit)	4807	5786
#有R&D活动的企业数　（个）	Number of Enterprises Having R&D Activities (unit)	1865	2349
有研发机构的企业数　（个）	Number of Enterprises Having Research and Development Institutions (unit)	2132	2620
R&D经费内部支出合计（万元）	Expenditure for R&D (10000 yuan)	2672706.7	2862407.1
按支出用途分组	Grouped by use of Expenditure		
经常性支出	Recurrent Expenditure	2369447.0	2702037.4
资产性支出	Capital Expenditure	303259.7	160369.7
按支出类型分组	Group by Expenditure Type		
基础研究支出	Basic Research Expenditure	1697.3	3106.7
应用研究支出	Applied Research Expenditure	35310.3	7914.0
试验发展支出	Experimental Development Expenditure	2635699.1	2851386.4
按资金来源分组	Grouped by Source of Funds		
政府资金	Government Appropriation Funds	75916.6	56003.7
企业资金	Self-raised Funds of Enterprises	2566339.6	2806330.0
境外资金	Overseas Funds	19971.8	
其他资金	Others	10478.7	73.4
R&D人员　（人）	R&D Personnel (person)	95562	99979
R&D人员折合全时当量（人年）	Full-time Equivalent of R&D Personnel (person-year)	69351	72877
企业办研发机构数　（个）	Number of Research and Development Institutions in Enterprises (unit)	2595	3040
研发机构人员　（人）	Personnel in Research and Development Institutions (person)	99492	109176
#硕士毕业及以上的人员	Personnel with Educational Background of Master and Above	8236	9668

17-9 资质以上建筑业企业研发情况

Research and Experimental Development (R&D) of Grade Construction Enterprises

项　　目	Item	2018	2019
资质以上建筑业企业数　（个）	Number of Grade Construction Enterprises (unit)	273	307
# 有R&D活动的企业数　（个）	Number of Enterprises Having R&D Activities (unit)	69	91
有研发机构的企业数	Number of Enterprises Having Research and Development Institutions (unit)	71	101
R&D经费内部支出合计　（万元）	Expenditure for R&D (10000 yuan)	318412.2	340333.5
按支出用途分组	Grouped by use of Expenditure		
经常性支出	Recurrent Expenditure	303327.0	329962.8
资产性支出	Capital Expenditure	15085.2	10370.7
按支出类型分组	Group by Expenditure Type		
基础研究支出	Basic Research Expenditure	484.8	
应用研究支出	Applied Research Expenditure	29169.4	12628.8
试验发展支出	Experimental Development Expenditure	288758	327704.7
按资金来源分组	Grouped by Source of Funds		
政府资金	Government Appropriation Funds	3325.9	561.9
企业资金	Self-raised Funds of Enterprises	313004.7	338814.3
境外资金	Overseas Funds	2081.6	957.3
其他资金	Others		
R&D人员	R&D Personnel (person)	6798	6816
R&D人员折合全时当量　（人年）	Full-time Equivalent of R&D Personnel (person-year)	5181	4927
企业办研发机构数　（个）	Number of Research and Development Institutions in Enterprises (unit)	102	138
研发机构人员　（人）	Personnel in Research and Development Institutions (person)	9528	12149
# 硕士毕业及以上的人员	Personnel with Educational Background of Master and Above	712	1187

注：本表中的建筑业企业指特、一级资质总承包、专业承包建筑业企业。

Note: Data in this table is the first-grade qualification of construction enterprise refers to the special and general contracting of construction enterprise specialized contracting.

17-10 规模以上服务业企业研发情况

Research and Experimental Development (R&D) of Service Enterprises above the Designated Size

项　　目	Item	2018	2019
规模以上服务业企业数　（个）	Number of Service Enterprises above Designated Size (unit)	1409	8088
#有R&D活动的企业数　（个）	Number of Enterprises Having R&D Activities (unit)	325	1094
有研发机构的企业数　（个）	Number of Industrial Enterprises Having Research and Development Institutions (unit)	373	1228
R&D经费内部支出合计　（万元）	Expenditure for R&D (10000 yuan)	908176.0	1048749.2
按支出用途分组	Grouped by use of Expenditure		
经常性支出	Recurrent Expenditure	880308.6	965805.3
资产性支出	Capital Expenditure	27867.4	82943.9
按支出类型分组	Group by Expenditure Type		
基础研究支出	Basic Research Expenditure	5979.5	6279.7
应用研究支出	Applied Research Expenditure	80334.0	87809.6
试验发展支出	Experimental Development Expenditure	821862.5	954659.9
按资金来源分组	Grouped by Source of Funds		
政府资金	Government Appropriation Funds	43020.9	41568.4
企业资金	Self-raised Funds of Enterprises	864797.6	1007122.8
境外资金	Overseas Funds	184.9	
其他资金	Others	172.6	58.0
R&D人员	R&D Personnel (person)	29790	36508
R&D人员折合全时当量　（人年）	Full-time Equivalent of R&D Personnel (person-year)	20707	25632
企业办研发机构数　（个）	Number of Research and Development Institutions in Enterprises (unit)	568	1547
研发机构人员　（人）	Personnel in Research and Development Institutions (person)	60081	96601
#硕士毕业及以上的人员	Personnel with Educational Background of Master and Above	10055	14055

注：1.本表中规模以上服务业只包含以下行业：交通运输、仓储和邮政业，信息传输、软件和信息技术服务业，租赁和商务服务业，科学研究和 技术服务业，水利、环境和公共设施管理业，卫生和社会工作，文化、体育和娱乐业。
2.2018年只调查大中型服务业企业，2019年统计范围扩大至大中小微型全部服务业企业。

Note: I. The service enterprises above the designated size in this table only includes the following industries: transportation, warehousing and postal service, information transmission software and information technology services, leasing and business services, scientific research and technical services, water environment and public facilities management, health and social work, culture and sports and entertainment.
II.In 2018, only large and medium-sized service companies were surveyed. In 2019, the scope of statistics was expanded to all service companies in large, medium, small and micro.

17-11 各区研究与试验发展(R&D)投入情况(2019年)
Research and Experimental Development (R&D) by District (2019)

地 区	Districts	R&D经费 内部支出 (亿元) Internal Expendi on R&D (100 million yuan)	研发强度(%) Percentage of R&D Expenditure in Provincial GDP (%)
全 市	**Total**	**677.74**	**2.87**
荔湾区	Liwan	12.74	1.15
越秀区	Yuexiu	60.47	1.93
海珠区	Haizhu	69.79	3.61
天河区	Tianhe	173.32	3.43
白云区	Baiyun	35.20	1.59
黄埔区	Huangpu	153.42	4.38
番禺区	Panyu	54.87	2.64
花都区	Huadu	36.58	2.34
南沙区	Nansha	50.63	3.01
从化区	Conghua	8.12	2.28
增城区	Zengcheng	22.62	2.24

注：本表研发强度数据按当年地区生产总值计算。
Note: The Percentage of R&D Expenditure in Provincial GDP data in this table is calculated based on the current year's Provincial GDP.

17-12 高新技术产品情况(2019年)
Statistics on High-tech Products (2019)

单位：万元 (10000 yuan)

项 目	Item	企业数 (个) Number of Enterprises (unit)	总产值 Gross Output Value	产 品 销售收入 Sales Revenue	出 口 销售收入 Sales Revenue of Export	实现利税总额 Total Profits and Taxes
合 计	**Total**	**5375**	**95186944**	**99199516**	**16483310**	**10834665**
#规模以上工业	Industries above Designated Size	1928	85198518	82890377	15522832	7787436
规模以上服务业	Service above Designated Size	961		9584425	197884	2634123

注：高新技术产品产值的口径不包含军工企业；不含军工企业的2019年规模以上工业总产值为194076433万元。
Note:The scale of output value of high-tech products does not include military enterprises; The total output value of industries above the scale in 2019, excluding military enterprises was 1940,764.33 million yuan.

17-13 规模以上工业企业高新技术产品情况（2019年）

单位：万元

项　　目	Item	企业数（个）Number of Enterprises (unit)	产品数（个）Number of Products (unit)
总　　计	**Total**	**1928**	**6407**
按地区分	By District		
荔湾区	Liwan	25	103
越秀区	Yuexiu	3	8
海珠区	Haizhu	24	119
天河区	Tianhe	71	485
白云区	Baiyun	273	882
黄埔区	Huangpu	519	2052
番禺区	Panyu	298	943
花都区	Huadu	279	717
南沙区	Nansha	179	435
从化区	Conghua	101	285
增城区	Zengcheng	156	378
按技术领域分	By Technological Circle		
电子与信息技术	Electronic and Information Technology		1310
机电一体化技术	Integration Technology for Machinery with Electronics		1233
生物技术	Biotechnology		1135
新材料技术	New Material Technology		1280
新能源高效节能	New Energy and High-efficiency Energy-saving		473
环保技术	Environmental Protection Technology		218
其他技术	Others		758

注：高新技术产品产值的口径不包含军工企业。

Statistics on High-tech Products of Industrial Enterprisesa Above the Designated Size (2019)

(10000 yuan)

总产值 Total Output Value	产品销售收入 Sales Revenue	出口销售收入 Sales Revenue of Exports	实现利税总额 Total Profits and Taxes
85198518	**82890377**	**15522832**	**7787436**
693508	679450	20432	188166
3232	3007		577
712098	704021	14939	70450
2256804	2200671	76479	178995
4139961	4059132	470372	470465
35502837	34046697	10738602	2094029
7414767	6995639	720215	606922
14233919	13910031	712904	1056066
13057669	13066805	1809963	2622796
1714208	1673646	366341	86660
5469515	5551278	592585	412310
15086142	14699990	7878165	860258
28244989	27544356	708353	3521138
4668487	4511233	160247	952144
11617524	10460972	1492859	741307
6599529	6539720	968986	675287
1697226	1772801	321596	142319
17284621	17361305	3992626	894983

Note: The scale of output value of high-tech products does not include military enterprises.

17-14 规模以上服务业企业高新技术产品情况(2019年)

单位:万元

项　　目	Item	企业数（个）Number of Enterprises (unit)
总　　计	**Total**	**961**
按地区分	By District	
荔湾区	Liwan	7
越秀区	Yuexiu	104
海珠区	Haizhu	64
天河区	Tianhe	446
白云区	Baiyun	27
黄埔区	Huangpu	205
番禺区	Panyu	74
花都区	Huadu	8
南沙区	Nansha	16
从化区	Conghua	3
增城区	Zengcheng	7
按技术领域分	By Technological Circle	
电子与信息技术	Electronic and Information Technology	961
机电一体化技术	Integration Technology for Machinery with Electronics	
生物技术	Biotechnology	
新材料技术	New Material Technology	
新能源高效节能	New Energy and High-efficiency Energy-saving	
环保技术	Environmental Protection Technology	
其他技术	Others	

Statistics on High-tech Products of Enterprises in Service Sector Enterprises above Designated Size (2019)

(10000 yuan)

产品数 (个) Number of Products (unit)	产品销售收入 Sales Revenue	出口销售收入 Sales Revenue of Exports	实现利税总额 Total Profits and Taxes
3419	**9584425**	**197884**	**2634123**
22	429596	1019	218510
390	647993	2136	111792
207	399475	3423	90739
1529	4653897	111841	775263
70	213448	30	31642
851	1442548	79236	283145
254	1634265	200	1086527
17	16671		1075
41	90708		26999
19	27971		4766
19	27854		3664
3419	9584425	197884	2634123

【研究与试验发展（R&D）】指在科学技术领域，为增加知识总量、以及运用这些知识去创造新的应用进行的系统的创造性的活动，包括基础研究、应用研究、试验发展三类活动。

【Research and Experimental Development(R&D)】 In the field of science and technology, comprise creative work undertaken on a systematic basis in order to increase the stock of knowledge and the use of this stock of knowledge to devise new applications. The term R&D covers three activities: basic research, applied research and experimental development.

第十八篇 CHAPTER 18

教育、文化、体育、卫生、社会福利和其他

EDUCATION, CULTURE, SPORTS, PUBLIC HEALTH, SOCIAL WELFARE AND OTHERS

第十八篇　教育、文化、体育、卫生、社会福利和其他

一、本篇资料反映广州市教育、文化、体育、卫生、社会福利及其他事业的发展情况。

二、本篇资料由广州市统计局人口和社会科技统计处整理提供。

三、教育部分包括高等、中等、基础教育、幼儿教育、各级成人教育。资料由省教育厅、市教育局、省人力资源和社会保障厅等相关部门提供。

四、文化部分主要包括文化机构、人员及业务活动开展情况等。文化统计资料根据省文化和旅游厅、市文化广电旅游局、省广播电视局、省委办公厅（省档案局）、市委办公厅（市档案局）等有关部门提供的统计年报加工整理。

五、体育部分主要包括体育行政部门主办的运动会和比赛活动、全民健身活动情况及运动竞技成绩等，资料由市体育局提供。

六、卫生部分主要包括卫生事业机构、床位及人员数、医院业务情况、妇幼保健情况等，资料由市卫生健康委员会提供。

七、社会福利部分主要包括社会福利事业的机构数、收养救济人数、婚姻登记状况等，资料由市民政局、市退役军人事务局、市应急管理局、市医疗救助服务中心提供。

八、社会保险部分主要包括五种险种的年末参保人数和全年享受人数。其中2019年的养老保险、失业保险、工伤保险和生育保险数据由广州市人力资源和社会保障局提供，医疗保险数据由广州市医疗保障局提供。

九、其他部分主要包括司法工作开展情况和刑事、交通、火灾事故发生情况等，资料由市司法局、市公安局、市应急管理局提供。

18 Education, Culture, Sports, Public Health, Social Welfare and Others

I. The data in this chapter show the development conditions of Guangzhou's education, culture, sports, public health, social welfare and others.

II.The data in this chapter are prepared and provided by the Division of Population, Social, Science and Technology Statistic of Guangzhou Municipal Bureau of Statistics.

III.The data on education cover the situations on higher education, secondary education, primary education, kindergartens and adult education at all levels. The data are provided by Guangdong Provincial Bureau of Education, Guangzhou Municipal Bureau of Education, Guangdong Provincial Bureau of Human Resources and Social Security, etc.

IV. The data on culture mainly cover the situations on institutes, employed persons and business activities of culture. The cultural statistics are processed according to the statistical annual reports provided by the Guangdong Provincial Department of Culture and Tourism, Guangzhou Bureau of Culture, Radio and Television Tourism, Guangdong Radio and Television Bureau, Guangdong Provincial Committee Office (Provincial Archives Bureau), Guangzhou Committee Office (Municipal Archives Bureau) and other relevant departments.

V. The data on sports mainly include the sports games and matches organized by sports administrative departments, mass sports and athletics sports. The data are provided by Guangzhou Municipal Bureau of Sports.

VI. The data on public health mainly include the number of institutions, hospital beds and personnel, hospital business, women and babies hygiene. The data are provided by Guangzhou Municipal Health Commission.

VII. The data on social welfare mainly include the number of institutions, the number receiving social welfare relief funds and marriage registrations, etc. The data are provided by Guangzhou Municipal Civil Affairs Bureau, Guangzhou Municipal Veterans Affairs Bureau, and Municipal Emergency Management Bureau and Guangzhou Municipal Medical Assistance Service Center.

VIII.The part of social insurance mainly includes the number of insurance participants at the end of the year and the number of people enjoying the whole year of five kinds of insurance. The data of endowment insurance, unemployment insurance, industrial injury insurance and reproductive insurance in 2019 are provided by Guangzhou Municipal Human Resources and Social Security Bureau, and the data of medical insurance are provided by Guangzhou Municipal Medical Security Bureau.

IX. The data on others mainly include the judicial conditions, basic statistics on traffic accidents and fires, etc. The data are provided by Guangzhou Municipal Bureau of Justice, Guangzhou Municipal Bureau of Public Security and Municipal Emergency Management Bureau.

18-1 主要年份教育事业基本情况

Basic Statistics on Education in Main Years

项　　目	Item	2018	2019
学校数　（所）	**Number of Schools (unit)**	**1731**	**1753**
普通高等学校	Regular Institutions of Higher Education	82	81
中等职业学校	Vocational Secondary Schools	82	82
技工学校	Technical Schools	55	56
普通中学	Regular Secondary Schools	527	534
高　中	Senior Secondary Schools	118	119
初　中	Junior Secondary Schools	409	415
小　学	Primary Schools	965	980
特殊教育学校	Special Schools	20	20
专任教师　（人）	**Number of Full-time Teachers (person)**	**178324**	**186174**
普通高等学校	Regular Institutions of Higher Education	62732	66773
中等职业学校	Vocational Secondary Schools	7866	7926
技工学校	Technical Schools	6128	6242
普通中学	Regular Secondary Schools	43519	44179
高　中	Senior Secondary Schools	14522	14475
初　中	Junior Secondary Schools	28997	29704
小　学	Primary Schools	57160	60035
特殊教育学校	Special Schools	919	1019

注：本表普通高等学校数据由广东省教育厅提供，技工学校数据由广东省人力资源和社会保障厅提供，其余数据由广州市教育局提供。

Note: The data of colleges and universities in this table are provided by the Department of Education of Guangdong Province, the data of technical schools are provided by Human Resources and Social Security Department of Guangdong Province, and the rest of the data are provided by the Bureau of Education of Guangzhou City.

18-1 续表 continued

项　　目	Item	2018	2019
招生数　　（人）	**New Student Enrollment　(person)**	**847467**	**902701**
普通高等学校	Regular Institutions of Higher Education	323605	356273
中等职业学校	Vocational Secondary Schools	66026	63309
技工学校	Technical Schools	76428	86561
普通中学	Regular Secondary Schools	174522	184705
高　中	Senior Secondary Schools	52401	53127
初　中	Junior Secondary Schools	122121	131578
小　学	Primary Schools	206514	210895
特殊教育学校	Special Schools	372	958
在校学生　　（人）	**Total Student Enrollment　(person)**	**3072572**	**3201170**
普通高等学校	Regular Institutions of Higher Education	1086407	1140949
中等职业学校	Vocational Secondary Schools	184094	180249
技工学校	Technical Schools	226342	244098
普通中学	Regular Secondary Schools	514428	526222
高　中	Senior Secondary Schools	163838	159355
初　中	Junior Secondary Schools	350590	366867
小　学	Primary Schools	1058455	1104714
特殊教育学校	Special Schools	2846	4938
毕业生数　　（人）	**Graduates　(person)**	**724389**	**730029**
普通高等学校	Regular Institutions of Higher Education	290395	286777
中等职业学校	Vocational Secondary Schools	67910	57941
技工学校	Technical Schools	67020	72854
普通中学	Regular Secondary Schools	159576	164047
高　中	Senior Secondary Schools	58514	56484
初　中	Junior Secondary Schools	101062	107563
小　学	Primary Schools	139039	147700
特殊教育学校	Special Schools	449	710

注：本表普通高等学校数据由广东省教育厅提供，技工学校数据由广东省人力资源和社会保障厅提供，其余数据由广州市教育局提供。

Note: The data of colleges and universities in this table are provided by the Department of Education of Guangdong Province, the data of technical schools are provided by Human Resources and Social Security Department of Guangdong Province, and the rest of the data are provided by the Bureau of Education of Guangzhou City.

18-2 主要年份每万人口在校学生数、每个教师负担学生数
Students Enrollment per 10000 Persons and Students Taught by Every Teacher in Main Years

单位：人 (person)

年 份 Year	平均每万人口在校学生数 Students Enrollment Per 10000 Persons			平均每个教师负担学生数 Students Taught by Every Teacher		
	普通高校 College and University Students	普通中学生 High School Students	小学生 Primary School Students	普通高校 College and University Students	普通中学 Regular Secondary Schools	小 学 Primary School Students
1978	44.94	795.85	1178.65	3.10	18.25	24.05
1980	54.28	598.04	1175.91	3.65	15.83	21.80
1985	94.77	456.79	993.46	4.83	15.15	20.43
1986	99.43	471.25	967.81	4.87	16.10	21.05
1987	103.35	487.88	938.26	5.18	16.40	21.04
1988	112.42	481.43	919.33	5.52	16.21	21.05
1989	116.10	463.41	941.98	5.74	15.44	21.93
1990	110.16	446.65	963.03	5.52	15.25	22.79
1991	106.92	446.28	985.58	5.58	15.56	23.24
1992	109.37	461.81	1009.11	6.04	15.99	24.16
1993	126.51	469.79	1034.06	6.87	15.94	24.52
1994	139.74	475.66	1058.77	7.75	16.20	24.62
1995	147.56	494.03	1073.74	8.13	16.42	23.90
1996	151.23	516.39	1074.82	8.23	16.53	22.77
1997	153.60	538.65	1085.07	8.72	16.79	22.24
1998	160.76	562.95	1087.87	9.33	16.99	22.14
1999	196.03	581.75	1083.13	10.83	17.25	22.81
2000	264.14	606.92	1080.31	13.95	17.59	22.16
2001	343.44	642.86	1106.66	16.48	17.60	22.04
2002	414.97	668.15	1133.21	14.40	17.38	22.04
2003	516.75	705.69	1168.69	14.48	17.21	21.76
2004	623.14	719.53	1185.82	15.45	17.28	21.88
2005	738.58	733.24	1203.62	15.89	17.09	22.02
2006	814.28	746.16	1174.64	16.22	16.89	21.85
2007	888.35	745.78	1149.31	16.33	16.38	21.24
2008	938.77	742.25	1100.35	16.90	16.07	20.45
2009	1001.75	723.94	1043.13	17.30	15.50	19.61
2010	1046.88	709.90	1023.16	17.32	14.97	18.88
2011	1100.10	689.46	1006.37	17.31	14.48	18.74
2012	1142.17	669.67	1000.36	17.49	13.74	18.43
2013	1181.11	657.14	1032.38	17.74	13.41	19.06
2014	1209.96	632.55	1068.44	17.82	12.84	19.00
2015	1221.30	603.18	1097.96	17.66	12.38	19.01
2016	1214.58	580.92	1112.63	17.71	12.07	18.60
2017	1188.74	567.37	1118.98	17.43	11.90	18.31
2018	1171.09	554.53	1140.96	17.32	11.82	18.52
2019	1196.32	551.76	1158.33	17.09	11.91	18.40

18-3 主要年份各级各类学校在校学生数

单位：人

年 份 Year	普通高等学校 Regular Institutions of Higher Education	中等职业学校 Vocational Secondary Schools	技工学校 Technical Schools
1978	21699		
1980	27239	18852	8273
1985	51647	48959	5615
1986	55223	61913	8670
1987	58402	69693	12479
1988	64859	78025	17225
1989	67969	84662	18514
1990	65465	95048	20319
1991	64389	103860	21692
1992	66958	113218	23842
1993	78901	141307	25242
1994	89019	154144	29742
1995	95429	182090	36078
1996	99214	212396	43446
1997	102372	210956	50566
1998	108378	210566	58396
1999	134283	227084	59779
2000	185078	219640	59570
2001	244736	209340	64008
2002	299037	200090	76660
2003	374742	200337	87878
2004	459676	184682	104317
2005	554327	191499	122108
2006	619442	216555	153175
2007	687115	237411	173413
2008	736152	244070	196197
2009	796006	251077	242085
2010	843934	248060	252812
2011	896123	248614	269188
2012	939208	239446	289967
2013	983051	240579	279329
2014	1019291	244585	240350
2015	1043221	237130	236323
2016	1057281	216974	222298
2017	1067335	196796	229651
2018	1086407	184094	226342
2019	1140949	180249	244098

Students Enrollment by Various Schools in Main Years

(person)

普通中学 Regular Secondary Schools	小　学 Primary Schools	特殊教育学校 Special Schools
384313	569165	326
300134	590146	289
248940	541420	372
261733	537528	481
275690	530189	546
277743	530368	651
271291	551458	724
265423	572286	854
268760	593537	949
282720	617779	1032
292991	644907	1680
303004	674464	3760
319493	694401	5411
338776	705134	6096
359000	723183	5977
379505	733375	5827
398499	741950	6106
425261	756961	5224
458099	788604	5877
481481	816617	5495
511756	847524	4947
530776	874749	5302
550320	903353	5010
567619	893575	5045
576845	888965	5340
582051	862859	5246
575252	828889	5131
572280	824807	5153
561618	819771	4527
550669	822594	4719
546941	859263	4389
532870	900072	4386
515228	937870	4281
505685	968531	2969
509427	1004695	2975
514428	1058455	2846
526222	1104714	4938

18-4 主要年份研究生基本情况

Basic Statistics on Postgraduates in Main Years

单位：人 (person)

年 份 Year	培养单位(所) Training Units (unit)	#普通高校 Regular Institutions of Higher Education	毕业生数 Graduates	#普通高校 Regular Institutions of Higher Education	#博 士 Doctors
1985	15	12	654	650	7
1990	25	13	1491	1438	101
1991	24	13	1272	1234	109
1992	19	13	947	917	76
1993	18	13	1025	1003	76
1994	18	13	1079	1064	142
1995	21	13	1259	1215	154
1996	21	13	1440	1396	188
1997	21	13	1770	1715	253
1998	21	13	1843	1759	420
1999	21	13	2168	2059	371
2000	21	13	2131	2028	417
2001	22	14	2753	2671	540
2002	20	12	3133	3022	574
2003	20	12	4439	4299	772
2004	24	16	6541	6303	1160
2005	24	16	9006	8699	1331
2006	24	16	11790	11360	1579
2007	26	18	12624	12170	1751
2008	26	18	14773	14286	2086
2009	26	18	15395	14969	2462
2010	26	18	16244	15828	2265
2011	26	18	18584	18155	2374
2012	27	19	20816	20372	2583
2013	27	19	21833	21382	2700
2014	22	19	22717	22636	2788
2015	22	19	23218	23132	2881
2016	22	19	24138	24057	2896
2017	22	19	24127	24044	2979
2018	22	19	25418	25315	3031
2019	22	19	26703	26599	2985

注：1.本表数据由广东省教育厅提供。
2.2014年起，中国科学院在我市研究所招收的研究生不再纳入全市教育事业统计，因此2014年及以后的研究生数据不含中国科学院在广州的数据。下表同。

Note: I.The data in this table are provided by the Department of Education of Guangdong Province.
II.Since 2014, Guangzhou education statistics does not include the recruit students of Chinese Academic of Sciences in Guangzhou. So since 2014 the statistic of graduates does not contain the graduates of Chinese Academy of Sciences in Guangzhou. The same as the following table.

18-4 续表 continued

单位:人 (person)

年 份 Year	招生数 New Students Enrollment	# 普通高校 Regular Institutions of Higher Education	# 博 士 Doctors	在校学生数 Students Enrollment	# 普通高校 Regular Institutions of Higher Education	# 博 士 Doctors
1985	1526	1518	74	2878	2859	92
1990	1113	1090	76	3355	3264	293
1991	1171	1157	167	3216	3149	338
1992	1258	1228	162	3492	3426	417
1993	1521	1490	201	3940	3865	533
1994	1866	1831	298	4656	4562	681
1995	1875	1782	407	5283	5080	935
1996	2367	2249	457	6162	5888	1192
1997	2387	2288	457	6696	6388	1391
1998	2997	2921	582	7821	7521	1539
1999	3673	3559	788	9253	8952	1933
2000	5435	5274	1048	12492	12135	2549
2001	7080	6837	1352	17150	16631	3421
2002	8245	7910	1596	20408	19674	4256
2003	10864	10403	2104	26294	25253	5499
2004	13642	13143	2656	34599	33302	7474
2005	15642	15140	2780	40594	39124	8980
2006	17093	16586	2672	45238	43725	9149
2007	18084	17578	2819	49838	48298	9846
2008	19298	18776	2893	53826	52313	10753
2009	22181	21684	3132	60129	58635	11530
2010	23390	22844	3059	65911	64321	11528
2011	24216	23690	3119	69825	68223	12125
2012	25042	24504	3195	73118	71484	12526
2013	26002	25457	3294	76193	74535	13389
2014	26524	26440	3463	77211	76943	13818
2015	27137	27037	3434	79547	79268	14085
2016	28563	28459	3617	82282	81979	14532
2017	34074	33963	3847	90716	90391	15171
2018	37356	37244	4580	101092	100757	16394
2019	39531	39395	5193	112432	112064	18460

18-5 普通高等院校各类专业本科学生数(2019年)

Students Enrollment in Regular Institutions of Higher Education by Field of Study (2019)

单位:人 (person)

项 目	Item	毕业生数 Number of Graduates	招生数 New Students Enrollment	在校学生数 Number Of Students Enrollment
合 计	**Total**	**150849**	**174474**	**666308**
哲 学	Philosophy	106	198	789
经济学	Economics	15941	15113	62403
法 学	Law	6242	6592	24974
教育学	Education	2955	4148	13313
文 学	Literature	17600	23186	82940
历史学	History	537	624	2305
理 学	Science	8093	10072	38090
工 学	Engineering	35293	48908	181920
农 学	Agriculture	1835	2517	8652
医 学	Medicine	9294	10288	49964
管理学	Management	42247	37270	150694
艺术学	Art	10706	13779	48485
财经商贸大类	Finance and Trade		239	239
装备制造大类	Equipment Manufacture		241	241
教育与体育大类	Education and Sports		308	308
土木建筑大类	Civil Engineering		244	244
旅游大类	Tourism		73	73
文化艺术大类	Culture and Art		103	103
电子信息大类	Electronics		542	542
轻工纺织大类	Light Industry and Textiles		29	29
土建施工类	Civil Construction			

注：1.本表数据由广东省教育厅提供。

2.2019年10月教育部对普通高校本科专业目录作出更新，新增9种大类专业，分别是：财经商贸大类、装备制造大类、教育与体育大类、土木建筑大类、旅游大类、文化艺术大类、电子信息大类、轻工纺织大类、土建施工大类

Note: I.The data in this table are provided by the Department of Education of Guangdong Province.

II.In October 2019, the Ministry of Education made an update to the directory of undergraduate majors of ordinary universities, adding nine new major categories, namely: finance and trade, equipment manufacture, education and sports, civil engineering, tourism, culture and art, electronics, light industry and textiles, civil construction.

18-6 普通高等院校专科分学科学生数(2019年)

Students Enrollment in Regular Institutions of Higher Education for Junior College by Field of Study (2019)

单位:人 (person)

项　目	Item	毕业生数 Number of Graduates	招生数 New Students Enrollment	在校学生数 Number Of Students Enrollment
合　计	**Total**	**135928**	**181799**	**474641**
农林牧渔大类	Agriculture,Forestry,Animal Husbandry and Fishery Category	1353	2265	5398
资源环境与安全大类	Resource Environment and Security Category	1343	2194	5130
能源动力与材料大类	Energy Dynamics and Materials Category	1281	1433	3567
土木建筑大类	Civil Engineering Category	10637	14794	37588
水利大类	Water Conservancy Category	360	569	1381
装备制造大类	Equipment Manufacturing Category	11607	16709	41087
生物与化工大类	Biology and Chemical Industry Category	1128	1267	3487
轻工纺织大类	Textile Category	1086	1273	3244
食品药品与粮食大类	Food,Medicine and Grain Category	2929	3755	10255
交通运输大类	Transport Category	8095	9321	25110
电子信息大类	Electronic Information Category	20993	32152	81593
医药卫生大类	Medical and Health Care Category	4972	13314	26091
财经商贸大类	Finance Category	37117	38921	113722
旅游大类	Tourism Category	3845	5317	14094
文化艺术大类	Cultural and Art Design Category	9637	11819	33032
新闻传播大类	Media Category	754	1714	4040
教育与体育大类	Education and Sports Category	13225	18848	48657
公安与司法大类	Public Security and Law Category	1825	2419	6266
公共管理与服务大类	Public Administration and Services Category	3741	3715	10899

注：本表数据由广东省教育厅提供。
Note: The data in this table are provided by the Department of Education of Guangdong Province.

18-7 普通高等院校本专科基本情况(2019年)

单位：人

院校名称	Name of Universities, Institutes and Colleges	毕业生数 Number of Graduates
合　计	**Total**	**286777**
中山大学	Sun Yat-sen University	7424
华南理工大学	South China University of Technology	5712
暨南大学	Jinan University	5391
华南农业大学	South China Agricultural University	8783
南方医科大学	Southern Medical University	2881
广州中医药大学	Guangzhou University of Traditional Chinese Medicine	3303
华南师范大学	South China Normal University	5904
广东工业大学	Guangdong University of Technology	9063
广东外语外贸大学	Guangdong University of Foreign Studies	4768
广东财经大学	Guangdong Business Institute	6770
仲恺农业工程学院	Zhongkai Agritechnical College	5222
广东药科大学	Guangdong Pharmaceutical University	3083
星海音乐学院	Xinghai Conservatory of Music	985
广州美术学院	Guangzhou Academy of Fine Arts	1317
广州体育学院	Guangzhou Institute of Physical Education	1749
广东技术师范学院	Guangdong Polytechnic Normal University	3946
广东金融学院	Guangdong Finance College	5542
广东警官学院	Guangdong Police College	1504
广州大学	Guangzhou University	9730
广州医科大学	Guangzhou Medical Institute	1808
广东白云学院	Guangdong Baiyun Vocational Technical College	4417
广东培正学院	Guangdong Peizheng College	3469
广东第二师范学院	Guangdong University of Education	2934
广州民航职业技术学院	Guangzhou Civil Aviation College	4155
广州航海学院	Guangzhou Maritime College	2362
广东轻工职业技术学院	Guangdong Light Industry Technical College	6245
广东省外语艺术职业学院	Guangdong College of Foreign Languages and Art	2610
广东机电职业技术学院	Guangdong Machinery and Electricity College	4281
广东工贸职业技术学院	Guangdong Vocational College of Industry & Commerce	4711
广东交通职业技术学院	Guangdong Communication Polytechnic College	4257
广东水利电力职业技术学院	Guangdong Technical College of Water Resources and Electric Engineering	4259
广东生态工程职业学院	Guangdong Eco-engineering Polytechnic	1850
广东司法警官职业学院	Judicial Police Officers' Professional Institute of Guangdong	1381
广东女子职业技术学院	Guangdong Women's Professional College	2005
广东农工商职业技术学院	Guangdong AIB Polytechnic College	5577
广东邮电职业技术学院	Guangdong Posts & Telecom Vocational Technology College	1228
广东建设职业技术学院	Guangdong Construction Vocational Technology Institute	2623
广东行政职业学院	Guangdong Vocational of Administration	1490

Basic Statistics on Regular Institutions of Higher Education (2019)

(person)

招生数 Number of New Entrants	在校学生数 Number of Enrolled Students	校本部教职工人数 Number of Teachers and Staff	# 专任教师 Full-time Teachers	# 正高级 Professors	# 副高级 Associate Professors	# 中 级 Lecturers
356273	**1140949**	**93506**	**66773**	**10477**	**18880**	**24925**
7756	32160	6184	4028	1655	1643	504
6412	25177	4170	2683	1002	1040	632
6263	25863	3888	2499	744	938	707
9807	37199	3286	2478	484	896	961
3152	13851	2781	2044	672	846	506
2958	12554	1853	1449	394	467	493
6965	25643	4764	2386	619	641	496
9319	36184	3276	2307	417	694	1083
4953	19749	2330	1588	338	422	586
5945	23829	1893	1595	227	435	612
5908	21097	1367	1053	129	295	457
3083	20858	1724	1410	204	427	777
1276	4818	651	378	46	129	109
1461	5427	929	546	77	174	266
1860	6622	642	437	68	117	186
7763	22805	1845	1037	142	322	478
3962	20916	1640	1335	102	281	579
1683	6718	674	327	38	109	101
9667	36369	3360	2301	388	718	633
2074	9004	1895	1343	467	586	96
6966	21223	1320	1048	101	218	465
4653	16572	914	726	48	77	392
3535	13202	963	651	50	141	248
4150	12363	715	553	19	166	282
2684	13682	801	618	51	165	303
8332	21495	1221	891	86	316	430
4156	10027	562	362	17	112	162
5614	15246	997	788	38	259	424
6759	16455	919	730	25	189	350
6703	15565	827	667	64	177	356
6338	15509	795	629	28	227	306
2585	6513	447	356	2	93	112
1874	4551	321	199	18	58	91
2878	6997	395	228	13	74	99
7652	20151	1196	1044	28	306	523
1755	4838	459	174	2	37	74
5435	11237	481	379	7	90	195
1004	3728	295	193	18	35	116

18-7 续表

单位：人

院校名称	Name of Universities, Institutes and Colleges	毕业生数 Number of Graduates
广东体育职业技术学院	Guangdong Sports Vocational Technical Institute	773
广东食品药品职业学院	Guangdong Food and Drug Vocational School	3911
广东文艺职业学院	Guangdong Vocational Literature and Art College	1077
广州工程技术职业学院	Guangzhou Institute of Technology	2351
广州番禺职业技术学院	Guangzhou Panyu Polytechnic College	4018
广州体育职业技术学院	Guangzhou Sports Training and Technical College	712
广东理工职业学院	Guangdong Polytechnic Institute of Technology	3734
广州城市职业学院	Guangzhou City Polytechnic College	2920
广东工程职业技术学院	Guangdong Polytechnic College of Engineering	3394
广州铁路职业技术学院	Guangzhou Railway Vocational Technical College	2759
广东科贸职业学院	Guangdong Vocational College of Science and Trade	3045
广州科技贸易职业学院	Guangzhou Polytechnic of Science and Trade	1701
广东青年职业学院	Guangdong Youth Polytechnic College	1803
广东舞蹈戏剧职业学院	Guangdong Dance and Drama College	765
广东南华工商职业学院	Guangdong Nanhua Vocational College of Industry and Commerce	2993
私立华联学院	Private Hualian University	2241
广东岭南职业技术学院	Guangdong Lingnan Polytechnic College	5655
广州康大职业技术学院	Kanda Vocational Technical College	
广州工商学院	Guangdong College of Technology and Business	5472
广州涉外经济职业技术学院	Guangzhou International Economics College	2939
广州南洋理工职业学院	Guangzhou Nanyang Institute of Technology	3479
广州科技职业技术学院	Guangzhou Vocational College of Science and Technology	3267
广州现代信息工程职业技术学院	Guangzhou Modern Information Engineering College	2158
广州华南商贸职业学院	South China Business Trade College	1547
广州华立科技职业学院	Guangzhou HuaLi Vocational College of Science and Technology	4138
广州珠江职业技术学院	Guangzhou Pearl-river Vocational College of Technology	2429
广州松田职业学院	Guangzhou Songtian Polytechnic College	961
广州城建职业学院	Guangzhou City Construction College	5755
广州华商职业学院	Guangzhou Huashang Vocational College	3248
广州华夏职业学院	Guangzhou Huaxia Technical College	4255
广州东华职业学院	Guangdong Donghua Polytechnic College	3214
广东工业大学华立学院	Huali College, Guangdong University	2618
广州大学松田学院	Songtian College, Guangzhou University	2418
广州商学院	Guangzhou College of Commerce	5051
中山大学新华学院	Xinhua College of SYSU	5401
广州大学华软软件学院	South Institute of Software Engineering	3826
中山大学南方学院	Nanfang College of SYSU	4528
广东外语外贸大学南国商学院	South China Business College, Guangdong University of Foreign Studies	2256
广东财经大学华商学院	Huashang College, Guangdong University of Business Studies	6380
华南农业大学珠江学院	Zhujiang College of South China Agriculture University	3645
广东技术师范学院天河学院	Tianhe College of Guangdong Polytechnic Normal University	2632
华南理工大学广州学院	Guangzhou College of SCUT	5104
广州卫生职业技术学院	Guangzhou Health Vocational and Technical College	1465

注：本表数据由广东省教育厅提供。

continued

(person)

招生数 Number of New Entrants	在校学生数 Number of Enrolled Students	校本部教职工人数 Number of Teachers and Staff	# 专任教师 Full-time Teachers	# 正高级 Professors	# 副高级 Associate Professors	# 中 级 Lecturers
1253	3561	254	189	13	55	88
8735	18543	1207	912	36	283	384
1201	3853	330	216	10	31	98
2775	8051	486	428	13	114	227
4378	12085	956	550	31	126	274
741	2244	470	182	3	42	93
4052	11922	734	471	29	107	295
3910	9126	633	422	16	117	217
7180	14038	646	582	16	162	317
3339	8420	557	372	17	94	156
6672	13290	735	599	15	109	210
3287	7481	418	304	6	74	156
1301	3961	244	166	8	15	81
1059	2667	334	188	2	38	48
4501	11337	537	446	8	60	210
3082	8800	505	362	12	48	160
6791	20451	1223	1021	43	162	356
668	1060	86	63	5	14	17
6656	24983	1581	1217	138	170	463
3868	10136	653	485	15	138	216
4068	11775	781	661	27	136	236
9823	18611	1352	1035	86	273	298
3370	8369	611	470	13	70	199
1700	6368	381	288	7	25	101
5339	14254	938	778	68	229	245
1739	7815	516	387	28	48	89
1582	4089	283	228	8	39	109
7010	19856	1113	895	38	256	321
4455	10682	556	460	51	88	174
4782	13469	772	597	34	92	203
1193	7348	607	452	3	89	117
5498	17858	978	755	29	264	324
3938	10534	501	432	17	39	260
4435	16799	998	777	78	156	341
5354	22721	1344	1040	186	222	399
3620	14284	887	639	58	154	332
5105	19590	761	646	52	97	320
2447	9242	764	437	82	100	183
7495	24095	1070	924	131	153	377
4070	12576	631	509	55	63	204
854	11097	603	511	68	88	258
5751	22232	1288	1014	86	254	479
1856	5079	402	203	8	66	100

Note: The data in this table are provided by the Department of Education of Guangdong Province.

18-8 高中、初中、小学毕业生升学情况

Statistics on Graduates of Senior, Junior Secondary Schools and Primary Schools Entering Higher Level Schools

项 目		Item		2018
高中毕业生数	(人)	Graduates of Senior Secondary Schools	(person)	58514
已升学人数	(人)	Students Entering Institution of Higher Education	(person)	54619
升学率	(%)	Percentage of Graduates of Senior Secondary Schools Entering Institution of Higher Education	(%)	93.34
初中毕业生数	(人)	Graduates of Junior Secondary Schools	(person)	101062
已升学人数	(人)	Students Entering Senior Secondary Schools	(person)	97120
升学率	(%)	Percentage of Graduates of Junior Secondary Schools Entering Senior Secondary Schools	(%)	96.10
小学毕业生数	(人)	Graduates of Primary Schools	(person)	139039
已升学人数	(人)	Students Entering Junior Secondary Schools	(person)	135864
升学率	(%)	Percentage of Graduates of Primary Schools Entering Junior Secondary Schools	(%)	97.72

18-8 续表 continued

项 目		Item		2019
高中毕业生数	(人)	Graduates of Senior Secondary Schools	(person)	56484
已升学人数	(人)	Students Entering Institution of Higher Education	(person)	52262
升学率	(%)	Percentage of Graduates of Senior Secondary Schools Entering Institution of Higher Education	(%)	92.53
初中毕业生数	(人)	Graduates of Junior Secondary Schools	(person)	107563
已升学人数	(人)	Students Entering Senior Secondary Schools	(person)	103695
升学率	(%)	Percentage of Graduates of Junior Secondary Schools Entering Senior Secondary Schools	(%)	96.40
小学毕业生数	(人)	Graduates of Primary Schools	(person)	147700
已升学人数	(人)	Students Entering Junior Secondary Schools	(person)	140216
升学率	(%)	Percentage of Graduates of Primary Schools Entering Junior Secondary Schools	(%)	94.93

注：本表数据由广州市教育局提供。

Note: The data in this table are provided by Guangzhou Municipal Education Bureau.

18-9 普通中学专任教师学历情况(2019年)

Diploma Qualifications of Full-time Teachers in Regular Secondary Schools (2019)

项　目	Item	人　数 (人) Personnel (person)	高　中 Senior Secondary Schools	初　中 Junior Secondary Schools
合　计	**Total**	**44179**	**14475**	**29704**
研究生毕业	Postgraduates	**4798**	2485	2313
本科毕业	Graduates Attending Regular College Course	**37459**	11959	25500
专科及以下毕业	Graduates Attending Specialized Subject	**1922**	31	1891

18-9 续表 continued

项　目	Item	构　成 (%) Composition (%)	高　中 Senior Secondary Schools	初　中 Junior Secondary Schools
合　计	**Total**	**100.00**	**100.00**	**100.00**
研究生毕业	Postgraduates	10.86	17.17	7.79
本科毕业	Graduates Attending Regular College Course	84.79	82.62	85.85
专科及以下毕业	Graduates Attending Specialized Subject	4.35	0.21	6.37

注：1.高中教师学历达标率为99.76%,初中教师学历达标率为99.99%。
　　2.本表数据由广州市教育局提供。

Note:I. The academic qualification rate of teachers in senior secondary schools is 99.76 percent, that in junior secondary schools is 99.99 percent.
　　II.The data in this table are provided by Guangzhou Municipal Education Bureau.

18-10 各类学校教职工人数及专任教师数

Staff and Workers and Full-time Teachers by Type of School

单位：人 (person)

项　目	Item	2018	2019
各类学校教职工人数	**Number of Staff and Workers by Type of School**	**228360**	**236951**
普通高等学校	Regular Institutions of Higher Education	89669	93506
中等职业学校	Vocational Secondary Schools	11391	11327
技工学校	Technical Schools	12493	12590
普通中学	Regular Secondary Schools	52566	54197
小　学	Primary Schools	61191	64154
特殊学校	Special Schools	1050	1177
各类学校专任教师数	**Number of Full-time Teachers by Type of School**	**178324**	**186174**
普通高等学校	Regular Institutions of Higher Education	62732	66773
中等职业学校	Vocational Secondary Schools	7866	7926
技工学校	Technical Schools	6128	6242
普通中学	Regular Secondary Schools	43519	44179
#高　中	Senior Secondary Schools	14522	14475
小　学	Primary Schools	57160	60035
特殊学校	Special Schools	919	1019

18-11 小学教育情况
Statistics on Primary Education

项　　目		Item		2018	2019
适龄儿童入学率	(%)	Percentage of School-age Children Enrolled	(%)	100.00	100.00
6-11岁学龄儿童数	(人)	Number of 6-11 School-age Children	(person)	1042345	1085795
#已入学人数	(人)	Number of Children Enrolled in Schools	(person)	1042345	1085795
毕业率	(%)	Percentage of Graduation	(%)	99.57	99.14
上学年预计毕业生数	(人)	Number of Graduated Pupils in Previous Year	(person)	139639	148986
毕业生人数	(人)	Number of Graduates	(person)	139039	147700

注：本表数据由广州市教育局提供。
Note: The data in this table are provided by Guangzhou Municipal Education Bureau.

18-12 成人高等教育基本情况
Basic Statistics on Adult Higher Education

单位：人　　(person)

项　　目		Item		2018	2019
成人高等教育		**Higher Education for Adults**			
学校数	(所)	Number of Schools	(unit)	9	9
教职工人数		Number of Teachers and Staff		3227	3284
#专任教师数		Number of Full-time Teachers		1977	1985
聘请校外教师	(人次)	Number of Teachers Engaged from Other Schools	(Person-time)	3614	3566
毕业生		Graduates		123934	134465
招生数		New Students Enrollment		206233	287260
在校学生数		Students Enrolled		458405	600354

注：本表数据由广东省教育厅提供。
Note: The data in this table are provided by the Department of Education of Guangdong Province.

18-13 成人高等教育在校学生数

Number of Students Enrolled in Adult Higher Education by Level

单位：人 (person)

项 目	Item	2018	2019
成人高等教育	**Higher Education for Adults**	**458405**	**600354**
成人高等学校	Institutions of Higher Education for Adults	84857	192277
广播电视大学	Radio and TV Universities	79628	185555
职工高等学校	Schools of Higher Education for Staff and Workers	5229	6722
管理干部学院	Colleges for Management Cadres		
普通高校附设	Departments Run by Regular Institutions of Higher Education	373548	408077
函 授	Correspondence Divisions	144337	145613
业 余	Evening Universities	229211	262464
脱 产	Courses in Form of Full Time for Adults		

注：本表数据由广东省教育厅提供。
Note: The data in this table are provided by the Department of Education of Guangdong Province.

18-14 民办普通中小学及幼儿园情况（2019年）

Statistics on Regular Secondary Schools, Primary Schools and Kindergartens Run by Society (2019)

单位：人 (person)

项 目	Item	学校数（所） Number of Schools (unit)	毕业生数 Number of Graduates	招生数 Number of New Entrants	在校学生数 Number of Enrolled Students	教职工数 Number of Teachers and Staff	# 专任教师 Full-time Teachers
合 计	**Total**	**1707**	**192773**	**233806**	**803577**	**87913**	**50818**
普通中学	Regular Secondary Schools	212	35910	44626	123892	16292	9448
高 中	Senior Secondary Schools	17	3678	4029	11674	2522	1105
初 中	Junior Secondary Schools	195	32232	40597	112218	13770	8343
小 学	Primary Schools	141	43588	63729	334171	19442	17128
幼儿园	Kindergartens	1354	113275	125451	345514	52179	24242

注：本表数据由广州市教育局提供。
Note: The data in this table are provided by Guangzhou Municipal Education Bureau.

18-15　幼儿园基本情况
Basic Statistics on Kindergartens

项　目		Item		2018	2019
幼儿园数	**（所）**	**Number of Kindergartens**	**(unit)**	**1846**	**1966**
公　办		Kindergartens Run by Government		557	612
民　办		Kindergartens Run by Society		1289	1354
教职工人数	**（人）**	**Number of Teachers and Staff**	**(person)**	**73617**	**79236**
#教　师		Teachers		35401	37912
在园幼儿数	**（人）**	**Number of Student Enrollment**	**(person)**	**498127**	**527648**

注：本表数据由广州市教育局提供。
Note: The data in this table are provided by Guangzhou Municipal Education Bureau.

18-16　体育事业基本情况
Basic Statistics on Sports

项　　目		Item		2018	2019
群众体育活动情况		**Mass Sports Activities**			
各级各类大型全民健身活动赛事	（项次）	Number of large-scale Body-building Activities Run by all kinds all levels	(item-times)	496	1184
举办国际级、国家级单项比赛次数	（次）	Number of international and national individual competitions	(times)	94	117
破纪录		**Records Chalked up**			
破世界纪录	（项、人次）	World Records Chalked up	(item, person-times)	1项1人次	
破亚洲纪录	（项、人次）	Asian Records Chalked up	(item, person-times)	1项1人次	5项6人次
破全国纪录	（项、人次）	National Records Chalked up	(item, person-times)	1项1人次	10项15人次
获得冠军		**Champions Won**			
广州运动员获世界冠军	（项、人次）	World Champions	(item, person-times)	37项39人次	15项17人次
广州运动员获亚洲冠军	（项、人次）	Asian Champions	(item, person-times)	26项31人次	15项19人次
广州运动员获全国冠军	（项、人次）	National Champions	(item, person-times)	120项171人次	40项70人次

注：本表数据由广州市体育局提供。
Note: The data in this table are provided by Guangzhou Municipal Sports Bureau.

18-17 文化主要指标

Main Indicators of Culture

项目		Item		2018	2019
电影、艺术		**Films and Arts**			
全年摄制完成影片	(部)	Film Production	(film)	1	4
#故事片		Feature Films		1	4
全年发行各种新影片	(部)	Release of Various New Films	(film)	555	542
#国产与合拍片		Chinese-made Films		426	351
进口片		Hong Kong-made and Import Films		129	191
艺术表演场馆	(个)	Art Performance Halls	(unit)	30	30
艺术表演场馆座席数	(个)	Seats of Art Performance Halls	(unit)	44749	44749
专业艺术表演团体	(个)	Specialized Arts Performance Troupes	(unit)	69	47
本团原创首演剧目	(个)	Premiere Performance of Original Play	(unit)	24	20
艺术表演团体演出场次	(万场)	Number of Performance for Arts Performance Troupes	(scene)	0.56	0.41
艺术表演团体国内演出观众人次	(万人次)	Number of Spectators for Arts Performance Troupes	(10000 person-times)	383	354
广播电视事业		**Broadcasting and Television Stations**			
广　播		Broadcasting			
广播电台	(座)	Number of Broadcasting Stations	(set)	2	2
节目套数	(套)	Number of Programs	(set)	17	17
中短波转播发射台	(座)	Medium Wave and Short Wave Broadcasting Transmission Stations	(set)	2	2
平均日播音	(时)	Broadcasting Hours per Day	(hour)	361	348
广播综合人口覆盖率	(%)	Listener Rating	(%)	100.00	100.00
电　视		Television			
电视台	(座)	Number of Television Stations	(set)	3	2
节目套数	(套)	Number of Programs	(set)	21	25
平均周播放时间	(时)	Broadcasting Hours per Week	(hour)	3909	3933
制作电视剧	(集)	TV Play Programs	(set)	735	116
电视综合人口覆盖率	(%)	Viewer Rating	(%)	100.00	100.00

18-17 续表 continued

项　　目		Item		2018	2019
图书、档案事业		**Books and Archives**			
公共图书馆	（间）	Public Libraries	(unit)	14	14
总藏量	（万册）	Total Collections	(10000 volumes)	3307	3638
#图　书		Books		2922	3243
阅览室座席	（个）	Seating Capacity of Reading Rooms	(seat)	26827	27207
#少儿阅览室座席		Seating Capacity of Children Reading Rooms		5605	6306
总流通人次	（万人次）	Total Number of Circulation	(10000 person-times)	3704	4170
书刊文献外借册次	（万册次）	Number of Books Borrowed by the Readers	(10000 volume-times)	3025	3666
国家综合档案馆	（个）	Number of National Comprehensive Archives	(unit)	13	13
馆藏案卷总数	（万卷）	Total Number of Collections	(10000 volumes)	521	528
图书销售量	（万册）	Number of Books Sold	(10000 volumes)	2513	2270
群众文化事业		**Mass Culture**			
群众艺术馆、文化馆	（间）	Units Responsible for Guiding Mass Art	(unit)	13	13
文化站	（个）	Cultural Stations	(unit)	169	170
举办展览	（个）	Number of Exhibitions	(unit)	967	993
组织文艺活动	（次）	Art Performances and Story-telling	(times)	9098	9848
举办训练班	（次）	Training Courses	(times)	13012	15501
文物事业		**Cultural Relics**			
博物馆、纪念馆及美术馆	（个）	Museums and Memorial Halls	(unit)	32	31
藏品数	（件）	Number of Cultural Relics Collection	(piece)	368024	381115
#一级品		Grade One		1062	1065
举办陈列展览	（个）	Number of Displays and Exhibitions	(unit)	115	104
参观人次	（千人次）	Number of Visitors	(1000 person-times)	12831	13617
文物商店	（间）	Cultural Relic Stores	(unit)	2	2

注：1．2013年起图书销售量不包括花都区、番禺区、增城区和从化区数据。
2．2018年起藏品数不含美术馆藏品，2018年藏品数同口径调整。

Note: I. Since 2013 number of books sold does not include Huadu, Panyu, Zengcheng and Conghua.
II. Since 2018, the number of cultural relics collection has not included art gallery collections, and the number of cultural relics collections in 2018 has been adjusted with the same caliber.

18-18 主要年份卫生事业基本情况

Basic Statistics on Public Health in Main Years

年 份 Year	卫生机构数（个） Health Care Institutions (unit)	#医 院 Hospitals	卫 生 技术人员（人） Medical Professionals (person)	#医 生 Doctors	卫生机构床位数（张） Hospital Beds (bed)	#医 院 Hospitals	每万人口医生数（人） Doctors per 10000 Population (person)	每万人口医院床位数（张） Hospital Beds per 10000 Population (bed)
1978	1589	140	31547	12014	17109	14382	24.88	29.78
1980	1802	141	35792	14566	17673	14747	29.02	29.38
1985	2098	163	42522	18079	23830	19439	33.17	35.67
1986	2319	165	44666	19152	25031	20020	34.48	36.05
1987	2173	174	45818	19557	26599	21544	34.61	38.13
1988	2387	182	46957	20094	27981	22663	34.83	39.28
1989	2409	186	47988	20913	28988	23458	35.72	40.07
1990	2353	190	48276	21015	29930	24395	35.36	41.05
1991	2347	194	48618	21026	31293	25286	34.91	41.99
1992	2323	200	49052	21304	32646	26901	34.80	43.94
1993	2094	210	50097	22153	32399	27339	35.52	43.84
1994	2131	216	50819	22401	33086	27871	35.17	43.75
1995	2238	221	52851	23321	34139	28721	36.06	44.41
1996	1987	222	52450	22384	34338	29728	34.12	45.31
1997	1989	224	53654	22829	35301	30067	34.25	45.11
1998	2013	224	54053	22817	35306	30791	33.85	45.67
1999	1670	250	54480	23068	36431	31284	33.68	45.67
2000	1703	252	55677	23503	38758	33716	33.54	48.12
2001	2257	253	56262	23949	39417	34558	33.61	48.50
2002	2265	196	54652	22169	40430	32736	30.76	45.43
2003	2349	183	57274	23464	42210	34140	32.36	47.08
2004	2443	188	59943	24493	45687	35979	33.20	48.77
2005	2517	211	64182	25852	47888	39359	34.44	52.44
2006	2603	223	69091	27338	50500	42821	35.94	56.29
2007	2543	225	76791	29056	52640	45209	37.57	58.45
2008	2388	218	80687	29953	54973	47128	38.20	60.10
2009	2341	224	89179	32926	59038	50367	41.44	63.39
2010	2387	216	95546	33575	62552	53227	41.65	66.03
2011	3459	207	100832	35638	65940	55429	43.75	68.05
2012	3511	224	106708	37442	70649	62194	45.53	75.63
2013	3729	222	114802	39694	73301	64864	47.69	77.93
2014	3749	224	120915	40715	77011	68685	48.33	81.53
2015	3724	229	126681	42499	82022	73313	49.75	85.83
2016	3806	243	137953	46791	87959	79037	53.75	90.80
2017	4058	243	145045	49747	90222	81747	55.41	91.05
2018	4598	255	156497	54134	95134	86011	36.32	57.71
2019	5093	269	168056	58671	100080	90940	38.33	59.41

注：1．从2016年起卫生指标按照新的《2016国家卫生和计划生育统计调查制度》统计。其中，医生为执业(助理)医师数。
2．从2004年起医院不包卫生院及社区卫生服务中心(站)。
3．2017年及以前年份，每万人口医生数和每万人口医院床位数用年末户籍人口计算，从2018年起用年末常住人口计算。

Note: I. Since 2016, the health indicators have been counted according to the new National Health and Family Planning Survey system 2016. Among them, the number of doctors practising (assistant) doctors.
II.The number of hospitals haven't included the township hospitals since 2004.
III.Doctors per 10000 population and hospital beds per 10000 population are caculated by the registered population.

18-19 医疗卫生机构数

Number of Health Institutions

单位：个 (unit)

项目	Item	2018	2019
各类医疗卫生机构合计	**Total Number of Health Care Institutions**	**4598**	**5093**
医院	**Hospitals**	**255**	**269**
综合医院	General Hospitals	140	143
中医医院	TCM Hospitals	29	28
中西医结合医院	Hospitals Which Integrate Traditional Chinese Therapeutics with Western Therapeutics in Practice	7	7
专科医院	Specialized Hospitals	74	84
护理院	Nursing Homes	5	7
基层医疗卫生机构	**Basic Health Care Institutions**	**4162**	**4651**
社区卫生服务中心(站)	Health Service Certers(Stations) for Community	331	325
社区卫生服务中心	Health Service Centers for Community	152	152
社区卫生服务站	Health Service Stations for Community	179	173
卫生院	Township Hospitals	31	31
村卫生室	Village Health Hospitals	928	931
门诊部	Outpatient Departments	1204	1381
诊所、卫生所、医务室	Clinics, Health Stations, Infirmaries	1668	1983
专业公共卫生机构	**Specialized Health Care Institutions**	**143**	**109**
疾病预防控制中心	CDC(Epidemic Prevention Stations)	17	17
专科疾病防治院(所、站)	Specialized Disease Prevention & Treatment Institutions	6	7
健康教育所(站、中心)	Health Education Stations(Centers)	3	3
妇幼保健院(所、站)	Maternity and Child Care Centers	12	12
急救中心(站)	First Aid Centers(Stations)	7	7
采供血机构	Blood Collection Agencies	5	5
卫生监督所(中心)	Health Supervision Stations	14	14
计划生育技术服务机构	Family-planning Technical Service Institutions	79	44
其他卫生机构	**Others**	**38**	**64**
疗养院	Sanitariums	7	7
医学科学研究机构	Research Institutions of Medical Science	5	6
医学在职培训机构	Training Institutions of Medical Science for Incunbent	1	1
临床检验中心(所、站)	Clinical Inspect Centers(stations)	14	34
统计信息中心	Statistical Information Centers	2	2
其他	Other Medical Institutions	9	14

注：本表数据由广州市卫生健康委员会提供。
Note: The data in this table are provided by Guangzhou Municipal Health Commission.

18-20 医疗卫生机构床位数(2019年)

Number of Beds in Medical and Health Institutions (2019)

单位：张 (unit)

项目	Item	2018	2019
各类医疗卫生机构床位	**Total Number of Beds in Health Institutions**	**95134**	**100080**
医　院	**Hospitals**	**86011**	**90940**
综合医院	General Hospitals	53516	57000
中医医院	TCM Hospitals	11175	11547
中西医结合医院	Hospitals Which Integrate Traditional Chinese Therapeutics with Therapeutics in Practice	2445	2687
专科医院	Specialized Hospitals	18234	19039
护理院	Nursing Homes	641	667
基层医疗卫生机构	**Community Medical and Health Institutions**	**5341**	**5116**
社区卫生服务中心(站)	Health Service Centers for Community	3257	3198
卫生院	Township Hospitals	2058	1892
门诊部	Outpatient Departments	26	26
专业公共卫生机构	**Specialized Public Health Institutions**	**3694**	**3686**
专科疾病防治院(所、站)	Specialized Disease Prevention & Treatment Institutions	106	106
妇幼保健院(所、站)	Maternity and Child Care Centers	3588	3580
其他卫生机构	**Others**	**88**	**338**
疗养院	Sanitariums	88	338

注：本表数据由广州市卫生健康委员会提供。
Note: The data in this table are provided by Guangzhou Municipal Health Commission.

18-21 医疗卫生机构工作人员(2019年)

Number of Employed Personnel in Medical and Health Institutions (2019)

单位:人 (person)

项　　目	Item	2018	2019
合　计	**Total**	**188695**	**202725**
# 卫生技术人员小计	Medical Technical Personnel	156497	168056
执业(助理)医师	Assistant Certified Doctors	54134	58671
# 执业医师	Certified Doctors	50584	54885
# 全科医生	General Doctors	5251	5536
注册护士	Registered Nurses	71740	77812
药　师(士)	Pharmacists	8804	9220
技　师(士)	Technicians	7658	8395
# 检验师(士)	Testers	5452	6089
其　他	Others	14161	13958
其他技术人员	Other Technical Personnel	5955	6868
管理人员	Managerial Personnel	8878	9081
工勤技能人员	Workers	16672	18101
乡村医生和卫生员	Rural Doctors and Medical Attendants	693	619

注：本表数据由广州市卫生健康委员会提供。2019年起全科医生数包含乡村全科执业助理医师人数。

Note: The data in this table are provided by Guangzhou Municipal Health Commission.

18-22 医疗卫生机构基本情况(2019年，按地区分)

Basic Statistics on Medical and Health Institutions (2019, by District)

地 区	District	卫生机构数(个) Number of Health Institutions (unit)	医疗机构数(个) Number of Medical Institutions (unit)	医院 Hospital	实有床位(张) Number of Beds (bed)	医院 Hospital
总 计	**Total**	**5093**	**4987**	**269**	**100080**	**90940**
荔湾区	Liwan	230	228	30	7121	6921
越秀区	Yuexiu	401	380	33	24777	22994
海珠区	Haizhu	328	321	18	10819	10235
天河区	Tianhe	776	769	46	13000	12596
白云区	Baiyun	734	708	52	21391	19787
黄埔区	Huangpu	368	353	21	4360	3975
番禺区	Panyu	521	514	24	6650	5839
花都区	Huadu	527	523	13	4148	2969
南沙区	Nansha	238	236	12	1437	1279
从化区	Conghua	382	371	8	2887	2057
增城区	Zengcheng	588	584	12	3490	2288

18-22 续表 continued

地 区	District	人员数(人) Number of Employed Personnel (person)	卫生技术人员(人) Medical Technical Personnel (person)	执业(助理)医师(人) Assistant Certified Doctors (person)	注册护士(人) Registered Nurses (person)
总 计	**Total**	**202725**	**168056**	**58671**	**77812**
荔湾区	Liwan	12514	10675	3904	4951
越秀区	Yuexiu	52538	44710	14252	21135
海珠区	Haizhu	21253	17781	6008	8356
天河区	Tianhe	33173	26667	9750	12512
白云区	Baiyun	30404	24444	8301	11662
黄埔区	Huangpu	9044	7141	2557	2813
番禺区	Panyu	15020	12700	4923	5553
花都区	Huadu	10669	9064	3416	4031
南沙区	Nansha	3629	2955	1156	1287
从化区	Conghua	5184	4139	1467	1940
增城区	Zengcheng	9297	7780	2937	3572

注：本表数据由广州市卫生健康委员会提供。
Note: The data in this table are provided by Guangzhou Municipal Health Commission.

18-23 民营医疗机构基本情况(2019年，按地区分)

Basic Statistics on Private Medical and Health Institutions (2019, by District)

地 区	District	医疗机构数(个) Number of Medical Institutions (unit)	床位数(张) Number of Beds (unit)	人员数(人) Number of Employed Personnel (person)	#卫生技术人员(人) Medical Technical Personnel (person)	#执业(助理)医师(人) Assistant Certified Doctors (person)	#注册护士(人) Registered Nurses (person)
总 计	**Total**	**3227**	**18346**	**46488**	**37381**	**15524**	**16833**
荔湾区	Liwan	162	719	2258	2067	948	908
越秀区	Yuexiu	260	605	4781	3709	1472	1886
海珠区	Haizhu	193	865	3109	2688	1199	1166
天河区	Tianhe	661	2766	12364	8969	3730	4200
白云区	Baiyun	495	9269	9940	8204	3157	3981
黄埔区	Huangpu	261	645	3110	2500	944	761
番禺区	Panyu	432	1447	4554	3814	1653	1547
花都区	Huadu	289	1011	2576	2293	1056	944
南沙区	Nansha	75	65	745	484	213	204
从化区	Conghua	112	404	609	542	233	269
增城区	Zengcheng	287	550	2442	2111	919	967

注：本表数据由广州市卫生健康委员会提供。

Note: The data in this table are provided by Guangzhou Municipal Health Commission.

18-24 医疗资源与服务情况（2019年，按经济类型和设置主办单位分）

Resources and Services on Medical Institutions (2019，By Economic Type and Setting Organizer)

项　目	Item	合　计 Total	公立医疗机构 Public Medical Institutions	#政府办 Operated by Governments	民营医疗机构 Private Medical Institutions
医疗机构数（个）	Number of Units (unit)	5093	1866	619	3227
总诊疗人次（万人次）	Patients Treated (10000 person-times)	16333.50	13815.17	12578.70	2518.33
#门　诊	Outpatient Visits	12805.43	11654.47	11074.89	1150.96
急　诊	Emergency Visits	1346.06	1274.22	1217.43	71.84
观察室留观病例数（万人次）	Number of Persons for Further Observation (10000 person-times)	95.73	94.74	94.21	0.99
健康检查人次（万人次）	Number of Persons for Health Examination (10000 person-times)	1081.22	821.72	737.41	259.50
入院人数（万人次）	Number of Inpatients (10000 person-times)	345.08	321.28	312.80	23.79
出院人数（万人次）	Number of Leaving Hospital(10000 person-times)	344.50	320.86	312.36	23.63
年底实有病床数（张）	Number of Beds at Year-end (unit)	100080	81734	77494	18346
病床使用率（%）	Utilization Rate of Beds (%)	84.75	89.89	90.01	61.22
病床周转次数（次/年）	Turnover Rate of Beds (times/year)	35.5	40.3	41.3	13.6
出院者平均住院日（日）	Average Hospitalization Period (day)	8.4	8.0	7.9	14.0
医师人均每日担负诊疗人次（人）	Average Daily For Per Doctor visited (person)	11.3	13.1	12.9	6.5
医师人均每日担负住院床日（人）	Doctor Responsible For Inpatient Bed Days Per Capita Daily (person)	1.8	1.8	1.8	1.9

注：本表数据由广州市卫生健康委员会提供。

Note: The data in this table are provided by Guangzhou Municipal Health Commission.

18-25　医疗资源与服务情况(2019年，按机构类型分)

Resources and Services on Medical Institutions (2019，By Organization Type)

项　　目	Item	医　院 Hospital	基层医疗卫生机构 Basic Medical and Health Institutions	社区卫生服务中心(站) Community Health Care Centers	卫生院 Health Center	专业公共卫生机构 Professional Medical and Health Institutions	其他卫生机构 Other Health Care Institutions
机构数　(个)	Number of Units (unit)	269	4651	325	31	109	64
总诊疗人次　(万人次)	Patients Treated (10000 person-times)	9962.40	5378.06	2921.00	517.43	974.02	19.02
#门　诊	Outpatient Visits	8853.97	3133.18	2746.81	386.01	799.74	18.54
急　诊	Emergency Visits	1009.37	198.06	76.64	121.42	138.14	0.49
观察室留观病例数　(万人次)	Number of Persons for Further Observation (10000 person-times)	86.16	9.46	4.03	5.43	0.11	
健康检查人次（万人次）	Number of Persons for Health Examination (10000 person-times)	606.32	325.96	138.42	35.10	85.96	62.97
入院人数　(万人次)	Number of Inpatients (10000person-times)	311.92	12.52	5.15	7.37	20.54	0.09
出院人数　(万人次)	Number of Leaving Hospital (10000 person-times)	311.23	12.65	5.25	7.39	20.52	0.09
年末实有病床数　(张)	Number of Beds at Year-end (unit)	90940	5116	3198	1892	3686	338
平均开放病床数　(张)	Average Number of Beds in Use (unit)	88087	4944	3020	1924	3667	338
病床使用率　(%)	Utilization Rate of Beds (%)	85.69	69.96	72.66	65.71	88.20	20.53
病床周转次数　(次/年)	Turnover Rate of Beds (times/year)	35.3	25.6	17.4	38.4	56.0	2.7
出院者平均住院日（日）	Average Hospitalization Period (day)	8.6	9.2	13.8	6.0	5.8	27.7

注：本表数据由广州市卫生健康委员会提供。

Note: The data in this table are provided by Guangzhou Municipal Health Commission.

18-26　村卫生室基本情况

Statistics on Rural Health Institutions

项　　目	Item	2018	2019
机构数　(个)	Number of Institutions (unit)	928	931
执业(助理)医师　(人)	Certified (Assistant) Doctors (person)	525	555
注册护士　(人)	Certified (Assistant) Nurses (person)	303	295
乡村医生和卫生员　(人)	Rural Doctors and Medical Attendants (person)	693	619
乡村医生数	Rural Doctors	657	590
卫生员	Medical Attendants	36	29
总诊疗人次　(万人次)	Patients Treated (10000 person-times)	318.04	282.82

注：本表数据由广州市卫生健康委员会提供。

Note: The data in this table are provided by Guangzhou Municipal Health Commission.

18-27 卫生事业其他指标

Other Indicators of Health Care

项目	Item	2018	2019
人均卫生资源	**Per Capita Health Resources**		
每万人口卫生机构床位数 (张)	Number of Hospital Beds per 10000 Population (unit)	63.83	65.39
每万人口卫生技术人员数 (人)	Number of Medical Technical Personnel per 10000 Population (person)	105.00	109.80
每万人口执业(助理)医师数 (人)	Number of Certified (Assistant) Doctors per 10000 Population (person)	36.32	38.33
每万人口注册护士数 (人)	Number of Registered Nurses per 10000 Population (person)	48.13	50.84
防病工作	**Disease Prevention**		
甲、乙类传染病发病率 (1/10万)	Incidence Disease Rate of type A&B Infectious Disease (per 100000 persons)	320.81	347.59
甲、乙类传染病死亡率 (1/10万)	Death Rate of type A&B Infectious Diseases (per 100000 persons)	1.01	0.87
儿童计划免疫接种率 (%)	Planned Vaccination Rate of Children (%)		
卡介苗基础免疫 (%)	BCG Basic Vaccination Rate	99.86	99.89
脊髓灰质炎基础免疫 (%)	Poliovirus Basic Vaccination Rate	99.84	99.82
百白破基础免疫 (%)	Pertussis, Diphtheria & Tetanus Basic Vaccination Rate	99.88	99.73
麻疹基础免疫 (%)	Measles Virus Basic Vaccination Rate	99.84	99.84
乙肝基础免疫 (%)	Hepatitis B Basic Vaccination Rate	99.84	99.83
乙脑基础免疫 (%)	Encephalitis B Basic Vaccination Rate	99.85	99.80
妇幼工作	**Women and Children**		
孕产妇保健系统管理率 (%)	Management Rate of Maternity Health Care System (%)	96.12	96.89
产前检查率 (%)	Medical Examination Rate before Birth (%)	98.23	98.41
住院分娩率 (%)	Hospital Childbirth Rate (%)	99.93	99.95
3岁以下儿童系统管理率 (%)	Management Rate of Children System at 3 Years Old and below (%)	93.65	96.14
7岁以下儿童健康管理率 (%)	Management Rate of Children Health Care at 7 Years Old and below (%)	98.46	99.22
新生儿遗传代谢性疾病筛查率 (%)	Screening Rate of Neonatal Genetic and Metabolic Disease (%)	99.64	99.70
新生儿听力筛查率 (%)	Neonatal Hearing Screening Rate (%)	99.00	99.18
住院分娩出生缺陷发生率 (1/万)	Birth Defect Rate at Hospital Childbirth (1/10000)	210.06	217.27
出生低体重儿发生率 (%)	Incidence Rate of Low Weight Infants at Birth (%)	5.98	6.20
5岁以下儿童中重度营养不良发生率 (%)	Incidence Rate from Medium and Serious Malnutrition of Children at 5 Years Old and below (%)	1.31	1.34
围产儿死亡率 (‰)	Death Rate of Perinatal Children (‰)	3.40	3.39
孕产妇死亡率 (1/10万)	Death Rate of Pregnant and Lying-in Women (per 100000 persons)	3.67	6.57
婴儿死亡率 (‰)	Death Rate of Infant (‰)	2.50	2.37
5岁以下儿童死亡率 (‰)	Death Rate of Children at 5 Years Old and below (‰)	3.41	3.26
生命指标	**Life Indicators**		
平均期望寿命 (岁)	Life Expectancy (year)	82.28	82.52
男性	Male	79.47	79.68
女性	Female	85.22	85.48

注：1.本表数据由广州市卫生健康委员会提供。
2.本表人均卫生资源用年末常住人口计算；
3.甲、乙类传染病发病率、死亡率用年平均常住人口计算。
4.平均期望寿命以死因统计年报计算。

Note: I. The data in this table are provided by Guangzhou Municipal Health Commission.
II. Per capita health resources is calculated by annual resident population.
III. The incidence disease rate and death rate of type A and B infections diseases are calculated by annual resident population.
IV. Life expectancy is calculated according to the statistical yearbook of death.

18-28 律师、公证、基层司法基本情况

Basic Statistics on Lawyers, Notarization and Grassroots Judicial Work

项目		Item		2018	2019
律师工作		**Lawyers**			
律师事务所	(个)	Number of Law Offices	(unit)	745	747
执业律师	(人)	Number of Certified Lawyers	(person)	14069	15880
担任常年法律顾问	(家)	Number of Units with Permanent Legal Advisors	(unit)	22181	23666
民事诉讼代理	(件)	Civil Case Litigation Agency	(case)	98057	147938
行政诉讼代理	(件)	Administrative Action Case Litigation Agency	(case)	3897	4837
非诉讼法律事务	(件)	off-court Case	(case)	44353	152980
刑事辩护及代理	(件)	Criminal Case Litigation Agency	(case)	21961	28167
公证工作		**Notarization**			
公证处	(个)	Number of Notary Offices	(unit)	11	12
公证人员	(人)	Number of Notary Personnel	(person)	492	532
办结公证总数	(件)	Number of Notary Documents	(case)	434865	439093
# 国内民事公证		Domestic Civil Notary		262689	255349
国内经济公证		Domestic Economic Notarization		86974	89326
涉外民事公证		Foreign-related Civil notary		83976	93214
涉外经济公证		Foreign-related Economic Notarization		1226	1204
基层司法工作		**Grassroots Judicial Work**			
司法所	(个)	Number of Law Services	(unit)	171	174
司法所人员	(人)	Number of Law Service Personnel	(person)	897	998
司法所兼职人员	(人)	Number of Units with Legal Advisors	(person)	13	5
司法助理员	(人)	Agent of Civil Cases	(person)	561	529
人民调解委员会	(个)	Number of People's Mediation Committees at Year-end	(unit)	3262	3299
调解人员	(人)	Number of Mediators at Year-end	(person)	15283	15656
调解纠纷总数	(件)	Number of Disputes Mediated	(case)	64332	59076

注：本表数据由广州市司法局提供。
Note:The data in this table are provided by Guangzhou Municipal Bureau of Justice.

18-29 社会治安主要指标

Main Indicators of Public Security

项　　目		Item		2018	2019
刑事案件		**Criminal Cases**			
立当年案数	(件)	Number of Cases Registered	(case)	111857	105997
破当年案数	(件)	Number of Cases Cracked in Current Year	(case)	31924	36916
破案率	(%)	Percentage of Cases Cracked to Total Criminal Cases in Current Year	(%)	28.5	34.8
治安案件		**Offense Cases against Public Order**			
受理数	(件)	Number of Cases Accepted to be Treated	(case)	152002	137220
查处数	(件)	Number of Cases Investigated and Treated	(case)	142750	132427
城市交通事故		**City Traffic Accidents**			
交通事故	(件)	Number of Traffic Accidents	(case)	2594	2506
死伤人数	(人)	Number of Deaths and Injuries	(person)	3246	2998
#死亡人数		Number of Deaths		738	735
损失折款	(万元)	Losses Converted into Cash	(10000 yuan)	883	740.5
火　灾		**Fires**			
火灾起数	(起)	Number of Fires	(case)	2181	32
死伤人数	(人)	Number of Deaths and Injuries	(person)	26	
#死亡人数		Number of Deaths		13	
损失折款	(万元)	Losses Converted into Cash	(10000 yuan)	2518	

注：1.本表刑事案件、治安案件、城市交通事故数据由广州市公安局提供。火灾相关数据由广州市应急管理局提供。

2.2019年火灾起数只包含森林火灾，与2018年数据不可比。

Note: I. This table provides data on criminal cases, public security cases, and urban traffic accidents provided by the Guangzhou Municipal Public Security Bureau. Fire-related data are provided by the Guangzhou Municipal Bureau of Emergency Management.

II. The number of fires in 2019 only includes forest fires, which is incomparable with the number of fires in 2018.

18-30　结婚和离婚对数

Couples of Marriage and Divorce

单位：对　　(couple)

地　区	District	2018 登记结婚对数 Number of Marriage Registration	2018 离婚对数 Number of Divorces	2019 登记结婚对数 Number of Marriage Registration	2019 离婚对数 Number of Divorces
全　市	**Total**	**77818**	**23275**	**73757**	**25298**
荔湾区	Liwan	4786	1466	4327	1318
越秀区	Yuexiu	9075	3433	8395	3538
海珠区	Haizhu	7056	2556	6299	2874
天河区	Tianhe	10209	2609	8834	2758
白云区	Baiyun	9372	2518	11359	3322
黄埔区	Huangpu	5413	1274	5382	1734
番禺区	Panyu	8449	2143	7443	2038
花都区	Huadu	6642	1958	6367	2509
南沙区	Nansha	3820	1193	3438	1232
从化区	Conghua	5016	1828	4388	1562
增城区	Zengcheng	7980	2297	7525	2413

注：1.法院判决解除和调解解除2019年3060对、2018年3097对。
2.从2018年起，涉外婚姻登记办理权限下放到各区。
3.本表数据由广州市民政局提供。

Note: I. Number of divorces by the court is about 3060 in 2019,and 3097 in 2018.
II. The authority for registration of foreign-related marriages has been delegated to all districts since 2018.
III. The data in this table are provided by Guangzhou Municipal Civil Affairs Bureau.

18-31 社会保险情况
Conditions of Social Insurance

单位：人 (person)

项目	Item	2018 年末参保人数 Persons Participating in Insurance at Year-end	2018 全年享受人数 Persons Enjoying Insurance
基本养老保险	Basic Pension Insurance	9283720	1666296
城镇职工基本养老保险	Basic Pension Insurance for Employed Persons in Urban Units	7835244	1092749
城乡居民养老保险	Pension Insurance for Urban and Rural Resident	1242198	432329
农转居养老保险	Pension Insurance for Resident transferred from Farmers	206278	141218
社会医疗保险	Social Medical Care Insurance	12476988	6177348
职工社会医疗保险	Employee Social Medical Care Insurance	7519504	4080869
城乡居民社会医疗保险	Social Medical Care Insurance for Urban and Rural Residents	4957484	2096479
失业保险	Unemployment Insurance	6087077	126681
工伤保险	Work Injury Insurance	6398682	15599
生育保险	Maternity Insurance	5852979	318328

18-31 续表 continued

单位：人 (person)

项目	Item	2019 年末参保人数 Persons Participating in Insurance at Year-end	2019 全年享受人数 Persons Enjoying Insurance
基本养老保险	Basic Pension Insurance	9090879	1721023
城镇职工基本养老保险	Basic Pension Insurance for Employed Persons in Urban Units	7689932	1142993
城乡居民养老保险	Pension Insurance for Urban and Rural Resident	1400947	578030
农转居养老保险	Pension Insurance for Resident transferred from Farmers	-	-
社会医疗保险	Social Medical Care Insurance	13022026	6801606
职工社会医疗保险	Employee Social Medical Care Insurance	8031247	4428028
城乡居民社会医疗保险	Social Medical Care Insurance for Urban and Rural Residents	4990779	2373578
失业保险	Unemployment Insurance	6442012	133120
工伤保险	Work Injury Insurance	7322657	15884
生育保险	Maternity Insurance	6281315	338646

注：1.从2018年起，养老保险、失业保险、工伤保险和生育保险数据由广州市人力资源和社会保障局提供，医疗保险数据由广州市医疗保障局提供。

2.从2018年起，城镇职工基本养老保险含机关事业单位养老保险，且其中的暂停缴费人数统计口径有调整，数据与2017年不可比。

3.职工医保享受人数仅统计享受医疗待遇人数，未包含医保个人账户注资人数。

4.自2019年8月1日起，我市原农转居基本养老保险参保人员并入我市城乡居民养老保险，按城乡居民养老保险制度统一管理。

Note: I. The data on old-age insurance, unemployment insurance, industrial injury insurance and maternity insurance are provided by Guangzhou Municipal Human Resources and Social Security Bureau, the data on medical insurance are provided by Guangzhou Municipal Medical Insurance Bureau, since 2018.

II. The basic old-age insurance for urban employees includes the old-age insurance for government and public institutions, and the statistical caliber of suspended contributions has been adjusted, since 2018. The data are incomparable with that of 2017.

III. Number of medical care insurance for employed persons only calculates the number of persons enjoyed medical treatment, excluding the number of personal capital account for medical insurance.

IV.Since August 1, 2019, former participants of the pension insurance for residents transferred from farmers have been merged into the city's pension insurance for urban and rural residents, which will be managed in a unified manner in accordance with pension insurance for urban and rural residents' system.

18-32 优抚和社会救助、福利事业情况

Statistics on Special Care, Social Relief and Social Welfare

项　　目	Item	2018	2019
优抚事业	**Special Care and Preferential Treatment**		
抚恤、补助优抚对象总人数(人)	Number of Persons Enjoying Regular Pensions and Allowances (person)	30422	31543
抚恤事业财政性支出 (万元)	Expenses on Special Care and Preferential Treatment (10000 yuan)	48298.86	52023.04
社会救助	**Social Relief**		
城市居民最低生活保障人数(人)	Number of Persons Enjoying Mininum living Security In Urbar Areas (Person)	21590	18742
城市居民最低生活保障户数(户)	Number of Households Enjoying Mininum living Security In Urbar Areas (Household)	14392	11640
农村居民最低生活保障人数(人)	Number of Persons Enjoying Mininum living Security In Rural Areas (Person)	26935	27370
农村居民最低生活保障户数(户)	Number of Households Enjoying Mininum living Security In Rural Areas (Household)	11953	12175
农村特困人员救助供养人数(人)	The Number of Relief Personnel in Rural Areas (Person)	4319	4024
资助参加医疗救助保险 (人)	Number of Persons Funded to Participate in Medical Care Insurance (Person)	171911	193364
直接实施医疗救助人次数(人次)	Number of Persons Direct Implementation of Medical Assistance(Person-times)	683847	1042976
# 住院救助人次数 (人次)	Number of Persons Enjoying Medical Assistance Intpatient Services (Person-times)	158562	366868
门诊救助人次数 (人次)	Number of Persons Enjoying Medical Assistance Outpatient Services (Person-times)	525285	676108
生活无着人员救助人次数(人次)	Number of Poor Persons Enjoying Relief (Person-times)	16853	23352
# 未成年人救济人次数 (人次)	Number of Child Enjoying Relief (Person-times)	461	332
社会救助事业财政性支出(万元)	Expenses on Social Relief (10000 yuan)	76712	86213
自然灾害生活救助财政性支出 (万元)	Financial Relief Funds for Disasters (10000 yuan)	7243	9
社会福利	**Social Welfare**		
社会福利收养性单位数 (个)	Number of Social Welfare Adoption Units (unit)	173	228
社会福利收养性单位床位数(张)	Number of Beds in Social Welfare Adoption Units (unit)	52490	63377
年末社会福利收养性单位在院人数 (人)	Number of Persons in Social Welfare Adoption Units at Year-end (Person)	28881	32306
社会福利事业财政性支出(万元)	Expenses on Social Welfare (10000 yuan)	221245	262010
城乡社区服务	**Grassroots Social Security in Urban and Rural Areas**		
社区服务设施数 (个)	Number of Community Service Facilities in Urban Areas (unit)	3329	4661
# 社区服务中心(站) (个)	Centers of Community Service	2212	2256

注:1.2018年，优抚事业数据由广州市退役军人事务局提供，医疗救助数据由广州市医疗救助服务中心提供，其余数据由广州市民政局提供。

2.从2018年起，社会福利收养性单位相关数据不含优抚及转隶单位数据。

3.抚恤事业财政性支出包含中央、市和区财政支出，统计口径包括优抚对象抚恤补助、慰问金、一次性抚恤金和义务兵家庭优待金等，2018年度统计数据同口径调整后，以此次报送为准。

4.2019年起，自然灾害生活救助财政性支出数据由广州市应急管理局提供，指救助经费，不含物资救助。因口径调整，与上年数据不可比。

Note: I. The data on preferential care are provided by Guangzhou Bureau of Veterans Affairs, medical assistance data are provided by Guangzhou Medical Assistance Service Center. Other data are provided by Guangzhou Civil Affairs Bureau, in 2018.

II. Since 2018, the relevant data of social welfare adoptive units do not include the data of preferential care and subordinate units,and the data of 2017 are adjusted according to the same caliber.

III. The financial expenditure on pension business includes the financial expenditure of the central government, municipalities and districts, and the statistical caliber includes pension subsidies, condolence payments, one-time pensions and preferential treatment for the families of conscripts，2018 statistical data of the same caliber adjusted to this report.

IV. Since 2019,the data of financial relief funds for disasters has been provided by Guangzhou Emergency Management Bureau,which includes only aid funding and does not include material relief. Because of the adjustment, it is incomparable with the data of the previous year.

18-33 社会组织机构情况

Social Organization Structure

单位：个 (unit)

项　　目	Item	2018	2019
社会组织机构数	**Number of social organizations**	**7861**	**8135**
# 社会团体	Social Group	3261	3423
民办非企业	Private non-enterprise Organization	4536	4633
基金会	Foundation	64	79
社会组织机构按行业分类	**Classified by Industry**		
1. 科学研究	Scientific Research	294	
2. 生态环境	Ecological Environment	47	
3. 教育	Education	2872	
4. 卫生	Hygienism	253	
5. 社会服务	Social Service	1110	
6. 文化	Culture	609	
7. 体育	Physical Education	654	
8. 法律	Law	34	
9. 工商业服务	Industrial and Commercial Services	782	
10. 宗教	Religion	16	
11. 农村及农村发展	Rural and Rural Development	99	
12. 职业及从业者组织	Organizations of Occupations and Practitioners	195	
13. 国际及涉外组织	International and Foreign Organizations		
14. 其他	Others	896	

注：1.本表数据由广州市民政局提供。

2.2019年“社会团体”不再进行行业分类统计。

Note: I.The data in this table are provided by Guangzhou Municipal Civil Affairs Bureau.

II.In 2019, "social groups" is no longer counted by industry classification.

【卫生技术人员】指卫生事业机构支付工资的全部固定职工和合同制职工现任职务为卫生技术工作的专业人员。包括中医师、西医师、中西医结合高级医师、护师、中药师、西药师、检验师、其他技师、中医士、西医士、护士、助产士、中药剂士、检验士、其他初级卫生技术人员。

【医生】指经卫生部门审查合格，具有执业资格的医疗专业人员。

【社会福利收养性单位在院人数】包括民政部门管理的和城镇及农村集体举办的社会福利事业单位中收养的老人、少年儿童、缺乏生活自理能力的残疾人员和精神病人。

【律师】指依法取得律师执业证书，为社会提供法律服务的执业人员。

【公证员】指符合《公证法》规定的条件，在公证机构从事公证业务的执业人员。

【办理公证文书】指公证处在一定时期内办结的公证文书件数。公证文书是按司法部规定或批准的格式制作。包括国内公证和涉外公证两部分。其中国内公证分为经济合同公证和民事法律关系公证两大类。

【调解人员】是经群众选举或者接受聘任，在人民调解委员会领导下，从事调解工作的人员。

【调解民间纠纷】指调解委员会依照法律规定，根据自愿原则，用说服教育的方法调解社会上发生的有关民事权利和义务的争执，促成相关当事双方达到协议和谅解，解决纠纷。包括婚姻家庭纠纷，财产权益纠纷等，不包括法院受理调解的民事案件数。

【Medical Technical Personnel】 refer to all permanent medical staff and workers employed by medical institutions, including doctors of Chinese and Western medicine, senior doctors who integrate traditional Chinese therapeutics with Western therapeutics in practice, senior nurses, pharmacists of Chinese and Western medicine, laboratory specialists, other specialists, paramedics of Chinese and Western medicine, nurses, midwives, druggists in Chinese and Western medicine, laboratory technicians, other technicians, other practitioners of Chinese medicine, nursing attendants, pharmacological workers of Chinese and Western medicine, laboratory workers, and other primary medical technical personnel.

【Doctors】 refer to qualified professional medical workers approved to practice by public health departments.

【Number of People Taken in by adoption units of Social Welfare Institutions】 refers to the number of old people, children, totally dependent handicapped people and mental patients taken in by social welfare institutions run by civil affairs departments and those run by collective units in urban and rural areas.

【Lawyers】 are certified legal workers according to law, and provide legal service to the public.

【Notary Personnel】 refer to judicial workers of the state notary offices handling notarization work according to law.

【Notarized Documents】 refer to the documents settled by notary offices in a year. The nutria documents are drawn up in accordance with the regulations of the Ministry of Justice, including domestic documents and foreign-related documents. Domestic documents are divided into two major categories: documents on economic contracts and documents on civil legal relations.

【Mediators】 refer to workers who are selected or employed by the masses under the lead of people's mediation committees responsible for mediating in civil disputes and cases of slight infraction of the law.

【Mediation of Civil Disputes】 refers to mediation committees' work in mediating in civil disputes concerning civil rights and duties through persuasion and education in accordance with the provisions of law on a voluntary basis, so as to solve disputes by helping the parties involved come to an agreement and understanding. These disputes include divorce cases and disputes over property ownership, but exclude the civil cases to be handled by the court.

附录 APPENDIX

附 1 全国国民经济主要指标

Appendix Ⅰ. Main Indicators of National Economy of China

项 目	Item	2018	2019
年末总人口 (万人)	Year-end Population (10000 persons)	139538	140005
国内生产总值 (亿元)	Gross Domestic Product (100 million yuan)	919281	990865
# 第一产业	Added Value of Agriculture	64745	70467
工业增加值	Added Value of Industry	301089	317109
全社会固定资产投资额 (亿元)	Total Investment in Fixed Assets (100 million yuan)	645675	560874
社会消费品零售总额 (亿元)	Total Retail Sales of Consumer Goods (100 million yuan)	380987	411649
货物周转量 (亿吨公里)	Total Freight To-kilometers (100 million ton-km)	204686	199287
旅客周转量 (亿人公里)	Total Passener-kilometers (100 million passenger-km)	34218	35349
邮政业务总量 (亿元)	Business Volume of Postal Services (100 million yuan)	12345	16230
电信业务总量 (亿元)	Business Volume of Telecommunication Services (100 million yuan)	65634	106789
货物进出口总额 (亿元)	Total Imports & Exports through Customs (100 million yuan)	305010	315505
进口总额 (亿元)	Total Imports through Customs (100 million yuan)	140881	143162
出口总额 (亿元)	Total Exports through Customs (100 million yuan)	164129	172342
实际使用外商直接投资 (亿美元)	Amount of Capital Actually Used in Foreign Direct Investment(USD 100 million)	1350	1381
一般公共预算收入 (亿元)	General Budgetary Expenditure (100 million yuan)	183360	190382
居民消费价格总指数（上年=100)	General Consumer Price Index (preceding year=100)	102.1	102.9
城镇非私营单位职工平均工资(元)	Average Wage of Fully Employed Staff and Workers in Urban Units (yuan)	82413	90501
城镇居民年人均可支配收入 (元)	Per Capita Annual Disposable Income of Urban Residents (yuan)	39251	42359
农村居民年人均可支配收入 (元)	Per Capita Annual Disposable Income of Rural Residents (yuan)	14617	16021
在校学生数	Number of Enrolled Students by Level of School		
# 普通本专科学校 (万人)	Undergraduate in Regular HEIS (10000 persons)	2831.0	3031.5
普通高中学校 (万人)	Regular Senior Secondary Schools (10000 persons)	2375.4	2414.3
普通小学 (万人)	Primary Schools (10000 persons)	10339.3	10561.2
医疗卫生机构床位数 (万张)	Hospital Beds (10000 units)	840	881
卫生技术人员 (万人)	Medical Technical Personnel (10000 persons)	953	1015
# 执业医师和执业助理医师	Doctors and Assistant Medical Practitioners	361	387

注：1．2019年为初步统计数据。

2．规模以上港口的统计范围为年通过能力在100万吨以上的沿海港口和200万吨以上的内河港口，以及从事外贸、集装箱装卸的港口具体范围由交通运输部划定。

Note: I. The figures of 2018 are preliminary ststistics.

II. Data on production capacity and handing capacity include the seaports handing cargo more than 1 million tons. Inland river ports with turnover over 2 million tons and ports with operation in foreign trade and containing shipping. The specific scope are decided by the Administration of Transportation.

附 2 广东省国民经济主要指标

Appendix Ⅱ. Main Indicators of National Economy of Guangdong Province

项 目		Item		2018	2019
年末常住人口	(万人)	Year-end Population	(10000 persons)	11346	11521
年末就业人员人数	(万人)	Year-end Employed Persons	(10000 persons)	7132.99	7150.25
地区生产总值	(亿元)	Gross Domestic Products	(100 million yuan)	99945.22	107671.07
人均地区生产总值	(元)	Per Capita GDP	(yuan)	88781	94172
社会消费品零售总额	(亿元)	Total Retail Sales of Consumer Goods	(100 million yuan)	39767.12	42951.75
货物周转量	(亿吨公里)	Total Freight To-kilometers	(10 million ton-km)	28644.77	29230.88
旅客周转量	(亿人公里)	Total Passener-kilometers	(100 million passenger-km)	4501.97	4764.98
港口货物吞吐量	(万吨)	Volume of Freight Handled at Ports	(10000 tons)	211037	191819
邮电业务总量	(亿元)	Business Volume of Postal and Telecommunication Services	(100 million yuan)	11010.28	16451.23
进口总值	(亿元)	Total Imports	(100 million)	28901.67	28068.35
出口总值	(亿元)	Total Exports	(100 million)	42744.06	43416.04
实际利用外商直接投资	(亿元)	Amount of Direct Foreign Capital Actually Used	(100 million)	1450.88	1522.00
地方一般公共预算收入	(亿元)	General Public Budgetary Revenue of Local Government	(100 million yuan)	12105.26	12654.53
地方一般公共预算支出	(亿元)	General Public Budgetary Expenditure of Local Government	(100 million yuan)	15729.26	17297.85
居民消费价格指数	(上年=100)	General Consumer Price Index	(preceding year=100)	102.2	103.4
工业生产者出厂价格指数	(上年=100)	Producer Price Index for Manufactured Goods	(preceding year=100)	101.8	100.2
工业生产者购进价格指数	(上年=100)	Producer Price Index for Purchased Goods	(preceding year=100)	102.5	99.2
城镇非私营单位就业人员年平均工资	(元)	Average Wage of Fully Employed Staff and Workers in Urban Units	(yuan)	88636	98889
城镇常住居民人均可支配收入	(元)	Per Capita Disposable Income of Urban Residents	(yuan)	44341	48118
农村常住居民人均可支配收入	(元)	Per Capita Disposable Income of Rural Residents	(yuan)	17168	18818
在校学生数	(万人)	Number of Enrolled Students by Level of School	(10000 persons)		
普通高等学校		Institutions of Higher Education		196.32	205.40
中等职业教育学校		Secondary Vocational Schools		86.73	85.97
普通中学		Regular Secondary Schools		556.18	572.77
小 学		Primary Schools		988.37	1033.43
医院及卫生院床位	(万张)	Hospital Beds	(10000 units)	47.75	50.39
卫生技术人员	(万人)	Medical Technical Personnel	(10000 persons)	75.78	79.51
# 医 生		Doctors		27.74	29.21

附 3 中国香港特别行政区主要统计指标

Appendix Ⅲ. Main Indicators of Hong Kong Special Administrative Region

项　　目		Item		2018	2019
人口及生命统计		**Population and Vital Events**			
总人口(年中数)	(万人)	Mid-year Population	(10000 persons)	745.1	750.7
男　性		Male		341.0	342.3
女　性		Female		404.1	408.4
粗出生率	(‰)	Crude Birth Rate	(‰)	7.2	7.0
粗死亡率	(‰)	Crude Death Rate	(‰)	6.4	6.5
劳动、就业		**Labor and Employment**			
劳动人口	(万人)	Labor Force	(10000 persons)	397.9	396.6
劳动人口参与率	(%)	Labor Force Participation Rate	(%)	61.2	60.6
失业率	(%)	Unemployment Rate	(%)	2.8	2.9
就业不足率	(%)	Underemployment Rate	(%)	1.1	1.1
本地生产总值		**Gross Domestic Product**	**(GDP)**		
本地生产总值(按2017年环比物量计算)	(亿港元)	GDP	(in chained 2017 dollars, HKD 100 million)	27355	27030
人均本地生产总值(按2017年环比物量计算)	(港元)	Per Capita GDP	(in chained 2017 dollars, HKD)	367130	360042
本地生产总值(按当年价格计算)	(亿港元)	GDP	(at current prices, HKD 1000 million)	28351	28682
人均本地生产总值(按当年价格计算)	(港元)	Per Capita GDP	(at current prices, HKD)	380503	382046
本地居民总收入(按当年价格计算)	**(亿港元)**	**Gross National Income (at current prices) (GNI)**			
本地居民总收入	(亿港元)	GNI	(HKD 100 million)	29699	30163
人均本地居民总收入	(港元)	GNI per capita	(HKD)	398597	401782
工业生产		**Industrial Production**			
工业生产指数	(2015年=100)	Index of Industrial Production	(2015 = 100)	101.3	101.7
工业电力消费量	(万亿焦耳)	Industrial Electricity Consumption	(Terajoule)	11081	10815
工业煤气消费量	(万亿焦耳)	Industrial Gas Consumption	(Terajoule)	1717	1824
对外商品贸易		**External Merchandise Trade**			
进口	(亿港元)	Imports	(CIF, HKD 100 million)	47214	44154
香港产品出口	(亿港元)	Domestic Exports	(HKD 100 million)	463	478
转口	(亿港元)	Re-exports	(HKD 100 million)	41118	39409

附 3 续表 continued

项 目	Item	2018	2019
对外服务贸易	**Trade in Service**		
服务输出 （亿港元）	Exports of Service (HKD 100 million)	8869	7939
服务进口 （亿港元）	Inports of Service (HKD 100 million)	6399	6191
房屋及物业	**Housing and Property**		
已登记物业买卖合约涉及的价值	Value of registered Agreements for Sale		
住宅 （亿港元）	Residential (HKD 100 million)	5593	5488
非住宅 （亿港元）	Non-Residential (HKD 100 million)	1821	1436
总计 （亿港元）	Total (HKD 100 million)	7414	6924
楼宇售价指数 （1999年=100）	Property price index (Year 1999=100)		
私人住宅单位	Private Residence	377.3	382.9
私人写字楼（甲级、乙级及丙级）	Private Office Building (Grade A, B & C)	554.7	542.8
运输、通讯及旅游	**Transport , Communications and Tourism**		
进出香港货物总量 （万吨）	Inward and Outward Movements of Cargo (10000 tons)		
总卸下	Total Discharged	17543	18584
总装上	Total Loaded	10975	10236
集装箱吞吐量 （万标准集装箱）	Container Throughput (10000 TEUs)	1960	1830
电话服务 （万条操作线路）	Telephone Services (10000 working lines)	410	406
访港旅客 （万人次）	Visitors Arrivals (10000 person-times)	6515	5591
酒店入住率 （%）	Hotel Room Occupancy Rate (%)	91	79
政府收支 （亿港元）	**Public Accounts (HKD 100 million)**		
政府收入(财政年度由4月1日至3月31日)	Total Government Revenue (Fiscal year: Apr. - Mar.)	5449	4913
政府支出(财政年度由4月1日至3月31日)	Total Government Expenditure (Fiscal year: Apr. - Mar.)	4607	5357
消费价格指数 （按年变动率）	**Consumer Price Indices (Oct.2014 - Sept.2015 = 100)**		
综合消费价格指数	Composite Consumer Price Index	107.0	110.1
教育程度 （万人）	**Education (Student enrolment by level of education) (10000 persons)**		
幼儿园学生人数	Kindergarten	17.62	17.43
小学学生人数	Primary	37.63	37.72
中学学生人数	Secondary	34.14	34.35
专上教育学生人数	Post-secondary	32.47	32.41

附 4 中国澳门特别行政区主要统计指标

Appendix Ⅳ. Main Indicators of Macao Special Administrative Region

项 目		Item		2018	2019
人口及生命统计		**Population and Vital Events**			
年中人口估计	(万人)	Mid-year Estimates of Population	(10000 persons)	65.9	67.2
出生率	(‰)	Crude Birth Rate	(‰)	9.0	8.9
死亡率	(‰)	Crude Death Rate	(‰)	3.1	3.4
劳动、就业		**Labour**			
劳动人口	(万人)	Labour Force	(10000 persons)	39.2	39.5
劳动力参与率	(%)	Labour Force Participation Rate	(%)	70.9	70.3
失业率	(%)	Unemployment Rate	(%)	1.8	1.7
就业不足率	(%)	Underemployment Rate	(%)	0.5	0.5
本地生产总值		**Gross Domestic Product**			
按2017年不变价格计算		At Constant Prices	(2017)		
本地生产总值	(亿澳门元)	GDP	(100 million MOP)	4295.0	4092.6
人均本地生产总值	(万澳门元)	GDP per Capita	(100 million MOP)	65.1	60.8
按当年价格计算		At Current Prices			
本地生产总值	(亿澳门元)	GDP	(100 million MOP)	4446.7	4346.7
人均本地生产总值	(万澳门元)	GDP per Capita	(10000 MOP)	67.3	64.5
对外商品贸易		**External Merchandise Trade**			
出口总值	(亿澳门元)	Exports	(100 million MOP)	121.9	128.0
进口总值	(亿澳门元)	Imports	(100 million MOP)	901.0	901.3
运输、旅游		**Transport &Tourism**			
进出澳门货运车数目	(万次)	Lorries Entering and Departing Macao	(10000 times)	34.8	34.1
访澳旅客	(万人次)	Visitors Arrival	(10000 person-times)	3580.4	3940.6
酒店入住率	(%)	Hotel Room Occupancy Rate	(%)	91	91
财政收支		**Government Accounts**			
公共财政总收入	(亿澳门元)	Total Government Revenue	(100 million MOP)	1413.1	1335.1
公共财政总支出	(亿澳门元)	Total Government Expenditure	(100 million MOP)	803.3	821.0
消费价格指数		**Consumer Price Index**			
综合消费价格指数(2018年4月至2019年3月=100)		Composite Consumer Price Index (Apr.2018 - Mar.2019 = 100)		99.05	101.78
教 育		**Education**			
小学生	(人)	Primary Education	(person)	32530	33961
中学生	(人)	Secondary Education	(person)	26022	26396
高等教育学生	(人)	Higher Education	(person)	34279	36107

注：2019年数据在日后得到更多资料时会作出修订。

Notes: Figures of 2019 are subject to revision as more data become available.